STALIN EMBATTLED 1943–1948

William O. McCagg, Jr.

Michigan State University

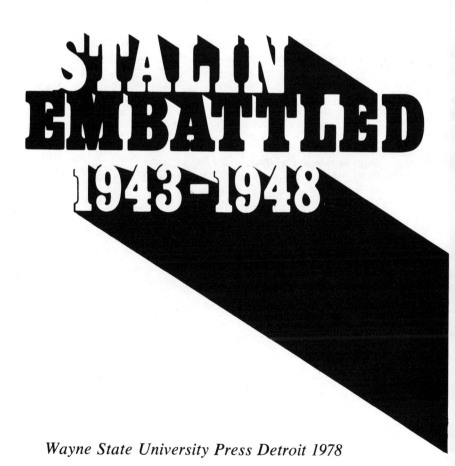

Wayne State University Press Detroit 1978

Library of Congress Cataloging in Publication Data

McCagg, William O.
  Stalin embattled, 1943–1948.

  Bibliography: p.
  Includes index.
  1. Russia—Politics and government—1936–1953.
2. Stalin, Iosif, 1879–1953. I. Title.
DK267.M28   320.9'47'0842   77-28286
ISBN 0-8143-1591-7

for my parents

Contents

Acknowledgments

SOME INITIAL RESEARCH for this study was done in Munich and London during 1960–61 under a Ford Foundation Foreign Area Fellowship. The Institute on East Central Europe at Columbia University funded a research trip to Eastern and Western Europe in 1964. The Inter-University Committee on Travel Grants made it possible for me to spend a total of twelve months in Budapest in 1966–67 and 1969: though I was working then on another subject, the experience was invaluable for deepening my understanding of the topic of this book. In more recent years Michigan State University has granted me relief from teaching obligations so that I might have time to work on this study. I am most grateful for all this institutional support, and also for the generosity and help I have received from the following libraries and their staffs: the Columbia University Libraries and the New York Public Library; the Library of Congress; the Widener Library and the library of the Russian Research Center at Harvard University; the libraries of Michigan State University, the University of Michigan and Yale University; the British

9

Museum and the Royal Institute of International Affairs in London; the library and archives at Radio Free Europe, the Institut zur Erforschung der UdSSR, the Institut für Zeitgeschichte, and the Südost Institut in Munich; the library of the Imre Nagy Institute, formerly in Brussels; and libraries in Budapest, Belgrade, and Novi Sad.

I am particularly indebted to the late Henry L. Roberts for his support and advice in connection with this project; and to my teachers, colleagues, and friends Arthur Adams, Zbigniew Brzezinski, Daniel Brower, Warren Cohen, Alexander Dallin, Herbert Dinerstein, P. R. Duggan, Vera Dunham, Donald Lammers, Marion Low, Alfred Meyer, Yaacov Ro'i, Robert Slusser, and William Zimmerman, all of whom have at one time or another read and criticized parts of the manuscript. Jonathan Harris has made an especially great contribution in many discussions over the years. Paul E. Zinner and György Heltai both gave me invaluable help at an early stage of my research. I have learned much from talks with Richard Lowenthal, Wolfgang Leonhard, Miklós Molnár, Gyula Schöpflin, and Péter Kende, and also from a number of persons in Belgrade, Budapest, Moscow, Prague, and Warsaw who prefer anonymity.

Two more debts must be mentioned: first to Jo Grandstaff and to Mary Patton, who typed several drafts of the manuscript, and to Jean Owen of the Wayne State University Press, who was enormously helpful in the editing of the final manuscript; and second, to my wife, Louise, and to my daughters, Alexandra and Dorothy, who have put up with Stalin beyond any call of duty or affection.

10

Names and Terms

Agit. Prop Administration	Propaganda and Agitation organization, Central Committee, CPSU
CCP	Chinese Communist Party
Cominform	Communist Information Bureau, 1947–56
Comintern	Communist International, 1919–43
commissariat	before 1946, a government ministry
CPBR	Communist Party of Belorussia
CPCz	Communist Party of Czechoslovakia
CPF	Communist Party of France
CPH	Communist Party of Hungary
CPI	Communist Party of Italy
CPInd	Communist Party of India
CPSU(b)	Communist Party of the Soviet Union(Bolshevik)
CPUK	Communist Party of the Ukraine
CPUSA	Communist Party of the United States
GOKO	State Defense Committee; from 1941 to 1945 supreme administrative organ of the regime
gorkom	city Party committee, CPSU
Gosplan	State Planning Commission
GPUKA	Main Political Directorate, Soviet Armed Forces; administrative organization in Central Committee, CPSU
Gulag	State Directorate for Camps; organization attached to the Interior Ministry; colloquial expression for the concentration camp system

11

kolkhoz	collective farm
Komsomol	Union of Communist Youth; organization affiliated with CPSU
krai	territory assigned to a nationality; equivalent of *oblast*
"link" (*zveno*) system	collective-farm reform focused on a small work unit
MGB	Ministry of State Security; before 1946 NKGB
MVD	Ministry of Internal Affairs; before 1946 NKVD
NKGB	People's Commissariat of State Security; after 1946 MGB
NKVD	People's Commissariat of Internal Affairs; after 1946 MVD
obkom	*oblast* Party committee, CPSU
oblast	province
Org. Instrukt. Department	administrative organization, Central Committee, CPSU; in 1947 became Administration for Checking Party Organs
Orgburo	Organizational Bureau, CPSU
partiinost, partiinyi	Party style; in the Party's style
plenum	Party Central committee meeting
Politburo	Political Bureau, CPSU
prikaz	order of the day
raikom	district Party committee, CPSU; inferior to *obkom*
Smersh	"Death to Spies"; wartime title of Soviet counterespionage system
Sovinformburo	Soviet Information Bureau; wartime information organization
Sovnarkom	Council of People's Commissars; acronym for the cabinet until 1946
Sovmin	Council of Ministers; the cabinet after 1946
Vozhd	"leader"; colloquial title for Stalin
Yezhovshchina	terror of the late 1930s; named after N. A. Yezhov
Zhdanovshchina	campaign for cultural conformity in the late 1940s; named after A. A. Zhdanov

1

Introduction

Stalin's "Statism"

"THE COMINTERN'S POLITICAL record . . . reveals . . . a basic characteristic of Stalin's way of thinking: he favored the instruments of state power; he allowed those instruments to carry over from the domestic political arena into international affairs and into the international revolutionary movement." An East European Communist formulated this judgment at a conference of Communist historians in 1966,[1] but few Western historians would object to it. The "statist" tag implies, quite properly, that Stalin's major accomplishments were his economic and political consolidation of the Soviet state and his abrupt retreat from the value system which Lenin's Bolshevik Party had propagated during the revolution of 1917. It hints also at the reasons why Stalin had so many Bolsheviks imprisoned or executed during the 1930s, and why he raised the banners of tsarist nationalism during World War II and again from 1949 until his death in 1953.

13

Mention of Stalin's statism highlights a paradox in the era we are about to discuss. At the end of the war, with Stalin still alive, his regime broke step with his statism, and the Communist Party briefly resumed its leading role within the Soviet system, encouraging the Red Army and the Communist parties abroad to press for revolutionary power. Their efforts created the illusion during 1948 that Stalin stood for worldwide revolution, in that very tradition of 1848 and 1917 which he had tried so hard to suppress before the war.

The paradox seems the greater because, as we now hear from his intimates, Stalin himself in those early postwar years was still quite as statist as he had been before the war. He was terrified of the Western Powers; he feared involving the Soviet Union in a new war and was hardly in a mood of revolutionary exaltation.[2] In virtually every one of his public statements after the war, as during it, he spoke of the possibility and desirability of peaceful coexistence between the Soviet state and the Western Powers. In 1947, in a statement clearly directed to Communists, he declared that "outdated" views of Marx, Engels, and Lenin must be criticized and discarded. A little later he called himself publicly a "businessman," as opposed to a "propagandist,"[3] and openly distanced himself from the then highly vocal spokesmen of the Communist movement.

How can one explain this contrast between the actual Stalin of the end of the war period and the image the world had of him, if not by studying the antagonistic political relationships which existed behind the monolithic facade of Communism? That is the objective of this book, and the results are enlightening. We find in the end that both the Communist movement and the Soviet state experienced domestic political traumas during the period under consideration, that these traumas dramatically affected Soviet behavior in the outside world, and that Stalin's paradoxical involvement in revolutions was not a function of his arbitrary will but of domestic political challenges to his power. Stalin, in sum, was a "force of order" (as opposed to a "force of movement"[4]) in the international political arena at the end of the war.

Communists at the end of the war, whether revolutionaries abroad or bureaucrats within the Soviet Union, had one thing in common: even the Titos and the Maos fervently believed that in their opposition to Stalin they were really doing what Stalin wanted—that somehow there *could* be no real conflict between their "revolution" and Stalin's.[5] They justified the paradoxical aspects of Stalin's behavior toward them by assuming that revolution could happen in new ways and in many ways. Historians of the period have not in general challenged this myth, particularly Soviet historians, for whom the hegemony of the Party within the Soviet system is axiomatic. By their account the Party built the Soviet state, the Party won the war, and the overt leadership of the Party just after the war is clear evidence that it was in fundamental control all along. They admit no possibility of conflict between Stalin and the Party. They compound this basic mythology, moreover, with the premise that in a socialist state ruled by a Communist Party there are no class distinctions, and that consequently domestic political conflicts over policy do not exist.

Western historians have been less dogmatic about these phenomena. They recognize that before 1948 many outsiders did tend to believe that Stalin had left the Party behind and was a businessman of their own sort. Most now acknowledge in general the existence of politics both within Soviet Communism and within the international movement, the intelligibility of these politics to outsiders, and certain interconnections between Soviet domestic and foreign policy. Western histories, however, frequently accept less than critically the Soviet myths about 1945. When it became evident after the war that Marxism was far from dead in Moscow, many of those outsiders who had taken Stalin at his word—as a "businessman"—felt profoundly bitter. They leapt to the conclusion that Stalin's prewar and wartime statism had been a trick designed to disarm them—that in reality all along he had been a Leninist out to conquer the world.[6] They came to believe that anyone who suggested that autonomous political forces existed within Communism under Stalin, or that such forces had an impact on Stalin's policies, was a victim of a naiveté which had been theirs.[7] Even the Western authorities who today admit the significance of Communist politics at this time still tend to assume that there was a bureaucratic insulation between such politics and the conduct of Soviet foreign policy.[8] To establish credibility for our thesis in the face of such assumptions, it is necessary to ask some basic questions: first, is there, in principle, anything objectionable about suggesting a primacy of Soviet domestic politics over foreign policy during and after the war? Were not the major problems of Soviet domestic policy and foreign policy closely intermeshed?

15

The Centralism of the Stalinist Command System

From 1941 to 1945 Stalin's state was engaged in a desperate war of survival. More than at any other time between 1920 and the present day, the foreign policy of the Soviet Union was completely subordinated to the domestic question of whether the Soviet state would survive. Correspondingly, in the era just after 1945, foreign policy was subordinated to the domestic question of how the state should reconstruct: as an industrial Great Power allied to the West but "catching up" with it; as a consumer state, neutral in international conflicts and devoted to improving the welfare of its exhausted people; or as a great military power, "backward" in its economy but prepared for any eventuality? At a time when such fundamental alternatives locked Soviet domestic and foreign policy together, foreign policy inevitably reflected domestic problems, and domestic problems could not be resolved without regard for the international situation.

Other ways of emphasizing this interrelationship lie on the surface of the history of the period. Let us look, for example, at the public discussion of Soviet foreign policy. During the war there was a political thaw, especially in 1944 and 1945, when even the official journals printed a considerable variety of opinion. One topic discussed was the relationship of the Soviet Union with the outside world and, in particular, with the Western Allies, whose virtues even Stalin lauded in public in the summer of 1944.[9] As numerous observers have recognized, many Soviet citizens came to associate friendliness with the Allies with the political thaw, and the West became popular.[10] Then came the *Zhdanovshchina*—the great domestic political campaign of 1946 for the revival of the Communist Party ideology—which takes its name from A. A. Zhdanov, a regional leader from Leningrad. One of the main results of the *Zhdanovshchina* was a violent change in the tone of Soviet discussions of the wartime alliance system: by 1947 the Soviet domestic press was no longer friendly to the Grand Alliance, the foundation of Soviet wartime foreign policy.[11]

Let us look next at the actual formulators of Soviet domestic and foreign policy. During the war and until September 1945, a small emergency committee known as the State Defense Committee (GOKO) coordinated all matters of policy. Its major members were Stalin; L. P. Beria, the internal security chief; K. E. Voroshilov, the defense commissar; G. M. Malenkov, the representative of the Party secretariat

16

and the industrial commissariats; and V. M. Molotov, the foreign commissar. All the organs of the government, the Army high command, and the Party were, by law, subordinated to this committee, which, so far as we can tell, had no subsections isolating foreign from domestic affairs.[12] When the war ended the command structure changed only slightly. The Party Politburo, which included most of the GOKO members, resumed its prewar function as the highest deliberative body within the Soviet system for problems both foreign and domestic.[13] At an early date, it evidently proved too large for Stalin's convenience, and he set up within it a six-man subcommittee for foreign affairs, but this separation of functions also proved inconvenient. In October 1946, just a year after the dissolution of the GOKO, Stalin appointed to this foreign policy subcommittee the chief of the State Planning Office, N. A. Voznesenky, who was a powerful domestic political figure, and then commissioned the resultant "septet" to take up matters of domestic as well as foreign policy, just as the GOKO had.[14] At this time, moreover, there came to light a considerable factional conflict between two of the most important Stalinist lieutenants, Zhdanov and Malenkov. In 1946 their disagreements seemed restricted to domestic policy, but in 1947 at the Cominform meeting and in 1948 the two men were pitted against each other over questions of foreign policy.

Fluctuation of the Soviet frontiers also blurred the boundaries between Soviet domestic and foreign affairs during and just after the war. When Germany invaded the Soviet Union in 1941, the boundary between domestic and foreign affairs in the western regions ceased to exist. In 1945, when the war ended, the Red Army, a Soviet institution neither exclusively domestic nor foreign, was in occupation of a huge belt of lands right up to and beyond the Elbe. Some of these lands—for example, the eastern part of Germany—would be ruled for some time by the Army and thus were objects of the attention of domestic agencies. All were targets for that unique Soviet domestic institution, the secret police. In Germany in particular, between 1945 and 1948 a broad range of Soviet domestic agencies competed with each other, with the army, and with the police for administrative primacy.[15] Under such circumstances, which were reproduced on a more modest scale in the Far East, it is obvious that in 1945 important areas of Soviet foreign policy were not insulated from domestic political interests.

Furthermore, in 1945, just as after World War I, Communists (as well as their ideological opponents all over the world) were wondering

17

whether Moscow was just the administrative center of a modern state or a breeding ground for international revolution as well. Lenin's Comintern, of course, was gone, and in most European and Asiatic countries the Communist parties were rapidly growing and, in varying degrees, were becoming popular political forces which could no longer be called mere instruments of Soviet state policy. But the cords to Moscow were by no means wholly cut. A section of the CPSU(b) (Communist Party of the Soviet Union[Bolshevik]) Central Committee Secretariat coordinated inter-party relations.[16] Many foreign Communist leaders had spent the war in Moscow and, after returning home in 1945, openly maintained relations with the Soviet embassies in their countries and (in Eastern Europe) with the Red Army. As will be seen later, the policies of international Communism were, in obvious fashion, coordinated with the foreign policies of the Soviet Union. In all of these senses, there were two foreign policies emanating from Moscow, one (that of the Foreign Commissariat) slightly more domestically oriented than the other. And the lines were all the more blurred because the less domestic of these spheres, that of international Communism, was the responsibility of A. A. Zhdanov, that leading figure of Soviet domestic politics mentioned above.

Wartime Relaxation

Let us turn now to the question of whether we can assume that there were significant political conflicts in the Soviet system after the war (conflicts within international Communism will be considered in later chapters). The Soviet Union in 1944 and 1945 was to an extraordinary extent politically relaxed. For four years, the entire energy of its peoples had been focused on the single goal of repulsing the German invader. In the struggle 20 million people died, a tenth of the entire population;[17] the country's most populous regions were devastated; and there was a mass movement of men into the armed forces, of women into war jobs, and of workers and technical experts from the western regions to the Urals and Siberia. Every citizen, young or old, suffered from privation and violent upheaval in his way of life. The experience was exhausting and completely distracted attention from the domestic issues which had created political tension before the war.

Of course the Party was still there; the police were still there; the concentration camps were still there; Stalin was still there. Aleksandr

I. Solzhenitsyn tells us how he was clapped into prison in the spring of 1945 for criticizing Stalin in a private letter written from the front,[18] but even this example suggests the change since 1941: Solzhenitsyn would hardly have written such a letter in the years just after the great purges. Moreover, the regime itself had encouraged relaxation. Il'ya Ehrenburg writes in his memoirs that over Radio Moscow during the war he used to promise the Soviet people a better future. As Stalin's spokesman, he urged them to fight hard for a world and life different from that of the years before the war.[19] Boris Pasternak reports the results: "Although victory had not brought the relief and freedom which were expected at the end of the war, nevertheless, the portents of freedom filled the air throughout the postwar period, and they alone defined its historical significance."[20] Stalin's regime still ruled by fiat—that was its style—but one may presume that there was far more doubt than before the war about how, and even whether, its dictation would be accepted. The measures which the regime took must be viewed not as the expressions of mere whim, but as steps considered necessary in the face of a revolution of rising popular expectations.

Within the regime itself, the war also wrought changes, the most important of which was a tremendous accretion of power to the armed forces. Before the war the Soviet armed services had been subject to very strict civilian controls. After the German attack in 1941, however, all that changed. The services grew immensely in size: by 1944 the Red Army's standing force was almost 12 million,[21] as opposed to 4 million before the fighting began, and the country's military leadership, in effect, controlled a considerable portion of the population. Further, the Army was temporary administrator of vast territories, was the major consumer of much of Soviet economic production, and in 1944–1945 was deeply involved in the governance of Eastern Europe and part of Germany—in other words, in foreign affairs.

Beyond this, even before the Stalingrad campaign began in 1942, the regime had specifically acknowledged, through Stalin's public speeches, its dependence on the military. After Stalingrad, Stalin and other civilian leaders donned uniforms and became marshals and generals. Epaulets and gold braid were restored for the first time since tsarist days, and Russia's military and national past was rehabilitated.[22] Meanwhile, the regime began to abandon the old system of political commanders and Party-run cadre selection within the Army[23]

19

and tolerated—indeed, encouraged—the emergence of *esprit de corps*. As outside observers, visiting foreign Communists, and insiders alike report, a certain self-conscious arrogance had appeared by 1945 among Soviet military commanders.[24] This arrogance was directed even toward Stalin himself and, like the revolution of popular expectations, was a factor which limited the freedom of action of his regime.

Other major shifts in the wartime Soviet regime took place within the Communist Party. Before the war, Stalin, for all his statism, had bowed to certain Party formalities. For example, the Party Politburo remained the leading decisionmaking body within the system. Further, in 1938 and 1939, after the great purges, Stalin reaffirmed the authority of the Party's ideology, in the sense that he published his own version of the Party's history and of dialectical materialism. Right up to the war, the Party played the role of a highly significant control apparatus separate from and overseeing the bureaucracy of the state.[25] Virtually from the day the war broke out, however, Stalin dispensed with such forms. For example, as noted above, the regime explicitly subordinated the Politburo, along with the government and the military high command, to the State Defense Committee.[26] Even Soviet Party historians, who have a strong interest in proving that the Party was in command all through the war, acknowledge that Stalin did not allow the Party to make ultimate decisions again until 1945 and, even then, did so sparingly.[27]

There is no question that certain Party organs—most notably the central secretariat—played a vital role in the wartime governance of the Soviet Union. But it is indicative of the real situation that the secretariat, run by G. M. Malenkov, once an organ distinct from the apparatus of state administration, became an integral link in the bureaucracy, substituting itself for state organs.[28] Malenkov himself emerged in 1942, 1943, and 1944 not only as the head of the Party's Secretariat but as a key leader of the state's war production bureaucracy and a representative of the economic ministries within the GOKO. A comparable mixture of Party and state functions fell into the hands of A. S. Shcherbakov.[29] By 1943 he was head of the Party's Moscow organization, was a member of the Central Secretariat, and was in charge of the Main Political Administration of the Red Army (before the war this was the only Soviet administrative apparatus in which Party and state functions were merged). In addition, as a general he played a major role on the Moscow front and was chief of the

20

Sovinformburo (during the war the main source of news about the Soviet Union), which was technically subordinate to the Foreign Commissariat. Comparable empires—and comparable "substitution" (*podmena*) of Party organs for wheels in the state bureaucracy—seem to have emerged throughout the Soviet administrative system during the war years.[30] Though outsiders may view them as ultimate evidence that the Party remained supreme all through the war, Party revivalists at the end of the war regarded such "substitution" as anathema, as do Party historians, who nowadays attempt to prove that the Party won the war.[31]

When Hitler attacked the Soviet Union in 1941, the All-Union CP claimed 3,870,000 members and candidates.[32] A majority of these seem to have been killed during the fighting, but wartime recruiting was so great that by May 1945 the Party could claim 5,760,000 members, about 3 percent of the Soviet population and almost 25 percent of all armed forces personnel. From the official point of view of the Party after the war, this development was no more desirable than the emergence of substitution. Even at the time, it was obvious that Party membership was often being awarded primarily for military valor. After 1945 Party spokesmen made it clear that the growth of the membership represented a diluting of the Party's strength. Today Party historians stress that cadre work during the war was very weak. On the home front, they indicate, the scarcity of trained Party members and massive turnover among those who remained led to a lapse of regular party activities in many places.[33] In the army, the Party's right to select cadres for promotion was expressly limited in November 1943 and not restored until mid-1946.[34] Further, the Party's network of cadre-training schools, which had broken down in the 1930s, disappeared entirely during the war, and after it even the regional Party high schools had to be re-established.[35]

The wartime shrinking of Party influence and activity was most conspicuous in the ideological sphere. In 1941 Stalin compounded his prewar retreat from the value system of the revolution by invoking Russian national heroes from the past. At the same time, his regime attempted to arouse support for the war effort among the component nationalities of the USSR through the use of nationalist symbols. In 1942, as the tide of official nationalism increased, the regime instituted an anti-sectarian campaign, which cast a pall over those aspects of Marxism-Leninism which might alienate its imperialist allies in the West.[36] A German Communist who spent the war years in Moscow says that from 1942 until the spring of 1945 even a joke about capitalism and imperialism was a political sin.[37] A leading general recalls that it was only in the late summer of 1944, when the Red Army had crossed the prewar Soviet frontiers, that he and his colleagues began to talk of the possibility that revolution might now spread.[38] Meanwhile, it became permissible, even at the upper levels of Soviet society, to speak with less regard for ideological correctness. Scientists and writers could publish much more freely in 1945 than they had been able to do before the war.[39] As late as 1947 a group of leading Soviet economists engaged in a markedly free debate about the nature of the capitalist world, and a transcript of the proceedings was published at the end of the year in the controlled press.[40]

Was Stalin's own power still intact at the end of the war? At first one might say yes because in 1945, just as before 1941 and after 1948, his authority was uncircumscribed: all of the elites acknowledged his leadership. The Supreme Soviet even conferred upon him the title of "Generalissimo." Yet power subsists not just in authority—in what outsiders and subordinates acknowledge—and in competence—in what decisions a ruler can make—but also in control. Although Stalin's authority and his competence were surely as great (if not greater) in 1945 as they had been in 1941, it is likely that his control had diminished. With the population undisciplined, with even the generals showing their arrogance, with the Party-state relationship within the huge governing bureaucracy drastically altered, one may guess that there was a major gap in 1945 between the competence of the *Vozhd* ("leader"), unchanged since 1941, and his lessened control.

Stalin himself frequently hinted to visitors during the war that his colleagues played more of a role in Soviet decisionmaking than outsiders supposed.[41] Press and diplomatic reports from Moscow were filled all through the late war and postwar years with tales of Stalin's impending retirement, his ill health, and his conflicts with his colleagues. These years were the heyday of the "prisoner of the Politburo" talk in the West. It is common nowadays to deprecate such talk as a symptom of that Western naiveté about Communism which, in the 1930s, led Western reporters in Moscow to accept what they were told about the great purge trials. However, in the 1930s, this naiveté was sustained by the all-embracing totalitarian terror which severely limited Western contacts in Moscow. In 1945, as we have seen, that terror no longer existed, and it was not the naive Joseph Davies who wrote home that Stalin's power was limited but the "hard-headed" experts. Late in 1945, for example, just a few weeks before George Kennan wrote his now famous "long telegram" warning the United States government not to trust the Russians, he wrote such things as:

> During the war Stalin has devoted a great deal of his own time to military matters.
>
> The safety of his regime, and his own personal safety, appear to have lain largely in the hands of such men as Beria, Malenkov, and—until his death—Shcherbakov. These men . . . are among the few people . . . Stalin can at least trust.
>
> This means [they] are very difficult indeed to replace.
>
> They can sabotage with impunity the major directives of Soviet policy, knowing that . . . Stalin will always back them up in the end.[42]

Kennan was not the only respected Western authority to report that Stalin's personal control was weaker than before the war.[43] Consequently, when Stalin himself intimated that he had to wrestle with his colleagues, he may well have been stating the obvious—something he felt he could not conceal. He may not have been a prisoner of the Politburo, but he was surely the prisoner of the no longer total control system over which he presided.

The Legitimacy of Relying on Communist Public Statements

Neither the publications of the Soviet regime nor the public statements of the postwar leaders of world Communism are extensive or, in the traditional sense of the word, reliable. Communists are notorious for lying. Stalin was particularly notorious for lying. One must ask, therefore, whether an outside historian can possibly trace the policy disputes inside Stalinist Communism. A Polish journalist suggested the answer to this question in the 1950s when he wrote:

> In our public, political and intellectual life, in our organizations and newspapers, there exists a special figurative speech. It consists in the usage of certain turns of phrase. . . . All that is needed is a clue. Those who have guessed that clue are able to read public utterances as if they were an open book and thus learn a lot of things. It goes without saying that one has to read between the lines, to follow hidden ideas. And this reading between the lines is not illegitimate: on the contrary, the texts are construed in such a way that reading between the lines is the only way to grasp their meaning. . . . Those who cannot read our special language are as naive as little children.[44]

A Hungarian former Communist agrees: "At top-level Party committee meetings, there was hardly ever any open clash; the disagreements were cautiously expressed by praising someone else's suggestion, then capping [it] with amendments so worded that they seemed logically to follow from the statements . . . although aiming at something quite different. Words and shades of opinion were loaded, and you had to develop a good ear to catch the undercurrents."[45]

Communism is an ideological movement.[46] Its followers subscribe to an extensive set of philosophical explanations of how the world goes round. Consequently, they possess a conventional language for communication with one another which, though mysterious to outsiders, is perfectly coherent—and thus reliable—to them. Since outsiders can learn this conventional language of Communism, as they can learn any other, it is entirely feasible to "listen in" to Communist communications. Of course, we are speaking here above all of those speeches and writings of top Communist leaders which may be regarded as *ex cathedra* because they are published in important journals. Further, we are speaking of an era relatively free of terror. We are assuming that the reader of these statements is judicious and will recognize that the Moscow journal *Pravda* is not a good source for the study of Tito's ideas; that though Andrei Zhdanov's speeches are revealing, those of his son, a minor official, are not; that *Pravda* tells far more about the development of Soviet foreign policy than the English translation of the Soviet Trade Union Organizations journal, *Novoe Vremya;* and that during the years of terror from 1950 to 1953 the press was generally unrevealing.[47]

To illustrate our point, let us recall Stalin's public statements of early 1947, cited above, to the effect that he was not a propagandist but a businessman interested in peaceful cooperation with the Western Powers. In the framework of Marxism-Leninism, did the literal meaning of this communication not count less than its lateral or implemental implications? Stalin really did not have to give his followers an articulated description of his goals, of the political situation in the Soviet Union in 1947, or of its relation with the West. All that was common knowledge and could go without saying so long as he, the leader, was willing to hint at how the understood goals should be accomplished. This he did. He left no doubt that in his opinion the best strategy for the moment was to seek peaceful cooperation with the West and to avoid the use of alarming revolutionary language.

To give another example, at the Yalta conference in 1945 Stalin told the Americans and the British that free elections would take place in Poland within a few months. For two years, however, elections did not take place, and when they did, early in 1947, they were, to Stalin's own knowledge,[48] not free. Westerners therefore assumed that Stalin lied at Yalta, as, indeed, he seems to have done with regard to the old Poland, which in 1945 he was cold-bloodedly raping with intent to destroy. But what about the new Poland? In 1945 Stalin installed Polish "national" Communists such as Władisław Gomułka at Warsaw, and in the following years he gave them such a free rein that by 1947 and 1948 he could perceive them as rebels against him. In 1945 they certainly did not intend to reduce Poland to the satellite-ship which that country achieved against its will in 1950. Did Stalin? And if he did not, did he lie at Yalta?

The meaning of such expressions as "democracy" and "free elections" is so different in Stalin's ideological language from our own that my inclination, even in the tangled business of Poland, is to posit that Stalin was mostly interested in tactics when he spoke—that when he promised free elections in Poland, he did so mainly for effect, without much precise thought about the distant future. The task of interpreting Stalin's words is made difficult, as we will see later, by confusion within the Communist movement which often prevented them from having the desired impact. But this does not mean that his statements were all lies or that outsiders cannot find in them a reliable index of his *tactical* intent.[49]

Furthermore, any top Soviet leader, even a Stalin, is obliged to use Marxism-Leninism for administrative purposes in running his bureaucracy, for the ideology is ultimately the source of his authority over the bureaucrats. This also makes Communist public communications useful as historical evidence. When such a leader speaks, particularly when he speaks on a solemn occasion such as 6 November, the eve of the annual celebration of the Bolshevik Revolution, he knows very well that the administrative bureaucracy he heads will be waiting expectantly for indications of where it stands in terms of Marxist-Leninist ideas. He knows, indeed, that the bureaucrats urgently need such indications to sanction their behavior vis-à-vis the rest of Soviet society. If only for this reason, one may presume that when such a top leader speaks, he is serious: he is not just making propaganda and telling lies to trick the enemy but is performing a vital governmental ritual.[50]

The evidence is strong that Stalin's public statements served such an administrative function. While he was in power, he spoke in public far less than the average Western political leader of his day.[51] In 1940, for example, though he was head of the Party and leader of the state, he published not a single word. During the war years he delivered a number of long speeches, but from 1945 to his death in 1953, he made only one lengthy public speech. Apart from some extensive theoretical writing published in 1950 and 1952, he depended on an average of four short "interviews" annually to satisfy the world's demand for his political views. Even these rare statements carried overwhelming political weight, however. A Soviet Central Committee directive of mid-1944 placed the reading of Stalin's collected war speeches among the primary obligations of Party organizers in the freshly liberated parts of the country, and advised: "This book gives our cadres the key to an understanding of the historical regularity [*zakonomernost*] of the course of the war and to the present war-political and international situations of the USSR. It arms our cadres with knowledge of the historic strength and power of the USSR and the Red Army. It directs us on the road to final victory over the enemy."[52] In February 1946 A. A. Kuznetsov, the first secretary of the Leningrad Regional Organization of the CPSU(b), announced at a meeting of Party activists: "Comrades: every speech of Comrade Stalin is a major event in the life of our country. . . . [Such a] speech is not just a report but a major programmatic document, a new general contribution to Marxist-Leninist science."[53] In May 1945 Mátyás Rákosi, the secretary general of the Hungarian Communist Party, claimed: "Stalin is a man of few words, who profoundly weighs everything he says. The whole world should hang on his every word."[54]

Finally, though it is clear that Stalin's Communist elites looked down upon "troglodyte" idealists[55] who took the ideals of the revolution quite literally, one must not underestimate the degree to which, in Stalin's day, the Soviet elite, like any other governing class, internalized its ideology. They were like the European bourgeoisies of the nineteenth century, who paid faithful lip service to the slogans of liberalism and even to those of the French Revolution but in practice were a most staid and conservative element in society. As a Polish sociologist has put it recently: "In common . . . with the petty bourgeoisie, the middle strata of the Communist organization establishment are nationalistic [in the sense that they are] easy prey to slogans calling for animosity and hostility against alien targets—targets which change with political exigency. . . . They adhere to Marxism, but in a simple-minded manner, and are knowledgeable of Marxist literature in the same way as devout Catholics are knowledgeable of their catechism.''[56]

One finds plenty of references in Soviet literature to such internalization of Marxist goals. Solzhenitsyn's *First Circle,* for example, describes a New Year's Eve celebration at which *partiinost* appears as a matter of "new class" day-to-day behavior. An editor of Serbian origin is arguing with a friend, a typically *spiessburger* Moscow public prosecutor, about the privileges of the Soviet elite. The prosecutor, feeling challenged, replies: "So what is there left to live for? What have we fought for? Don't you remember Engels? 'Equality does not mean the equality of everything with zero. . . . ' Well, go on and finish what you had to say. . . . You mean the Fascist regime in Yugoslavia [this is 1949] is a socialist government? You mean what we have here is an aberration?" The Serb replies: "No, no, of course, not! . . . The capitalist world is doomed by incomparably worse contradictions [than ours]. And as everyone in the Comintern predicted, I believe firmly that we will soon witness an armed conflict between America and England for world markets.''[57] Such "propagandistic" talk, according to Solzhenitsyn, was typical of after-dinner conversation among the Soviet elite. If this is true—to make our point—then Communist public documents, with their special language, are not just propaganda for the benefit of outsiders but reflect the mentality of their writers.

It is important to point out that the Communist public documents on which this book is based may reflect not just the mentality of Stalin's followers but also that of the *Vozhd* himself. Stalin was statist not only because he favored the instruments of state power and spent much of his later life building them up, but also because he favored them within a party system. He was not a Napoleon, who felt free from the ideological synthesis of the revolution which had made his power possible. As he admitted at Lenin's bier in 1924, he thought of himself as a high priest guarding a cult which someone else had created.[58] He composed prayers for the Communist movement. He conducted rites. He anathematized from the altar. But never did he transform himself formally, as did Napoleon, from a republican general into the sort of emperor his republic had sought to abolish. Until his death he remained simply Lenin's successor, a hero, according to the Marxist view of history, but no more than a caretaker of the

27

Marxist-Leninist creed.[59] It seems that he always dreaded that someone would accuse him of being a false priest, a betrayer of the revolution, and a liar in the eyes of his god.

Some historians have ascribed this lack of boldness in Stalin to what they call the "conscience" in the Bolshevik Revolution.[60] Others have seen in it a reflection of the psychological scar created by his childhood conflict with his father.[61] But certainly it was Stalin's peculiarity as a historical figure that, while always fighting the Marxist explanation of reality, he never broke away from it.[62] Because the language of Communist public documents in Stalin's day reflected his own mentality as well as the mentality of his petty bourgeois underlings at home, they may be accepted as reliable historical evidence.

Conclusion

Until the end of the war in 1945, Stalin's goal seemed to be establishment of a world system of cooperating states in which the socialist Soviet Union might play a major part. He resumed pursuit of this unrevolutionary goal after 1949 and up to his death. But in 1945 Soviet policy began to revert to the revolutionary models of 1917, and by 1948 Stalin seemed to be behaving almost in the barricades tradition of 1848. Our book attempts to explain this paradox through study of antagonist political relationships within the Communist world, proposing that domestic traumas in the Communist movement forced distortions in Stalin's foreign policy at the end of the war. We have seen that Soviet domestic politics easily could have had such an effect on foreign policy because of the centralism of the Stalinist decision-making apparatus at the end of the war. There was also room for significant domestic political activity both within the Soviet state and within the Communist movement, and we have reliable tools for documenting such activities. Our project is not impossible. Let us therefore proceed to Stalin's battles with Communists between 1943 and 1948 in greater detail.

I

The First Battle:
Against the Insurrectionists

2

The Emergence of "New Type Government" in 1944

A Great Leap

AT LIBERATED ALGIERS on 6 April 1944, the French Communist Party entered the provisional coalition government of General Charles de Gaulle. The Party received only two posts in the cabinet, neither of which could be regarded as crucial for gaining control of the state. However, Party members had very considerable power in the underground in France, won while fighting the Germans. Even with a weak position in the De Gaulle government, therefore, the CPF could—and did—play a dramatic role during the crisis of liberation, which in France began in June 1944, and during the three years of reconstruction which followed.[1]

The 6th of April was a key moment in the history of all Europe in the postwar era because the French Communists set a precedent for

31

many other Communist parties. In the past, Communists had often contemplated entering coalition governments as equal or weaker partners with the bourgeoisie, but they had almost never done so. Such coalitions had seemed too unrevolutionary—too much like the "opportunism" which Lenin had derided in the turn-of-the-century French Social Democrat Millerand and in the Second International.[2] As recently as December 1943, the Czech Communists in Moscow piously refused a place in the government-in-exile of President Edvard Beneš, even though Beneš was a good democrat.[3] Now, however, only a few days after the French Party had joined De Gaulle's distinctly conservative regime, the Italian Communists made a sharp political turn and joined the regime of Marshal Badoglio, a Fascist collaborator whom most Italian democrats deeply resented.[4] In subsequent months the Greek Communists, radical revolutionaries who were tremendously strong in the underground resistance movement, agreed to join a coalition organized by the British around exiled bourgeois political elements.[5] During the autumn of 1944, as the Red Army crashed through the Balkans and the Americans and British rushed to complete their liberation of France and Belgium, Communists all over Europe entered coalitions. Even the Chinese Communist Party accepted coalitionism in principle.[6] In October a British Communist leader gave this system the name of "new type government."[7] From the strongholds which these Communist parties established within coalition governments in 1944 and 1945, world Communism made its momentous acquisitions of power during the next few years.

If the Communists had not joined bourgeois forces in coalition governments in 1944, the era which followed would have been full of confrontations, less dominated by ideals of international unity, and probably much more realistic about the vast social and political problems which faced the world. "New type government" is thus a logical initial focus for our attempt to determine why, after the war, Stalin came to seem so much more revolutionary than he actually was.

Strategy versus Tactics

Major clues to Stalin's understanding of the "new type governments" of 1944 are found in his speeches of the period, in particular, a speech of 6 November 1943 in which he memorialized the Bolshevik Revolution. As was his custom in these ceremonial, *ex cathedra* orations, Stalin opened liturgically:

32

Comrades: The nations of the Soviet Union are celebrating today the twenty-sixth anniversary of the great October socialist revolution. For the third time, our country is marking the anniversary of its national revolution under conditions of a patriotic war. In October 1941 our Motherland experienced difficult days. . . .

In October 1942 the peril of our Motherland grew even greater. . . . Yet even in those serious days, the armies and the nation did not lose heart. . . . Immediately after the October days of last year, our forces went on the offensive.[8]

However, the body of the speech was wholly pragmatic, in no way reflecting revolutionary and Party attitudes. Stalin recalled how the Red Army had counterattacked near Stalingrad in November 1942, surrounded huge German forces, driven the Germans to the Don, and then stopped the enemy summer offensive of 1943 in a great tank battle at Kursk. Then he praised the home front's contribution to the military exploits of the state, reviewing the contributions of industry and the workers, of agriculture and the peasants, of the transport system, of the intelligentsia, of the nationalities, and of the Party.

In the third and final section of the speech, Stalin spoke of the anti-Fascist alliance the Soviet Union had formed with the United States, Great Britain, and other states in the West. He reminded his listeners that in October 1943, just a few weeks prior to the celebration of the anniversary of the Revolution, the foreign ministers of the three great allies had conferred in Moscow, and that the Western Powers were this year materially contributing to the cause of defeating Hitler. The Americans had landed troops in North Africa, cleared it of the enemy, and then invaded Sicily and Italy proper, toppling Hitler's major European ally, Mussolini. The Allies, he said, were regularly providing the Soviet Union with weapons and raw material. He noted that the operations in southern Europe were still not a second front, but he called them "something resembling a second front" and, noting that such a second front was no longer "out of sight," he admitted that "the anti-Hitler coalition had shown itself a firm union of nations established on a strong foundation." At the end of the speech, he listed a set of goals which were all consistent with continuation of the Grand Alliance: "together with his allies," he wished to liberate the captive nations of Europe from Germany, give them freedom to "resolve the question" of their political systems, take measures to suppress Fascism and to prevent further aggression,

33

and establish a long-term system of European "economic, political, and cultural cooperation."

Although Stalin's reference in this speech to the Communist Party of the Soviet Union was striking, he described it pragmatically as a subsidiary organ of the Soviet state system.[9] Of foreign Communism and world revolution, he said only that "a general explosion of resentment" was brewing in the occupied lands of Europe. Otherwise, the speech was among the most statist, anti-sectarian statements he published during the war. In historical perspective, it fits very well with the ostentatious dissolution of the Comintern six months earlier, and with the Allied summit meeting at Teheran a few weeks later. If, therefore, one takes this speech to be a directive or guideline issued by the leader of world Communism to its followers, the implications seem transparent. The goal was defeat of the Fascist foe. The chosen strategy was alliance with the Western Powers and with all anti-Fascist forces in all countries. This strategy would carry over into the postwar period. Followers should not make themselves conspicuous through crude revolutionary activity but should accommodate themselves to the policies of the Soviet state.

A certain parallel exists between this speech and the "new type governments" which European Communist parties were entering the following year. If Stalin's state was allied with the bourgeois states of the West, analogy suggested that Communist parties abroad should ally themselves with the bourgeois anti-Fascist forces of their own countries.[10] Stalin himself had recently specified such behavior. In May 1943, after the Comintern dissolution, Stalin explained that action as necessary first of all to refute "Hitlerite lies" about Soviet interference in the domestic affairs of other countries. Second, he said, the dissolution would "simplify the work of freedom-loving patriots in all countries in the unification of the progressive forces of their countries, independently of party and religious persuasion . . . against Fascism." As the third reason, he declaimed with deliberately parallel language: "it will simplify the work of patriots in all countries who seek the unification in one international camp of all freedom-loving peoples . . . against Hitlerism."[11] Here was an explicit parallel between the Western alliance of the Soviet state and the political alliances which Stalin expected freedom-loving patriots—in other words, Communists—to pursue within their respective national political frameworks. The "new type governments" of 1944 were, in such terms, merely foreign Communist imitations of Stalin's statist strategy of 1943.

34

Yet there is a problem here. Stalin was a Communist. He issued his political directives, even during the great anti-sectarian campaign, in the structured language of Marxism-Leninism. According to the assumptions built into that language, the goal of all Communist political activity is not just the winning of a war between states but the furthering of revolution in all parts of the world. Even if Stalin himself saw the "new type governments" of 1944 as just a peripheral reflection of his state's general wartime strategy, his language implied that they represented tactical moves in the central struggle of the Communist movement to further world revolution. As it happens, many Communists outside the Soviet Union interpreted the "new type governments" of 1944 in precisely this fashion. The wartime attitudes of these foreign Communists have been described by a former secretary general of the Finnish Communist Party in a memoir about the war: the leaders of the Danish CP "had been given Moscow's solemn assurance that the Second World War would bring about the final victory of the Soviet Union and Communism throughout the world. Thus the resistance movement, as far as the Danish Communists were concerned, was nothing but a struggle for world revolution. [I know this] because . . . [as] an executive of the Comintern . . . I was one of the relayers . . . of the assurances."[12]

Moreover, the urge to make revolution was particularly strong in 1944 because Marx had predicted that revolution was inevitable, and Lenin had asserted that revolutions follow inevitably and immediately in the wake of the wars which are unavoidable in an imperialist system.[13] All through the interwar period, Communists had been predicting another great imperialist war and, in its wake, the collapse of world capitalism, opening the way for world revolution. In 1944, therefore, when the end of the war was visible and "new type governments" were appearing in Europe, most Communists believed that the moment of revolution was at hand. No matter what Stalin said about the necessity of the Grand Alliance, many foreign Communist listeners regarded the coalitions less as strategy than as tactics.

Mátyás Rákosi, the Stalinist leader of postwar Hungary, describes this divergence rather well:

> The greater part of those comrades who were not acquainted with . . . our strategic plan devised during the war were surprised in 1944–1945 at such a broad coalition . . . and treated it with antagonism.
> How often during those weeks were we reproached by good comrades: "This is not what we expected of you." And they told us what

they wanted: "In 1919," they said, "the imperialists used arms to destroy the Hungarian Soviet Republic and reinstated the dictatorship of the great landowners and capitalists. Now the Red Army has liberated us. Let us profit by this opportunity to restore the proletarian dictatorship." At the time of the liberation, we did not explain this problem soon enough to the broad masses of the Party. In 1945 it was tackled only in the intimate circles of the Party because even a theoretical suggestion of a goal of proletarian dictatorship would have created upheaval in the ranks of our coalition partners.[14]

"Nineteen-nineteenism" was probably not as strong in Hungary in 1944 as Rákosi suggests here. The importance of his account, however, lies not in its exact substance but in the relationship it recalls. Even in 1952, at the height of his power, Rákosi felt constrained to admit that there was a split, during the crisis of the liberation in Hungary, between his own Stalinist point of view and the revolutionary expectations of Communists inside Hungary. When one looks back, moreover, to what Rákosi actually said in the inner circles of his Party in 1945, one discovers not only a flamboyant condemnation of alleged advocates of proletarian dictatorship but effective denial that "new type government" was a matter of tactics. In 1945 Rákosi informed his comrades that Stalin, for strategic reasons, wanted to delay a Communist assumption of power in Hungary for ten to fifteen years.[15]

Stalin's View of the Grand Alliance

In proposing that Stalin and the foreign Communists had divergent political views in 1944, it is important to stress that Stalin's commitment to the Grand Alliance with the West had nothing to do with love and affection. Stalin's wartime allies were the staunchest representatives of what he knew as imperialism, and from his early years in politics, he worked with all his strength and energy for the overthrow of that system. During the Russian Civil War, for example, when he was still a minor and parochial Bolshevik leader, he had seen the United States and Britain, for all their Wilsonian hyperbole, intervene in Russia on the counter-revolutionary side.[16] As he rose to power during the 1920s, developed his thesis that socialism could be built in one state, and then proceeded to act upon it, Stalin in general accepted rigid isolationism as the best of foreign policies.[17] But in the 1930s he presided (reluctantly) over normalization of relations with the outside world.[18] In 1934 and 1935 Moscow joined the League of Nations; entered treaty relationships with France and with France's eastern ally, Czechoslovakia; took an ideological stand against the Fascist foes of Western liberalism; and led international Communism into a tactic of popular front. This general retreat from the revolution occurred at a time when the Soviet leadership was demonstrably nervous and deeply suspicious. The start of the great purge came in September 1936, just after the Falange rebelled against the popular frontist republic in Spain. During the ensuing period, when Soviet nerves were particularly strained, Stalin saw the Western democracies, which had urged him into the popular front, abandon first Spain, then Austria, and finally democratic Czechoslovakia. In this light, it seems understandable that when opportunity came his way in 1939, Stalin turned away from the laggard British and French and toward the Germans.[19] Among imperialists, they seemed at least predictable. Geographically they were closer to him and thus all the more dangerous as enemies, and from them his state could receive certain concrete material rewards—the Baltic lands, the western Ukraine, and Bessarabia—and relief from waging a war with Japan.

It was indicative of Stalin's thinking that until 22 June 1941 he was more wary of the British than of the Germans.[20] He rearmed the Soviet Union, of course, and in April, when an anti-German coup took place in Yugoslavia, Moscow greeted it eagerly, as if to stave off the German conquest of the Balkans, which followed immediately. In this sense, Stalin was preparing for a German assault on Russia. Meanwhile, however, he spoke repeatedly of his fear that all the information about Hitler's impending attack had been manufactured in London to provoke him into war with Germany and thus relieve the West of Hitler's pressure.[21] In May 1941 he issued a public statement reaffirming his belief that the war was a struggle to the death between imperialists, a struggle from which the Soviet Union could and should remain aloof.[22] A danger he seemed to feel then, with Rudolph Hess in England and the Germans attacking the British imperial lifeline in Crete, was that London would somehow seek a breathing space by guaranteeing Hitler spoils in the East. This attitude of distrust persisted: after 22 June 1941 Stalin did accept alliance with the Western Powers, but when he first spoke of the alliance in public, he made no attempt to conceal the imperialist nature of his partners. Instead, he depicted Hitler's Germany as worse than the "tsarist reaction" of the past—in other words, worse than the imperialists.[23] Only after a year of war were his suspicions somewhat allayed. In 1942 he introduced the anti-sectarian campaign at home, imposed a rule of silence on the subject of imperialism, and publicly described the alliance as a Soviet-British-American front with a common "action program" against the "bestial" enemy, world Fascism.[24]

Even in 1943, after the victory at Stalingrad, Stalin and his regime continued to talk of the possibility of negotiating with Berlin.[25] Late in January 1943, Roosevelt and Churchill met at Casablanca without Stalin. On 23 February, the *Vozhd* issued a *prikaz* ("military order of the day") in which he described the task of the Red Army only as that of clearing the enemy out of the territory of the Soviet Union.[26] Coinciding, as it did, with the Western leaders' call for unconditional German surrender and with impatient Soviet calls for a second front, Stalin's statement was read even in the West as a hint of a separate peace.[27] When, in the summer, the Allies belatedly told him that there could be no second front that year, Moscow set up a German National Committee and recruited a League of German Officers from the POW camps.[28] These organizations appealed openly to Germans of all political complexions within Germany to dump Hitler and—implicitly with neither revolution nor defeat—to negotiate a peace. It now appears that secret diplomatic contacts actually took place during these months, and that at one point an armistice may have been in the making.[29] Even in mid-January 1944, *Pravda,* the most official of all Soviet journals, published materials justifying a separate peace: it reported rumors from Cairo that the Allies were engaged in secret conversations with the Germans.[30] But by then the basic prerequisite of a separate Soviet peace with Berlin was fading. Next to Germany, the Western Allies were the world's leading military and industrial powers. The United States was virtually undamaged by the war. If the Soviet Union were to leave the alliance, therefore, it would have to depend on the Germans for protection from retribution by the West, and by early 1944 the German ability to provide such protection was in doubt. Unrest was increasing on the Continent. At Teheran Stalin ascertained that the Allies were in earnest. It was symptomatic of this fading of the German option that early in January 1944 Moscow began to play down the League of German Officers and adjusted its propaganda to reflect the goal of unconditional surrender.[31]

Thus when "new type government" appeared in Europe early in

1944, Stalin stood not at the culmination of a long, happy love affair with the Western Powers but in a reluctant, unnatural, forced union with them. In expediency, however, there is often benefit. And in observing the benefits Stalin could derive from his alliance with the West in 1944, one may judge why he committed himself to it and why he advocated "new type government" to Communists abroad. The Soviet Union still had resources: the war had forged a Red Army far more powerful than the Soviet armies of the past, but even it was receiving a fair proportion of its supplies from the West,[32] and with the invader still inside Soviet territory and the entire military might of industrial Europe still behind Hitler, the Western Alliance was certainly advantageous. A second front in France appeared imminent, and there was also the possibility of absolute victory in Europe over Germany, eliminating, once and for all, Russia's most traditional European foe. And of course, if the Soviet Union were within the Alliance, the danger that not Stalin but Hitler would find an opportunity to jump out of the war would be avoided.

Besides, by the first months of 1944, Stalin could see that at least one extremely knotty problem might be resolved through continued good relations with the West. Even in the darkest days of 1941, he never concealed his ambition to retain, after the war, the frontiers he had worked out with Hitler in 1939 and 1940, frontiers which restored to Russia most of the territories she had lost after World War I. In his "separate peace" statement of 23 February 1943, he made this point explicit,[33] and in the ensuing months the difficulties of the position became apparent.[34] Great Britain had entered the war because of her obligations to Poland. Since 1939, a Polish government-in-exile with a strong following in the homeland had existed in London. In 1941 this government gained the backing of the United States, yet it refused to accept the validity of the frontiers which Stalin demanded, and by March 1943 it was willing to credit allegations from German sources that the Russians had murdered thousands of Polish officers. In April the Soviet government broke diplomatic relations with the "London Poles." In May, Moscow permitted Polish Communists in Russia to set up a Union of Polish Patriots, which thereupon endorsed the Soviet-favored Polish-Soviet frontier. It now became obvious that Soviet insistence on that frontier might provoke an open political confrontation with the Western Powers.

At Teheran in December, however, Stalin received private assurances from the Western leaders that they might agree to his demands on the Polish issue.[35] A month later, Soviet troops crossed the prewar Polish-Soviet frontier. The Polish government published a comment on this, and the Soviet government then launched a public polemic against the London Poles.[36] This polemic evidently reflected a major foreign policy debate among the Soviet leaders, for it coincided with the "rumors from Cairo" report and the end of the effort to negotiate with Germany. The results of the debate appeared in the order of the day which Stalin issued on Red Army Day, 23 February 1944, six weeks before the emergence of "new type government" in France. Stalin spoke first of the immense task the Soviet state and the Red Army were accomplishing. Then he noted German diplomatic efforts to divide the Grand Alliance and achieve a separate peace—if not with the Soviet Union, then with the Western Powers. He mentioned in passing, as he had in his November oration, that the war would involve the liberation not just of Soviet territory but also of the occupied countries of Europe. At the climax of his order of the day he emphasized: "Never in history has an enemy run over the precipice all by itself. To win a war, it is necessary to force the foe to the precipice and push him over."[37] From the urgency of this appeal for continuation of the Grand Alliance, one may deduce that Stalin now recognized that he might obtain from the West what he had once thought could only be gotten from Hitler.

The Futility of Annexationism

Until 1939 the policies of the world Communist movement were worked out separately from the policies of the Soviet state.[38] Indeed, between 1928 and 1934, when the decisionmaking power in the Comintern was already decisively under Soviet control, there was a clear contradiction between the revolutionary intransigence which the Comintern professed and the seemingly open foreign policy of the Great Socialist Fatherland. With the introduction of the popular front after 1934, however, this split disappeared.[39] Late in 1938, for example, the Comintern dissolved the Communist Party of Poland.[40] Coincidentally, most of the Polish Communists in the Soviet Union fell victim to the great terror. Since the CPP was illegal inside Poland, the dissolution meant that when, in September 1939, the partition of Poland took place and the country's eastern half was annexed to the Soviet Union, there existed—by Communist definitions—no internal revolutionary force to carry the country to socialism. As a concession to revolutionary tradition, Moscow labeled the annexed lands "Western Belorussia" and "Western Ukraine," the implication being that the Belorussian and Ukrainian divisions of the CPSU(b) had provided an element of popular revolutionary action. But the Soviet state alone had initiated the revolutionary progress towards socialism, despite the fact that orthodox Marxists believed it would come from within a given country and from below. As a result, observant Communists trying to justify their subservience to the Soviet Union could guess that henceforth the Soviet state might provide everywhere the "initiative towards socialism."[41]

Upon the outbreak of the "winter war" between the Soviet Union and Finland late in November 1939, "annexationism," as a theory of socialist expansion, received another push: a "popular" Finnish government was instituted at Terijoki, behind Red Army lines, headed by a Finnish member of the Comintern Executive Committee (who, it was later revealed, was also a member of the Soviet CP).[42] Then, in the summer of 1940, Estonia, Latvia, and Lithuania all became socialist, with only the most perfunctory internal popular action, through absorption into the Soviet Union.[43] At the same time the Soviet Union, in the interests of its foreign policy, was encouraging separatist tendencies in the Czechoslovak and Yugoslav parties,[44] the Rumanian Party received instructions from Moscow to abandon all opposition to the Rumanian Fascist movement,[45] and the Soviet leadership was discussing whether the Comintern should be disbanded altogether.[46] Consequently, in Communist circles in Europe annexationist explanations became commonplace. Not Stalin but events seemed to dictate this analysis.

When the dissolution of the Comintern actually took place in May 1943, the Soviet Union was engaged in the Great Patriotic War; by then the whole question of world revolution had come to occupy a rather small place in the minds of the Soviet leadership. Yet it seems clear that, in general, Moscow still held to the annexationist views of 1940. Many of the foreign Communists in the Soviet Union were now busily at work organizing ethnic military units of their compatriots which could fight the German foe as part of the Red Army.[47] In January 1944 the Communist Party of the United States acknowledged the impossibility of a Red Army liberation of America and offered instead a highly revisionist plan for dissolving itself and helping the existing American political parties work toward socialism.[48] Then just three weeks before Stalin's Red Army Day appeal for support of the Grand Alliance, the Soviet leadership organized a peculiar little drama which reminded its audience of the leading role of the Soviet state in the march toward world revolution. On 28 January 1944 the highest legislative body of the Soviet Union, the Supreme Soviet, convened, ostensibly to approve an annual budget law. It had convened only once since before the war, and then in mid-1942 it was to formalize the treaty of alliance with Great Britain. Consequently, the budget did not seem the real reason for the meeting, and attention was drawn to a new law now submitted which created separate foreign and defense commissariats for the major constituent republics of the USSR. In retrospect, many historians have seen in this new law an adumbration of Stalin's subsequent request that those republics, especially the Ukraine and Belorussia, be granted membership in the United Nations Organization.[49] At the time, however, the new law seemed to emphasize the compatibility of the Soviet Union's federal framework with the existence of national political entities—in other words, it seemed to suggest that new nations could easily join the USSR.[50] As V. M. Molotov, the Soviet foreign commissar, who sponsored the law, said: "Who does not understand by now that the Red Army fulfills its mission of liberation not only with regard to its own motherland, but also with regard to all democratic countries?"[51] This was close to saying that the Red Army would initiate a revolutionary process abroad when it passed beyond the Soviet frontiers—which it was in fact about to do.

These persistent hints of annexationism need not, however, obscure three factors which, early in 1944, were making Molotov's rhetorical question meaningless. The first factor was the intellectual and political sophistication of the Comintern veterans in Moscow—men and women who still headed the most important Communist parties of the world. The ranks of these Muscovites reflected the history of world revolutions since the turn of the century.[52] The Bulgarian Vasil Kolarov participated in the violent struggles before World War I which gave the leftist faction of Bulgarian social democracy a claim, second only to that of Lenin's Bolsheviks, to being the original Communists. Mátyás Rákosi was a deputy people's commissar in the Hungarian Bolshevik Republic in 1919. Wilhelm Pieck and Walter Ulbricht "bolshevized" the German Communist Party during the late 1920s and, by obeying Stalin and fighting "social fascism," helped pave the way for its downfall in 1933. Georgi Dimitrov was world-famous for his role in the Reichstag fire trial of 1934. Dolores Ibarruri

42

was an inspiration of the left during the Spanish Civil War. Klement Gottwald led the popular-frontist Czechoslovak Party to its doom in 1938–1939. Maurice Thorez, the head of the French Communist Party, fled to Moscow in 1939 when faced with criminal charges at home after the Nazi-Soviet Pact was signed.

The list of Muscovite Communists included Wanda Wasilewska, the Polish writer, and György Lukács, the Hungarian philosopher. It included men such as Imre Nagy, who came to Moscow as prisoners of war in the first world war, and others who were prisoners in Soviet concentration camps during the purges of the 1930s. It included such men as Palmiro Togliatti, Communists who fled to Moscow when their countries fell to Fascism and dictatorship between the wars, and men who became Communists in Soviet prisoner-of-war camps after their capture on the Russian front in World War II. It even included the children of older Cominternists who had spent almost all their lives in the Soviet Union.

These Muscovites were Stalinists. All of them were sensitive to the peculiarities of Soviet political life and no longer worried about departures from purist revolutionary behavior, the absence of egalitarianism, and the presence of Beria's secret police. They understood the subtle language of *Pravda,* where a slight change of ideological emphasis might herald major political events and where a portrait of a Stalinist leader constituted a political document. Few of their contemporaries believed that these men and women could in any way be a threat to Stalin. They appeared to be his craven tools.

Yet it was precisely the sophistication and diversity of their Stalinism which made many of these Muscovites an obstacle to the further expansion of socialism through Soviet annexation of new nations. They were intelligent and could rationalize all the twists and turns of Stalin's political line and reconcile it with their own revolutionary ideals, and they were thus incapable of accepting the dictates of the leadership of the socialist fatherland simply because they represented Stalin's orders. When orders came, these people obeyed them scrupulously, on the understanding that in some esoteric fashion obedience was necessary for the furthering of socialism in their own country. One could say that they were craven for a reason.

That important Muscovites were versatile rationalizers was no secret in Moscow during the war. In 1944 Stalin himself told a visiting representative of the underground Yugoslav Communist Party, Milovan Djilas, that the dissolution of the Comintern had not taken place at his dictation but was the result of pulling and tugging between his regime and the Muscovite foreign Communists:

> The Westerners are so sly that they mentioned nothing about it to us. And we are so stubborn that had they mentioned it, we would not have dissolved it at all! The situation with the Comintern was becoming more and more abnormal. Here Vyacheslav Mikhailovich [Molotov] and I were racking our brains, while the Comintern was pulling in its own direction—and discord grew worse. It is easy to work with Dimitrov, but with the others it was harder. Most important of all there was something unnatural about the very existence of a general Communist forum at a time when the Communist parties should have been searching for a national language and fighting under the conditions prevailing in their own countries.[53]

Later, after the liberation of Europe, many of these Muscovites demonstrated to the world their subtle and profoundly rationalistic approach to the problems of constructing socialism. Dimitrov in Bulgaria and Gottwald in Czechoslovakia both proved to be master theorists who could explain the grim realities of postwar Eastern Europe in populist terms acceptable to their countrymen. Later, Imre Nagy and György Lukács in Hungary and Palmiro Togliatti in Italy became popular heroes because they clearly understood that socialism is not just a matter of the imposition of proletarian dictatorship by the Red Army but is something far more complex.

When Stalin let the Comintern dissolve itself in 1943, he deprived the Muscovites of even a name. He put some of them to work organizing ethnic regiments for the Red Army; he employed others at institutes in Moscow which were known only by numbers like "99."[54] From a Leninist point of view, this was the most degrading moment in the history of Bolshevism. Yet the Muscovite Communists kept on scheming and planning the paths which their countries would follow toward socialism. There in Moscow, under Stalin, they developed an elaborate tactical methodology which their parties could use even if the Red Army did usurp the leading role in revolutionary progress.[55] In this sense, they may be said to have kept alive in Stalin's world the idea of the independent national movements toward socialism and to have made impossible any Soviet project for furthering socialism by means of the Red Army alone.

The second factor which made annexationism impractical early in 1944 was the activist tactic which, ever since 22 June 1941, the Soviet Union had been urging on its sympathizers abroad.[56] During the Nazi-

Soviet period, Communists abroad had been told not to fight—indeed, they were told to collaborate with the Fascists in their countries until the annexationist moment approached. But by mid-1941 in some countries (China,[57] Poland,[58] and Yugoslavia[59]), some Communists had returned to activism. After 22 June, all of them did so. By 1944 Communists were playing a role in the underground resistance to Fascism in almost all the war-zone countries, and, as a result, a change occured within world Communism. A few parties remained in the weak, anemic condition to which almost all had been reduced by the bloodletting in Moscow in the 1930s: for example, at the end of the war, most of the Canadian CP members were still, more or less explicitly, paid agents of the Soviet diplomatic and secret police establishment.[60] But in the countries in the war zone, the underground Communist parties became more popular, organizationally stronger, and politically more influential than they had been before the war. This was particularly true in France, northern Italy, the Balkan lands Yugoslavia, Albania, and Greece, and, of course, in China, where the CP had long had a full-scale army of its own.

The directives which came to the European underground Communist forces from the Comintern beginning in 1941 warned against provocative behavior.[61] Indeed, they stressed the need for the broadest possible anti-Fascist front and passed silently over the whole question of future progress toward socialism. But here lay the difficulty. What Communist in the underground fighting for his life each day against a Fascist foe could be expected simply to forget about the socialist future—about revolution? Such a Communist might understand perfectly why Moscow radio was silent about revolution: he would know that Stalin had to worry about his Western Allies. But the more such a Communist sacrificed himself and his comrades to the common anti-Fascist struggle, the more he would be inclined to use his own and his party's opportunities to move toward socialist goals.[62]

Extraordinary diversity of view prevailed among the Communists in the Eurasian resistance movements during World War II. In Axis Hungary, for example, the underground Communists, who were without guidance from Moscow, believed (as did those in the United States) that the dissolution of the Comintern in 1943 meant the opening of some sort of new era in the history of socialism. They guessed that national Communist parties would no longer be needed and dissolved their organization.[63] In Western Europe, on the other hand,

45

especially in France, communications with Moscow were never interrupted, and the bulk of the underground Communists stayed in line. Insurrectionism became popular primarily among Communists in lower-level provincial organizations.[64] But in China, engaged in a war with Japan which the Soviet Union was not fighting, the Communists got firmly into the habit of making their own plans, and in the Balkan countries, where the Communists were much influenced by the mountain tribalism of their peasant recruits, insurrectionism was poorly concealed.[65]

Late in 1943 and early in 1944 this diversity—indeed, this rank disorder in the underground Communist parties—was coming rapidly to the surface. Even in February 1943, before the Comintern dissolution, Greek Communists had played an important part in a mutiny of Greek military units in the Middle East against the British-supported Royal Greek government-in-exile.[66] In September and October 1943, when Italy surrendered to the Allies, Greek Communists underground engaged in more or less open civil war with British-supported anti-Communist resistance forces. Coincidentally, French Communists on Corsica seized that island from the Italians and had to be suppressed by Allied troops.[67] And then, late in December 1943, on returning from the Teheran Conference, Stalin received news that Yugoslav resistance Communists at Jajce had publicly announced their deposition of the British-sponsored Yugoslav royal government-in-exile. Stalin's annoyance at this step is a matter of record.[68] These developments demonstrated to one and all that the Communist parties of the world were not prepared to wait for the Red Army to initiate the process of liberation. Annexationism, in this sense, had ceased to be a practical explanation of the development of socialism by the start of 1944.

The third and decisive factor which made the annexationist policy inoperable in 1944, however, was its incongruity with the revolutionary explosion which Communists now anticipated. During 1939 and 1940, when annexationism developed, world revolution had clearly not been brewing. Precisely for that reason, it seemed probable that further progress of nations toward socialism might take place only through the expansion of the Soviet frontiers. By 1944 Communists were prepared to believe that a world revolutionary moment was again imminent, and not just near the Soviet frontiers but in all the countries of the Eurasian war zones, and perhaps even beyond. It seemed improbable that in such a widespread crisis the Soviet state, through the Red Army, could or would initiate revolution everywhere. Early in 1944 no one knew how far the Red Army would actually be able to penetrate into Europe and eastern Asia at the end of the war, but the odds were already strong that it would not join the Allied armies in the liberation of Italy or precede them into France, so that, in Italy and France at least, moves toward socialism would have to be initiated by forces from within.

Annexationism did not die all at once. Even after Stalin had angrily rebuked the Yugoslav partisans for the Jajce declaration in the last days of 1943, he did not force the Czechoslovak Communists to enter the coalition government of President Beneš, who was then visiting Moscow;[69] in August and September 1944, Tannu Tuva, a nominally independent People's Republic on the Soviet-Mongolian frontier, "requested," and was granted, admission to the Soviet Union.[70] Nonetheless, annexationism was clearly on the way out in those last days of 1943 when Beneš was in Moscow, for it was then that the whole problem of the Communist role in postwar Europe was first openly discussed by Stalin with his state's allies, and the Czechoslovak Communists were the first to promise to enter a coalition government with the bourgeoisie after the war.

"New Type Government" Is Born

Examination of Soviet policy toward France helps to explain why "new type government" in Europe emerged first in that country, and why it did so precisely in April 1944. During 1943, after the Allied invasion of northern Africa, Moscow sought to influence France's future through extraordinarily aggressive diplomatic activity. For example, in the spring, when the Allies, after much bickering with each other and with various French political groups, finally allowed General De Gaulle's Free French leadership to move from London to Algiers, Moscow managed to move an ambassadorial representative there too.[71] This gentleman, A. G. Bogomolov, promptly made himself a focus of political activity by opening discussions with the French CP and indulging in a variety of intrigues. To the considerable annoyance of the Allies, he even developed a special relationship with De Gaulle. As a representative of the Soviet state, Bogomolov seemed prepared to direct the entire range of future French politics. The French Communist Party, despite its strength in the underground resistance within metropolitan France, stood almost modestly behind

47

Bogomolov and rigidly refused to collaborate with De Gaulle except on Bogomolov's rather stiff terms.

Early in 1944, however, it became obvious that Bogomolov's activities were ineffective. The planned American and British landings in northern France were approaching. It was to be anticipated that De Gaulle, backed by the Allied armies, would return to the motherland in their wake. Moscow heard in February 1944 that De Gaulle was scheming with the Americans to form an anti-Soviet postwar Western bloc.[72] These reports implied that if the Communists did not enter De Gaulle's government before he returned home, their influence over the future of France, and Moscow's, might not be great. There is evidence that Stalin took these warnings to heart.[73] Moreover, it was logical for him to think that if the Communists were not in the government by the time the liberation began, there would be nothing to inhibit a confrontation between Gaullists and insurrectionist Communists in the underground.

Events in Italy strongly suggest that this was Stalin's reasoning when he countenanced the French Communists' abandonment of their scruples and entry into the De Gaulle regime on 6 April.[74] Late in the summer of 1943, when Italy defected from the Axis, Moscow sought (as in France) to dominate matters through diplomatic activity.[75] Stalin requested that a special tripartite Allied military-political commission be set up to direct Italian politics. Then he dispatched no less a figure than Deputy Foreign Commissar A. Y. Vyshinsky to be his representative to the commission. Vyshinsky, like Bogomolov, indulged in an extraordinarily broad range of activities, among them negotiating behind the backs of the Western Powers with the turncoat Marshal Badoglio in Naples to establish a special relationship between Moscow and liberated Italy. Moscow even extended diplomatic recognition to Badoglio. Early in 1944, however, it became evident that, as in Algiers, such Soviet diplomatic maneuvers would not work. Badoglio proved unfaithful, the Allies limited Vyshinsky's contacts, and not only the Communists in the resistance but also the socialists and the leading bourgeois political parties found Moscow's chosen partner politically repulsive. Thereupon, late in March, Palmiro Togliatti, the exiled chief of the CPI, returned from Moscow. He threw all his energies into dragging the Italian political left into a coalition government under Badoglio with Communist participation. His efforts were supported by Vyshinsky at a hortatory press conference in Moscow on 16 April.[76] The coalition government formed on

22 April showed clearly that Stalin was worried about the Communist left.[77]

The character of the change which began in Soviet foreign policy at this time was most clear in Eastern Europe. During the first months of 1944, as the Red Army broke the siege of Leningrad, burst into Estonia and Poland, and in the south approached the Dniestr, Moscow was negotiating secretly with the German satellite government of Finland, demanding of it not unconditional surrender but a change of sides in the war, combined with territorial concessions.[78] Similar terms seem to have been available at this time to Rumania.[79] On 22 March, however, the Soviets announced that the Finns had rejected a settlement. On 2 April, Soviet Foreign Commissar Molotov issued a statement in honor of the Red Army's arrival at and passage over the Soviet-Rumanian frontier of 1940: "The Soviet government states that it is not pursuing the aim of acquiring any part of Rumanian territory, or of changing the social order of Rumania, and that the entry of Soviet troops into Rumania is dictated exclusively by military necessity and by the continuing resistance of enemy troops."[80] This statement was widely taken in non-Communist circles at the time as an indication that the Soviet Union was forswearing the cause of spreading socialism outside its borders. The real interest of the statement, however, lies in Molotov's flat contradiction of the claims he had made on behalf of the Red Army just two months earlier. Then he promised in strong terms that the Red Army would pursue a mission of liberation, which meant to Communists that socialism would expand through the agency of the Soviet state. Now, as Communists in the Soviet Union recognized,[81] Molotov was paving the way for a new official Soviet concept of liberation whereby forces other than the Red Army might take the initiative in introducing social change. Stalin himself confirmed this shift in a statement on 1 May 1944: "It is hardly to be expected that the present governments of the Axis satellite countries are capable of breaking with the Germans. One must suppose that the peoples of those countries will themselves have to take into their hands the cause of their emancipation from the German yoke."[82] Coincidentally, the Soviet political leadership was convening an assembly of Red Army commanders and "for the first time"— as one of them put it—discussing with them the "world historic" significance of the advance beyond the pre-1941 frontiers.[83]

These statements show that in April 1944, Stalin was willing to admit that annexationism was no longer useful as an explanation of how socialism would henceforth expand. It follows that "new type government"—the core of his postwar political stance—was for him not a conspiratorial tactic directed against his imperialist allies—at least not *just* such a tactic. At its inception, it was a device for protecting the strategic alliance with the unloved West against the Communists of the underground, who, he now admitted, would of necessity play an important role in the liberation process. This explanation is strengthened by the fact that on 31 March 1944 the danger of confrontation between foreign Communists and Stalin's allies became manifest once again in a fresh anti-British mutiny among the Greeks.[84]

3

The Great Deception

Stalin versus Tito

JOSIP BROZ TITO, Comintern bureaucrat turned guerrilla, returned to Moscow on 21 September 1944, for the first time since the war, eager to pluck the fruits of the Yugoslav Communists' wartime struggle and to establish socialism in his country forthwith. Stalin demurred. He thought it better to set up a coalition government and to trick the West by including not only Communists but also representatives of the exiled royal Yugoslav government from London. He even advised Tito to allow the king of Yugoslavia to return to the throne: there would be plenty of time later on to slip a knife into his back. Up to this point Stalin's behavior was consistent with his effort, earlier in the year, to protect the Grand Alliance by encouraging "new type government," but now he added something new. As Tito tells it: "Just then Molotov came back into the room after being called out for a minute. He had with him a report from some Western news agency that the British had landed in Yugoslavia. I exclaimed: 'That's impossible.' Stalin replied: 'What do you mean—impossible? It's a fact!' I explained. . . . Stalin then asked me directly: 'Tell me, Walter [Tito's Comintern name], what would you do if the British did invade Yugoslavia?' I told him we would offer determined resistance.''[1] With this information in hand, Stalin prepared a surprise for Tito. Within days, he was dropping hints to British (and later American) military men that the Western forces should head for the Ljublana Gap.[2]

This incident makes Stalin seem virtually anti-Communist and quite different from what he had been in the spring. He seems to have been provoking the very confrontation between insurrectionist Communists and the Western Allies which earlier he had sought to avoid. As we will see, the incident was not even unique: Stalin was unhelpful to other Communist parties as well late in 1944. This chapter will inquire, therefore, whether something between April and October 1944 could have changed Stalin's outlook and made him more resentful of revolutionaries abroad.

A New Balance of Power

The course of the war was one factor which could have changed Stalin's political outlook during 1944 and made him doubly distrustful of Communist insurrectionists abroad. In the West during May the Allies ended the winter-long stalemate which had held up their forces in Italy, and on 4 June they captured Rome. On 6 June they at last attacked Normandy. Despite massive German resistance, their beachhead was secure within two weeks. On 15 June the Americans launched a seaborne attack on the Japanese-held island of Saipan in the Mariannas and conquered it by early July. At the end of June the British began a land offensive in Burma. On 25 July American tanks broke the German lines near Saint-Lô, and by early August they were rapidly advancing into central France. On 14 August a landing was made on the Riviera. On 20 August Paris rose up against the Occupation, and by the 24th the city was in Allied hands. By mid-September, when Tito reached Moscow, the Allies had liberated most of France, were deep into Belgium and Lorraine, had entered Germany, and had launched an air attack north of the Rhine into Holland.

Militarily, the supremacy of the Western Powers had never seemed clearer than in the summer of 1944, and they were obviously using their military weight to affect the future of Eastern Europe. In

April the British suppressed the Communist-led revolt within the Greek forces in the Middle East.[3] In May they made overtures to Moscow about spheres of influence in Europe.[4] In mid-summer Churchill held discussions with Tito in Italy.[5] In July the Americans attempted to mediate the Polish problem; early in August, when the London-influenced Polish Underground Army precipitated a revolt against the Germans in Warsaw, the Western Powers requested Moscow to let them operate an airlift to the city.[6]

On 14 June, Stalin publicly acknowledged the power of the Allies:

> It is impossible not to recognize that the history of warfare knows no enterprise comparable in breadth of conception, grandiose scale, and masterly execution [to the Normandy landings]. As is well known, invincible Napoleon in his time failed ignominiously in his plan to force the Channel and occupy the British Isles. A hysterical Hitler . . . likewise dared not risk trying to carry out his threat to force the Channel. Only the British and Americans succeeded in realizing a plan to force the Channel. . . . History will record this event as an achievement of the highest order.[7]

Milovan Djilas, the first representative of the underground Yugoslav Communists to visit Moscow after the war, held political discussions with the *Vozhd* just prior to D-Day and the publication of this statement. He reports that Stalin then showed no lasting affection for the West. Indeed, he said to Djilas privately: "Perhaps you think that just because we are allies of the English . . . we have forgotten who they are and who Churchill is. They find nothing sweeter than to trick their allies."[8] From this, Djilas realized that Stalin's public emphasis on the power of the West was intended as a warning to foreign Communists to follow the Soviet example and to enter bourgeois coalition governments. Djilas indicated that "new type government" eventually took shape in Yugoslavia because of Stalin's warning, but, as we have seen, Tito was very reluctant and delayed the final negotiations into November. Perhaps, therefore, Stalin's provocation of Tito in October stemmed from heightened fear of the West; exasperation that a "peanut"[9] such as the Yugoslav leader should endanger the interests of the Soviet Union; and resignation to the probability that Tito would confront the "imperialists" no matter what Stalin did. "Best get it over with" may have been Stalin's thought.

There is a major flaw in this explanation, however. Not only the Allies but also the Russians were victorious during the summer of 1944. In April and May the Red Army liberated the Black Sea littoral,

Odessa, and the Crimea. In June it recaptured Vyborg and Karelia, then attacked in Belorussia. By late July it had completely cleared the enemy from Belorussia and had reached the Vistula in central Poland. In August the attack continued in the south, completing the liberation of the Ukraine, whereupon, on 24 and 25 August, the king of Rumania decided that his country should change sides in the war. By late September, most of the lower Danube was in Soviet hands, and the battle of Hungary had begun. In the north, on 3 and 4 September, Finland sued for peace and left the war. On 5 September a Soviet invasion of Bulgaria led to its collapse.

These military and political developments resolved a complex of problems that had hitherto dominated Soviet relations not just with the West but with the entire outside world. Since 1939, and especially since 1941, the Soviet frontier in Eastern Europe had been subject to negotiation. Now that frontier was solidly in Soviet hands; indeed, Moscow could now extend it even farther. The Soviet government moved with alacrity in the autumn of 1944 to remove all doubt about what had happened, and extracted from the Rumanians,[10] the Poles,[11] the Finns,[12] and the Czechs[13] recognition of the unification of the Soviet Ukraine, Belorussia, and Karelia. This solution to the frontier problem transformed Stalin's relation with the Western Powers from that of a client to that of an equal. The disparity between Western and Soviet power remained, but the disability represented by the alienation of soil claimed by the Soviet Union was gone.

At this time also, a most difficult aspect of the Polish question resolved itself. As everyone knew, the resistance within Poland was very strong and overwhelmingly accepted the authority of the exiled government in London, which had Western backing and refused to sanction Soviet territorial designs. Until August 1944 these resistance forces constituted a Western bulwark blocking whatever plans Moscow had for postwar Eastern Europe. On 21 July, as the Red Army advanced, the Russians allowed a Polish Committee of National Liberation to emerge behind the lines and settled it at Lublin; on 27 July they assigned this committee governmental powers in the liberated areas. But until 1 August the main problem, the underground army, remained wholly unresolved. Then light dawned. As Soviet forces approached Warsaw from the east, the underground army launched an uprising within the city in hopes of seizing the credit for its liberation.[14] At almost the same moment, S. Mikolajczyk, the prime minister of the London government, arrived in Moscow under heavy pressure from Roosevelt and Churchill to negotiate a settlement. At this point the Germans brought in reinforcements, and the Soviet troops, overextended and worn out, halted their advance. Stalin then personally sought to blackmail Mikołajczyk into accepting a coalition with the Lublin Committee—a coalition in which London would have only a 20 percent representation. Mikołajczyk refused.[15] By mid-August Stalin had labeled the uprising an "adventure" and a "provocation" which the Red Army could not support.[16] In the weeks that followed, the Germans pounded the Polish capital into submission, and the core of the underground army ceased to exist.

From Stalin's point of view, the situation was all the brighter because this happened virtually with Allied consent. In November 1943 at Teheran Roosevelt and Churchill had intimated their willingness to cooperate with Moscow in Poland. Although in August 1944 the Western Powers sought permission to start an airlift to Warsaw, they gave up the notion when Stalin blocked it.[17] In October, two weeks after Warsaw collapsed, Mikołajczyk returned to Moscow, this time with Churchill at his side, and Stalin had the pleasure of witnessing an angry attempt by the prime minister of England to browbeat the Pole into accepting Soviet demands.[18] When, on this same visit, Churchill once again raised the question of spheres of influence in Eastern Europe, yet claimed a dominant role for the West only in Greece, it must have been clear to Stalin that Moscow's interests in the Grand Alliance were not definable merely in terms of Soviet industrial weakness and Allied military might.[19] It was obvious that the Allies were, for some reason, weak in will.

Why, therefore, did Stalin think it desirable in October 1944 to provoke a confrontation between Tito and the Allies? Surely not just because, out of heightened fear of the Allies, he was exasperated over Tito's reluctance to accept "new type government." This problem seems all the more troublesome because outside Yugoslavia during the autumn of 1944, as the reasons for coddling the West became less pressing, Soviet advocacy of foreign Communist participation in coalition governments increased. Even in conquered Rumania, Bulgaria, and Finland, this was the tactic which the Red Army imposed.

In Rumania, of course, local conditions may explain why, in 1944, Moscow encouraged not a Communist seizure of power but CP acceptance of a decidedly minor role in a coalition government run by generals of the old regime.[20] It was, after all, the king and the old political parties who delivered their country into Soviet hands and legitimized Soviet territorial demands. Besides, the armistice agreement allowed for Red Army occupation of the country, the Communists were extremely weak and, by tradition, unpopular, and it probably seemed wiser not to press the issue of Communist progress toward power at the moment.

In Finland, however, such explanations do not apply.[21] There the Soviet Union had no reason to be grateful to the existing regime: Finland's surrender was inspired by sheer necessity, and the old government had a long record of anti-Soviet feeling. Further, the Communist Party was almost as weak and unpopular there as in Rumania. It needed help, yet, ostensibly out of respect for the Western Powers, Moscow did not insist, in the armistice agreement of 19 September, that the country be put under military occupation. The Soviet government did send an important political representative, A. A. Zhdanov, to Finland, and Zhdanov inaugurated a policy whereby Finland would be "educated for socialism." But in concrete matters of political power in 1944, Moscow was so careless of Communist Party interests in Finland that when the hour of decision came three and a half years later, Finland's Communist Party (alone among the East European parties) lost its bid for power.[22]

In Bulgaria, Dimitrov's country, Moscow was more aggressive in the early autumn of 1944.[23] Here the old regime, because of Slavophile tradition, had never declared war on the Soviet Union. Nevertheless, Moscow invaded Bulgaria, and a coalition government emerged. It was from the first dominated by Communists and, in the presence of the Red Army occupation, accepted a severe armistice agreement and instituted a singularly brutal purge of non-Communists throughout the public administration. Here, more than anywhere else in Eastern Europe, the Western Powers found proof over the next few months that the coalition government system was intended to exclude them.[24]

Yet even in Bulgaria one may question whether the policies of the Soviet government were identical with local Communist interests. It soon became evident that the Bulgarian coalition had been designed by underground Communists who had seized power before Soviet troops arrived in Sofia. The purge which soon took place was the work of the underground, not of Moscow, and Moscow soon let it be known that the Bulgarians were being decidedly too violent and anti-Allied to please Stalin.[25]

Other developments in this period suggest that Stalin was attempting to prevent Communist underground forces from openly seizing power anywhere. At the time of the insurrection in Paris in August, for example, some French Communist Resistance members felt that the Party should make a bid for power before the Americans arrived in the capital, and certainly the Communist position in the underground was strong enough to justify such an attempt.[26] Yet the Party leadership in Moscow stalled, called repeatedly for a broad anti-Fascist front, and may even have warned against "adventurism."[27] As a result, the moment passed, and De Gaulle smoothly assumed the leadership of the country. In October, when De Gaulle demanded that the Resistance forces surrender their arms, Moscow again cooperated. The Communists of the Resistance, for obvious reasons, wanted to stay armed, but the Party leader, Maurice Thorez, came home from Moscow as opportunely as Togliatti had, in the spring, and imposed a policy of disarmament.[28]

Meanwhile, an equally odd development occurred in Slovakia. There, as in France, the Communists were quite strong in the underground, for they could count not only on the pro-Allied disposition of the exiled Czechoslovak government in London but on the anti-Czech sentiments in the population, which Stalin had flattered in 1940 when he recognized Fascist Slovakia's independence. Yet early in August 1944, when these Communists sent an emissary to Moscow to prepare the ground for a nationalist uprising, they found Stalin cool to the enterprise.[29] Indeed, he seems to have invoked the wholly irrelevant example of what he called the "adventurism" of the anti-Communists in Warsaw.[30] As a result, the revolt in Slovakia broke out spontaneously, without Communist leadership, late in August. The Red Army did not spring to its aid, and it was all the Czechoslovak Communist leaders in Moscow could do to elicit Moscow's verbal approval and some tardy supplies. Initially successful, in October the Slovak revolt fell victim to the same sort of heavy-handed German repression that had destroyed Warsaw. In November Stalin's message to the underground Communists in Europe finally became explicit: when the Red Army approached Budapest, the Communists there received instructions from Moscow not to be "sectarian" by staging a revolt.[31]

People's Democracy

On 28 September 1944, while Tito was in Moscow, Georgi Dimitrov, the Bulgarian who had been secretary general of the Comintern, published an open letter to the Bulgarian CP Central Committee in Sofia. He wrote that in his country, which had just been liberated by the Red Army, the Communists had an obligation to join with other established political parties in governmental coalition in order to move toward a political form he dubbed "people's democracy."[32] This seems to be the first use of this famous tag in Communist public documents, and a study of how it became popular in the following months reveals another explanation of why Stalin seems to have been so unhelpful to foreign Communists.[33]

For three reasons, Dimitrov's people's democracy formula made sense when applied to Bulgaria.[34] First, the Communists there were still not strong enough to seize state power outright (though some of them were trying to do so). Second, an action by the Soviet state had actually initiated the process of liberation, and with classic simplicity. Third, because of the Red Army occupation, the Communists could afford to dally on the road toward socialism and join in a coalition with other political parties.[35] For similar reasons, Dimitrov's people's democracy thesis seemed attractive to Communists in most other East European countries.

In Yugoslavia, however, the formula did not make sense. There was a governing political front, the so-called AVNOJ (Anti-Fascist National Liberation Council of Yugoslavia), but in it no party, not even the Communist Party, which controlled it from behind the scenes, was distinct.[36] Further, the Red Army had not liberated Yugoslavia, although on 29 September Moscow did announce that the AVNOJ had granted it passage through Yugoslav territory,[37] and it participated in the liberation of Belgrade on 20 October. And though the Yugoslav Communists were as intent as the Bulgarians on "progress," they were vigorously advancing toward the Party goal of socialism rather than toward some ambivalent intermediate stage called "people's democracy." They did not need coalition and intermediate stages; they had already defeated their domestic foes. They were adopting a model of behavior that was honest, direct, pure, and native, and were not loath to boast about it to Communists from other lands or even to Russians.

Dimitrov's people's democracy thesis was thus tantamount to negation of the Yugoslav model of progress toward socialism, and the Yugoslavs could not ignore it. Only ten days earlier, a Yugoslav Communist delegation appeared in liberated Sofia, attended a Central Committee meeting of the Bulgarian CP, and, boasting of the Partisans' exploits against the Germans, extracted the consent of the Bulgarians to the retrocession of Serbian Macedonia. The Yugoslavs even demanded the cession of part of prewar Bulgaria.[38] Tito's subsequent visit to Moscow was designed, inter alia, to obtain Soviet sanction of such imperialist designs, and all through the autumn the Yugoslav and Bulgarian Communists were in intense negotiation (often in Moscow) about the possible founding of a Balkan federation. Inevitably, the question of socialism was also discussed. Since Dimitrov had spent the war in Moscow, had Stalin's ear, and possessed great prestige as the former leader of the Comintern, his formulation of the people's democracy slogan had the effect of impeding Yugoslav imperialism, and of doing so in Stalin's name. When Communists elsewhere in Eastern Europe—in Finland[39] and Hungary[40]—also began to talk about people's democracy, one could safely deduce that, using Dimitrov's theory, Stalin was trying to prevent foreign Communists from taking the exciting Yugoslav path.

One of the most memorable published accounts about Stalin at this time is told by Djilas:

> At one point [Stalin] got up, hitched up his pants as though he was about to wrestle or to box, and cried out almost in a transport, "The war shall soon be over. We shall recover in fifteen or twenty years, and then we'll have another go at it." There was something terrible in his words: a horrible war was still going on, yet there was something impressive, too, about his cognizance of the paths he had to take, the inevitability that faced the world in which he lived and the movement that he headed.[41]

This anecdote suggests the boldness, the military bravery, and the clarity of perspective with which Stalin faced the perils of the world in the period we are studying. Yet we cannot overlook the fact that in this same period he was striving, not like a lion but like a spider, to catch the admiring foreign Communists in a Marxist-Leninist web.

All through the winter of 1944–45, the Russians vigorously attempted to erase the memory of the greatest difference which distinguished the Yugoslav performance during the liberation process from the performances of the East European countries liberated by the Red Army.[42] Soviet military commanders in Belgrade insisted that it was the Red Army, not Communist-led Partisan resistance forces, which played the principal role in the liberation. They said that the Red Army had freed Belgrade. When the Yugoslav Party countered with complaints about Red Army excesses, they then created an atmosphere of crisis by alleging that the Red Army's honor was under attack. Stalin himself made invidious comparisons between the Partisans and the army in Dimitrov's Bulgaria, which the Russians had liberated. The Bulgarian army, according to Stalin, was "very good, drilled and disciplined."[43] The Partisans he called "unfit for serious front-line fighting."[44] The reason for all this is self-evident. The less important the internal liberation of Yugoslavia could be made to appear, the more Yugoslavia, with her special forms, would be isolated in an Eastern Europe increasingly populated by countries striving toward people's democracy.

In March 1945, when Tito visited Moscow a second time, the pressure on him became intense. As Djilas recalls it:

> At one point Tito brought out that there were new phenomena in socialism and that socialism was now being achieved in ways different from those of the past. This gave Stalin an opportunity to say: "Today socialism is possible even under the English Monarchy. Revolution is no longer necessary everywhere. Just recently a delegation of British Laborites was here, and we talked about this in particular. Yes, there is much that is new. Yes, socialism is possible even under an English king."[45]

What could have been more blunt than this effort to get Tito to admit community not with the Russian CP, which had attained socialism, but with the British Laborites, who, in insurrectionist Communist eyes, were among the least principled and militant parties on the face of the earth? "In the course of the conversation about this, I [Djilas] interjected that in Yugoslavia there existed in essence a Soviet type of government; the Communist Party held all the key positions, and there was no serious opposition party. But Stalin did not agree with this. 'No, your country is not Soviet—you have something in between De Gaulle's France and the Soviet Union.' "[46]

Stalin did not completely condemn the Yugoslav model in this period: indeed, in a public statement of 18 May 1945, he recommended it to the Polish Communists.[47] But he did repeatedly compare the Yugoslav achievement to the (far lesser) achievements of other East European Communists, and, behind the scenes, generated strong pressure to make Tito admit Yugoslavia's community not just with the embattled Poles but with "new type governments" in countries elsewhere in Europe, governments which were lurching, by clearly non-insurrectionary methods, toward conspicuously hazy democratic goals.

On 7 July 1945 Tito finally gave in. Perhaps impressed by the imminent Potsdam Conference of the victorious Allies, he announced that Yugoslavia was a people's democracy: "Naturally, we cannot agree with that type of democracy which exists in certain other countries, for we believe that the democracy which we have is a higher type of democracy, a democracy of the popular masses. . . . We reject the advice of those who want a democracy of the Western type in Yugoslavia. . . . Here there is a democracy of a people's type wherein those people have freedom who actually fought for freedom."[48] When Tito admitted this, Stalin was ready for him. Two days later the Muscovite leader of the Czechoslovak CP, Klement Gottwald, made a parallel pronouncement: "Today there is a people's democracy in Czechoslovakia, not a formal democracy. . . . We are experiencing in our republic our own peculiar development which cannot be squeezed into any pattern, and in the course of which we must seek our own paths, our own method, our own Czech and Slovak policy. . . . Our regime is the regime of a national democratic revolution, a regime of a peculiar, specifically Czechoslovak type."[49]

Hitherto, the non-violent Communists of Soviet-dominated Eastern Europe had depicted people's democracy as a goal to be attained in future,[50] but now Gottwald put it decisively in the present tense. Presumably when Tito announced the presence of people's democracy in Yugoslavia it was not his intention to retreat from his advanced position on the road to socialism. He recognized only two roads to socialism, his own and that of the Russians, and he saw them as equally valid. Gottwald, however, forced him to retreat: he not only applied the "people's democracy" tag to his own coalition government, which was among the most Western and least insurrectionary in all Eastern Europe at that time, but also described a community among any and all national democratic systems, irrespective of exact political forms. For Gottwald (just as for Stalin in March) every nation had a separate path to socialism. All were equal, all were different, and none had a claim to be more advanced and admirable than the others, except, of course, the original one.

One may see Stalin's hand behind this theoretical bludgeoning, just as one may deduce that Stalin was the inspiration for Dimitrov's original use of the term people's democracy.[51] And Stalin, we know, had other embarrassments in store for Tito. For example, after Tito accepted people's democracy, Soviet authorities began to ask questions which had practical implications for Yugoslavia. If Yugoslavia were a people's democracy, then should it not conform to generally accepted definitions of the term, which assumed separate political parties united in a coalition front? Should not Tito abandon the anonymity of his Communist Party, reorganize his AVNOJ, and accept the presence of a real political opposition? Such questions became a major feature of the discussion between the Soviet and Yugoslav parties which culminated in 1948. And if Tito's Yugoslavia *was* a people's democracy and thus not in a stage of socialism, should Tito not eschew crude leaps toward socialism which might disturb and alarm the imperialist West? This question became a second major theme in the postwar Yugoslav-Soviet debate.[52]

Through manipulation of the people's democracy formula in 1944 and 1945, Stalin was trying to throw the Yugoslav Partisan Communists off balance, just as he had tried earlier to disrupt the West European underground Communists by sending Maurice Thorez home to France. Further proof that in the latter part of 1944 and in 1945 Stalin was deeply interested in establishing control over the insurrectionists in the Communist movement seems unnecessary. This may explain why at times he seemed almost anti-Communist.

6 November 1944

On 6 November 1944, as in all the war years, Stalin delivered the oration commemorating the Bolshevik Revolution. His speech attracted little attention in the West because in form and literal statement it seemed no more than a repetition of his "statist" speech on the same occasion a year earlier. Now as then, in a first section Stalin told of the exploits of the Red Army; in a second section he focused on the home front; in the last part of the speech he spoke about foreign policy. Outwardly, the only changes from his 1943 speech were that he recorded more military victories, including the opening of the second front in France, and that in the final section he took up the now topical subject of a postwar United Nations Organization and endorsed it heartily. Western listeners were satisfied that this was no more than an elaboration of the pro-Alliance interview after D-Day.[53] Read in context and in detail, however, the speech seems as important as any Stalin delivered in the entire period from the start of the war until his death in 1953, and it affords us another sort of explanation, apart from a naked desire for control, for his apparent anti-Communism in 1944.

Stalin called attention to a major difference between this speech, and his speech a year earlier, with his opening words: he began by announcing (untruthfully) that the fourth year of the war was "radically different" from the first three because the Red Army had won "decisive" victories.[54] Then all through the speech, he used heavy-handed expressions redolent of the determinist ideology of Bolshevism: "It must be recognized," "there can be no doubt," "it cannot be considered an accident." He did not mention the Communist Party this year (as he had in 1943), but in his references to the army—within the wartime Soviet system, the alternative to the Party as a source of power—he spoke now with sharp deprecation.[55] At the end of the second section of the speech he declared: "The Hitlerites have suffered not only a military but also a moral and political defeat. The ideology of the equality of all races and nations which has taken firm root in our country . . . has won a complete victory over the Hitlerite ideology of bestial nationalism."[56] In this hour of approaching victory, when Communists everywhere were attuned to the prognosis of world revolution, these words in the context of Stalin's jargon were certainly suggestive. He said nothing specific about Marxism-Leninism, but subtly he made one think of it.

The important part of the speech was the section dealing with foreign policy, which began:

> The year just over . . . was a year of consolidation of the unity and coordinated operations of the three main powers against Hitler's Germany.
> There is talk of differences between the three powers on some questions of security. There are differences, of course. . . . Differences occur among people in one and the same political party. All the more must they occur among the representatives of different parties. . . . It is known that these differences were resolved ultimately in a spirit of complete agreement. . . . *This means that the foundation of the alliance between the USSR, Great Britain, and the USA lies not in chance and passing considerations but in vitally important and long-term interests.*[57]

This was strong language for a Marxist-Leninist who knew very well that the Grand Alliance was the union of a socialist state with two leading imperialist capitalist states precisely because of the "chance and passing" need to defeat their common enemy, Fascist Germany.

A Communist, on reading this passage, would be virtually forced to ask why Stalin, as high priest speaking *ex cathedra,* referred so pointedly to the unequal stages of political development within the Grand Alliance and then denied their importance. The denial, indeed, was particularly conspicuous because in his 6 November speeches of 1941 and 1942 he had gone to considerable lengths to hide the truth about his alliance with the imperialists. In 1941 he compared Hitler's Germany to the "medieval reaction" of tsarist Russia—something far worse than ordinary imperialism—in order to justify Soviet Russia's emerging alliance with Great Britain, which might otherwise have struck orthodox Leninists as reprehensible.[58] In 1942, to the same end, he put forth a pseudo-Marxist thesis whereby the Soviet Union and the Allies shared a "program of action" comparable in strength and dimension to the "ideology of racial hatred" characteristic of the "second camp."[59] Coincidentally, discussion of Lenin's theory of imperialism had become the principal victim of a great anti-sectarian campaign—an explicit ban on the use of the language of revolutionary Bolshevism.[60]

At the climax to his 1944 speech, Stalin gave an answer to the great questions he had raised. Turning to the problem of European security after the war, he mentioned the recent United Nations Conference at Dumbarton Oaks. Then, at length and most explicitly, he proposed perpetuating the Grand Alliance in the form of a United Nations Organization for the purpose of peacekeeping after the war:

> As history shows, aggressive nations being the attackers are usually more prepared for a new war than the peace-loving nations, who, not being interested in a new war, are usually late in preparing for it. . . . [This] is natural and comprehensible. If you like, *it is a law of history* which would be dangerous to ignore. . . .
>
> Apart from the complete disarmament of the aggressor nations, only one means exists [to ensure the suppression of aggression in the future]. A special organization must be founded . . . by the representatives of the peaceable nations. The controlling body of that organization must have the minimal armed forces essential for averting aggression. . . .
>
> Can one reckon upon the actions of such an international organization proving sufficiently effective? *They will be effective if the Great Powers, who have borne on their shoulders the main burden of the war against Hitlerite Germany, will continue to act in the future in a spirit of unanimity.*[61]

Stalin here invented a "law of history" in order to justify some extraordinary assertions. By his account, the Grand Alliance would not have to fall apart after the collapse of Germany but could and should survive because it could serve as a device for protecting the victory (already described as ideological) of the union of states and peoples forged during the war. Here were hints, first, that through continued Soviet participation in the Grand Alliance with the imperialists wars which, according to Lenin, were inherent in the structure of imperialism might be postponed, and second, that through Soviet manipulation of this same instrument, the sacred cause of progress, socialism, and, implicitly, revolution might be advanced. Stalin's speech adumbrated a vast strategic plan.

A word of warning: Communist public statements should be read first of all as implying a tactical direction rather than as literal expressions of direct intent: in this speech the tactical direction was very evident. During the preceding weeks at Dumbarton Oaks in Washington the conference held to design the postwar United Nations Organization had failed to reach agreement on many important points. As Stalin knew, the leaders of the West were extremely anxious to obtain Soviet participation in the United Nations but were hesitant to accept Soviet demands for a veto within it. By means of this speech Stalin appeased them and lured them on to further negotiations without, of course, any direct and permanent commitment of his country.[62] In fact, he was being about as truthful about his direct intention of realizing the ideological goals of Marxism-Leninism as Franklin Roosevelt was when he composed the Atlantic Charter—Stalin intended not to limit future policy but to move men. It is vitally important to make this distinction because it is a key to what happened later. Because he did not intend to pursue ideological goals in detail, he exposed himself, through his hints about them, to pressure from his movement's followers to explain why not.

A second warning: in analyzing this speech the reader should be aware that Stalin was swayed not only by his recognition of new opportunities abroad but also by domestic policy considerations. In January 1944, as will appear in later chapters, he had initiated the revival of the Soviet Communist Party, the focal political phenomenon studied in this book. The great Soviet foreign policy debate of that month coincided closely enough with this change in domestic policy to suggest a connection between the two. In September and October 1944, along with the appearance of the new opportunities abroad, there were major domestic policy changes which advanced the revival of the Party and heralded the postwar decline of the Soviet

Army. Stalin's deprecatory remarks about the military in his speech clearly suggest his approval of those changes, as does his renewed use of Marxist jargon.

One may, indeed, go farther in pointing out the domestic political inspiration of this oration, which was outwardly concerned mainly with foreign policy. In the summer of 1944, Andrei A. Zhdanov, who was to figure as the primary spokesman for the Party revival in 1946 and 1947, left his wartime post at Leningrad.[63] He was known at the time for his public advocacy of the Nazi Soviet Pact of 1939.[64] As we will see later, the theoretical attitudes he expressed in foreign policy statements of 1946 and 1947 were not dissimilar to those found in Stalin's speech. Zhdanov returned to the limelight in October 1944 as the architect of the post-surrender political situation in Finland. It is possible that Zhdanov started his postwar domestic political career in the autumn of 1944 by whetting Stalin's enthusiasm for Communist foreign policy explanations, and that Stalin's speech reflects, accordingly, his domestic as well as his foreign policies.

A third warning: Stalin spoke in subtle and guarded terms. Nonetheless, he was evidently hinting in this speech at a coming end of the anti-sectarian campaign which during the war had inhibited open Marxist-Leninist talk within the Communist movement. He encouraged Communists the world over to look at things in a more explicitly Marxist perspective. He encouraged a more direct communion between the followers and the source of authority within the movement. From the point of view of his control, this was dangerous. It meant that the movement could take its directives once again, as in the pre-Stalinist past, not from him but from Leninist ideological imperatives. It was predictable, given the disordered condition of the movement in 1944, that the result was bound to be at the least confusion. As a prominent Hungarian ex-Communist, György Heltai, described it: "When Stalin said something Communist, we rejoiced and obeyed him. When he said something nice about the Allies, we presumed he was tricking them; we tricked them too, and we became even more revolutionary."[65] Stalin's return to jargon opened the way also to questioning of his role within the Communist movement—to measurement of his record against the yardstick of Marxist ideals and to the consequent attack upon his ideological purity that took place in Yugoslavia and in China.[66] Comparable difficulties, as we shall see, arose even at home as a result of this speech.

Stalin, as is well known, was altogether unsentimental. His behavior during the Warsaw uprising shows that in 1944 he was still the tyrant whose stubbornness and iron will ten years before had caused the death of millions of Soviet peasants. Consequently, it is extremely difficult to explain why Stalin should have exposed himself to these predictable dangers save in terms of his enthusiasm. The speech exultantly told of the opportunities the Soviet Union and the Communist movement faced in the world. Stalin's whole emphasis was on the glorious prospect that in the exciting, tumultous moments of liberation and victory the world's first socialist state and its following might break away from the past and create a peaceful, fresh, and bright new world. Was not this adequate ground for enthusiasm? Khrushchev, who met him at about this time, even says he was "in the highest spirits, . . . strutting around like a peacock with his tail spread."[67] Here is another reason for not taking the speech too literally as a precise statement of Stalin's intentions.

With this said, it remains evident that Stalin's speech evinced awareness of the emerging configuration of Soviet power in postwar Eurasia and of the remarkable pliability of the great imperialist powers in the West. It is fact also that in the aftermath of the speech many foreign Communists started talking about Stalin's "great strategic plans" for the postwar world—plans which apparently called for long-term concerted action with the Soviet state by Communist parties operating within coalition governments abroad, manipulating the Western Powers within the framework of a United Nations Organization dominated by the "Big Three."[68] Stalin's speech fell decidedly short of the "blueprint plan" which Western cold warriors and a recent major Soviet history have attributed to him (and to his Communist Party).[69] But the sum of his attitudes in the speech may well explain his seeming treachery toward and lack of support for foreign Communist insurrection then: from his point of view, there may have been no place for foreign revolutionaries who, with their vulgar, old-fashioned notions of insurrection, were eager to upset his applecart.

Such an interpretation is supported by events. In October 1944 British troops landed in Greece in the wake of a German evacuation and brought with them a coalition government to which the Communists of the resistance had made a commitment.[70] The coalition broke down within a month, when its bourgeois majority insisted that the resistance forces surrender their arms, as they had in France. On 3 December the Communists confronted the British, launching a civil war. Who started the conflict is still in doubt, but it seems clear that the Communists did nothing to avoid it and acted on their own initiative after receiving direct advice from Tito, but not from Moscow. When the conflict erupted, Stalin showed his disapproval. He did not protest the British suppression of the revolt, and the leading Soviet political journals likewise failed to speak out.[71] In subsequent months, the Western Powers received the impression that Soviet tolerance of the suppression of the Greek civil war was the quid pro quo for Allied tolerance of Soviet domination in Central Europe.

Coincidentally, early in December Stalin revealed the sort of Communist tactic of which he approved. Hitler's "last ally in Europe," Hungary, was just then suffering national catastrophe. The Germans had occupied the country, and the old regime had failed miserably in its attempt to get Hungary out of the war. Ferenc Szálasi, a demented Fascist, headed the government, and the Germans and Russians were about to start a month-long artillery battle inside Budapest. There was no good reason for the Communists to pamper the remnants of old Hungary, but in conversations in Moscow about the composition of a liberated government, Stalin intervened and personally recommended great caution. (This record appears in the Epilogue to this book.) Consequently, on Christmas day the formation of a coalition government was announced in Moscow, which was most picturesque. It contained only three Communists; along with them were three generals of the old regime, one count, and, in the ministry charged with the police, a populist writer. So that the cabinet might appear more democratic, one of the generals and one of the Communists dubbed themselves Social Democrats.[72] In Hungary, as in Greece in December 1944, Stalin sacrificed the immediate interest of Communists in seizing power in order to pursue a higher revolutionary scheme.

Stalin's Foreign Policies Assessed

In this and the previous chapter we have seen Stalin begin to move away from statism toward a more revolutionary foreign policy—the beginning of the paradox to be examined in this book—and we have seen that he took those steps not just, as outsiders often suppose, because of revolutionary hatred of the West but, above all, because of fear of revolutionary insurrection in the liberated lands of Eurasia and a desire to preserve the wartime Grand Alliance and to convert it into an instrument of peace. Was Stalin irrational and paranoid in so doing? Was his speech of November 1944, with its great strategic vision, utterly out of touch with reality? These are questions which must be resolved because we know that there were actually very few insurrectionist Communists for Stalin to fear in the world in 1944, and that the Western Allies were actually far stronger than Stalin suggested in November 1944.

Was Stalin irrational in his dread of insurrection in 1944? Clearly not, unless one labels as irrational the entire Soviet world view and that of the movement which he headed. One must remember that a generation of Marxists had been looking forward to a new outbreak of revolution in the wake of the second great imperialist war. The end of that war was now approaching. The crises of liberation in Europe and Asia were at hand. Anyone who was following Greek, French, Italian, or Yugoslav affairs could have seen that some Communists in the resistance were eager to seize the moment for revolutionary insurrection, against the interests of the Allies. In addition, Stalin was aware of the constant push and pull between his state and the foreign Communist parties. Further, he was in a position of responsibility: he had to defend the security of the world's first socialist state. Under such circumstances, he would have been irrational had he ignored the signs of conflict between his movement's followers and his state's allies— had he not attempted to inhibit, indeed, to squash, the budding insurrection of the foreign Communist parties.

One may go farther in stressing the rationality of Stalin's move to the left in foreign policy during 1944. In many ways he was correct, even from a proper revolutionary point of view, to insist within the movement in 1944 that insurrectionism was anachronistic and that entirely new understandings of revolution had to be developed to fit the new international political situation. Unlike World War I, this was was not just an imperialist war—in other words, just a war between nationalistic superpowers without implications for the ideology of progress. The peculiarity of this war was that the Axis superpowers went so far out on the limb of ideological nationalism that all the other superpowers were forced to join in an ideological program not just to oppose Fascism but also to establish democratic freedoms on a worldwide scale. This was an unprecedented development. Since 1789 Europeans had been talking about the virtues of world revolution, but not once before 1944 had there been a chance of realizing such a revolution because not once had the powerful states of the Western world—not to speak of the democratic political movements—come near agreement on such a goal. Now, as Stalin seemed to recognize, there was such an agreement. The head of the Republican Party in the United States had written a programmatic book entitled *One World.* The president of the United States had told Stalin he thought well of having a general transformation of India according to the Soviet revolutionary model.[73] From the point of view of socialism, it would have been most injudicious at such a time to waste these opportunities.

If one wished for the greatest possible extension of Communist power after the war and its most effective consolidation, the logical policy for the movement in 1944 was not to grab immediately and indiscriminantly for power but to hold back, in countries where it was readily available, to see what could be done by parliamentary means in countries beyond the reach of the Red Army, and above all to educate—to prepare the societies of the war-torn Continent for the new social order which the Communists hoped to build.

Stalin was remarkably perspicacious when he told Djilas in June 1944 that it was somehow "unnatural" to have a Comintern forum in existence at a time when "Communist parties should . . . be searching for a national language and fighting under the conditions prevailing in their own countries."[74] The most admirable aspect of Stalin's policies within Communism was his encouragement of separate national paths to socialism in all countries. Objectively, it was thanks to this Stalinist policy of "separate roadism" (of which more in later chapters) that the socialist world of today owes its shape and expanse. If the Communist parties of Europe and Asia had turned directly to insurrectionism and bolshevization in 1944 and 1945, not only would the French, Italian, Finn, and Greek parties have failed but perhaps many of the Central European and East Asian movements as well.

Though it was broadly revolutionary and rational, however, Stalin's new leftist foreign policy of 1944 had recognizable and very serious flaws. He himself suggested one of them in 1952, in his *Economic Problems of Socialism in the USSR,* when he raised the question of whether wars are still inevitable. As in 1944, he said that they *were* still inevitable but could be postponed if an international peace movement were effectively organized. But he then went on: "It is possible . . . that in one place or another the struggle for peace can turn into a struggle for socialism; but that would no longer be the same thing as the present struggle for peace, but a struggle for the overthrow of capitalism."[75] These words recall that in 1944 Stalin himself did not keep the struggle for peace separate from the struggle for the overthrow of capitalism but deliberately and systematically mixed the two. In order to protect the peace, he induced his movement's followers to pursue a cleverer sort of revolution.

Had Stalin been honest, this first flaw in his policy—this mixing of the struggle for peace with the struggle for the overthrow of capitalism—might be chalked up to the necessities of the moment: one might say that Stalin had to mix the two struggles because the Soviet socialist state was central to both. But Stalin was not honest, and this was the second and fatal flaw in his policy. Even in 1944, when he was apparently filled with enthusiasm for the future, he let no one know what he was doing and played tricks. He manipulated the Allies; he deceived the foreign Communists; he even tricked his own colleagues within the Kremlin, as we will shortly see. So much deceit was bound to lead to tangles. In addition, one must recall that Stalin's style was rough: he had a tendency to dictate, to oversimplify issues, and to be undeviating beyond reason. It was not necessary, even in the name of a far-sighted and clearly conceived foreign policy, to wrap so many matters so tightly together as he did in his speech of 6 November 1944. Finally, one should recall that his political instruments were crude: in 1944 he commanded no smoothly oiled, modern, peacetime, technocratic state machine but a Red Army "replete with rapists" (as the East Europeans might say) and foreign Communist parties filled with peasant revolutionaries.

In sum, Stalin's foreign policy in 1944 did not take into account the presence of the man himself or of his tools. For that policy to have been truly effective, Stalin and all he stood for would have had to fade away. It was unreasonable to anticipate that he would do that. Consequently, in assessing the policy, one may judge that it was unrealistic. One may judge that it would have been better if he had showed the face his enemies knew him to possess; if he had played fewer tricks and come out openly as a force of order in the postwar world; if, instead of pretending still to be a revolutionary, he had pursued forthrightly and without cowardice a more imperial path.

II

The Second Battle: Against Commanders and Managers

4

Soviet Domestic
Political Trends

Stalin's Toasts

WHEN STALIN, STANDING among
the commanders of the Red Army at a banquet in May 1945, toasted
the Russian people, he was preparing a fraud. He praised the Russians as the leading nation and leading force within the USSR. With
seeming affection he called them "clear in intellect, steadfast in character, and patient,"[1] thus belying the baleful spirit of autocracy he
had long stood for and hinting a promise of a new life. Then nine
months later, when the excitement of the victory had died down,
Stalin announced that the little people, the Russian people, would
gain no respite, but for reasons of state would have to toil on harder
than ever, not just for one five-year period but for two and maybe
three such periods, before a time of rest would come.[2]

Stalin's toast was more than a trick on the common people, however: it was also the key to a peculiar drama within the Soviet regime.

As mentioned earlier, there are good reasons for believing that Stalin's power over his elites was lessened during the war. He still possessed immense authority, but his actual control was probably a good deal less than before 1941. In his toast he made striking references to the elites. In his view, for example, it was a major virtue of the Russian people that in 1941 and 1942, despite the mistakes of the government, which had led to a desperate situation, and despite the abandonment by the army of city after city, they had not lost faith. They had not angrily expelled their government, he said, and their faith (not the skill of the commanders) had been the decisive factor in the victory over Fascism. A month later, at another military banquet, Stalin went further and toasted the "common people, those who have little rank and unenviable title, . . . the cogs in the great machine of state without whom, to be brutally frank, all of us marshals and front and army commanders are not worth a cent."[3] With these toasts Stalin deprecated the accomplishments of his military and bureaucratic commanders, pointedly distanced himself from them, and prepared the way for systematic campaigns during the following months to restore his control over them.

Stalin's campaigns against the wartime commanders and bosses were not all equally successful, but together they constitute the substance of Soviet politics at the end of the war and provide an essential background for understanding the Bolshevik Party's paradoxical revival, which is the actual subject of this book.

Stalin and the Armed Forces

Almost from the moment of the Red Army's creation, in the first winter of the Russian Revolution, Soviet politicians regarded it with suspicion.[4] Some saw it as a vehicle of counter-revolution—an instrument through which remnants of the old tsarist regime might infiltrate and recover power. Others saw it more as a weapon through which one of their own number might, Napoleon-like, usurp political power and negate the Revolution. Suspicion of Trotsky's involvement with the army contributed to his fall, and even after Stalin grabbed power from other Bolsheviks and was accused of "Napoleonism" by the entire spectrum of the defeated Russian Marxist movement, the Kremlin continued to distrust the Army as an institution. Under Stalin, a Party organ functioned as the Main Political Directorate of the Red Army [GPUKA], a unique case of open usurpation by a Party

76

organization of state administrative functions. Stalin's regime also planted political commissars beside military commanders at many levels, and for a time in the late twenties the regime ordained that command decisions should be collegial, shared by political and military officers. In the middle 1930s Stalin did allow a professional army to re-emerge, reflecting Soviet concern over the growing political disorders in Europe and the Far East. By 1937 the reintroduction of fixed ranks, emphasis on discipline, professional emoluments, and regular recruiting had restored a degree of respect to the Army it had not known since the Revolution. But in June of that year, reportedly[5] because of false documents planted by the Gestapo, the secret police attacked the central Soviet military command. In August 1938 this purge struck the Far Eastern command at the very time when it was actively defending Soviet territory against Japanese incursions. Eighteen months of purge virtually destroyed the Soviet officer corps at the top, seriously depleted it at lower levels, and deluged it with police and Party controls.[6]

As noted in an earlier chapter, the European war forced the Soviet political leadership to relent in its attitude toward the Army. In 1939 universal military service was instituted, allowing the military to play a sharply increased role in Soviet civilian life. Then the winter war with Finland showed the dangers of dispensing with professionalism. In 1940, therefore, the regime deposed the political commissars and re-established unity of command, introduced the titles of general and admiral, reinforced discipline more sharply than at any time since 1917, and gave precedence to combat training over political indoctrination. Then, after the German attack of June 1941, the Army in effect swallowed the regime's political arm, as Party members in huge numbers all over the country became the Army's first recruits—and first casualties.[7]

Convulsively, in the opening days of the war, the regime restored the political commissars but at the same time placed the entire Soviet system under the State Defense Committee (GOKO), which operated as a clearinghouse for provisioning the army.[8] In October 1942 the political commanders were again removed. In May 1943 the deputy commanders for political affairs followed them, with the result that the Party staff in the military was cut in half.[9] At the same time, because of the huge influx of battlefield recruits to the Party, Party organizations were set up for the first time at company level. But six months later, in November 1943, Party supervision of cadre affairs in the Army was officially limited.[10] Meanwhile, in April 1943 Soviet military intelligence had been detached from the secret police and incorporated into the defense structure.[11]

As a result of these and many other measures, the Soviet military, as mentioned earlier, came to occupy a highly visible and uniquely independent position in the political system by the end of the war. Moreover, there is undisputed evidence that the leaders of the Red Army developed an arrogance and self-consciousness which amounted to *esprit de corps*. It was no secret that the regime had abolished the political commanders because of the professional military officers' resentment of them.[12] In Berlin in 1945, Soviet officers freely told German Communists how much they resented even the non-Party, civilian ministerial teams which had been sent into the military's bailiwick for the purpose of looting Germany's industrial wealth.[13] At the end of the war Soviet marshals jubilantly paraded through Moscow, arrogantly cast the banners of the fallen enemy at the base of the Kremlin walls, allowed their wives to display the jewels and furs they had brought home from Europe,[14] and boasted of the superiority of Russian military science. Generals such as G. K. Zhukov and I. S. Konev spoke openly with foreigners, even, in the case of Zhukov, held conferences with the foreign press, and allowed it to be known that they did not consider Stalin, for all his genius, to be the Soviet Union's greatest expert on military affairs.[15]

Stalin, from the beginning to the end of the war, displayed a peculiar dread of armies. It was characteristic that in 1941 he tried to treat the German attack as a provocation staged by certain German generals who allegedly had some sort of interest in a war.[16] One month later, he had the astounding notion of urging Churchill to open a second front so as to please the British army.[17] In May 1945 he told Harry Hopkins of his abiding fear of Bonapartism in armies.[18] Meanwhile, early in the war, he took steps to turn himself into a military genius.[19] He assumed the office of chief of the Supreme Headquarters staff and of defense commissar.[20] He took steps to shift responsibility for the initial disasters from his own shoulders to those of the military, and had certain officers shot.[21] Early in the war he sometimes deferred to technicians such as Zhukov,[22] but by late 1941 he had laid down what he called the "permanently operating factors" in modern warfare.[23] By the end of the Stalingrad campaign he seemed in fact much more conversant in military matters than he had been in 1941. In 1943 he became marshal of the Soviet Union. By the final campaigns before Berlin, in the spring of 1945, he had mastered military affairs sufficiently to win the respect of his commanders and—perhaps more important—to set them against one another.[24] In June 1945 he allowed himself to be named Generalissimo. In August the Soviet Party, just then reviving, eulogized M. I. Kutuzov, the tsarist general who allegedly lured Napoleon deep into Russia in order to defeat him.[25] This, the Party spokesmen asserted, was the highest achievement of pre-revolutionary Russian military science, and they noted that Stalin had presided with genius over a similar retreat in 1941.

Many of the measures which affected the fate of the Soviet armed services in 1945, after the victories in Europe and the quick war against Japan, would have been taken under any political regime. On 4 September, for example, the Supreme Soviet abolished the GOKO and restored civil jurisdiction throughout most of the country.[26] Not to have taken these measures, which ended the wartime political hegemony of the army, would have been extraordinary: it would have meant that some sort of military dictatorship was being established. In June the government had announced demobilization plans, and between late 1945 and 1947 the Soviet forces were reduced from about twelve million to somewhat under three million.[27] In March 1946 there was a general reorganization of the high command; at the same time the various service commissariats were reconstituted as peacetime ministries.[28] In every country after the war, similar measures took place. No country wanted to stay on a war footing—all wanted to prepare for peace and reconstruction.

In the Soviet Union, however, these normal peacetime measures were turned by Stalin to a political use. As early as October 1944, the CPSU(b) Central Committee, in one of the earliest decrees of the Party revival, stopped granting Party membership as a reward for military accomplishment and launched a campaign for indoctrination of Party members already in the army.[29] A recent Soviet historian calls this "the turning point" in the postwar relations between Party and army.[30] All through 1945 the Party directed propaganda at the army and discussed the need for Party ideology in military circles.[31] As the army demobilized in 1946, the Party stepped in. On 22 August 1946 the Central Committee ordered that Party secretaries in the army be independent of the military command system. Henceforth, Party secretaries were to be elected, not appointed.[32] As a result, within little more than a year a system of political commanders had been reintroduced. Discipline and the military chain of command were not

79

decisively interrupted, as they had been during the onslaught of 1937, but political instruction at all ranks was enormously stepped up. By 1948 an entirely new set of political schools had been introduced for the training of officers. At the end of 1948 "there were in the armed services 2,640 polit-schools, 4,250 circles for studying the biography of V. I. Lenin, 6,200 circles for the study of the Party's history, 690 Party active schools on the divisional level, and 142 evening universities for studying Marxism-Leninism. All in all 270,170 Communists of the army and the fleet were enrolled in these."[33] There is universal agreement among those who have studied the matter that by such means the army's wartime institutional independence from political controls was effectively eliminated.[34]

Especially on the high command level, Stalin acted in this period as if the army were his enemy. The story begins with the sudden rise of a political general, N. A. Bulganin, who began his career as a Chekist in the young Red Army during the Russian Civil War.[35] During the 1930s Bulganin made a name for himself as an economic administrator in the city of Moscow and the Russian Republic. In 1941 he was chairman of the USSR State Bank, but after the outbreak of hostilities he returned to the army as a political commissar at the Military Council for the Western front. Subsequently, he filled the same function at the headquarters of the first Belorussian front. Late in July 1944 he was appointed chief Soviet political representative to the Polish Committee of National Liberation at Lublin, an office he held all through the siege of Warsaw. Evidently he served well, for early in November, just after Stalin's speech, he was made a general; on 21 November he became Stalin's deputy as commissar for defense; the following day he replaced Marshal Voroshilov as chief representative of the armed services in the GOKO. Bulganin did not assume the leadership of the key Main Political Directorate of the Red Army: upon the death of A. S. Shcherbakov in May 1945, this was transferred to I. V. Shikin, a Party revivalist functionary.[36] But Bulganin was Stalin's main factotum in the Army from 1944 until the purge of the Party revivalists in March 1949. In March 1947 he even succeeded Stalin as minister of defense.

The promotion of Bulganin was an insult to the professional general staff.[37] His primary institutional affiliation was symptomized in March 1946 and later, in January 1948, by his admission to the Politburo, first as a candidate and then as a full member. He was a watchdog, pure and simple, and through him Stalin found it possible to displace the more distinguished combat generals after the war. A well-known example is the case of Marshal Zhukov, who was named chief of the Allied Control Commission in Berlin in 1945.[38] Zhukov disappeared from that position suddenly in June 1946. He was temporarily commandant of the Odessa Military District, but he lost his seat in the Party Central Committee, dropped from notice in the Soviet press, and in 1948 was relegated to the obscure Urals Military District. Regime spokesmen now unanimously attributed to Stalin the contribution Zhukov had made to saving the country during the battle of Moscow in 1941 and during the Berlin campaign in 1945.

Zhukov was not alone in this eclipse. Some Soviet generals ended up in prison, and from 1945 until Stalin's death promotions at the higher levels in the armed forces virtually ceased.[39] The atmosphere Stalin and Bulganin cultivated in the army officer corps in these years was symptomized by the announcement on 2 August 1946 that General A. A. Vlasov, the hero of the battle of Moscow, who was captured by the Germans in 1942 and collaborated with them, had not been shot, as befitted his rank, but hanged.

Was Stalin's attack on the generals necessary? The worst criticism made by a recent Party historian regarding the military authorities at the end of the war is that they displayed a certain snobbery toward Party workers.[40] Apparently, in a large number of cases the military chain of command, which until 1946 still controlled cadre selection in the services, neglected to replace transferred Party workers with their deputies—that is, with other Party workers. Was this so great a sin? Furthermore, in 1945 and 1946, three-quarters of all commanders in the army held ranks appropriate to the posts they actually filled, but only 7.5 percent of the political functionaries in the army had appropriate ranks. Moreover, in the first six months of 1946, before the Party offensive in the Army was launched, not a single such *politrabotnik* ("political worker") was promoted to the rank of major or lieutenant colonel, and no *politrabotnik* was made a full colonel from the end of the war until after the middle of 1946. To an outsider, this list of charges suggests at most that professional military commanders may have looked down on Party workers. It also suggests, by analogy, that Stalin's offensive against the generals after the war was inspired above all by ingrained distrust or, as Khrushchev tells us, by his obsession with the idea that no-one but himself should have credit for leading his country.[41]

On the other hand, one should not forget that Stalin and the

Soviet Army coexisted in a political system of the type which has been called "totalitarian." In such a system, enormous, bureaucratized central institutions emerge, drastically curtailing the independent activities of individuals without enlarging the society's ideological superstructure correspondingly. In fact, in the original totalitarian systems of the 1920s and 1930s, and particularly in Soviet Russia, bureaucratization was accomplished by a sharp reduction in the complexity of the ideological superstructure. Some observers feel that, as a result of this ideological dysarticulation, totalitarian systems are characterized by problems of control over, and conflict among, the central bureaucracies. And if this is so, it may mean that the Soviet Army by its very existence constituted a threat of sorts to Stalin's power, and that its wartime prominence, *esprit de corps,* and independence represented so clear an alternative to his own authority that he had to suppress it.[42]

Regardless of one's interpretation, however, it seems clear that Stalin did attack the army, and this is what is relevant here. He evidently began his attack in the latter half of 1944, coincident with the emergence of the new foreign policy described in the preceding chapters. The victory toasts of 1945 told openly where he was headed. In 1946 and 1947 he used the opportunities afforded by the transition to peace to wage a vast offensive against the generals as individuals and the army as an institution. His effort at re-establishing civilian hegemony within the system was a principal feature of the entire late Stalinist era, and it succeeded. The Army swallowed his bitter pills.

Stalin and the Police

In so far as Stalin played Napoleon in the revolutionary upheaval in Russia, he did so through adulation not of the army, as happened in France, but of another type of disciplined and uniformed corps, the secret police. It was not he, of course, who established the Soviet secret police.[43] Lenin and the Bolsheviks did that late in 1917, in a country whose former regime was characterized by an extraordinarily powerful secret police. It seems that the Soviet secret police was not exclusively under Stalin's control until the Party's March plenum of 1937 opened the gates to the *Yezhovshchina.*[44] Until then, under Dzherzhinskii, Menzhinskii, and Yagoda, a certain idealism, whereby the secret police was seen as an especially pure instrument of the highest Party collective, apparently remained. But from the 1920s on, Stalin, as general secretary of the Party, was able to use the secret police against his Bolshevik foes. After March 1937, his autocracy rested on direct control over the police. Characteristically, he needed no Central Committee approval when he decided to stop the purges and, by fiat, replaced N. I. Yezhov with L. P. Beria late in 1938.

Under Beria in the last years before the war the police ceased to terrorize the population on the same scale as it had under Yezhov, but it now reached its apex of power as a state within a state. It included not just a small army of armed and uniformed men located in strategic positions all over the country but also an extraordinarily widespread secret political police with its host of spies, a military police service with branches in every military unit, a counterintelligence service directed against foreign spies, and an apparatus for espionage abroad. Correspondingly, in the economic area there was not only an administration for supervising the entire economy and for enforcing the laws against speculation but also a separate transport police force to guard the railroads and the notorious GULAG (Concentration Camp Administration), with its vast army of forced laborers[45] and numerous economic enterprises. The most extensive statistical documentation of this economic empire which we possess, the detailed state plan of 1941, indicates that the police supervised at least 3.5 million laborers; received approximately 18 percent of the civilian budget; and were responsible for 40 percent of all chrome ore mining, 3 percent of all coal mining, 2.7 percent of all oil production, 12 percent of all timber production, 4 percent of all fish production, and 1.3 percent of all cement production in the USSR.[46] This vast empire was thus far greater in importance than many of the economic commissariats, and between 1938 and 1941 Beria instituted reforms designed to provide it with *esprit de corps* and systematic training.

Even before Beria took power, moreover, the police empire had a certain territorial aspect: the Soviet frontier guards were under the command of the NKVD (the Commissariat of the Interior), and in the north of both European Russia and Siberia the GULAG administered vast regions. In the Komi *oblast* in 1941, for example, the police administration was responsible for some 50 percent of all production. To this territorial character Beria added a sphere of influence of his own in the Caucasus.[47] Before coming to Moscow, he had been first secretary of the Georgian Party, and he left it in the hands of men he found reliable. During the war he was given special responsibility for the defense of the southern Caucasus and its frontier, and though certain inroads were evidently made into his general control of that area after the war, until 1951 it remained distinctly "Beria's region."

Despite Beria's slavish adulation of Stalin's person, there were signs before the war that Stalin in some fashion feared the size of the police organization. The most marked of these was a reform early in 1941 which split the police commissariat in two by assigning most of the economic functions to the NKVD and the security functions to a Commissariat for State Security (NKGB), and which gave Beria direct charge only of the latter[48] (the regime rescinded this reform soon after the war started).

When Beria became a founding member of the GOKO, the powers of the police expanded still further. Some police units, the frontier guards, took their place at the front. The police played a major role in organizing partisan groups at the enemy's rear. Beria assumed control of some sectors of munitions production, at times challenging the Army's priority in weapons deliveries.[49] In 1944 he became deputy chief of the GOKO.[50] His organization played a major role in handling prisoners of war. During 1943 and 1944, the police carried out the deportation of various nationalities which Stalin considered traitors.[51] In 1945 the police took responsibility for the repression of guerrilla activities of nationalists in Lithuania and the western Ukraine—activities which for a time assumed the scope of a civil war. At the end of the war the police undertook the vast task of screening (and often imprisoning) not only the millions of Soviet citizens who had been under German rule or who had been deported by the enemy but also the Red Army personnel who had served abroad. At the moment of victory, the ranks and uniforms of the police were made equivalent to those of the regular army, and Beria was made a marshal of the Soviet Union.[52] This last development, like Stalin's toasts, heralded the precipitous attack on the army.

At the end of the war, however, there were renewed and even more urgent signs that Stalin was bothered by Beria's power. Early in 1943, as soon as the front stabilized at Stalingrad and long before the Party revival had begun, Stalin re-established the division of police functions which had been tried briefly in 1941. Beria retained under his command only the NKVD. Then in 1945, when the country's economic planners started converting war production commissariats to peacetime duties, Beria's munitions industries were shaken up along with the rest. Early in 1946 he was removed from direct supervision of the NKVD (just then renamed Ministry of the Interior [MVD]). In October, at the height of the Party revival, a new commander appeared in the MGB also.[53]

As with the reorganization of the army, these measures can be partly accounted for as normal in a transition from war to peace. But one aspect of them is peculiar. During the war the regime had centralized its counterespionage activities in a new organization within the defense structure, Smersh ("death to the spies"). Its commander was V. S. Abakumov, reputed to be one of the most treacherous and sycophantic of all Soviet secret police leaders. His deputy was S. N. Kruglov. In 1946 it was decided to dissolve Smersh, whereupon first Kruglov and then Abakumov appeared as the new ministers of Internal Affairs and State Security, respectively. Beria's official empire had fallen to men who possessed an organization of their own.[54] Meanwhile, the Communist Party reactivated its supervision of police activities; indeed, in 1947 this function fell into the hands of A. A. Kuznetzov, one of Zhdanov's principal associates who had been prominent in Leningrad during the war.[55] Coincidentally, it would seem, A. N. Poskrebyshev, the head of Stalin's personal secretariat, began to take an active role in supervising police affairs.[56] The stage was now set for traumatic events. Zhdanov died in August 1948, the Party revival came abruptly to a halt, and Beria led a particularly ferocious purge of Party revivalists, especially of the Leningrad Party organization.[57] Abakumov turned out to be among the leading prosecutors of that purge, but Kuznetsov was one of the two principal victims.

For a short time after this Leningrad affair and the coincident rumination of Tito (within the framework of international Communism) and of the Jews (both at home and abroad), Beria may have become more secure. In 1950, according to Khrushchev, Beria was the only person Stalin consulted about foreign policy.[58] In 1951 he delivered the annual ceremonial oration of 6 November, but he again encountered trouble suddenly the same month, when a purge affected the Caucasian republics, which, as mentioned above, represented Beria's power base.[59] The trouble spread, and by early 1953, just before Stalin's death, Beria himself seems to have been about to fall.

We are by no means so well informed about these matters as about Stalin's relations with the army, but as in the case of the army, Stalin evidently came to feel threatened by his commanders during the war and from the very moment of victory began to manipulate the

Party revival against them. In the army he seems to have achieved a massive victory in short order, in the sense that there was no resistance from the generals, while his success may have been more limited with the police. Perhaps the difference was that the army demobilized, whereas the police did not. At any rate, the sheer bitterness of Beria's attack on the Leningraders in 1949 suggests that he was unwilling to accept defeat: he fought back, not directly against Stalin but against those who carried out Stalin's commands.

Stalin and the Managers

The words "industrial managers" indisputably describe an important group of individuals whom Stalin brought to power in post-revolutionary Russia. The captains of Soviet industry were, broadly speaking, Stalin's "new class."[60] Yet it is equally indisputable that they were not a "class," even in his last years, when compared with any recognized Western model. First the Revolution, then repeated and massive purges, had destroyed any ties some of them may have had with the pre-revolutionary Russian administrative and business intelligentsia. They consciously prided themselves not on their acquired status but on their proletarian or peasant background (and this of course is the case even today). Geographically dispersed throughout the urban centers of the world's largest territorial state, they lacked professional coherence. They were in no way even a corps, in the sense of having received uniform training.[61]

It must be admitted that before the war Stalin to some extent encouraged a certain class-consciousness among industrial managers, finally disposing of the leveling policies of the Revolution. His great retreat[62] left the managers set off from the rest of the Soviet population by their very great material privileges, by public respect for their technocratic approach to practical problems, and by their inclusion in the self-contained communications system of the commissariat structure. In 1941, on the eve of the war, Stalin allowed G. M. Malenkov, one of his principal aides, to express in programmatic form a philistine dislike of revolution characteristic of a middle class. Malenkov attacked as "talmudists" and "troglodytes" people who continued to invoke the words of Marx and Lenin as guides to action.[63] Nonetheless, in discussing Stalin's relations with the industrial managers before the war, it is really more useful to employ a model not of a sociological class but of a centralized bureaucracy.[64]

With the war, however, the structure and coherence of the Soviet managerial world changed drastically. First, and perhaps most important, the tremendous tasks which faced the country after the German attack brought an end to the administrative separation of powers between Party and state. On the top level, the GOKO emerged as a central clearinghouse in matters of military supply; it stood absolutely above all organs of Party and state. Lesser GOKO committees with similar authority appeared in the major provincial industrial centers of the rear area.[65] Even before this, in a strikingly spontaneous fashion, the Party and state administrative organs began to merge both in the center and the provinces, in the interests of efficiency. Sometimes a Party secretary would take on direct economic functions: a top-level example of this was the appearance of CPSU(b) Secretary A. A. Andreev in southern Siberia and the Urals in the summer and autumn of 1941 as a plenipotentiary of the GOKO concerned with converting the economy to war. More often, the merger seems to have led to a virtual withering away of the Party as a supervisory factor in the economy. Again and again one finds functions which had formerly belonged to separate Party and state organs accumulating in the hands of men who, regardless of their formal office, were effective administrators.

The second notable factor in the coalescence of Soviet managerial strength during the war was a matter of the movement of population. In 1941, 20,000 Communists were evacuated from the West to Chelyabinsk; 15,000 went to Novosibirsk; 53,000 went to Kazakhstan; and a total of 350,000 went to the rear.[66] Judging from available accounts, some of these were skilled workers and leaders of cultural institutions, but a large number were economic specialists, enough of them to maintain the size of the Party organizations of the Urals and Siberia, alone in the whole country, during the mobilization of Communists in the first year of the war. These figures suggest that the industrial managers and engineers did not go into the army, and the mobilization figures themselves confirm this assumption. It appears that whereas in agrarian regions such as Belorussia and Omsk or Kursk the local Party organization sent three-quarters and more of its membership to the army, in Moscow, a huge administrative and industrial center, only 48 percent went to the army. From the industrial Ukraine, despite the invasion, only 43 percent of the Communists entered the army, and from industrial and administrative Leningrad, despite the siege, only 44 percent of the Communists went to the army.[67] These figures certainly suggest that a substantial portion of

87

the managerial personnel of Soviet industry either went East in 1941 and 1942 or remained in civilian life. There, it can easily be shown, they were caught up in a rush of activity wherein singular stress was laid on efficiency (in the sense of "getting things done") and technical expertise. One of the peculiarities of the great process of converting the country to war was, indeed, that local academic technical specialists were brought into the planning of operations. By 1943 the nation's planning chief, N. A. Voznesensky, was seeking out academics to help plan the economy, even on the highest levels, thus challenging the hold of Party theorists.[68] Such evidence suggests that as a result of the wartime experience a highly visible civilian technocratic social element had formed within the Soviet elite. There are clear signs that in the period just after the war this element formed a sharp contrast to the soldiers coming back from the front.[69]

Third, a broad shift in both locus and purpose of Soviet industry during the war encouraged the emergence of a specifically industrial elite. The western lands, which had been by far the most important industrial centers in the prewar period, were captured by the enemy and devastated. The Urals and Siberia, on the other hand, became an arsenal, in an exciting great economic leap forward. In his book on the subject, Voznesensky estimated that the total industrial output of the regions of the Volga, the Urals, western Siberia, Kazakhstan, and central Asia was 2.9 times higher in 1943 than in 1940, and that the share of these regions in the total industrial output of the USSR increased more than threefold.[70] The development of the Urals was particularly spectacular, with overall production almost quadrupling by 1943. This region, centering on Sverdlovsk and Chelyabinsk, was the destination of almost a third of the industrial plants evacuated from the west and the focus of state industrial investments all during the war. The Urals became the source of 40 percent of all war industrial output, what Voznesensky called "the basic and most powerful industrial region in the country."[71] Many branches of industry were developed there which had not previously existed.

This tremendous success could hardly leave the country's economic managers unaffected. The Hitlerite challenge led to the disintegration of the administrative system which had formerly held them apart and cast a great many of them into a geographically unified economic locus—one can call it the "Moscow-Ural axis" to denote the central ministries on the one end and the eastern industrial complexes on the other. The war also eliminated many conflicting claims on their attention—calls for consumer production, agricultural production, and so on. Under such conditions, they must have felt a sense of group triumph, and in fact expressions of such a feeling are easy to find. In February 1944, for example, the party secretary of Chelyabinsk *oblast,* N. S. Patolichev, addressed the Supreme Soviet in the following terms:

> Comrade Deputies! The role of the Stalinist Urals in the war is well known. Not without reason do people call it the "metal fulcrum of the front"! The Urals will self-denyingly serve the Fatherland even after the war. . . . The Urals will also prove themselves a great industrial base for the future development of the national economy. . . . For such reasons, we consider that the industrial development of the Urals should be intensive in 1944 as in 1942 and 1943.[72]

With this introduction, he then asked for a large chunk of the national budget for the Urals in 1944, despite the growing need to reconstruct the western regions. Nor was his the only such selfish voice in 1944,[73] and in the Supreme Soviet budget debates after the war, many representatives of the heavy industry ministries and the war industrial *oblasty* endlessly recited statistics to justify further demands: "During the Great Patriotic War the production of diesel motors was highly developed in the tank industry. More than 44 million horsepower in such motors was given to the Red Army. In the new Five Year Plan we count on producing some 35,000 motors of different diesel models for the use of the national economy. The transport machinery plants require, therefore, very great quantities of metal."[74] Occasionally these spokesmen would admit that the thousands of workers evacuated to the Urals during the war still did not have decent housing or adequate supplies of consumer goods. In passing, they would say: "Alas, the constructors have fulfilled the housing plans badly. . . . During the war they lost the taste for such matters."[75] But this did not prevent them from making arrogant and ruthless demands on the budget for investment in their own eastern, non-consumer industries.

During the eventful last two years of the European war, the locus and personnel concentration of the Soviet industrial empire was modified. In August 1943 the government issued a decree under which the new industrial centers of the east were made responsible for initial reconstruction work on certain old industrial centers being liberated from the Germans.[76] By the end of the war, this decree had resulted in a substantial dissipation of the power of the eastern regions. Eventually many plants evacuated from the west in 1941 were shipped back to their original locations, and investment patterns favoring the east were modified. In particular, large numbers of technical specialists from the eastern wartime establishment were sent back to the Ukraine and Leningrad, whence they had come.[77]

Although these measures generally modified the Moscow-Urals axis as a geographically united phenomenon, it is important to observe some factors which counterbalanced these changes. One was a clear tendency of managers who returned from the eastern regions to the Ukraine and other industrial centers of the west to annex their new charges to the axis. They simply took command of the western mines and plants in which they were interested and rebuilt them, without much attention to the needs of the western regions as a whole.[78] The process resembled internal colonization. The other factor was the rise of Georgi M. Malenkov as an industrialist leader.

Malenkov, after Beria the most important of Stalin's aides during the post-purge, war, and postwar periods, made his name as chief of Stalin's private secretariat in the late twenties and early thirties.[79] At the Eighteenth Party Congress in 1939 he became the cadre chief of the Party and a member of the Secretariat. At the Party's conference in February 1941, he emerged as spokesman for a "defensist" and "practical" line in opposition to the "theory-oriented" policy line which had been dominant since 1939 (These expressions are defined in later chapters). In June 1941 he became one of the five original members of the GOKO and a deputy chairman of the Sovnarkom (Council of Commissars), but in the first period of the war, despite his towering influence with Stalin, his power base seems to have remained the Party Secretariat, and his function seems to have been trouble-shooting at the front, rather than economic affairs.[80] In 1943, however, Malenkov took over the committee under the GOKO for reconstruction of the western regions. He assumed special responsibilities for the aircraft and tank industries and became the main economic specialist in the Secretariat.[81] Moreover, certain leaders who had been important on the economic front early in the war now took on sharply specialized assignments. A. A. Andreev, the Party secretary who countersigned the major economic decrees in 1941 and 1943 and was the GOKO plenipotentiary during the evacuation to the east in 1941, suddenly became commissar for agriculture.[82] N. A. Voznesensky, the chief of the Gosplan (State Planning Office) and the most critical figure in the conversion of the economy to war in 1941, joined the Academy of Sciences and had the chance to do lots of planning for the postwar era. A. N. Kosygin, another key figure in the industrial evacuation of 1941 and in the creation of the Siberian arsenal, became chairman of the Council of Commissars of the Russian Republic in 1943. A little later, V. V. Kuznetsov, the deputy chairman of the Gosplan, was reassigned to the wholly political post of chairman of the Council of Trade Unions. In the wake of these shifts, Malenkov emerged with a reputation for being the dominant figure behind the whole industrial empire, the master of the Soviet home front, and the personification of managerial rule.

The conversion from wartime to peacetime production began with the announcement of the demobilization in June 1945, a call for a reconstruction Five Year Plan in mid-August,[83] the dissolution of the GOKO early in September, and a large-scale reorganization of the economic commissariats in the winter of 1945–1946.[84] Outwardly all this was routine. Indeed, as if to emphasize the routine aspects of the great transition to peacetime production, the Soviet regime, going out of its way to restore the appearances of legitimacy within and around the political system, organized an election campaign for the Supreme Soviet during that winter.[85]

Under this cloak of legitimacy, however, a tremendous change, which would affect directly the life of every home-front manager in the country, was taking place. The Party revived, and its agitators began to insist, first of all, that Party leaders at all levels of the bureaucratic hierarchy look into the economic process and make sure that the industrial managers were politically correct. In 1945 and 1946 in the Urals and Siberia, as all over the country, the Party organizations revived, doubled and tripled in size, and absorbed the huge influx of Communists, new and untrained, returning from the front.[86] In 1946 all the energy of these swollen organizations was directed toward demolishing the wartime system whereby on the local level the Party secretary and the industrial managers collaborated in the interest of efficiency, sharing responsibilities and involvement. A typical Central Committee criticism of September 1946, declaimed that the Party committee of a certain factory had physically "substituted for the regular administrators, studying and deciding many lesser economic questions: but at the same time it simply did not take under consideration many basic questions of the plant's activity."[87] Another resolution claimed: "In the conditions of the war, Party organizations quite often made decisions on many economic questions and in fact assumed administrative and managerial functions. True Bolshevik leadership consists in systematically helping the [Soviet and governmental] organizations, but *not* in substituting for them."[88] These and many other pronouncements of the period represented attempts to restore the prewar arrangements whereby the Party over-saw or controlled *all* activities and decisions, technical and otherwise, of the industrial sector but left actual day-to-day responsibility to the state administrators.[89]

The effort at disassociation of the Party from administration of industry was, of course, accompanied first by a massive step-up in ideological work and then systematic involvement of all Communists in specifically Party activities—meetings, reading groups, agitation, election campaigns, etc. In the Moscow city districts during the first year after the war, 109 plena and 120 activist meetings were held. In the districts of the Moscow *oblast* in the same period, there were 320 plena.[90] In the Sverdlovsk *oblast,* 14,837 persons were engaged in regular Party agitation work in 1946. Between March 1946 and Febru-ary 1947 the Party organization there sponsored 108,000 lectures and speeches on the subject of the Five Year Plan alone.[91] These humor-less boastings are the material with which Party historians prove that the Party's drive on the home front after the war was a success.

Yet, in perspective, one may guess that so far as Stalin was concerned, the objective of the Party revival was less a step-up in agitation than an attack on substitution—in other words, on the war-time coalescence of managerial power. This guess is confirmed by a study of upper-level organizational patterns: for example, between October 1944 and June 1946 the Party first secretaries of no less than twelve industrial *oblasty* in the Urals-West Siberian area changed office, implying a managerial shakeup in those regions coincident with the shakeup implied by the rearrangement of the central commissari-ats.[92] Further, one of the earlier announcements of the Party's organ-izational revival, which appeared in December 1944, mentioned the removal of one of the greatest home-front industrial potentates, Polit-buro member L. M. Kaganovich, from direct supervision of the Rail-roads Commissariat.[93] The GOKO, abolished "routinely" in Septem-ber 1945, just happened to be a major power base for G. M. Malen-kov; and in 1946 he lost other loci of power. In March, just after the reorganization of the war production commissariats, he surrendered his post as deputy chairman of the Council of Commissars. In Oc-tober he resumed that post on paper but was deposed from the other pillar of his power, the Party's Central Secretariat. Third (and coincidentally), his hold on the apparatus through which he had originally risen, the Central Committee's Cadre Administration, was challenged (this will be discussed in detail below).

The pattern of this attack on the wartime industrial managers is identical with the attack on the police and on the army. An explanation, moreover, now seems clear. If the industrial managers, like the wartime police and army, struck Stalin as some sort of threat to his power, then at the moment of victory he had special reason to move against them. His authority (as distinguished from his control) was then at its peak. Never before or after was he so close to popularity. In this sense, he was free to use his opportunities, and, as it happened, opportunity beckoned to seize the political initiative during the period of the conversion to peace. The army was about to be demobilized, thus releasing millions of Communists and non-Communists for reintegration into the home-front regime. The economy itself was about to endure a transformation which inevitably would involve redefinition of every function of the regime. If Stalin could somehow steal from the Malenkovs and Berias, his wartime home-front lieutenants, the governance of this gigantic bureaucracy, then his personal control could be re-established on a considerable scale. Such an opportunity might indeed never recur, and the Party revival was perfectly designed to give Stalin the political initiative, for no one in the bureaucracy could deny the need for some sort of new Party activity, given the troubling revolution of rising expectations in the population as a whole.

The difference between Stalin's attacks on the industrial managers and his other campaigns of the same period lies in the results. The managers evaded his blows. In September 1947, hardly a year after his eviction from the Secretariat, Malenkov appeared at the Cominform meeting in Poland with Zhdanov, and delivered the main report on Soviet domestic affairs. When Zhdanov died in August 1948, Malenkov suddenly reappeared again, this time as the leading and seemingly unchallenged power (with Beria) in Soviet domestic politics. In terms of results, Stalin's attack on him thus failed. One finds this same seeming imperviousness to the end-of-the-war shakeup in the leading ministerial ranks: despite the Party revival, the same names which filled the economic slots in the cabinet of 1941 are found in the cabinets of 1946, 1949, 1951, and 1953.[94]

Some details will suggest how Malenkov evaded his demotion.

The Central Committee's Cadre Administration, through which he originally climbed to power, was a controversial organization.[95] It was set up in 1939, apparently as a device for establishing central control over the nation's managers. It proved unworkable during the emergency of the first months of the war and for a time was replaced by a series of central industrial departments at the Central Committee. But in 1943 and 1944, Malenkov and his deputy, N. N. Shatalin, managed to re-establish it. However, in the early autumn of 1946, there were signs that Shatalin no longer controlled all the important appointments being made. First, N. S. Patolichev, Malenkov's successor in the Secretariat, installed a political associate as Shatalin's deputy, and a number of *oblast* Party secretaries were appointed (two of them from Leningrad) who would disappear in the purge of 1949.[96] Next, a section of the Central Committee which had hitherto been rather unimportant, the Department for Checking Party Organs,[97] was suddenly expanded, given equal status with the Cadre Administration, and assigned a number of functions which up until now had probably been the Cadre Administration's. Yet Malenkov was not ruined. On the contrary, when he reappeared in power in 1948 he himself attacked the Cadre Administration. Late that year, the administration and the subsidiary cadre administrations and cadre departments at lower levels of the CPSU(b) were summarily abolished (as were those in some Communist parties in the East European satellites, for instance, Hungary), and Malenkov became the patron of the Central Committee's industrial departments.[98]

The explanation of this extraordinary pattern of events seems to be that at the end of the war Malenkov and hundreds of other home-front industrial potentates like him no longer depended on any specific organizational form but on their contacts and personal influence. Attacked on one front, they were entirely capable of ducking out of that situation and surfacing again with undiminished power in some other place.

Stalin's attack on the industrial managers at the end of the war did have one effect. When Malenkov returned to power in 1948 and 1949, he was an investigator of the Leningrad affair along with Beria.[99] Whereas in that investigation Beria was at least functioning within his official police authority, Malenkov, an industrial manager, far exceeded his normal role. Does not this suggest that in 1946, when challenged, he grew scared, and that next year mounting fear drove him to murder? Surely it is indicative of the results of Stalin's attack in 1945 on the Soviet managers that those of Malenkov's known enemies who did not fall victim to his vengeance (for example, Patolichev and V. N. Andrianov) also became purgers after 1947, Patolichev in the Ukraine, Rostov *oblast,* and Belorussia, and Andrianov in Leningrad.[100]

By 1945 it was evidently too late for Stalin to achieve a victory over the industrial managers proportionate to his victory over the wartime generals. They, like the generals, proved compliant, indeed, slavish and cringing, under his attack, but the war had cemented a vast web of personal relationships among them. They were no longer just a group of officials: they had developed some attributes of a ruling class, and even Stalin could not fragment them again, as he had before the war, just by evicting them from office. It is indicative, indeed, of his defeat in this attempt that he did not renew it after 1950, as he did his campaign to harness the police. On the contrary, he himself took the lead in publicizing the philistine ideas of the new class.[101] Now he was the one attacking "talmudists" and "troglodytes," and he pursued the chauvinist notion that Russian could be the universal language of a universally socialist world.[102] Further, in the last year of his life, preparing a new great purge, he seemed prepared to spare the new class, indeed, to liberate it.[103] So far as one can tell, the Jews were to be the victims of that purge, and Beria and the security organs were supposed to fall, as were the surviving sponsors of the postwar Party revival, the members of the Politburo. In 1952 the word "Bolshevik" actually disappeared from the Party's name, and Communists were purged in great numbers. But the managers as a class do not seem to have been among the designated victims: on the contrary, Malenkov, so far as one can tell, was supposed to be chief beneficiary.

Of Fear and Economics

Stalin's craving for power and control is a tempting explanation for the vast domestic political operations of 1945, and many historians have depicted them in just such terms. Given the Soviet regime's past record of indifference to the welfare of the population, its obsession with public order, its evident dread of spontaneity, and its presumption of hostility at the very threshold of its bureaucratic strongholds (and inside them too), one may not dismiss this explanation out of hand. Presumably Stalin's first steps away from statism at home and

95

toward revival of the Party in 1944–1945 were taken in part because he was afraid.

However, it would be unjust to Stalin's capacities for leadership—indeed, his greatness—were historians not to recognize also that he was caught in an economic dilemma at the end of the war which forced his hand. During the war he had rallied the population to a national cause and loosened the reins on the agencies of the state in order to hold the regime together. But as the end of the war approached, it was doubtful that the ravaged Soviet land could satisfy all the expectations which had been roused. Bad harvests in 1946 and 1947 disastrously widened the gap between the regime's promises and its ability to fulfill them. Despite one great belt-tightening measure after another in those years, there was starvation in the fatherland of world socialism.

Stalin's initial steps away from statism at the end of the war and his launching of the Party revival were a response, at least in part, to this vast economic problem. If the regime had kept its promises to the population, if the Army had maintained its wartime hegemony within the system (much less its wartime manpower), if every managerial branch of the economy had indulged its cravings for expansion, there would have been an impossible squeeze on the meager resources available—indeed, one may wonder whether the regime could have survived. It was not necessary, of course, for Stalin to resolve the competition for resources precisely as he did, through cheats and stealthy manipulations. It was probably not economically absolutely necessary in the midst of the reconstruction to launch the campaign of building more heavy industry and "catching up" with the West which Stalin began in March 1946. But one must admit that strong measures of some sort were necessary at the end of the war if, in the midst of starvation, the regime was not to fall apart. It was Stalin's virtue that he managed to reassert control, that he forced the many arms of the Soviet state into a semblance of cooperation, and that he had the courage in adversity to launch the "catch-up" campaign of 1946, which, after all, was not unsuccessful in the long run.

5

The Revival of the Party: Moscow, 1944

Khrushchev's Recollections

IN HIS "SECRET SPEECH" to the
Twentieth Congress of the Communist Party of the Soviet Union in
1956, Nikita S. Khrushchev made the following remarks:

> After the conclusion of the patriotic war . . . the country experienced a
> period of political enthusiasm. The Party came out of the war even
> more united: in the fire of the war, Party cadres were tempered and
> hardened. Under such conditions, nobody could have even thought of
> the possibility of some plot in the Party.
>
> [Yet] it was precisely at this time that the so-called "Leningrad
> affair" was born. Facts prove that the Leningrad affair [was] the result
> of willfulness which Stalin exercised against Party cadres. . . . [Stalin's]
> unbelievable suspiciousness was cleverly taken advantage of by the
> abject provocateur and vile enemy, Beria, who had murdered thou-
> sands of Communists and loyal Soviet people. . . . The Party's Central

97

Committee has examined this so-called Leningrad affair; persons who innocently suffered are now being rehabilitated and honor has been restored to the glorious Leningrad Party organization. Abakumov and others who had fabricated this affair were brought before a court; their trial took place in Leningrad, and they received what they deserved.[1]

Khrushchev could hardly have made it clearer that somehow the purges of 1949 were justified in terms of controversies between Stalin and the Party which began in 1944 and 1945.

After perusing the preceding chapter, the reader may feel inclined to find Khrushchev in error. It seemed evident that, far from fighting the Party in 1945, Stalin deliberately revived it in order to undermine the wartime powers of the army, the police, and the home-front industrial managers. Further, as seen earlier, the Party was demoralized and in decadent condition during the war, so one may guess that it had little strength in 1945 for controversies with Stalin.

Yet Khrushchev was there and in a position to know, and his words merit at least a hearing. Further, other sources confirm the presence of "enthusiasm" in the Party then,[2] and, as has been pointed out, there was a certain paradox in the emergence of a Party revival under Stalin. All through his career, so far as one can tell, Stalin favored the state. His lasting view was that "it is necessary to increase the role of the state vis à vis the Party; that it is necessary to place the government more in the foreground in the interest of wider and more direct connections with the masses."[3] Precisely in 1944, as we have seen, Stalin acted in the theater of international Communism against traditional Party forms of action. How can we reconcile these apparently divergent sets of evidence regarding the postwar Party revival?

The Propagandists

The Soviet Party's revival effectively dates from an announcement on 27 January 1944 of a Central Committee plenum;[4] a series of local Party conferences in the Moscow area;[5] a public criticism of recent writings of the Leningrad satirist Mikhail Zoshchenko;[6] and Stalin's conventional inclusion in his military *prikaz* on 23 February 1944 of a reference to the Party as "the inspirer and organiser of the Red Army's great victories." In the following months, there were further such measures. The most typical were a Party criticism of a *History of West European Philosophy,* recently published by the So-

98

viet Academy;[7] an attempt to assert control over Soviet science;[8] and a vigorous campaign in Moscow to make sure that local Party units held regular meetings. Then, in mid-September, the Central Committee published two resolutions dated 9 August attacking local nationalism in the Tatar ASSR (Kazan) and lax Party discipline in Belorussia.[9] It followed these up on 27 September with two very far-reaching resolutions on educational propaganda in general and on Party political work in the liberated areas of the country.[10] At the same time it made the decision to cut down on Party admissions in the army and to step up Party education there—this was the "turning point" in the history of the postwar relation between the Party and the army mentioned earlier.[11] In October 1944 there were more initiatives from the Moscow Party organization. Finally, on 6 November, the first phase of the revival came to a climax with Stalin's jargon-laden speech about the United Nations which we discussed in an earlier chapter.

At first sight, this record affords no suggestion of the enthusiasm mentioned by Khrushchev in 1956, much less of any controversy between Stalin and the Party. The record suggests that Stalin deliberately and for utilitarian purposes of his own initiated the revival; and initially this is confirmed by the fact that the principal Party revival spokesmen were actually the Central Committee's professional propagandists.

The Party's propagandists were grouped under the Propaganda and Agitation Administration (Agit-Prop). Its chief during the war and until 1947 was G. F. Aleksandrov, a professional philosopher not noted for his strength of character.[12] The deputy chief was P. N. Pospelov, the editor of *Pravda*, a journalist and historian with no reputation as a political strongman.[13] Especially during the war, Agit-Prop was hardly a major executive organ. It had a permanent staff which organized conferences and meetings in all areas of Soviet culture.[14] It worked out and transmitted directives from the Party political leaders to cultural specialists at lower levels of the Party organization, and it supervised the Party schools and the press. It also coordinated the publication of *Pravda*, the Party's daily newspaper; *Bol'shevik*, the monthly theoretical journal; and *Partiinoe Stroitel'stvo*, the monthly journal for provincial Party activists. But even these journals were officially described then as attached to the Central Committee, not to Agit-Prop. Moreover (until 1946), the Moscow, Leningrad, and major republican Party organizations each had their own largely independent daily and monthly journals, all locally managed. Even in editorial matters, the activities of Agit-Prop were limited at this time.[15]

What is more, very important propaganda functions during the war were directed from outside the framework of Agit-Prop by several top Party political leaders. For practical purposes, the most important of these was A. S. Shcherbakov, the first secretary of the Moscow Party organization.[16] In 1941 Shcherbakov was appointed chief of the Sovinformburo, which controlled all press releases during the war.[17] This role seems to have meant that he was the immediate supervisor of the entire Soviet press. In 1942 he was made head of the Chief Political Directorate of the Red Army (GPUKA) and deputy commissar for defense.[18] GPUKA was the Party's control center for all political activities in the army, not least of all agitation and propaganda. Given the extraordinary prominence of the army in Soviet life during the war, his position as GPUKA director made Shcherbakov in effect Soviet propaganda dictator. And he was not the only top political leader who had a finger in the propagandist pie outside the framework of Agit-Prop. Within GPUKA, for example, Politburo member M. I. Kalinin was responsible during the war for Party educational activities in the army.[19] A. A. Zhdanov was responsible for educational activities within the fleet.[20]

Superficially, it seems improbable that in the power-oriented Soviet political arena the propagandists could have mustered enthusiasm or strength enough to argue with Stalin or, even in his most suspicious moments, to worry him. But one further question can provide clues about the enthusiasm Khrushchev mentioned in his speech of 1956 and understanding of how the conflict between the Party revival and Stalin during 1945 may have arisen.

If the propagandists were not an important power group, can it be said that they were a group at all? As soon as one tries to identify in detail the propagandists, one finds oneself talking not just about Agit-Prop people but about many others as well. Some Western authorities lump all Soviet journalists under such a label. And what about Soviet philosophers, writers, film-makers, radio people, and politicians? In effect, the propagandists disappear into the larger group of the entire Soviet professional intelligentsia.

It is helpful here to cite some evidence from 1941. A great number of witnesses have recorded as scandalous the evacuation of Moscow in September and October of that year. Apart from the general confusion of the operation, the major complaint is that the evacuees were somehow "parasitic" and predominantly "political bureaucrats," whose "main occupation was in organizing meetings and briefing selected orators with 'facts' to suit the spirit of the time."[21] They are described, in these accounts, as people whose language and behavior remained unchanged despite the catastrophe which had affected the country. When these Party demagogues arrived at their destinations in Ufa, Alma Ata, or Novosibirsk, it is said, they behaved with outrageous disregard for the population: they requisitioned the best housing, ate well, and continued their ritualistic prewar political behavior undisturbed. One may link such descriptions with the evidence in certain obscure Party journals that some propagandists at the Party center simply never stopped using Party jargon and making plans for a Party revival at the end of the war[22] and with the hints in various memoirs that some people near the top were, even in the worst moments of the war, concerned with the most trivial sort of *partiinost,* or "Party style."[23] Yet in reality the evacuees of 1941 were not just Party demagogues but included a substantial section of the Soviet elite, including the academic elite, with their wives and children, who were acting under orders which could not be disobeyed. Though reviled as a group by the poorer elements in the population, most of them had no choice in the matter. Their alleged "differentness" is largely explicable in terms of their educated status. Such witnesses as Il'ya Ehrenburg and Wolfgang Leonhard, who participated at the time in *partiinyi* activities in the eastern regions, say that it was not a particular group of propagandists that kept *partiinost* alive but the willingness of the entire emergent Soviet ruling class to accept the traditions and behavioral norms of Party institutions.[24] Svetlana Alliluyeva strongly suggests in her memoirs that *partiinost* was to some extent a matter of "new class personality." She contrasts the style of life of her husband's family (the Zhdanovs), which she dubs *partiinyi,* with the allegedly more free, honest, and sincere manners of the old Bolsheviks among whom she grew up.[25] So also, as we have seen, in Solzhenitsyn's *The First Circle,* one encounters *partiinost* as a matter of new class behavior and Party jargon as the normal social language of the Soviet elites.

In the previous discussion of the coalescence of the Soviet industrial managers into a new class, we attributed to them a philistinism which Stalin from time to time encouraged, with his attacks on "talmudism," that is, with his public derision of pure Marxist-Leninist ideas. That discussion did not imply that the new class in some fashion was against *partiinost,* although by definition this seems a cult of Lenin and Marx. Against philosophy, against Marxism-Leninism, yes. But against *partiinost,* no. Marxism-Leninism is concerned with the idea of freedom from social dogma. Stalin, in attacking talmudism, was encouraging the new class to detach itself from such an idea and to be conventional. But *partiinost* is a search for social security through dogma. Neither Stalin nor the new class were seeking the elimination of this search—on the contrary. The inner contradiction within Stalinism seen here is that in fact it cultivated bourgeois conventionalism, but in word it claimed to be a revolution against that conventionalism. Indeed, the more self-righteous and Stalinist the Stalinist bourgeoisie became, the more it waved its revolutionary banners.

The Agit-Prop propagandists were weak as a power grouping in 1944, but they performed a function of immense importance for the Soviet elites: they vented its egotism. It follows that when Stalin launched the Party revival, he did not merely encourage these writers to use more jargon and slogans: he deliberately excited the *partiinost* of the entire top stratum of Soviet society. In this light, neither the Party enthusiasm mentioned by Khrushchev in 1956 nor the possibility of propagandist controversy with Stalin seem incongruous.

In his memoirs, George Kennan cites an interesting and relevant conversation he had in 1944 with a Soviet friend. In a wholly private context, this friend suddenly said: "Our people must not be allowed to forget that they live in a capitalist world, that a friend may be a friend today and an enemy tomorrow. We cannot permit you foreigners to associate closely with them. You will tell them all sorts of things about your countries, about your higher standard of living, about what you consider to be your happier life. You will confuse them. You will weaken their loyalty to their own system." Even in his private life, this Soviet official evidently identified with the elitist and xenophobic aspects of the Party revival—with its ostensible purpose of preserving the control of the regime in the face of rising popular expectations. The revival expressed not just propaganda from above, but his internalized goals. He went on: "We are very successful these days. The more successful we are, the less we care about foreign opinion. This is something you should bear in mind about the Russian. The better things go for him, the more arrogant he is. That applies to all of us, in the government and out of it. It is only when we are having tough sledding that we are meek and mild and conciliatory. When we are successful, keep out of the way."[26] From this example, one can sense the kind of enthusiasm Khrushchev described in 1956—aggressive, *partiinyi* enthusiasm, not easily subject to control.

Relevant also is the plot of a novel published in 1963 under Khrushchev about soldiers returning from the front at the end of the war to civilian life. The book has two motifs. One concerns the freezing of popular hopes for a better life and centers on Sergei Vokhmintsev, the son of a Moscow Party administrator. Sergei, an officer and war hero, is demobilized late in 1945. He honestly admits that behind his bravery lay a fear of death, and remarks to a friend: "I'd like the prewar era to come back. But without the hurrahs! I'd just like to live normally with my buddies."[27] This proves impossible. In 1949 his father is arrested. Sergei chooses not to denounce him to his Party cell at the university. As a result, Sergei himself is subjected to a self-criticism session and can save his freedom and honesty only by volunteering to become a factory worker in Siberia. Thus he fails in the postwar job market because he rejects *partiinost*.

The second motif of the book concerns the victory of opportunism, and focuses on Uralov, another returning officer, whom Sergei knows was a coward at the front and was responsible for the destruction of a whole company of men. At first Uralov is apologetic and attempts to let bygones be bygones. But then he busies himself with his career. At a gay New Year's Eve party, he avoids a confrontation with Sergei by aggressively proposing a toast to Stalin. By 1949—through smooth *partiinost,* systematic acceptance of Party slogans, and one-upmanship—he becomes a leader in the Party. At the climactic self-criticism session, though Sergei denounces Uralov's cowardice at the front, Uralov, by mouthing Party cant, obtains Sergei's exile.

This novel tells us that, along with the enthusiasm of Kennan's friend, natural in a moment of victory, there was a second sort of enthusiasm burgeoning in the Party revival at the end of the war. This was the enthusiasm of the opportunists, stirred by the great upheaval which was taking place in the Soviet bureaucratic system—an upheaval in which *partiinost* was the key to success.[28] And this sort of enthusiasm may have been even less subject to control than the enthusiasm of the victory.

Shcherbakov and Zhdanov

In its original form in 1944, the Party revival seemed an orderly, well-controlled, and overtly Stalinist campaign conducted not only by

Agit-Prop propagandists but also by the Moscow city and *oblast* Party organization headed by A. S. Shcherbakov. But this leadership did not last, and an examination of the circumstances of its removal can give historians much insight into Khrushchev's remarks in 1956 about the Leningrad affair.

During the war, the home-front leaders of the Soviet system, particularly Shcherbakov, had developed a positive image of the Party's function, which was close to what had actually come to exist but which was distinctly different from the Party of prewar times.[29] This wartime Party was comparatively tolerant of the thousands of new, untrained members. It laid less stress on ideology. Much of its activity consisted of agitation among the masses. Through the organization of a Slavic committee, youth and women's organizations, and even a Jewish committee, it tried to keep up the spirit of the people and to alert the regime to the problems of the civilian population. It sought also to fill a concrete function on the factory level. Its secretaries were middlemen—the "substituters" in the state administration mentioned elsewhere—who helped with technical questions of planning, did specified work in the procurement of raw materials and especially of labor, and were a major communications link in the wartime economy. As on the home front, so in the war zone this new Party dropped its standing challenge to the industrial bureaucracy and pitched in to help the state fight the external enemy. In the war-affected regions, it claimed to play a vital role in the organization of partisan resistance to the occupation authorities—a practical undertaking in which the home-front Party organizations took great, though distant, pride.

The Party ideology which circulated on the home front and especially in Moscow during the war was no less different from prewar times than the new practices. Following the pattern of Stalin's own speeches, the ideology had grown nationalistic. Even Kalinin, one of the most *partiinyi* of the Soviet leaders during the war, declared early in 1944 that *partiinost* lay not just in the keeping of the Party's rules and in dogma but in "understanding" and in extensive education.[30] He ridiculed people who studied Marxism without learning Russian history. In this connection he even recommended that Party agitators leave Marxism to professional philosophers—an injunction which sounded at least ambiguous in a party whose Central Committee had just dropped the "Internationale" as the Soviet Union's national anthem.

Shcherbakov's own speeches of the midwar period were models of how to avoid sectarianism—reference to traditional Leninist themes—and how to merge a Marxist thought structure with a Soviet patriotic content.[31] The Moscow Party organization under Shcherbakov is rumored to have become so Russian in character that Jews were evicted from its apparat.[32] This last flourish should not be over-stressed because GPUKA, Shcherbakov's other main power base, became famous during the war as the fountainhead of the virulent "hate the Germans" propaganda led by the writer Il'ya Ehrenburg, a Jew.[33] Shcherbakov's Sovinformburo dealt with the foreign press through S. A. Lozovskii, also Jewish.[34] But of the fervent nationalism current in the organizations which Shcherbakov headed during the war there can be no doubt.

As the Party revival got under way early in 1944, the hand of these new-style home-front Party leaders became very obvious. For example, there was a certain turnover problem in factory leadership at this time. In one home-front *oblast* in 1943, fifty district Party secretaries were shifted in seven months, and the leadership of eighteen districts changed completely in the course of the year.[35] In Moscow in 1942 and 1943, 38 percent of all the regular Party *apparatchiky* were shifted; similarly, 61 percent of the regular Party personnel in one major *raikom* (district Party organization) and 42 percent in another were shifted.[36] From every corner of the Party there were reports of district committees never holding elections, seldom holding activist meetings or committee plena, and generally doing little.[37] The Party revivalists of 1945 and 1946 attacked such lassitude as an attack on Party control. Shcherbakov, in a long speech of November 1943, depicted it as an interruption of production.[38] The early part of the Party revival in 1944 concentrated on the economic damage resulting from the Party's weak cadre work.[39]

In ideological matters the hand of the home-front Party leaders was no less evident in the early phases of the revival. Their nationalism was not systematically developed; it grew up gradually and spontaneously during the war. It needed a firm underpinning, such as increased Party theoretical work could afford. And in effect, the Party's cultural interventions of early 1944 established such underpinnings. For example, the attack on the writer Zoshchenko in January was not based on questions of traditional Leninism but on how a National-Marxist Party should control culture. In 1943 Zoshchenko began to publish a series of autobiographical essays which, with their

105

introspection and Freudian overtones, contrasted with the general preoccupation of Soviet writers with the war. The Party attacked him specifically for concerning himself with personal matters while the nation was straining to evict an invader, re-establishing its prewar cultural prerogatives without insisting on a return to prewar ideological themes.[40]

Similarly, when the Party journal *Bol'shevik* criticized the *History of West European Philosophy* in April 1944, a nationalist motif predominated. It was alleged that the philosophers responsible for the book had sinned in two ways. First, they failed to make a clear distinction between Marx and his German predecessors, Hegel, Kant, and Fichte. They ignored the fact that Marx (and Stalin) sharply distinguish the Marxist dialectic and view of history from the Hegelian dialectic and view of history, and that Marx and Engels attack Hegel, Kant, and Fichte as reactionaries. Second, the authors neglected to identify Hegel with anti-Slavic Prussianism and failed to connect German philosophy in general with Germany's colonial oppression of the Slavic people.[41] When one considers that Soviet Party propagandists, and even Stalin himself, were (as Marxists) unable to attack those other Germans Marx and Engels directly, one may guess that this early work of the Party revival came perilously close to installing anti-German nationalism as the ruling ideology of Stalin's Soviet Union.[42] In the Party's third ideological initiative, the scientific conference of June 1944, the defense of nationalism was explicit. The theme was "we know well that Russian science, like all Russian culture, has always been original and independent from European science."[43] Thus the Party revival at its inception had the character of a consolidation of the wartime home-front status quo. This revival could be, and was, used against the army, but there are no signs that Shcherbakov had any intention of loosing the runaway internationalist and anti-substitutionist force which the Party revival on the home front became in 1945, 1946, and 1947.

During 1944, however, two things happened to change the character of the revival radically. The first of these was the recall of A. A. Zhdanov from his wartime post in Leningrad. Zhdanov was one of the most distinctive of Stalin's lieutenants.[44] Born in 1898, the son of a provincial school inspector, he studied for the priesthood before the Revolution, and when he joined the Party in 1917 he was in many ways a typical old-Russian *intelligent,* a true product of a social formation which had contributed perhaps more than any other group to Russian political radicalism in the nineteenth century. He rose to prominence in 1934, when he was the leading Stalinist spokesman at the great Soviet writers' congress of that year, purveying the notion that writers should be "engineers of the spirit"; then he succeeded S. M. Kirov, who had been murdered, as secretary of the Leningrad Party organization. In his joint role as cultural specialist and Leningrad chief, he was prominent all through the purge period. In 1939 he achieved even greater notice when, at the 18th Party Congress, he was named one of the five members of the Party Central Secretariat. He was also the leading exponent of the reasons why the purging should stop,[45] and in June 1939 he became the major public spokesman for the new foreign policy of rapprochement with Nazi Germany.[46]

Naturally Zhdanov was by no means the only person responsible for either the pact or its "failure" in 1940 and 1941. Foreign Commissar Molotov was at least as responsible for the rapprochement with Germany as Zhdanov was, and Stalin himself was the first major Soviet leader known to have hinted in public that such a rapprochement might be in order. But of these three, Zhdanov was the most forceful supporter of the somewhat esoteric official theoretical justification of the pact—that Moscow should make friends with the German imperialists lest the British and French imperialists join with their German opposite numbers in an all-imperialist, anti-Comintern war. Furthermore, Molotov had diplomatic skills which Stalin could use during the war, and thus made a poor scapegoat. Consequently, Zhdanov became the scapegoat. Even before the war broke out in 1941, he had become notably less conspicuous in Soviet politics; as noted earlier, he spent much of the war fairly narrowly confined to activities in Leningrad and turned over most of his cultural responsibilities in Moscow to Shcherbakov.[47]

His disgrace ended in 1944. His last appearance in Leningrad was in April, three months after the siege of the city was broken. By October he had a new office, that of Allied high commissioner in occupied Finland. Then in January 1945, on the eve of the Yalta Conference, the Soviet press announced that he had been recalled from Leningrad to "responsibilities" at the Party center in Moscow. There, in 1946, he was to become the leading public spokesman for the Party revival. But long before that, it is reported, he began to use the revival as a vehicle to further his own political career.

What led Stalin to recall Zhdanov to Moscow in 1944? Possibly a series of international events just then may have made Zhdanov's foreign policy theories (discussed in a later chapter) particularly attractive. Perhaps also his educational theories were relevant to the problems of building socialism in Eastern Europe. At this point, however, we can suggest a third reason for the recall. In the preceding chapter, it was noted that Stalin's first major step in his attack on the army was his rapid promotion of N. A. Bulganin in the autumn of 1944. Correspondingly, the first visible step in his attack on the home-front "substituters"—the Malenkovs—was his removal of one of them, L. M. Kaganovich, from the Transport Commissariat in December 1944. There were also signs that month that Stalin was attempting to hem in Shcherbakov. The Moscow Party organization then re-elected its leadership at all levels. The result was a 50 percent turnover in personnel[48] and installation of a colorless bureaucrat, G. M. Popov, as Shcherbakov's new deputy.[49] In such a context, it may be suspected that Stalin originally called Zhdanov back to Moscow to watch over Shcherbakov in propaganda matters.[50]

It does not seem likely that Stalin intended Zhdanov to become his premier lieutenant in 1944. The signs and reports of Zhdanov's disgrace persisted as the war drew to its close: one recurrent rumor had it that in April 1944, after the relief of Leningrad, a triumphal march of the partisan units of the area into the city ended in a riot, and that Beria used the occasion to intervene and to lay that disgraceful event at Zhdanov's door.[51] It was shortly after this that Zhdanov left Leningrad.[52] In September 1944 he was made head of the Allied Control Commission for Finland, a responsibility which required his regular appearance in Helsinki during 1944–1945 and which is reported by some to have been a real "promotion downstairs." In March 1945, as we shall see in the next chapter, Zhdanov's Leningrad Party organization was publicly and severely criticized by a leading journal of the Moscow Party.[53]

Nonetheless, the very fact that he was back in Moscow gave Zhdanov considerable power in *apparatchik* circles. One must recall that even in disgrace he had retained the title of secretary of the Central Committee and was, along with Stalin, Malenkov, Beria, and Shcherbakov, one of the system's five most distinguished leaders. Further, because of his *intelligent* image, because he was an inventor of socialist realism—officially still the basic standard of all Soviet culture—because of his power base in Leningrad, the country's second largest city; and because he had actually been at the front,

Zhdanov had great prestige. It was his weight and influence which gave *éclat* to the second major development in the Party revival in 1944. This was the collapse and death of Shcherbakov. The Moscow leader made his last recorded public appearance in December 1944. He died on 8 May 1945, the eve of the German surrender. *Pravda*'s announcement of Zhdanov's recall on 27 January 1945 is perhaps the best indication of when Shcherbakov actually became ill.[54]

In 1952 Stalin accepted the charge that Shcherbakov and Zhdanov had been murdered.[55] In both cases the charges are now considered unjust: both men, it seems, died of drink and in their beds. But there was a difference between the two cases. Zhdanov was out of favor and deep in conflict with the secret police when he died in August 1948. Since Stalin's agents were involved in at least two well-known political murders in 1948,[56] one may understand why he could later talk of the murder of Zhdanov, but of Shcherbakov this cannot be said. There is simply no evidence, nor even rumor, that an atmosphere of murder prevailed in political circles in Moscow in 1944 and 1945. Perhaps Stalin's later suspicion reflected not his memory of a murder but his intense shock and surprise over a death which caught him unawares.

In effect, Shcherbakov's death caused Stalin major political problems, and herein lies its relevance to Khrushchev's remarks in 1956 about the Leningrad affair. Stalin launched the revivalist movement early in 1944, despite his long prewar record of struggle against the Party. One may deduce that he had confidence that under Shcherbakov's management this revival would accomplish his manipulatory purposes without getting out of control. Now the main prop of this confidence was destroyed. Suddenly Stalin had to find a new leader for the revival, as well as new men to fill the posts in Moscow, the army, and the Sovinformburo which were essential to it. And he had to do this in the presence of Zhdanov, a skillful and experienced politician who was at bay, who was the archtype of the new-class Soviet propagandists discussed earlier in the chapter, and whom Stalin had already admitted to the revivalist stage for very different purposes. At no other time during Stalin's years in power was there a clearer opportunity for the *partiinyi* enthusiasm of the Soviet elites to get out of bounds.

Printsipnost

Even before Shcherbakov's death, a change was affecting the work of the Party propagandists because of the spread of what they called *printsipnost,* or cult of principles. After Shcherbakov grew ill, this cult spread wildly in Party circles and came to threaten Stalin in distinctive ways. In September 1944 a well-known Party philosopher, M. Mitin, published an essay in the theoretical journal *Bol'shevik* that suggests what *printsipnost* was.[57] Writing of the role of Marxist doctrine in Communist political practice, Mitin described two distinct understandings. One he called "creative." He reminded his readers that Lenin had "frequently pointed out that Marxism is creative theory," "a guide to practice" which was most effective when its followers did "independent work on original problems." In this connection, he warned against treating Marxism as a bundle of immutable slogans. Yet, on the other hand, he emphasized "farsightedness." In approaching this second understanding of the relation between theory and practice, he again started with an anti-nominalist position: he stressed that Marxism is not in its own terms an ideology but a scientific, empirical insight into objective laws. In Marxism, he recalled, the laws lie in the facts, not in the words describing the facts. But from anti-nominalism, he then leapt far into nominalism by writing that our perceptions of the objective laws—i.e., our *words*— should be treated with peculiar respect and should be accepted as guides in practice. In defense of this view, which he obviously favored, Mitin recalled that Lenin had "protected Marxism against the opportunism of social democrats" and that Marx and Lenin had both been far-seeing, as, he claimed, was Stalin's Bolshevik Party, whose "granite base" was Marxism even today.

Mitin's contraposition of creative thinking with farsightedness symptomized an emerging official sanction in the autumn of 1944 for the practice of reading everything as a fulfillment of Marxist and Leninist principles—hence, *printsipnost.* The latent threat to Stalin which this practice posed came to light dramatically immediately after the *Vozhd's* own greatest contribution to the Party in 1944, his speech of 6 November. In that speech, it may be recalled, he dropped a number of strong hints that in current events there was *zakonomernost,* a "reflection of laws," and he even spoke specifically of one "law of history." In the following days and weeks, his Party's propagandists went to remarkable extremes to explain what Stalin really meant, and in many cases they ended up by almost completely transforming the subtle points which he had made. For example, at a key place in his speech, Stalin made a pronouncement on an alleged ideological character of the war: "In the course of the war the Hitlerites have undergone not only a military defeat but also a moral-political defeat. The ideology of the equality of all races and nations which has become firmly established in our country, the ideology of the friendship of nations, has gained a full victory over the Hitlerite ideology of bestial nationalism and race hatred."[58]

It is important to recognize here that Stalin did not state that Marxism-Leninism was winning the war or that it was even contributing to the victory. He certainly implied it, but he did not say it. Yet when *Partiinoe Stroitel'stvo,* the Party's principal journal for activists, some weeks later[59] published this speech, its lead-off editorial read as follows: "The ideology of equality of all races and nations, the ideology of friendship between nations, has established itself in our country. In the course of the war, this ideology has won a full victory over the ideology of bestial nationalism and race hatred kindled by the Hitlerists."[60] So far so good. This was exactly what Stalin had said. But then the editorial went on: "This very great victory in the area of ideology was prepared for by the long and successful struggle of our Party for the solution of the nationality question. The friendship of nations, the supreme achievement of our country, did not fall full-grown from the heavens: it grew strong in the fire of the common struggle of nations for the independence of the Fatherland, in the common front for consolidation of a socialist system."

Now Stalin had not said this. He hardly mentioned the Party in his speech, and he said not one single word about socialism. This was an addition by the propagandist who wrote the commentary. Yet the following lines were: "The Party always bears in mind the words of Comrade Stalin about how 'the survivals of capitalism in the consciousness of men burn with greater vitality in the area of the nationality question than in any other area. The more they can mask themselves well in national costume, the more vitality they have.' The Party has unceasingly unmasked the fact that hatred of man by man is the essence of any kind of nationalism." Here the editorialist was using an old quotation from Stalin to make his own interpolation seem to be a direct consequence of what Stalin had said in his speech, and to identify his own version of Stalin's idea with what the Party had "always" been doing.

As a result of this manipulation, the Party's leading journal for activists all over the country ended its discussion of Stalin's speech with the words:

> The Lenin-Stalin nationality policy led to the result that all the nations of the Soviet Union unanimously undertook the defense of the Fatherland, counting the present patriotic war as the common cause of all workers, without national differences. We are reaping the fruits of the wise policy *of our Party,* and of *its* work in teaching Soviet patriotism. The Party organizations should carefully explain the meaning of friendship among nations as the source of the strength of the Soviet state and educate the masses *in the spirit of Leninist-Stalinist internationalism.*

Again, this was entirely different from what Stalin had said, yet it was attributed to him in a most respectable source, and one can well imagine that, as a result of reading this bit of propaganda, Party activists all over the country indulged in a little *printsipnost* on their own.

This editorial was far from the only specimen of the new sort of work the Party's professional propagandists were doing in the last months of 1944. An entire issue of *Bol'shevik* published in December was given over to such disquisitions on what Stalin really meant on 6 November, some of them more venturously *partiinyi* than *Partiinoe Stroitel'stvo.*[61] Further, in the first issue of *Partiinoe Stroitel'stvo* for 1945 (published on 1 February 1945), the attempt to find meanings in what Stalin said was carried a great step further. Under the title "Unceasingly Spread Leninist Propaganda in the Ranks of the Party," the lead-off editorial began:

> In the past year our armies have inflicted shattering blows on the enemy . . . under the leadership of our leader and captain, Comrade Stalin. In order to comprehend the enormous *meaning* of these events *it is necessary to know how to see* their links with all past developments. . . . These successes were obtained above all on the basis of the correct policies of the Bolshevik Party, the leading force of the Soviet people. In *all* our military victories, just as in *all* the other victories of the socialist state and in the moral triumph of the Soviet people in the patriotic war, *we may see the all-conquering power of Leninism, the ideological banner of our Party.* We conquer through the correctness [*vernost*] of Leninism.[62]

The propagandists who wrote this editorial were no longer as constrained as they had been in the editorial on the November speech, cited above, in which they simply twisted Stalin's words into endorsements of Party views. Now they were, in the broadest possible fashion, directing Party activists to find lessons in events without reference to Stalin, through direct communion with the lasting ideas of Marxism-Leninism. And this was not all. They proceeded to issue the following extraordinary directives: "Our state is coming out of the war stronger than ever. . . . If we want our state to go forward to yet further victories, . . . to its goals in the future, . . . it is necessary that [Party] cadres, the decisive backbone of our state, unceasingly follow Leninist teaching."[63] At this point, a quotation from Stalin was still considered necessary: "Comrade Stalin has said that the most important tasks of the Party organization in the area of ideological-political work are 'unceasingly to spread Leninist propaganda in the ranks of the Party.' "[64] But then, in the followup, the propagandists in effect did away with Stalin altogether:

> The significant book of Comrade Stalin, *Problems of Leninism,* is a further development of Marxism-Leninism in new conditions. . . . Comrade Stalin's book *On the Great Patriotic War of the Soviet Union* [the collection of his war speeches] summarizes the tremendous experience of the Soviet people's struggle for the honor, freedom, and independence of their country. Every book, article, and speech of Lenin and Stalin . . . is urgent with its deep *ideinost.* Herein lies their great educational value.

This was nothing more nor less than a suggestion that Party activists go about reading Stalin's sayings with an eye not for their literal meaning but for their *ideinost,* or ideological content, in other words, for what he did not say, for what he may not even have hinted, but for what could be construed through reference to the correct notions of Marxism-Leninism—that is, the Party's slogans.

Later in this same issue of the activist journal, the point was put even more forcefully: " 'The value of the Communists lies in the fact that they know how to defend their beliefs,' says Comrade Stalin. Bolshevik *printsipnost* means a complete rejection of every slightest deviation from Marxism-Leninism."[65] Here, through a quotation from a speech Stalin made in the 1920s, the editorialist made him the defender of reliance on abstract Marxism-Leninism in 1945! And he went on: "Comrade Stalin has shown more than once that [Party] leaders have to know how to 'speak out their opinion . . . with the frankness which is characteristic of Bolsheviks.' . . . Public opinion in the Party has always sharply condemned every sign of ideological [*ideinoi*] unsteadiness, of lack of principle [*bezprintsipnost*], of toadyism, which lead Party workers to shallow compromises with their consciences." Here a comment of Stalin's made in the 1930s is used to make him the advocate, in 1945, of direct reliance by Party workers on the Bolshevik conscience. The editorial carried the general title "Lenin and Stalin on the Qualities of Bolshevik Leadership." This was the voice of the Party Central Committee telling its agents throughout the Soviet Union how to behave.

By 1946 the editorialists of *Partiinoe Stroitel'stvo* had carried their theses to the ultimate conclusion:

> Of [Party] leaders who fail to learn from practical errors . . . it may be said that they grow like grass, thinking not of the past and gazing not into the future. Comrade Stalin has compared such workers to oarsmen who row honestly, spare no effort, and flow through the water smoothly following the current, but who neither know, nor care to know, where it is taking them. Work without perspective is work without a rudder and without a sail—that is what floating with the current leads to. And the results? The results are clear. At the start [these leaders] limit themselves, then they become dullards, then they get sucked into the darkness of philistinism, and finally they get transformed into deluded philistines themselves.[66]

Here in an absolute and explicit sense the Party workers of the CPSU(b) were instructed, apparently by the highest authority, to trust in what they themselves conceived to be a proper Marxist-Leninist perspective. For this Stalin's high-priestly mediation was wholly unnecessary.

How was it that the Party propagandists in 1944 and later came to take these and (as we shall see) many other enormous liberties with Stalin's meaning? One obvious and probably very important answer relates to Zhdanov. He was back on the scene. He and Shcherbakov were the only cultural leaders of the Party prestigious enough to authorize such trifling with Stalin's words. Attached to his Moscow bailiwick Shcherbakov had an activist journal, *Propagandist,* which propagated a far less *partiinyi* line (and, as we will see later, even criticized Zhdanov's coterie in Leningrad in the winter of 1945). Perhaps *Partiinoe Stroitel'stvo* was Zhdanov's organ. It is notable that it did not change its editorial board when Zhdanov's influence in the Party's propaganda apparatus rose in the summer of 1945, whereas both *Propagandist* and *Bol'shevik* did come under new management.[67]

To blame Zhdanov for all the daring work of the Soviet propagandists in that period is to miss seeing other and probably much more important reasons for what happened. For example, it is probable that Stalin himself recognized the inconvenience of his anti-sectarian wartime nationalism to the project of reviving the Party, and decided to tolerate a little monkey business. Certainly, it was he above all who, with his jargon in the 6 November oration, precipitated the revival of *printsipnost* and *ideinost*. In deducing this, of course, we obtain another confirmation of his belief, even late in 1944, that Shcherbakov would keep the Party revival in hand. It is hardly credible that Stalin would have opened the door to *printsipnost* if he had thought his words would become distorted beyond all recognition, as in the end they were.

In all probability, a practical consideration was as important as Stalin's own tolerance of *printsipnost*. The Party "propagandists"—and we use the expression narrowly here to mean professional editorial writers—had a difficult task from 1944 on. Stalin was their leader. He had started a Party revival which entailed a very considerable quantity of fresh work for them.[68] A good quantity of this work necessarily consisted of proving to Party activists and the masses that Stalin, the leader of the Party and the main authority within the state, had authorized a Party revival. Yet for years Stalin had said very little—during the war most of his sayings were most un-*partiinyi*—and even the speech of 6 November 1944 was less than explicit in its *partiinost*.[69] Under these circumstances, the men who had to write long articles explaining the supreme qualities of what Stalin had said may have decided that their easiest way out was to fill the lacunae between Stalin's recent jargon hints with explicit references he had made in the past to the commonly known theoretical structure of Marxism-Leninism.

How were these propagandists to know that Stalin and Shcherbakov could conceive of stopping halfway between nationalism and *partiinost*? We are not even sure that Stalin and Shcherbakov themselves had a clear idea of what stopping halfway might mean. Indeed, it is objectively difficult to conceive of, and one must suppose that Stalin and Shcherbakov could do so only because they were so deeply engrossed in the weighty affairs of running the wartime Soviet state that they had no time to worry about it. The propagandists, moreover, had a natural bias on this question. They were professional Marxist-Leninist-Stalinists. To them, presumably, wartime nationalism had been from the start nothing but a propaganda tactic which they were only too happy to cast aside. They had never moved toward nationalism, so naturally it was difficult for them to stop halfway back from it.

To this we must add a last vital fact: we are speaking of 1944–

1945, when the war was approaching a victorious end and the Soviet elites were exuberantly and freely expressing their enthusiasm for the victory. It was only natural, in that winter pregnant with joy, that Stalin's propagandists should be a little heavy-handed in explaining what their leader meant—that even they, sycophantic as they were, should become enthusiasts.

Counterattack

When Khrushchev hinted in 1956 that a conflict between Stalin and the Party in 1945 may have led to the Leningrad purge of 1949, he touched upon reality. In 1945 Party propagandists, through the liberties they took with his speeches, stole from Stalin the most direct and vital control he had over those of his followers whom he did not know personally—his high-priestly control. This is not to suggest that Stalin could not dominate those followers through his administrative system; clearly he could, but that was an indirect sort of control, dependent on the goodwill of the men who dominated the administration. In the high-priestly speeches, on the other hand, Stalin exerted a direct and entirely personal control over every one of them. As long as it was recognized that he meant exactly what he said, *and only what he said,* these speeches enabled him to communicate over the heads of his administrators. With the revival of *printsipnost* and *ideinost,* however, this possibility was gone. Once having hinted that his followers should refer to the structure of Marxism-Leninism to understand his meaning, it was virtually impossible for him now, as high priest of ideology, to tell them that, after all, they should not read his words in the light of that structure. As Stalin knew well from prewar experience, no Marxist-Leninist can tell other Marxist-Leninists, in Marxist-Leninist terms, not to be Marxist-Leninists. Before the war it had taken him years to turn the Bolshevik ideological labels upside down and to terrorize his followers into thinking Marxism was only what he, Stalin, said. All he could do after legitimizing direct references by his followers to their ideology was to hint that they should be quiet about their thoughts. Until they were quiet, he stood the chance of having the wildest of their *partiinyi* slogans put into his mouth.

The proof of the matter is that Stalin fought back in 1945 as if faced with exactly this sort of challenge. As early as 1934, he had been highly critical of people who relied on slogans to bring about the spontaneous emergence of socialism.[70] In 1941, at the eighteenth

CPSU(b) Conference, his lieutenant, G. M. Malenkov, launched a violent two-pronged attack, first against "windbag-like" use of *partiinii* slogans to evade responsibility, and then against a "know-nothing" reliance on slogans to win political power.[71] A "windbag" manager, he explained, would reply to questions from his superiors about deficiencies in his factory not with precise details but with a quotation from Stalin about "putting the pressure on." A "know-nothing," on the other hand, would use a quotation from Lenin to reject technical advice and criticism of his own performance. In both cases, the slogans would be empty of meaning and would be called into play only to place the entire weight of the Party dictatorship behind the windbag or know-nothing.

During the summer of 1945, this sort of attack began again in some of the organs of the Soviet Central Committee. As we will see later, the initiative came from Stalin. Such attacks culminated in February 1946, when Malenkov again spoke out in an election speech:

> Creative leadership consists of following Marxist teaching [while] studying present-day experience in construction . . . and letting [such experience] be reflected in everyday practice. We have people justly referred to as pedants who [instead] have . . . quotations from Marx and Engels ready for every possible occasion. . . . They have only one standard: either "Marx said—" or "Marx never said—." Daily, comrades, we come across [such] routine and stagnation. . . . Our most important task lies in merciless struggle against it.[72]

Far more explicitly than he had in 1941, Malenkov was identifing the know-nothings and windbags as Party enthusiasts. This campaign against pedants remained focal to Stalin's personal political line from 1946 until his death in 1953.

Under these circumstances it may hardly be doubted that Stalin was aware of the new *printsipnost* of 1944 and 1945 and recognized the danger it posed to him. The Party legions on whom he was relying in his great campaign against the commanders and managers were escaping his control. Within a few months of the start of that campaign, Stalin had overreached himself.

117

6

The Leningrad Affair

A Question of Robbery

HOW SERIOUSLY did Stalin overreach himself in his campaign against his commanders and managers at the end of the war? The preceding chapter shows that some sort of overextension occurred. The Party revival, which Stalin started in 1944 in order to attack the managers, did get out of control in the enthusiasm of the victory in 1945, and its supporters did attack him at his point of greatest weakness—his inability to deny Leninism as the source of his authority. Yet anyone who witnessed Stalin's power will want to probe further to discover what the argument between him and the Party revivalists was all about. Stalin, after all, stayed in power for several years after the war and managed before his death to obscure the very memory of the Party revival of 1945. Does not this record suggest that the Party's challenge to Stalin was somehow negligible?

Our weightiest official source for such matters, Khrushchev's "secret speech" of 1956, gives only one hint of the substance of the argument between Stalin and the Party in 1945. Midway through the speech, Khrushchev started talking about who within the Soviet system actually won the war:

> All the more shameful was the fact that, after our great victory over the enemy which cost us so much, Stalin began to downgrade many of the commanders who contributed so much. . . . Stalin very energetically popularized himself as a great leader; in various ways, he tried to inculcate in the people the version that all the victories gained by the Soviet nation during the great patriotic war were due to the courage, daring, and genius of Stalin and no one else. . . . Let us recall the film, *The Fall of Berlin.* Here, only Stalin acts: he issues orders in a hall in which there are many empty chairs and only one man approaches him and reports something to him—that is Poskrebyshev, his loyal shield-bearer. (Laughter in the hall.) And where is the military command? Where is the Politburo? Where is the government? . . . There is nothing about them in the film. Stalin acts for everybody.

Hereupon Khrushchev interjected: "Not Stalin. . . . The main role and the main credit for the victorious ending of the war belongs to our Communist Party, to the armed forces of the Soviet Union, and to the tens of millions of Soviet people raised by the Party."[1]

It was in this context that Khrushchev went on to talk of the persecution of the Leningrad Party organization in 1949. Since we know that objectively neither Stalin nor the CPSU(b) was in any way singlehandedly responsible for the victory, we can see that the debate Khrushchev refers to was important: it was a debate between robbers over who would get the loot. Still, was it important enough to make the overreach in Stalin's campaign against the commanders and managers a major historical event?

To resolve this problem, we will in this chapter identify the "victims" of the Leningrad affair of 1949 and then inquire systematically what they were doing during the Party years at the end of the war. In adopting this deductive approach, we will be abandoning the inductive historical method used elsewhere in this book, but there seems no other effective means of getting to the heart of the paradox which this book is intended to investigate.

The Liberated Territories

It is well known that the Leningrad affair entailed the downfall of A. A. Kuznetzov, Zhdanov's successor in 1945 as the chief of the

Leningrad city and *oblast* Party organizations and of perhaps two to three thousand other leaders of the Leningrad Party.[2] Less widely recognized is the fact that the Ukrainian Party organization also suffered. In the Ukraine, the postwar purging began during 1947 and only intensified in 1949, when the Leningrad purge broke.[3] Practically unknown, moreover, is the fact that these purges of 1947, 1948, and 1949 affected not only the Ukraine and Leningrad but virtually all the Party organizations in the territories liberated from the foe. The war-zone *oblast* Party first secretaries were purged between 1947 and 1950 at the rate of about 70 percent, whereas the average rate among home-front *oblast* first secretaries was 43 percent. If one discounts new men installed during the Party revival, the home-front rate is considerably lower.[4]

When one asks whether the Party organizations of the liberated territories—the largest contingent of victims in the Leningrad affair—played some special role in Soviet politics in 1945, it appears that they did. In the first place, these organizations had a common interest in a Party revival. In April 1944, shortly after the siege, the Leningrad organization no longer had 151,000 members, as in 1941, but 16,241.[5] In October 1943 the Ukrainian Party counted not half a million members but 16,816, scattered among not 33,000 but 1,611 local organizations. Even on 1 January 1945, six months after the liberation of Ukrainian territory was complete, the Ukrainian Party had only 164,743 members.[6] For other liberated *oblasty* the tale was even worse. In August 1944, for example, six months after the liberation, the Pskov *oblast* had only 1,470 Communists (compared to 10,000 before the war), and most of them were wartime recruits.[7] Because of such depletions, one may assume that the Party organizations of the liberated territories had a much greater need for a Party revival than the organizations of the home-front provinces.

To this, one may add that the Party in the liberated areas needed a revival because the structure of society and the apparatus of Soviet control had been either destroyed or, in the case of Leningrad, terribly shaken. Party revival here was not simply a matter of building up one of the several branches of the Soviet governmental system in competition with others; it was a matter of setting up the entire system anew. In so far as the Party was at all times the recruiter and trainer of reliable cadres for the system, reconstruction of the Party was the first step toward restoration of Soviet control. Then, of course, there was the problem of purifying those regions where the window to the West had been opened wide—which had been exposed, in fact, to Fascist propaganda. Here organizational control had to be supplemented with ideological control if Soviet rule were to be restored, and ideology was the Party's responsibility. On the home front, revival of the Party was a matter of important concern to the leadership, but it was conceivable that some leaders might be indifferent to it or actually oppose it, for Soviet control had not been really disturbed. In the liberated territories, however, virtually every single person involved in the re-establishment of the Soviet regime had to take an active part in the Party revival and to declare it his own cause.

One further common experience made the Party organizations of the liberated territories particularly susceptible to revivalist spirit. The Party here had gone to war in 1941 not just by sending its leading cadres to the army, which was done by all the Party organizations in the Soviet Union, but also by organizing and helping the partisan movement behind the enemy lines.[8] The home-front Party organizations could claim to have been the inspirers and organizers of the victory only on the basis of some of Stalin's anti-army homilies, but the war-zone organizations could boast that they had actually fought. The first secretaries of the Bryansk, Novgorod, Orel, and Velikie Luky *obkomy* (*oblast* Party committees) in the Russian Republic at the end of the war are known to have been partisans,[9] as were the first secretaries of the Bobruisk, Brest, Grodno, Minsk, Molodechno, and Pinsk committees in Belorussia.[10] The head of the Belorussian Party, P. K. Ponomarenko, had been head of the partisan staff at general headquarters during the war.[11] In the Ukraine, fewer partisans became *obkom* first secretaries at the end of the war (only two are known), but this seems to reflect a definite policy in the Ukrainian Party of not sending higher Party officials behind the German lines.[12] The lower officials in the Ukraine often were partisans, and Khrushchev, the first secretary of the Ukrainian Party, together with a considerable group of his aides in the central and provincial leadership of that Party, were active at the front between 1941 and 1943,[13] as were the postwar Party secretaries in the Kursk, Pskov, and Stalingrad *obkomy* of the Russian Republic.[14]

The partisan Communists were heavily infiltrated by the NKVD. Most marked in the Belorussian Party after the war, this seems to have put a brake on the development of a specifically Party spirit.[15] Nor did the partisans always make a satisfactory transition into peacetime Party organizers. The *obkom* histories of the liberated territories abound with references to dictatorial practices left over from the war, and in the Ukraine it is reported that certain ex-partisan elements actually had to be liquidated in the late 1940s.[16] However, it may be noted that in 1942, when Stalin abolished political commissars in the army, a parallel measure for partisan units was violently objected to by those units and had to be withdrawn,[17] and in both the Ukraine and Leningrad the cult of the partisans was strong all during the Party revival.

In recording these possibilities for explicitly Party solidarity in the liberated territories at the end of the war, one must be cautious. The Communists of Stalingrad were liberated early in 1943, and by 1945, when the western Ukraine and western Belorussia became free, they were, from all we can tell, substantially reintegrated into the home-front Party. The Communists of the North Caucasus regions had far fewer physical and moral problems to face after the Red Army returned than did those of Novgorod or the Crimea. Odessa was nowhere nearly so badly hurt as Minsk. Further, the presence of pressing needs in the liberated territories does not mean that the Communists of these areas received no help or sympathy from the home front. As early as the middle of 1943, the Soviet government and the Party set up an aid program whereby the home-front regions would help reconstruct the liberated territories. In March 1944 the government and the Party even set up a special program for the reconstruction of Leningrad.[18] During the latter months of 1944, the Party center in Moscow investigated each major organization of the liberated territories and issued long and detailed instructions about how the local Communists should mobilize the general population, what kind of newspapers and journals they should set up, what kind of lectures they should give and to whom, how they should train new recruits, how they should handle the vital problems of agriculture and industry, and so forth.[19] There was nothing unique about the need to rebuild the Party in these areas: only the urgency of the task was unique.

There were also aspects of the Party's task in the liberated territories which may have inhibited the emergence of any sort of enthusiasm about the common task. For example, in Estonia, Latvia, Lithuania, the Western Ukraine, and Moldavia, which were centers of strong, popularly based, anti-Russian nationalism, the regional Party organizers, when they were natives, had the appalling task of suppressing the independence of their own countries. No matter how fervent their internationalism, this was a task hardly designed to stir their enthusiasm. And, more important, the Soviet police led them in their task, and in Lithuania its brutality engulfed them in a civil war. In the records of the CPSU(b) revival, the reports of the Baltic Communists—of Karotamm from Estonia, of Kalnberzins from Latvia, of Snieckus and Suslov from Lithuania—are prominent. But one may suspect that these reports were more important as confirmations of the Party's success, which the revivalists in Moscow could read with satisfaction, than as expressions of real enthusiasm from the harried Party members on the scene.

In addition, factors which led to revivalist enthusiasm among some Party members in the liberated territories may have left others indifferent. Judging from his speeches, for example, Khrushchev was highly enthusiastic about the revival at the end of the war, not least of all because he saw in it a means of solving the agricultural problems of his area. To some extent, perhaps, he was right. The Ukraine, the breadbasket of the Soviet Union before the war, suffered more during the fighting than any other part of the country. In 1944 the sown area of the Republic was only one-third of what it had been in 1940. Even in 1945, barely 60 percent of the prewar sown area was cultivated.[20] Livestock had been massacred on a vast scale. Agricultural machines were virtually nonexistent. Those peasants who remained in their villages were demoralized by the German occupation and paralyzed by the destruction. Khrushchev, though ostensibly the ruler of the forty million people in the Ukraine, possessed, in effect, no instrument for reaching the villagers because the regime's local instruments of control had simply ceased to exist.[21] Consequently, when faced with the problem of meeting Moscow's demand for grain, Khrushchev had much to gain from a restoration of the village Party organizations and of the *kolkhoz* system. In that way he could obtain agents in the villages who could talk to the peasants and could set up a framework within which he could supervise the peasants' work. The alternative—abandoning the *kolkhoz* system—may well have seemed to a Politburo member and an experienced Stalinist entirely too innovative and risky to be worth attempting.

Khrushchev also had strong faith, often expressed in later years, that Party workers in villages could with a little effort be as interested in and sympathetic with the peasantry as he was himself. In May 1944 he summed up his views in an anecdote about an old, illiterate peasant whose son went away to work in a factory, got sick, and wrote home for money. When the father got the letter, he had a neighbor read it to him. The reading was faulty, and only the part about money was clear. The father grew angry and refused to help his son. But then the following week another neighbor, more literate, looked at the letter. This time the news of the illness was underlined, the father dissolved in tears, and the money was sent immediately. The moral, said Khrushchev with evident sincerity, is that in the villages people can and must be helped to see things the right way.[22]

Despite Khrushchev's confidence, it is clear that restoration of Party rule in the villages was far from universally accepted either as the best way to restore agricultural production or as a source of *partiinyi* enthusiasm. At least one *obkom* secretary from the liberated territories, P. I. Doronin of Kursk, made a name for himself in the postwar years as an advocate of a general loosening and reform of the *kolkhozy* through introduction of the so-called link system and new pay scales,[23] and it is a matter of record that even in the Ukraine the Party's cadres simply would not go out into the villages until they were forced to do so in 1947.[24]

In the spring of 1945, however, a major integrative factor countered the fragmentation of the Party organizations in the war-zone provinces. A confrontation over economic priorities took place between them and the great industrial *oblasty* of the home front. During the war years there had been no such confrontation because the entire country's first interest was in increasing the production of the war industries on the Volga, in the Urals, and in western Siberia. At the Supreme Soviet meeting which passed the national budget in February 1944, no one blinked when the representative from Chelyabinsk suggested that his *oblast* be once again a scene of intensive state industrial investments.[25] When the Supreme Soviet convened to consider the budget in April 1945, however, peace was clearly at hand, and it was necessary to decide whether intensive development should continue in the eastern region or whether reconstruction of the liberated provinces should take priority.[26]

In the published minutes of the budget debate of April 1945, virtually all the speakers mentioned came from the liberated territories; only one, the representative from Tomsk, could in any sense be described as a representative of the war industrialists. This emphasis radically distinguished this Supreme Soviet meeting from that of 1944, when almost all the speakers were from the industrial Urals. Further-

124

more, the most important speakers from the western regions, A. A. Kuznetsov from Leningrad, L. R. Korniets, the Ukrainian finance commissar, and members from Kursk and Stalingrad all sharply criticized the alleged selfishness of the representatives of various industrial commissariats in their areas.[27] Kuznetsov in particular made it clear that he was speaking for all the areas of the country which had been devastated by the war.

The outcome of this confrontation is by no means clear from the available sources. We know that in the later months of 1945 the government issued a number of decrees which promised financial favors to the devastated western regions. Moreover, in the All-Union budget for the year 1945, the Ukrainian Republic received almost one-third of the sum assigned to the Russian Republic, and the Belorussians received substantially more than any of the Central Asian or Caucasian republics.[28] In the Russian Republic budget published in June, Leningrad, while receiving only a third of the sum alloted Moscow, got four times the sum assigned to the Urals and Volga industrial centers.[29] Against these successes, however, one must balance the fact that at the end of the debate over the budget of the RSFSR, the delegate from Sverdlovsk declared himself "perfectly satisfied"[30] and the far more important fact that the Leningrad leaders got much less than they had publicly requested[31] and had to scale down drastically their grandiose projects for making their city "a very strong industrial and cultural center of the Soviet Union"—a "metropolitan" (*stolichnaya*) city.[32] Further, one may recognize that the Soviet state in 1945 could not possibly have satisfied all the legitimate demands of the devastated liberated regions even if the government had been willing to sacrifice the interests of the home-front industrialists altogether.

From the available sources, nonetheless, one may conclude that in the spring of 1945, the Leningraders and the Ukrainians were officially encouraged to lead the Party elites of the liberated territories in a more or less open and united attack on their opposite numbers in the industrial east. The reason for this is not hard to guess. Stalin at that time was starting his sabotage of the wartime home-front industrial empires. As we have seen, he methodically used the Party revival in this attack and in his other coincident attacks on the army and the police. From Stalin's point of view, the formation of a war-zone pressure group with a common economic interest may have seemed all the more advantageous because it was based on ravished, needy, and thus politically weak territories. Wherever the truth lies, this new interest group of 1945 was clearly not simply the tool of Comrade Stalin, but was a channel for real enthusiasms from deep within the Soviet regime, and it had a valid claim to rewards for wartime accomplishments. Herein lies its relevance to Khrushchev's allegation that behind the Leningrad affair lay an argument in 1945 about who had won the war.

Leningrad and the Ukraine

The two Party organizations which suffered most conspicuously in the purging of 1949 were those of Leningrad and the Ukraine. Both organizations, but especially that of Leningrad, were conspicuous at the end of the war for their cult of the Party. In the Leningrad case, the reasons for this cult are obvious. In 1941 a very large portion of the civil administrators of the city went into the Army, and its economic experts were evacuated to the eastern regions. Consequently, the task of administering the city during the long siege fell largely to the local Party leaders. Soviet historians call Leningrad a classic example of how the Party, in the emergency of the war, abandoned its traditional hands-off stance vis-à-vis the state administration system and took up the role of deciding technical administrative problems.[33] During the long siege, the Party grew accustomed to ruling directly. It established liaison with the command centers of the Leningrad military front and with the partisan units of the entire northwestern region.[34] It made itself, as far as possible, the focus of the hopes of the depleted and starving population. In the relative isolation of those years, it developed a certain mystique. The fact that the chief of the Leningrad Party was the top-level Stalinist Zhdanov contributed, as did the energy and ability of his two main assistants, A. A. Kuznetsov, the party secretary, and P. S. Popkov, the city Soviet chairman, or mayor.[35] But the main contribution to the Leningrad Party's new mystique was the city's history as the administrative and cultural capital, and particularly the revolutionary capital, of tsarist Russia. Leningrad was the home of many Russian revolutionaries of the past century. It was the main scene of the Bolshevik Revolution, and even after the imposition of Stalinism it had had a Stalinist minister of its own, S. M. Kirov, who was murdered in 1934.[36]

At the end of the siege the local Party not only did not abandon this mystique but capitalized upon it. The Party organized a victory

126

parade for the partisans; it disseminated visionary plans for the recon-struction of the city;[37] it boasted of the city's history and heroism;[38] in December 1944 it criticized the city's literary journal, *Zvezda,* for not publishing enough poems and stories about local themes; and, with the obvious intent of keeping up the spirits of the still-starving inhabitants, it cultivated the theme: "We, the Party [that is, we the Leningraders], are the people who really won the war."[39]

The sources of the Ukrainian Party organization's self-adulation were somewhat different. Although far larger than the Leningrad Party, the Ukrainian Party failed to remain in place during the war and in 1943, at the liberation, was a mere skeleton, without even its leadership in one location.[40] It had none of the cohesiveness that characterized the Leningraders at the end of the war. Yet structurally it was more independent: it held its own congresses, had its own press, and even in cadre affairs was less subject to arbitrary interfer-ence by Moscow than was the Leningrad *obkom*. Furthermore, Khrushchev, its chief, was a more attractive character than Zhdanov. Where Zhdanov overawed or scared people with his intellectual man-ner, Khrushchev was clearly a man of the people and made friends easily.[41]

The Ukrainian Party could hardly boast, as the Leningraders could, that it had preserved the independence of its region. The pre-war Party had delivered a temporarily independent Ukraine into the Great Russian embrace after 1917.[42] It also had to combat the anti-Soviet Ukrainian nationalism which was expressed in the Republic during the German occupation,[43] and in the postwar years it was engaged in a small war with the Ukrainian nationalist underground movement in Galicia.[44] The Ukrainian Party had no such glorious Russian revolutionary nineteenth-century history as the Leningrad Party, and in the more distant past, the Ukraine had been anti-tsarist and anti-Russian to an extent that was rather awkward for twentieth-century Ukrainian Communists.

Nonetheless, the Ukrainian Party, far more than the Leningrad Party, reaped the benefits of Stalin's tolerant nationality policy during the war. Early in 1944 it obtained separate Ukrainian defense and foreign commissariats, the latter headed by D. Zh. Manuilsky, the former Comintern leader.[45] At the end of the war, it was responsible for unifying all Ukrainian-inhabited lands in one polity for the first time in centuries—indeed, in history.[46] Although Khrushchev did not obtain the formal diplomatic bonds with the East European states which he sought,[47] his government did obtain a seat in the United Nations Organization. All this was clearly designed to have an effect on the Ukrainian national ego. In addition, Ukrainian Communist writers and academics were given considerable freedom to express themselves according to Ukrainian traditions and in the Ukrainian language.

During the war, a number of Ukrainian Communist intellectuals were so certain that cultural liberalization was permanent that they were willing to display it to the non-Soviet world. For example, Aleksandr Korniichuk, the writer and first Ukrainian foreign commissar, impressed President Beneš of Czechoslovakia with his sincere Ukrainian patriotism in December 1943,[48] and Maksim Rylskii, a good poet, though a member of Stalin's Slavic Committee, composed a quantity of decidedly patriotic Ukrainian verse in the last years of the war. In 1944 he even made a trip to Leningrad, and came home delighted with the "brotherly" (as opposed to "filial") relationship of Leningrad and Kiev to Moscow.[49] In the spring of 1945 the Ukrainian *Pravda,* like that of Leningrad, was busily encouraging the cult of local heroes and regional tradition.[50]

To some extent, this wartime cultural Ukrainianism was purely tactical. According to one report, for example, in November 1944 Khrushchev himself attended the funeral of the Greek Uniate Metropolitan Sheptytskii at Lvov and presented a wreath from Stalin.[51] The same year, he carefully distinguished in his speeches the abhorrent anti-Soviet "Banderist" leaders and "Ukrainian-German nationalists" from their popular following in the anti-Soviet underground.[52] Such cultural tolerance began to wane in the Ukrainian Party long before Stalin's Russian toast of 24 May 1945 precipitated the matter. Nonetheless, the feelings it encouraged in Khrushchev's Party may not be dismissed as false or fleeting. Regional patriotism contributed so much to the special spirit in the Ukrainian Party that it became an issue in the purge of Communists in the Ukraine in 1947, of which Rylskii was a main victim.[53]

Did this sort of Party nationalism or *esprit de corps* in Leningrad and the Ukraine give Stalin trouble? Some peculiar incidents point to affirmative answers. In January 1945, for example, the Leningrad city and *oblast* Party committees held a plenum at which they accepted criticism for their wartime policies.[54] They found it necessary, in particular, to end certain "undemocratic" practices of the wartime leadership, to hold long-overdue elections of local Party officers, to restrict admission to the Party, to reimpose candidacy for new members, and to give up mass or group admissions. Zhdanov was officially removed as first secretary in Leningrad. The meeting, from the record published in the journal of the Moscow Party Organization, sounds most dour.

Within days, however, the Leningrad Party *esprit de corps* showed itself in a most striking fashion. The Supreme Soviet had awarded Leningrad the Order of Lenin. On 27 January 1945 M. I. Kalinin, the chairman of the presidium of the Supreme Soviet and thus technically the Soviet chief of state, visited the hero-city to present the award. This was the occasion for a widely publicized celebration, and Kalinin used it to do more than just hand over a medal.

An aged politician, Kalinin was one of the loudest spokesmen for the Party revival during these months.[55] At Leningrad he made a characteristically garrulous speech in which he declared that the holiday was not just for the Leningraders but "for the country and for the whole of progressive humanity."[56] He then romantically told Leningrad's story. The Germans, he claimed, wanted to settle accounts with "Lenin's city" because it was a generally recognized "nest of revolution." The German "imperialists," in particular, had a personal hatred for Leningrad because after the October Revolution many German "hirelings of tsarism" there had been thrown out of the country. The confrontation of Leningrad with Fascism, therefore, according to Kalinin, represented a confrontation between "the forces of progress and the forces of barbarism," with the result a victory for "progress." "Was it an accident," he asked, "that all Leningrad was filled with patriotism and revolutionary fire?" His answer to this leading question was "Absolutely not! Leningrad is the cradle of the October Revolution . . . and of Russian revolutionary thought." Kalinin, perhaps through some instinctive caution, hardly mentioned the Party in this speech, but this lacuna was quickly filled by Soviet Chairman Popkov, who formally accepted the award, and by A. A. Kuznetsov, who on this occasion replaced Zhdanov as joint first secretary of the Leningrad *obkom* and *gorkom*. "The soul of the heroic defense of Leningrad," said Kuznetsov, "was the Party organization led by the *oblast* and city Party committees under Comrade Zhdanov."[57] It took little imagination, when Kalinin closed with vapid predictions about how the revolutionary spirit of wartime Leningrad would continue in the years of peace, to see that he was actually boasting about how the Party had won the war. This euphoric celebration was publicized all over the Soviet Union. Despite the harsh criticism they had had to accept inside their Party committees, the Leningrad leaders made their celebration a focal point of the entire Party revival.

Later on, especially during 1946, attacks on Leningrad from the Party center in Moscow became decidedly more vehement. For example, when Zhdanov launched his well-known campaign against the Soviet intelligentsia, he lashed out in particular against the intellectuals of Leningrad.[58] At the same time, the Leningrad leaders were compelled to admit that their own organization during the war had been an outstanding example of the "harmful" practice of substitution.[59] Further, it became more and more evident that the Soviet government was not going to underwrite the mighty plans for Leningrad's reconstruction.[60] Meanwhile, the Party organization of the Ukraine, around which there was also a local Party mystique, got deeply in trouble for tolerating local nationalism. All through the autumn of 1946, the central Party press howled about the erroneous policies of the Ukrainian Party. In February 1947 the Central Committee sent out a special team of strongmen, reminiscent of the purge era, to "help" Khrushchev put his region in order.[61] In September 1947 Stalin himself entered the fray. On the occasion of the eight hundredth anniversary of the founding of Moscow, he issued a statement, one of only four published that year. In it he stressed over and over again the virtues of Moscow in the Russian past, in the Russian Revolution, in the winning of the war, and in the world peace movement at that time.[62]

One might imagine that such symptoms of central Party opposition to local patriotism would have terminated expressions of the spirit of Leningrad. On the contrary, in 1946 the divergence between the spirit of Leningrad and the directives from the Party center became even more pronounced. One incident involving the Leningrad Party secretary, A. A. Kuznetsov, is illustrative of the trend. Comparatively young—he was only forty in 1945—he was bold.[63] He made a name for himself before the war as an outspoken defender of the Molotov-Ribbentrop Pact of 1939. In 1945, as Leningrad Party secretary, he became as voluble as Kalinin in favor of *partiinost*, of the needs of Leningrad, and (often more than implicitly) of the virtues of his own organization. In 1946 and 1947, when he became a secretary of the Central Committee, he was so foolhardy as to interfere with the political police,[64] and in February 1946 he took some liberties with Stalin.

In his election speech of that month, Stalin denied that the war had been "accidental" and thus confirmed the Marxist view that the struggles within capitalism had led inevitably to it. He then gave a report on the Party's accomplishments. Kuznetsov, in reporting on the speech to his Leningraders, added some embellishments. While dubbing the speech "a major event in the life of the country, . . . a new general contribution to Marxist-Leninist science," Kuznetsov attributed to Stalin the notion that *all* the people's victories were Party victories and that war is the "*inevitable* accompaniment of imperialism *even now.*" Stalin, of course, had not said this. Indeed, in March 1946 (in his interview with E. Gilmore) he denied it. In all probability many Soviet leaders thought war was inevitable and thought that Stalin also thought so, but only Kuznetsov seems to have been so bold as not only to say so but to attribute the thought to Stalin.[65]

Nor was this the only such incident. In 1946, 1947, and even 1948, the Leningrad leadership lost no opportunity to recall their city's heroic and revolutionary exploits. Ignoring the unhappy fate of the patriotic Ukrainian Party and of Khrushchev, the Leningraders, turning and twisting with every political wind, kept talking about Leningrad. For example, in a new journal which Zhdanov organized in 1946, *Partiinaya Zhizn'*, there were full-length articles either about Leningrad or written by prominent Leningraders in ten out of twenty-four issues in 1947, whereas only five such articles related to Moscow (including three about Stalin's statement). These boasts did not stop after Stalin's intervention but continued into 1948, when the storm clouds were clearly gathering around Zhdanov's head. They ceased only when *Partiinaya Zhizn'* itself abruptly ceased publication in April of that year.[66]

One may hardly argue from the evidence just cited that the Leningrad and Ukrainian Party organizations were in any conscious sense opposed to Stalin at the end of the war. To the contrary, it is perfectly clear that the men and women of these organizations were filled with idealism about Stalin. Khrushchev, whose career was made by his role in the great purges, claimed credibly in his de-Stalinizing public statements and in his memoirs over and over again that he believed absolutely in Stalin's virtue and saw no contradiction between objective morality and Stalinism.[67] Roy Medvedev, a strongly anti-Stalinist Soviet historian, speaks similarly of the Leningraders:

> Many of the officials who were cut down in 1949–1952 belonged to the new generation of leaders who rose to prominence after 1936–1937. They were significantly different from the preceding generation. As a

131

rule they completely accepted the cult of Stalin's personality. As their careers progressed, some of them acquired the characteristic features of Stalinists: rudeness and unjustified abruptness in their treatment of subordinates, dictatorial manners, vanity. But many of these younger officials had not yet perceived the grave consequences of Stalin's cult and knew little of the lawlessness he had created. They were basically honorable people who tried to do their jobs as well as possible.[68]

Yet Milovan Djilas tells how just such idealism in another regional Party organization at the end of the war created a sort of political blindness. Writing of the Yugoslav-Soviet dispute, he says: "What happened to the Yugoslav Communists is what has happened to all who throughout the long history of man have subordinated their own fate and the fate of mankind to one idea: unconsciously they described the Soviet Union and Stalin in terms required by their own struggle and its justification."[69] Djilas claims that Yugoslav Communists, in a sense, attached Stalin's name to their own ideas and that, after the war, they took all sorts of actions under its authority, without any sense that this might be displeasing to him. Perhaps when the Leningrad Party organizers boasted in 1945 that the Party, not the army or Stalin alone, had won the war, they were doing the same thing.

The Politburo Majority

The Leningrad affair of 1947–1949 involved not only the Party organizations of the liberated territories and the Ukrainian and Leningrad organizations but also a number of prominent individuals. One was Zhdanov, whose death in August 1948 signaled the beginning of the purge. Another was Khrushchev, who suffered political eclipse before Zhdanov's death but then recovered and late in 1949, at the height of Leningrad's travail, became the head of Moscow's Party organizations. Less drastically threatened were three major Politburo members: V. M. Molotov, the foreign minister, N. A. Bulganin, the minister of defense, and A. A. Mikoyan, the minister of foreign trade. All three were removed from control of their ministries in March 1949 when the Leningraders were arrested, and all three are reported to have remained in political limbo from then until Stalin's death.[70] One may also place in this category A. N. Kosygin, the minister of finance in 1948,[71] and G. M. Popov, the head of the Moscow Party organization in the postwar years, although both retained minor ministries after 1949.[72] Finally, there were the men who actually figured in the Leningrad affair trials. Among these were N. A. Voznesensky, the head of the State Planning Office and author of the postwar five-year plan; his brother A. A. Voznesensky, minister of education in the Russian Republic; M. I. Rodionov, Kosygin's successor in 1946 as chairman of the Council of Ministers of the Russian Republic; A. A. Kuznetsov, from 1946 until 1949 secretary of the CPSU Central Committee; and I. V. Shikin, head of the Political Directorate of the Red Army after Shcherbakov's death in 1945. Of this last group, all but Shikin were shot.

Remarkable numbers of personal and political bonds linked these various men with one another toward the end of the war. Zhdanov, for example, had had his power base in the Party organization at Leningrad since 1934. Voznesensky was chief of the Leningrad City Soviet Planning Commission from 1935 until the end of 1937, and in that period formed lasting associations with the economists at the Leningrad Financial-Economic Institute.[73] Kosygin received some of his higher schooling in Leningrad and between 1935 and 1939 started his career in the Leningrad city and Party administration.[74] Kosygin, Mikoyan, and even Molotov were involved in the evacuation of Leningrad in 1941.[75] Voznesensky's brother was rector of Leningrad University from 1944 until 1948. General Shikin was military commissar of the famous "ice road" to Leningrad across Lake Ladoga in the winter of 1941–1942 and, at the same time, chief of the political administration of the Leningrad front.[76]

There are several flaws in this pattern of associations. Mikoyan and Molotov, for example, were sent to Leningrad in 1941 as part of a task force which, by all acounts, was not appreciated by Zhdanov and the city's Party organization.[77] One can argue that Voznesensky's association with Leningrad was no more critical to his career than his subsequent tenure in the State Planning Office in Moscow or his vitally important tour of duty in the Urals in 1941–1942. One of the principal figures in the Leningrad affair, M. I. Rodionov, has no record of having served in Leningrad, although he may be linked with Zhdanov through their joint service in another city (Gorky) during the late 1920s.[78] Kosygin and Rodionov, indeed, seem to have been involved in the group through their association with Voznesensky during the period of industrial transformation in the Urals in 1942.[79] One may also wonder whether patterns of friendship—much less political alliances—among the Soviet leadership can be deemed "proved" just because various leaders at one time or another served in the same large city. Nonetheless, the available Soviet sources do emphasize the Leningrad background of the group,[80] and even Rodionov can be drawn into it on the basis of his pointed references to "Lenin's city" in writings of 1947.[81]

Some of these top-level victims of the Leningrad affair, moreover, were linked in 1945 by a common approach to practical economic problems. Of this grouping, the most important was N. A. Voznesensky. Although as a theoretician Voznesensky had (as we shall see below) a strong voluntarist bent, in administrative matters he had a practicality which won him the respect of economic rationalizers.[82] He was not content simply with drawing great Marxist schemes in the air, as were some of his colleagues. As planning chief, he attempted to articulate the various long-range and short-range functions of the planning apparatus. He insisted that the central planners go beyond issuing edicts to and receiving statistics from the national economic administration, and look into the instrumentation and results of the plan decrees on the local level. He stressed regional planning. He tried to give concrete emphasis to the problems of agriculture and consumer goods. Above all, he tried to refine Soviet planning techniques, seeking the advice of scientists, and especially mathematicians, from the academic world. In other words, though a voluntarist in theory, Voznesensky was a technical modernizer in practice, and herein lay his association with Mikoyan, Kosygin, and Rodionov.

Contemporary evidence suggests that Voznesensky, Mikoyan, Kosygin, and Rodionov came together in 1945 explicitly as a managerial grouping which favored establishing a place in the peacetime economy of the Soviet Union for light as well as heavy industries. Voznesensky published little in the daily press, so he is difficult to pin down, but his Five Year Plan speech of March 1946 assigned priority on the immediate level to reconstruction tasks, civilian housing, and consumer goods.[83] Mikoyan's rationalizer position is confirmed by an article in *Pravda* dated 19 May 1945. In the Supreme Soviet meetings of 1944–1945 Kosygin and Rodionov were the two leading advocates of satisfying civilian consumers.[84] In 1945 and 1946 consumer demands were of course urgent, and nearly all the leading economic personnel in the government on one occasion or another made some comment about satisfying them. But Voznesensky's group and the Party revivalist Molotov (in his election speech of February 1946[85]) were responsible for the most explicit of these remarks.

During the war itself, these men had not stood out as a "group." The home-front economy of the Soviet Union was characterized during the war, as we have noted elsewhere, by a stress on efficiency. That label covered both the technical efficiency that Voznesensky stood for and the application of Stakhanovite methods to the tasks of building regardless of a balanced economic emphasis. At the close of the war, however, when the complexities of managing a peacetime economy once again came to the fore, the efficiency camp evidently split. The industrialists who favored Stakhanovism preferred to keep things as they were. They grouped themselves around Malenkov,[86] who in his election speech of February 1946 firmly identified the road to efficiency with purge. "Our most important task," he declared, "lies in waging a merciless struggle against stagnation. . . . The organizers who fail to understand this must be replaced."[87] The Voznesenskys, on the other hand, were anxious to find new ways to deal with new problems.

There is some evidence that after 1945 this group, and particularly Rodionov, was involved in political intrigues. In 1944 Rodionov was first secretary in the Gorky *oblast*. At no time after the war was he outspoken in favor of reviving the Party—on the contrary, from his writings one might judge that he was a Russian nationalist[88]—but during the revivalist months he seems to have become known as an associate of Voznesensky and of Kosygin. In 1946 he succeeded Kosygin as chairman of the Council of Ministers in the Russian Republic. Once he was near the top, distinctive projects evolved under his aegis. For example, in the Russian Republic a number of administrative reforms to increase consumer production seem actually to have been carried out,[89] and as the political pressures increased in 1946, there was talk of holding an international Russian fair at Leningrad and of transferring the capital of the Republic from Moscow to Leningrad.[90] Even after Stalin pointedly toasted Moscow as the historic center of all Russia in September 1947,[91] Rodionov published in *Bol'shevik* some quotations from the martyred Bolshevik S. Kirov stating that Leningrad was "a great forge of cadres for our new socialist system" and that "in industrial affairs Leningrad plays a uniquely responsible role."[92]

Under Stalin, this sort of empire-building by a man who had not even been close to the real seats of power was truly risky and may have justified the consequences. After Rodionov's purge on 11 March 1949, the Central Committee charged him with insulating the Russian Republic *oblasty* from the directives of the Moscow Party and government agencies and with encouraging local leaders, particularly those in the Gorky Party, to develop tendencies so incorrect that they could be labeled "parasitism" (*izhdivenchestvo*).[93] All this might suggest that the Leningrad affair was not (as Khrushchev tells us) just the result of Beria's provocation. Along with the smoke there may have been fire.

However, a healthy perspective on the Politburo-level victims of the Leningrad affair is offered in a report by Vladimir Rudolph, a former official in the Soviet economic administration of postwar Germany.[94] He gives the history of a committee which GOKO member G. M. Malenkov set up late in 1944 under the Soviet Council of Commissars (Sovnarkom) to coordinate the activities of those Soviet governmental organs participating in the rapid looting of parts of Germany captured by the Red Army (Malenkov apparently did not expect the occupation of Germany to last long). Rudolph devotes most of his memoir to the story of how the committee found favor in some quarters of the Soviet state apparatus and resistance in others. The heavy-industry commissariats for aircraft and for tank construction, for example, favored the dismantlement project because they were subordinated to the committee's chairman, Malenkov, and expected that he would get them a lion's share of the spoils. The police and slave-labor apparatus controlled by Beria approved of the committee because it also, through Beria's political influence, believed that it would acquire a major share of the spoils. The state planning apparatus under Voznesensky was less pleased, however; the state planners were interested in a unified chain of command and soon discovered that Malenkov's special committee was in practice simply a smoke-screen to conceal uncoordinated and competitive booty-seeking by the major Soviet economic commissariats. The planners also had begun to recognize the advantages of leaving Germany in a condition to pay extensive reparations: they preferred assured income to hastily gathered loot. For similar reasons, the Commissariat of Foreign Trade, headed by A. I. Mikoyan, was also opposed to the Malenkov committee. Once the committee began operations, both Mikoyan's apparatus and the military occupation authorities grew indignant at its appalling waste and interference with their own operations.

According to Rudolph's account, in 1945 the Soviet Party, as personified by Zhdanov, managed to politicize the affairs of this special committee and to turn such administrators as Voznesensky and Mikoyan against the established economic power represented by Malenkov and Beria. By the middle of 1945, Malenkov's prestige had been seriously undermined, and in 1946 Voznesensky and Mikoyan managed to turn the scales decisively against the special committee. Then, Rudolph reports, these two leaders came forward with an alternative project of their own. They continued to assume that the Red Army would be obliged to withdraw from Germany eventually, but they sought to counter this eventuality, not by de-industrializing their former enemy (the Malenkov solution of 1944) but by establishing Soviet ownership of key German industries. To this end, they set up joint Soviet-German stock companies and assigned them huge industrial assets. Only in 1947, when it became evident that the Soviet grip on eastern Germany might be lasting, did these Party administrators go on the defensive. Malenkov seized upon the implication that Moscow had an interest in keeping the occupation zone economically strong. He counterattacked, and gradually the Voznesenskys and Mikoyans were compelled to hand over their joint stock companies to the German Communists.

Rudolph's report clearly suggests that the Leningrad grouping at the Party center in 1945 was not engaged in a struggle for Stalin's power. Its members had come together because of the great campaign which Stalin himself organized against the managers of the wartime home front. They hoped to seize managerial power for themselves, but under Stalin. And in this connection one may well remember all those present at Stalin's court who have told how servile Stalin's aides were—how they would accept even public humiliation at his hands without protest.[95]

Nonetheless, the top-level victims of the Leningrad affair did come together at the end of the war in one fashion which one must presume was offensive, and even alarming, to Stalin. The most important records we possess of top-level Soviet political opinion in that period are the programmatic election speeches which the principal leaders delivered in January and February 1946. Among the Polibuiro-level politicians who spoke, only one of those who particularly stressed the virtues of the Party is absent from the list of Leningraders. This exception is M. I. Kalinin, who died in June 1946. Further, of the men on the list who spoke in 1946, only two, Kosygin and Rodionov, did not speak out loudly in favor of the Party. It

137

follows that men who were purged in 1949 were, in the main, the leading advocates of Party revival in the top Soviet leadership during 1945 and 1946. The significance of this group is heightened by the fact that they commanded a majority of the votes in the wartime GOKO and the restored Politburo of late 1945—in the GOKO, they represented half the membership: in the Politburo, they had a flat majority[96]—and from the start of 1944, one of their major projects in the Party revival was fulfillment of the Party statutes.[97]

This project hardly affected Stalin as long as it was simply a matter of making sure Party members paid their dues, local organizations held regular meetings, and lower-level Party officials were properly and periodically re-elected. But when the top levels of the Party began humming with talk about the purity of the rules, Stalin *was* affected. Strict adherence to the rules at this level meant that the country would be governed through the Party's Politburo, its Secretariat, and its operational arm, the Orgburo. It also meant quarterly plena of the Central Committee and triennial congresses. Since 1941 Stalin had ruled not through the top Party organs but through the GOKO. Since 1941 the Central Committee had met perhaps once, and there had been no congress since 1939. We do not know precisely how much talk there was of such matters in the upper regions of the Party in 1945, but we do know that there was some talk because in September 1945 the GOKO was abolished; in January 1946 the functions of the Politburo, Orgburo, and Secretariat were discussed and eventually redefined;[98] and in March 1946 the Central Committee did at least meet. Meanwhile, there were rumors that a congress would be held.[99]

Perhaps Stalin had nothing to lose through enforcement of the rules. However, one can guess from his long record of not observing them that he found them at least inconvenient. Pressure for this sort of reform from Party revivalists in the Politburo in 1945 would have disturbed the atmosphere which Stalin cultivated in his regime from his assumption of power late in the twenties until his death in 1953. And from his point of view in 1945, this group must have seemed all the more dangerous because it joined the burgeoning enthusiasm of the Party revival with the struggle for the interests of the liberated territories and the *esprit de corps* of Leningrad and the Ukraine.

The Politburo-level victims of the Leningrad affair probably threatened Stalin in another way also. One may most easily approach the evidence about this through study of a public lecture delivered on

23 October 1944. K. V. Ostrovityanov, a professor of economics at the Moscow State University, spoke of what he called the "basic regularity [*zakonomernost*] in the development of the economy of socialism." Ostrovityanov was primarily concerned with the success of the Soviet planners who in 1941 supervised the evacuation of huge industrial installations to the rear and the transformation of the whole economy to a war footing. He claimed that there was "meaning" in this titanic economic feat, which, he professed, had made possible the survival and victory of the Soviet Union. It showed, he said, "the specific character of the economic laws of socialism": these laws "exert their influence not as laws spontaneously ruling over people, but as recognized laws continuously *used and applied* in the practice of the Socialist system."[100] Ostrovityanov claimed that because the Soviet state planners of 1941 recognized this specific character of the economic laws and built upon their knowledge, they had been able to perform economic miracles.

This was a voluntarist line of argument.[101] By declaring that the wartime accomplishments of the state planners were the rational results of the economic laws operating within socialism, Ostrovityanov could deduce that whatever project the Soviet planners projected was practicable. By this standard, it did not matter how miraculous such projects might appear. They would emerge from the drawing boards of the Soviet planners, who were socialists, as functions of the specific character of the economic laws of socialism and therefore would be possible. Clearly, Ostrovityanov was aware that if carried to an extreme his arguments might displease Stalin, to whom overt voluntarism was a cardinal sin associated with Trotsky. Consequently, he sharply criticized the "leftist voluntarism" of any assertion that "under socialism economic laws lose their force of objective necessity and that we can at will create them." But the brunt of his attack was on a "so-called theory" of Karl Kautsky that "socialism is the passive product of economic forces."[102]

The importance of Ostrovityanov's lecture derives in part from its clear affinity with the ideas of Voznesensky, who was starting work late in 1944 on a book on the war economy of the USSR.[103] In that book he took the same generally voluntarist approach as Ostrovityanov and chose the same topic—the "miracle" of 1941. In his Five Year Plan speech of March 1946, moreover, he openly declared that under socialism the state's economic plans "possess the force of economic laws."[104] Since Ostrovityanov became chief of the Institute of

Economics at the Soviet Academy under Voznesensky's aegis in 1946 and in 1947 stage-managed the Zhdanovite attack on the work of the economist E. Varga, one may suspect that his lecture of 1944 was in effect a testing ground for Voznesensky's ideas.[105]

Ostrovityanov's lecture is important most of all, however, for its departure from the spirit of a famous anonymous essay on political economy, which appeared in 1943 and gained world renown as an expression of wartime pragmatism in Soviet economics.[106] Whereas Ostrovityanov clearly admired the beautiful *zakonomernost* of economic events, the essay opens with a bitter attack on people who, before the war, allegedly "transformed political economy from a general, historical science which explores the living web of real actuality into a collection of anti-scientific abstractions and lifeless schemes." Whereas Ostrovityanov clearly idealized the institutions of socialist state planning, the essay begins with a frontal attack on all sorts of idealization within Marxism. Whereas Ostrovityanov stated in his lecture that "in our economy the law of value is a tool of the planning leadership," the earlier essay contains a massive polemical attack on the "mistaken view" that "in socialism there are not and cannot be any economic laws such as dominate capitalism" and on the "deeply mistaken approach to the law of value" which claimed it does not apply in socialism. On a technical level, it is possible to discover many elements common to both Ostrovityanov and the essayist of 1943. This is natural, since both writers were products of the same school of Marxist-Leninist economics.[107] But within that school they represented divergent attitudes.

The voluntarist arguments of Ostrovityanov's lecture probably account for the coming together, in 1945, of Zhdanov with Voznesensky himself and with the various economic rationalizers who later became victims in the Leningrad affair. The Kosygins and Rodionovs, though interested in consumer production and the like at the end of the war, were in no position to push for it unassisted. Until 1946 Kosygin was chairman of the Council of Commissars of the Russian Republic, a position of no great political leverage. Rodionov was Party secretary in the Gorky *oblast*. Even Voznesensky, the head of the Gosplan, had been pushed by Malenkov out of the dominating position in the home-front economy which he had held in 1941. Nor would the argument that consumer goods might please the population carry much weight among the arrogant Soviet elite if it were presented (as it would be in a rational budget) as an alternative

140

to heavy industry and military power. But through *partiinyi* voluntarism the consumer goods argument took on greater significance. If it were true that the state planners could, as Ostrovityanov and Voznesensky argued, manipulate the law of value to achieve economic miracles—if a balance between income and output was, in fact, irrelevant to the planning of Soviet investments—then a choice between heavy industry and consumer goods need not be made: if the planners in peacetime, as during the war, were capable of miracles, then the Soviet state could push both heavy industry and consumer goods.[108] This was the argument which Voznesensky, supported by Zhdanov, presented in 1945 and 1946. As Western observers, to their considerable bewilderment, immediately recognized, Voznesensky's Five Year Plan was drawn up with regard almost exclusively to needs, as opposed to capacities. To use Naum Jasny's expression, this was the "Stalin-has-everything-his-own-way" plan par excellence.[109]

Voluntarism was also a connecting link in 1945 between all the top-level people discussed thus far and the most significant Soviet leader who fell with them in 1949, V. M. Molotov.[110] In his election speech of February 1946, Molotov's major flight into domestic policy at the end of the war, he said: "Some people still dream that it would be well if our country's leadership passed to some other, non-Communist Party. We can answer them with the simple Russian proverb: 'If only beans grew in one's mouth!' . . . The world, my friends, does not just turn around: one can affirm that it turns purposefully and that it has its own forward course toward its own better future." He followed this affirmation of his faith in the laws revealed by Marxism-Leninism with as explicit a statement of philosophical voluntarism as we possess from a top Soviet leader of the period: "A great deal depends, of course, on whether people know how to work well, but even more depends on their having the will to learn how to work."[111] Perhaps when Molotov said these things he was trying above all to make a point of foreign policy: the atomic bomb was exploded in mid-1945; Molotov for several months thereafter was the Soviet leader who publicly suggested most frequently that the bomb was a "paper tiger"—that it would not diminish the importance of traditional statecraft.[112] Nevertheless, in February 1946, he was clearly indicating that political success in general depended on form—on accomplishing a task through proper Party channels—and on will.

Such voluntarism could be a source of considerable political power if seriously argued on the Politburo level of the Stalin regime. We have noted elsewhere that sloganism at lower levels of the system was useful to opportunists because a slogan mobilized the Party's organization behind whatever project the sloganeer might be promoting. In the Politburo, that particular sort of one-upmanship would work less well because the Politburo itself was the seat of Party authority, and slogans there would evoke no fear—they might even sound hollow. But if one of Stalin's colleagues, someone politically impeccable in the Politburo, were to use voluntarist Marxism seriously to press a policy line, he might attain much the same effect as sloganism could at lower levels. Marxism was the political language of Stalin's circles, and such a rationale would easily gain a hearing. Because a voluntarist interpretation of reality afforded extraordinary policy freedom, it would be especially appealing. In effect, its proponent could promise anything he chose, thus outbidding his opponents on the practical level. And if such a comrade could once win Stalin's acceptance of a policy so argued, then he could use comparable arguments to place the *Vozhd* subtly on the defensive in other policy matters as well.

It is known that Stalin did approve such an argument in 1945. On 18 August the regime commissioned the State Planning Office to produce a new Five Year Plan. In March 1946 Voznesensky came forward with the voluntarist document mentioned above. One may assume that Stalin approved the matter in principle long before its publication,[113] and one may also guess why. The plan was a splendid lever for pushing aside the home-front managers of the war era, the pragmatic Stakhanovites, and the Malenkovs. It allowed Stalin to side both with old-fashioned Marxism and with modern technological science in an attack on the pragmatic but crude methods of the bureaucrats he wished to depose.

One may guess also that once Stalin approved this plan, he was in trouble. It was basic to Voznesensky's argument that miracles were possible because the system was socialist. This meant that the Party was the inspiration, that the Party stood at the center of the system, and that the Party had won the war. Consequently by sanctioning this plan, Stalin was subtly sanctioning the principle that whatever the Party decided should be done. Thereafter, even within the Politburo, if he felt a Party policy to be impractical, the burden of proof lay not with the proponents but with him.

142

Who Won the War?

A mass base in the Party organizations of the liberated territories, well-integrated vanguards of middle-level cadres, a powerful grip on the central political institutions of the Soviet state system, and a fresh way of making political decisions—these are the ingredients of the Party revival of 1945 which this analysis of the Leningrad affair has uncovered. One may readily perceive now why they could have alarmed Stalin when they became apparent, perhaps quite suddenly, in the early months of 1945. He could hardly have anticipated so vigorous a rally in 1944, when he launched his campaign against the commanders and managers. Yet to grasp his consternation in full, one must go on to observe the outcome of his first efforts to still the swarm.

Stalin probably realized that his campaign had overreached itself when Shcherbakov fell ill in January 1945, when Leningrad celebrated late in the same month, and when the liberated territories prepared their demands for the Supreme Soviet session in April. He knew it for certain by the time Shcherbakov died early in May, at the time of the collapse of Germany. Just after that, on 9 May, Stalin spoke over the radio in the following terms: "Comrades! Fellow countrymen and countrywomen! the great day has arrived. . . . Comrades! Fellow countrymen and countrywomen! The Great Fatherland War has ended with our complete victory. The period of the war in Europe has ended. The period of peaceful development has begun. The victory is yours, my dear countrymen and countrywomen."[114]

Just as he came down from his Party pedestal in his first wartime speech and appealed to "citizens, brothers, and sisters," now at the end Stalin spoke in Old Russian, nationalist terms, not to the Party but to the people—as if he and they alone had won the war. During the following weeks, he pressed the argument further, in a flurry of short statements. In two of these he mentioned the importance of the Party,[115] but neither received wide circulation, and in the statements of this period which did receive attention—statements for which he is still remembered today—he made it plain that the people had won the war. His toast to the Russian people of 24 May 1945 and his toast to the "cogs" of 26 June raise the same questions Khrushchev asked in 1956: "Where is the military command? Where is the Politburo? Where is the government?" These statements signaled not only (as suggested elsewhere) Stalin's intention to displace the wartime political command but also his firm desire to counter the new cult of the Party.[116]

Hereupon, the extent of his trouble appeared. Despite his coldness to the Party, the editorialists of *Partiinoe Stroitel'stvo* found it possible to comment officially on his recent statements as follows:

> The complete rout of the Hitlerite state, the Hitlerite army, and the Hitlerite party, which was the party of the most gangster-like imperialists of all the imperialists of the world—this rout is the glorious consequence of the bitter struggle the Soviet people has carried on for almost four years under the leadership of the Lenin-Stalin Party.

The editorialists continued with page after page of praise not of the country and Stalin but of the Party:

> Humanity knows no other political party which could have played so well a liberationist role in the history of its country and people as the All-Union Communist Party of Bolsheviks. . . .
>
> "The outcomes of wars are decided in the long run . . . by correct policy" (Stalin). The most important virtue of our Party is that it always translates into reality the correct policy, that it knows which way things are going and leads successfully forward. . . .
>
> Inside the Soviet land the noble and lofty aims of the war gave birth to that historically unparalleled mass heroism with which our people brought fame to themselves in the struggle with the German-Fascist aggressors. The Party inspired the people in their feats of arms and labor. . . . The Communists in the Army not only showed themselves fearless soldiers, but also revealed their organizational talents and their knowledge of how to lead. . . .
>
> The Party, although it had been in power for more than a quarter of a century, did not lose touch with the glorious traditions of its past. The heroic professional revolutionaries of the first generation of Bolshevism can note with pride . . . that thousands of Communists proved themselves outstanding organizers of the national partisan struggle. . . .
>
> The organizational skill of the Bolshevik Party showed itself in the days of the patriotic war in all its manysidedness . . . in the adjustment to a powerful war economy, without which any victory would have been inconceivable. The socialist system conceals enormous possibilities within itself. But the advantages of the Soviet system reveal themselves only because the party of Lenin and Stalin knows how to steer by means of the laws of socialism.

These editorialists of the Party's leading activist journal even managed to conclude their paean to the Party's victory with a direct reference to Stalin's highly nationalistic toast to the Russian people:

> A clear intellect, a steadfast character, and patience—these, according to Comrade Stalin, are the distinguishing features of the Russian

144

people. These national features, spiritualized by means of Communist *ideinost* and by wholehearted devotion to the cause of Lenin and Stalin, result in the superiority of the Bolsheviks, the best sons of our Fatherland, fearless soldiers, tireless workers, the noble educators of the Soviet people. Hail to the Bolshevik Party, the inspirer and organizer of the victory! Hail to the great Bolshevik Stalin![117]

This was not what Stalin had said in May 1945, nor did it resemble anything he even implied then or for a long time theretofore. This was open transformation and perversion of Stalin's words and name for Party purposes.

One might ask whether, with forceful action, Stalin could not have silenced the Party in the spring of 1945. His prestige was then at its peak, his person almost popular. Indeed, probably at no other time in his career were circumstances more favorable for getting rid of the Party altogether, for banishing the Zhdanovs for good, and for admitting openly and bravely that he, Stalin, sat on a throne. Yet even while suggesting such a putsch, one must acknowledge its impossibility. Stalin had grown up with Marxism. He had given his life to a Party-led revolution. He was only a man, with inhibitions and foibles. It is simply not reasonable to propose that at the age of sixty-five he should have had the distance and perspective necessary even to conceive of such a putsch.

Further, there were practical difficulties. To have banished the Zhdanovs for insubordination in the middle of 1945 would have forced Stalin once again to lean upon the wartime commanders and managers. No one man can rule a great country without managers, any more than one man can win a great war without commanders. In the heady months of his victory over Hitler, such a retreat on the domestic political front could well have struck Stalin as a heavy price to pay for silencing the Leninist rhapsody. After all, he had attacked the wartime powerholders for good reason. During the war, his personal administrative controls had grown flaccid, and the bureaucratic upheaval and demobilization inevitable at the end of the fighting afforded a unique opportunity to re-establish them. If he retreated now, if he turned against the Party revivalists and fell back on Malenkov and Beria before the transition to peace had demolished their power, it was improbable that such an opportunity would come again.

There is yet another consideration: the men of the Party revival—the Kuznetsovs, the Rodionovs, the Voznesenskys—were on the whole new men, fresh faces, young, dynamic, attractive. The energy of

145

their revivalism may have been a shock to Stalin. Their *partiinost* and especially their voluntarism in policy debates invoked the abstract authority of Marxism which he feared. But the stakes were very great. And is it not the function of a great leader to encourage such men—to bring new blood into the leadership, even if this entails a certain risk to oneself in one's old age?

Stalin was seriously overextended in his campaign against his commanders and managers by the spring of 1945, yet there were good domestic political reasons why he should not give up the enterprise he had undertaken. It is not surprising, therefore, that one must look beyond the domestic political arena to foreign affairs for clues about how he brought the Party revival to its knees.

III

The Third Battle:
Against the Party

7

The Theory of Imperialism

Revival of the Theory

ON 6 NOVEMBER 1944 Stalin said it might be possible in the future to avoid wars, that if the great powers who were defeating Germany held together after the war and formed the core of a new United Nations peacekeeping organization, future war-like enterprises of aggressive countries might be nipped in the bud.[1] Stalin laced his speech with Party jargon, so it is not difficult to deduce his explanation of this wonderful new possibility. The inevitability of wars stemmed, according to Lenin, from the struggles between the various imperialist states over the distribution of raw materials and colonial territories. Stalin's major allies in World War II were among the greatest of the imperialist states, and after the war, it was predictable that they would be the only two of any account. Since Great Britain, the weaker, possessed by far the largest number of colonies, whereas the United States, the new world colossus, was conspicuously lacking in colonies, a Marxist could easily predict that

149

conflict between the two of them would be the source of the future imperialist wars. If, however, the two countries remained bound in a peacekeeping alliance with the world's first socialist state, then a mechanism would exist for forestalling such wars. Such a mechanism, moreover, would afford the Soviet Union splendid opportunities for manipulating the Allies in the interests of the socialist cause.

Stalin did not spell out this explanation in his speech, which, as indicated elsewhere, was less a "blue-print plan" replete with time-tables and specific goals than an expression of attitudes. However, his attitudes soon hardened into a basis for tactical operations. By May 1945 at least one group of East European Muscovite Communists—the Hungarians—were using his unspoken argument to justify the moderate coalition tactic they were foisting on their native comrades. By their account, Stalin's manipulation of the Grand Alliance was to continue for ten to fifteen years.[2] Meanwhile, the great wartime anti-sectarian campaign ended inside the Soviet Union, and late in April 1945 the Soviet Party's theoretical journal, *Bol'shevik,* for the first time since 1941 discussed Lenin's theories about just and unjust wars. With specific reference to Stalin's speech, *Bol'shevik* explained that wars were no longer so inevitable as in the past.[3] In October 1945 it discussed anew the theory of imperialism, again in the context of Stalin's speech, and made a striking reference to the nature of the peace. Out of the war of liberation, wrote the editorialist, would come a "peace of liberation" if the Grand Alliance endured.[4] Finally, in February 1946, Stalin himself, in his well-known election speech, made explicit reference to Lenin's theories about war (and thus to the two articles just mentioned), indicating that they were the theoretical basis for Soviet foreign policy.

One may add that all through the years 1946 and 1947, less important Soviet journals were filled with speculation about the coming crisis of capitalism, which would fling the United States and Great Britain into conflict.[5] Stalin's own brief public statements of those years all concerned a supposed absence of "real" danger of a new war—he hinted broadly that the Western imperialists could not afford to do without the Grand Alliance because of their quarrels with one another.[6] Even in 1952, when it had been clear for some time that the main political split among the world's states was between the Soviet East and a united Western bloc, Stalin insisted that it would be erroneous not to anticipate splits within the imperialist camp.[7] Finally, all Soviet historians of the postwar period write as if the splits between the Allies at that time were important and worthy of Soviet manipulation.[8]

Stalin's transition from hints about the theory of imperialism late in 1944 to implicit acceptance of it as a basis for policy early in 1946 was his single most overt departure from statism in the period discussed in this book. We have touched elsewhere on some of his earlier motives. In the revolutionary moments toward the end of the war he felt a need to hem in the more radical Communists abroad. He was enthusiastic, moreover, about the vast foreign policy prospects open to his country now that the Red Army had entered Europe. The purpose of the present chapter, and of those which follow, is to specify his other motives. Ultimately we will demonstrate that during 1945 Soviet foreign policy became the main battleground between Stalin and the runaway Soviet Communist Party. This battle above all, I propose, accounts for Stalin's sharply increased reliance on Lenin's theories just when the war in Europe and Asia was coming to its close.

Lessons of Experience

At the end of the war, a number of Western observers were well aware of the trend in Soviet political analysis of the outside world but thought it irrational. For example, in April 1945, just after President Roosevelt's death, the United States ambassador to Moscow, Averell Harriman, reported to the new president, Truman, "that some quarters in Moscow believed erroneously that American business needed as a matter of life and death the development of exports to Russia. Mr. Harriman said that this was of course not true, but that a number of Russian officials believed it."[9] In May 1945, George Kennan wrote incredulously from Moscow: "No one in Moscow believes that the Western world, once confronted with the life-size wolf of Soviet displeasure standing at the door and threatening to blow the house in, would be able to stand firm. And it is on this that Soviet global policy is based."[10] In March 1946, Kennan cabled home that Soviet policy toward the West involved questions "so intricate, so delicate, so strange to our form of thought that I cannot compress the answers into a single brief message. . . . Please note that the premises on which the Party line is based are for the most part simply not true."[11]

In retrospect, historians must admit that this Western astonishment about Soviet views was misguided, for in 1945 there was strong evidence that splits between the imperialist Allies existed then and had existed since America entered the war.[12] Even in 1942, when Molotov traveled to Washington to establish personal contact between Stalin and Roosevelt, the Americans were dropping hints regarding the desirability of dissolving the British Empire.[13] In the spring of 1943, when the question of East-West summit meetings arose, Roosevelt attempted to meet Stalin privately, behind Churchill's back. The salient political development at the Teheran Conference late in 1943 was not an East-West disagreement but an American-Russian combination designed to thwart a British invasion of southeastern Europe, which would have preserved the eastern Mediterranean as a British sea. In their first private encounter, Roosevelt even startled Stalin by proposing that British power be removed from India through "reform from the bottom, somewhat on the Soviet line."[14] After Teheran, moreover, while East-West relations within the Grand Alliance reached an unprecedented level of warmth, considerable squabbles broke out between London and Washington over oil interests in the once British-dominated Middle East and over Argentina, where Britain possessed large investments before the war. Disputes also arose over British wishes regarding the regime in defeated Italy, and many other topics. Meanwhile, both Washington and London were bickering with the newly established De Gaulle regime at Algiers, refusing to recognize French pretensions to equality as a great power, and hedging over French colonies. In October 1944 Roosevelt ostentatiously refused to let Churchill speak for him when the prime minister visited Moscow.[15]

All this was not foolishness: for America, a fight against British subjection of the Third World in Asia was consistent with a fight in Europe for Britain against Hitler. And even if we assume that Stalin and his colleagues were relatively free of Marxist-Leninist bias, an improbable assumption, this spectacle of discord could very easily have led them by November 1944 to believe that the Western imperialists were engaged in a struggle for the control of the colonial lands. Moreover, after Stalin's speech the signs of discord in the West multiplied. On 2 December 1944 General De Gaulle arrived in Moscow for the purpose of negotiating a Soviet-French treaty which would be independent of London and Washington. When Stalin proposed instead a tripartite pact including Britain, De Gaulle balked. When Stalin asked about a Western bloc, De Gaulle became confused.

When Stalin asked about French conflicts with Britain and America, De Gaulle acknowledged their existence.[16] Coincidentally, in Greece, the traditional Mediterranean lifeline of the British Empire, the British Army abandoned all pretense of neutrality and vigorously suppressed a Communist-led uprising. As a result, on 5 December the newly appointed United States secretary of state, Edward Stettinius, publicly criticized British interference in the internal affairs not only of Greece but also of Italy.[17]

There is circumstantial evidence that at the end of 1944, four months before the official revival of the "imperialist wars" theory in April, Moscow sought to "test" it by manipulating the splits between the Allies to extract concessions in Poland. We have observed earlier how great an obstacle the political situation in that country was to Moscow's interests. By late 1944 the catastrophic Warsaw uprising had greatly weakened the London Polish government, but major difficulties still existed, for the London Poles still had Western backing, still commanded public opinion inside Poland, and, despite public British pressure, still rejected Soviet territorial demands. Six months of occupation of eastern Poland had shown the Russians how inconvenient it was to deal with a hostile population.[18] With the approach of the conference at Yalta, the time seemed ripe to press for transformation of the Lublin Committee of National Liberation into an official government. Further, the possibility of splits among the Western Powers was strong. After their successes in France in mid-1944, their armies had bogged down at the German frontier. Indeed, in December they had suffered military reverses, and had fallen to squabbling about military priorities. Accordingly, on 5 January 1945, in open defiance of the Allies, Moscow allowed a Polish provisional government to be formed at Lublin and granted it diplomatic recognition.[19]

The Soviet government sought, as much as possible, to cushion this outright defiance of Allied wishes in Poland. When General De Gaulle came to Moscow in December 1944 to sign a Franco-Soviet treaty of alliance, for example, Stalin and Molotov almost let the opportunity slip through their fingers in their anxiety to obtain French recognition of the Lublin Committee in the bargain.[20] During December 1944 and January 1945, Moscow corresponded urgently with Washington and London in an attempt to get their consent to Soviet recognition of Lublin.[21] Coincidently, *Pravda* published the news that a beautifully "democratic" new type government had emerged in Hungary, as if that were evidence of Soviet democratic intentions in Poland also.[22] And it was generally believed at the time that Stalin's silence on the subject of the British involvement in the Greek civil war was designed to obtain a free hand in Poland.[23] Only after these efforts had failed to elicit Allied consent did Moscow finally act. Even then, Moscow went out of the way to placate Polish opinion: once the deed was done, the newly recognized Polish government sent a delegation to Moscow, where Stalin promised financial assistance for the reconstruction of Warsaw and, apparently, support for an Oder-Neisse frontier in the West.[24]

Despite this show of concern for the sensibilities of outsiders, there were clear signs that the Polish coup was designed to probe, on the broadest scale, the question of future Soviet relationships with the Western Powers. For example, the Lublin Committee precipitated the crisis with a public demand for recognition on 31 December 1944, a warning to the whole world of what was coming. On 1 January Stalin personally wrote Roosevelt and Churchill to say that the Soviet Union had promised the Lublin Committee to grant recognition, and refused their request for a month's delay. On 3 January, while the Allies, presumably, were worrying about what to do, Molotov, in a most extraordinary break with diplomatic protocol, handed the American ambassador in Moscow an aide-mémoire stating Soviet readiness to place $6 billion worth of orders with American industry in the first years after the war.[25] Molotov made the meaning of this overture quite explicit: his note referred to the "transition period" during which the economy of the capitalist United States was expected to go through a "crisis of overproduction," face diminishing markets, and suffer mass unemployment.[26] In his verbal explanation, he even excused his departure from protocol by saying that American industry "must be interested" in knowing in advance the dimensions of Soviet needs. The proposed financial arrangements make it amply clear that the Russians thought they were doing the United States a favor, rather than the other way around, and, of course, the proposed purchases were on a scale which could have solved the problems which were anticipated for American business.

There is little documentary evidence that Soviet diplomacy in the first weeks of 1945 was based on Lenin's theory of imperialism. At that time, the great anti-sectarian campaign had for two years banished discussion of that doctrine from Soviet public life. Although we know that it had been privately discussed since the spring of 1944 among the top leaders,[27] the only recent public references to it were the hints in Stalin's speech of 6 November. Further, it seems reasonable to think that the Soviet Union did urgently need the credits Molotov requested so peculiarly on 3 January 1945, and that accordingly the request was more than just a diplomatic ploy. Nonetheless, both its timing and its form suggest it was designed to make American capitalists and imperialists think of their own interests at a time when Moscow, with the *fait accompli* in Poland, was primarily defying Britain, which had gone to war over Poland.[28]

If indeed the circumstances just reviewed were a deliberate testing of Allied responses, then the Soviet leaders may well have found the results gratifying. On 6 January, the day after the Soviet Union granted official recognition to the Lublin Poles, Churchill in a cable to Stalin made his famous plea for an offensive on the Eastern front to take German pressure off Allied troops in the Ardennes.[29] The Western Powers swallowed the Soviet coup in Poland without much further protest, and they did not interrupt the plans for the conference at Yalta, which was then in the offing. In such terms the Soviet leaders may well have thought that the Allies had proved soft.[30]

Early in February, the Yalta Conference again forced Moscow to face the question of how the Allies would respond to pressure, and it signaled, more distinctly than in January, that the Russians were systematically testing the Alliance. From the very start of the conference on 4 February 1945 Stalin and Molotov seemed to be acting according to a careful game plan.[31] In the first meetings they took defiantly uncompromising stands on the necessity of dismembering Germany, of keeping France out of the occupation councils, and of establishing an absolute great power veto in the United Nations Organization. They encountered united Allied opposition to these positions but did not retreat until a divergence between British and American positions on the Polish question had become apparent. In his initial presentation of American policy, Roosevelt stressed the desirability of Russia's making concessions on Poland's eastern frontier, rather than the necessity of bringing the London emigré group into the new Polish government.[32] Churchill, on the other hand, tended to stress the governmental question above all.[33] On the second evening of the conference, Roosevelt heightened this appearance of divergence by addressing to Stalin a letter about Poland which, although Churchill had seen its contents, bore only one signature.[34] Immediately after receiving this letter, Stalin dramatically accepted the American version of the

155

UNO voting system and came forward with what were obviously well-prepared compromise demands on the UNO membership question.[35] He also reduced his demands on Germany from dismemberment to massive reparations. Then he and Molotov hinted that the Westerners should compromise also, and on this basis they bargained for the remainder of the conference.

One should recognize that this seeming pattern in Soviet diplomacy at Yalta was substantially a matter of diplomatic formalities and that statesmen normally prepare themselves carefully for important conferences.[36] But one may recognize also that at Yalta, perhaps more than ever before, the Russians received signals that the Allies were seriously divided over imperial questions.[37] At his very first encounter with Roosevelt there, Stalin heard the American president express, more viciously than he had at Teheran, his dislike of British imperialism. Roosevelt even told Stalin that Britain was urging America to rebuild France so that France could later become a British satellite.[38] In the famous private meeting during which he and Stalin discussed the price of Soviet participation in the Far Eastern war, Roosevelt attributed his Eastern policy largely to a desire to get the British out of Hong Kong and other colonies.[39] That Stalin and Molotov took these words seriously is clear: during the conference they repeatedly baited Churchill about the British Empire.[40] And the Russians had more than a little success in their fishing. We know from Vladimir Rudolph's report that as late as November 1944 some members of Stalin's entourage still expected the Western Powers to end the Soviet occupation of eastern Germany at an early date. Now at Yalta he obtained guarantees of a prolonged occupation of Germany, reluctant assurances of extremely large reparations, expressions of willingness to accept the status quo in Poland if Western face could be saved, and promises of territorial acquisitions in the Far East. These were no small gains. They were elicited through diplomatic manipulations in a context of inter-imperialist splits. Experience thus could have prompted the Soviet regime to consider Lenin's theory of imperialism indeed far-sighted and reliable as a guide to foreign policy practice early in 1945.[41]

A Question of Hope

An authoritative book by the Soviet economist Eugen Varga suggests indirectly another factor which lent the theory of imperialism operational value in Soviet eyes at the end of the war. Varga's book concerned changes in the economy of capitalism as a result of World War II. Chapters of it were published in the leading Soviet economics journal early in 1945, and discussion of the completed work was possible by autumn.[42] Varga's major message was that the world outside the Soviet Union was infinitely more complex than it had been in Lenin's day or even before the war. As suggested by his title, his main conclusion was that the economic mechanisms of capitalism might not conform to older Soviet prognoses. Through extensive empirical use of statistics, he demonstrated that, even in terms of population, there had been leveling tendencies in the European countries which might neutralize the chronic swings from underproduction to overproduction which had been characteristic of capitalist societies so often in the past. He stressed the enormous role that the state administrative structures had assumed in the management of the national economies in both the Axis and the Allied capitalist countries during the war and predicted that since these structures would not wholly disappear in the postwar era, the capitalist states might to some extent limit the "anarchy of planlessness" which, according to Marx, had hitherto characterized all the national economies of the bourgeois world.

In many ways, of course, Varga was a dogmatically orthodox economist who clung to many of the standard assumptions, although he criticized others. Every hint of redemption for capitalism that he found in his statistics was offset by a dour catalogue of growing unemployment and the greed of private business, which, he claimed, would in the long run inevitably drive the bourgeois system into collapse. He was confident that in all conflicts between the new Western state bureaucracies and the "monopoly corporations" the latter would always win. Even though the capitalist states could now manage their economies, according to Varga, the result was merely a postponement of the inevitable crisis of the system. He rested his entire argument on an analysis of the imbalance of colonies between newly great America and exhausted Britain and France, which, he judged, inevitably would lead them into internecine imperialist conflicts, if not to war. So dogmatic was Varga's work that the Western economists who read it at the time found it uninteresting and could not understand the considerable attention given it in the Soviet Union.[43]

However, in the eyes of Stalin and his colleagues Varga's work was to be compared not to that of contemporary Western economists but to that of the official economists of prewar Stalinism, who responded to the Great Terror with wholly schematic predictions of the immediate death of capitalism. In the Soviet world in 1945, Varga's stress on the eventual doom of capitalism and even his old-fashioned Leninist terminology would not have seemed odd. What was new in his work, however, was its reliance on Western statistical material, its generally empirical approach to objective phenomena, and, above all, its realistic view that capitalism might not collapse right away.

We can see why the theory of imperialism was so appealing to Soviet leaders in 1945. In Varga's realistic study of world conditions, only the theory of imperialism offered a ray of hope: only his reference to the imbalance in the distribution of colonies among the imperialists offered the slightest assurance that Russia might after all come out on top. His pragmatic demonstration that capitalism might live on, and that the trying interwar conditions of "encirclement" would probably return, was depressing, unsettling—indeed, alarming—to anyone with a realistic evaluation of conditions in the war-torn, wreckage-strewn, starving Soviet Union.

The other major book on political economy published in the Soviet Union just after the war was Voznesensky's *War Economy of the Soviet Union in the Period of the Great Patriotic War*. Mention of it here confirms our point. It did not concern the outside world but focused almost exclusively on the performance of the Soviet economy after 1941. The author begins by recalling the prewar years of socialist construction in the USSR, the gathering war clouds as the conflicts within imperialism grew more severe, and the low opinion imperialist observers had of the Soviet economy. He then discusses branch after branch of that economy during the war in order to show that, because the system was socialist, the prognoses of outsiders had proved wrong. In the fire of the war, he claims, the planned Soviet state economy had accomplished miracles. One must therefore conclude that the system is by nature superior, that Leninism is far-sighted and correct, and that a leader of that system who has faith and a strong will can overcome any problem. At the end of his book Voznesensky makes shining forecasts for the postwar Soviet economy and repeats the prediction that imperialism will soon collapse because of its internal flaws. Hope radiated from everything he said, and both his own political success in these years and the Stalin Prize immediately awarded to his book attest to the interest of the Soviet leadership in such optimism. From the Soviet leaders' perspective, the realities of

158

the world around them were in those years not especially bright. The alternative to the wishful optimism of theory was pessimism and despair. The theory of imperialism was attractive because it showed a way out.

The Challenge of Isolationism

One more factor may have strengthened Stalin's own tendency to see the Western Powers as manipulable allies late in the war. One may ask whether anyone among the Soviet leadership was then inclined to a policy of cooperation with the West. The best evidence of Soviet leadership opinion at the time is the galaxy of top-level election speeches of February 1946. There, surprisingly, we discover that apart from Stalin, Molotov, and Zhdanov, only old Kalinin made more than a passing reference to the wartime alliance with the West. The dominant tone of the other speeches was one of isolationism and thinly veiled distrust of outsiders. The home-front industrial troubleshooter L. M. Kaganovich, for example, stated that although Hitler's Germany and imperialist Japan had been defeated, eliminating the closest and most dangerous links in the prewar "capitalist encirclement" of the USSR, that encirclement still remained.[44] Beria likewise stressed that "it would be erroneous to think that the necessity for further strengthening of the military-economic power of the Soviet Union had disappeared." According to him, "the black forces of Fascism still hide in many countries."[45] And Malenkov lent his prestige to these premises:

> There have been cases in history when the fruits of victory escaped the victors. It is up to us so to conduct matters and so to work as to secure the fruits. To do this, we must continue, first of all, to strengthen the Soviet state created by Lenin and Stalin. . . . The weak are not respected, and what is more, it has been frequently demonstrated that the weak are thrashed. . . . We already represent a very great power. Let us not forget that we are strong enough to maintain the interest of our people. If necessary, we can wait until all concerned realize that we have achieved victory for ourselves and wish to safeguard our Motherland against any eventualities. We do not wish to pull chestnuts out of the fire for others. If we have the chestnuts, let us use them for the benefit of our own glorious Soviet people.[46]

We may note that in 1947 again it would be Malenkov (far more than Zhdanov) who would talk of the two great "tendencies" in the world as though they were geographically defined blocs.[47] Such evidence suggests that a very substantial segment of the home-front industrial leadership of the Soviet Union was thinking at the end of the war in terms of indifference, if not outright hostility, to their wartime imperialist partners.

Nor was this all. There was also a strong strain of antagonism to the West among the Party revivalists. For example, A. A. Kuznetsov, the leader of the Leningrad Party organization, used the occasion of Stalin's election speech in 1946 to make Stalin himself seem to say that there was a present danger of a new war.[48] Kalinin chattily told a conference of agricultural leaders in August 1945 that the defeat of the Fascist imperialists had not ended the threat from imperialism.[49] As early as April 1945 the editorialists of *Partiinoe Stroitel'stvo* declaimed that true vigilance involved Bolshevik knowledge that "as long as capitalist encirclement exists there will be spies from foreign states in the Soviet rear."[50] Furthermore, one may judge from the recent spate of military memoirs in the Soviet Union that even in the army there was strong distrust of the West.[51]

What may one deduce from this pattern of indifference or outright hostility to the Western Powers, which ran from one end of the Soviet political spectrum to the other in 1945 and 1946? The inference seems justified that the Western Powers had very few real friends in the top circles of the Soviet elite. This is not to say that all these leaders wanted war or were set on offending the West. The home-front leaders in particular, as noted above, seem to have been largely isolationist. They simply wanted to be strong and uninvolved; probably the Party revivalists did not actually want more war. But there was a universal bias against the outside world, and the more the traditional view of Marxism-Leninism was strengthened by the emergent Party revival, the more this bias tended to crystallize into an express rejection of binding commitments to the outside. This was not as unnatural or abnormal a development in Soviet attitudes as Westerners of the time often thought. Given the history of Russian xenophobia and the Marxist-Leninist revolutionary traditions of the Soviet elite, this anti-Westernism was entirely natural. What was unnatural was the opposite phenomenon—the existence of some pro-Western sentiments among the Soviet elite.

In October 1945, when Ambassador Averell Harriman visited Stalin at Gagry, where he was vacationing, Stalin said that there was an alternative to the foreign policy of participation in the Grand Alliance which he was then pursuing.[52] He called this alternative "isolationism," and suggested that hitherto he had opposed it. Presumably what he told Harriman was carefully weighed to leave the impressions intended, and this seems especially true of the rationale he gave now for considering a shift in his position. He claimed that he was being driven toward a new policy by continued Western opposition to Soviet political objectives. Examples included the American refusal to let Soviet troops land on the home islands of Japan; American insistence on bringing the French and the Chinese into the Big-Three peace discussions; and other signs of blocism in the West. These excuses aside, however, we can see in this talk of isolationism a major factor which could have strongly inclined Stalin personally toward a Marxist political analysis which stressed the possibility and desirability of maintaining the Grand Alliance in times of peace.

Stalin was more directly responsible for the preservation and security of the Soviet state than any other single leader or group of leaders in the country. Because of the nature of his dictatorship, he alone had to decide, on the basis of the available facts, what was and was not necessary to the state's security. Even Molotov, the actual administrator of foreign policy, was only a functionary compared to Stalin and had only a limited view of the problem. Stalin alone could recognize that, despite all its victories and its effective army, the Soviet state in 1945 probably could not afford another war right away and should, therefore, shrink from even the possibility of new confrontations abroad. Stalin also had to bear in mind the Leninist teaching that under certain conditions imperialists are quite likely to avoid conflict with each other by forming a united front against Communism and attacking the world's first socialist state.

If under such circumstances Stalin saw that virtually all his circle of advisers was taking an anti-Western stand, he had to act. No leader can afford to be surrounded just with arguments against a policy which, in terms of objective realities, is wise. In such terms Stalin was obliged, from the very dawn of the peacetime era, to commit himself publicly to a specifically Marxist-Leninist defense of the Grand Alliance such as he hinted at in November 1944.

"Anti-Blocist" Participationism

As mentioned earlier, two major second-level Soviet leaders did refer to the wartime alliance with the West in their election speeches of early 1946. These were Molotov and Zhdanov. They were the two Politburo members most directly responsible for foreign policy, although in different spheres. One may deduce that it was in part because of the offices they held that they referred to the Alliance, and did so approvingly. But this was not the only occasion on which they took such an approving stance, and in order to get a complete view of Stalin's conversion to the theory of imperialism during these years, it is useful to review their overall record.

Molotov made his most important policy speech of the entire postwar era on 6 November 1945 when he delivered the annual celebratory oration memorializing the Bolshevik Revolution. He opened with the remark that the war had been against Fascism and had been won by the "peoples."[53] He then went on to say that the Soviet "people" had established a new state in 1917, and that this people's state had not only stood up against Hitler's assault but had also saved European civilization. In the major foreign policy section of his speech, he said that the peace achieved would be a continuation of the war, that it would be characterized by participation of the peoples in the realization of their interests, and that the Grand Alliance, which derived (as Stalin said a year earlier) from the union of the "peoples" of Britain, America, and the Soviet Union, would protect the peace in the form of a United Nations Organization. At this most conspicuous point, Molotov described a sort of political formation which might obstruct Stalin's project:

> There has been considerable talk about founding either blocs or groupings of states as a means of ensuring protection for common external interests. The Soviet Union has never participated in groupings of powers directed against other peace-loving states. In the West, as is well known, this sort of thing has happened more than once. The anti-Soviet character of many of these groupings in the past is also well known. The history of blocs and groupings among the Western Powers shows that in all cases these served less to ward off aggressors than to give birth to aggression; this happened above all with Germany. This is why the vigilance of the Soviet Union and other peace-loving states in this respect cannot be relaxed.[54]

Molotov's main thesis was that the Soviet Union opposed blocs.[55]

Molotov's vision of what was happening in the world was not explicitly Leninist in this speech, nor did it become so in later ones. Some of his phrases sounded indeed almost populist. The only division he allowed in the world was horizontal, that between the peoples on the one hand, and elements (such as the Fascists in Germany), on the other hand, which existed within various states and which were capable of seizing and misusing power in their state. A point he stressed in 1945 and would continue to stress right through 1948 was that the peoples of the world were peace-loving, that they did not want war, and that consequently the states (now controlled, as Stalin has suggested in November 1944, by the peoples) could not make war.[56]

A certain lack of realism in what Molotov said, however, indicates that his populism camouflaged his real views. When he spoke, after all, the wartime Grand Alliance had already ceased to function, and it was coming to seem, objectively, as though there *were* two great blocs of states in the world, East and West. Shortly after Molotov spoke, moreover, one of the most heretical members of the Soviet regime, Duputy Foreign Commissar Maksim Litvinov, told Ambassador Harriman that there had been a change of policy in Moscow, and that the wrong people were now in charge.[57] Later he expanded this by saying that the "root cause" of the trouble between East and West was the "ideological conception prevailing here that conflict between Communism and capitalism is inevitable."[58] Litvinov's gloomy words are very puzzling unless one assumes that behind Molotov's populism lay a Leninist structure, and this is also suggested by Molotov's other major public statement of the winter of 1945–1946, his election speech. As noted elsewhere, Molotov was Leninist in that speech to the point of being voluntarist. He advised that by looking at a Leninist reality—by probing deep below the surface to find "real" popular movements and "real" alignments—one could see the bright future.

What then lay behind Molotov's "anti-blocist" Soviet foreign policy? Litvinov's indiscretions again afford us our best clue. In June 1946 he told an American correspondent that Molotov's rigid stands must not intimidate the West, in fact, that if the West made concessions, Molotov would merely make more demands.[59] The implication is clear: in supporting an "anti-blocist" continuation of a Grand Alliance between the Soviet Union and the Western Powers after the war, Molotov anticipated that the West, inevitably divided, could be forced by hardheaded diplomatic tactics to comply with the Soviet will.

Zhdanov, as has been noted, spoke even before 1941 about emphasizing the deeper realities of international politics and of basing Soviet foreign policy systematically on a Leninist analysis. His justification for the treaty with Germany in 1939 was based on a Leninist denial of qualitative differences between Fascist Germany and the Western democracies. After the war, he addressed himself even more vigorously to this thesis. In his speeches on literature in August 1946 he said:

> It does not really matter how beautiful the outside of the work of fashionable contemporary bourgeois . . . writers is. . . . They cannot preserve and elevate the standards of their bourgeois culture because it is based on a rotten foundation and has been placed in the service of private capital and ownership. Bourgeois writers . . . are trying to divert the attention of the progressive part of society from the important questions of the political and social struggle and to direct their attention to the sphere of vulgar literature and art, without ideals, filled with gangsters, robbers, glamor girls, adulterers, and low adventurers. We, the representatives of progressive Soviet culture, Soviet patriots, cannot really debase ourselves to the point of admiring bourgeois culture and its disciples.[60]

Zhdanov's views on Soviet culture, in contrast, were enthusiastic in 1946: "Our literature, which reflects a state order of much higher standards than that of any bourgeois country and a culture which is much more advanced than that of bourgeois countries, has the right to instruct others in a new public morality. Where can you find such a nation and such a country as we have? Where can you find such splendid human qualities as were shown by our Soviet people in the Fatherland war? . . . Every day our people are rising higher and higher."[61] In his speeches on philosophy in June 1947 and on music in January 1948, his abhorrence of the West grew even more violent and his adulation of Soviet culture more passionate.[62] It was this combination of vitriol and optimism that earned him his postwar reputation as a "hard-liner" about the Grand Alliance.

Yet Zhdanov's foreign policy theses in 1946 were not aimed at discarding the Grand Alliance (as is often claimed): they were exact parallels to the "anti-blocist" theses Molotov had propounded in 1945.[63] Even in the speeches on literature, for example, he spoke out decisively in favor of viewing the world not in terms of a vertical division, between blocs of states, but in terms of a horizontal division:

> As a result of the Second World War, the position of socialism was strengthened . . . [for] the question of socialism was placed on the [political] agenda in many European countries. This displeases the imperialists of all shades. They are afraid of socialism and [especially of

164

the fact that] our our socialist country an example to all mankind. The imperialists and their ideological henchmen, their writers and journalists, their politicians and diplomats, are trying by every means to slander our country and to present it in a wrong light—in other words, to vilify socialism.

In such circumstances, the task of Soviet literature is not only to parry these slanderous and base attacks on our Soviet culture but to hit back and also boldly to attack the state of miasma and degeneration of bourgeois culture itself. . . . No matter what efforts the bourgeois politicians and writers are making . . . to erect an "iron curtain" which will prevent the truth about the Soviet Union from penetrating beyond Soviet frontiers . . . they must be doomed to failure. . . .

Soviet writers and all-out ideological workers are at present in the front line. [We must recognize that] in the conditions of peacetime progress the tasks of the ideological front grow rather than diminish.[64]

With these words, Zhdanov justified the whole great public education campaign which he was just then introducing not as a response to internal Soviet needs but as counter-propaganda aimed at foreign imperialists, whom he saw not as nations but as elements within nations. He clearly indicated that the states of the world did not have to worry about war—that the war talk was a propaganda matter which writers could handle well enough.

What is more, he repeated this general line of argument three months later, on 6 November 1946, when he, in his turn, delivered the annual revolutionary oration:

What is the reason for the different views in several countries on the postwar settlements? World War II had an anti-Fascist liberating character to people who fought against the Fascist bloc. . . . One might anticipate that . . . general peace and security would [therefore] be achieved now without much difficulty or argument. But this has not happened. To the contrary, the peace program [of the Soviet Union] has met with organized resistance from *reactionary elements* in a number of states, especially in Great Britain and the United States. These *elements* have been using as camouflage a number of small countries which are willing to follow in their wake. . . . These anti-democratic tendencies became particularly evident at the [Peace Conference]. . . . [Imperialist circles are interested] in having their hands free to win world supremacy. . . . [Their] campaign for undermining international peace is accompanied by a furious anti-Soviet effort. . . . It is impossible not to notice that the *slander campaign* waged against the Soviet Union and the people inhabiting it has recently gained particular impetus. It is being conducted on a large scale and is calculated to undermine the increased . . . authority of the Soviet Union among the peoples of the democratic countries. . . . When our blood was flowing, . . . our high moral qualities . . . evoked

universal admiration. . . . Now that we wish to realize in collaboration
with other peoples our equal right to participate in international affairs,
we are drenched with streams of invective. The war . . . has failed to
teach anything to those people.[65]

With these words, Zhdanov again indicates that the East-West split—
by then in reality far advanced—is little more than a conspiracy of
warmongering and reactionary elements, armed with propaganda,
against the united peoples of the world. Far more explicitly than in his
August speech on literature, the split in the world is made to seem not
vertical, between East and West, but horizontal, between "isolated
imperialists" and the "peoples."

Why Zhdanov committed himself to these remarkable foreign
policy theories in 1946 is a question which can only be resolved in
part in terms of his voluntarism and of the euphoria of victory. By
1946 and 1947 the emergent Cold War had made insistence on "anti-
blocism" and horizontalism extremely awkward. But another reason
for Zhdanov's commitment strongly suggests itself. Just a few weeks
prior to his oration, on 24 September 1946, Stalin issued the following
statement:

> I don't believe there is a real danger of new war. The noisy people on
> this subject are mostly military and political scouts [*razvedchiky*] and
> their few adherents in civilian ranks. . . . One must make a strict dis-
> tinction between the noise about a new war, as conducted at present,
> and real danger of new war, which at present does not exist. . . . I do
> not think the governing circles of Great Britain and the United States
> could create a capitalist encirclement of the Soviet Union even if they
> wished to, which, however, I cannot assert.[66]

Stalin himself was to such an extent relying on a Leninist perception
of reality that Zhdanov could hardly do otherwise.

Stalin's obvious role in encouraging Zhdanov to stand by "anti-
blocism" in the years after 1945 suggests a final explanation of the
Vozhd's increased reliance on the theory of imperialism in that year.
From Stalin's point of view this theory may have had concrete domestic political advantages. Most of the isolationists were the wartime managerial "substituters" whom Stalin at just this time was
moving to unseat. Molotov and Zhdanov, on the other hand, were
leaders of the Party revival through which Stalin was launching his
domestic policy attack. By encouraging the esoteric foreign policy
theses of those two men, Stalin could further his attack on the man-

agers and oppose isolationism while in a sense muzzling the isolationist impulses in the revival itself. This was a tempting combination,
and historians who are aware of Stalin's cravings for control will be
unwise to overlook its attractions.

Conclusions

The evidence is strong that the Soviet leadership revived Lenin's
theory of imperialism in 1944–1945 and made it a basis of their foreign
policy for empirical, psychological, and practical reasons. Looking
out from Moscow in the exciting last months of the war, one could
legitimately believe that Leninism was coming true—that the imperialists really were deeply divided in a moment of revolutionary challenge. Psychologically, the Soviet leadership had an obvious and
deep-seated need for optimistic political prognoses, for the present
reality was very grim indeed. And in practical terms, given the deep-
rooted anti-Westernism and isolationism of most of his colleagues at
this time, Stalin could hardly afford not to encourage the members of
his entourage who argued in favor of continuing the Grand Alliance.

The question remains as to which of these various factors played
the greater role. In the following chapters we will review the international political developments of 1945 in the hope of finding an answer.

8

Rebuttal

Vyshinsky's Intervention in Rumania

TOWARD THE END of January 1945, just before the Yalta Conference, the Communists in Rumania began to agitate for a leftward shift in the political direction of their country. The far from progressive Rumanian government, perhaps reassured by Western advisers, refused to budge. There was bloodshed in Bucharest during huge demonstrations on 24 February. On 27 February, A. Y. Vyshinsky, the chairman of the Allied Control Commission, descended upon the Rumanian capital and demanded that King Michael replace the regime of General Rădescu with a "democratic front" government headed by a leftist peasant party leader, Petru Groza. When the king procrastinated, Vyshinsky gave him a two-hour ultimatum and, as he left, slammed the door so hard that the plaster on the ceiling cracked. The king gave in.[1]

168

Partial explanations of Vyshinsky's intervention were readily visible on the Rumanian scene. The Soviet Union had gained a great deal under the armistice arrangements of September 1944: retrocession of Bessarabia and the Bukovina, expulsion of the Germans from the lower Danubian region, a change of sides by the Rumanian army, which now fought the Germans, acceptance of the Rumanian Communists into the Bucharest government, and a Red Army occupation of the entire country. But in February 1945 there was room for Soviet complaints because the traditionally Russophobe political structure of the old regime had been left largely intact. In December 1944 the Rumanian Communists, who were few in number and very unpopular, had tried to bring about a change with a first wave of demonstrations, but had failed. In February King Michael's choice as prime minister publicly characterized the Communist leaders as "hyenas" and "foreigners without God or country" (a reference to the Jews among them). Moscow could hardly tolerate this sort of name-calling in a Soviet-occupied country where anti-Bolshevik nationalism was deeply ingrained in the minds of the population. Besides, considerable social disorder was breaking out in the countryside, brought on by the conflict between the Communists and the government, and this also was undesirable in the Red Army's rear.[2]

Despite these objective factors, Vyshinsky's ultimatum and door-slamming remain a mystery. His action was among the crudest examples of Soviet political meddling in Eastern Europe in the entire postwar period, a blatant violation of the Yalta agreements signed just a few weeks earlier. It was also a direct affront to the Western Powers, for Vyshinsky acted in their name against their known desires, and did so with deliberate éclat. The contrast with the Russians' outward cordiality to the Allies at Yalta was unmistakable. Further, one could wonder whether the change in Rumania's political direction had to be brought about in this particular way. Massive purges which were just then affecting neighboring Bulgaria showed clearly that when the Red Army was in occupation of a country, the local Communists did not need spectacular Soviet political interventions to get rid of their enemies. Only a few months after Vyshinsky's action, Moscow highlighted its artifice by awarding King Michael the Soviet Order of Victory. For such reasons contemporaries tended to look outside Rumania for explanations of this first East-West confrontation of the Cold War, and Western historians follow suit.[3]

A Case of Nerves?

It has been tempting to seek the deeper motives for Vyshinsky's intervention in discords which were just then emerging within the Grand Alliance. On 23 February, Soviet Foreign Commissar Molotov met with the Allied ambassadors to Moscow to work out the details of the Yalta agreements about Poland.[4] The meeting was relatively cordial: Molotov even invited the British and Americans to send observers into Poland to assess conditions there. But at a second meeting on 27 February he withdrew his invitation, and the atmosphere changed. The Russians now claimed that the Yalta conference had accepted the Lublin government, which they were sponsoring, whereas the Allies argued that the London government should be saved.[5] To some extent the trouble was that the text of the Yalta agreements concerning Poland was vague. But Molotov proved both rigid and rude in the face of the difficulties,[6] and meanwhile trouble was brewing for Western interests inside Poland.

In January and February, the Red Army finally liberated Warsaw and western Poland. In mid-March the London-affiliated remnants of the Polish underground army acknowledged their helplessness by agreeing to meet with Soviet negotiators. Moscow responded by arresting them, despite the protection they enjoyed in the West.[7]

Coincidentally, two other storms blew up, the first over the Turkish straits. At Yalta, Stalin expressed the view that the Montreux Convention of 1936 had to be revised, and Roosevelt and Churchill agreed in principle, though not in detail. Late in February the Soviet press drummed up a campaign against Turkey, and on 19 March Moscow denounced the Soviet-Turkish Treaty of 1925. There was also talk of changing Turkey's frontiers, which caused dismay and protest in Allied circles.[8] On 14 March Harriman told Molotov that Western military authorities were in contact with German officials in Berne regarding a surrender of Axis forces in Italy. Harriman assured Molotov that Soviet observers would be welcome once the negotiations reached matters of substance, but Molotov took it for granted that the talks were closed to the Russians altogether and concerned a separate peace. A few days later, Stalin withdrew Molotov from the Soviet delegation that was to attend the United Nations Conference at San Francisco. By early April, Stalin was hurling rude and angry charges at Roosevelt and Churchill, claiming that the West was about to make a separate peace with the enemy.[9]

During March the military situation in Europe began to shift radically. The great Soviet winter offensives, which in the days of the Yalta Conference had reached the Oder River, one hundred miles from Berlin, ended in hard-fought battles in Silesia and Pomerania and the western Danubian plain, but in the West the German front collapsed. After a long, slow battle in February, the Allies captured a bridge over the Rhine at Remagen on 7 March. Cologne fell on 10 March, Worms on 21 March. Three days later great offensives eastward from the Rhine began and the end of the war approached, with the Allies, not the Russians, the obvious winners. It was this breakthrough which Stalin attributed to Allied collusion with the foe.

Had Vyshinsky's intervention in Bucharest been delayed only a few weeks, one could easily attribute it to this complex of roughly coincident discords which marred inter-Allied relations in March 1945. Perhaps the Soviet leaders felt excessively optimistic after Yalta, which represented a dazzling rise in Soviet status in the world. Disillusionment may have come thereafter, with the discovery that the Polish controversy was still unsettled—indeed, that the Allies were apparently backing away from promises they had made. Perhaps in their disappointment the Soviets felt only within their rights in truculently starting a campaign against the Turks. Perhaps they had real feelings of suspicion mixed with jealousy over the Allied breakthrough on the Rhine. In such a context, Vyshinsky's action might seem the result of a crisis of nerves in Moscow.

But Vyshinsky acted on 27 February, and on that very day the Allied ambassadors in Moscow first discovered the depth of the split between the two sides on the Polish question. All the other disagreements of the following month arose after the Bucharest coup. As for the military situation, on 27 February the Western Allies were still encountering enemy resistance quite as determined as that in the east. Thus Vyshinsky's coup cannot be explained as the result of a build-up of Soviet disappointment and nervousness. It seems, rather, the opening salvo of a Soviet barrage which, as if deliberately, produced bad feeling among the Allies. One must ask here once again why Vyshinsky's vehemence seemed necessary to Moscow as the end of the war approached.[10]

A Further "Test"?

The very form of the Rumanian coup suggests an explanation. In all but one respect, this coup was comparable to the one in

Poland in January 1945. In both Rumania and Poland, for example, Moscow needed, and through these actions attained, a shift toward "friendliness," defined according to Soviet standards. In both cases there was direct defiance of the known positions of the Western Allies. Furthermore, there were remarkable parallels in the propaganda accompanying the two coups. In December 1944, before the Polish action, *Pravda* presented the newly announced government of Hungary as a sort of guarantee that Soviet intentions were democratic. Now, on the eve of the Rumanian intervention, *Pravda* pointed to the Soviet-sponsored free elections in Finland as further evidence.[11] In January, after the Polish coup was over, Stalin promised the new Polish government both German land and Soviet money for the reconstruction of Warsaw as a sop to Polish national pride; on 9 March Stalin himself, with great fanfare, handed over to the Groza regime the administration of northern Transylvania, which the Germans had returned to Hungary in 1940, and which the Russians had not given back to Rumania after the liberation in October 1944.[12]

The vital respect in which the Rumanian intervention seems different from the one in Poland was the obvious attention the Russians paid to the position of the Allies. In the Polish case, Stalin personally made a great effort to win Allied consent before he acted. In the Rumanian case, he made no such attempt. However, his insult to the Allies was as pointed as the attempt to placate them had been in the case of Poland. And there is confirmation that this is a valid way of reading the facts. At the time of the Polish coup, it may be recalled, Molotov made a crude attempt at bribing the Americans with promises of huge Soviet purchases of American goods. He implied that the Allies were imperialists, dependent on Soviet favors because of the chaos of their capitalist economies. In a comparable way, at the height of the Berne affair, in his last letter to Franklin Roosevelt Stalin pointedly set forth a quid pro quo for ending the crisis, as if the Western Powers were somehow at his mercy: "The Polish question has reached an impasse. What is the reason? The reason is that the US and British ambassadors in Moscow . . . have departed from the instructions of the Crimea Conference. . . . In order to break the deadlock and reach an agreed decision the following steps should, I think, be taken."[13] Molotov repeated this ultimatum in his initial discussion of the Polish problem with President Truman on 22 April, as did Stalin in his first letter to Truman on the subject.[14] Evidently, they felt free to gamble the whole unity of the Grand Alliance on the imperialists' willingness to swallow the Soviet interpretation of the extremely unclear Yalta agreement.

To sum up, through a process of comparison, one may deduce that the Rumanian coup of 27 February 1945 was the beginning of a deliberate Soviet test of the political responses of the Allies. Just as earlier in Poland and in the stylized diplomatic maneuvering at Yalta, Moscow seems to have been trying to find out whether Allied behavior would fit the Leninist theory of imperialism. The novelty of this new Soviet testing of the mettle of the Allies lay in its conspicuous lack of caution. Earlier in the year Moscow still seemed to be worried about the stability of the Grand Alliance and the security of the Soviet state. Now it seemed so confident that the Allies were split that it pressed forward ruthlessly and recklessly.

Anti-Blocism Begins

Major shifts in Soviet foreign policy just after the death of Roosevelt tend to confirm the suggestion that both Vyshinsky's coup in Rumania and Stalin's behavior in the Berne affair were part of a deliberate reliance on Lenin's theory of imperialism. On 16 March *Pravda* published an editorial which reflected many of the statist attitudes of the war era. The subject of the editorial was a new book by the well-known American columnist Walter Lippmann, which speculated, among other things, on the probable postwar complexion of Europe and proposed that Germany, because of her cultural traditions, should fall into a Western, not a Soviet, sphere of influence. *Pravda*'s criticism was not of the idea that Europe might be divided into spheres of influence; Lippmann's error, according to *Pravda,* was his indulgent attitude toward the enemy. Less than eight weeks before the fall of Berlin, *Pravda* still felt it dangerous to even think of coddling the hated Fascist foe.[15]

The Berne affair reached its peak a few days later. On 12 April Roosevelt died without having decisively refuted Stalin's allegations of treachery. Hereupon, on 14 April, G. F. Aleksandrov, the chief of the Agit-Prop Administration of the CPSU(b) Central Committee, published in *Pravda* a sharp criticism of Il'ya Ehrenburg, the most strident anti-German voice raised in the Soviet Union during the war.[16] This article was immediately recognized as stemming from the highest official circles.[17] It called first for a reduction of the essentially nationalistic anti-Germanism of the past few years and thus, in a sense, advocated a return to the Party's traditional internationalism. But this was not the significant part of the article, if only because now, when the occupation of Germany was beginning, the Soviet regime may have been forced to lower its propaganda level so that the occupation could go smoothly. The meat of the article lay in its second section, in which Aleksandrov took issue with Ehrenburg for explaining the desperate German resistance on the Eastern front in terms of German hatred of Russia and preference for the Allies. Such an explanation, according to Aleksandrov, could only play into the hands of the "expiring Hitlerites" by feeding suspicions within the Grand Alliance. Since the suspicions in question were obviously not Allied suspicions of Russia but Soviet suspicions of the Allies, it follows that Aleksandrov supported the unity of the Grand Alliance and opposed any suggestion that its members might betray the Soviet Union to the foe.

Six days later *Pravda* once again took up Walter Lippmann's book but from an entirely different point of view. Now Lippmann's error lay in his blocism and in his alleged failure to support the unity of the United Nations Organization.[18] The shift in *Pravda*'s position makes it clear that it was after the Berne affair that the Soviet foreign policy line moved decisively away from the statist views of the war period to the anti-blocism which, Molotov would boast in November, "had always been" at the heart of Soviet policy because imperialist power blocs had been the source of the century's major wars.

There is other evidence that it was just after the Berne affair that the Soviet leadership decided to rely on Zhdanov's reading of the theory of imperialism. For example, Wolfgang Leonhard recalls that on 29 April he heard an anti-Western joke for the first time in Moscow since early in the war. This, he suggests, was when the anti-sectarian campaign effectively ended.[19] On the same day the CPSU(b) theoretical journal *Bol'shevik* went to press with its first article in years about the "Lenin-Stalin Teaching about Just and Unjust Wars."[20] As mentioned earlier, this article frankly admitted that the key to understanding war was class analysis of the competing powers, a direct allusion to Lenin's theories about imperialism. The article went on to quote from Stalin's speech of November 1944 indicating that despite the continued existence of imperialism, wars would no longer be inevitable if the Grand Alliance held together.

Furthermore, on 1 May 1945 Stalin himself confirmed the gist of

Aleksandrov's article, reverting to a more Communist way of looking at the German question. He said: "Lying Fascist propaganda is intimidating the German population with nonsensical tales that the armies of the United Nations want to wipe out the German people. The task of the United Nations is not to destroy the German people. The United Nations will destroy Fascism and German militarism, and they will severely punish war criminals. . . . But the United Nations are not harming and will not harm the peaceful population of Germany."[21] With these words, Stalin removed the stigma which in Communist circles had hitherto placed the German people outside the Pale[22] and readmitted the Germans to the family of nations which had the capacity to proceed toward socialism.

The effects of Stalin's words were soon visible in terms of German Communist Party policy. Until now, the KPD had been assuming that the German people would for a long time not be capable of normal democratic political activity. But according to a new Party line published in June 1945, the German people were as capable of democracy as any other people, and Party policy became identical with the coalitionist policies of the other European Communist parties.[23] The effects of Stalin's statement were also visible in Soviet state policy regarding Germany. Beginning in May Moscow began to premise that Germany would not be partitioned but would remain a single political entity. At this same moment the Allies cut Germany up into occupation zones. In practice, over the next few years the Russians did not seem eager to reunify the country on any terms but their own. Consequently, outsiders tended to disregard the expressed theoretical base of Soviet policy. It is clear today, however, that from 1945 until the beginning of 1948 Stalin favored reunification, indeed, envisaged the emergence of an all-German leftist coalition government as a concrete possibility, and for this reason blocked the establishment of a regional German government in the Soviet zone.[24]

In April 1945, Stalin decisively restated his allegiance to the keystone of the Zhdanovite foreign policy theses of the next few years—the notion that the Grand Alliance could form the core of an effective United Nations peacekeeping organization. During the March crisis, he had announced that Molotov would not attend the foundation conference of the United Nations scheduled in San Francisco. But on 13 April, in response to a plea from President Truman, he changed his stance. On 21 April, in a speech on the occasion of the signing of a state treaty with Poland, he sought to cover up the emer-

175

gence of a Soviet bloc in Eastern Europe. The new Slavic pro-Soviet regimes constituted, he said, a bloc against Germany, but they were not *just* an East European bloc but were part and parcel of the world-wide anti-Fascist bloc of the United Nations.[25]

This awkward top-level "blocist denial of blocism" was paralleled by a fresh and authoritative statement of the international Communist line. At the end of April Jacques Duclos, a prominent figure in the French Communist Party who had visited Moscow in March, published an attack on the allegedly anti-Party and un-Communist behavior of the wartime leader of the CPUSA, Earl Browder.[26] In 1944 Browder had dissolved his Party on the then perfectly acceptable Stalinist grounds that since the United States was allied with the socialist Russian state, it could progress toward socialism without the intervention of a Communist Party. Now Duclos charged that Browder was terribly at fault. No country, he claimed, could possibly progress toward socialism without Communist leadership. So vigorous was his attack on Browder that it has been called the first salvo of the Cold War. But actually the model with which he confronted Browder was that of his own party in France. Fourteen months earlier, the CPF, with its neighbor in Italy, had pioneered Stalin's "new type government" tactic—that bourgeois participationism which for half a century in the eyes of European leftists had been the most execrable aspect of social democracy's decay. Since then, moreover, Duclos's party (on Stalin's urging) had been the first resistance Communist Party in Europe to surrender its arms to a primarily bourgeois coalition government, and in April 1945, it was seeking power not through insurrection in the style of Tito, Lenin, or Marx but through a Machiavellian coalition with the bourgeoisie and democratic popular elections.

All these shifts in the Soviet attitude toward the outside world in April 1945 confirm the presence of deliberate Soviet testing in the crisis of the Grand Alliance during March; some material from recently published Soviet military memoirs may settle the matter. It seems notable, for example, that V. I. Chuikov, then a general, now a marshal of the Soviet Union, has accused Stalin of deliberately delaying the end of the war for political purposes. On 4 February 1945, according to Chuikov, Stalin, who was at Yalta, telephoned Marshal Zhukov, the Soviet commander-in-chief in the West, whose troops were then approaching the Oder. Chuikov claims that Zhukov could have plunged through, seized Berlin, and brought about the collapse of the enemy then and there, but that Stalin ordered him to stop. Zhukov has denied this report, and Soviet historians have also decided to reject it. But the mere fact that the allegation has been made and that it seems to the Russians worth denying suggests that Stalin's intimates did not put any limits on the scope—or the grossness—of his manipulations.[27]

More directly relevant to our problem is the evidence which has been released about the planning in the Soviet General Staff of the final Berlin offensive. Marshal Zhukov claims that on 29 March 1945, six weeks after he had halted his offensive at the Oder, he was called to Moscow and received by Stalin, who showed him a letter from a "foreign well-wisher" concerning the Berne affair. According to the letter, the Allies would not make a separate peace with the Germans, but were sorely tempted to accept a German offer of free entry into Berlin before the Russians. Stalin told Zhukov that the German military had indeed suggested such an offer. His opinion was that the British, though not the Americans, might accept it, and he ordered Zhukov to prepare for final decisions about a new Soviet offensive on 1 April.[28] The next day he called General Konev, the other major Western front commander, to Moscow to attend the decisive meeting.[29]

Just at this point, the unexpected happened. On 28 March, with the Rhine breached and the Ruhr virtually surrounded, General Eisenhower, the supreme allied commander in Western Europe, decided that Berlin was no longer a top military priority for his forces, shifted various army units from the British front in northern Germany to the American-commanded center, and, without consulting the Joint Chiefs of Staff, cabled Stalin directly to ask where in Saxony Western and Soviet troops could meet. His decisions seemed a major change in the Western battle plan.[30] They caused a tempest of resentment in England,[31] and, of course, when his cable was handed to Stalin in Moscow late on 31 March,[32] it altered the entire scenario in which the Russians had been planning the urgent attack on Berlin. If, as Stalin was clearly given to understand by the bearers of the Eisenhower message, the West would leave him Berlin, then there was no urgency.

Stalin's response was, first of all, to cable Eisenhower early on 1 April that he agreed that Berlin was now a secondary objective and that the next Soviet offensive would head for Saxony and a meeting with the Americans.[33] Second, he spent two long days with his generals as if nothing had changed, planning an immediate attack on Berlin to keep the British out. He used the respite Eisenhower had given him only to play a trick on Zhukov and Konev. He knew the two men were rivals. He made no demarcation line in the Berlin area between their two fronts. He told a colleague: "Let the one who is first to break in, take Berlin," turning the offensive into a competition.[34]

Stalin's main response to the Eisenhower telegram, however, was another sort of provocation—a new testing of the Grand Alliance. On 3 April, he sent an insulting telegram to Roosevelt:

> You are quite right in saying, with reference to the talks between the Anglo-American and German commands in Berne or elsewhere, that "the matter now stands in an atmosphere of regrettable apprehension and mistrust." You affirm that so far no negotiations have been entered into. Apparently you are not fully informed. . . . My military colleagues . . . are sure that negotiations did take place and that they ended with an agreement with the Germans, whereby the German Commander on the Western Front, Marshal Kesselring, is to open the front to the Anglo-American troops and let them move east, while the British and Americans have promised, in exchange, to ease the armistice terms for the Germans. . . . I realize that there are certain advantages resulting to the Anglo-American troops from these separate negotiations . . . but why conceal this from the Russians?[35]

Here once again Stalin acted as if Eisenhower's message were a trick or never existed, and, as he had done earlier in the war when he had wanted to get something from the Western leaders, he insulted them.[36]

In interpreting anecdotal materials in Soviet memoirs, one must be continuously alert for the traces of latter-day politics. These particular stories have survived the test of time, however, and we are entitled, therefore, to point to their lesson: Stalin's extreme rudeness in his letter to Roosevelt on 3 April indicated his full awareness that he was playing a game—throwing insults at his partner for no other reason than to elicit a convincing response.

This finding leads us to a speculative interpretation of the entire March crisis of 1945. Perhaps after the Allied concessions at Yalta, Stalin wanted to establish once and for all the strength or weakness of the West. It was safer to do this now in March 1945, while the war still continued, than it would be later. If the Allies did turn out to have some muscle, Stalin could still anticipate that in order to finish the war they would avoid a final break with him, even if he tested their patience. As long as Hitler was alive, Stalin, in a sense, had an insurance policy against the collapse of the Grand Alliance. Later on, after the end of the war, this insurance would disappear.

An Inspired Debate

In view of the absence of firm documentation of Soviet motives, any analysis of the March crisis must be as speculative as the above. But this one has a fault in addition to being speculative: it is too neat. It conceals the variables which, unknown to the Russians, determined American and British behavior during the closing months of the war, and makes it seem as if the Western Powers naively blundered into an all-knowing Politburo's trap. It is necessary, therefore, to note some further evidence about the March crisis of 1945 which suggests that in moments of excessive cleverness even Stalin might be foiled.

As pointed out earlier, there was a great celebration at Leningrad on the very eve of the Yalta Conference. The chairman of the Presidium of the Supreme Soviet, M. I. Kalinin, was present and awarded the hero-city the order of Lenin for its bravery during the three-year siege. The celebration was a major symptom of the radicalization of the Soviet Party's revival at that time. Some peculiar developments just after this celebration suggest that even then Stalin was in a sense rebutting the Party revivalists by re-emphasizing nationalist themes of the war era. On 31 January, for example, after long preparations, the Holy Synod of the Russian Orthodox Church convened in Moscow to elect a new patriarch. On 2 February the synod unanimously elected Alexis, metropolitan of Leningrad, a man of great popularity because he had remained in the city throughout the siege; on 4 February the synod, with considerable ceremony, crowned him. Although representatives of the foreign press were in attendance, there had been virtually no publicity in the Soviet press about these events. But on 5 and 6 February, not only the government organ *Izvestiya* but also the Communist Party's *Pravda* devoted their front pages to such detailed coverage of both the coronation and the synod's appeal to Christians throughout the world that observers began to wonder if some real reconciliation between church and state might be at hand.[37]

Nothing suggests that these church ceremonies were linked with the celebration at Leningrad by anything but sheer coincidence. Administratively, the two celebrations were quite separate. But the same cannot be said of the reportage, which was sudden and surprising. It could have been arranged in connection with the reports on the Leningrad ceremonies, and it certainly would remind readers of that earlier publicity. It is interesting, therefore, that the news of the church ceremonies sharply contrasted with the *partiinyi* image of Leningrad, which dominated in the publicity about the celebration.

In the following months the nationalist symbols which had emerged during the war were reactivated on a large scale. In April, for example, Stalin himself held talks with the heads of the Georgian church, who were visiting Moscow.[38] The Orthodox church, moreover, was given an extraordinary opportunity to participate in Soviet foreign policy operations: at the end of May 1945, Patriarch Alexis toured the Near East with the express purpose of re-establishing the church's influence in Alexandria, Damascus, and the Holy Land, and in September a church mission went to the United States to establish the Moscow patriarch's authority over the important Orthodox branch there. On 27 November, the patriarch of the Armenian church joined in, demanding that Turkey turn over to the Soviet Union Kars and Ardahan, ancient Armenian lands taken from Russia at the end of World War I.[39]

Meanwhile the Panslavic Committee went into action. This committee had been established during the war by East European émigrés living in Moscow. It published a journal, was apparently run from behind the scenes by Beria's secret police, and seemed mainly intended to convince outsiders that Soviet foreign policy fitted into a statist, nationalist mold. It was perhaps not surprising that the committee turned out in full force in March 1945, when President Beneš of Czechoslovakia returned there on his way to his liberated homeland: by Soviet standards, Beneš was "bourgeois" and susceptible to nationalistic appeals. But the committee figured prominently also in the reception early in April of Marshal Tito of Yugoslavia, a good Communist. On 21 April, during a state visit by members of the Polish Provisional Government, Stalin himself described Slavism as a movement to ensure the peace and security of Eastern Europe far into the future.[40] He was beginning to sound as nationalistic again as he had been during the war. Then on 24 May Stalin published his toast to the Russian people, from which we have quoted elsewhere.[41] In this toast, as in the public pronouncements he delivered during the summer of 1945, we hear of nothing but the people and Stalin, bound together not by any Marxist-Leninist bond but by faith and an explicitly pre-Soviet nationalism. This return to national motifs again must have reflected decisions by Stalin himself. It counterweighed the rapidly spreading enthusiasm of the Party revival.

A remarkable hint of a connection between the March foreign policy crisis and Stalin's undercutting of the Party revival came in April, when, amidst all those signs of a major shift in Soviet foreign policy cited earlier, *Pravda* published a double article by Vyshinsky, who had just returned from Bucharest.[42] Vyshinsky clearly delineated Stalin's thinking on the state. He indicated, above all, that the Soviet state had not come into being as a result of some inherent mechanism of socialism; over and over again he emphasized that Lenin and Stalin had "renewed" Marxism on the basis of "practical experience" and had "created" the state in forms which Marx had not predicted. Lenin, for example, allowed no withering away of the state in the immediate wake of the Russian Revolution, as many pre-revolutionary Marxists had expected; he did not exclude the peasantry and the nationalities from representation in this state; he did not wait for the world-wide revolution which many Marxists thought would be necessary to the construction of socialism. According to Vyshinsky, Lenin and Stalin had built socialism not through passive attention to ideological dogmas but pragmatically, through "learning from experience": without Lenin and Stalin there would have been no socialism. Vyshinsky's essay sharply contrasted with the theses of the Party revivalists.

This essay was not disregarded. Published to memorialize the anniversary of Lenin's birth, it was reprinted within a few days even in the journal *Partiinoe Stroitel'stvo,* which was the major purveyor of *partiinost* at this time, and within a few months Vyshinsky emerged as editor-in-chief of a new journal, *Sovetskoe Gosudarstvo i Pravo,* which became notorious in the later years of Stalin's life as the organ of the state's administrative functionaries.[43]

The aftermath of this domestic policy follow-up of Vyshinsky's foreign policy coup at Bucharest suggests the connection between Stalin's March crisis and the Party revival. On 22 April the editor-in-chief of *Pravda,* P. N. Pospelov, juxtaposed Vyshinsky's views and a *partiinyi* essay of his own which neatly refuted them.[44] Pospelov opened with this sentiment: "Lenin wrote: The teachings of Marx are all-powerful because they are reliable [*vernyi*] beyond doubt." Then he presented almost the same subjects as Vyshinsky had, but with different interpretations. In describing, for example, the birth of

181

the Soviet state, he wrote not as though it had been the brainchild of Lenin and Stalin but as though it had been implicit in Marx's ideological scheme from the start, and Lenin and Stalin had only "realized" it. Socialism in one country likewise became something implicit in Marxism long before the Russian Revolution, rather than an enrichment of Marxism drawn by Stalin from experience. Pospelov added:

> After the death of Engels, the social-democratic parties of Western Europe became parties of social reform. . . . Lenin, Stalin, and the Bolsheviks saw and understood that such opportunism . . . was unhealthy for the proletariat. That is why the Bolshevik Party became a "party of the new type." . . . The Party of the Bolsheviks managed to inspire and organize our people to accomplish three revolutions, . . . and managed to found the great Soviet Power. The Party was able to do this above all because with unswerving leadership it steered itself according to the correct concepts of the advanced theory of Marxism-Leninism. The victory in our country confirms especially strongly the words of Marx: "Theory becomes material force in proportion as it gains mastery over the masses."[45]

Vyshinsky had asserted that the power of the Marxist ideology derived from its "creative" application by Lenin and Stalin, while Pospelov was insisting that the power of the ideology was essentially far-sighted—true—and could be relied upon by Bolsheviks who possessed the proper will.

The Vyshinsky-Pospelov exchange was the start of a long and highly stylized but nonetheless significant debate between high Soviet personages in the pages of Party theoretical journals all through 1945. The major spokesman for one side was G. F. Aleksandrov, the head of the Agit-Prop Administration who signaled the new foreign policy line on 14 April with his attack on Ehrenburg. Aleksandrov took up Vyshinsky's cudgels. On the other side, the main figure was Pospelov. In August 1945, in a widely published lecture, Alexsandrov put forth at length the view that theory is but an aid to thinking, not a substitute for it: "Lenin teaches that . . . ideologies can be proven . . . only through life. . . . History gives many examples of how each and every theory which has arisen in the past, no matter what the system of social views on which it is based, underwent the severe test of life: either it disappeared, . . . or it took on *new* strength, drew from life *new* proof of its correctness and truth."[46]

Aleksandrov then followed Vyshinsky's reasoning and suggested that Lenin and Stalin had always "learned from experience" in improving Marxism, and asserted that ideology "is not a dogma, but a method." Later in the year, he went further: "Everyone who seriously tries to study Marxist-Leninist theory must, like Lenin and Stalin, enrich his memory from the history of the social sciences and learn also to criticize the unscientific idealistic theories of the development of society."[47] Consequently, he explained, it is incorrect and unMarxist to study Marxism without reference to bourgeois ideas. Learning comes first, criticism second. In his speech delivered on the anniversary of Lenin's death in January 1946, he declaimed:

> The founders of the scientific world outlook of the worker class, Marx and Engels, used to laugh at those bookworms who tried to view the revolutionary theory as a collection of dogmas. . . . Lenin was a real Marxist who understood in a constructive way the revolutionary essence of Marx's teaching. . . . Lenin developed the thought that Marxists must not view Marx's theory as something forever completed and inalterable. . . . The theory has to absorb new historical experience and thereby influence society.[48]

This was the signal for Pospelov to speak. In January 1946, in direct riposte to Aleksandrov, Pospelov wrote: "The Soviet people converted a once backward country into a powerful socialist state and achieved a historic victory of world import *mainly* because they were led by the Lenin-Stalin Party."[49] Dogmatically he then explained the arguments for *printsipnost,* using an old quotation of Stalin's: "Our Party is a party on the ascent, a Party which is powerful because its deeds do not contradict its words. It does not deceive the masses. It tells them nothing but the truth. It builds its policy not on demagogy, but on scientific analysis of class forces." With his position thus unassailably defended, Pospelov outlined in some detail a proposal for solving all of the country's ills by instituting the massive, Party-administered educational program which was subsequently realized during the *Zhdanovshchina.*

In the passages just cited, this debate between "creative thinking" and "far-sightedness" seemed to leave the former more voluntarist than the latter. But the fundamental difference between the two sides came out clearly in February 1946, when all the top-level politicians of the Soviet leadership spoke to their electorates. Two of these leaders—Malenkov and Molotov—were granted far more publicity than any others. The former, in his speech of 7 February, picked up

Aleksandrov's attack on "bookworms" almost word for word and argued the importance of "knowing how."[50] Molotov, on the other hand, defended the Party's great educational scheme and gave this as his basic reason for doing so: "A great deal depends, of course, on whether people know how to work well; but even more depends on their having the will to learn how to work. As is well known, it is never to late to learn."[51] Although Aleksandrov and Vyshinsky sounded at times more voluntarist than Pospelov during this long debate, they argued for only a limited freedom of the will—a freedom to interpret Marxism-Leninism in practical matters. Molotov showed that behind Pospelov's argument for following Marxist-Leninist precepts lay the enormously greater freedom of will which we have encountered earlier in Voznesensky's work—freedom for a socialist to follow his own will *because* he is a socialist.

This debate is the main published index of the conflict between Stalin and the Party revivalists during 1945. It connects the March foreign policy crisis of 1945, which Vyshinsky launched on 27 February in Bucharest, with Stalin's counterattack against the revivalists at home. Consequently, some other symptoms of a relationship between Soviet domestic and foreign policy at this time should be noted. First, in the March crisis, it was the Soviet state, not the Party, which aggressively asserted its interests. Vyshinsky, remembered for his role as chief prosecutor in the great purge trials of the 1930s, was in some ways the most typical public figure of the Soviet state,[52] and in both the Polish and the Rumanian affairs, the role of the Soviet state in advancing socialism outshone by far the role of local Communist parties. Further, the diplomatic demarche against Turkey in mid-March was intended to recall tsarist and Russian Orthodox claims to Constantinople. It was pressed in particular by Beria's strongholds in Armenia and Georgia, which started publishing demands for the "unification of their ancient lands."[53] At the time of the Berne affair, for what it is worth, Stalin wrote that his suspicions of the West had been fanned by his "military" advisers.[54] The crisis in the Grand Alliance prompted a campaign inside the Soviet Union for vigilance against foreign spies and for a brief moment late in March sharply reduced political enthusiasm within the Soviet elite.[55] To Tito, early in April, Stalin exclaimed: "This war is not as in the past; whoever occupies a territory also imposes on it his own social system. Everyone imposes his own system as far as his army can reach." No room for popular insurrection here! And then with statist gloom Stalin added: "The war will soon be over.

We shall recover in fifteen or twenty years, and then we'll have another go at it.''[56]

If the March crisis of 1945 represented deliberate reliance on the voluntarist theses of Molotov and Zhdanov, the leaders of the Party revival, and if Stalin wished to tame the revival, then all the statist overtones of the crisis are explicable. Molotov and Zhdanov had achieved a striking political success at Yalta, and as a result the tide of revivalist enthusiasm was mounting fast on the domestic political front. By involving his country in a new foreign policy adventure, and then employing statist agents like Vyshinsky and the anonymous "military advisers" to stir up a war scare—indeed, to endanger the entire operation—Stalin may have hoped to deflate the balloon. In the history of European diplomacy, manipulations of this kind are not unknown: Bismarck had done as much.

The Western Powers did not respond vigorously to Vyshinsky's coup or to the violence of the March crisis, and before he died Roosevelt even indicated a willingness to overlook Stalin's insulting letters.[57] Thus from a Soviet point of view, this testing may have proved once again that the West was weak, which may explain why in April the voluntarist, anti-blocist theories of the Party revival became the basis for Soviet foreign policy, and why Stalin coincidentallly started making nationalistic public statements which strikingly distanced his person from the new voluntarist Party line. The Party's demonstration of the weakness of the West had succeeded, but he, Stalin, had failed.

Stalin the Victor

There is only circumstantial evidence of a connection between Stalin's domestic and foreign policies in March 1945. Documents are unavailable to historians, and one may wonder whether, even if they were available, they would be helpful, for, after all, Stalin was an autocrat who played his cards close to his chest and is not likely to have put his various manipulations onto paper. Perhaps historians will forever have to work only with coincidences.

However, it is useful here to review Stalin's calendar in the critical days of March and April 1945. On 27 March the Polish Home Army leaders were arrested. On 28 March Stalin attended a state funeral for Marshal Shaposhnikov, a former Soviet Chief of Staff, and a state banquet for President Beneš.[58] On 29 March he wrote a sharp letter to Roosevelt about the Berne negotiations.[59] The next day the Americans and British completed the encirclement of the Ruhr. On 31 March Beneš left Moscow, and Eisenhower's cable was delivered. On 1 April Stalin received a strong letter from Roosevelt regarding the deterioration of Allied relations over the Polish question.[60] On 1 and 2 April Stalin presided over the staff meeting of his leading generals and, while fomenting the jealousies existing among them, made the basic decisions regarding the final assault on Berlin.[61] On 3 April Stalin dispatched his most outrageous letter to Roosevelt about the Berne affair.[62] On 5 April the USSR abrogated its fishing treaties with Japan and thus signaled its eventual decision to enter the Far Eastern war; and Marshal Tito arrived in Moscow on a state visit. On 6 April the annual state plan for Soviet agriculture was published, and the Red Army reached Vienna. Meanwhile, the great domestic policy debate continued over whether the liberated territories or the home-front industrialists should receive the most investments in the first peacetime budget, which would be considered by the Supreme Soviet on 24 April. On 15 April President Truman's first messenger to Stalin, American ambassador to Chungking Patrick E. Hurley, forced the *Vozhd* to consider the whole vast complex of problems which would emerge later in the year during the crisis of liberation in the Far East.[63] Then decisions had to be made about whether to sign a state treaty, in the face of opposition by the Western Powers, with the Lublin Poles, whose delegation arrived in Moscow on 19 April, four days after the Aleksandrov-Ehrenburg affair.

When United States Ambassador Averell Harriman visited Stalin on the morning of 13 April to tell him of Roosevelt's death and to persuade him to send Molotov to the founding conference of the United Nations Organization at San Francisco, Molotov, despite the emotion of the moment, kept mumbling in the background: "Time, time, time."[64] It is credible under such circumstances that Stalin, the great manipulator, mingled domestic and foreign policy during the March crisis of 1945. This is suggested also by the absence of any convincing explanation of that crisis based on objective foreign circumstances alone, and by the emergence, just after it, of the foreign policy theories of the Party revivalists as the foundation of Soviet foreign policy.

9

A Gamble

The Conference at London

ON 9 MAY 1945, hostilities against Germany came to an end and peace arrived in Europe. From 17 July until 2 August, Stalin, Harry S. Truman (the new American president) and the prime ministers of Great Britain (Churchill and, after the election of 26 July, Clement R. Attlee) met at Potsdam in good spirits. On 6 August the Americans dropped an atomic bomb at Hiroshima, on 8 August the Russians entered the war against Japan, and on 14 August Japan capitulated, surrendering formally on 2 September. On 11 September the foreign ministers of the principal victorious powers gathered in London to begin the process of writing treaties of peace. The conference was unsuccessful, and on 2 October they adjourned, unable to agree even upon the text of a communiqué.

The London Conference marked the shift in East-West relations from the public friendship of the war to the public antagonism, if not hostility, which marked the next quarter century.[1] This alone makes it

187

notable, all the more so because the issues were so petty. This was not a conference to consider the peace treaty for Germany but for the small European countries which had been Germany's allies—Italy, Bulgaria, Finland, Hungary, and Rumania—and it broke up not because of disagreements over substance but because of procedural issues. On 22 September the chief Soviet delegate, Molotov, announced that the whole conference had been organized incorrectly. He refused to budge from his technically proper but very belated position until the other foreign ministers decided to go home. The failure of this conference, like Vyshinsky's coup seven months earlier at Bucharest, stands out as unnecessary and thus irrational. Contemporaries outside of Russia found themselves unable to understand what could have aroused the display of Soviet temperament. Historians, who know that then as on 27 February, there was still much for the Russians to gain from the Grand Alliance, are no less puzzled.

A Question of Resentment?

Molotov arrived at London with a long list of Western offenses against the Soviet Union.[2] It was still on his mind that the Americans had been singularly inconsistent during the UNO conference in San Francisco, seeking to admit large numbers of Latin American countries to assure themselves a ready majority in the UNO General Assembly, yet vigorously rejecting Soviet efforts to include constituent Soviet republics and representatives from the Soviet-backed regime in Warsaw, which, whatever its faults, had been unmistakably anti-Axis. Beyond this, both Western Powers had remained unenthusiastic about Soviet policy in Poland, even after they agreed in June to a merger of the rival London and Warsaw regimes. When the Russians organized a coalition government in Austria under the respectable old Social Democrat Karl Renner, the West on principle refused to cooperate with it.[3] The Westerners also rejected Soviet demands for high reparations from Germany, haggling over the assurances they had allegedly made at Yalta;[4] their complaints about Communist aggression in Soviet-occupied Bulgaria, Rumania, and Hungary had increased.

All this could suggest that the Western Powers were deliberately trying to roll back Soviet power. Molotov was bitter about such a possibility: "Apparently . . . in Greece the Western newspaper correspondents are happy, but the people are not; whereas in Rumania the people are happy, but the correspondents are not. The Soviet government attaches more importance to the feelings of the people."[5] On another occasion he charged: "The Rumanian government is liked by the Rumanian population but not by the American government. What should be done? Should we overthrow it because it is not liked by the United States government and set up a government that would be unfriendly to the Soviet Union?"[6] He considered the idea of a roll-back of Soviet forces in Eastern Europe a bad idea, and if there were a Western attempt to do this, was it not necessary at the London Conference for him to stand fast?

One may add that at the time of the London Conference, the United States, in general, had become an enigma. The presidency had fallen to a man neither known in the great world nor particularly knowing of it. There had been three secretaries of state in nine months, and Harry Hopkins had been replaced as the real power behind the scenes in the making of American foreign policy, first by Joseph Grew and then in August 1945 by Dean Acheson. This turn-over could hardly have been reassuring to the Russians.[7] Besides, in the summer of 1945, Americans were going through a painful transi-tion from war to peace curiously similar to the experience in the Soviet Union. In America, as in Russia, some home-front industrial-ists worried about how to avoid losing military contracts, and others worried about how to ensure markets for a reconversion to consumer goods. In America, as in Russia, there were generals with an eye for politics, and politicians, long tolerant of war-enforced compromises, suddenly concerned for the sanctity of the "system." In America, as in Russia, the elite was aware that the population might expect more "peace" than the politicians could produce, and that demobilization entailed certain dangers. As in Russia, American leaders were firmly convinced that somehow the "system" had won the war—that the United States had saved European civilization and that progress was on its side. And in America there was the same faith that in the outside world everyone but a few wicked politicians really saw things "our way." America even had its Leningrad—London, filled with the piety of martyrdom—and its Ukraine—Western Europe, in ruins.

Seen from Moscow, moreover, American behavior was wholly inconsistent. One day it conspired with Russia against imperialist En-gland; the next day it halted, without warning, the flow of Lend-Lease industrial equipment to Russia as well as to Britain.[8] One day it broadcasted its hopes that one world of equal and united nations would emerge to keep the peace; the next it proposed a brutal solution to the German problem—keeping Germany forcibly demilitarized through a great power consortium formed outside the United Nations.[9] It kept the Russians and the British out of conquered Japan, yet complained in tones of moral outrage about the exclusion of American commercial interests from Poland, Hungary, Rumania, and Bulgaria.[10] It manufactured the atomic bomb, by far the most powerful weapon known to humanity, and then spoke of voluntarily sharing the discovery with all the world, while tacitly using it as a threat to achieve political gain.[11]

Perhaps from the Soviet point of view one could only ask of this America what it really wanted and hope to reach a compromise.[12] It was too dangerous to treat it as an enemy, too volatile to treat as a friend. In this sense, a rational alternative for Soviet policy in the late summer of 1945 was to stand firm against America until one found out what America was.

Though it is not difficult to explain Molotov's obduracy at the London Conference in such terms, the problem remains: why did he accept a rupture in the Alliance? If he and Stalin were resentful and uncertain about the West in September 1945, it would surely have been wiser not to give up the military security represented by the Grand Alliance. Russia needed the West. The country was in ruins; the people were exhausted and starving. America was fresh, rich, and vigorous, and possessed the atomic bomb. This question seems the more pressing because in terms of the theory of imperialism put forth in the early months of 1945 and adopted as state policy in April, the Soviets had every reason not to break with the West.

Perhaps earlier, in April and in May 1945, Moscow may still have had doubts about the viability of a transformed Grand Alliance as a peace-keeping institution. During the March crisis, Stalin had withdrawn Molotov from the Soviet delegation to the San Francisco conference, which was to effect the transformation by establishing the United Nations. The first request of President Truman when he took office, however, was that Molotov come to San Francisco after all. Stalin relented, but then when Molotov arrived in America on 23 April, he found grounds for regret. Truman greeted him with a sermon about the limits of American tolerance[13] and, after he reached San Francisco, took steps suggestive of a new anti-Soviet United States foreign policy—steps which culminated in the cutting off of Lend-Lease to the Soviet Union early in May. It was then that Molotov first displayed in public the rigid negotiating tactics he later used at London. He insisted that the United Nations include the Soviet-sponsored Polish government. He protested the American sponsorship of Latin American countries—especially Argentina—which had not fought against Hitler. He stood fast on the principle of a Great Power veto.[14]

Since the end of May, however, the profitability of anti-blocism had become more and more evident as the Americans indulged their anglophobia.[15] This was as true in the Istrian dispute and in Austrian and German affairs as it was in the Near and Middle East and in Japan. In May Truman dispatched Joseph Davies, Roosevelt's onetime ambassador to Moscow and a notorious Russophile, to London to lecture Churchill about the dangers of following Hitler's anti-Russian path.[16] By midsummer, Roosevelt's aide Harry Hopkins, who was by no means pro-British, could write of the atmosphere in Washington: "To hear some people talk . . . you would think the British were our political enemies!"[17] Meanwhile, Washington dropped all show of anti-Soviet sentiment.[18] Late in May, Truman dispatched Hopkins, as a symbol of the Soviet-American friendship which had flourished under Roosevelt, on a mission to Moscow. Hopkins carried with him the president's assurance that Soviet-American relations would in no way be contingent upon or less important than America's relations with Great Britain.

In the face of this show of American friendliness, Stalin proved willing to let Washington think he would reconsider his views about the UNO,[19] and for a month before the Potsdam Conference, despite British protests, Soviet-American cooperation was the order of the day. The Americans even withdrew from the parts of the proposed Soviet occupation zone in Germany which they had captured during the final weeks of the war. In return, the Russians withdrew from the western zones in Austria.

At Potsdam, the Americans and British cooperated with each other more effectively, in some respects, than they had at Yalta. Nonetheless, Soviet satisfaction with apparent splits between the Western Powers became very obvious. When Stalin met Truman for the first time, for example, he hinted that the British might make trouble for the peacemakers.[20] In his private talks with Churchill, however, he complained that the Americans were breaking the Yalta agreements.[21] During the plenary sessions, particularly in the earlier stages of the conference, he continually needled the British about their imperialism while avoiding disputes with the Americans.[22] By so acting, on more than one occasion he provoked an Anglo-American dispute over colonial issues.[23] Molotov achieved the same result in the foreign ministers' meetings. Meanwhile, both Stalin and Molotov made demands on the Alliance which were unexpected. No longer were they interested simply in a private political preserve in Eastern Europe and in enormous reparations from Germany, as had seemed the case at Yalta. Now they were grabbing for the Turkish straits, requesting footholds in Tripoli, Tangier, and even the Congo, asking for the German fleet, trying to persuade the Western Allies to break off relations with Spain, increasing their territorial demands in the Far East, and expressing a permanent interest in the Middle East.[24] They acted, in a word, as if they had a basis for expecting the Western Powers to accept them as equal partners in what had traditionally been British preserves.

The results of the Potsdam Conference may have been as confusing to the Soviet leadership as they were to the other powers. Those were bewildering days. Britain, the birthplace of modern capitalism, had voted a socialist government into power, and Japan, the superpower of the Far East, was rapidly collapsing. Yet for all the rush of events, some things were clear. Above all, the Western Powers were not challenging Soviet participation in the peacemaking. Further, they were evidently willing to accept a permanent Soviet presence not only in Europe but in the Far East as well. Stalin could see that the Western leaders were still worried by the prospect of Soviet domination of all Eastern Europe, but, as at Yalta, he could judge that their concern was not with the existence of Soviet power but with the technicalities of saving face. To the members of Stalin's entourage, who, as recently as November 1944, had considered an early and forced Soviet evacuation of Germany most likely, the manipulation of the Allies must have seemed highly successful.

To support this analysis, one may note that in September 1945 the Soviet Party theoreticians went a step further in reviving Lenin's theses on imperialism. In the lead article of its August issue (to press on 9 October), *Bol'shevik* discussed, at far greater length than it had in May, the imperialistic origins and character of modern wars.[25] P. Fedoseev, who wrote the article, scornfully derided the notion that wars could arise over questions of a "racist," "chauvinist" ideology such as Fascism. Such ideologies, he wrote, were no more than propaganda, through which capitalist interest groups deceived the people. He said that World War II had begun as a result

192

of conflicts among imperialists and was only transformed into a European "struggle for national liberation" with the entry of the Soviet Union into the war. This "completely confirmed" Lenin's statements of some twenty years earlier and Stalin's "foresight" before June 1941. After quoting Stalin's prediction that the UNO would work, Fedoseev wrote: "Leninism teaches that the only complete guarantee of peaceful construction by the peoples is liquidation of the exploitation of man by man, of one nation by another. But Leninism does not consider war to be unavoidable even in the present state of affairs. Wars can be avoided if peace-loving nations act in agreement in the interest of peace and take effective measures (in advance) against possible aggressions."[26] He then cited a famous maxim: "Marxism-Leninism proceeds not only from the fact that all wars are a continuation of previous policy, but that peace is an extension of the policy carried out in the time of war. The goals which states pursue in war by fighting also define the policies of these states after the war."[27] According to Fedoseev, World War I, an imperialist struggle, ended in an imperialist peace. World War II, which had become a war of liberation, could correspondingly end in a peace of liberation.

During the first two days of the London Conference, Molotov, the chief of the Soviet delegation, raised a cloud of procedural issues which were bound to make difficulties between the Americans and the British but might form the basis for agreements between the Americans and the Russians. On the third day, when work began on the treaty for Italy, on which the Western Powers had a certain unity of view, Molotov injected a demand for a Soviet trusteeship in Tripolitania, appealed for American aid in breaking the British domination of the Mediterranean, and engaged in a series of private conversations with the American secretary of state, James Byrnes, in which he made obvious his availability for a deal. On 22 September, at a further meeting with Byrnes from which he ostentatiously excluded the British Foreign Secretary, Ernest Bevin, Molotov introduced the question of Japan, where the Americans, by excluding both the Russians and the British, were establishing a monopoly of power comparable to that of the Russians in Eastern Europe.[28] Byrnes rejected a deal. It was then that Molotov denounced the organization of the conference, raising points of procedure designed to alienate the Americans and British from the French and the Chinese and the British from their Commonwealth partners.[29] Molotov's tactics were a logical continuation of the divisive tactics he and Stalin had employed so successfully at Potsdam. That he used them implies that he recognized the value of the Grand Alliance—and makes all the more puzzling his willingness to kill the goose that laid such golden eggs.

The Liberation of China

When Molotov raised Far Eastern issues at the London Conference, he reflected the problems Stalin had faced during the crisis of liberation in China—problems rooted in the long and difficult Soviet relationship with the Chinese Communist Party which, because of the size and geographical importance of China, may easily have affected the entire pattern of Soviet world diplomacy.

The CCP had been in more or less active rebellion against the republican government of China since the late 1920s. During the war it had built up an army in the remote hills along the Mongolian border that was more powerful than any Communist-dominated resistance force in Europe. Yet for reasons of state the Soviet Union maintained friendly relations with the Kuomintang through all those years, and gave the Communists only nominal support. Furthermore, although the Chinese of all political complexions were at war with the Japanese, who by 1942 had occupied the greater part of northern and eastern China, the Soviet Union made peace with Japan a cardinal point of its wartime foreign policy. A common political line was therefore impossible for the Soviet and Chinese Communists, and much unpublicized mutual recrimination took place.[30] Moreover, Mao Tsetung, isolated at Yenan, developed theories regarding the possibility of working toward revolution in cooperation with the Chinese peasantry, and Stalin took to calling the CCP leaders "margarine" (fake) Communists.[31] As late as January 1945 the Moscow-Yenan relationship was perforce as distant as the link between Moscow and the French Communists had been in 1940.

In November 1944 Stalin spoke slightingly about Japan in a speech on the anniversary of the Bolshevik Revolution. On 5 April 1945 Moscow announced the lapse of the Soviet-Japanese fishing treaties. One could guess by then that after the defeat of Hitler the Soviet Union would join the war in the Far East and that the liberation of China would ensue. The Chinese Communists, bolder than any of their European comrades, responded by making public their dialogue with Stalin. For two years they had been negotiating at Chungking for the formation of a government of Chinese national unity. Now they trumped up an excuse for breaking off the discussions.[32] At the same time they made friendly overtures to the United States.[33] Then on 24 April, at the first CCP congress in several years, Mao Tse-tung enunciated a remarkable policy line. First he endorsed "new type government" in principle, showing his willingness to remain within the general framework of Stalin's world strategy. He even went so far as to say that national coalition was "the only course China can take. . . . This is an historical law, an inexorable trend which no force can resist."[34] But then he added, pointedly, that coalition in China would never mean compromise: "We Communists do not conceal our political views. Definitely and beyond all doubt, our future or maximum program is to carry China forward to socialism and communism." He went on:

> Some people are suspicious and think that once in power, the Communist Party [of China] will follow Russia's example and establish the dictatorship of the proletariat and a one-party system. Our answer is that a new democratic state based on an alliance of the democratic classes is different in principle from a socialist state under the dictatorship of the proletariat. Beyond all doubt, our system of new democracy will be built under the leadership of the proletariat and of the Communist Party, but throughout the stage of new democracy, China cannot possibly have a one-class dictatorship and one-party government and therefore will not attempt it. . . . The Chinese system for the present stage is being shaped by the present stage of Chinese history, and for a long time to come there will exist a special form of state and political power, a form that is distinguished from the Russian system but is perfectly necessary and reasonable for us—namely, the new-democratic form of state and political power based on the alliance of the democratic classes.[35]

These statements indicated that Chinese Communist willingness actually to enter a coalition government might depend on Stalin's tolerance of CCP formulas for China's special and specifically non-Russian road to socialism. To bolster the point, the Congress was told that Mao was "a creative Marxist of genius, linking as he has the universal truths of Marxism, mankind's superior knowledge, with the concrete practice of the Chinese revolution."[36] In other Communist parties of the day, such things were said only of Stalin.

Stalin well deserved such a challenge. At the Teheran and Yalta conferences he had committed himself secretly to a policy of postwar collaboration with the Kuomintang government and with United

States interests. At Yalta he had even extracted promises that Washington would bludgeon Chungking into ceding some Chinese territory to Russia. He knew by April 1945, from his experience with the Yugoslavs, that purist foreign Communists equipped with armies were no longer likely to accept without protest his peculiar notions about keeping their revolutions "peaceful." In a talk with United States Ambassador to China Patrick Hurley on 15 April, therefore, even before Mao's speech, he enthusiastically went along with Hurley's plans for excluding the CCP from the spoils of victory.[37] Late in May, when Harry Hopkins visited him, he stated his interest in a pact with Chungking, promising to enter the Pacific war once it was signed and enthusiastically supporting America's vision of the Kuomintang's future. He specifically rejected the CCP's hopes of dominating postwar China. So convincing and far-reaching were his promises to Hopkins (and to Harriman, who was also present) that many historians see his performance as the "greatest bluff and deception" of the emerging Cold War.[38] In July, Chiang Kai-shek's foreign minister came to Moscow, and negotiations regarding the fulfillment of the Yalta agreement began. It seemed likely that Stalin might manage to enter the Japanese war as the avowed ally of the Chinese Nationalist government, in which case Mao would have had few options. Had Stalin's plan succeeded, Yenan would have had to accept coalition government essentially on Chungking's terms (as the French and Italian Communists had done in March and April 1944) or to attack the considered foreign policy of the world's first socialist state. For the Communists of that day, this was no choice at all.

But the course of events interfered with Stalin's scheme. The Kuomintang procrastinated, unwilling to accept Moscow's greedy demands without a struggle. In mid-July Stalin and Molotov had to break off the negotiations in order to attend the meeting at Potsdam. By 2 August, when the Potsdam Conference finally ended, the atomic bomb was almost ready to be dropped. Stalin tried to persuade the Americans to delay,[39] but the blow was dealt Japan on 6 August, and to get in on the spoils he had to declare war before he had completed his negotiations with Chungking.[40] Hereupon, Mao acted on his own. On 13 August, a week after Hiroshima and five days after the Soviet declaration of war, he broke with the coalition government line. He charged that Chiang Kai-shek was a "Fascist chieftain," that the Kuomintang had frustrated all the CCP's moves toward coalition government, and that it was initiating a civil war. He declared that the

Chinese people's democratic forces would consequently endeavor to free as much of China from the Japanese as they could.[41] Mao's declaration did not gain much world attention at the time. The international press was far too concerned with the atomic bomb and with the collapse of Japan to feature the sayings of Chinese Communists. However, this declaration symbolized a rebellion of the colonial peoples against European hegemony which was to transform the world in the postwar era, and it was assuredly a defeat for Stalin.

Mao's pronouncement was not published in *Pravda,* but within three weeks Stalin issued three public statements stressing a strictly statist view of events in the Far East.[42] On 10 August he warned the Nationalists to hurry up lest the Communists get into Manchuria.[43] On 14 August he completed his negotiations with them and published the Sino-Soviet treaty on the 24th. Meanwhile, his feelings could be seen in the behavior of his troops. The Red Army embarked on a large-scale invasion of China, heading first for the north Chinese corridor, through which Mao's forces would have to pass on their "liberationist" campaign, nor did it stop promptly upon the capitulation of Japan. As a Soviet chronicler has remarked, its advance was so massive and swift that the participation of the Chinese Communists in the death blow to Japan was not needed.[44] Mao got the point. On 28 August he changed course and left his wartime hideout in Yenan to participate in fresh negotiations at Chungking.[45] Stalin had won the round after all.

Stalin's efforts to inhibit Communist insurrectionism in China had clear repercussions in other countries. For example, in Outer Mongolia during August the Soviet Union vigorously dramatized the benefits which non-Soviet Communists could derive from passive collaboration with the Soviet state. Outer Mongolia had once been part of the Chinese empire. Detached during the 1920s, and guided by Communists into a Soviet pattern of development, it was technically still not independent. Under the Sino-Soviet treaty of 14 August, the Chinese made a declaration of relinquishment of Chinese rights, subject to the results of a plebiscite. The Mongolian regime responded with loud rejoicing, even before the almost unanimous vote for independence on 23 October. The Red Army underlined the lesson for the Chinese Communists by allowing Outer Mongolian military units to participate in the disarming of the Japanese, while paying practically no attention to those unhappy Inner Mongolians who wanted to unify Mongolia by popular movement but who were close to Yenan.[46]

197

In Korea no such elaborate drama was possible. But in August, before the break with Japan, Soviet consular personnel in Seoul reportedly went about instructing the Communists underground that they should operate within an all-Korean democratic coalitionary front, and that the Red Army would occupy the entire country.[47] One may infer that a Communist bid for power was not needed. During Japan's collapse it actually became possible for the Russians to occupy the entire peninsula, but they did not do so. Instead, they welcomed the Americans and quietly accepted an American plan for a long-term joint occupation and for preventing any sort of unsupervised political development.[48] As for Japan, Stalin personally intervened in August through November to obtain a partition and a role for the Soviet state in the occupation regime, though Communist insurrections were not even in question there.[49] In Sinkiang, where there had been tribal disorders on the Sino-Soviet frontier for many months and an "East Turkistan Republic" had emerged during the summer, Stalin openly collaborated with Chungking in September, pulling the rug out from under the feet of Mao's possible allies.[50]

While Stalin was thus vigorously pressing the Chinese Communists to eschew insurrection, odd things were happening in Eastern Europe, where the Communists were usually sensitive to his moods.[51] First, the Hungarian CP decided to go so far in appeasing Western observers as to tolerate free popular elections. These took place in the autumn. The decision reflected in part a romantic, Zhdanovite euphoria among the Hungarian Moscovites, which made them think that they could win (and they were sorely disappointed when they lost). But one may recognize also that Stalin had a part: the decision coincided with the return from Moscow of Marshal Voroshilov, the chairman of the Allied Control Council in Budapest, and with Allied complaints, transmitted through Moscow, about Communist behavior in Hungary.[52] In Rumania, King Michael went on "strike," refusing to sign any legislation until the Groza government resigned. The Rumanian Communist Party had frequently gone to the street earlier in the year when things did not go its way. Now, however, there was no protest. Instead, the top CP leaders went to Moscow for consultation.[53]

Most peculiar of all, the Bulgarian Communists, who by violent, less-than-democratic means were preparing to hold an election, agreed on the eve of the election, in the face of Allied protests transmitted through Moscow, to postpone the voting. It may be that Stalin

198

himself ordered this decision.[54] A comparable show of Soviet-inspired CP abstention from insurrectionary methods occurred in Austria.[55] All this "moderation" on the part of the East European Communists was obviously related to the London Conference of Foreign Ministers on the satellite peace treaties, as well as to the crisis in China, and demonstrates how intimately all the far-flung aspects of Soviet world strategy were interrelated.

For this reason it is relevant to note that while the London Conference was in session, Stalin was reaping the bitter fruit of his flamboyant efforts to check the CCP. Within a few days of the Red Army invasion of northern China and Manchuria, Soviet economic agencies instituted a policy of removing the area's industrial wealth. In Europe this sort of systematic looting had been reserved for the defeated enemy. Even Axis satellites in Europe were subjected only to Red Army rape, not to industrial looting, and European countries which were technically Soviet allies—as China was—were spared. The looting of Manchuria can only be explained if one assumes that Stalin was planning to hold to his pact with the Chinese Nationalists, expected to withdraw the Red Army within a few weeks or months, and decided, therefore, to gather the "captured enemy property" as quickly as he could.[56] That policy of collaboration with Washington and Chungking proved a disastrous mistake. The Chinese Nationalists and their American backers could not even supply the troops to take over the countryside around Peking from the Japanese, much less to replace the Russians in Manchuria. Not until early October did Chungking make its first request to the Russians for admission to the northern regions. The hasty looting had not even been necessary. Meanwhile, the Communists had appeared. In the liberation of Europe, the advancing Red Army never had to hesitate before greeting armed Communists of the resistance as brothers-in-arms. Even in Yugoslavia it had been able to cooperate with the Communists, though Stalin, on the diplomatic level, was stabbing Tito in the back. Yet now in a thousand different localities in China Red Army commanders, because of Stalin's treaty with Chungking, had to refuse to collaborate with native armed forces carrying revolutionary banners and displaying the red star. They had to face the question: was Moscow as revolutionary as its ideology?[57]

Stalin did not stand firm. In September it became clear that the Red Army was accommodating the Communists, handing over to them administrative functions in Mukden and the Yellow Sea ports.

This cooperation was at first not universal. As late as early October, the Red Army command graciously admitted a large contingent of Nationalist Chinese officials who arrived by air at the Manchurian capital, Changchung. But on 6 October, that same command refused permission for a sea-borne landing of Nationalist troops at Dairen, and during the following six weeks the Russians systematically obstructed the extension of Kuomintang power in their occupation zone, a clear violation of the Sino-Soviet treaty.

These disillusioning events during the London Conference of Foreign Ministers call one's attention to some remarkable confidences Stalin imparted to Ambassador Harriman a few weeks later. As James Byrnes, the newly appointed United States secretary of state, describes the talk in his memoirs:

> [I] asked Ambassador Harriman to request an interview with Generalissimo Stalin who was then on vacation at Gagry. . . . The result was a revelation. When the Ambassador started to present our views on European questions, Stalin interrupted to say that what he wanted to hear about was our view on the control of Japan. Mr. Harriman was as surprised as he was unprepared. . . . At London when Mr. Molotov had raised the question of Japan at the same time that he was killing days discussing procedural questions, we had concluded it was simply part of his war of nerves. . . . Now we suddenly realized that . . . the remarkable performance that had led to the breakdown of the London Conference had been stimulated by the Russians' belief that they were not being consulted adequately by our officials in Japan.[58]

Stalin did not mention China in his conversations with Harriman, but the debacle of both his own and of United States policy in that country was so clear that no comment was really necessary. From Stalin's perspective, the Americans had let him down badly. His demands for a role in the occupation of Japan implied a strong desire for reparation; perhaps we may explain the rigidity of Molotov's diplomacy at London comparably, in terms of sudden Soviet anger over developments in the Far East. Perhaps Molotov allowed the break in the Grand Alliance to occur at London because Stalin felt, impulsively, that the goose with the golden eggs deserved to be squeezed.

Yet even this explanation of the London Conference has limits, as may be judged from another set of events in Asia at about the same time. In 1941, in coordination with the British, the Red Army had "provisionally" occupied northern Iran. By 1944, with the end of the war in sight, the Soviet government was asking Iran for long-term oil concessions and, to generate pressure, was allowing Azerbaijani and Kurdish nationalists and "democrats" in the frontier provinces to organize themselves politically. Since Iran had a long history of regional secessionism, one could hardly miss the menace in this development, even if one did not know about the large-scale shifting of ethnic groups which Beria was then sponsoring inside the USSR, the annexation of Tannu Tuva, and the nascent rebellion in Sinkiang. Next, in August 1945, the Communist-run Tudeh ("masses") Party in Iran helped its Azerbaijani colleagues set up a Democratic Party in the north and, about 30 August, issued in their name a public appeal for Azerbaijani autonomy within Iran. The alarmed Iranian government on 12 September called Moscow's attention to the treaty which obliged the Red Army to withdraw at the end of the war. Two days later *Pravda* gave special coverage to the Democratic Party's appeal.[59]

At first glimpse this development seems to represent an exception to the rule of moderation which Stalin had been imposing on the non-Soviet Communists during his duel with Mao and a step-up in pressure on the Western Allies, foreshadowing Molotov's obstinacy at London. Iran before the war had been a weak link in the chain of British economic control over southern Asia. British capitalists owned the oil, but the Shah kept trying to attract competitors. The Anglo-Russian occupation of Iran in 1941 had finally evicted the German competitors whom the Shah favored. But by 1943 Teheran had brought the Americans into the picture, their interest in oil was legendary, and in September 1945 they were forcing the British to let them share in oil explorations throughout the Middle East.[60] As any Marxist could guess, therefore, political disturbances in Iran at this time would produce signals about how far the Americans would go in robbing their English allies. As we have seen, it was just such signals that Soviet diplomats were looking for in London.

Study shows, however, that the events in Iran were not a contradiction of Stalin's general policy of anti-insurrectionism. Azerbaijan at this time was one of two regions in Asia occupied by the Red Army in which "popular forces" were on the march against the will of the native central government of the country. The other was Manchuria. Whatever happened in Iran, therefore, was bound to be watched by the theoreticians of the CCP and to provide useful "analogies" for them (such as the models which the Bulgarian Communists gave the Yugoslav partisans late in 1944). The nature of these analogies is not hard to discover. The Communists of Iran did not even use their party name in public, much less command an army, as the Chinese Communists did. In Azerbaijan the Communists acted exclusively through a coalitionary front with tribally based ethnic parties, and their objective was regional autonomy—not the capture of a centralized state, but its breakup. The Azerbaijani Communists were thus the antithesis of the overtly Communist, peasant-based militarists whom Mao Tsetung, for over seventeen years, had thrown into a struggle to capture the whole of China. Were these Azerbaijani to succeed, with Soviet help, in bringing Iran quickly to socialism, piece by piece instead of all at once, the feat would put Mao's titanic battle in the shade. Stalin was probably inhibited from pressing such a lesson in Sinkiang, where the ground was better prepared, because there he wished to dramatize his treaty obligations to Chungking—and also because his efforts there might have helped Mao.[61]

The events in Iran in September 1945 thus marked no break in the spirit of Stalin's general anti-insurrectionist policy of the preceding months nor, one must add, did they represent any sudden, impulsively violent step-up in pressure on the Western Allies comparable to the break at London. In mid-September the Soviet ambassador to Teheran returned to duty after several weeks in Moscow and did generate a little pressure. On the 25th he called on the United States ambassador and, for the first time in two years, engaged him in a discussion of policy. In a two-hour talk he revealed that in Soviet eyes the Iranians were being "treacherous" toward both the Russians and the Americans, and that they were inspired by the British. His effort to split the West was transparent.[62] But there the matter rested. At the London Conference itself Molotov seems to have made no reference to Iran—a striking omission, considering his other divisive moves. Further, while the London Conference was in session, for over a month the Iranian scene was quiet, as if the Soviet advisers of the Azerbaijani democrats wished not to disturb the Great Powers in their deliberations. Herein lies the great weakness of any explanation of the break at London in terms of a sudden, angry fluctuation of Stalin's general line, sparked by the debacle in China. Away from London there was no such fluctuation.

Stalin's Retreat

In September 1945, as during the crisis in March, domestic political developments may have determined Soviet foreign policy. A first sign of this was the essay in *Bol'shevik* mentioned above about the Leninist theory of imperialist wars. Written by a leading propagandist, P. Fedoseev, it was no insignificant scribbling. Fedoseev became, with this issue of that leading Soviet theoretical journal, its editor. A short time later the Central Committee sharply criticized the former board of editors for having paid insufficient attention to the fundamentals of Marxism-Leninism.[63] The article on imperialism was thus an inaugural essay, and, more than any other published tract of the day, it pulled together, and gave coherence to, the voluntarist arguments of the Party revival. A program for the Party revival, it went to press just one week after the London Conference collapsed and four days after Molotov's return to Moscow.[64]

One may recall that at this same time other changes took place: the call for a new Five Year Plan, the abolition of the GOKO, and the demobilization of the army. On 6 October, the day after Molotov's return from London, the regime launched the great election campaign in which the Party reasserted authority over the whole vast organizational superstructure of Soviet society. The London Conference thus coincided exactly with the major Soviet domestic political turning point of the whole era we are studying in this book. The chief Soviet delegate to the London Conference was Molotov, a leader of the Party revival at home, and the questions of peace-making considered at the London Conference were central to the theoretical program of the Party revival. Such coincidences alone make probable an interrelationship between Molotov's obstinacy at London and what was happening at home; other details make the relationship even clearer.

On 7 August *Pravda* greeted the atomic bomb not with pragmatic admiration for the technological breakthrough it represented, but with hints that it was a "paper tiger"—that wars in the future, as in the past, would be won by the forces of history, not by technology.[65] These hints were taken up in conversation during the following months even by Molotov. They symptomized the overriding *partiinost* which now flooded the Soviet official media. "Staleness," George Kennan called them, because they were reminiscent of the Stalinist "realism" of prewar days,[66] but they were also reflections of elite enthusiasm over the victory, as appeared, for example, from some remarks by Chairman M. I. Kalinin in August at Leningrad: "Even now after the victory, we cannot for a moment forget the basic fact that our country is the only socialist state on the globe. Victory does not yet mean that all danger to the existence of our state and its socialist system is past. Only the most concrete and immediate danger which threatened us from Hitlerite Germany is gone."[67] Here was an expression of enthusiastic Party isolationism in its crudest form. It was by no means the only one. One Party journal came out with this warning: "In the closing stages of the war, when the Red Army is completing the collapse of Hitlerite Germany, only naive persons can think that the subversive spy activity of the enemy has somehow stopped being a danger to us. To the contrary . . . Comrade Stalin says: 'It is necessary to recall that the nearer our victory comes, the greater our vigilance and the stronger our blows against the enemy must be.' "[68]

To Soviet ears, this warning had an especially authoritative sound because this was precisely the law of history which Stalin had used to justify the great purge of the 1930s. Having thus caught the reader's attention, the editorialists of this enthusiastic journal went on: "The basis for high vigilance is Bolshevik *ideinost*. He who thoroughly understands what capitalist encirclement is—he who takes into account that as long as capitalist encirclement exists there will be spies from foreign states in the rear areas of the Soviet Union . . . will not give himself over to complacency and trustfulness." This was as explicit an expression of anti-Westernism as had been published in the Soviet Union since the start of the war. Apparently it came from Stalin himself and was printed in a journal distributed to all the country's leading home-front Party activists. In the exciting weeks at the end of the war, its certain result would be to encourage an explosion of anti-Allied sentiment among the Soviet elites.

As it happens, we can determine Stalin's attitude toward such outpourings and perhaps toward the entire Party revival at this time. In his radio broadcast of 2 September announcing the end of the Far Eastern war, he reviewed the course of Russo-Japanese relations since the turn of the century. This itself signaled his outlook. According to Marxism-Leninism, the Bolshevik Revolution marked a new stage in world history and interrupted every stream of historical events. Stalin spoke, however, as though, from 1904 to 1945, Russia and Japan had simply carried on a traditional type of conflict. Then he pushed the point home at the climax of his speech: "The defeat of the Russian armies in 1904 . . . left a sad burden on the conscience of the nation. It left a dark blot on our country. Our people, however, trusted and waited for the day when Japan would be defeated and the blot would be eradicated. We of the older generation have waited forty years for that day. And now that day has come."[69] As Isaac Deutscher pointed out years ago, this was equivalent to an insult to the Party.[70] The Russian defeat by Japan in 1904 was not a sad moment in the history of Russian socialism, as everyone knew. From the Party's point of view, it was a joyous event that made possible the revolution of 1905 and the first step in the destruction of tsarism. When Stalin said that he and the older generation were sad because of the 1904 defeats, he was indicating even more clearly than in his toasts of May and June 1945 that he had no use for the rantings of the Kalinins and the Party propagandists.

Those rantings nonetheless reached the public. Perhaps this is the most significant aspect of the revivalist victory, which coincided with the London Conference of Foreign Ministers. Stalin's toasts had not stemmed the tide of Party enthusiasm; perhaps they had even fanned it. By September 1945 his published words were being ignored by the movement's following. This created and brought to maturity the dilemma described in a previous chapter. If Stalin wished to achieve the home-front upheaval which had been his goal for a year, he had to rely on the Party and encourage *partiinost,* yet the more he gave the Party a free rein, the more it escaped his control and challenged his authority within the political system.

In this context, consider some peculiar aspects of Stalin's behavior during these months. Suddenly, he began to confess that he belonged to an older generation, that he was tired, sick, and thinking of retirement. He was sixty-five at the time of the victory. His hair had been gray since the 1930s. He had not had a vacation since 1941, and, in view of the enormous burden of work which fell to him during the war, he was surely tired. One witness said later that he was senile.[71] But one must recall that though he had been visibly old for a long time, until 1945 he did not talk about his age. Indeed, until 1944, all official photographs of him made him seem a young man, and as late as the end of July 1945 his photograph appeared on the front page of *Pravda* without gray hair or wrinkles.[72] Now, however, he himself initiated a discussion of his age and health.[73]

On 25 June at the reception in the Kremlin following the Red Army's great victory parade, Stalin made an impromptu speech to his assembled generals, admirals, and Party and government leaders in which he remarked on his age and said he would have to retire after two or three more years.[74] In the following weeks, his visitors from abroad learned the same thing.[75] In July he pointedly refused to take direct command over the coming military operations in the Far East;[76] in the middle of the month, he arrived a day later than his announced schedule at the Potsdam Conference, allegedly because of his health.[77] On 1 August *Pravda* published a snapshot of him at the Potsdam Conference which had not been retouched, and thereafter all the official portraits of him reflected his age. Five days after Molotov's return from the London Conference, on 10 October 1945, *Pravda* announced that Stalin had gone on vacation. United States Ambassador Harriman, who visited Stalin late in October at Gagry, reported nothing unusual about his health, but Stalin's daughter Svetlana, though she did not see him for many months after August 1945, thought that the "vacation" was occasioned by sickness.[78] Moscow was full of rumors about the illness. Because censorship was relaxed, gossip about his ill health and coming retirement filled the world press.[79]

Moreover, a number of administrative reforms at this time affected Stalin's personal role. The GOKO, the State Defense Committee, which all through the war had been the central organ of Stalin's authority in the Soviet Union and had been supreme over the Council of Commissars, the General Staff, and the Party Politburo, was dissolved on 4 September.[80] A month later, when Stalin went on vacation, the press as much as stated that Molotov would act as his replacement. Stalin seldom even announced his vacations, and this was the only time that his duties were so formally reassigned.[81] On 6 November there was another innovation. Molotov instead of Stalin delivered the annual revolutionary oration. When Stalin came back from his vacation in December, the Politburo asserted itself as the leading organ of the whole political system. It began to meet regularly every two weeks.[82] Meanwhile, it was decided to hold the long-overdue elections for the Supreme Soviet.[83] These took place on 11 February 1946. The newly elected soviets of the Union and the republics convened on 12 March, and on 15 March Stalin formally submitted his resignation as head of the Soviet government and those of all his commissars. On 19 March it was announced that the Party Central Committee had met and had renewed the membership of the Politburo, Secretariat, and Orgburo.[84] At the same time, the Politburo decided that the Orgburo would be the effective supervisor over all Party affairs and would meet at least once a week. In August the Politburo defined the role of the Party Secretariat by assigning it only the tasks of preparing the questions to be submitted to the Orgburo and of making sure that the Politburo and Orgburo decisions were carried out.[85] With this, Stalin's functions were for the first time in many years circumscribed, at least on paper.

These reforms probably affected Stalin little. The same session of the Supreme Soviet which accepted his resignation, for example, commissioned him to form a new government, which he promptly did. The only real changes in the government at this time were a shift in names—the People's Commissariats were now given the tsarist appellation "ministry"—and the consolidation of an inner council of eight deputy chairmen within the Council of Ministers, whose membership was increased from twenty-three to thirty-six.[86] The regular bi-monthly meetings of the Politburo were far too infrequent to affect Stalin's day-to-day command of the affairs of state, and, as we know, he did not allow the reform to take permanent root.[87] Of interest to us here, however, is not whether the reforms of 1945 and 1946 were effective but the fact that, at the time of the London Conference, Stalin went through these motions of reform in such grand, theatrical style. It was as though he wanted to impress upon the world that he was only human, unable to supervise everything, and, more important, that he was above it all—the undisputed master who was not responsible for the foibles of the system.

The London Conference is not a popular subject among Soviet historians, nor, indeed, is any of the diplomacy of the Stalinist years just after the war—a remarkable fact in view of the so-called victories which outsiders so often attribute to Soviet diplomacy at that time. The most recent Soviet monograph, furthermore, attributes the breakdown of the conference to American rattling of the atomic bomb and to a "reactionary conspiracy," organized by Churchill, to interrupt Soviet-American friendship. Then, with characteristic evasion, it revives the old notion that Soviet policy relied on a "democratic plan" worked out by the CPSU(b) during the war.[88] But an older account by a well-known Stalinist historian, G. A. Deborin, discusses the conference in terms that are extraordinarily interesting, in view of the peculiar retreat by Stalin which we have just described. Deborin suggests that for the Soviet regime the London Conference represented a gamble on the power of history.[89] He claims that in the late summer of 1945 the "forces of progress" all over the world were sweeping away the debris of the past. Unfortunately (in his view), the Americans and especially the newly elected British socialists were ignoring these portents and resisting the direction in which history was carrying them. Consequently, the Soviet government accepted the mission of forcing the reluctant West to obey. Through the agency of Molotov and in the framework of the Council of Allied Foreign Ministers, Deborin alleges, the Soviet government revealed to the Allies history's terms for a just peace and then, when the Allies refused to concede, it allowed the conference to break up without agreement.

This explanation is certainly exotic. Yet it is consistent with what went before: these Soviet tactics were, in effect, a test of the Grand Alliance in the tradition of Vyshinsky's coup at Bucharest and the Berne affair. Even contemporary Westerners sensed that the Russians seriously expected America and Britain to do their bidding at the London Conference and were extremely surprised when Byrnes and Bevin stuck together.[90] Further, in the light of the domestic policy dilemma in which Stalin was caught and his retreat from responsibility at the time of the London Conference, the explanation is plausible.

In the early months of 1945 Stalin had conducted the testing of the Grand Alliance himself. When his success at Yalta fanned excessive enthusiasm among the Party revivalists, he took the risk of drumming up a war scare in order to dampen them, and failed. Although he tried to do so with vigorous expressions of nationalism all through the spring and summer, events continued to betray him. The revivalists usurped his name and egregiously claimed that what he did and said, he did and said in the interests of their party—of their ideals. As a result, Stalin had to bear the responsibility for what they did spontaneously, thoughtlessly, and irresponsibly in the name of the Party. If Soviet policy at the London Conference constituted a great gamble, it enabled Stalin to turn the tables. He had established his own line firmly and distinctly for all the world to see—a line which deprecated the Party. Now he made Molotov, the leader of the Party revivalists, go abroad, and there, without Stalin, rely on revivalist theory in a gamble with the highest of all stakes, the security of the Soviet state. One is reminded of Zhdanov's imagery in his speeches on literature in August 1946: "The task of every conscientious Soviet writer is to depict the new high qualities of the Soviet people, to show the life of our people today, and to throw light on the road to the future. [But] the writer cannot follow events. He must be in the first ranks of the people, showing them the way of progress, being guided by the methods of socialist realism."[91]

To follow, and yet to lead—this was the impossible task with which Stalin burdened Molotov at the London Conference: to be correct, and yet to take enormous risks. When Molotov complied, Stalin ostentatiously went on vacation, leaving his foreign commissar to accept the consequences. To Stalin, these must have seemed predictable. Despite recent Allied behavior, it was hardly credible that the Americans, with their atomic bomb and their industrial wealth, and the British, with their empire and their victory, would accept Molotov's obstinacy without protest. It was predictable that in this test the revivalists would lose, and Stalin would be able to claim that though the waves of history were strong, they were dangerous and navigable only by Stalin.

Separate Roads to Socialism

Developments in the theater of international Communism confirm our analysis that, in late 1945, Stalin made a theatrical retreat from political involvement and took a vast gamble in foreign policy. As the reader may recall, he launched his postwar Communist policy early in 1944 by taking a strong stand against any revolutionary upheaval erupting during the liberation of Europe. Faced with the possibility that disturbances might interrupt his war effort, faced with the certainty that Communists would be involved in such disturbances and that they might end up by attacking his allies, Stalin insisted that Communists join coalition governments. But this open intervention in the affairs of foreign parties was only part of Stalin's new international Communist policy. Once the crises of liberation were over, he changed his tack. When foreign Communists requested orders from him now, as had been customary in the Comintern, he would no longer oblige. As Milovan Djilas reports, he said, "No. I do not [have comments on your work]. You yourselves know best what is to be done." Djilas reported to Tito after this: "The Comintern factually no longer exists, and we Yugoslav Communists have to shift for ourselves. We have to depend primarily on our own forces."[92] This was not the only such case. In December 1944, during the negotiation in Moscow concerning the formation of a new government for Hungary, Stalin prevented Molotov and other Soviet leaders from imposing their views on the Hungarian Communists. "Beyond question," he said, the Hungarians "know better than we what the situation is, and we must accept their point of view."[93]

We have seen elsewhere that Stalin knew quite clearly what he was doing when he gave such free rein to the Communists of Eastern

Europe. Recognizing that there were some Communists whom he could not control, he commanded them all to be free and independent and then used the tame ones to lure the wild ones back into the fold, a tactic analogous to his activity at the time of the London Conference of Foreign Ministers in September and October 1945.

From the Communist point of view—perhaps even objectively—a revolution occurred in the war zones of Eurasia in that year of victory. This is not to say that the populations of the war-zone countries were all rushing to the barricades. Most Europeans were far too exhausted, dulled with suffering, too hungry for that sort of revolution. But everywhere in the war zones, there was disorder. Governments had collapsed. Armies were going home. Millions of people were roofless and wandering. Hope was in the air. Opportunities were at hand. Nobody knew what the future would be. Above all, there was no control, and anything could happen.

Furthermore, even those foreign Communist parties which Stalin dominated in 1945 were enduring transformations. The obedient Hungarian Communist Party, which had had a few hundred members in 1943, claimed more than 300,000 by the autumn of 1945.[94] The French Party, which in 1943 had no way to count its ravaged membership at home, was approaching one million members by mid-1945 and received some five million votes in a free election the following October.[95] The unpopular Polish CP rose from 20,000 members in 1944 to 235,000 members by December 1945 and to more than 500,000 members in 1946.[96] Many of the new Communists were hardly likely to run amok.[97] They were a motley crowd, including fellow travelers of every stripe—idealistic scholars, adventurous youths, public-spirited housewives, petit bourgeois opportunists, terrified ex-Fascists, and lumpen proletarians hoping to gain social mobility—both the cream and the scum of the world's war-torn society. Such people could be counted on to do what they were told. But they were not the only recruits. There were also people who had benefited from the liberation and knew something of what they wanted—for example, victims of Fascism, men of the prewar political left, workers, and peasants. Many of these were militants who wanted revenge. Others wanted distinct forms of social legislation or massive land reforms which would entail virtual transformation of the societies in which they lived. Even if we presume that the famed democratic centralism of Leninism was effective under such conditions of tremendous growth and political change, it can be seen that the administrative

210

problems Stalin faced in obtaining obedience from such Communist parties were not of the same sort as he faced in 1943. He could not stick to the old methods if he wished to remain in charge.

Change occurred first in China. By November, the negotiations between the Communists and the Nationalists at Chungking were deadlocked, and the whole scenario of the original Soviet intervention had vanished, leaving the Red Army close to becoming a participant in a Chinese civil war. Worse, in southern Manchuria the Red Army now found itself standing by while Chinese Communist troops prepared to resist by force the landing of Nationalist troops from American vessels, with American marines not far away. Stalin's brotherly help to China was leading him dangerously close to military confrontation with his allies in the West. Hereupon, on 17 November the Soviet ambassador to Chungking proposed the basis for a general settlement to the Chinese Nationalists. His note denied that the Soviet government wished to help the Communists, blamed all that had happened since the occupation on the Nationalists' inability to appear in Manchuria in adequate force, suggested that Chungking legitimize the continued Soviet presence in Manchuria, and offered to facilitate the entry of Chinese government forces there when they were ready to appear. The Nationalists accepted, and in January 1946 the Russians gave them control of the principal Manchurian cities. After much procrastination the Red Army finally evacuated in April.[98]

Meanwhile, Moscow worked out new arrangements with the CCP. Mao set up a Northeastern Bureau for Manchuria within his party and instructed it to concentrate on the countryside, avoiding the big cities, which were to be handed over to Chungking. This must have been a bitter pill for him because the Northeastern Bureau was given considerable political autonomy, including the right to maintain regular and separate liaison with the CPSU(b), as well as the Red Army. It became, in a word, a Soviet Trojan horse within the CCP.[99] Further, Mao apparently agreed to conform, at least verbally, to Stalin's coalitionary line. Regularly over the next two years, despite the emerging civil war in the field and the CCP's obduracy at the negotiating table, Mao continued to promote the virtues of coalitionism. But for all this he received much in exchange. Before the evacuation of Manchuria, the Red Army gave the Northeastern Bureau the captured Japanese military materiel which eventually made possible the CCP's victory in the Chinese civil war. Second, Mao received Stalin's recognition of China's separate road to socialism. Stalin's stated opinion was, of course, that the Chinese revolution should proceed slowly, but he acknowledged Mao's peasant doctrine—this was explicit in the instruction that the Manchurian Communists avoid the cities and thus the proletariat.[100] And since he could not do so, he did not insist that Mao conform. Stalin, who until September had fought so hard to stop or at least to limit Mao's independent revolution, now ended his intervention, indicating as he had to the Yugoslavs eighteen months earlier, "You yourselves know best what is to be done."[101]

Stalin's retreat, after the London Conference of Foreign Ministers, into tolerance of Chinese Communist "separate roadism" was no isolated instance. Every fluctuation in his relationship with the CCP then was reflected in his relationships with the Communists of other countries—these were fluctuations in his general line. In Iran, for example, beginning early in November, the Red Army command let the local "democrats" run free. The latter still denied that they wanted to destroy the Iranian state, demanding only the establishment of autonomous regimes in certain provinces. But they raised a cry for revolutionary elections—plebiscites. On 15 November the Red Army started to provide these local forces with weapons. By the 20th it was systematically protecting them from interference by the Teheran forces. On 12 and 15 December, after elections, new parliamentary assemblies proclaimed an "Autonomous People's Democratic Republic" in Azerbaijan and a "People's Republic" for the tribal Kurds.

These picturesque activities won immediate attention in the world press and thus formed the background for the negotiations regarding the Soviet evacuation of China, which began on 17 November and culminated with Mao's directive of 28 December to the Northeastern Bureau of his party. The lesson could hardly be missed: if Mao would only heed Stalin, he also might enjoy Soviet bounty. The Iranian events also served a clear function in the development of Soviet foreign policy. Three weeks after Stalin went on vacation, at a time when Molotov, in charge of the government, was waiting for the Western responses, they renewed the challenge of the London Conference. If the Americans were interested in breaking the imperial power of the British, here was a golden opportunity. Washington had only to cooperate with the Russians, and British-dominated Iran would be no more.[102]

These non-Iranian functions of the events in Azerbaijan in November and December 1945 should not distract one, however, from their message regarding Stalin's stance toward Communists abroad. He was theatrically withdrawing from a supervisory role, just as in China and in such distant colonial regions as the Dutch Indies[103] and Indo-China,[104] where in an absolute sense Moscow had little opportunity to control the course of events. But the clearest examples of the Stalinist retreat now appeared in Europe. During November 1945, for example, in Soviet-occupied Eastern Germany, the overwhelmingly Muscovite CP leadership began abruptly to enunciate the thesis that Germany should follow its own "separate road" to socialism. In March 1946, these Communists carried their new line so far as to break ranks with all the other European Communist parties by forcing a merger on the East German Social Democratic Party, a move which was alleged to show respect for "special German conditions."[105] This happened in a country which did not possess a national government and in a zone directly ruled by the Red Army. Coincidently, in Soviet-occupied Hungary, Mátyás Rákosi, that Muscovite first secretary of the Communist Party who took pride in his reputation as Stalin's most subservient servitor, developed a theory of Hungary's separate and special road to socialism. Together with his Muscovite colleagues, he developed tactics for seizing power which were said to be especially tailored to Hungarian conditions.[106] The Poles, the Czechs, the French, and the Italians also emerged with their national democratic roads.[107] Some parties, most conspicuously the Rumanian CP, neglected such esoteric theoretical work.[108] But in February 1946, Dimitrov (whom Stalin had finally sent home) generalized in Soviet-occupied Bulgaria that "*every* nation will effect the transition to socialism now, not by the Soviet road, but by its own realistic, painless path."[109] And later in 1946 Stalin himself told at least one group of visiting East European Communist leaders:

> As experience shows and as the classics of Marxism-Leninism teach, there exists no single road [to socialism] leading through soviets and the dictatorship of the proletariat. Under certain conditions there may be another way. . . . Especially now after the defeat of Hitlerite Germany—after the Second World War, which on the one hand has led to so many sacrifices, and on the other has swept away the ruling classes of so many countries—the consciousness of the broad popular masses is high. In the presence of this kind of historical circumstance there are many possibilities open to the socialist movement—many paths. In Yugoslavia, Bulgaria, Poland and [Czechoslovakia] a special

213

road to socialism is possible. . . . It need not pass through the soviet system and the dictatorship of the proletariat, but can follow other channels.[110]

A conversation Stalin had in April 1945 when the leaders of the Yugoslav partisan movement journeyed to Moscow shows what was involved in Stalin's "separate roadism" apart from acknowledgment of the revolutionary conditions of the time. When Tito "brought out that there were new phenomena in socialism and that socialism was now being achieved in ways different from those of the past," Stalin retorted: "Today socialism is possible even under the English monarchy. Revolution is no longer necessary everywhere. Just recently a delegation of British Laborites was here, and we talked about this in particular."[111] Tito was trying to suggest that since more than one road to socialism was now open, the Yugoslav model was as good as the Soviet model and thus, by implication, that he was not far behind Stalin. Stalin countered by indicating that if there were two roads, there were a hundred, and that one must not insist that the barricades-type of revolutionary action, in which the Yugoslavs took such pride, was needed to reach socialism. Stalin's "separate roadism" here was an instrument for making sure that the Yugoslav-model road to socialism would seem no better than those of the Germans, the Hungarians, and the French and that the Soviet model remained, as a result, supreme.

A modest but significant theoretical development during the autumn of 1945 confirms that *divide et impera* was Stalin's motive when he encouraged "separate roadism" and, by extension, when he withdrew from direct administrative supervision at home and encouraged Molotov in London. Early in the autumn, the Soviet theoretical journal *Bol'shevik* published Stalin's adaptation, dating from 1924, of a well-known Leninist premise: "The working movement without socialism [that is, without Marxism-Leninism] is trade-unionist blundering, which *never* leads the proletariat to victory and which leaves the proletariat in the embrace of bourgeois ideology."[112] This statement had obvious implications for the possibility of any country achieving progress without Communist Party leadership. Therefore, it was important that in November *Bol'shevik* issued a "correction," stating that Stalin had "really" said: "The worker movement without socialism is trade-unionist blundering which *sometimes, it can be seen,* leads to socialist revolution, though at the price of long suffering to the proletariat."[113]

214

The point of this correction was emphasized by its appearance in the issue of *Bol'shevik* which contained the first Soviet endorsement of Marshal Tito's theses on people's democracy and on Yugoslavia's special road to socialism.[114] It was intended to rebut Tito's claims of having reached socialism in Yugoslavia by suggesting: "Revolution is no longer necessary everywhere. . . . Yes, socialism is possible even under an English king."[115]

Stalin's retreat from responsibility within international Communism during the late autumn of 1945 existed, and there was method in it—of this there seems no doubt. A similar tactical retreat in the sphere of Soviet domestic politics at the time of the London Conference is not, therefore, improbable.

Stalin's Style

Early in September 1945, Stalin took aside George Kennan, secretary at the American embassy in Moscow, at the end of a meeting and assured him: "Tell your fellows not to worry about those East European countries. Our troops are going to get out of there and things will be all right."[116] Kennan hardly knew what to make of this surprising intimacy save that Stalin was more tractable than other Soviet leaders. A month later at Gagry, when Ambassador Harriman came to see him, Stalin went further. He hinted ever so gently that it was not he but his Politburo colleagues who would force the Soviet Union into an isolationist stance if the West did not help him out. Harriman was inclined to believe him.[117]

All through the war Stalin had been accessible to foreign leaders. By 1945 he had developed a real intimacy with some of them—with Churchill, Roosevelt, Harry Hopkins, and Harriman in particular; they as a result had come to feel that with Stalin, as opposed to Molotov and his other lieutenants, one could negotiate effectively and accomplish something. But seldom before August, September, and October 1945 did he so deliberately cultivate an attractive "prisoner of the Politburo" image among his foreign associates. Just when he was pressing Molotov into accepting responsibility for a diplomatic break with the Western Allies at London, tricking the Party revivalists on a massive scale, he was keeping a private line of communication open to the enemy abroad.[118] Clearly he was an extraordinarily devious man; this is the lesson also of a peculiar incident which, more than any other, confirms our interpretation of Soviet behavior at the London Conference of Foreign Ministers.

When Stalin went on vacation, there was a relaxation of the Soviet censorship.[119] We do not know why this was done, although it may be relevant that Zhdanov once said: "No matter what efforts the bourgeois politicians and writers are making . . . to erect an 'iron curtain' which will prevent the truth about the Soviet Union from penetrating beyond the Soviet frontiers . . . they must be doomed to failure."[120] Perhaps the censorship was raised to test this optimistic notion. At any rate, the major result was that the world press had a chance to air the news about Stalin's age, sickness, and coming retirement. Later the censorship was reimposed, and in his talk with Harold Stassen early in 1947 Stalin said:

> it would be difficult in the USSR to do without censorship. Molotov tried a couple of times to do without it but failed. Each time the Soviet government attempted to change the censorship rules, it came to regret it and reintroduced them. In the autumn of [1945], the censorship was changed in the USSR. He, J. V. Stalin, was on vacation, and the correspondents began to write about how Molotov had forced Stalin to go on vacation, and afterward they wrote that he, Stalin, had returned and chased Molotov out. In such fashion the correspondents made it seem that the Soviet government was some sort of bestiary. In the end, [we] Soviet people were repelled and were forced to reintroduce the censorship.[121]

In the light of the circumstances described in this chapter, one can respond to this pious statement with a sigh: "poor Molotov!" One is reminded of Eisenstein's film *Ivan the Terrible,* first shown in January 1945. At its climax, Ivan leaves Moscow in a theatrical gesture so that his subjects may learn their helplessness without him and implore him to return and institute his *oprichnina*—secret police control.[122]

10

Fireworks

The Election Speech

JUST FOUR MONTHS after the London Foreign Ministers' Conference, on 9 February 1946, Stalin caught the ear of the world by declaiming:

> It would be a mistake to consider that the Second World War broke out by accident or as a result of errors of one or another statesman, although such errors indubitably did take place. Essentially, the war broke out as an inevitable result of the development of the world's economic and political forces on the basis of contemporary monopoly capitalism. Marxists have more than once pointed out that the capitalist world economic system contains in itself the seeds of a general crisis and of warlike clashes.[1]

Western observers took this resurrection of the theory of imperialism as a sign that Stalin and his colleagues no longer regarded the West in

217

the same friendly spirit as they had during the war. They were surprised and horrified by the contrast between the ideological stance Stalin adopted on this occasion and the Russian nationalism he had espoused a few months earlier. They asked why, as we have throughout this book.[2]

The mystery of Stalin's speech is all the greater because on the diplomatic front very little happened during the early winter of 1945–1946 to explain such a radical shift. After the London Conference most governments settled down to face the domestic problems they had neglected during the war. East-West diplomatic contacts in general lapsed, and the few diplomatic contacts which took place were friendly. Indeed, when Ambassador Harriman visited Stalin late in October at his vacation spot in the Caucasus, the conversations were extremely cordial.[3] In December the Allied foreign ministers met in Moscow and resumed the deliberations broken off in London in an atmosphere quite lacking in recrimination.[4] They agreed on procedures for the occupation of Japan and Korea, resolved some Western objections to developments in Soviet-occupied Rumania and Bulgaria, and discussed China and Iran. Differences remained: in January 1946, for example, the British and the Russians exchanged accusations of imperialism at the UNO session in London, and by February Soviet reluctance to evacuate the Red Army from northern Iran was threatening to bring on an international crisis (which in fact erupted in March). But until Stalin's speech the reconciliation achieved at Moscow still seemed sound.[5]

Now Stalin publicly reaffirmed the validity of the theory of imperialism, describing the Western Powers as his ideological enemies. In March, moreover, in his reply to Winston Churchill's "Iron Curtain" speech, he specifically endorsed the rebirth of revolutionary Communism: "Mr. Churchill is near the truth when he talks of the growth of Communist Party influences in Eastern Europe. One must point out, however, that this is not the whole truth. The influence of the Communist parties has grown not only in Eastern Europe, but in nearly all the European countries. . . . The rise of the Communists cannot be considered fortuitous. It represents a phenomenon based on laws of development."[6] Even if he was justifiably angry at Churchill when he said this, and even if he made up for it a few days later with a public reaffirmation of his United Nations speech of November 1944 and his faith in the Grand Alliance,[7] one must still ask why he adopted so strong an ideological stance.

218

The Moscow Conference

In October 1945 Stalin let Averell Harriman feel that Soviet foreign policy was not pragmatically construed in each country according to local conditions. By balancing Far Eastern issues against European issues, he made it as clear as he could that Moscow followed a highly analytical, world-wide policy, and that there was linkage among all its various ramifications. He also intimated that he was hovering between a general policy of participationism and one of isolationism, and that his choice would depend on Western behavior.[8] These warnings offer a first clue to his "Communist" speeches of February and March 1946.

After such warnings (and regardless of their objective truth), the United States should have acted with great caution, especially when, in the middle of November, the people's democratic rebellions against the Iranian government began in Azerbaijan. The Americans, however, were not cautious.[9] They may have been focusing on domestic affairs after the long wartime involvement abroad; they may have been bewildered by the catastrophic situation in China.[10] At any rate, in the face of this systematic Soviet testing of American mettle, Secretary of State James Byrnes acted as though all the issues facing the Grand Alliance could be considered separately, and as though international diplomacy were, to quote Kennan, "simply a rough and tumble" in which a participant's overall image made no difference.[11] Byrnes describes events as follows:

> A few days later it was Thanksgiving Day [actually 23 November], and I was alone in my office taking advantage of the holiday quiet to think over several problems. Suddenly I recalled that at Yalta it had been agreed that the three foreign ministers should meet every three months. . . . A meeting of the three foreign ministers might get the peace-making machinery in motion again. I thought it was worth a try, so next morning a cable was sent to Mr. Molotov. . . . I suggested . . . that a meeting be held in the Russian capital. I felt sure that Russian hospitality being what it is, the Soviet government would extend the invitation, and I believed that if we met in Moscow, where I would have a chance to talk to Stalin, we might remove the barriers to the peace treaties. Of course, a proposal for a meeting under such circumstances was in violation of accepted diplomatic procedure. . . . Against the advice of the diplomats and the columnists, I went to Moscow.[12]

Even from this passage it is clear that the American government responded to the Soviet gambit at London in a way which invited misreading in the Kremlin. Further, Byrnes fails to mention facts which may have seemed extremely important to the Russians. In London at this very time negotiations were in progress for a massive United States loan to the British, and the Americans were driving a very hard bargain, blatantly attempting to introduce American trade into Britain's empire. Yet Byrnes did not even consult the British about his overture to the Russians, which came at a critical moment in the loan negotiations, and his action touched off an explosion of indignation in London.[13] A leading British statesman of the day recalls that the Labor government seriously considered breaking economic relations with the United States and adopting a "go-it-alone" policy because of the selfishness of Byrnes' foreign policy.[14] It follows that the Soviet recipients of the secretary of state's cable would have been justified in thinking that they were witnessing a major split among the imperialists, and Byrnes' report on the Moscow meeting of the Council of Foreign Ministers leaves no doubt that he pushed Stalin and Molotov even further toward such an assumption:

> The meeting opened at 5:00 p.m., December 16. . . . Our proposal on peace conference procedure was based on our last position at London. . . . The following day Mr. Molotov presented his counterproposal which failed to advance the situation beyond the London stand of the Soviet delegation. . . . Ambassador Harriman, Mr. Bohlen and I went to the Kremlin for the first of our meetings with Generalissimo Stalin.[15]

> I . . . sketched the discussions with Mr. Molotov on our proposed list of states [to be admitted to the peace conference]. . . . I pointed out that if India and the three Baltic states were admitted to the peace conference, "this would mean that Britain would be there with five dominions and the Soviet Union would be there with five republics. It would be difficult for me to explain such a decision in the United States," I told him. . . . Molotov interjected that even if India were dropped, Britain would still have four dominions represented. . . . I replied, "We have made important concessions in this matter of peace treaties, and it is not too much to ask that our list for the conference be approved." . . . The next afternoon Mr. Molotov . . . said that the Generalissimo had just telephoned to inform me that he would accept our list of states. . . . [16]

> With this agreement reached, we turned again to the question of Rumania and Bulgaria. . . . Once again it appeared that the only hope was to take up the matter directly with the Generalissimo, and I went to see him the following night. . . . We first discussed the question of withdrawing all foreign troops from Iran, and then I expressed a desire to talk about the Balkans "as I have been having a difficult time with Mr.

Molotov on this subject.'' Stalin smiled broadly and said that this was unexpected news. . . . Since elections had been held in Bulgaria it was impossible to ask for reorganization there, but he finally agreed it would be possible to advise [the Bulgarians] to include in the government two representative members of two important political parties not then represented. . . . In the case of Rumania, he conceded, it would be less difficult to make changes. After considerable discussions it was agreed to send a commission composed of the American and British Ambassadors to Moscow, and [of] Mr. Vyshinsky to Bucharest to work out with the government . . . the restoration and maintenance of civil liberties. Stalin asked me to convey his acceptance of this proposal . . . to Mr. Bevin. I agreed to inform the British Foreign Minister and added jokingly that even though we were supposed to have a bloc with Britain I had not informed Bevin about my proposal to Mr. Molotov for this meeting in Moscow as soon as I should have. The Generalissimo smiled and, in the same spirit, replied that this obviously was only a cloak to hide the reality of the bloc.[17]

From Byrnes' account one may see that the two major European agreements made at the Moscow Conference were hammered out by the USA and the USSR in an atmosphere of conscious independence from the British. If this were not enough to confirm Stalin and Molotov in their impression of United States treachery toward Britain, Byrnes behaved quite oddly with regard to the blossoming crisis in Iran, where Britain's imperial interests were very much at stake. This behavior is evident even in his less than candid account:

We discussed Mr. Bevin's proposal that a Three-Power Commission be appointed to go to Iran. [Stalin] was noncommittal regarding the Bevin proposal, and I said once again that we hoped no action would be taken in Iran that would cause a difference between us. To this the Generalissimo replied: ''We will do nothing to make you blush.'' . . . [The next day] Molotov offered several amendments to Mr. Bevin's proposal. Bevin accepted all but one which left in doubt the date for the withdrawal of troops. . . . In view of our private conversation I thought Molotov would finally agree to Bevin's language. However when we met the afternoon of December 26, it was clear that the Soviet High Command had changed its attitude. Molotov announced that the Iranian case was not properly on the agenda and ''cannot be considered.'' Bevin complained. . . . ''What is my next step?'' Bevin asked. ''You know that well,'' Molotov answered. . . . [Then] I suggested that we resume, [later] in London, consideration of pending problems.[18]

The postponement of ''pending problems'' lightly referred to by Byrnes here in fact represented a major American concession to Russian wishes at British expense in Iran, an important area of British interest. As Byrnes well knew, although he does not mention it, the British were extremely unhappy over this betrayal of Western solidarity.[19] One may judge what the Russians thought from an article which the Stalinist economist Eugen Varga published early in January 1946 about the recent Anglo-American financial conversations. Varga's argument was based entirely on the thesis that the United States was exploiting its advantageous postwar position to gain entry to Britain's colonial markets.[20]

Byrnes says that at the end of the Moscow Conference

> members of the staff were asked to prepare the protocol to be signed by the three foreign ministers. . . . Mr. Bevin signed first and the papers were passed to me. After signing, I arose to say good-bye. . . . Suddenly Mr. Molotov sent one of his aides to me. . . . He said that his staff had, "by mistake," included the Soviet document on Bulgaria in the Russian text of the protocol. He asked if, after all, it could not be accepted. We promptly said it could not. He then suggested that we might combine the first half of my proposal with the second half of his draft. I told him we could not do things by "halves"; that since he had come half way, he should accept the American proposal. To my amazement, he did. Mr. Bevin then facetiously asked him to look in his pocket to see if he could not find another "mistake" that would satisfactorily end our discussions on Iran. In good humor, Mr. Molotov said he could not.[21]

Molotov clearly intended to exacerbate the supposed splits among the Allies. One could hardly ask for better evidence that he and Stalin felt that the West was gullible and that therefore the Grand Alliance was worth preserving.

In so far as Stalin in the autumn of 1945 was betting against a Leninist prognosis that the Allies would split in the face of an implacable Soviet stand, apparently he lost; in so far as the Soviet Party revivalists bet on such a split, apparently they won. There is no proof of these matters, and there will be none until the Soviet archives are opened. But the assumption that a mighty and successful gamble characterized Soviet foreign policy at the London and Moscow conferences accounts for more of the known and puzzling facts than the other explanations which have been offered. Above all, it suggests a first reason why Stalin on 9 February 1946 publicly acknowledged that Lenin's theory of imperialism might still be true. The Moscow Conference had proved it true.

A Defense of Stalinism

Apart from the opening paragraphs on the theory of imperialism, just discussed, Stalin devoted his entire election campaign speech to current domestic problems. The Soviet Union was just then in transition from wartime to peacetime activity. Since the end of the war with Japan, the government had begun demobilizing the army, converting the national industrial plants from production of tanks and guns to peacetime purposes, and supervising the return of millions of people from the Siberian arsenal and German captivity to their homes in the western regions of the country. The government had announced the preparation of a new Five Year Plan and had called elections. Furthermore, and very important in connection with the interpretation of Stalin's speech, the wartime high command structure, the GOKO, had been dissolved, and, the Politburo had resumed its function as the supreme political organ within the system, meeting frequently and keeping minutes of its decisions. It had given *partiinost* full rein, was preparing a huge Party-run educational campaign to put the nation's affairs to rights, and was allowing the voluntarist Party economic theorist N. A. Voznesensky to play a dominant role in the formation of the peacetime economy.

In his speech Stalin showed full awareness of these mighty changes and made it clear that he was in favor of them. He spoke to his audience not in his role as head of the Soviet government but as secretary general of the Party. Much of his speech was in the form of a report on Party activities. His endorsement of the theory of imperialism at the beginning of the speech represented a Party point of view. From that endorsement he proceeded to summarize the results of the war: the Soviet social system and the Soviet states system had proved to be valid, and the army had proved to be a first-class force. This he cited as evidence of the Party's prewar foresight. Then, in a report on the Party's plans, he said:

> for the more distant future, the Party has taken steps to organize a new great development of our national economy which could enable us, for example, to triple our industrial production over the prewar level. We must reach a point where our industry can produce annually 50 million tons of pig iron (prolonged applause), 60 million tons of steel (prolonged applause), 500 million tons of coal (prolonged applause), and 60 million tons of oil (prolonged applause). Only under such conditions can we assure that our Fatherland will be guaranteed against all eventualities

223

(enthusiastic applause). This may take three new five year plans, if not more. But it can be done, and we must do it (enthusiastic applause).[22]

Stalin's lofty production goals were fully worthy of the Party revivalist Vosnesensky, who outlined the same goals in greater detail to the Supreme Soviet some weeks later.[23] Given the ruins left by the war, these were a voluntarist's goals (albeit they were less unrealistic and unexpected than Western observers judged).[24]

Stalin's deliberate favoritism toward the Party was nowhere more obvious in his election speech than in his comments about the army, whose wartime *esprit de corps,* as we know, he was systematically undermining. In November 1944 he installed the political general N. A. Bulganin as his military deputy in the GOKO and the Armed Forces Commissariat. In the final battles of the war in Germany, he created dissension among his leading generals.[25] In January and February 1946 the pages of the army journal *Krasnaya Zvezda* carried a sharp argument between those who suggested a resumption of Party influence within the armed services and those who simply praised Stalin's state.[26] Now Stalin, speaking in the name of the Party, announced that "it would be . . . a mistake to affirm that we gained victory thanks just to the bravery of our soldiers. Without bravery, of course, it is impossible to gain victory. But bravery alone is not enough to defeat an enemy who has a huge army and first-class weapons. . . . For that it is necessary to have . . . up-to-date weapons and effective supply."[27] This was a nasty shock to an army which had become accustomed to public praise. Stalin followed up this comment with a *prikaz* (Order of the Day) on Red Army Day (23 February) in which he emphasized that the army's most immediate task was to ensure the political as well as the military toughness of its soldiers and that the victory "must not lead to conceit and complacency."[28]

A deluge of changes followed. On 25 February the separate army and navy commissariats were abolished, giving place to a new united Armed Services Commissariat, under Stalin.[29] A month later this was renamed a ministry, and six deputy ministers were appointed. Five of these—Marshals Vasilevskii and Zhukov, Admiral Kuznetsov, and Generals Vershenin and Khrulov—were professional soldiers, and each was given specific responsibility for a particular service. Obviously, they would compete with one another. The sixth minister, N. A. Bulganin, the political general, was named first deputy minister, given responsibility for general questions, and made a member of the

Party Orgburo. His authority over the others was clear. General Shikin, who would be involved in the Leningrad affair three years later, emerged as the replacement for Shcherbakov in the Political Administration of the Armed Service, the GPUKA.[30] In the following months, as the demobilizations drastically depleted the strength and dimensions of the military, the Party organizations in the services were systematically strengthened; political education was drastically stepped up; war heroes like Marshal Zhukov were quietly shuttled off to obscure commands; and political controls were reintroduced.

These circumstances underline the extent to which Stalin's election speech was a delicate instrument through which he deliberately pressed his domestic policy goals, and they make one wonder why some other Party political activities going on at this time did not receive comparable open endorsement. Investigation reveals a problem which Stalin faced as he composed his speech and points to the reason why he now invoked the theory of imperialism in foreign policy.

As mentioned elsewhere, the main wartime power base of the great home-front leaders Beria and Malenkov was the GOKO. It fell away in September 1945, and they were not long in feeling the restoration of Politburo authority. On 14 January 1946 Beria was removed from direct command of the NKVD. Six months later his wartime deputy in the other police ministry, the MGB, was replaced.[31] Beria was elected a full member of the Politburo in March 1946 but was given no position in the Party executive organs. Indeed, the slot in the new Orgburo which evidently involved supervision of the police fell to M. I. Suslov, who was not a "Beria man."[32] As secretary in the Stavropol *krai* of the northern Caucasus during the war and in Lithuania during 1944 and 1945, Suslov acquired considerable police experience, but it is as an ideologist and as an associate of the one figure in Stalin's entourage who dared oppose Beria—Stalin's secretary, A. N. Poskrebyshev—that he has figured in history. Moreover, Poskrebyshev himself now emerged from his obscurity (although it was only in 1947 that he became chairman of the Supreme Soviet Committee on Draft Legislation).[33] As we know, Beria's power survived this challenge, but for the time being, it was clearly reduced.

Meanwhile, on 19 January 1946 the Chief Administration for War Industry, a Malenkov stronghold, was abolished, giving place to a series of new commissariats.[34] On 7 January the Ammunition Commissariat was abolished; on 17 February the same fate attended the commissariats for Mortar Armaments and Medium Machine Construction. Coincidentally, the Coal and Oil commissariats were split into eastern and western divisions. All these had been under Malenkov's general supervision during the later war years, and presumably his authority suffered in the shakeup. What is more, in the first year and a half of the Party revival the Party secretaries for nine of the most important industrial *oblasty* of the home front were removed.[35] Most of them were given new jobs in the Party center in Moscow, so it may hardly be said that they were purged. One must recognize, nonetheless, that all of these *oblasty,* which were Malenkov's particular responsibility during the latter stages of the war, did undergo a shakeup in our period, and five of the nine replacements became victims of the purge of 1949, which, it was popularly believed, Malenkov administered.

Malenkov, as it happens, was made a full member of the new Politburo in March 1946 along with Beria, but he was conspicuously absent from the list of deputy chairmen of the Council of Ministers in that month. In effect, he was cut out of the government altogether for a time, and in October 1946, when he was finally made a deputy chairman of the Council of Ministers, he was evicted from his position as a secretary of the Party,[36] the original base of his power. By the latter half of 1946, Malenkov had been as conspicuously and thoroughly degraded as Zhdanov had been during the war.

The Party-led assault on Beria and Malenkov was patently useful to Stalin, for, as we have seen elsewhere, their power had begun to threaten him, but in his election speech of February 1946 he did not endorse the attack. On the contrary, the speech in many ways seemed almost a defense of what Malenkov and Beria stood for. As Stalin reviewed the record of what he called the Party's past activities, he singled out as correct the decisions to industrialize the Soviet Union, collectivize its agriculture, and wage war on the "Trotskyites and rightists" who (allegedly) had opposed industrialization. Was not this a defense of Malenkov's industrial empire and of Beria's police regime? But there was a striking logic in what Stalin did. If he had openly abandoned Beria and Malenkov and all they stood for in his speech, he would have exposed himself to attack. Their accomplishment, after all, was Stalinism and, in particular, the industrialization, the collectivization, and the purges of the prewar era. On the occasion of their fall, therefore, he had to ensure that he himself did not go down with them. This was surely his main purpose in delivering the speech of February 1946 in the form he did, declaring over and over again that Russia's industrial growth was the Party's achievement, that the country's socialized agriculture was an example of the Party's foresight, and that the war against Stalin's domestic foes had been led by the Party. In this way he united his own prewar record, with all its failings and lack of *partiinost,* with that of the Party.

Let us return now to the question of why Stalin opened this speech with an endorsement of Lenin's theory of imperialism offensive to the Western Allies. Perhaps the answer lies in his conflicting purposes in making the speech. On the one hand, he wanted to encourage the Party revival, and to that end, it was essential that he insert somewhere in his speech an endorsement of Marxist-Leninist theory. On the other hand, in his discussion of domestic affairs he could not afford to let himself sound too *partiinyi* but had to make the Party sound Stalinist. He could not end his speech as Voznesensky would a month later, declaring that the state's economic plans "possess the force of economic laws"—in effect, giving the Party and the Planning Office a free rein[37]—nor could he echo Molotov's voluntarist enthusiasm, saying, "a great deal depends, of course, on whether people know how to work well: but even more depends on their having the will to learn how to work."[38] Stalin's tone and message had to be pragmatic: "It can be done and we must do it."

In what connection, therefore, was Stalin able in this speech to symbolize his endorsement of the Party's cause, if not in connection with foreign affairs? No doubt he well knew that his endorsement of the theory of imperialism would offend the Western Powers. But if, as may have seemed the case after the Moscow Conference, the Western Powers were divided and gullible, why not offend them? In any event, it was surely far less dangerous for him to offend the West than to risk disassociating his name from the victorious Party at home.

Teasing

One explanation of Stalin's endorsement of the theory of imperialism in February 1946 is that it then seemed true. A second is that he felt obliged to insult the West in order to preserve his power at home. A third is that he was growing extraordinarily devious and insulted the West in order to trick the Party revivalists at home. We have observed some of the organizational changes which affected the Soviet leadership during the winter of 1945–1946 and have seen that outwardly their main direction was replacement of the wartime command structure with a revived Party. The Army, Beria, and Malenkov were all, as the Kremlinologists say, on the decline. The Party, on the other hand, seemed on the ascent. Closer study shows, however, that things were not so simple.

If the Party had truly been on the ascent, for example, one might anticipate that the leaders of the Party revival would acquire considerable new power. But this did not happen. On the contrary, the only decisive *eviction* of a top political leader from the seat of power in this entire shakeup of February and March 1946 was that of a Party revivalist, M. I. Kalinin, who was abruptly replaced as chairman of the Presidium of the Supreme Soviet by the colorless trade union executive N. Shvernik.[39] Since Kalinin died in May 1946, one may presume that age and incapacity precipitated his fall. But it is of interest that in 1944 and 1945 he had been by far the most outspoken of the leading Party revivalists. Of comparable interest was the composition of the new Politburo, as shown in the table which follows. As noted elsewhere, that institution had a clear revivalist majority in 1945. After the promotions of March 1946, that majority ceased to exist. Even more interesting is the failure of any new center of power to emerge from the ruins of the wartime empires which the Party was destroying. The first of the great wartime power nuclei to disintegrate was, of course, Shcherbakov's. It consisted of the Moscow Party organization, extensive propaganda power, and control of the Party organizations in the armed forces through the GPUKA. Remarkably enough, not one of Shcherbakov's offices fell to another top Soviet leader when he died in May 1945. The Sovinformburo, a wartime institution, was apparently abolished. The Moscow Party organization was given to a politically unknown functionary, G. M. Popov.[40] Although Popov became a member of the Party's influential Secretariat in March 1946 and fell from office with the Zhdanovites in 1949, there is little suggestion either in the press of the time or in the revelations of later years that he was a Party revivalist or, in fact, anything but a colorless bureaucrat. The GPUKA fell, as noted above, to General I. V. Shikin, who seems to have been closely associated with Zhdanov at one point and who spoke out publicly in the following years for the Party revival. Yet Shikin, like Popov, was essentially a little man; in the affairs of the army he was wholly outweighed by Bulganin. In general, one may say of his appointment that it kept both Bulganin and Zhdanov from replacing Shcherbakov. Zhdanov, in particular, received only one minor new office in 1945 and 1946.[41]

The Politburo

	1941–1945		1946	
	members	candidates	members	candidates
chairman	Stalin		Stalin	
"statists"	Andreev	Beria	Andreev	Shvernik
	Kaganovich	Malenkov	Beria	
	Voroshilov	Shcherbakov[1]	Kaganovich	
		Shvernik	Malenkov	
			Voroshilov	
"revivalists"	Kalinin	Voznesensky	Kalinin[2]	Bulganin
	Khrushchev		Khrushchev	Kosygin
	Mikoyan		Mikoyan	Voznesensky
	Molotov		Molotov	
	Zhdanov		Zhdanov	

[1]Died May 1945.
[2]Died May 1946.

The Orgburo, 1946

Secretariat Members	Office or Function	pre-1946 Office
Zhdanov	supervisor of Agit-Prop affairs and of Foreign Department in Central Committee	
A. A. Kuznetsov	Leningrad representative	first secretary, Leningrad Party Organization, 1945–1946
Popov	Moscow representative	first secretary, Moscow Party Organization, 1945–1949
Stalin	secretary general	
Malenkov	supervisor of economic and cadre affairs	

229

The Orgburo, 1946

Other Members	Office or Function	pre-1946 Office
Aleksandrov	chief, Central Committee Agit-Prop Administration	
Andrianov	chief, Central Committee Org-Instrukt. Department (in 1947, Administration for Checking Party Organs)	first secretary, Sverdlovsk Party Organization, until 1946
Bulganin	first deputy minister of Armed Forces	
V. V. Kuznetsov	secretary general, Trade Union Organization	
Mekhlis	minister of State Control	
Mikhailov	secretary general, Komsomol	
Patolichev	chief, Central Committee Economic Departments	first secretary, Chelyabinsk Party Organization, until 1946
Rodionov	RSFSR minister president, after June 1946	first secretary, Gorky Party Organization, 1943–1946
Shatalin	chief, Central Committee Cadres Administration	
Suslov	probable chief of "Special Department" in Central Committee (police)	first secretary, Stavropol *krai*, 1943–1945; chief, Lithuanian section of Central Committee, 1945–1946

Another interesting pattern appears in the list of personnel of the Orgburo elected in March 1946, as shown in the organizational table. The Politburo had just then redefined the Orgburo as the decisive administrative center of the Party.[42] Stalin, Malenkov, Zhdanov, Popov, and A. A. Kuznetsov, the five new Party secretaries, were now all made members of it. Included also (following the model of earlier Orgburos) were leading Party figures from the army, the Ministry of State Control, the Komsomol, the trade unions, and the Central Committee's Agit-Prop and Cadre administrations. The fascinating feature of this new Orgburo, however, was the presence in it of no less than six men who still were—or who until very recently had been—regional Party secretaries. This suggests that the various regions of the country were now to be given much more recognition than before. This suggestion is strengthened by the fact that two of the six former secretaries, Kuznetsov and Suslov, were from the liberated territories, and that two others, Patolichev and Andrianov, were from the Urals. The last two were Popov, from the Moscow center, and Rodionov, from Gorky, one of the vocal advocates of increased consumer goods production.

The new Orgburo, in a word, was, on the face of it, a remarkable indication that Stalin was instituting several attractive reforms which had been proposed within the Party over the past year: it was both more functional and more "regional" than its predecessor. But a closer look suggests that the reforms lacked substance. First and foremost, the new Orgburo contained fifteen people, each of whom had an important executive office to administer. It is simply not probable that such a cumbersome group would convene once a week or that, if it did, it could give anything resembling adequate attention to the many problems which faced the Party as a whole at such meetings. The probability that it operated efficiently seems even less when one considers that for the first three months of its existence some of its members were still posted as far away from Moscow as Leningrad and Chelyabinsk; that until the latter months of 1946 several of them were new to their very formidable jobs; and that during and after the autumn of 1946 some of them were purged. In sum, if the new Orgburo was not a trick on the Party, it was at least a deception.

There is one more, and perhaps the most important, organizational example of how Stalin tricked his Party in the reform era of 1945 and 1946. The personal rivalry between Zhdanov and Malenkov is said, in all Western histories of the period, to have dominated

231

Soviet politics after the war.[43] This rivalry followed a peculiar course. It seems to have begun in the events of 1940 and 1941, when, as Zhdanov's star went down, Malenkov became more and more clearly Stalin's number one home-front lieutenant. Until the end of the war, however, whatever was personal in the rivalry was obscured by the great institutional issues of the day. Even in Vladimir Rudolph's report of bureaucratic struggles in the Kremlin in 1945, Malenkov figured not as a personality but as the representative of the various home-front industrial elements which had been successful during the war, whereas Zhdanov was simply a representative of the Party. The little that we know from the public statements of various Soviet leaders prior to March 1946 indicates that Malenkov then, as the defender of certain well-entrenched interest groups, was pitted not against Zhdanov but against Molotov, the spokesman of other interest groups.

In the early months of 1946 a change occurred. In the speeches of the election campaign, each of the major leaders expressed different points of view within a common framework, as if they were speaking for themselves. On this occasion, for the first time in the postwar period, Malenkov and Zhdanov visibly assumed divergent positions. Coincidentally, new political arenas were set up in which they had opportunity for frequent face-to-face contact. The Politburo was restored to supremacy in the system, and after it had demolished Malenkov's wartime "empire," he was admitted to it as a full voting member. At the same time, Zhdanov's position in the Party Secretariat was reaffirmed, and his Leningrad aide, A. A. Kuznetzov, was installed in that body with him. Together they could challenge Malenkov's wartime hegemony. Under these circumstances, for whose emergence Stalin was patently responsible, Malenkov and Zhdanov could hardly help but clash, and, as we will see, they did.

These organizational changes in the Soviet leadership require attention because they reveal so clearly that Stalin was actively manipulating—and thus playing tricks on—his colleagues. Pretending to side with the Party against the army, Malenkov, and Beria, he was in reality doing what he could to make sure that the Party revivalists failed to get a solid power base. With this pattern of manipulations in mind, let us note some highly peculiar statements which Stalin made at this time. One of these was an introduction he wrote for the volume of his collected works in January 1946, a few weeks before his election speech.[44] In this document, he discussed a number of occasions before the Russian Revolution when Lenin said things which, in terms of latter-day Stalinist Marxism-Leninism, were not correct, and Stalin asked how one could account for this apparent fallibility of Lenin. At one point he simply proclaimed that Lenin had "not yet discovered" the laws of imperialism when he made his incorrect statements. His major explanation, however, was that "practical" Party workers in general had "inadequate theoretical training" to understand political situations, and had to be tricked by their leader. He demanded rhetorically: "Was it not because [Lenin] believed the question was not yet ripe, and because he did not expect the majority of the Bolshevik practical workers . . . to be sufficiently equipped to understand and accept the [correct] theory . . . that he refrained from advancing these arguments?"[45]

To enjoy the full flavor of this explanation, one must recall that publication of Stalin's *Collected Works* was commenced early in 1946 as one of the principal undertakings of the great educational campaign through which the Party revivalists hoped to restore order to the Soviet Union. Before the war, the ideological foundation of the Soviet regime had been a short collection of Stalin's speeches entitled *Problems of Leninism* and the famous *Short Course.*[46] Now the Party revivalists proposed to replace those books with millions of copies of *Collected Works,* a complete record of all that Stalin had said. His "introduction" was thus no insignificant document, and in it, Stalin said, on the eve of his election speech, that sometimes a Leninist leader might have to take the enormous risks of deceiving even Party insiders about his real ideological position.

Were this the only suggestion that Stalin was being deceitful when he endorsed the theory of imperialism in his election speech, historians might ignore it. But there is other evidence. A document published in February 1947, a year after the election speech, but dated 23 February 1946, two weeks after that speech,[47] took the form of a reply by Stalin to questions about whether or not one should still accept Lenin's dicta regarding the nineteenth-century German military reformer Clausewitz. The questioner, an army officer named Razin, felt as a Party member that he should respect Lenin's words, but at the same time he suspected that "German militarist doctrine" was false in all its parts, including the work of Clausewitz. How to get around this contradiction, Razin wanted to know. Stalin replied first by confirming a well-known premise: "Lenin admired Clausewitz because Clausewitz confirmed the thesis, correct from a Marxist point

233

of view, that retreat in unfavorable conditions is as valid a form of fighting as attack"[48] (was this what Stalin himself had done when he wrote the introduction to his *Collected Works*?). Stalin then went on to attack what he called "pedants":

> It follows that Lenin approached Clausewitz' works not as a soldier, but as a politician. . . . Thus in criticizing Clausewitz' military doctrines, we, the followers of Lenin, are not bound by any teaching of Lenin limiting our freedom of criticism. And from this it follows that your judgment that [an article condemning Clausewitz] is an "anti-Leninist onslaught" and a "revision" of Lenin's evaluation has no application. . . . Is it necessary to put an end to the [old] useless evaluation [of Clausewitz]? It is necessary! And . . . it is necessary particularly for us, who have defeated Germany, to criticize him. . . . It is impossible to move science forward without subjecting the outdated positions and sayings of well-known authors to critical analysis. This applies not only to military views but to the Marxist classics also. For example, Engels once said that among the Russian generals of 1812 only Barclay de Tolly was capable as an army leader. Obviously Engels erred because in reality Kutuzov was two heads above Barclay as an army leader. Yet one finds even today people who with foaming mouths defend Engels' incorrect stand.[49]

To understand the "Reply to Razin" one must recall the distinctive theoretical discussion which raged in the Soviet Party in 1945. In proportion to the exuberant growth of enthusiasm within the Party, certain prominent personalities in Stalin's entourage had started speaking out as if in opposition to *partiinost*. In particular, they attacked "people who have quotations ready for every occasion."[50] One of the more vigorous of these attacks went as follows:

> The founders of the scientific world outlook of the worker class, Marx and Engels, used to laugh at those bookworms who tried to view the revolutionary theory as a collection of dogmas. . . . Lenin was a real Marxist who understood in a constructive way the revolutionary essence of Marx's teaching. . . . Lenin developed the thought that Marxists must not view Marx's theory as something forever completed and inalterable. . . . The theory has to absorb historical experience and enrich itself . . . and thereby enrich society.[51]

These had not been unheard-of imprecations in the Soviet Union before the war: on the contrary, such repudiation of pedants had been a constant theme among Stalin's followers at least since the early 1930s. But, as recounted in an earlier chapter, the Party revivalists fought back against these slurs in 1945. In the election campaign of January and February 1946, virtually all the top Soviet leaders publicly took one side or the other in the debate over pedantry. Stalin's own election speech, coming at the climax of that debate, was in an obvious sense a decision in favor of the "bookworms," for he explicitly affirmed the continuing validity of a well-known Marxist-Leninist doctrine. But the "Reply to Razin," dated only two weeks after the election speech, was at least a reversal of Stalin's decision and perhaps was intended to suggest that he had never really made it. In this sense, it seems to confirm the hint in the introduction to the *Collected Works* that he was somehow, in February and March 1946, undermining the Party revival.

A New March Crisis

By the end of February 1946, two important changes had taken place in the international situation. First, in the wake of Stalin's election speech, the official Russophilia of the more important Western governments withered. The Americans in particular abandoned the optimism of 1945 and decided to join the British in firmly resisting Soviet encroachments in Iran. On 5 March Churchill fired the spirit of Western solidarity with his "iron curtain" oratory, and by mid-March, it was very difficult to believe that just a few months earlier the Western Powers had been quarreling with each other over their divergent colonial interests. Second, in Iran the political situation which had inspired Soviet moves changed. Until mid-February, the Iranian government had pursued a pro-Western course and resisted all Russian efforts to obtain a permanent political foothold within the country. But then the government fell, and the new premier accepted Communists into his cabinet and seemed tolerant of the Soviet-inspired separatist movement in Azerbaijan. He even went to Moscow to negotiate whatever Stalin wished to negotiate.[52]

In this situation, had Stalin been just a builder of empires for the sake of either national or revolutionary expansion, it seems almost certain that he would have reassessed his position and judged that for the time being the mood of the West was dangerous, and that with some prime objectives achieved in Iran it would be sensible to stand still, avoiding a crisis. Instead, he embarked on a two-pronged manipulation and stirred the murky waters even further.

At the Moscow Conference of December 1945, Stalin personally acquiesced to Western requests for a 15 March date for the evacuation of Soviet troops from Iran;[53] even Molotov held back, willing to accept the principle involved in setting such a date but reluctant to put the matter in writing. In effect, at Moscow Stalin and Molotov kept their hands free, probably in order to extract the sort of concessions which the Iranians made in March. Yet in March, with the game won, Stalin persisted in refusing to evacuate Iran, trying, it seems, for more and more concessions, risking the peace of the world for the sake of petty greed. On 13 March, while Western indignation was fast rising over this refusal, he published his reply to Churchill. In that statement he confirmed Churchill's worst fears regarding the rise of Communism in Europe and explicitly acknowledged for the first time in many years the "laws" which were dragging the world toward revolution. He also insulted Churchill personally, comparing him to Hitler, calling him a racist and a liar, and rubbing in the fact that the "little people" of England had rejected him at the polls in 1945. Since the start of the war, Stalin had become adept at making both insulting and flattering remarks to Westerners for political effect, and he must have been aware of the inflammatory response this would arouse in the capitalist world. Moreover, he knew that the Labor government in Britain thought well enough of Churchill to continue his foreign policies and that an attack on him would inevitably displease Truman, who was present during the "iron curtain" speech. One may judge, accordingly, that Stalin was deliberately stirring up a hornet's nest with his reply.[54]

Thereupon, on 23 March Stalin published a second press interview, responding this time to questions posed him by United Press correspondent Eddie Gilmore. Now, at the very peak of the Iranian diplomatic crisis which he had exacerbated, Stalin announced that there was no real danger of "new war": "Neither the nations nor their armies are aiming at new war. . . . The present fear of war is caused by the actions of certain political groups which are busy with propaganda. It is necessary for the public and the ruling circles of the states [of the world] to organize a broad counterpropaganda against the propagandists of a new war and for the safeguarding of the peace."[55]

This was no more nor less than the voluntarist theory with which Andrei Zhdanov in the following months justified the great public educational campaign which bears his name.[56] Consequently, though we do not know the details, circumstances make it seem that Stalin was opening the door to Zhdanov's educational campaign on condition that it be posed in terms of "the public and the ruling circles of the various states," launching a "counterpropaganda" which could make the "war-mongers" fall back in disarray. More simply put, it seems that Stalin was pushing Zhdanov into a commitment to the United Nations thesis of November 1944 as the quid pro quo for launching the educational campaign. Here he set a trap. His first public statement had caused an outbreak of criticism in the West. This second one suggested, with Leninist optimism, that the critics were "paper tigers"[57] who could not bite. Stalin left it to Zhdanov to defend that point.

Conclusion

Stalin, it follows, did not deliver his election speech in February 1946 just because he was for some reason confident enough in his arbitrary power to reveal the Leninist truth (as many Westerners decided). This was not evidence that he had been a statist for so many years only in order to deceive outsiders. His purpose in this speech was above all to escape the domestic political dilemma which plagued him all through 1945. On the one hand, he was embarked—justifiably, one may recall—on a massive campaign to shake up the home front. To complete it he required the services of the revived Party. On the other hand, the more he encouraged the Party, the more it escaped his control and threatened to restore the Bolshevism of the pre-purge years which he hated so much and found so restrictive to his freedom.

Through the speech Stalin allowed the Party revivalists an illusion of victory: he let them purge certain enemies and institute certain surface reforms. But he gave them nothing tangible, nothing lasting in return save the hatred of those they purged. Then on the foreign policy battlefield, where they had been so successful all through 1945, Stalin once again—as during the March crisis of 1945—provoked the West, now visibly at the end of its patience, and then once again, by relying on Zhdanov's foreign policy theses, induced the revivalists to accept responsibility. The retaliation, which was now virtually certain, would prove them wrong, and thus place them in his hands. Stalin's retreat from statism during 1945 was above all an exercise in control. If in the process he risked war abroad, one must suppose that his fear of war was less than his fear of losing control at home.

IV

The Fourth Battle:
The Insurrectionists Again

11

Did Stalin Want Peace?

A Debate

IN MARCH 1946, in his interview with Eddie Gilmore, Stalin publicly reiterated the United Nations foreign policy scheme, first described in November 1944, whereby despite the survival of imperialism, peace might be preserved under the blanket of a Grand Alliance-based United Nations Organization.[1] In September 1946, in an interview with Alexander Werth, he went on to assert that there was no real danger of new war because no one wanted it save a few "military political scouts and their civilian supporters" in certain countries abroad.[2] On 23 January 1947 he published an interview recently granted to Elliot Roosevelt, the son of the late president.[3] Roosevelt's first question was whether Stalin thought it possible for the United States and the Soviet Union to coexist without interfering with one another, despite their differing political systems. Stalin replied: "Yes, of course! It is not only possible. It is reasonable and entirely realizable!" Stalin went on not only to reiter-

241

ate his faith in the UNO but also to resurrect the project for an effective UNO international peace force. He said that the success of the UNO depended on harmony between the three great powers, emphatically denied that relations between the Russian and American peoples had deteriorated,[4] and declared that, despite Soviet unhappiness about the "failure" of denazification of the Western zones of Germany, there was no serious anxiety in Moscow.

Yet Westerners had to heed some circumstantial factors. In Manchuria in the spring of 1946 the Red Army abandoned quantities of Japanese weapons to the Chinese Communists, who then proceeded to engage in civil war with the Kuomintang on an ever-increasing scale. In the eastern Mediterranean during the summer, while the Soviet government stepped up diplomatic pressure on Turkey and Greece, Tito's forces in Yugoslavia attacked two American planes, grounding one and destroying the other, and in Greece the Communists turned toward armed resistance to their country's government. In Soviet-occupied Poland on 19 January 1947, just four days before the publication of the Stalin-Roosevelt interview, the Communists in effect "fixed" the election which Stalin had promised the Western Powers at Yalta would be "democratic." This disparity between what Stalin said and what his "followers" did persuaded more and more Westerners that Stalin was lying, concealing under a barrage of statist peace talk the reality of his Leninist drive. They began to compare him to Hitler, insisting that he must want war.[5]

In retrospect one may see flaws in the Western reconstruction of Soviet motives. The Chinese and Yugoslav Communists were not under Stalin's control and in 1946 acted against his advice. Even the Greek Communists disregarded his warnings against civil war and pursued an independent policy,[6] and in Poland the clear interests of the Soviet Union and the Communist Party made a free election impossible.[7] Historians now argue also (as I have in earlier chapters) that the Soviet state may be presumed peaceful at the end of the war because of its desperate economic condition. They point out that the whole terminology of the peace-or-war debate in 1946 and 1947 was borrowed from the discussion in the 1930s about Hitler, whereas after 1945 the Soviets acknowledged (as Hitler did not) the obsolescence of war and the advantages of peaceful imperialism. Finally, Stalin's statements should really be read for their instrumental meanings, rather than as truth or lies.

Nonetheless, the disparity between Stalin's word and Soviet

deed increased with time, becoming one of the most startling features of the early Cold War period. This was as true of his interview with Harold Stassen early in April 1947[8] as it was of his two public statements in 1948 insisting that cooperation would be possible if only the British and the Americans wanted it.[9] In his interview of 28 October 1948, during the Berlin blockade, he was still putting forth the notion that all might be well if only "rightist circles" in the West would drop their efforts to hide the possibilities of cooperation between systems: "More than anything, the incendiaries of war . . . dread [actual] agreements and cooperation with the Soviet Union." To Western observers at the time, these statements seemed no more than sand thrown in the eyes of the gullible and naive.[10] This chapter addresses the problem of Stalin's intentions by constructing a framework for assessing what he "wanted" in the areas of agriculture and culture, and then (by process of analogy) in international affairs.

Stalin's Agricultural Policies

The first year of the new Five Year Plan, 1946, was not a catastrophe for Soviet industry, despite the difficulties and delays inherent in any massive conversion of a vast industrial plant from war to peacetime purposes. By November the Soviet press was optimistically projecting early fulfillment of the plan; by 1948 many Soviet industrial sectors were allegedly attaining or surpassing prewar levels of production.[11] In agriculture, however, a disaster did occur.

The difficulties of Soviet agriculture were in part, as Khrushchev has told us, the result of the war.[12] The agricultural labor force had been drastically diminished by the mobilization in 1941, and since then the government had paid for the war by cutting off agricultural investment. For years the fields, even in the rear areas, had not been adequately worked or enriched. Equipment had deteriorated, livestock had been slaughtered and farm organizations had disappeared. In the territories occupied by the Germans both armies had wrecked the land, much of which was the most fertile in the country, and ravished the villages. The damage was not easily or quickly repaired, despite some postwar government encouragement, for there was virtually no new equipment, seed, or fertilizer available, and many returning soldiers were reluctant to go back to the collectivized fields.[13] In 1945, 75 percent of the land cultivated in 1940 was sown, but in 1946 only 76 percent was sown.[14] Conditions

243

were so bad that, even at the start of 1946, there was a threat of starvation in some villages.

But true disaster was brought on by the worst drought in living memory in the Ukraine and southwestern Russia, the most ravaged territories. By midsummer, the lack of enthusiastic reports on the harvest was a clear indication that the government knew a catastrophe was in the offing. By autumn it was evident that a famine might occur. The grain harvest of 1946 was eight million tons (one-sixth) lower than that of the previous year.[15] This meant misery, not only in the villages but also in the recovering cities. And it meant budgetary disaster: there could be no exports of grain, and imports might be needed.

In this situation, the government took steps, many of which were clearly only temporary and remedial. The rationing system was continued; prices were raised in order to restrict purchases; a certain quantity of UNRRA grain was accepted from abroad;[16] Professor Varga, the economist, was allowed to suggest publicly that the United States and Canada were artificially withholding grain from the starving world markets in order to keep prices high.[17] But the government evidently did not allow the harvest catastrophe to interfere with its own desire to make political capital by exporting grain,[18] and its main emergency measure was a decree enforcing the Statute of the Collective Farm.

On 19 September 1946 Stalin, for the government, and Zhdanov, for the Party, signed a decree entitled "On Measures for the Liquidation of Abuses of the Statute of the Agricultural Artel and Collective Farm."[19] It was published on 20 September, together with a decree of 1939 defining the defense of *kolkhoz* property. It outlined two general sorts of reform. On the one hand, it ordered the elimination of "incorrect" calculations of the work day—in other words, "excessive" payments to the peasantry—and the recovery of alienated *kolkhoz* lands and property. On the other hand, it ordered a restoration of *kolkhoz* democracy, which meant a general shakeup of the leadership structure of all the collectives. The decree was described as a "return to Leninism" and was to be carried out within two months, along with a check to establish that grain deliveries to the state were being made in full.

On 8 October the government set up a Council for *Kolkhoz* Affairs to enforce the decree. The charter of this new organization was not unrealistic.[20] It allowed for consultation with agricultural experts and even with representatives of the collective farms themselves regarding the desirability of modifying the statute, particularly in the matter of introducing labor incentives. But this council threatened to add chaos to disorder because it became the fourth overlapping central administrative organization created within a year to handle farm problems,[21] and in composition it was not overly suggestive of sympathy for the peasantry. It was headed by A. A. Andreev, the Politburo industrial troubleshooter of 1941, who was commissar for agriculture from 1943 until December 1945. On its presidium were four Party secretaries from agricultural areas (including Khrushchev, from the Ukraine) and Andreev's successor as minister.[22] But the two deputy chairmen, the men who apparently characterized the council, were N. S. Patolichev and V. M. Andrianov, the new members of the Party Orgburo who made their reputations as *oblast* Party secretaries in the industrial Urals during the war.[23]

In Western literature on the subject, these agricultural measures of September 1946 are almost invariably depicted as resulting from Stalin's decision to reimpose control on the Soviet village. To a large extent they certainly were,[24] but they had another equally notable aspect which was probably more striking to Soviet observers of the day: they reflected a conviction that the most efficient way to handle the practical crisis in Soviet agriculture was to restore Leninist norms—a conviction which rested on Voznesensky's analysis of history. As a leading reformist historian of the Soviet peasantry put it:

> A series of works [on agriculture were] published immediately after the war. [Under the influence of N. A. Voznesensky, the authors] adhered, whether they wished to or not, to the notion that during the war, despite the sharp cutbacks in material and labor resources, Soviet agriculture developed successfully. It followed from this view that all the problems with which the Party is still today [1963] struggling were resolved during the war exclusively through an intensification of effort and the general outburst of patriotic enthusiasm. It is completely obvious that, whether or not there was great patriotic enthusiasm, . . . modern agriculture could not possibly . . . have *not* been damaged during the war years. To overlook such obvious facts is characteristic, so to speak, of the ideology of the Chinese pseudo-Marxists with their speculations about revolutionary spirit and their contemptuous aristocratic disregard of the significance of real conditions, material factors, and professional and technical knowledge. This typically idealistic interpretation of history . . . was based on inadequate statistical calculation. [Nevertheless, it served] to substantiate voluntarist administrative methods of doing things.[25]

In effect, the new decrees on agriculture sought to resolve the crisis of the harvest by stirring revolutionary enthusiasm within the peasantry comparable to the allegedly successful patriotic enthusiasm of the war era.[26] These were doctrinaire decrees filled with the voluntarism of Zhdanov, who signed them, and of Voznesensky, who provided the statistical data.[27]

The results were in some respects impressive. Within five months, 14 million hectares of land were recovered from peasants who, through one subterfuge or another, had taken them over during the war;[28] 456,000 *kolkhoz* members were shifted from administrative to productive work, and another 182,000 were removed from *kolkhoz* payrolls; 140,000 head of cattle and 15 million rubles were recovered. In general, however, as one may imagine, the result of the effort was disorder. One agrarian specialist reported later that in the late 1950s many of the lands recovered from private use in 1946–1947 were still lying fallow because the collective farms had no men or machines to till them.[29]

Within a few months of these voluntarist decrees of September and October 1946, the regime returned to the problems of agriculture and instituted reforms of a different tenor. It recentralized the Ministry of Agriculture so as to eliminate bureaucratic overlap.[30] From 21 to 26 February 1947, the Party Central Committee discussed a speech on agriculture by Andreev[31] and retreated from the unadulterated Party voluntarism of September 1946. Andreev called for pay benefits within the collective farms proportionate to work done; for establishment of the so-called "link" system of labor organization; for varying agronomic techniques according to soils and climate; for relaxation of current marketing regulations; and, above all, for consultation with technical experts on all levels of agricultural administration.[32] The Central Committee endorsed much of what he said. The reader should bear in mind that many of his projects were never effected under Stalin,[33] but this failure should not obscure the fact that the reforms of the February plenum were substantially different in spirit from the decrees of September 1946.

This was also the lesson of other developments at the February plenum. Apparently at this point the pseudo-scientific theories of T. D. Lysenko and V. R. Vil'yams came under serious consideration.[34] To Westerners, advocacy of the universal introduction of winter planting for spring wheat and of grasslands crop rotation, and so on, seem as Marxist as Voznesensky's calls for subjecting everything to the correct Party forms. However, as David Joravsky has pointed out, Lysenko was not a Party member and his theories were justified in terms of technology, not of scientific Marxism, although they made the same voluntarist promise. Further, in 1947 Lysenkoism was backed by political elements within the Soviet regime which opposed Zhdanov. It became the basis for official agricultural policy in August 1948, quite literally over Zhdanov's dead body.[35]

The third major development at the February meeting also suggested change. The committee pilloried Khrushchev for the agricultural difficulties in the Ukraine and seemingly gave Malenkov responsibility for the management of Soviet agriculture.[36] Khrushchev's fall opened a new chapter of the great late Stalinist purge: after an attack on the wartime statist "right," there was an attack on the Party revivalist "left." Stalin punctuated the turn on 23 February by publishing his letter to Razin attacking "pedants" and "bookworms" who "have a quotation from Marx for every occasion."[37] This letter effectively reversed his February 1946 endorsement of the Party revival.

Did Stalin want Soviet agriculture to be productive after the war? One approach to an answer stresses the disastrous results of his policies. In 1946 in the Soviet Union, there seem to have been about 66 million peasants living in the most wretched conditions.[38] Even before the war there was little food and few consumer goods available in the villages. During the war, according to a recent study, matters became far worse. The peasantry during the war ate only two-fifths as much bread and eggs per person and only half as much meat as in 1940. Manufactured goods, sugar, and medicines virtually disappeared from the market, as did cloth and every variety of factory goods. Only potatoes and, to some extent, milk were available in any quantity to stave off starvation.[39] Given this situation, one might well judge that the first step in any effort to improve productivity of agriculture should have been attention to incentives. Grain will not grow, one may moralize, unless there are people willing to grow it.

The Zhdanovite "Liquidation of Abuses" decree, Lysenkoism, and increased taxes[40] were the most far-ranging measures through which the Soviet regime undertook to raise agricultural productivity after the war. These measures did not improve the material lot of the peasants or cause a dramatic rise in productivity, even though shortly before Stalin's death, at the 19th Congress of the CPSU, Malenkov boasted that the Soviet grain problem was solved for all time.[41] We know now that Malenkov was deceived. The peasants had balked under Stalin. Soviet grain production in 1952 was barely a quarter of what Malenkov claimed and did not even suffice to meet the needs of

247

the state. If one assumes that Stalin knew that the road to agricultural productivity entailed pleasing the peasant, one must recognize that he completely failed, and doubt whether he *wanted* to improve agricultural productivity after the war.

There is another approach to an evaluation of Stalin's agricultural policies, however, equally strong in logic, which leads to quite different conclusions. This approach begins with a recognition that the problems Stalin faced in agriculture at the end of the war were insuperable. The regime he headed came into existence in large part through a war against the peasantry. From the start, it was Marxist—in other words, urbanist and anti-peasant.[42] Before the revolution of 1917, Lenin opened the door to an alliance with the peasantry, and during the New Economic Policy period in the 1920s the Leninists compromised with the peasants. But in order to preserve its existence during the Civil War of 1918–1920, the Bolshevik regime systematically looted the villages, and the Stalinist revolution of the 1930s began with the great collectivization campaign during which the peasantry was starved into submission to the cities. Despite the detente during World War II, the attitudes of both bureaucrats and peasants—of slavedrivers and slaves—were irreconcilable; there was no practical possibility of making the peasantry happy through use of the particular instruments of state—the bureaucrats and their policies—which Stalin possessed in 1945. Further, even if this had been feasible in terms of available human material and ideas, it was not in terms of physical resources. In the wake of the war, with the cities ruined and the countryside consumed by drought, Stalin and his regime, even with the best will in the world, could not have improved the material lot of the 66 million illiterate, antagonistic people in the countryside.

In the light of this set of arguments, it seems clear that the key question facing agricultural policymakers in 1946 was not how to make the peasants happy but how to build a bridge over these chasms. To this question the voluntarist policies of 1946 and 1948 provided answers. They institutionalized relationships between bureaucrat and peasant. They let the regime carry out its central function of feeding the urban population and proceed without hindrance on its chosen path of industrialization. These policies were, of course, very one-sided: Stalin came down entirely on the side of the bureaucrats and not at all on the side of the peasants. One may also recognize that these policies were crude and that they failed. An improvement in agriculture did not result during Stalin's lifetime. But granted the insuperability of the problems faced, its one-sidedness, crudity, and eventual failure does not mean that the policy was irrational or that it failed just because of its crudeness. From a certain perspective, it might even be deemed a necessity.[43]

Stalin's Cultural Policies

A second area of domestic policy loomed large in the Soviet Union during 1946 and 1947: cultural policy. Discussion of it will be useful here to underline the lesson just learned: an evaluation made from the point of view of the Soviet regime may differ fundamentally from one made by outsiders in the West. From a Western point of view, the Soviet cultural outlook was relatively bright at the end of the war because there was hope and freedom. Ehrenburg writes: "Yes, I must admit that I believed in the wonderful future. Otherwise it would have been difficult to carry on."[44] He then quotes from editorials he wrote as early as 1942 in which he rejected "the narrow-mindedness, the indifference, the shirking of responsibility," and, of course, the fear prevalent in the Soviet Union before the war and in which he told of the men at the front, who "are thinking why yesterday's operation was unsuccessful and why there are so many things they had not been taught at the ten-year school. They think about the future and the wonderful life the victors will build . . . [when] people will live differently and work differently. The war has given us initiative, discipline, and an inner freedom."[45]

In this atmosphere of relaxation, Russian culture to some extent recovered from the blight of the thirties.[46] In music and film, works of lasting creative value appeared, such as Shostakovich's Eighth Symphony and Eisenstein's *Ivan the Terrible*. The poets began to speak bravely again. More important, they could publish. In May 1944 there was a poetry reading in Moscow during which the audience ignored the official poets of the Party but wildly applauded Pasternak and Akhmatova.[47] Official novelists conscientiously sought spontaneous popularity with tales of "true love" in natural settings with nationalistic themes—for example, Konstantin Simonov's *Days and Nights*. Even in Aleksandr Fadeev's *Young Guard* of 1946—the typical epic novel of the early Party revival—spontaneity and melodramatic excitement were at a premium.[48] Meanwhile, the cultural interests of the Soviet nationalities were still receiving attention, and cultural intercourse with the outside world was allowed, in the form of American films and literary and scientific contacts with the West, and even some trips abroad. The pall of socialist realism was by no means gone from Soviet culture. The intelligentsia shared the depressed standard of living of everyone else, and many still suffered directly from restrictions imposed during the purge era—witness the case of Nadezhda Mandelstamm. By Western standards, however, Soviet culture seemed very much alive.

In this setting, the Soviet regime launched the *Zhdanovshchina*. All through 1945 there had been talk in Soviet Party journals of the need for reconsolidation within the Party and for increased *partiinost*. The result was a series of practical reforms prepared with obvious care. In the spring of 1946, for example, republication of Lenin's *Collected Works* and of Stalin's *Short Course* began, as did the publication of Stalin's own collected works. Late in June a new Party journal, *Kultura i Zhizn'* ("Culture and Life"), designed to glorify the Party's ideological supervision of Soviet civilian life, appeared.[49] At the same time the Party initiated a major organizational challenge to the command system on all levels of the armed forces.[50] On 26 July 1946, the CPSU(b) Central Committee issued an epochal decision tightening admissions to the Party and increasing scrutiny of the membership,[51] and on 2 August it issued a major decision regarding the reform of the Party educational system.[52]

However, the *Zhdanovshchina* involved more than this sort of carefully prepared administrative reform. Judging from the discussions of 1945, the main feature of the great education campaign was to be a deliberate effort to raise Soviet morale by an act of will. Zhdanov explained this in two speeches on literature in mid-1946:

> It is not for us to bow low to everything foreign or to take up a passive and defensive position. If the feudal system and the bourgeoisie in their periods of greatest progress were able to create a literature and art which asserted the establishment of a new regime and its prosperity, we, who are building a socialist order which represents everything that is best in the history of human civilization and culture, have an even better opportunity to create a new, progressive world literature. It will leave far astern the best work of the past ages.[53]

With this basic hypothesis in mind, he sketched the tasks ahead:

> Our literature, which reflects a state order of much higher standards than that of any bourgeois country and a culture which is much greater than that of bourgeois countries, has the right to instruct others in a

new public morality. Where can you find such a nation and such a country as we have? Where can you find such splendid human qualities as were shown by our Soviet people in the Fatherland war? . . . Every day our people are going higher and higher. . . . The task of every conscientious Soviet writer is *to show the new high qualities of the Soviet people,* to show the life of our people today, and to throw light on the road to the future. The writer cannot follow events. He must be the first in the ranks of the people; he must show them the way of progress but be guided by the methods of Socialist Realism, study our reality conscientiously, and try to understand the basis of our growth and development.[54]

In the pursuit of this lofty objective, Zhdanov and his followers precipitated a deluge in the Soviet cultural world. Early in August, at a Leningrad Party activists meeting, Zhdanov launched a bitter and violent attack on two local literary journals, *Zvezda* and *Leningrad,* for their tolerance of non-*partiinyi* themes, and on the satirist Mikhail Zoshchenko and the aging "acmeist" poetess Anna Akhmatova for their individualism and allegedly admiring attitude toward the bourgeois culture of the West. On the basis of this speech, on 14 August 1946 the Central Committee issued a decree demanding Party-imposed discipline in all literary matters.[55] At Zhdanov's bidding, the Leningrad Party organization precipitated a witch hunt among the intellectuals of the city, even depriving Zoshchenko of his ration card—in those days almost a sentence of death—for a short time.[56] On 26 August a decree appeared demanding an end to laxity in the theater and, in particular, an end to the presentation of Western plays in the Moscow repertory houses. On 4 September another decree condemned the excess of "vulgarity" and *tsiganshchina*—"gypsy stuff"—in recent Soviet films and demanded more *partiinyi* plots.[57] All through the autumn, *Kul'tura i Zhizn'* lambasted the leading figures of the Soviet intelligentsia, thus bringing to an end the relatively spontaneous creativity of the war era.

The arbitrary and—in Western terms—irresponsible character of this onslaught was probably greater than Zhdanov planned, for there are signs that the entire campaign was subject to Kremlin politics. In February and March 1946, it may be recalled, Stalin allowed the Party revivalists to appear successful but did not give them the great wartime bureaucratic power bases from which he was removing the Malenkovs and Berias. Instead, he broke up those bases and in addition established on the Politburo level a balance of forces less favorable to the revivalists than before. Since March, while the cultural *Zhda-*

251

novshchina brewed, reports spread that within this new organizational framework Zhdanov was struggling with Malenkov in particular. Thereupon, at the start of Zhdanov's cultural campaign, hints
were dropped that both men had suffered setbacks. In July, for example, the Politburo defined and limited the powers of the Party
secretariat, long a Malenkov stronghold. At about the same time Malenkov began to lose his place in the listings of the top Soviet leaders.
By autumn he seems to have dropped out of the secretariat altogether.[58] Meanwhile, early in August, just as the cultural campaign
erupted, Zhdanov lost the inner Party journals on which he had based
his comeback in 1945: all were engulfed in a general reform and
ceased publication.[59] Moreover, Zhdanov obviously had to pay a
price for the opportunity to preach that Soviet intellectuals, by an act
of will, could go higher and higher simply because they were socialist:
Zhdanov had to launch a Central Committee attack on his own bailiwick, Leningrad,[60] and coincidentally had to precipitate an organizational shakeup in the Leningrad Party.[61] In September, just before
Pravda finally published his speeches on literature, Zhdanov embarked upon an adventure so dangerous that it suggests he acted
under pressure. On 19 September he attached his signature to the
"Liquidation of Abuses" decree: he hitched his political wagon to the
notoriously unreliable star of Soviet agriculture—and this at the start
of a famine.

On 3 October 1946, Stalin issued the following order, which
Khrushchev published in 1956 as an example of a major violation of
Central Committee legality:

> 1. The Political Bureau Commission for Foreign Affairs ["sextet"]
> is to concern itself in the future, in addition to foreign affairs, also with
> matters of internal construction and domestic policy.

> 2. The sextet is to add to its roster the chairman of the State
> Commission on Economic Planning of the USSR, Comrade Voznesen-
> sky, and is to be known as the "septet."[62]

This order usurped, for a small group within the Politburo and for
Voznesensky, who was still only a candidate member of the Politburo, virtually the entire range of Politburo affairs. One may deduce
the reason. Three members of the original foreign affairs sextet were
presumably Molotov, the foreign minister; Zhdanov, the Central
Committee secretary responsible for foreign Communist affairs; and

Mikoyan, the minister of foreign trade. Judging from their speeches during the 1946 election campaign, these three were all backers of the Party revival, and so of course was Voznesensky, who now joined them in the septet. In the full Politburo of nine members and four candidates, these four did not have a majority. Indeed, Voznesensky was not even a full member of the Politburo. But in the septet they had four votes out of seven.

The effects of the creation of the septet were immediately visible. On 15 October a postponed session of the Supreme Soviet convened.[63] Its main business was approval of the "Liquidation of Abuses" decree regarding the collective farms and the institution of the *kolkhoz* council, mentioned earlier. But it also approved the only published indication that Malenkov's job was changing,[64] and just two weeks later, on 2 November, *Pravda* reported for the first time that there was a new man in the Party secretariat.[65] Coincidentally, on 18 October a change in the national police command limited the powers of Malenkov's peer on the wartime home front, L. P. Beria.[66] It can be judged from this that the first undertaking of the illegal septet was a purge of the main obstacles to the Party's progress on the domestic scene, Malenkov and Beria.

In 1945 the Soviet Party revivalists stood for reform, for an escape from the Stalinism of the 1930s and a return to the pure system of Lenin and his revolution. Now, evidently in order to realize their great voluntarist cultural revolution, they accepted the revival of the most impure aspect of Stalinism, the purge. Only Stalin stood to benefit from this corruption of the Party revivalists. Accordingly, one may regard the eruption of the *Zhdanovshchina*—their apparent victory—as an outward sign of Stalin's victory over them. This supposition seems confirmed by the fact that after the broadside against Leningrad the next step in Zhdanov's cultural onslaught was the suppression of Party revivalist nationalism in Khrushchev's Ukraine. Early in November 1946 Party officials reorganized the press in the Ukraine along centralist lines, subordinating it to Moscow much more than before.[67] On 15 November Maksim Rylskii, the patriotic Ukrainian Party poet, was ousted from the chairmanship of the Ukrainian Writers' Union. By the end of that month, a vicious campaign for eradication of alleged nationalistic deviationism in Khrushchev's Ukrainian Party and in the cultural institutions under its care was in full swing.[68] By February 1947, as we have seen, this campaign had spread to agriculture. The united revivalist front of 1944–1945 thus split in the autumn of 1946 at the very moment of Zhdanov's apparent success. Once again, only Stalin stood to gain.[69]

The record of Soviet cultural policy in 1946, like that of agricultural policy, reveals, first of all, a huge gulf between Stalinist and Western values. It is as clear that Stalin wanted peace with the Soviet intelligentsia as it is that he wanted productivity in agriculture. But equally, he had no interest in the spirit of artistic exploration, spontaneous and individualistic creativity, and the freedom which emerged in the war era. All these qualities seem valuable to Western observers of Soviet culture, but to Stalin and his colleagues in 1946 they were deplorable, disorderly, if not disreputable, and unproductive.

Was the policy course which Stalin followed in cultural affairs in 1946 effective from his own point of view? Before the war Soviet intellectuals, even when living in an atmosphere of terror, continued to produce paintings, novels, poems, operas, symphonies, and epic films—all to the specifications of the Party. In 1946, from the regime's point of view, it was necessary to re-establish order and control so that the intellectuals would again further the national production effort. Since Stalin's policy did this, it was by his own standards sensible. Despite its politicization, moreover, it was most effective. As proof, one has only to read Ehrenburg on the period after 1946:

> What sustained me at the time? I wrote about this later: . . . "How could [outsiders] possibly guess, even briefly, even for a minute, even in their sleep, by accident, what it means to think about the spring, what it means during the chill of March, when despair grips one, to wait and wait for the heavy ice clumsily to start to move. But we knew such winters; we became inured to such chill so that there was not even sorrow, only pride and trouble. And in the hard icy pain, blinded by the dry snow-storm, we saw, without seeing, the green eyes of the spring."[70]

There can be no better testimony that the Westernized, creative Soviet intelligentsia between 1946 and 1953 had nothing to hang onto except hope. This, we may judge, was just as Stalin wanted it to be.

Did Stalin Want Peace?

In the spring of 1946, as noted earlier, relations between the Soviet Union and the Western Powers went from bad to worse. In March, the Americans joined the British in a successful diplomatic effort to compel Soviet troops to evacuate northern Iran. The resultant crisis left indelible scars on the East-West alliance. It was followed by further trouble. In May the Americans cut off reparations to the Soviet Union from the Western zones of Germany. They had never effectively replied to the Soviet inquiries of 1945 about extensive postwar economic credits, and now they decided they had no intention of sharing their atomic secrets except under conditions which, from the Soviet point of view, were unacceptable. Next, clear signs of Western blocism appeared. At the foreign ministers' conferences which met in May and June to prepare peace treaties for the former German satellites in Europe, the Americans and British acted together. At the peace conference, which met from 26 July until 15 October, and at the UNO meeting, which lasted from 26 October until 15 December in New York (coincident with another meeting of the Council of Foreign Ministers), the Americans and the British mobilized massive majorities of small countries against the Soviet point of view. Meanwhile in China General Marshall's mediatory mission to cement a coalition between the Nationalists and the Communists failed; in Yugoslavia, as noted earlier, the Communist-run regime caused a crisis by shooting down American planes.

In this increasingly tense atmosphere Soviet diplomacy faltered. For example, by June America had become the principal Western target of Soviet propaganda. During 1945 the decaying imperialism of Great Britain had been the main target, and the change suggested a reconsideration of the world situation.[71] Late in June, when stubbornness on both sides in the Council of Foreign Ministers jeopardized the calling of a broader peace conference on the satellite treaties, Molotov abruptly made a series of concessions on points he had previously treated as essential and thus eased the log jam.[72] In August, with the opening of the peace conference, the Russians once again, as in 1945, launched a diplomatic offensive. Moscow sent a strong threatening note to Turkey demanding concessions on the Black Sea straits.[73] It was accompanied by intensive propaganda and loud protests against the British decision to tolerate a Greek referendum on 2 September on the question of restoring the monarchy.[74] This Soviet offensive miscarried. The Western Powers encouraged both the Greeks and the Turks by sending warships into the Aegean. On 31 August Molotov returned to Moscow from Paris to consultations, and after a few days his government not only announced the postponement of a scheduled meeting of the Supreme Soviet until mid-October but also asked that the coming session of the UNO be postponed for a month.[75] All this suggested considerable hesitation and uncertainty in Moscow.[76]

At this point the unexpected happened. On 7 September the American secretary of state, James Byrnes, made a policy speech at Stuttgart declaring the intention of the two major Western Powers to merge their zones in Germany and generally to encourage the economic and social recovery of the former enemy, with or without Soviet cooperation. The speech precipitated a crisis in the United States government. On 12 September Henry Wallace, the last remaining Roosevelt cabinet appointee, publicly called Byrnes anti-Soviet and demanded a return to the Grand Alliance policies of the war era. On 20 September, after much procrastination, President Truman requested Wallace's resignation.[77] These events are worth mentioning here because on 18 September *Pravda,* which had been violently criticizing Byrnes, broke silence about the Wallace affair and announced with thunderous enthusiasm that at last the "peoples" were moving within the United States against the "warmongers" who had been conspiring to block Soviet plans for world peace.[78] On 23 September Stalin issued the remarkable interview with Alexander Werth described earlier, in which he stated that there was no real danger of new war, doubted that the United States and Great Britain either wanted to or could encircle the Soviet Union, and implied that Wallace's analysis of Soviet intentions was correct and that the atom bomb was a paper tiger.[79]

It has been pointed out that Stalin's interview served the purpose of calming world public opinion during a war scare. President Truman also made a calming statement at this time.[80] Nonetheless, as we have seen elsewhere, the views Stalin reconfirmed were those same anti-blocist views which had been behind the testing of the Grand Alliance in 1945. They had seemed highly credible in February 1946, but now, after a summer of East-West strife and Wallace's resignation, they were dubious. Could one still seriously argue, even in Moscow, that the Soviet state should rely on "popular forces" within the United States to beat back and isolate the "imperialist elements" there, as the anti-blocists hoped? That Stalin chose now to reiterate those views suggests politics, and so do other actions—the publication on 20 September of the "Liquidation of Abuses" decree, signed by Zhdanov, and on 22 September of Zhdanov's speeches on literature, the core of the cultural *Zhdanovshchina.* Further, while the Soviet press predicted that, despite the fall of Wallace, the American people would show their agreement with him—would move—in the forthcoming congressional elections, on 30 September (just before Molotov paid a second quick

256

visit home from Paris) Stalin created the foreign policy "septet." The immediate result, as we have seen, was the purge of Malenkov. This extensive pattern of coincidences suggests that Stalin issued his Werth interview in connection with the provocation against the Party revivalists which he was just then staging.

On 6 November, speaking about the anniversary of the revolution, Zhdanov restated the anti-blocist foreign policy position with great vigor.[81] It sounded more unrealistic than ever, for just two days earlier the Republican Party had won a smashing victory at the polls in the United States, and immediately thereafter the Zhdanovite attack on nationalism in the Ukraine suggested the debacle of the Party revival. Three weeks after 6 November anti-blocism finally became absolutely untenable, for Washington threatened to let the whole machinery of peacemaking collapse unless Moscow came around to the American point of view. Accordingly, on 29 November, Molotov dropped the obstructionism which, since the London Conference in the autumn of 1945, had been the outward manifestation of his adherence to anti-blocism. He made concessions. The peace treaties with Hitler's former satellites were rapidly completed and signed, and an East-West "thaw" of sorts set in. Stalin preached to Elliot Roosevelt about the triviality of the East-West misunderstandings. On 19 December *Pravda* criticized a Soviet naval journal for its unfair depiction of the British effort to help Russia during the war. There was apparently a reduction of Soviet occupation forces in Eastern Europe, and several diplomatic gentilities took place.

These circumstances suggest that Stalin was playing domestic politics with his foreign policy in the middle of 1946, as earlier. Apparently, he let the Party revivalists assume power at home on condition that they commit themselves to a participationist foreign policy thesis. As this became more and more clearly wrong, he apparently used it as a tool to get them to purge Malenkov, and then to cause a split between Zhdanov and Khrushchev, before finally calling them to heel.

As noted at the start of this chapter, Western observers did not take Stalin's peace talk of late 1946 very seriously. By their standards, the Soviet Union was in general not respecting the independence of her borderlands, was not abstaining from the propagation of Communism abroad, and was not living up to the democratic promises that Stalin had made in public and private during the war. Early in February 1947 an American official for the first time publicly labeled the Soviet Union as aggressive;[82] in tangible ways, one must admit, the "thaw" did not consist of much—by the end of January 1947 it was already over.

This contemporary Western assessment presumed, however, that a peace, in the Western sense of the term, was attainable after the war. But what if the problems Stalin faced abroad at the end of the war were as insuperable as those he faced in agriculture, and a peace such as the Americans wanted could not be obtained under any circumstances? This is not an improbable assessment. There was a vast reservoir of political hostility among the members of the wartime anti-Fascist alliance: indeed, the wartime friendship was a radical departure from the norm, and a relapse into traditional antagonisms was entirely natural. Further, it is more than arguable that a peace such as the Americans wanted was absolutely unacceptable to the Soviet regime—and it was with that regime, after all, that whatever peace came about had to be made. The Western Powers could afford a laissez-faire peace. They were economically the strongest and richest countries in the world. They had populations long accustomed to modern urban life, democratic procedures, and rule by law. They did not have border problems. They were not dictatorships. They could leave their economies in private hands and their frontiers open because they knew that their populations would not rise up against them. The regime in Moscow could not afford such luxuries. The Soviet industrial economy was developing but not mature. In comparison with the colonial lands of Asia, Africa, and Latin America, it was advanced, but it was hardly competitive in a world of free markets. Further, it did have border problems and neighbors who by tradition were unfriendly, and the regime did not have the domestic security to brave a world of open frontiers and free elections. There were too many blatant lies, too many injustices, and too much poverty and social hatred to allow the Soviet government to attempt a peace in the American style.

It follows that when Stalin spoke of peace after the war, he meant not the open door for world-wide social and economic integration to which the Americans aspired but, at most, a continued effort at building limited bridges across the profound natural cleavages in a divided world—institutionalization of conflicts, one might call it.[83] Stalin's own definition was not inept: he labeled his objective "peaceful cooperation," which is something more than just coexistence but decidedly less than laissez faire. In such terms the state of international affairs at the end of 1946 was not disastrous. The ideals of the war era had been shattered, that was certain. Yet, as we know, from Stalin's point of view this may not have been a bad thing, and though in Europe, especially in Germany, the Western Powers were acting unitedly against Soviet desires in worrisome fashion, it is entirely possible that Stalin saw this—as he told Roosevelt—as a matter of "misunderstandings" between governments which could easily be ironed out.

One may argue, indeed, that from Stalin's point of view his politicization of Soviet foreign policy during 1945 and 1946 had brought him much closer to realizing East-West cooperation than he had been, in the sense that he had regained the initiative at home. Perhaps he ceased to be a "prisoner of the Politburo"—certainly he became less one than at the time of the wartime victories in 1945. His manipulations were confusing to outsiders. One may label them extremely clumsy methods if one choses to measure them by comparison with the polished methods of European diplomacy. But their real measure is in terms of his task, which was to attain a balance between all the competing Zhdanovs and Molotovs, Malenkovs and Berias, in his regime and among the "rapists" in the Red Army, the bureaucratic looters, and the unruly variety of foreign Communists through whom he had to work.

In such perspectives the "thaw" of late 1946 was a step in the right direction, a sign that there was a new opportunity for building bridges between East and West. The best evidence that it was serious—that this was indeed how Stalin viewed it—lies in the continuity of his line. After his showdown with the anti-blocists, Stalin did not break with the policy of participationism.[84] He stressed regularly in his public statements over the next year that "peace" was what he wanted with the West, and that in his belief cooperation between differing governmental systems was entirely possible, if the desire was there.

The American Challenge

Late in January 1947 rigged elections took place in Poland. On 21 February the British informed Washington that within six weeks it would have to stop its financial and military aid to the Greek government, which was menaced by Communist rebellion. On 26 February Soviet troops in Hungary arrested Béla Kovács, a leading non-Communist politician. But it was not just because of these external stimuli that on 12 March President Truman, in a speech messianic in its broad and all-encompassing ideological anti-Communism, requested congressional approval for a program of aid to Greece and Turkey. A profound internal transformation had overtaken the United States. The introspection of the past was resurgent, but no longer did it move the country to isolation from the political currents of the outer world. Americans were aware that isolation in the old sense was no longer possible because of advancing technology. They were proud—perhaps too proud—of their unique power and wealth. They were insulted by the humiliations they felt they had suffered since Yalta and fearful of Communists of any complexion. They had therefore elected a Republican Congress and made Truman, in effect, a prisoner of *his* Politburo. To win congressional backing for his policies after November 1946, Truman had to use the jargon of the Republicans—he had to crusade.

One may readily perceive the irony of this development. Until the end of the peace conference in December 1946, Stalin was wrestling with the Politburo and for that reason was unable to extend a friendly hand to the West. Yet it was only until November that Truman was free to extend a hand in return. Afterwards he not only took a hard line (as he could have in 1945, but did not) but became, of necessity, belligerent and unfriendly, making agreements with the Russians difficult indeed.

But let us look at matters another way. Assessing Stalin's foreign policies in an earlier chapter, we criticized him for being too full of hope late in 1944—for being unrealistic because his coalition scheme did not take into consideration either his own character or that of the Soviet Union and the Communist movement. We predicted that his concept of a new, peaceful, pluralized, world-wide revolution after the war might fail in practice because it was too "tricky" and because it was not openly imperialistic enough. This was indeed the case. By the start of 1947 the foreign policy devised in late 1944 was falling apart. But its failure left the way open for the more realistic imperialistic policy which he might have followed three years earlier. Was the outlook for realism hopeless in 1947, even after the Truman Doctrine? This is the basic problem of the postwar era.

12

Realism, 1947

A Question of Explanations

FROM 22 TO 27 SEPTEMBER 1947, representatives of eight European Communist parties (those of Bulgaria, Czechoslovakia, France, Hungary, Italy, Poland, Rumania, and Yugoslavia) met with two Soviet leaders in Polish Silesia at the elegant *schloss* at Szklarska Poręba (Schreiberhau).[1] Most of these men and women had achieved power and influence in their native lands since 1945. Many of them knew each other from the old days when they were all poor, working for the Comintern in Spain, France, and Moscow. Accordingly, the meeting was an occasion for celebration, and the excitement was heightened by the business. In their view, Stalin, their hard-eyed leader, had been challenged by the Western imperialists as he guided the victory over Hitler into revolutionary channels. It was now their task, they thought, to help him respond.

For outsiders, too, the Szklarska Poręba meeting seemed an action aimed at the outside world. For thirty months, ever since the Yalta

261

Conference in 1945, tensions had been rising among the Allies. Many Westerners had tended to blame the Russians, but the case had been cloudy. Now it appeared that A. A. Zhdanov, the leading Soviet representative, had spoken of division of the world into two vigorously opposed camps and had initiated the establishment of an international organization for Communists—a "Communist information bureau," or Cominform. The Western response was immediate. On 6 October, even before *Pravda* commented editorially on the meeting, a United States State Department spokesman deplored the action of the nine Communist parties. Ever since, Westerners have called the Szklarska Poręba meeting "Stalin's answer to the Marshall Plan" and a "Soviet decision to cut Europe in two."[2] Clearly, this first meeting of the Cominform is a useful focus for this chapter, whose purpose is to see whether Stalin attempted to halt the drift toward Cold War in 1947.

A Puzzle

Stalin's response to the Truman Doctrine of March 1947 was notably mild. Truman proposed to Congress that the newly acquired Soviet zone of influence in Eastern Europe should be contained, if not rolled back. A year earlier, when Winston Churchill, who had no official status at the time, said far less violent things, Stalin had countered loudly and bitterly. This time he stayed silent for a month, and then in a calm interview with Harold Stassen, a member of the Republican Party and his ideological enemy, he described himself as "a businessman, not a propagandist"; denied that capitalist encirclement of the USSR made war inevitable; and declared: "Let us not be sectarians."[3] Meanwhile, in the Council of Allied Foreign Ministers, which was then meeting in Moscow to consider peace terms for Germany and Austria, Molotov did nothing to break the vicious circle of conflicting interests which separated the Allies. Acidly he invoked the Potsdam "agreements" about keeping Germany economically unified, rigidly insisted that the Soviet Union must receive $20 billion in reparations from the defeated enemy, and quibbled over seemingly minor procedural questions. But after Truman's insults one could perhaps not expect more, and Stalin set the tone of the meeting on 15 April when, after an extraordinarily long and irate reprimand by George Marshall, the new secretary of state, he quietly advised patience.[4]

During the Marshall Plan crisis in June 1947, the Soviet Union again acted with restraint. It accepted the Anglo-French invitation to a preliminary discussion of Secretary of State Marshall's proposals of 5 June, and on 26 June Molotov arrived in Paris with no less than eighty-nine economic advisers in tow. After some days of talk, of course, he decided to reject the plan, and did so on the high principle of preserving Soviet national sovereignty. There is a possibility, moreover, that the trip to Paris was a ruse, and that Stalin planned to reject the project from the start.[5] But many observers felt that Moscow was genuinely interested still in the possibility of obtaining American financial credits. Certainly Molotov's questions at Paris about whether he could obtain a blank check and about Germany's role in the proposed plan attested to such interest; and his excuse for departing was ultimately trumped up at the last minute: on the basis of a state secrets decree, enacted by the Supreme Soviet just a few weeks earlier, he declared that the American demand for Soviet economic data would violate Soviet law.[6]

Furthermore, until Molotov left Paris, there was a complete absence of Soviet directives to the East European Communist parties, and their governments, about how they should treat the invitations to the Marshall Plan conference. On 7 July, the Czech Communists agreed to accept the invitation.[7] The Polish, Hungarian, and Rumanian Communists were prepared to do the same.[8] Only on 9 July did Stalin intervene and angrily compel the Czech Party and government to reverse their decision. From these circumstances (which had parallels in Western Europe[9]), it seems clear that Stalin felt no compunction about giving orders to European Communists in such matters, but was having trouble making up his mind. Evidently, he was hesitating in June and July 1947, delaying foreign policy decisions until the last possible moment.

The Cominform meeting in September produced a declaration which at first sight did suggest that the Soviet leadership was trying to formulate a hard foreign policy line in the face of Western attacks. Published on 5 October, it opened with these ringing phrases: "Fundamental changes have taken place in the international situation. . . . These changes are characterized by a new disposition of the basic political forces operating in the world arena, by a change in the relations among the victor states in the Second World War and their realignment."[10] This was clear enough. The declaration went on to indicate that even during the war some members of the Allied camp had been democratic whereas others had not, and that even then there had been differences with regard to war aims:

> The Soviet Union and other democratic countries regarded as their basic war aims the restoration and consolidation of democratic order in Europe, the eradication of Fascism and the prevention of the possibility of a new aggression on the part of Germany, and the establishment of a lasting all-around cooperation among the nations of Europe. The United States of America and Britain in agreement with them, set themselves another aim in the war: to rid themselves of competitors on the markets (Germany and Japan) and to establish their dominant position. This difference in the definition of war aims and tasks of the postwar settlement grew more profound after the war. Thus two camps were formed—the imperialist and anti-democratic camp, having as its basic aim the establishment of world domination for American imperialism and the smashing of democracy, and the anti-imperialist and democratic camp, having as its basic aim the undermining of imperialism, the consolidation of democracy, and the eradication of the remnants of Fascism.[11]

This appearance of a clear hard line dissolved, however, in the latter parts of the declaration. After talk of saber-rattling by the United States and betrayal of the democratic cause by rightist Social Democrats, the declaration took a stand on the notion, proved inadequate almost a year earlier, that there was no real danger of new war:

> It is essential to bear in mind that there is a vast difference between the desire of the imperialists to unleash a new war and the possibility of organizing such a war. The nations of the world do not want war. [If] the forces standing for peace . . . display stamina and resolution, the plans of the aggressors will meet with utter failure. It should not be forgotten that the war hullabaloo raised by the imperialist agents is intended to frighten the nervous and unstable elements and, by blackmail, to win concessions for the aggressor. The principal danger for the working class today lies in underestimation of their own strength and in over-estimating the strength of the imperialist camp.[12]

Here, quite as clearly as in the Stalin-Zhdanov statements of fall 1946 (and as in Mao Tse-tung's coincident but more famous "paper tiger" interview), it appeared that the present danger to peace was propaganda. The Cominform Declaration thus did not respond to the American challenge by rejecting in principle the Grand Alliance (now UNO) peacekeeping organization. It confirmed that the world system of 1945 could work if everyone wanted it to work, and it ended, of course, with a resolution to organize counter-propaganda—to set up a bureau for distributing information among Communists, who were considered the leading force in the democratic camp.

This both hard and soft declaration in many ways simply

reflected the proceedings at Szklarska Poręba. On 22 September, the first day of the meeting, Zhdanov and Malenkov, the Soviet delegates, addressed the assembly. Zhdanov reported on the international situation, Malenkov on the activities of the Soviet Party since the war. On the 23rd and 24th there were a series of reports, two each morning and two each afternoon,[13] from the other parties on their activities since the war. On the morning of the 25th, the Yugoslav delegate, Edouard Kardelj, probably prompted by Zhdanov,[14] viciously attacked the French and Italians for "errors" which allegedly led to the recent expulsion of these two Communist parties from the coalition governments of their countries. On 26 September, Zhdanov and Malenkov themselves told Duclos and Longo, the delegates of the French and Italian parties, to exert self-criticism. Zhdanov demanded of them "not a change of detail, but a change from top to bottom of their whole policies." After his victims made suitably abject apologies, he said that Stalin personally was satisfied with the "debate."

As in the declaration, however, this hard line was only superficial. In closing the meeting, Zhdanov was extremely ambiguous. He wanted a "change from top to bottom" in French and Italian Communist policy, but he did not want these parties to call for insurrection or to give up the coalition government line.[15] Meanwhile, he stressed that Stalin's own "policy of peace" would remain unchanged. If his purpose was to meet American economic power with Communist insurrection, this was surely an unconvincing way of going about it. Further, the record of the conference was oddly treated. The news of what had happened trickled out in *For a Lasting Peace, For a People's Democracy,* the new Cominform paper, during November and December. It revealed that representatives of the nine parties had met, compared experiences, and agreed to set up a supranational organization. But the attack on the French and Italians was not mentioned. On the contrary, even though this was the "directive" leading to the most dramatic consequences of the meeting—a great wave of strikes in Western Europe late in the autumn—it remained a profound secret until one of the Italian delegates published his notes in 1958.

Nor are these the only confusing aspects of the Cominform meeting. A Communist international organ for the exchange of information existed even before the founding of the Cominform: Jacques Duclos started a journal of this nature named *La démocratie nouvelle* early in

1946.[16] Was not the Cominform Bureau thus superfluous from the beginning? Also, one must ask why only nine Communist parties attended a meeting which seemingly concerned all the Communists in Europe, and why the Cominform was limited to Europe, when Communism, after all, was a world-wide movement opposed to a world-wide foe.

As a response to a challenge from the West, the Cominform meeting was no more immediate, urgent, or clear than had been Stalin's responses to the Truman Doctrine in March and to the Marshall Plan in June. Indeed, it delayed so with respect to the Western challenges and was so confusing in its outward forms that it raises questions for historians which contemporary Westerners would hardly have suspected. Was Stalin in the doldrums? Was he sick? Why was he so cryptic? It seems relevant that in his interview with Stassen, he made a direct comparison between his situation in 1941, when Hitler did not want to cooperate with him, and in 1947, when his allies were the Americans and the British.[17] Was he alluding to his inability to make up his mind about policy then, and hinting that a comparable, almost paralyzing indecision was afflicting him now? This is possible, for Khrushchev in his memoirs depicts Stalin as trembling with fear of the West in 1947, as in 1941; and in 1947 rumors circulated in Moscow again about Stalin's illness and growing senility.[18]

Insurrectionism Again

In 1944 and 1945 Stalin responded very strongly to the possibility that in the crises of liberation the Communists of the Eurasian war zones might make trouble for him. He developed the coalition government tactic as a device for inhibiting them. Once the crisis of liberation was over in the Far East, he strengthened the coalition tactic by insisting that each Communist Party follow a separate road to socialism, and he evidently expected, through the use of this all-embracing doctrine, to obscure the independence and individuality of the few parties which were beyond his control. It is relevant to recall these matters here because in the months prior to the Cominform meeting, the coalition system of 1944 ceased to function, and there was no lethargy in Stalin's response to this at Szklarska Poręba.

The coalition system never had become as universally accepted in practice as in theory. By late 1946 the Communists of China, Vietnam, and Greece, though still paying lip service to Stalin's coalition

266

line, were in fact engaged in a revolutionary struggle,[19] and though in Eastern Europe, outside Yugoslavia, the coalition tactic proved very advantageous to the Communists initially, by mid-1947, as the Cominform meeting would reveal, most East European Communist parties were actually in power and found the coalitions a burden. In March 1947 the Belgian Communists were forced out of the coalition government. In May the French and Italian Communists suffered the same fate. These last two parties had spearheaded the introduction of the coalition tactic in 1944. After their fall, there remained only a few countries—Finland, Germany, Austria, Czechoslovakia—where the coalition tactic was really needed. Everywhere else, it seemed more useful to turn to the traditional "pure" tactics, which many Communists instinctively preferred. By September 1947, in this sense, Stalin had lost his reins.

What was worse, throughout the Communist movement in 1947 there was ebullient enthusiasm for socialist activity. For example, in the American Communist Party the leadership fell in 1945 to a narrow-minded one-time Cominternist, William Z. Foster, who felt that all Communists should fortify themselves for intensive battle against United States imperialism. Given the obvious peril in which such a battle would place Foster's own party, one might think that he might at least have held his tongue until Stalin chose the time and the place of battle. Instead, he published his ideas and went on to criticize other Communists for their indifference to the danger of war—this at the London Conference of Communist parties of the British Empire early in 1947 and in various European capitals, West and East, so inevitably Stalin heard about it.[20] Another sort of impatience was visible in France, where, early in 1947, that same Jacques Duclos who in 1945 had publicly condemned the wartime dissolution of the CPUSA now told American visitors: "It is quite clear that the one means whereby the danger of a third world war can be eliminated is by giving us in Europe time to show that the tremendous human advance achieved by the peoples of the USSR on the ruins of Czarism can be surpassed by the peoples of Europe building on the ruins of Hitlerism."[21] Duclos did not support Foster's calls for immediate confrontation with imperialism. But, like Foster, he claimed to speak not just for himself or for the Communists of his country but for international opinion, and he boasted that his rush toward socialism showed a greater wisdom than the Russian course.

Communist enthusiasm for an immediate push toward socialism

burst forth in 1947 even in Soviet-ruled Eastern Europe, and probably explains one of the most blatant examples of Soviet intervention in East European politics in the entire postwar era. During 1945 and 1946 in Hungary the leader of the Communist Party, Mátyás Rákosi, committed himself to long-term governmental cooperation with the centrist Small Landholder Party, which had won a national election late in 1945. The Soviet military authorities did the same.[22] But inside the CPH an anti-Muscovite radical wing developed around the minister of the interior, László Rajk. These predominantly "native" Communists recognized that their party's power was much greater than it appeared on the surface. They considered the coalition "corrupt," and they craved a cleaner break with the past than Rákosi was offering.[23]

Late in 1946 a section of the Communist-dominated police discovered evidence that certain members of the Smallholder Party were conspiring against the regime. It became apparent that the police could manipulate the evidence to destroy the Smallholders and thus open the road to Communist power. The investigation proceeded in spurts, erratically; rumor soon had it that a struggle was going on between branches of the police loyal to Rákosi and those loyal to Rajk. Finally, in February, the affair culminated with the arrest of Béla Kovács, one of the leading Smallholders, and the sequestering of all the evidence by Soviet forces. Outsiders at the time were shocked and horrified by the brutality of the Soviet action, but they noted, to their surprise, that only one major politician had been arrested; that Rákosi continued the coalition with the Smallholders for many more months as if nothing had happened; and that Rajk continued to be a focus of radical Communist discontent. One may guess that the arrest of Kovács was to some extent a preventive action designed to slow down and control the collapse of the coalition system in Hungary. In such fashion, six months before the Cominform meeting, Communist radicalism in Eastern Europe lured Stalin into a major foreign embarrassment, for, after all, the Béla Kovács episode made Stalin's "thaw" of early 1947 seem a mockery and, as much as anything else, destroyed his credibility in the West.

In effect, confusion reigned in the world Communist movement in 1947.[24] Stalin had told every party to take a separate road to socialism. He spoke in public hardly at all, so in the prewar sense there was no general line. As a result the movement was proceeding under its own steam (of which there was plenty), with Communists in different countries beginning to take their line from each other, sometimes even downplaying what little Stalin did say. It was now, as noted earlier, that Communists began to take Stalin's words seriously only when he said something "Communist." When he said nice things about peaceful cooperation with the West, Communists took it for granted that he was tricking the West and followed suit.[25]

These circumstances explain several peculiarities of the Cominform meeting in September. First, they suggest why only nine European Communist parties were invited. Had there been a world conference of Communists in 1947, the East Asians and the southeast Europeans could have made the advantages of insurrectionism seem great, and together they could have formed a "leftist" alternative to Stalinism such as finally emerged within the movement in 1961. By excluding the East Asians and by cutting off the Yugoslavs from contact with the Albanians and Greeks, Stalin postponed this alternative.[26] By inviting the French and Italians while excluding the lesser West European parties and even the Germans and the Finns, Stalin gave the impression that the Szklarska Poręba meeting would not be a "Millerandist" morass but a meeting which might endorse the Yugoslav special model. At the same time, by packing the meeting with five East European parties, Stalin could expect that the conference would help him tie the Yugoslavs down.

Recognition of the crisis of the coalition government tactic sheds light also on the Soviet-Yugoslav intrigue at Szklarska Poręba. The Yugoslavs advocated a turn to insurrectionism there, but this was not the tactic which dominated. Instead, first the Bulgarians and then the Rumanians, the Czechoslovaks, the Poles, and the Hungarians boasted that because of the Red Army, revolution of the old type was no longer necessary. Their emphasis was on their adroit manipulation of the coalition government tactic. What is more, the French and the Italians also limited their discussion to the coalition tactic. Indeed, because Zhdanov's report omitted any reference to the shifts of Soviet policy in 1944, these West Europeans could not discuss the fact that it was Stalin who had kept them from insurrection in 1944, and instead were forced to discuss their eviction from the government in terms of incompetent manipulation of the coalition. In the end, even Zhdanov came down on the side of coalitionism. He recommended that the French and Italians basically rethink their policies, but he also prepared them for new coalitions.[27] Continuity, not change, was Zhdanov's line, and the Yugoslavs were dragged toward a new endorsement of the general policy they had resisted even in 1944.

Part IV: The Insurrectionists Again

As for the idea of an information bureau, it was not welcome to many of the parties represented. The French, in particular, had reason to oppose it: as noted above, they were already publishing the journal *Démocratie nouvelle*. Nor did the Poles, the hosts of the Cominform meeting, welcome the new organization. Their chief representative, Władisław Gomułka, let the conferees know that every suggestion of a revived Comintern should be avoided. One may suspect that other East European Communist leaders privately felt the same way, and, judging from its later fate, the Russians had no need of the Cominform Bureau. The idea of an information bureau was welcomed, however, by the Yugoslavs. In fact, they had been advocating it for two years and were well content when it not only came into existence in the autumn of 1947 but was based in Belgrade.[28] This fact strongly suggests that the bureau was founded so that the Yugoslavs would not drop out of the group after the conference intended to blunt their claws ended.

This analysis of the Cominform meeting does, of course, raise one major problem. The major victims of the proceedings appear here to be the Yugoslavs, whereas in reality we know that they escaped without criticism and actually dominated the meeting. There are two simple explanations of why this happened. First, it seems probable that Stalin was trying to kill more than one bird with his stone and consequently missed his mark. In Poland "separate roadism" had by 1947 brought the Communist Party leadership, and especially Gomułka himself, to the point of voicing certain Polish nationalist motifs which in the past had connoted anti-Sovietism.[29] Indeed, just at this time Gomułka was preparing for a merger of the Polish Communist and Social Democratic parties by claiming to stand in the tradition of the latter party, profoundly anti-Russian though it had been before 1944, and Gomułka was known to be against Soviet-style collectivization of Poland's agriculture. From the Soviet point of view, Poland was the most vital of the East European countries, certainly more so than Yugoslavia. The very staging of the Cominform meeting there suggests that Stalin was aware of these trends, and it is known that, shortly after the meeting, the merger movement lost momentum, not recovering until late in 1948 after Gomułka's fall. It follows that the Soviets encouraged the delegates at Szklarska Poręba to force the Poles as well as the Yugoslavs into line, and that the resultant confusion made possible the escape of the latter.

The other explanation of why the Yugoslavs escaped criticism is apparent from the course of the debate. On the first day Zhdanov and Malenkov addressed the assembly. On the second morning the real drama of the conference began when Vlko Chervenkov, the brother-in-law of the famed Cominternist Georgi Dimitrov, rose to boast of the activities of the Bulgarian Communist Party since the war. Chervenkov started with an account of the liberation of his country through a combination of a Red Army invasion and a Communist-led popular insurrection in September 1944. He then told how the Communists, as leaders in a national front, had organized a coalition government just after the liberation; how they had used this as a cover for seizing key positions of power throughout the country, especially in the army and the police; and how they had isolated one opposition element after the other until finally, in the most recent election, their forces had obtained 52 percent of the vote and a majority in the parliament. There had been difficulties and mistakes, Chervenkov admitted, but the victory was now clear.

The next rapporteur, Jacques Duclos of the French CP, accepted the same values. Although objectively the French CP record was not shameful, Duclos made it seem so. As recently as June 1947, Maurice Thorez, the CPF leader, was still boasting that the Party was "governmental" in the sense of having proved itself "worthy of trust." But Duclos was a veteran of the Leninist Comintern who had fought personally in the wartime underground and had aggressively attacked other Communist parties in 1945 for their lack of revolutionary vigor. Here at the meeting he was filled with the same enthusiasm for revolution as was Chervenkov. His report was therefore apologetic from the start.[30] He accepted the idea that his Party had somehow failed and that socialism had been ill-served in France.

Two further reports on this day were filled with this same excited awareness of revolution. Gheorghe Gheorghiu-Dej told how the Rumanian Communists, after repeated Soviet interventions in their country, had maneuvered within a coalition government to seize the principal organs of state power. Rudolf Slánský of the Czechoslovak Party then described how, with skill and careful planning, his Party also had out-maneuvered the other political parties, grabbed the instruments of state power, and organized great worker enthusiasm for further steps toward socialism. When Dej and Slánský had finished, one could agree that Duclos' apology for his Party's failure was appropriate. Czechoslovakia, after all, was a westernized country like

France, and though Soviet troops were not in occupation there, the Communists had done very well.

On the following two days, it came to seem as though the main purpose of the conference was criticism of the French. First Gomułka stressed the great difficulties his party had faced in a traditionally Russophobe, "backward," and war-wrecked country. But, he went on, through coalition government the Communists in Poland now had state power in hand. Next Luigi Longo presented a report comparable to Duclos': he apologized for his party, which had been evicted from a coalition government by the bourgeoisie. Thereupon Kardelj told how the Yugoslav Communists had fought so well during the war that they had hardly needed a coalition government. The national committees on which the Yugoslav government now rested were nothing more nor less than soviets, in Kardelj's depiction, and the socialization of the economy was well under way. Finally, József Révai, the Hungarian, reported that within the framework of a coalition government, his Communist Party had seized almost total power for itself. As proof of the cleverness of his party, Révai announced that half of the cabinet ministers from the other coalition parties were secret Communists.

By this time, the meeting had fallen into the pattern, very familiar to Comintern veterans, of a self-criticism session, and the revolutionary zeal of the delegates carried them away.[31] On the morning of the 25th, the Yugoslavs openly criticized the Italians and the French for errors. Kardelj prescribed to the Italians a civil war such as the Greek Communists were fighting, even if this meant splitting Italy permanently in two. Milovan Djilas told the French that they would have served Soviet interests had they fought the Americans in 1944. The Hungarian, Mihály Farkas, advised applying his party's famed "salami" tactic to the French bourgeoisie. Ana Pauker, the Rumanian, commanded the French and the Italians alike to stop their parliamentary "pirouetting."

Zhdanov rigged the meeting at Szklarska Poręba—of that there can be no doubt. But behind the criticism of the French and the Italians was the spirit of revolutionary optimism which filled the Communists of the day. One may predict that Kardelj and Djilas would have condemned the West Europeans as failures even without Soviet encouragement, for they had been privately critical of them ever since the war.[32] One may also guess that the Italian and French parties were in a mood to apologize for not having been more aggressive and would have done so anyway in the autumn of 1947, albeit perhaps not with the same violence.[33] And finally, one may guess that it was because of the revolutionary exaltation which prevailed among the Communists in Europe that Stalin's project for reining in the Yugoslavs failed. The assembled delegates did not criticize the Titoists, but shared their mood; and when Stalin suppressed the record of the attack on the French and Italians, he presumably showed his real opinion of what happened.

Soviet Titoism

On 9 September 1947 *Pravda* published a large photograph of Stalin aboard a ship on the Black Sea in the company of A. N. Kosygin, the consumer goods advocate, and A. N. Poskrebyshev.[34] To the knowing few in Stalin's entourage the photograph was politically significant because Poskrebyshev, the head of Stalin's private chancellery and a man of incalculable power behind the scenes, had seldom until recently been mentioned in the press. For historians it is doubly significant. They know that Poskrebyshev became in these years Stalin's main agent in his secret battle with the police, and they may conclude, therefore, that on the eve of the Cominform meeting Stalin stepped up that battle.[35] And the photograph can lead historians to other bureaucratic struggles within the Soviet regime which played as significant a role at the Cominform meeting as did the squabbles among the foreign Communists.

On 24 September, while the Cominform meeting was in session, *Pravda* revealed that M. A. Suslov was a member of the CPSU(b) Secretariat and had responsibilities involving communication with foreign Communist parties.[36] This revelation was important because it affected Zhdanov, who was widely known as the Party secretary responsible for international Communism. It prompted the question why a new man was needed to perform Zhdanov's functions in the Party's (very narrow) highest administrative body, and it compounded a recent blow to Zhdanov's prestige. The cult of Leningrad was one of the major features of the Party revival: over and over again in Zhdanov's Party education journals during 1945 through 1947 Leningrad was praised, while very little mention was made of Moscow. On 7 September, however, Stalin issued a toast celebrating the eight hundredth anniversary of the founding of Moscow. He told how the city had three times rescued the Russian people from the horrors

273

of foreign oppression. He also stressed the theme of centralization: "Only a country united into a single centralized state can count on the possibility of serious cultural and economic growth and of maintaining her independence. The historic service of Moscow is that she has been and remains the foundation and initiator of a centralized state among the Russians."[37] The city, he said, became the capital of Russia after the revolution, and was thus a "herald of the liberation movement of laboring humanity from capitalist slavery." It was an example for all capital cities in the world through its elimination of slums. It was also the spokesman of the fight for a lasting peace against the incendiaries of new war. All these last phrases sounded vaguely internationalist, but Stalin concluded by saying: "Those are the services for which our Motherland today celebrates the eight hundredth anniversary of Moscow with such love and reverence for its capital city. Hail to our powerful, native [*rodnaya*] Soviet Socialist Moscow."[38] Stalin's toast strongly recalled the Russian nationalism of the war period—a nationalism which disappeared during the *Zhdanovshchina* of 1946 but which soon reappeared in strength as Zhdanov's star declined.

Apart from its slap at Zhdanov, the announcement of Suslov's new appointment was an important symptom of a surprising sort of political adventurism which emerged in the top Soviet administrative levels at this time, when Stalin was clamping down on the police and Zhdanov. As indicated elsewhere, in March 1946 Suslov became the member of the Party Orgburo in charge of police affairs. It is known that A. A. Kuznetsov, Zhdanov's aide from Leningrad, at some time before 1948 assumed responsibilities for supervising the police. One may deduce that he did so when Suslov moved on.[39] Kuznetsov was a younger man whose career had taken shape since the great purges under Zhdanov in Leningrad. He came to the center of the Party only in March 1946, when Zhdanov brought him into the Secretariat. He was thus an outsider to the whole central regime, not to speak of the police. Granted the notorious danger of getting in Beria's way, historians must ask whether September 1947 was the optimum moment for such a new man in the Kremlin, inexperienced in the ways of Stalin's court, to take on his police assignment. With Zhdanov, his protector, visibly insecure, it required bravery for Kuznetsov to assume such a role. Yet we know he did it, and he was not the only one to be so bold.

As mentioned elsewhere, the Party educational journals kept

274

right on praising Leningrad, not Moscow, in the autumn and winter of 1947–1948. Suddenly, in April 1948, *Partiinaya Zhizn'*, Zhdanov's new journal, ceased publication, not to resume until after Stalin's death.[40] How could this have occurred, if not through some lack of caution among the editors of those journals and the leaders of Leningrad, comparable to the boldness of Kuznetsov? Equally astonishing was the behavior of M. I. Rodionov, the young Russian nationalist leader of the Gorky *oblast* Party organization, who in 1949 became, with Kuznetsov and Voznesensky, a principal victim of the Leningrad purge. Late in 1947 he publicly linked his campaign for reform in the Russian Republic with the cult of Leningrad.[41] One may assume that these fresh cadres had some sort of tangible assurance that they were carrying out Stalin's wishes when they acted so boldly in 1947. It seems clear, however, that they were consciously and deliberately playing with fire—and that in their boldness they were willing to ignore or to overlook Stalin's published hints that his support of them might wane. Perhaps, therefore, one may characterize them as Soviet Titoists. Under the conditions of terror then emerging in the Soviet Union, perhaps they were acting as Tito was doing at the same time abroad, pursuing their own revolution on the idealistic assumption that it was identical with Stalin's.[42]

In many ways this kind of middle- and upper-level political jousting in the Soviet bureaucracy hardly affected foreign policy. It did not, for example, generate pressures comparable to the pressure for revolutionary action which was coming from within international Communism. But it did affect foreign policy through one of the great "scholarly debates" of the period: the debate about the nature of democracy. These debates were extraordinarily complex. Although bureaucratic political forces continually intervened and attempted to control the conclusions reached, these were not staged debates but sprang from deep and spontaneous sources in Soviet society and historians who summarize just their political aspect miss the reality of what happened. In this particular debate, however, the political aspect was from the start so important that a brief summary of it seems permissible.

The debate about democracy began with a lecture by G. F. Aleksandrov at the Party High School in Moscow in the autumn of 1946 entitled "On Soviet Democracy."[43] Aleksandrov, it may be recalled, was then chief of the Party's Agit-Prop Directorate and the principal spokesman for those bureaucratic elements who defended "creative

Marxist practice'' against the ''far-sighted reliance on Marxism'' advocated by the Party revivalists. His lecture coincided with Stalin's victory over the revivalists, and its major theme was that there were only two types of democracy in the world—the Soviet type and the bourgeois type. In such fashion Aleksandrov tended to contradict the Zhdanovite foreign policy thesis that the basic division in the world now was not vertical, between Soviet and Western blocs, but horizontal, between ''isolated imperialist elements'' inside some states and the popular progressive forces inside *all* states.

In the wake of Aleksandrov's widely published lecture, a number of other prominent theoreticians took up the question of democracy and emphasized that in fact there were not just two types any more. Since the war, they pointed out, a new type of democracy had appeared in Eastern Europe which was neither capitalist nor socialist but somewhere in between, the people's democracies. The problem of defining these democracies was of course one of the principal questions then facing Soviet Marxists and was made even more complicated by the fast pace of political change in Eastern Europe. One may hardly claim, therefore, that these particular essays were in any way merely bureaucratic replies to Aleksandrov. It seems hardly accidental, however, that some of these essayists were propagandists who had been most vocal in favor of the Party revival and thus opposed to Aleksandrov in 1944 and 1945.[44] One may note also that they were fighting a rear-guard action, for in 1947 the political *Gleichschaltung* in Eastern Europe was beginning—''people's democracy'' was beginning to be less different from the Soviet form of government.

One of the scholars who addressed himself to the people's democracy question early in 1947 was Eugen Varga. Varga's book, published a year earlier, had not been a revivalist document, optimistic in all things. He was very much the economist of doom: he found that capitalism had not conformed to the prognoses of ''primitive Marxism'' but had changed and proved capable of postponing for at least a short while the ''inevitable crisis'' on which the Party revivalists were relying. He had also declared, as Aleksandrov did now, that there were only two kinds of democracy, that the emergent people's democracies were specimens of ''state capitalism'' which were moving toward socialism but were not yet there. On a certain level of understanding, therefore, it could be claimed that Varga had made mistakes in his book; that the article on people's democracy which he now published constituted acknowledgment of his mistakes; and that consequently the entire book should be subjected to scrutiny. Here was a fine way for the revivalists to hit back at Aleksandrov. The bait was all the more tempting because Varga headed the Institute on World Economy and World Politics, the principal Soviet economics institute, and edited its prestigious journal. The bait was taken. The Economics Section of the Soviet Academy of Sciences decided in March 1947 to hold a conference on Varga's book.[45]

Hereupon, Stalin himself unexpectedly thrust Varga into the political limelight. On 9 April he talked at length with Harold Stassen about the economy of contemporary capitalism, drew him into a discussion of the possibility of a new depression in the West, referred to the ability of the United States to "regulate" its economy, and then, when Stassen affirmed that through such "regulation" a sensible and strong American government could effectively avoid depression, Stalin replied, "*eto pravil'no*" ("that's right").[46] This was precisely what Varga had written in 1945, and it was a challenge to the optimistic prognoses of the Party revivalists, who claimed that the imminent crisis of capitalism would soon solve all Stalin's problems.

On 7 May 1947 the Economics Section held the first of the three sessions of its conference on Varga's book. To underline his personal interest in the proceedings, Stalin published his interview with Stassen on 8 May, and Varga himself defended his empirical findings so valiantly that no one was able to find any significant chink in his armor. He was nonetheless viciously attacked over and over again for "errors." For example, his opponents found that in 1942 he had predicted Germany's collapse from economic exhaustion. This, they said, was "obviously" wrong, or the Soviet government would not be demanding $20 billion worth of reparations from Germany now, at the end of the war. It was indicative of the proceedings that Varga had to publish a formal apology for having "failed" in 1945 to assess correctly the "new type" of democracy which had then not yet emerged in Eastern Europe.[47] The reasons for the attack were clear: that in his main theses he had been right; that Stalin, in an anti-revivalist mood, was backing him up; and that the revivalist bureaucrats, unable because of Stalin's position to attack the major theses, felt bound to prove him wrong on minor points in order to hide their loss of Stalin's favor.

Varga resisted the revivalist onslaught of May 1947 and survived, although on 8 September, two weeks before the Cominform meeting, he lost the leadership of his institute and its journal and eventually had to rewrite his book. But meanwhile the debate about democracy entered a new stage. In June, as noted earlier, Molotov and his economic experts at the Paris consultation about the Marshall Plan attempted to avoid the division of Europe into East and West blocs, failed, and thus made it predictable that the "new type" democracies of Eastern Europe might all too soon become democracies of the Soviet type, proving Aleksandrov correct. Only Zhdanov's intervention saved the day. Perhaps foreseeing the outcome of Molotov's trip, Zhdanov attended a conference of Soviet professional philosophers just after Molotov went abroad. There he attacked Aleksandrov for alleged errors in a philosophy textbook published in 1944 and thus managed to dislodge him from the Agit-Prop Directorate.[48]

At the Cominform conference in September the foremost protagonists in the Soviet bureaucracy entered the debate. On the first day of the meeting Malenkov described an "anti-imperialist democratic tendency" (*napravlenie*) emerging in the world as the group of states which would subsequently form the Soviet bloc. Moreover, he suggested that the assembled Communists reply to the imperialist challenge by organizing an information bureau, whose functions sounded identical with those of the old Soviet-dominated Comintern. In his view, evidently, there were only two types of democracy, the Soviet type and the bourgeois type, and the world had to choose between them.[49]

It was Zhdanov who introduced at the Cominform meeting the word "camp" (*lager*), much more definite than "tendency," who actually said that there were only two "camps" in the world, and who spoke most virulently against the West. However, Zhdanov took every opportunity to stress that his new terminology did not imply a break with his earlier advocacy of anti-blocism. He included in the anti-imperialist camp not only the Soviet Union and the "lands of the new democracy" (Bulgaria, Yugoslavia, Czechoslovakia, and Poland) but also Rumania, Hungary, and Finland, which were allegedly "developing along democratic lines";[50] Indonesia and Vietnam, which were allegedly "associated" with the anti-imperialist camp; India, Egypt, and Syria, which were allegedly "sympathetic"; the worker movement in all countries; the national liberation movements in the developing countries; and the "progressive and democratic forces present in every country." In the imperialist camp Zhdanov included two governments, those of the United States and Great Britain. But according to Zhdanov, this camp consisted above all of the Wall

Street capitalists and their propagandists—in other words, "elements" inside certain states, not the states themselves.[51] Zhdanov, in sum, still sought to describe the world as divided horizontally between peoples and isolated war-monger elements. His line sharply contrasted with the verticalism propagated by Malenkov. What is more, when Zhdanov discussed the nature and functions of the information bureau which was to be set up, he specifically denied any intention to re-establish the Comintern and stressed looseness of organization and an informational rather than coercive function. Here in particular his words contrasted sharply with Malenkov's.

The great Soviet debate about the nature of democracy carried on after the Cominform meeting into 1948. It did not really end until December 1948, when, with the *Gleichschaltung* of Eastern Europe in full swing, Dimitrov, Rákosi, and Bierut, three East European Communists whose parties had most actively spoken for "separate roadism" in 1945, 1946, and 1947, simultaneously pronounced that they had been wrong: that people's democracy was really nothing else but dictatorship of the proletariat, for which the Soviet democracy was the standing model.[52] Our discussion of the first part of the debate has been relevant, however, as evidence of how the bureaucratic struggles of Soviet domestic politics dramatically influenced foreign policy in 1947. At the Cominform meeting, Stalin was face to face not only with the danger of insurrectionism among the foreign Communist parties but also with the panicky adventurism of his lieutenants at home. Indeed, it seems not too much to suggest that this adventurism was responsible for the miscarriage of his plan for reining in Tito. How can one explain Zhdanov's allowing such a miscarriage save in terms of his eagerness to use every opportunity to find allies in his struggle against Malenkov?

The Cult of Personality

Before the war, Stalin adapted the doctrines of Marxism and rewrote the history of Lenin's party in order to establish his own high-priestly authority. But as underlined at the start of this book, his theoretical work of the 1930s actually enshrined Marxism-Leninism more firmly than ever as the backbone of the Soviet administrative system. In those last years before the war Stalin ruled not, as often supposed, merely through administrative organizations but also through a sort of personal contact with each member of the bureaucracy. He conveyed authority directly by means of his pseudo-Marxist public line.

During the war, despite the campaign against sectarianism, Stalin re-emphasized this personal sort of control. He spoke more frequently in public then than he had during the years before the war. He let the lesser Stalinists explain: "Comrades: Every speech of Comrade Stalin is a major event in the life of the country, . . . not just a report, but a major programmatic document, a new general contribution to Marxist-Leninist science."[53] Or: "Stalin is a man of few words who profoundly weighs everything he says. The whole world should hang on his every word."[54] But then at the end of the war, Stalin, for one brief moment in his speech of 6 November 1944, relaxed his grip on the Party's ideology, spoke enthusiastically in Marxist-Leninist terms, and encouraged *partiinost* among his elites, and the vast edifice of his personal control system came tumbling down. Hence his fear.

When enthusiasm swept the victorious Soviet elites in 1945 and the reviving Party in Stalin's name preached "far-sightedness" and "principled" return to Marxism-Leninism in its pre-Stalinist forms, suddenly Stalin was not the ultimate authority any more. Ideological imperatives that did not stem from him governed the bureaucrats. Under the guise of *partiinost,* reform became the order of the day. Stalin, as we have seen, fought back, and did so successfully, but in the process he developed a new political language of sorts, and this is what concerns us here. The new language explains why he let Zhdanov make a mistake at the Cominform meeting and the seeming lethargy of his foreign policy in 1947.

Before and even during the war Stalin had spoken in a Marxist framework with relatively little objectivity toward his ideology. After the war he let his underlings organize a debate about Marxism-Leninism, which he in the end could judge, and then with his election speech of 19 February 1946 he perceptibly turned on his Marxism, publishing statements which indicated he had done so for a purpose. This objectivity toward his ideology was the first characteristic of his new political language. A second characteristic was the medium through which he communicated his line to the bureaucrats. As noted elsewhere, before and during the war he had customarily delivered long and programmatic speeches, but now he restricted himself to very brief interviews and toasts. Although these statements made sharp points, only one—the response to Razin's questions about

280

Clausewitz—related in any way to Marxism-Leninism. Meanwhile, he brought into use the peculiar signs and symbols called kremlinological evidence. Through hints in the Party press late in 1945 and early in 1946, he encouraged the bureaucrats to watch the great debate between his lieutenants. At the climax of the election campaign in February 1946, Stalin most theatrically arbitrated between the Malenkovs and Berias, on the one hand, and the Zhdanovs and Molotovs, on the other. Finally, during 1946 a conflict between personalities, Malenkov and Zhdanov, became the leading index to Stalin's line.

In 1952 a prominent British political scientist explained that the signs and symbols in the Soviet press reflected an "artificial dialectic" through manipulation of which Stalin attempted to rule.[55] This seems too tendentious. What Stalin was developing was something more like a kind of history which he could use for his own purposes because it was not subject to great dialectical laws, as Marx's history was. For this innovation it seems best to use the conventional Communist term "cult of personality." It did not prove ultimately satisfactory to him as a language of control. In 1950 he reverted to Marxism itself and published the essays entitled "Marxism and Linguistics." In 1952 he reverted even further by publishing a cryptic rehash of his postwar debate with Voznesensky—*Economic Problems of Socialism in the USSR.* One can only speculate why he abandoned the cult, but historians may recognize that during the immediate postwar period the "kremlinological evidence" was a very real instrument of Stalin's control.[56]

Two weeks before the Cominform meeting Stalin published his toast to Moscow, whose statist and nationalistic themes had negative implications for the Party revival and for Zhdanov's cult of Leningrad. There is substantial evidence that the details of the meeting were worked out virtually at the last minute, perhaps even after the toast.[57] In terms of Soviet politics the most remarkable feature of the meeting was the appearance of Malenkov. It marked his recovery from the political disgrace into which he had fallen almost exactly one year earlier, when Stalin created the Politburo "septet" for the Party revivalists (Stalin, it may be remarked, adored anniversaries).[58] The significance of Malenkov's appearance was underlined by *Pravda*'s announcement during the meeting of Suslov's official duties in Zhdanov's bailiwick, and, of course, by the blandness with which Malenkov's speech reflected Stalin's statism and nationalism. One is reminded of an anecdote told by Stalin's daughter: "Knowing that Zhdanov suffered from recurrent heart attacks, my father, angered by Zhdanov's silence [at a lunch in the early autumn of 1947] . . . turned on him viciously: 'Look at him, sitting there like Christ, as if nothing were of any concern to him! There—looking at me now as if he were Christ!' Zhdanov grew pale, beads of perspiration stood out on his forehead. I was afraid he might have an attack and gave him a glass of water."[59] Clearly, Stalin used Malenkov and Suslov at the time of the Cominform meeting to torment Zhdanov, deliberately manipulating the events around him for the edification of his bureaucrats.

But why? Svetlana Alliluyeva's story gives a clue. In effect, after the defeat of anti-blocism in November and December 1946, Zhdanov was silent in public about foreign policy. Particularly in his speech at the philosophy conference in June 1947, he carefully ducked any sort of general definition of the Soviet position in the world such as had characterized his speeches on literature in 1946; one may note that Zhdanov's cautious Party revivalist comrade, Molotov, avoided such general definitions from the time of his evasive "populist" speech of 6 November 1945. Consequently, since Stalin himself had provided no such definition, the Soviet Union through much of 1947 lacked any authoritative theoretical formula to guide its foreign policy.

Now at the Cominform meeting, despite the signs of Stalin's disfavor, Zhdanov was the master of ceremonies. The first to speak, he delivered the report on the international situation to which all the other reports at the meeting, including Malenkov's, related. Zhdanov was also the last to speak, summarizing what the meeting had accomplished. Stalin was conspicuously absent (although, as Zhdanov privately informed the delegates, he kept in touch daily by telephone), and Zhdanov had sufficient freedom of action to collude with the Yugoslavs and thus made a mistake. Such circumstances suggest that at the Cominform meeting, Stalin set up a confrontation, inducing two notoriously rival personalities to present opposite foreign policy theses in public, so that in the ensuing debate a new foreign policy definition might emerge which he could publish as the Party line.

Stalin and Failure

But why did not Stalin himself speak out forthrightly and give a new definition? Why did he resort to this Byzantine ritual of a staged debate between his lieutenants, instead of giving a programmatic

282

speech befitting his role as autocratic leader of the Soviet state and the world Communist movement? One answer may be, as suggested earlier, that somehow he could not make up his own mind—that in 1947, as in 1941, he was almost sick with fear in the face of an external danger which he had not foreseen. In his speech of 6 November 1944 and at the inter-Allied conferences of 1945 he committed himself to the notion that the Soviet state could work with the Western Powers safely, just as he had committed himself in 1939 to the idea that it was safe to work with Hitler. Despite his efforts at aloofness from anti-blocism in 1945, ultimately he was responsible, and by 1947 anti-blocism was just as demonstrably wrong as the collaboration with Hitler had been in the spring of 1941. Perhaps Stalin, when caught thus in between policies, lost his ruthlessness, became indecisive and lethargic, and needed an elaborate ritual and someone to blame, in order to make a decision. As Herbert Dinerstein has pointed out, there are parallels between the way Stalin changed policy as far back as 1934 and the change of policy in 1947.[60]

In addition, however, Stalin's foreign policy lethargy in 1947 and the ritual at the Cominform meeting may be seen as a matter of control. In 1944 he had undertaken to resume the leadership of the world Communist movement and to ride on the crest of what he perceived as a revolutionary wave. In 1945 he chose to regard the enthusiasms of his followers in the Soviet Party as a similar wave: instead of resisting the revivalists he used them to accomplish his political ends. By 1947 the real power of the Communists abroad had grown immensely as a result of Stalin's guidance, and for this very reason, far more than in 1944, they were threatening his control. At home the energies of the Party bureaucrats were by no means exhausted, despite Stalin's victory over Zhdanov, and because of the difficulties in the West xenophobia was running wild. Under such circumstances, perhaps it seemed to Stalin that he could save the peace only by moving as slowly as possible and by deliberately trying to force his underlings, both at home and abroad, to be responsible. He had attempted to impose such responsibility through his "retreat" in the autumn of 1945 at home and through his "separate roadist" tactic in the Communist movement abroad. By means of the staged debate at Szklarska Poręba he may have hoped to repeat the performance.

This latter explanation of the Cominform meeting in particular hints that Stalin in 1947 was genuinely concerned for the peace of the world and attempted to stop the drift toward hostility between East and West. But it suggests also the narrowness of his methods—he was obscure, excessively manipulative, too indirect—and it makes the aftermath comprehensible. What happened at Szklarska Poręba did not calm the waters but made them more stormy than ever. Even Stalin had to recognize the extent of the disaster. On 14 October 1947, after the publication of the Cominform declaration and just before the release of Zhdanov's speech, Stalin granted an interview to a British left-wing Labor Party member of Parliament, Konni Zilliacus, in which he spoke openly. He now said that any effort to revive the old Comintern would be a "utopian enterprise," "quixotic" and "stupid," even had the Comintern not long since outlived its purpose. He stated further that the nine Communist parties at the Cominform meeting simply wanted "to work together . . . in order to improve the condition of the working class and the common people . . . and to defend the independence of their countries." He flatly denied that the Cominform meeting meant a change in Soviet state policy, and he called anew for an improvement in political and economic relations between the Soviet Union and all countries, "beginning with Great Britain and the USA."[61]

Unfortunately, Stalin had no credibility abroad by this time. The Western world largely ignored this interview while giving headline attention to Zhdanov's speech.[62] The Communists likewise, baffled by the details of the meeting, decided that Zhdanov's socialist fervor was what counted. The Cominform meeting did not delay but rather precipitated the confrontation of 1948. Stalin had failed.

13

Confrontation, 1948

The Onset of the Cold War

IN THE YEAR after the Cominform meeting, the Berlin blocade began what almost became a hot war between the Soviet Union and the leading Western Powers. It was a year of extraordinary political turbulence from one end of Eurasia to the other, and ended with Communists in power at Prague and approaching the gates of Peking. Was Stalin responsible for this disintegration of the peace which had been won in 1945? Many Western observers judged immediately that he was: and even if one shies away from such a hasty answer, one may recognize the existence of a real historical problem here. From Stalin himself we possess virtually no documents for 1948—only some letters to the Yugoslav Communists, a few diplomatic notes, and four very short public statements. Few foreigners got to talk to him, moreover, so we lack even the eye-witness accounts which abound for earlier years. The very dimensions of his political decisions are consequently unclear to historians, and as

285

for interpretation, what is one to make of a world leader in the middle of the twentieth century whose most visible activities in a year of international crisis are to besiege a city, as in ancient times, and to descry a heretic in the midst of the revolution, as in the Middle Ages?

Korea and Palestine

In Korea in September 1947, at almost exactly the same time as the convening of the Cominform meeting in Poland, the Soviet Union changed policy. For the first time anywhere since the war it rejected the idea of working in cooperation with the West and adopted a "bloc-ist" doctrine like that it followed in many other countries by the middle of 1948. In microcosm, therefore, Stalin's decision in this small country may give a clue to his larger decisions elsewhere later on.

A first factor in the change was certainly the incongruity between what had actually been happening in Korea since 1945 and what should have been happening according to the theses we have labeled as "anti-blocism." In 1945, one may recall, Korea was not a defeated enemy but a liberated nation. According to the anti-blocist schema, "popular forces" should have progressed there, as in the liberated countries of Europe, toward "peaceful transformation" of the country, while the Soviet Union, through the Grand Alliance, kept "imperialist elements" in America and Britain split and at bay. But this did not happen. During the war the Americans decided that the Koreans, because of their long history of repression by Japan, were not ready for independence and should be put under a Great Power trusteeship.[1] Stalin, in his efforts to inhibit the Chinese Communists in 1945, accepted this notion. In December 1945, at the Moscow Conference of Allied Foreign Ministers, the Great Powers set up a Soviet-American Joint Commission to work out the political future of the country, which was meanwhile governed by the Soviet and American military occupation authorities. Korea had thus become, with Germany, the only portion of Eurasia which had no indigenous government and which was clearly divided into Eastern and Western halves. The incongruity between theory and practice was the greater by 1947 because, in their efforts to limit Chinese Communist influence, the Russians were encouraging a Communist Party consolidation in the north of Korea along statist and military lines. Kim Il Sung, their favorite in northern Korea, possessed a regular army to which there was no parallel in eastern Germany.[2]

Until the summer of 1947 the fundamental inapplicability of Soviet anti-blocism to what was happening in Korea remained inobtru-
sive, although progress in the Joint Commission toward establishing
a provisional all-Korean government was very slow. As in Germany,
Moscow insisted that it stood for reunification of the country and
blamed the existing division, and the occupation regime, on the
West. The Koreans themselves, however, grew more and more frustrated, as did Washington, which allowed them to protest in public
and therefore felt their pressure. Finally, on 26 August 1947, the
United States brought the matter to a head, and this was the second
factor which influenced Stalin's decision. The Americans proposed
in the Joint Commission that the entire Korean question be returned
to the foreign ministers of the Great Powers. On 4 September (three
days before Stalin's toast to Moscow), the Soviet Union rejected
this proposal. Thereupon, on 16 September, despite Soviet protests,
the United States submitted the Korean question to the United Nations. In so doing Washington was determined to avoid just such a
Great Power commission as the anti-blocists admired. It wished also
to prove that the UNO was not subject to Soviet manipulation; in
fact, it expected the UNO presence to undo the consolidation of
Communist power in the north, which Kim Il Sung was touting as
the first stage in Korea's special path to socialism.[3] The American
move was thus a more localized but a far more determined challenge
to Soviet anti-blocism than the Marshall Plan had been earlier in the
summer.

The Soviet response to the challenge was formulated by 22 or 23
September, the first days of the Cominform meeting.[4] It was a proposal to end the occupation of Korea forthwith through simultaneous
withdrawal of all American and Soviet troops. From the Soviet point
of view, this was a practical suggestion: in the north the Communist
army was strong, whereas in the south the Americans, through their
denial of Korean readiness for independence, had made themselves
decidedly unpopular. There was thus little doubt as to who would win
if the occupying forces withdrew. But the theoretical aspect of the
Soviet response is what concerns us here, and it was decidedly one-
sided. The new proposal implied outright abandonment of the notion
that "progress" might be achieved through manipulation of the Grand
Alliance. It implied policymaking according to the theory of "two
camps" which Zhdanov reluctantly, and Malenkov eagerly, advocated at the Cominform meeting on 22 September. The Soviet press

was not slow in spelling out the meaning of the shift.[5] This brings us to the third reason for Stalin's decision in Korea: sheer coincidence suggests a relationship between this decision in the theater of inter-state relationships and Stalin's intricate domestic political manipulations at Szklarska Poręba. Indeed, the shift to overt blocism in Korea was as a whole akin to the announcements in *Pravda* with which Stalin prodded Zhdanov during the Cominform meeting.

Important developments in another part of the world confirm the subjection of Soviet foreign policy to Stalin's domestic political manipulations during 1947. On 26 September, four days after the policy shift in Seoul and one day after Zhdanov allowed the "mistake" to occur at Szklarska Poręba, the British announced that they would withdraw from their mandate in Palestine. Earlier in the year, having decided against "going it alone" with a socialist economy at home, the British recognized that in free market terms they were almost bankrupt. Their military empire, it followed, was too expensive. In February they announced their decision to leave India and abandoned to the Americans the defense of Greece and Turkey. Until autumn they were undecided as to which part of the Middle East they would keep and which they would give up, but now they decided to leave Palestine, where they were having great trouble acting as a buffer between the Arabs and the Jews.[6] The Soviet government in its turn now had to make a choice. On the one hand, it could stand aloof and curry favor in the Moslem world by opposing the partition of Palestine and by insisting, as before the war, that the Zionist dream of a Jewish state in the Middle East was pure imperialism of a retrograde nineteenth-century type. Such a course had disadvantages, however. It would place the Soviet state on the side of religious Moslem masses who, as experience had shown, were almost impervious to the appeals of Marxist socialism. It would also be unpopular among Soviet sympathizers in the European and American political left, where there was great sympathy for the Jews, and it offered no possibility for a Soviet intrusion into the Middle East. On the other hand, if the Soviet Union opted to support the partition of Palestine, the emerging anti-Communist trend in Western public opinion might be halted, and through the United Nations Moscow might step in when the British stepped out.[7]

A choice was made by 13 October 1947, the day before Stalin's reassuring talk with Konni Zilliacus about the Cominform meeting. On that day, a Soviet delegate to the United Nations revealed that his country would support the partition of Palestine and would not insist on the continued frustration of Zionist political objectives. For the Middle East this decision was a bombshell, equivalent to the Molotov-Ribbentrop pact of 1939 in its reversal of prior Soviet policy. As one may see from the alternatives just mentioned, the decision reflected Soviet domestic political interests. To have opposed partition would have implied isolationism and disregard of public sentiment abroad—in other words, adopting the position of Malenkov. To support partition meant participation in the great world and popularity in leftist circles abroad, the position of Zhdanov and Molotov. The anti-blocists had recovered, it seemed, from their setback in Korea.

In the following months the advantages of the new Middle Eastern policy from the anti-blocist viewpoint became more evident. At the United Nations in October and November, it led to a very real official collaboration between the governments of the Soviet Union and the United States. The result was the UNO's Palestinian partition plan of 29 November, with its implied recognition of Soviet involvement in the Middle East. Had it not been for a coincident escalation of political tensions in Western Europe and the failure of a new Council of Foreign Ministers' Conference on Germany, the advantages might have been greater still. Furthermore, by the end of the year, the independence struggle of the Jews meshed with the enthusiasm for "movements of peoples" which Zhdanov had tolerated at Szklarska Poręba. In late December 1947 and early January 1948, civil war broke out in Palestine between the Jews, who were supported by the European left, and the Arabs, who got their weapons from the British. The Jews in Palestine thus became (by Soviet definitions of the day) the enlightened vanguard of a great revolutionary movement of all the Middle Eastern people against a most benighted form of imperialism—a coalition between Whitehall and the Mullahs.[8]

These changes in Soviet policy in Palestine and Korea at the time of the Cominform meeting tell us much about Stalin's methods. At issue in Palestine and in Korea were a great number of weighty local questions. Stalin no doubt was conversant with many of these issues, for he impressed visitors with his mastery of detail,[9] and his decisions were not irrational in the sense that they completely ignored objective facts and external challenges. But judging from the pattern here, his decisions were not just pragmatic—based on local conditions. They evidently reflected choices between alternative courses which would fit in with his highly distinctive theoretical approach to world politics, and they were evidently subject in part to his policies at home and to the ongoing effort to control the international Communist movement which occupied the center of his political stage.

The Shift to Blocism in Germany

Stalin was almost certainly under pressure to extend his blocist decision from Korea to Germany in the autumn of 1947. As noted above, both countries were divided between East and West, neither had an indigenous coalition government, and if in Korea the Communist consolidation of the Soviet zone was more advanced, in Germany the machinery of Allied military government was more fractured. It was logical, therefore, to treat them in the same way; in addition, Germany was so much the center of the international stage that even the most faithful Stalinist Communists had to look at reality. In August 1947 a group of East German Communist leaders were embarrassed when Stalin himself told them that the premise of Soviet policy in their country was unified political development under the Grand Alliance aegis—in other words, anti-blocism.[10] There is evidence that other East European Communists expressed doubts about Stalin's German policy.[11] Nonetheless, even in Korea during the autumn the shift to blocism proceeded at a snail's pace, and in Germany anti-blocism prevailed unchanged.

The Council of Allied Foreign Ministers was scheduled to meet on 25 November, this time in London, to wrestle anew with the problem of carrying out the Potsdam agreements and to prepare a peace treaty for Germany. On the very eve of the conference, the East German Communists began hastily to organize an all-German popular representative body—a Volkskongress—at Berlin, which would generate pressure upon the Allies to set up an all-German regime.[12] They took this step even though the Americans and the British had been attempting to merge their occupation zones for nine months, consolidating West Germany administratively, and even though it was clear in advance that the principal West German political parties would not participate. Grasping the slogan *"Wiedervereinigung,"* they were battling for anti-blocism in the face of all the observable facts. Moreover at the Foreign Ministers' Conference Molotov himself acted as if anti-blocism were unchallenged. He reiterated all his well-known arguments about Soviet loyalty to the Potsdam agreements and Allied betrayal of Yalta. Just as he had in the oration on the anniversary of the revolution on 6 November,[13] he now insisted that only the West had changed—that Stalin and the Soviet Union remained steadfast. Despite the taunting and even anger of his Western colleagues, he demanded that the Allies abandon Bizonia and go back to the arrangements of 1945. In the end, on 15 December, he allowed the conference to break up *sine die,* just as in October 1945, as though he still believed that the forces of history would compel the imperialists to abandon their points of view.[14]

After this, of course, Stalin did decide to adopt a blocist definition of his policies in Germany and throughout Europe. Beginning in January 1948, Moscow imposed state treaties of mutual assistance against aggression on Hungary, Rumania, and Bulgaria, the former Axis satellites. Comparable treaties already existed with Poland and Czechoslovakia. They marked the birth of the Soviet bloc.[15] In February the Communists seized power in Czechoslovakia. In March the Allied Control Council for Berlin broke down, and the Russians began interrupting Western communications with the former Axis capital. By late June Stalin's army was risking war by blockading the Western sectors of Berlin. One could hardly ask for clearer evidence that Stalin was no longer basing his foreign policy on the denial of the existence of state-led blocs in the world.[16] In the meantime, moreover, the clearest imaginable Western challenge had emerged, virtually forcing Stalin into a blocist policy in Germany. Even before the Council of Foreign Ministers adjourned in December, Secretary of State Marshall and Foreign Secretary Bevin decided to move toward the establishment of a West German government. Promises about this were made to the Germans at a meeting of Bizonal officials on 7 and 8 January. Then on 21 January, Bevin, speaking in Parliament, involved France and the Low Countries by proposing the military, political, and economic consolidation of Western Europe. On 17 March his appeal resulted in the signing at Brussels of a military pact covering Western Europe, which in turn led to the negotiations during the summer of 1948 for a North Atlantic treaty. This was signed in April 1949. Meanwhile between 23 February and 5 March 1948, and again between 20 April and 2 June, representatives of the United States and the five West European countries hammered out their disagreements over Germany and decided to go ahead with the plan for a separate West German regime.[17] Not even the blindest Party revivalist could insist, in the face of this challenge, that the Western imperialists were fundamen-

291

tally at odds with one another and about to come groveling for favors to the Soviet door.

Nonetheless, it is a central mystery of Stalin's foreign policy in the postwar period that we do not know, and cannot perceive clearly from the available documents, the moment of the shift to blocism in Germany. Apparently he had made his decision by 12 or 13 January 1948, when Djilas visited him and heard him say: "The West will make Western Germany their own, and we will turn Eastern Germany into our own state."[18] At about the same time the Russian officials at the Control Council in Berlin began complaining (as could be expected) about the Western moves toward German consolidation in their zones.[19] In February, the Soviet forces in East Germany let the German Communists take some first secret steps toward constructing the administrative apparatus which, in the autumn of 1948, would emerge as the East German state machine.[20] But there was no public announcement of a change in the Soviet Union's German policy, and in March, when the East-West military confrontation at Berlin began to blow up, the German Communists convoked another Volkskongress, as if they still stood for an all-German political development.

Stalin himself helped to conceal the moment of his shift to blocism in 1948. In January and February, for example, while he was calling the East European governmental delegations to Moscow to sign the treaties which established the Soviet bloc, he stressed the "consistency" of his policies, his desire now as ever for peace, his faith in the "possibility" of cooperation and coexistence among states, and his view that the "imperialist" elements in foreign states could be isolated.[21] In August 1948, with the Berlin blockade in full swing, Stalin informed a group of visiting Allied diplomats: "After all, we are still allies!"[22] In November 1948, Molotov made the continuity and consistency of Soviet foreign policy since the war the major theme of his speech on the anniversary of the Bolshevik Revolution.[23] Judging from such indicators, one might well decide, as many confused contemporaries did, that Soviet policy had been blocist without interruption since the war.

Changes on the Home Front

If it can be argued that, despite Korea, Stalin remained outwardly a defender of established foreign policies well beyond the end of 1947, on the home front this was not so. All through the autumn there were signs of intense political struggle over a matter of vital national interest. At the Cominform meeting Malenkov announced that the Soviet Union could and would revise its Five Year Plan goals upward "to ensure the peace," with the heavy industrial *oblasty* of the east taking the lead.[24] This sounded very like the decision to rearm, which, as we now know, must have been taken at about this time.[25] But it was never published as such, and Malenkov's speech itself was suppressed until 9 December (more than a month after the publication of Zhdanov's speech), when *Pravda* released it in a modified version.[26] One may guess at an explanation: public admission of a need to rearm, and of the existence of a blocist challenge from the West, would have implied the bankruptcy of Zhdanov's foreign policy.

By mid-November *Pravda* was mentioning Malenkov with admiration for the first time in over a year and published an adulatory biographical sketch of Suslov, who, one may recall, had intruded onto Zhdanov's administrative territory during the Cominform meeting.[27] Hereupon the pace of the Soviet economy changed. Early in 1947 the press began to feature "appeals" from various worker groups offering to labor harder for the success of the Five Year Plan. Late in November a Leningrad group seized the initiative and challenged the nation to complete the plan in less than the scheduled five years.[28] At this point the cult of the Party revivalist economic planner N. A. Voznesensky reached new heights. As first deputy prime minister, Stalin is supposed to have placed him in virtually full charge of the Soviet government[29] and gave him permission to publish his voluntarist book *The War Economy of the USSR*. The first review appeared on 12 December in Zhdanov's *Kul'tura i Zhizn'*, and it praised the book to the skies. A flood of such reviews followed, lauding Voznesensky as if he were Stalin or Lenin. Meanwhile, Voznesensky's revivalist allies in the Soviet academic world had managed to oust Eugen Varga, the empiricist, from his leadership of the principal institute of economics. They now used citations from Voznesensky's book to initiate a witch-hunt against Varga and his friends.[30]

On 15 December, the day the Foreign Ministers' Conference adjourned in London, the Soviet regime published a decree signed by Stalin, for the government, and by Zhdanov, for the Party, which went far toward preparing the economy for a major rearmament drive such as Malenkov had mentioned. The decree revoked the existing national currency and established a new one at rates highly unfavorable to private hoarders. At the same time much of the rationing system was abolished, and prices were lowered in the state markets. The result was disaster not only for the black market but for all those citizens who, since 1941, in one fashion or another had managed to accumulate some cash. Particularly hard hit were peasants who sold their produce privately; the inhabitants of the Western territories who had earned currency issued by the German occupation authorities; and returning soldiers who had collected the freely minted Soviet occupation rubles in Europe. The reform placed the entire consumer economy at the regime's disposal, eliminating the last vestige of war-time laxity.[31] Such a decree was surely desirable from a fiscal point of view in Soviet ruling circles because of the long-standing corruption of the ruble. What is more, as a substitute for an explicit announcement of rearmament it had the advantage of not alarming the external world. Politically, its virtue was unmistakable: it gave enormous power to Voznesensky's Central Planning Office; it reflected his theories about how socialist planning could accomplish miracles—simultaneous reconstruction, catching up with the West, consumer goods production, and rearmament too.[32]

The 1947 currency reform was Voznesensky's equivalent to A. A. Kuznetsov's coincident challenge to Beria and the police and to M. I. Rodionov's collusion with the Leningrad Party. It was a bold political challenge to Malenkov, one of the major figures of the Stalin regime and a man who knew all the ropes, by a political neophyte. The reform, thus seen, explains why a year later Voznesensky, with Kuznetsov and Rodionov, fell to Malenkov's and Beria's vengeance in the Leningrad purge.[33] Such adventures were a bureaucratic phenomenon, no doubt encouraged by Stalin but truly originating from below. They represented nervousness—jitters, so to speak—at times when pressure from above was increasing and political tensions were high.

On the home front, as in foreign policy, a major change affected Stalin's line in early 1948. But here there was far less vagueness, far less of an attempt to cover up what happened. One of the first signs appeared late in December when the journal *Kul'tura i Zhizn'* criticized the novelist Aleksandr Fadeev for the novel *Young Guard*, published in 1946 and one of the most characteristic expressions of the victorious Party revival. Fadeev, it was alleged, had paid too much attention to the spontaneous Party enthusiasm of young Communists in the war areas and not enough to the indispensable work of the *apparatchiky* back in Moscow.[34] The criticism was in threatening contrast to Zhdanov's anti-nationalist, *partiinyi* attacks of 1946 on such popular novelists as Konstantin Simonov, who had expressed nationalistic proclivities during the war.[35] At about the same time the anti-blocist decision to back the partition of Palestine proved to be a two-edged sword. Russia was the home of one of the largest Jewish communities in the world.[36] The revolution of 1917 had eased some of the tensions which surrounded the Jews under the tsarist regime. In the 1920s Trotsky, a Jew, was a leading figure in the Bolshevik government, and Jews, insofar as they were not capitalists or religious, enjoyed relative freedom. There were projects to give them a national homeland in the Crimea or in Birobidzhan. But after the great purges destroyed many of the old Bolsheviks and made the rest public enemies, the new elites began to internalize the notion that the revolution of 1917 represented a victory of nationalities and Jews over the Russians. Even during the war against Hitler, the "bestial" destroyer of the Jews, one could hear that Shcherbakov had "cleaned out the Yids from the CPSU."[37] Jews remained prominent as individuals: Kaganovich was a member of the Politburo, and Molotov's wife was a Jew, as was Voroshilov's. The Jewish Anti-Fascist Committee was one of the most useful propaganda organs of the regime.[38] But there was silent resentment, and hate-filled jokes could be heard even in Stalin's inner circle. The Soviet decision to support the Jews in Palestine in 1947 evidently politicized this anti-semitism at home.

Early in January 1948, when Milovan Djilas arrived in Moscow, he encountered Soviet bureaucrats boasting of their anti-semitism. On 12 January, when Stalin and Beria made their attempt to recruit Djilas as a spy, they used anti-semitism as part of the bait. On 13 January at Minsk, political thugs murdered the head of the Jewish Anti-Fascist Committee, Solomon Mikhoels. This murder heralded the end of the freedom which the Jews had enjoyed in the Soviet Union since 1941; Stalin evidently connived in it, thus encouraging a variety of nationalism which was antipathetic to the Party revivalism of the preceding three years.[39]

In mid-January, just after the Mikhoels murder, Zhdanov presided over a hastily convened conference of Soviet musical figures. He was accompanied by Suslov, who by now had become the successor of G. F. Aleksandrov as chief of the Central Committee's Agit-Prop Directorate, intruding into Zhdanov's second major field of responsibility.[40] There had been trouble with a new opera which had been commissioned for the fortieth anniversary of the Bolshevik Revolution and which stressed Party virtues.[41] Zhdanov used the occasion to reverse the cultural line he had set in August 1946 in his speeches about the writers of Leningrad. He was no longer worried by the lack of *partiinost* in cultural works and the excess of naturalness: the "mistakes" he attacked now were "formalism," excess of "cosmopolitanism," and inadequate attention to Russian folk themes.[42] A Central Committee resolution based on the speech was formulated on 10 February and published on 15 February. But unlike Zhdanov's other speeches, this one was not considered worthy of publication in the important Party journals.[43] Evidently he was on the decline.

On 24 January Molotov took up the new line. In Kiev he delivered a speech to the Ukrainian Supreme Soviet filled with strong Russian nationalist sentiments.[44] In February the campaign against "cosmopolitanism" and "formalism" became general, extending even to propaganda aimed at industrial workers. Functionaries in the factories were ordered to stress economic productivity: the Party supremacy of the past three years began to fade from sight.[45] And then came signs of purge. In December 1947 the disgrace which Zhdanov had generated for Khrushchev in 1946 came to an end.[46] On 9 January a major organizational shakeup began in Voznesensky's Planning Office, and in February there was a change of personnel in the Politburo.[47] The stage was set for the debacle of Zhdanovism which occurred during the following summer.[48]

Traditional analysis of Soviet policies has stressed the insulation of the various theaters of Stalin's operations from one another. Any shift in Stalin's foreign policy, it is assumed, was motivated by his struggle with the West over foreign policy objectives; if we lack exact knowledge about these objectives, or about the moment of a policy change, it is because we lack access to the documents, not because Stalin may have been disinterested in foreign policy. However, our review of the background of his change to blocism in Germany in 1948 belies any such assumption. It makes the shift in Germany seem a confused reflection of an earlier domestic political decision to rearm, and the important issues behind it, battles fought in domestic political terms by Stalin's lieutenants. The imbalance of the traditional perception of Stalin's priorities appears even more striking, moreover, when one studies developments in the theater of international Communism during the winter of 1947–1948.

Insurrectionism

In October 1947, after the announcement of the Cominform meeting, the European Communists made the best of the unintelligible in Stalin's meanings: they decided he intended them to consult more with each other and to move more rapidly toward socialism. In this spirit the Communist parties of France and Italy began to put pressure on their governments to take them back into the cabinet and to abandon the essentially pro-American and anti-Soviet foreign policy courses then being followed. The pressure came to a head late in November in a series of mighty strikes which, particularly in France, almost toppled the regime. These strikes failed, of course. By 7 December even Soviet analysts showed signs of recognizing this,[49] and by 9 December the strike wave in France was ending.

Judging from the political aftermath in Moscow, the lesson of the strikes was that the solutions Zhdanov had formulated at the Cominform meeting would not work—that he had failed. But, paradoxically, outside the Soviet Union the strikes probably contributed to a sense of growing excitement throughout the world Communist movement. Events in Greece in particular suggest this. There the Communist Party, which was heavily influenced by Tito, decided in mid-September (and announced on 8 October) that the time had come to resort to all-out civil war. For a year it had been organizing a guerrilla movement but, with one eye on Moscow, at the same time continued legal political activity. Now the Party leader, Nikos Zachariades, announced the Party's abandonment of legal work and went abroad. Perhaps because of a deep split in the Party leadership over tactics, there was no action along Zachariades' line for almost two months. But after the West European strikes (and despite their failure), the opposition swung into step, and on 24 December its leader, Markos Vafiades, announced from the mountains the establishment of a "temporary democratic government" in Macedonia and launched an offensive to capture a "capital city" in northern Greece.[50]

This was by no means the only sign of extraordinary excitement in the Communist movement as a result of the strikes in the West. In Yugoslavia Tito indulged in some remarkable adventures. Ever since 1944 one of his major political objectives seems to have been a Balkan federation uniting Yugoslavia and Bulgaria. This effort failed, so far as one can tell, at a conference at Bled in the summer of 1947.[51] Thereupon he attempted a flanking movement on a Danubian scale,

297

designed to capture what the Bulgarians had refused him. He bid first for a customs union with Albania. This led to a split in the Albanian Communist leadership and the suicide in protest, early in December, of one of its members.[52] Next a similar union was proposed to Bulgaria, and late in November Tito made a trip to Sofia to sign a military alliance and a customs agreement. Capitalizing on his alleged prestige in Moscow, he managed to turn the visit into a triumphal march, making it seem as if he were Stalin's second-in-command within the Communist movement. On 2 December he announced in the Yugoslav Skupshchina (parliament) that "the borders in essence have disappeared," and turned north. On 6 December he arrived in Budapest to sign a pact similar to the one with Bulgaria.[53] On 17 December he appeared in Bucharest for a similar purpose, spreading rumors everywhere of a coming Danubian federation of some sort. His boldness not only did not abate but mounted after the failure of the West European strikes: just after Christmas he removed from office Andrije Hebrang, Stalin's principal spy in the Yugoslav Party leadership.[54]

In Asia at almost the same time there were equally remarkable signs of Communist enthusiasm. For over a year, it may be recalled, Mao Tse-tung had guided the CCP away from coalitionism into overt civil war, but, because of Stalin, he had avoided theoretical rejection of the coalition line. In the autumn of 1947, however, a CCP representative visited Belgrade and wrote reports in his Party's daily newspaper.[55] Then came the French and Italian strikes, and on 25 December (the day of the Greek Communist declaration of civil war) Mao announced to a CCP Central Committee meeting that the struggle with Chiang Kai-shek was openly a "people's liberation war," and that it had reached a turning point—that victory would come soon.[56] Late in December the Communist Party of India likewise turned to radicalism: its newly installed leadership denounced the long-standing CPInd policy of support for Nehru's Indian national coalition and proclaimed a struggle for a people's democracy in India which would be aimed against the so-called national bourgeoisie.[57] This action threatened the coalitionary movement throughout the colonial and recently colonial Third World, with all that such a breakdown would imply for worsening relationships between the Soviet Union and the West,[58] and there were widespread rumors that Yugoslav influence lay behind the Indian Communists' shift.[59]

To a man of Stalin's ideological bias and strategic vision, the meaning of these developments must have seemed unmistakable. He knew perfectly well that Tito enjoyed great influence in the Greek Party. The suicide in Albania could have recalled to him some of the "suicides" he himself had engineered during the 1930s among colleagues in the Soviet Party who had turned against him. Tito's triumphant travels and the removal of Hebrang could have seemed a direct challenge to his own role as leader of the Communist movement, and to his suspicious eye their coincidence with the emergence of radicalism in the Communist parties of Asia bespoke a conspiracy against him. His response was electric. Neither his change from anti-blocism to blocism in foreign policy nor his shift away from *Zhdanovism* on the domestic political scene could be pinpointed, but one may be precise about when he started his offensive against the insurrectionists abroad.

Within days of the deposition of Hebrang in Belgrade, Stalin invited the Yugoslav Communists to send one of their leaders—Djilas was suggested—to Moscow "for discussions." Djilas arrived in the Soviet capital about 12 January, the day before the Mikhoels murder. Stalin received him immediately, an extraordinary event (most visitors had to wait several weeks before being received), and attempted to recruit him as a spy to replace the deposed Hebrang.[60] Meanwhile, he began an attempt to isolate the Chinese from other radical Communists of the world. On 6 January 1948, *Pravda* published the gist of Mao's speech of 25 December without commentary, but juxtaposed it to a TASS denial of Western reports that the Soviet Union was sending aid to the CCP.[61] When talking to foreign Communists, Stalin now made no secret of the fact that the Chinese Communists had declared war without his approval.[62] *Pravda* throughout 1948 showed general lack of interest in China.[63] What happened there was Chinese business, it seemed, and it was to be made clear to all that the emerging revolution there was *not* a signal from Stalin for spontaneous revolution around the world.

Stalin used rougher tactics in the Balkans. First, in rapid succession he summoned top-level delegations from Poland, Rumania, and Hungary to Moscow to sign the state treaties of mutual assistance mentioned earlier. Then he attacked. On 21 January Georgi Dimitrov, on a visit to Bucharest, held a press conference during which he spoke favorably about Tito's federation projects. *Pravda* reported this without comment on 23 January but on 28 January called Dimitrov sharply to heel, pronouncing that no federations were needed at all. At a congress of the Bulgarian Communists early in February, Dimitrov retracted his statement, but it was clear that Stalin's interest was in Tito. He summoned the top Yugoslav and Bulgarian leaders to Moscow. On 10 February he organized a new seminar of leading Communists, and there he personally tried to extract from the Yugoslav leaders the self-criticism which Zhdanov had spared them at Szklarska Poręba.[64] He told them also that the civil war in Greece had to be "rolled up."[65]

Just at this time in Czechoslovakia the struggle for power between Communists and non-Communists was becoming acute. In that country, almost alone in Eastern Europe, the outcome was not foreseeable, and a deadline loomed, for national elections were scheduled for the late spring, and there were indications that the Communists would lose ground heavily if the elections were free. By mid-January an atmosphere of crisis was observable within the CPCz. On 3 February Rudolf Slánský delivered a speech which was widely interpreted as heralding political action. On 7 February the trade union organization scheduled a congress which would bring very large numbers of Communist-organized workers to Prague on 22 February.[66]

Whether and, if so, to what extent the Communist seizure of power during the February crisis in Prague was "planned in Moscow" is still not clear. There is a good deal of evidence that after the Cominform meeting the Czechoslovak Party leadership, like the others discussed, simply assumed from Zhdanov's ambiguities that it should step up its battle for power, and that during the early winter it was swept along by radical elements in the Party's ranks. Indeed, the February crisis may have been sparked by some junior Communists in the police, who staged a provocation without the permission of Gottwald and Slánský,[67] and no tangible evidence came to light, even in 1968, of Soviet "directives" ordering a seizure of power.[68] Once the crisis was under way, however, Stalin seized his opportunity. Abandoning the caution which he had shown in Eastern Europe since 1945, he allowed the Red Army to request passage through Czechoslovakia for Soviet military units. With much fanfare he dispatched a Soviet deputy foreign minister, V. Zorin, to Prague to investigate some "economic matters" just as the Communists went into action: and in other ways, both subtle and blatant, he let it appear that Soviet armed might was at the disposal of revolutionary forces abroad.[69] Under his aegis the Czechoslovak Communists slipped into power. By March, therefore, it was clear that revolution might well proceed just as in the past, not separately in every country but coordinated with and supervised by the world's first socialist state. Tito had been outflanked.

The Berlin Crisis

Challenged from the West during the final months of 1947, Stalin displayed far more interest in matters of domestic policy than in foreign affairs. His foreign policy stance was clearly defensive until the wave of insurrectionism broke in the Balkans and the Far East at the turn of the year. Then his interest in the external world picked up, he leapt into action, and singlemindedly grasped every opportunity which came his way to contain the radical Communists. The American political theorists of the Kennan school, who were just then preaching containment to the West, would have been abashed had they recognized that Stalin was a master at their game.

Was Stalin then altogether free of responsibility for the debacle of the peace and the start of the Cold War in 1948? To find the answer, it is worth while to look further into the events of 1948. On 22 February, at the very height of the crisis in Czechoslovakia, Stalin wrote a letter (published on the 28th) to J. Paasikivi, the president of Finland, inviting Finland to sign a treaty of non-aggression and mutual assistance with the Soviet Union similar to those just signed with Rumania and Hungary.[70] The letter constituted a demand that Finland, like the rest of Eastern Europe, join the Soviet bloc. If ever there was a clear sign that Stalin himself was pressing for change in the status quo abroad, the start of his action in Finland was it.

Not Finland, however, but Berlin is the true measure of whether or not Stalin acted responsibly in international affairs during 1948. Indeed, the Finnish action was sidetracked (perhaps for Soviet domestic political reasons)[71] late in the spring, and its outcome can be cited as proof of how "reasonable" Stalin was in that year of crisis. But the same may not be said of events in Germany, where the Soviet security agencies acted during the spring in curious synchronism with Stalin's campaign to topple Tito.

On 1 March 1948 the Yugoslav CP Central Committee pointedly ignored the spectacle of Stalin's statist patronage of revolution in Czechoslovakia and his invitation to the Finns, and indicated its solidarity with Tito by expelling Andrije Hebrang from the Party.[72] Less than three weeks later, on 18 and 19 March, the Soviet government abruptly withdrew its military and civilian advisors from Belgrade.

And on 27 March, after the Yugoslavs protested the withdrawal, Stalin sent the first of his now famous sneering and bitter letters to the Yugoslav Communist leadership. As it happened, exactly coincident with these events came the first escalation of the military confrontation at Berlin. On 10 March V. D. Sokolovsky, the Soviet member of the Berlin Allied Control Council, violently declared that all further discussion about Western policy in Germany was useless. On 20 March he closed down the council. On 31 March Soviet forces began their harassment of Allied communications with Berlin. During April, therefore, when Stalin circulated his letter to the Yugoslavs among the leading Communists of Eastern Europe requesting their support, the Berlin action was firmly underlining his worth as a revolutionary.

On 13 April the Yugoslavs wrote to Stalin refusing to submit. On 4 May Moscow threatened to take up the controversy at a forthcoming meeting of the Cominform. On 19 May the Yugoslavs received a message from Suslov by special courier, inviting them to the Cominform meeting; another letter of 22 May confirmed that at the request of the Hungarians and Czechoslovaks the meeting would take place in the latter half of June. The Yugoslavs decided not to attend, and the showdown began. Meanwhile, clouds were gathering in Germany, despite occasional signs of a Kremlin desire for relaxation of the tensions. By the end of May the Western forces in Berlin were already seriously embarrassed by Soviet interruption of land communications. As recounted earlier, the Western Powers early in June agreed among themselves to put Western Germany on its feet— specifically, to institute a currency reform as a basis for economic recovery and to convoke a West German constituent assembly. The East German Communists responded with a massive protest, but soon began openly organizing a government of their own. The Russians in turn let it be known that they also would institute a currency reform. The Western Powers were not deterred but on 18 June issued their new deutsche mark. On the 23rd the East Germans and Russians issued an East German currency; on the 24th the Soviet army imposed a complete land blockade of the Western zones of Berlin; and it was to this action that the Americans responded on the 26th with their airlift.

On 19 June a Soviet cable to Belgrade renewed the invitation to the Cominform meeting and commanded the Yugoslav delegation to appear at Bucharest no later than the 21st. Once again the Yugoslavs declined to attend. Only then did Stalin go into action. The Cominform delegates who were convened in Rumania under the leadership of Zhdanov and Suslov decided that Tito was a deviationist of "rightist," even "counter-revolutionary," inclination. They then expelled the Yugoslav Communist Party from their organization.

Both for Stalin (who, as noted elsewhere, loved anniversaries) and for the Yugoslavs, the most delicious touch in this theatrical performance was the publication of the Cominform declaration on 28 June. The day was Vidov Dan, the anniversary of the battle of Kossovo and of the assassination of 1914, the Serbian national holiday. This is the surest sign that Stalin at least synchronized the Berlin confrontation with the climax of his battle with Tito, starting a war scare, just as he had in March 1945 and March 1946, so as to emphasize his domestic political manipulations.

14

Epilogue

Deluge

IN THE KREMLIN a deluge followed
Tito's resistance to the Cominform. On 20 July, three weeks after the
Cominform meeting, *Pravda* published a telegram from the CPSU(b)
Central Committee to the Central Committee of the Communist Party
of Japan, signed by Malenkov, who was identified as a member of the
Secretariat. This marked Malenkov's decisive return to the seat of
power from which he had been ousted during the *Zhdanovshchina*,
and suggested Zhdanov's loss of control over the development of
Communism in the Far East (which was just then, of course, in the
forefront of the world revolution).[1] Meanwhile great events were
brewing in Soviet agriculture, which Malenkov had been supervising
in the Council of Ministers for over a year. During the spring
Zhdanov had inspired (through his son, Yurii, the head of the Central
Committee's Division of Science) an attack on the pseudo-genetics of
T. D. Lysenko. The latter, though not a Party member, apparently

had access to Stalin's ear, and fought back by seeking to pack the Lenin All-Union Academy of Agricultural Sciences with his adherents. On 15 July the Council of Ministers approved this operation. On 31 July the Academy's annual meeting began, and Lysenko staged a putsch. He announced that his report had been approved in advance by Stalin, the entire Soviet press came out in support of him, and Yurii Zhdanov had to publish a letter (dated 10 July) apologizing for having supported Mendelian genetics. By the end of August, the Council of Ministers was imposing Lysenkoism by decree throughout the Soviet state educational system and in all agricultural institutions, and the press was heralding the agrarian plans which were later known collectively as "The Great Stalin Projects for Remaking Nature."[2] Lysenko's "voluntarist" technology was replacing the "voluntarist" *partiinost* of N. A. Voznesensky through the action not of the Communist Party, but of the state.

On 30 August Zhdanov died. He received a magnificent Party funeral, but very shortly numerous figures in the Soviet political world who in one way or another could be associated with him fell on hard times. On 21 September Il'ya Ehrenburg published an article in *Pravda* which raised the question of divided loyalties among Jews, a clear menace to the Soviet policy of supporting Israel. In October, when the first Israeli ambassador arrived in Moscow, the Jews of the city demonstrated their delight in the streets. In November, one after the other, the flourishing Jewish political and cultural organizations of the Soviet Union were systematically abolished, most of their leaders were arrested, and their membership was terrorized. Even Molotov's wife, who was Jewish, was sent to a camp.[3] Meanwhile, a massive reorganization hit the Party's central secretarial apparatus, and a new regime was introduced which emphasized Party subordination to the state's economic interests.[4] In December, A. A. Kuznetsov was mentioned for the last time in the press. In January a purge was instituted among Zhdanov's former followers at Leningrad. In March Molotov was relieved of his post as foreign minister, Zhdanov's other top-level allies—Bulganin, Mikoyan, and Voznesensky—also lost their posts and the Central Committee started a vicious attack on M. I. Rodionov of Gorky. By the time this "Leningrad affair" was wound up in 1950, Voznesensky, Kuznetsov, and Rodionov had all lost their lives, as had hundreds of former Party officials from Leningrad.[5]

So tight were the walls of secrecy and fear which surrounded the Soviet world from 1948 until after Stalin's death in 1953 that few

Westerners heard about the Leningrad affair until years after the event. But outsiders knew there was terror and, in part because they could only see the exterior of the system, they came to judge that Stalin's power was as total as Hitler's had been in Germany and certainly more so than Mussolini's, though the latter had invented the term "totalitarianism." In the fifties it was regularly implied in the United States that Stalin ruled without problems from the apex of the system, in absolute control. Laughter greeted memories of the "prisoner of the Politburo" illusions of the postwar years.

The fear was certainly there, Soviet society was ice-bound, and Stalin was adulated beyond measure. But if everything went exactly his way, how can one explain the fact that at the height of the Leningrad purge in the spring of 1949, Stalin's daughter married Zhdanov's son, with her father's approval, and that she remembers him as having actually liked and respected Zhdanov?[6] Further, as we have observed in earlier chapters, Stalin developed a rarified system for political control after the war—manipulation of the personality cult—and until 1948 Zhdanov played a crucial role in the system. He was one of the two "poles" through which Stalin sought to activate the vast bureaucracies of the Party and the state (the other was Malenkov). Clearly Stalin was pressing Zhdanov rather hard at the time of the latter's death, but one may question whether Stalin would willingly have liquidated the entire system by having Zhdanov murdered (even though in 1953 it was implied that Zhdanov had been murdered).[7] It seems more reasonable by far to construe that Zhdanov's death took Stalin by surprise, and if that was the case, then all that followed appears not as a reflection of deliberate, specific decisions by an all-powerful dictator totally in control but as the result of an accidental, sudden imbalance in a vast system of conflicting bureaucracies.[8] Stalin appears as the victim of that "nature" which his propagandists claimed he was about to transform, and the prosecutors of the Leningrad affair turn out to be Malenkov and Beria, just as Khrushchev tells us, moved by their own sudden excess of power and their own fear, not by Stalin's commands.[9]

In effect, the more one learns about the central workings of the Soviet system during the final years of Stalin's life, the more one may be impressed not by the freedom of his power but by his frustration. The whole society was "gasping for air" under the weight of the bureaucracy—of this there can be no doubt. But the atmosphere was quite different from the mass hysteria which had convulsed Moscow during the 1930s: the purging of the 1950s seemed much more purposeful. The Leningrad affair reflected the vengeful feelings of Malenkov and Beria as they returned to power. It was followed by surprising moves on Stalin's part: late in 1949 he called Khrushchev, who had been a Party revivalist in 1945, to an eminent position in Moscow.[10] Next, despite all the objectivity he had displayed toward Marxism-Leninism in 1945 and 1946, Stalin returned to its use as the vehicle for his line. In 1950 he published a series of papers regarding Marxist theory and linguistics, manipulating references to "pedantry" and "far-sightedness" to suggest political directions.[11] There followed a new series of political purges which particularly affected the Caucasus, which seemed to be directed against the head of the secret police, Beria, himself, and which by their very existence suggested that in 1950 and 1951 Stalin's power was limited—that Beria was somehow able to resist.[12]

Beria's strength is suggested also by the denouement of Stalin's career in 1953, the "doctors' plot," an affair which (it now seems) was directed against the police chief and which almost destroyed him—at a price. The price was a compromise with the Malenkovs— with the former home-front industrialists of the war era, with the bureaucrats of the new class, and with the generals of the army. In 1952 at the Nineteenth Congress of the CPSU(b) Stalin placed these people at the head of the system, at last removing the word "Bolshevik" from the Party masthead and abandoning the silent threat of any new *Zhdanovshchina*. Only then did the campaign against Beria show signs of bearing fruit, and we may assume, accordingly, that within the inner realm of Soviet power during Stalin's last years, despite all the groveling before him, the praise of his name, and the prisons for the common people, he had limited control. Perhaps Stalin's daughter sensed his frustration when she recalled, "He was seventy-two by this time (1951) but his stride was brisk as he walked through the park with the fat generals of the bodyguard panting to keep up with him. Suddenly he would change course and run right into them. It made him explode with anger, and he scolded the first one who happened to be handy on some trivial pretext or another."[13]

Revolution

The Cominform's expulsion of Tito stunned the Communists of Europe. All of the parties for three years, some for four, had been caught up in the enthusiasm of battling on separate roads to socialism. The struggle had not always been smooth. In the Western countries for a year the specter of failure had loomed. But in the East the Communist parties had been successful in seizing power. An unheard-of expansion of socialism had actually occurred. The Yugoslavs had increasingly seemed to be the finest example of how the new revolution had been fought. They were Zhdanov's allies, Stalin's apparent favorites among the Communists abroad. Now at the moment of victory they were in disgrace, and the whole doctrine whereby different countries might proceed by new methods and new national patterns was clearly suspect. The shock was so great to some of the leaders of the Yugoslav Party that they became ill—one actually lost his hair.[14] Gomułka, the most powerful Communist in Poland, lost his self-control in public a few months later, when he was forced to acknowledge the consequences of Tito's disgrace for his own illusions.[15] For thousands of lesser Communists across the continent there was a reckoning and psychological agony: all they had fought for seemed at stake.[16] For the Muscovites, who had had some warning of the coming fall of Tito early in the year, there was an additional shock, even more stunning, at the end of August, when Zhdanov died and the world of the Kremlin to which they had grown accustomed fell into disarray.

For European Communists outside Yugoslavia, however, there was no choice of alternatives after 28 June 1948. To condemn Tito might be bad, but to defy Stalin and to join Tito was morally impossible—incomparably worse. The success which Stalin had achieved in mastering the revolutionary movements in Europe over the past three years is indicated by the fact that there were almost no defections to Yugoslavia from the European Communist parties, east or west, in 1948 and after. Stalin issued no more policy statements in 1948 and 1949 than he had in 1947, but his enigmatic silence at last paid off: his manipulations proved to be, in effect, extraordinarily responsive to the alienated mentality to which the Communist movement appealed in Europe.

In the East European countries, one might say, it was not psychology but force which produced the "captive mind" among the Communists.[17] As noted elsewhere, in September 1948 Gomułka, the leading "separate roadist" Communist in Poland, was, in effect, deposed. In December 1948 and January 1949, Dimitrov in Bulgaria, Rákosi in Hungary, and Bierut in Poland publicly denied the doctrine of "separate roadism" and identified people's democracy with a dictatorship of the proletariat of the Soviet type. In June 1949 "Titoists" were placed on public trial in Albania. In October in Hungary the Communist Party, which had already shown its cleverness by extracting a public confession from a cardinal of the Roman Catholic Church, put its own most prominent "separate roadist," the former minister of the interior, László Rajk, on trial as a Yugoslav-American spy, and he confessed his "guilt," just as had the victims in the Soviet purge trials of the 1930s. Meanwhile, in almost all the East European countries the Communist parties introduced measures which in short order "sovietized" their political systems, economies, and cultural life. Only the Czechoslovak Party was backward, but after 1950 it too caught up, and in Prague in the last month of 1952 the most vicious of all the Stalinist political trials in Europe took place. Spontaneous as all this purported to be at the time, we know today that much of it was directly stage-managed by the Russians.[18]

Yet if one can argue that Red Army guns and Beria's police were in part responsible for these horrifying excesses in the East, one must recognize that in the parties of the West the same thing happened— the same "state of siege" mentality, the same quasi-ecstasy of belief in Stalin appeared—for exclusively psychological reasons. In 1949 the chief of the French Communist Party, Maurice Thorez, declared publicly that his followers would fight against their country if the Red Army invaded it—and yet the Party remained strong, an island as immune to the temptations of the democratic society around it as the Western island at Berlin was to the attractions of the Communist East.[19] Stalin had entirely mastered the Communist mentality in Europe, and until his death his control remained firm in both East and West.

In Asia, Stalin's mastery of what he viewed as "the revolution" was far less complete after 1948. As in Europe, of course, Communists glorified the name of Stalin in all the Asiatic countries, but, as we have seen, Soviet attention to the affairs of Asia tended to be sporadic, intensive only during crises such as the moment of Japan's collapse in 1945 and of Mao's turn to civil war late in 1947. It is not really surprising, therefore, that in 1948 and 1949 the Communists of Burma, Malaya, Indonesia, Vietnam, and the Philippines resorted to armed warfare—or abstained from it—in ignorance of Stalin's line.[20] The Tito crisis and the Cominform were too far away for them, too European. Even after the Communist victory in China during 1949,

309

these Southeast Asian Communist parties took their cues at least as much from Peking as from Moscow and waged battles of their own.[21]

In Korea, of course, where Soviet troops were an occupying force, and to some extent in Japan, the Communists followed the European model of submission to Stalin, but even here the determining factor in their behavior was not psychological subjection to Stalin's line but consciousness of Chinese Communist power, and in China, as is now known, Stalin met his equal. When Mao was in trouble in 1947, Stalin did nothing to help. When Mao went to war in 1948, Stalin ignored him. But in 1950, when Mao was victorious, Stalin, despite his efforts to pretend the victory was unimportant, had to make concessions, withdrawing from the territories he had acquired from Chiang Kai-shek in 1945.[22] Many authorities feel that world Communism's great political adventure in 1950—the Korean war—was, if not instigated,[23] at least tolerated by Stalin because it might involve the Chinese Communists in a direct military confrontation with the West which the Chinese might well lose.[24] In his last years, in this sense, Stalin was still dependent on the provocateur tools he had employed in Europe in 1945, 1946, and 1948. On the whole, however, even in Asia Stalin's success at controlling the Communists was remarkable, for Mao in the long run accepted Stalin's authority, used many of his political models in the construction of socialism in China, waited until he was dead before attempting to assert his own ideal for the world movement, and then, during Moscow's destalinization campaigns, kept Stalin's name in the Marxist pantheon.

To paraphrase Henri Pirenne, without Stalin there would have been no Eisenhower. Without Stalin's insistence that communism labor for peace instead of insurrection, the bourgeoisies of the West would have been far less triumphant in the decade after 1948, their social consciences far less clear, and in the Third World the revolt against colonialism could not have been postponed.

Peace

In February and March 1948 some Communist veterans of the wartime resistance movement in France organized a movement called Combattants de la Liberté, whose goal was to mobilize the general public for peace. In August, six weeks after the expulsion of the Yugoslavs from the Cominform and at the height of the crisis over

Berlin, a world congress of intellectuals for peace assembled at Wrocław (Breslau) and attracted a considerable number of non-Communists. Aleksandr Fadeev, the leader of the Soviet delegation, almost caused a walkout by delivering a tirade against both "American war-mongers" and Jean-Paul Sartre. But this crisis was avoided, and after Stalin issued a statement favoring peace in October, and Molotov on 6 November declared that the constant and unwavering goal of Soviet diplomacy since the war had been peace, a world peace movement began to mushroom, controlled from Moscow but with its center in France.[25]

At Paris in April 1949 the first World Peace Congress met. In the summer of 1950, even before the start of the war in Korea, the peace movement launched an appeal from Stockholm; by the end of the year the petition had 500 million signatures. In November 1950 a second World Peace Congress met at Warsaw and launched a "peace appeal" which, in the course of a year, attracted 562 million signatures (a quarter of the world's population, although 90 percent were from behind the iron curtain). This peace movement became one of the principal features of late Stalinist Soviet foreign policy and has led even Western historians to grant that in the 1950s, as after the war, Stalin's goal was, in the long run, some kind of peace—some kind of stable system of interrelations whereby his state could coexist and even cooperate with the imperialists of the West.

But peace did not come. Stalin strove so hard throughout his career to escape the revolution and to build a great state that one may suppose that this is in fact what he wanted. As the leader of the Soviet state he offered his friendship to Hitler in 1939 and was rejected in 1941. He gave his friendship to the West during the war, and after 1947 the Allies also rejected him, with results so disastrous that during the last years of his life he existed as an abnormality in the world political arena.

The reasons for this failure were in part no doubt structural. The Soviet state was in too may respects incongruous with the foreign states with which Stalin attempted to deal. It was overheavy with bureaucracy, whereas they were decentralized; it was a backward and impoverished country, where they were rich; it could not afford to grant its peoples freedom, whereas they by their nature insisted on open frontiers. So great were the structural differences between the Soviet Union and the Western Powers in the postwar period that one may seriously wonder whether any accommodation between them

311

was possible at all. Even such phenomena as Stalin's war scares and Molotov's insulting diplomacy in the years just after the war can be chalked up to structural differences between the Soviet Union and the West. If one is a pessimist, if one believes that there may be no peace without control, that there could have been no peace without stability inside the Soviet Union and controls on the Communists abroad, then the whole story told in this book is evidence that Stalin worked for peace. Certainly all of his policies from 1944 to 1948 were directed ultimately toward achieving control.

To suggest the other side of the question of why Stalin's peace drive failed, let us conclude by pointing to one thing that might have been different. Stalin's public silence was of great utility to him, as we have seen repeatedly, in his efforts to control foreign Communists. Had he spoken as glibly and freely as Harry Truman did, he could not have sustained the illusion that he was really a revolutionary, a fitting heir to Lenin and Marx, worthy of homage from insurrectionists all over the world. Correspondingly, Stalin's silence at the end of the war was, as far as we can tell, a matter of sheer necessity to him at home. Had he spoken out against the Party in the hour of victory, there was a very real danger that his authority would have been undermined, and that he might have been forced to retire.

In the conduct of the foreign relations of the Soviet state, however, this silence was extremely harmful to Stalin's interests. Diplomats cannot grasp the intention of a statesman when it is not voiced. Though he wanted peace, he did not explain to outsiders the methods he would use to attain it, apart from some coy asides in the period of the Potsdam and London conferences in 1945. As a result, outsiders disregarded his statements altogether, and put him in the group of forces of disorder which they wanted to contain, judging his intentions from the actions of foreign Communist insurrectionists and Soviet bureaucrats. The excess of cleverness and the obsessive fear which kept Stalin silent in public after the war, it seems, prevented him from attaining the successful peace which might have been his.

Epilogue

Addendum to Chapter 3:
Excerpts from Ernö Gerö's Memoir

Some recently published notes by Ernö Gerö, who was second in command in the Hungarian Communist Party in 1944, cast sharp light on the beginnings of Soviet rule in East Central Europe. Gerö's notes confirm that Stalin initially regarded the countries of that region as subject to the same conditions of development as the West European countries liberated by the Americans and the British and that he was not always honest with his fellow Communists.

Gerö's notes require some explanation. On 15 October 1944 Admiral Horthy, the regent of Hungary, attempted unsuccessfully to follow the example of King Michael of Rumania and to "jump out" of the German into the Allied camp. Some military representatives of his regime thereupon proceeded to Moscow to negotiate an armistice with the Russians, but in Budapest an overtly fascist government under Ferenc Szálasi emerged, and the Red Army overran eastern Hungary. Early in November, Gerö and other Muscovite Hungarian Communists arrived at Szeged, behind Soviet lines, announced the re-establishment of the Hungarian CP, and published an "action program," of which they sent a copy to Dimitrov, their contact in Moscow. This program gave the Allied governments a free rein in the selection of a government for liberated Hungary, but envisaged the emergence, alongside that government, of a "constitutional assembly" to "consolidate" a new democratic order which the Communists would found. During November, as the front advanced toward the Danube, the Russians sought to establish a government based on elements of the Horthy regime, but no one with an adequate power base could be found to lead it. Finally, on 20 November, the CPH chief, Rákosi, called Szeged from Moscow to say that the Soviet Union had decided to form a government based in part on popular forces inside Hungary. The Gerö group at Szeged now hastily arranged for the emergence of a "Hungarian National Independence Front" composed of several political parties, elicited from it a proposal for the establishment of a coalition government, and dispatched a delegation to Moscow to join the Horthyist generals. The delegation was small, but it included Gerö and another important Muscovite Communist, Imre Nagy. Between 1 and 5 December these Communists met two or three times in Molotov's Kremlin office with Rákosi, Molotov, the latter's deputy commissar, V. G. Dekanozov[1] (an asso-

313

ciate of Beria's), and G. M. Pushkin, who was later the political adviser of the Allied Control Commission in Budapest. There was one meeting at which Molotov was absent, chaired by Dekanozov; once or twice Stalin came in from a neighboring room to participate.

Gerö wrote down Stalin's words in Russian immediately after the meetings. His notes are preserved in the MSzMP Party History Institute at Budapest and are supplemented by a memoir which he wrote many years later. The following is a translation of the published excerpts from the memoir, together with quotations from the notes, and a bracketed synopsis of the unpublished material.[2]

> When we discussed the question of Hungary with Molotov in his office, we saw that he was well acquainted with the [CPH action program, as was Stalin. Gerö deduced for the first time then that Dimitrov had shown the documents to the Soviet leadership.]
> When we brought out [that the CPH had changed position, and that in place of a legitimate government] we wanted to establish a Provisional National Government and a Provisional National Assembly, we encountered sharp opposition from Molotov's deputy, Dekanozov. Dekanozov referred to the French model and wanted us to establish a National Liberation Committee and an Advisory Body. Just as I was speaking against Dekanozov's project, Stalin entered the room. He asked what we were discussing. I summarized the discussion and the arguments for our point of view. Stalin supported the Hungarian Communists: "A Provisional Government must be established, not a National Committee." His reasons were as follows: 1. If the Szálasi people have a government, why should the patriots have only a Liberation Committee? 2. The Hungarian comrades say that the situation is ripe for a Provisional Government. They surely know the situation better than we, so we must accept their point of view. [Stalin then went on to say:] "But people will ask where this government comes from. We would have accepted Horthy, but the Germans took him away and forced him to sign documents. Horthy is morally a corpse, but the Szálasi people nonetheless have a point. The generals [who came to Moscow] have nothing. It is necessary to establish a source of authority [*Neobkhodimo sozdavati istochnik vlasti*]. This has been done actually or for form's sake in every other country. De Gaulle started with his Advisory Assembly. Let the Hungarian comrades think about their proposal in this context. Look at history."
> [In such fashion Stalin entirely closed the government-or-committee question. A final decision against "legitimacy" followed only later, however. The decisive factors were] first of all, naturally, the emergence on liberated territory of a broad revolutionary movement. Second, Horthy's behavior—the fact that even though under pressure he himself signed the nomination of Szálasi as prime minister. In this connection, Stalin

said: "Horthy committed political suicide [*On policheskii (sic) rasstrel-yal sebya*] when he named Szálasi." For the Russians, this was the main reason for rejecting Horthy. The Hungarians simply accepted this thesis. Finally, naturally, our own theories played a role. Stalin carefully listened to them, approved what we said, and supported us—not just with regard to the government and national assembly, but with regard to the entire character of the new power. [Stalin also said:] "As far as the Provisional National Assembly or Advisory Body goes, it is important that according to the Hungarian comrades there is a tradition behind a National Assembly, whereas an advisory body would have none. The French analogy doesn't hold because De Gaulle was in northern Africa, not on French soil, and was forced to establish an advisory body. The Hungarian comrades are on native soil so they can go further. It's better to do the job more broadly and more democratically."

[On 1 December, the first day of the discussions, the Russians still insisted:] There has to be a manifesto or announcement and it must contain something about Horthy. [On the first day, likewise, Stalin said:] "The National Council must be put together from representatives of the urban and rural institutions of local government. If there are trade unions, without fail their people must be brought in too; so also, representatives of cooperatives and other social organizations. The Party— not at the start." [On the first day the Hungarians mentioned that the new government would need an armed force. It was agreed that this could be organized either in the Western Ukraine or in Hungary. The Soviet Union would release any Hungarian prisoners of war who proved willing to participate in the fight against the Germans.] They would wear national uniforms. [They could use captured German weapons or Soviet weapons. The problem of a currency for the new regime was discussed. It was decided that the manifesto] must absolutely mention the question of land reform. The great estates must be given to the peasants. One cannot hold back the land from the peasants just in Hungary while land reform is being instituted in neighboring countries. [The Soviet leaders mentioned the Polish land reform in this connection.]

[Gerö's notes read:] "One mustn't bring into the government the exchangees [the Hungarian Communists who were ransomed to the Soviet Union in 1940]. They'll be considered Moscow puppets. At home this will be a different question. But let the people elect them." [This shows Moscow's extreme caution in all these discussions vis-à-vis the Hungarian public and the Western Allies.]

[The notes also say:] "You have to call in [the Horthy generals] and speak squarely to them. The best policy is a direct policy. Tell them it's time to pay. Tell them that if they won't participate [in the government] then others will come and the government will be more leftist. [This shows how important Moscow considered the question of legitimacy.]

[At the end, while promising the Soviet government's far-reaching assistance to the Hungarians, Stalin spoke emphatically:] "But Soviet power cannot do everything for them. Let them do some struggling, let they themselves do some work!"

[The discussions with Molotov and Stalin were interrupted between 1 and 5 December by General De Gaulle's visit to Moscow. In the interval, the Hungarians decided to argue for a Provisional National Assembly to be elected, not just selected, and for representation not just of the old-regime institutions of local government but also of the national committees which were being set up in the liberated territories. By this plan the Assembly would then elect the Provisional Government. Meanwhile,] the Soviet comrades proposed [three Horthyist generals] as prime minister, war minister, and minister of food. They explained that a war was on, and that the government must include generals respected by the Hungarian officer corps. The Hungarians proposed [the Communists] Imre Nagy for agriculture and József Gábor for transport. We left the other portfolios open, but agreed that we would fill out the list at Debrecen so as to give the Smallholder, Social Democratic, and National Peasant parties suitable representation. [The 5 December meeting ratified these modifications of the 1 December decisions. In practice, the elections were carried out mainly by the national committees.]

[Most of the 5 December meeting was devoted to the draft of the new government's manifesto, which derived from the action program of the CPH.] During the last discussions with Molotov, Stalin came into the office. Among other matters Stalin spoke about our program, saying that it was on the whole good, but that in his opinion we ought to underline more strongly the defense of private property and the preservation and development of private enterprise [*Po gushche o chastnoi initsiative*]. We took this to heart and guessed [*megértettük*] why Stalin thought these matters important. [Gerö's notes read:] "More flexible formulas. Declare especially clearly that private property remains. Parallel the Polish manifesto. There must be nothing scary in the formulas. Make the formulas about private property more like the Polish model. More elasticity in the land question. Don't talk about size. Here also use the Polish model. Speak more squarely about private property. Speak more flexibly about the purge of the administrative apparatus. . . . Don't be stingy with words. The government should make an armistice its first task. Mobilize as many people as possible to help."

[During the evening of 5 December, the Gerö group held its discussions with the Horthyist generals. The latter, when they saw the manifesto, exclaimed that it was exactly what they had been saying all along! When all the Hungarians met with Molotov late that evening, the generals again raised the question of legal continuity with the old regime. Molotov now cut them off, saying that as far as the Soviet government was concerned the Horthy regime no longer existed. The generals, the Communists, and a number of high Soviet officials thereupon proceeded by train to Debrecen, where the Provisional National Assembly convened on 24 December.]

316

Selected Bibliography

General Sources

GUIDES TO THE STUDY of Stalin's Soviet Union are John A. Armstrong's "An Essay on Sources for the Study of the Communist Party of the Soviet Union, 1934–1960," mimeographed (Washington, D.C.: Divison of Intelligence and Research, U.S. Department of State, 1961); and John Erickson, "The Soviet Union at War, 1941–1945. An Essay on Sources and Studies," *Soviet Studies,* Vol. XIV (1963), pp. 249–79. A useful general bibliography is Thomas Hammond, *Soviet Foreign Relations and World Communism* (Princeton: Princeton University Press, 1965).

The following are useful in locating Soviet work: E. V. Bazhanova et al., *Narodnoe khozyaistvo SSSR. Bibliograficheskii ukazatel' knizhnoi i zhurnal'noi literatury na russkom yazyke* [The national economy of the USSR. A bibliographical directory to books and journal literature in the Russian language], Vol. II: *June 1941–May 1945* (Moscow: Nauka, 1971); V. N. Egorov, ed., *Mezhdunarodnye otnosheniya. Bibliograficheskii spravochnik,* 2 vols. (Moscow: Izdat. Mezhd. Otnosh., 1961–65); Leo Okinshevich, *United States History and Historiography in Postwar Soviet Writings* (Santa Barbara, Calif.: Clio, 1976); G. P. Polozov, "Partiinoe rukovodstvo deyatel'nostyu intelligentsii v gody Velikoi Otechestvennoi Voiny. Istoriografiya i istochnikovedenie" [The Party leadership of the activity of the intelligentsia during the Great Patriotic War. Historiography and sources], *Voprosy Istorii KPSS,* no. 9 (1976), pp. 116–25. One must refer also to the following Soviet historical periodicals which regularly discuss the war and postwar periods and provide bibliographical data: *Istoriya SSSR* [History of the USSR]; *Novaya i Noveishaya Istoriya* [Modern and recent history]; *Voenno-Istoricheskii Zhurnal* [Military-historical journal]; *Voprosy Istorii* [Problems of history]; and *Voprosy Istorii KPSS* [Problems of the history of the CPSU].

For East and West European work, the following journals are indispens-

319

able; all publish bibliography regularly: *Dzieje Najnowsze* [Recent history] (Warsaw); *Est et ouest* (Paris); *Europa Archiv* (Frankfurt); *Jahrbücher für Geschichte Osteuropas* (Munich); *Osteuropa* (Stuttgart); *News from behind the Iron Curtain* (after 1959 title changed to *East Europe;* published by Radio Free Europe, ceased publication in 1970); *Párttörténeti Közlemények* [Party history reports] (Budapest); *Příspěvky k Dějinám KSČS* [Contributions to the history of the Czechoslovak Communist Party] (Prague) (after 1967 title changed to *Revue Socialismu*[Review of socialism], repressed in 1970); *Revue de l'histoire de la deuxième guerre mondiale* (Paris); *Soviet Studies* (Glasgow); *Südosteuropa* (Munich); *Z Pola Walki* [From the battlefield] (Warsaw).

For American work, one should consult Robert F. Byrnes, *Bibliography of American Publications on East Central Europe. 1945–1957* (Bloomington: Indiana University Press, 1957); *The American Bibliography of Russian and East European Studies,* annual volumes, 1958–67 (Bloomington: Indiana University Press, 1959–73); computerized volumes for 1968–69, 1970–72, 1973, and 1974–75 (Columbus, Ohio: AAASS, 1974–76); Jesse J. Dossick, *Doctoral Research on Russia and the Soviet Union* (New York: Garland, 1960); Jesse J. Dossick, *Doctoral Research on Russia and the Soviet Union, 1960–1975* (New York: Garland, 1976). The journals *Slavic Review* and *Studies in Comparative Communism* are also indispensable.

The Radio and the Press

The single most important tool for studying the political history of the Soviet Union and international Communism in the period at the end of the war is the record, printed daily, of BBC monitorings of Soviet, East and West European, and Far Eastern broadcasts. In those years there was no *Current Digest of the Soviet Press* nor Radio Free Europe and Radio Liberation weekly reports on the Soviet and East European press; the FBIS and CIA monitorings were not yet regular. Further, many Soviet and East European newspapers were published irregularly and were not sent to Western libraries. For practical purposes, therefore, the BBC record, available at the Royal Institute of International Affairs, is the only convenient tool by which the Western historian may gain a rapid overview of international political affairs.

The *Times* of London and the *New York Times* are the most valuable Western newspapers for the period under consideration because of their comprehensive coverage of Eastern Europe and the Soviet Union and their published indexes. I have used other contemporary Western newspapers primarily through an extensive clipping file at the Royal Institute for International Affairs. The Russian-language monthly *Sotsialisticheskii Vestnik* [Socialist herald], published in New York, has been very useful, as has *Posev* [Sowing], an émigré journal published in West Germany.

I have referred extensively to the following Soviet and East European journals published from 1943 to 1949:

Agitator i Propagandist Krasnoi Armii [Agitator and propagandist of the Red Army] (Moscow)
Bol'shevik (Moscow)
Démocratie Nouvelle (Paris)
For a Lasting Peace, For a People's Democracy (Belgrade-Bucharest)
Izvestiya [News] (Moscow)
Krasnaya Zvezda [Red Star] (Moscow)
Kul'tura i Zhizn' [Culture and life] (Moscow)
Leningradskaya Pravda (Leningrad)
Mirovoe Khozyaistvo i Mirovaya Politika [World economy and world politics] (Moscow)
Novoe Vremya [New times] (Moscow); also published in English as *New Times;* before 1945 *Voina i rabochii klass* [War and the working class]
Novyi Mir [New world] (Moscow)
Nowe Drogi [New paths] (Warsaw)
Partiinaya Zhizn' [Party life] (Moscow)
Partiinoe Stroitel'stvo [Party-building] (Moscow)
Planovoe Khozyaistvo [Planned economy] (Moscow)
Pod Znamenem Marksizma [Under the banner of Marxism] (Moscow)
Pravda [Truth] (Moscow)
Propaganda i Agitatsiya [Propaganda and agitation] (Leningrad)
Propagandist (Moscow)
Rudé Pravo [Red right] (Prague)
Sputnik Agitatora [Agitator's companion] (Moscow)
Szabad Nép [Free people] (Budapest)
Társadalmi Szemle [Social review] (Budapest)
Vechernyaya Moskva [Evening Moscow] (Moscow)
Voprosy Filozofii [Problems of philosophy] (Moscow)
Zvezda [Star] (Leningrad)

Documentary Collections and Official Histories

The following lists collections and official publications referred to in the notes and reference works which were especially useful in the preparation of this study.

Andreev, P. P. *Kommunisticheskaya partiya v period Velikoi Otechestvennoi Voiny* [The Communist Party in the period of the Great Patriotic War]. Moscow: Party High School, 1959.
Biegański, S., ed. *Documents on Polish-Soviet Relations, 1939–1945.* 2 vols. London: Heinemann, 1961–70.
Bol'shaya sovetskaya entsiklopediya [Great Soviet encyclopedia]. 2d ed., 1949–58. 3d ed., 1970–. Moscow: BSE, 1970.
Canada. *Report of the Royal Commission Appointed Under Order in Council P. C. 411 of February 5, 1946, to Investigate the Facts Relating to and the Circumstances Surrounding the Communication, by Public Officials and Other Persons in Positions*

Selected Bibliography

of Trust, of Secret and Confidential Information to Agents of a Foreign Power, June 27, 1946. Ottawa: Edmond Cloutier, 1946.

Chandler, Alfred D., et al., eds. *The Papers of Dwight David Eisenhower.* 5 vols. Baltimore: Johns Hopkins Press, 1970.

Clissold, Stephen, ed. *Yugoslavia and the Soviet Union, 1939–1973. A Documentary Survey.* London: Oxford University Press, 1975.

Coakley, Robert W., and Leighton, Richard M. *The United States Army in World War II. The War Department. Global Logistics and Strategy 1943–1945.* Washington, D.C.: U.S. Government Printing Office, 1968.

Communist Party of the Soviet Union. *Istoriya KPSS* [History of the CPSU]. Moscow: Politizdat, 1970.

———. *KPSS v rezolyutsiyakh i resheniyakh s'ezdov, konferentsii i plenumov ts. k.* [The CPSU in the resolves and decisions of its congresses, conferences, and the plena of the CC]. 7th ed., 5 vols.; 8th ed., 10 vols. Moscow: Politizdat, 1954, 1973.

———. *XVIII s'ezd VKP(b). Stenograficheskii otchet* [18th Congress of the CPSU(b). Stenographic record]. Moscow: Gospolitizdat, 1939.

———. *Resheniya partii i pravitel'stva po khozyaistvennym voprosam* [The decisions of the Party and the government in economic affairs]. 5 vols. Moscow: Politizdat, 1968.

———. *Soveshchanie deyatelei sovetskoi muziky v ts. k. VKP(b)* [Meeting of active figures in Soviet music at the CC of the CPSU(b)]. Moscow: Politizdat, 1948.

———. Marx-Engels Institute. *I. V. Stalin. Sochineniya* [J. V. Stalin. Collected works]. 13 vols. Moscow: Gospolitizdat, 1946–52.

———. Marx-Engels Institute. *V. I. Lenin. Sochineniya* [V. I. Lenin. Collected works]. 4th ed. 35 vols. Moscow: OGIZ, 1946–51.

Crowley, E., et al. *Party and Government Officials of the Soviet Union, 1917–1960.* Metuchen, N.J.: Scarecrow Press, 1969.

Degras, Jane, ed. *The Communist International, 1919–1943. Documents.* 3 vols. New York: Oxford University Press, 1956–66.

Dér, László, et al., eds. *Felszabadulás, 1944, szeptember 26–1945, április 4. Dokumentumok hazánk felszabadulásának és a magyar népi demokráciának megszületésének történetéből* [Liberation, 26 September 1944–4 April 1945. Documents from the history of our country's liberation and of the birth of the Hungarian people's democracy]. Budapest: Szikra, 1955.

Dilks, David, ed. *The Diaries of Sir Alexander Cadogan, 1938–1945.* New York: Putnam, 1972.

Dimitrov, Georgi. *S'chineniya* [Collected works]. 14 vols. Sofia: BKP, 1951–55.

"Diskussiya po knige E. Vargy, 'Izmenenie v ekonomike kapitalizma v itoge vtoroi mirovoi voiny,' 7, 14, 21 maya 1947 g. Stenograficheskii otchet" [The discussion of the book by E. Varga, 'Changes in the economy of capitalism resulting from the Second World War.' 7, 14, and 21 May 1947. Stenographic record]. *Mirovoe Khozyaistvo i Mirovaya Politika,* no. 11, 1947.

Ehrman, John. *Grand Strategy, 1943–1945.* 2 vols. London: Her Majesty's Stationery Office, 1956.

Ellis, L. F. *Victory in the West.* 2 vols. London: Her Majesty's Stationery Office, 1962–68.

Esherick, Joseph W., ed. *Lost Chance in China. The World War II Dispatches of John S. Service.* New York: Random House, 1971.

Gabrielov, L. B., and Pintkovska, V. V., eds. *Borba KPSS za vosstanovlenie i razvitie narodnogo khozyaistva v poslevoennyi period. 1945–1953 gg. Dokumenty i materialy* [The struggle by the CPSU for the restoration and the expansion of the national economy in the postwar period. Documents and materials]. Moscow: Gospolitizdat, 1961.

Gomułka, Władisław, *W walce o demokrację ludową* [In the struggle for peoples' democracy]. 2 vols. Łódz: Książka, 1947.

Gottwald, Klement. *Deset let* [Ten years]. Prague: Svoboda, 1947.

———. *Spisy* [Writings]. 15 vols. Prague: SNPL, 1955–57.

Gromyko, A. A., et al., eds. *Istoriya diplomatii* [History of diplomacy]. 5 vols. Moscow: Politizdat, 1974.

Hungary. Ministry of Justice. *Laszlo Rajk and His Accomplices before the People's Court*. Budapest: State Publishing House, 1949.

Informatsionoe soveshchanie predstavitelei nekotorykh kompartii v Pol'she v kontse sentyabrya 1947 g. [Briefing conference of delegates from a number of Communist parties in Poland at the end of September 1947]. Moscow: Gospolitizdat, 1948.

Institut zur Erforschung der UdSSR. *Materialy konferentsii instituta po izucheniyu istorii i kultury SSSR* [Materials from the conference of the Institut zur Erforschung]. Munich: Einheit, 1953.

———. *Porträts der UdSSR Prominenz*. Munich: Einheit, 1960. This publication has been continued quarterly as *Portraits of Prominent USSR Personalities*. Metuchen, N.J., 1968–.

Kalinin, V. B., and Konyukhov, B. N. *KPSS—Vdokhnovitel' i organizator pobedy sovetskogo naroda v Velikoi Otechestvennoi Voiny* [The CPSU—inspirer and organizer of the Soviet people's victory in the Great Patriotic War]. Moscow: Moscow University Press, 1961.

Khrushchev, N. S. *Stroitel'stvo kommunizma v SSSR i razvitie sel'skogo khozyaistva* [The construction of Communism in the USSR and the development of agriculture]. 6 vols. Moscow: Politizdat, 1962–64.

Klimeš, Miloš, et al., eds. *Cesta ke květnu. Vznik lidové demokracie v Československu* [The road to May. The origin of people's democracy in Czechoslovakia]. Prague: Akademia, 1965.

Leningrad. Entsiklopedicheskii spravochnik [Leningrad. Encyclopedic reference book]. Moscow: BSE, 1957.

Loewenheim, Francis L., et al., eds. *Roosevelt and Churchill. Their Secret Wartime Correspondence*. New York: Saturday Review Press, 1975.

McNeal, Robert H., ed. *I. V. Stalin. Sochineniya* [J. V. Stalin. Collected works]. 3 vols. Stanford, Calif.: Hoover Institution, 1967.

———. *Resolutions and Decisions of the Communist Party of the Soviet Union*. 4 vols. Toronto: University of Toronto Press, 1974.

Malaya sovetskaya entsiklopediya [Small Soviet encyclopedia]. 3d ed. Moscow: BSE, 1968–.

Mao Tse-tung. *Selected Works of Mao Tse-tung*. 4 vols. Peking: Foreign Languages Publishing House, 1961–64.

Mástný, Vojtěch, ed. "The Beneš-Stalin-Molotov Conversations in December 1943: New Documents." *Jahrbücher für Geschichte Osteuropas*, Vol. XX (1972), pp. 367–402.

Meissner, Boris. *Das Ostpaktsystem: Dokumentensammlung*. Frankfurt am Main: Metzner, 1955.

Millis, Walter, ed. *The Forrestal Diaries*. New York: Viking, 1951.

Molotov, V. M. *Voprosy vneshnei politiki. Rechi i zayavleniya, 1945–1948* [Problems of foreign policy. Speeches and statements]. Moscow: Gospolitizdat, 1948.

Morača, Pero, ed. *Narodni front i komunisti. Jugoslavija, Čehoslovačka, Poljska, 1938–1945* [National front and the Communists. Yugoslavia, Czechoslovakia, Poland, 1938–1945]. Belgrade: Kultura, 1968.

Nagy, Imre. *Imre Nagy on Communism*. New York: Praeger, 1957.

Nicolaevsky, Boris, ed. *The Crimes of the Stalin Era. Special Report to the 20th Congress of the Communist Party of the Soviet Union by Nikita S. Khrushchev*. New York: New Leader, 1962.

323

Selected Bibliography

Pelikan, Jiří, ed. *The Czechoslovak Political Trials, 1950–1954*. London: MacDonald, 1971.

Pogue, Forrest C. *The Supreme Command*. Washington, D.C.: U.S. Government Printing Office, 1954.

Ponomarev, B. N., ed. *Politicheskii slovar* [Dictionary of politics]. Moscow: Gospolitizdat, 1958.

Pospelov, P. N., et al. *Istoriya Velikoi Otechestvennoi Voiny Sovetskogo Soyuza, 1941–1945* [History of the Great Patriotic War of the Soviet Union]. 6 vols. Moscow: Politizdat, 1960–65.

Prečan, Vilém, ed. *Slovenské národne povstanie. Dokumenty* [The Slovak national uprising. Documents]. Bratislava: Akademia, 1965.

Rákosi, Mátyás. *A magyar demokráciáért* [For Hungarian democracy]. Budapest: Szikra, 1947.

———. "Népi demokráciánk útja" [The path of our people's democracy]. *Társadalmi Szemle*, Vol. VII (1952), pp. 115–50.

Reale, Eugenio. *Avec Jacques Duclos au banc des accusés à la réunion constitutive du Kominform*. Paris: Plon, 1958.

Révai, József. *Élni tudtunk a szabadsággal* [We made the best of freedom]. Budapest: Szikra, 1949.

———. "Népi demokráciánk jellegéröl" [Concerning the character of our people's democracy]. *Társadalmi Szemle*, Vol. IV (1949), pp. 161–67. (Translated as "The Character of a People's Democracy" in *Foreign Affairs*, Vol. XVIII [1949], pp. 143–52.)

Royal Institute of International Affairs. *The Soviet-Jugoslav Dispute: The Published Correspondence*. London: Oxford University Press, 1948.

Sanakoev, Sh. P., et al., eds. *Tegeran, Yalta, Potsdam. Sbornik dokumentov* [Teheran, Yalta, Potsdam. Collection of documents]. 2d ed. Moscow: Izdat. Mezhd. Otnosh., 1970. (Translated into German, with detailed footnotes to the American protocols of the conferences, by Alexander Fischer as *Teheran, Jalta, Potsdam. Die sowjetische Protokollen von den Kriegskonferenzen der "Grossen Drei"* [Cologne: Wissenschaft und Politik, 1968].)

Smith, Jean E., ed. *The Papers of General Lucius D. Clay: Germany 1945–49*. 2 vols. Bloomington: Indiana University Press, 1974.

Stanojević, T., ed. *Josip Broz Tito. Govori i članci, 1941–1957* [J. B. Tito. Speeches and articles]. 12 vols. Zagreb: Naprijed, 1959.

Tel'pukhovskii, Boris. *Velikaya Otechestvennaya Voina Sovetskogo Soyuza, 1941–1945* [The Great Patriotic War of the Soviet Union]. Moscow: Politizdat, 1959. (Translated into German, with detailed evaluation and commentary, by A. Hillgruber and H.A. Jacobsen as *Die sowjetische Geschichte des grossen vaterländischen Krieges, 1941–1945, von B. S. Telpukhowski* [Frankfurt: Bernard und Graefe, 1961].)

Thorez, Maurice. *Oeuvres*. 23 vols. Paris: Éditions Sociales, 1960.

Union of Soviet Socialist Republics. Central Statistical Administration. *Narodnoe khozyaistvo SSSR. Statisticheskii spravochnik, 1965*. [The national economy of the USSR. Statistical handbook]. Moscow: Gos. Stat. Izdat., 1965.

———. Ministry of Foreign Affairs. *Perepiska predsedatelya soveta ministrov SSSR s presidentami SShA i premer-ministrami Velikobritanii vo vremya Velikoi Otechestvennoi Voiny, 1941–1945* [Correspondence of the chairman of the council of ministers of the USSR and the presidents of the United States and the prime ministers of Great Britain during the Great Patriotic War]. 2 vols. Moscow: Politizdat, 1956. (Republished in English by the Foreign Languages Publishing House in Moscow in 1957.)

———. *Sobranie postanovlenii i rasporyazhenii pravitel'stva SSSR* [Collection of the USSR government decisions and decrees]. Irregular. Moscow: Sovnarkom, 1938–46.

324

General Sources

———. *Sovetsko-bolgarskie otnosheniya, 1944–1948* [Soviet-Bulgarian relations]. Moscow: Politizdat, 1969.

———. *Sovetsko-chekhoslovatskie otnosheniya vo vremya Velikoi Otechestvennoi Voiny, 1941–1945. Dokumenty i materialy* [Soviet-Czechoslovak relations during the Great Patriotic War]. Moscow: Gospolitizdat, 1960.

———. *Sovetsko-frantsuzskie otnosheniya vo vremya Velikoi Otechestvennoi Voiny, 1941–1945. Dokumenty i materialy* [Soviet-French relations during the Great Patriotic War]. Moscow: Gospolitizdat, 1959.

———. *Sovetsko-vengerskie otnosheniya, 1945–1949. Dokumenty i materialy* [Soviet-Hungarian relations]. Moscow: Politizdat, 1969.

———. *Vneshnyaya politika Sovetskogo Soyuza. Dokumenty i materialy* [The foreign policy of the Soviet Union. Documents and materials]. *1945* (1 vol.); *1946* (1 vol.); *1947* (2 vols.); *1948* (2 vols.). Moscow: Gospolitizdat, 1949–51.

———. *Vneshnyaya politika Sovetskogo Soyuza v period Otechestvennoi Voiny. Dokumenty i materialy* [The foreign policy of the Soviet Union during the Great Patriotic War. Documents and materials]. 3 vols. Moscow: Gospolitizdat, 1944–47. (Andrew Rothstein has published a convenient English translation of Vols. I and II as *Soviet Foreign Policy during the Patriotic War. Documents and Materials* [London: Hutchinson and Co., n.d.].)

United States. Department of State. *The Conference of Berlin (Potsdam)*. 2 vols. Washington, D.C.: U.S. Government Printing Office, 1960.

———. *The Conferences at Cairo and Teheran, 1943*. Washington, D.C.: U.S. Government Printing Office, 1961.

———. *The Conferences at Malta and Yalta*. Washington, D.C.: U.S. Government Printing Office, 1955.

———. *Foreign Relations of the United States. Diplomatic Papers. 1943* (6 vols.); *1944* (7 vols.); *1945* (9 vols.); *1946* (11 vols.); *1947* (11 vols.); *1948* (9 vols.). Washington, D.C.: U.S. Government Printing Office, 1963–76.

———. *Nazi-Soviet Relations 1939–1941. Documents from the Archives of the German Foreign Office*. Washington, D.C.: U.S. Government Printing Office, 1948.

———. *United States Relations with China*. Washington, D.C.: U.S. Government Printing Office, 1949.

Varga, E. *Izmenenie v ekonomike kapitalizma v itoge vtoroi mirovoi Voiny* [Changes in the economy of capitalism as a result of the Second World War]. Moscow: Gospolitizdat, 1946.

Vasilenko, V. S., and Orekhova, E. D., eds. *Kommunisticheskaya partiya v period Otechestvennoi Voiny* [The Communist Party in the period of the Patriotic War]. Moscow: Gospolitizdat, 1961.

Vedomosti Verkhovnogo Soveta SSSR [Supreme Soviet records]. Moscow: Supreme Soviet, 1941–50. (Issued irregularly.)

Vladimirov, Peter. *The Vladimirov Diaries. Yenan, China, 1942–1945*. Garden City, N.Y.: Doubleday, 1975.

Voznesensky, N. A. *Voennaya ekonomika SSSR v period Otechestvennoi Voiny* [The war economy of the USSR in the period of the Patriotic War]. Moscow: Gospolitizdat, 1948.

Woodward, Llewellyn. *British Foreign Policy in the Second World War*. 5 vols. London: Her Majesty's Stationery Office, 1971–76. (A condensed one-volume edition was published in 1962.)

Zasedaniya Verkhovnogo Soveta SSSR. Stenograficheskii otchet [Sessions of the Supreme Soviet of the USSR. Stenographic record]. (Published irregularly from 1938 to 1953.)

Selected Bibliography

Zbornik dokumentata, podataka o narodno-oslobodilačkom ratu jugoslovenskih narodu [Collection of documents concerning the war of national liberation of the Yugoslav peoples]. Belgrade. (Published irregularly beginning in 1949.)

Memoirs and Biographies

The publications listed here are of three types: memoirs by foreigners about personal encounters with Stalin between 1943 and 1948; memoirs by Soviet generals and by foreigners who did not meet Stalin but who, for one reason or another, had special insight into the closed world of international Communism between 1943 and 1948; and official biographies of selected Soviet and international Communist personalities. No attempt has been made to give a publishing history of these works, although in some cases several editions of an item have appeared.

Acheson, Dean. *Present at the Creation: My Years in the State Department.* New York: New American Library, 1970.
Aczél, Tamás, and Méray, Tibor. *The Revolt of the Mind.* New York: Praeger, 1959.
Akshinskii, V. S. *K. E. Voroshilov. Biograficheskii ocherk* [Biographical sketch]. Moscow: Politizdat, 1974.
Alliluyeva, Svetlana. *Only One Year.* New York: Harper, 1969.
—— *Twenty Letters to a Friend.* New York: Harper, 1967.
Attlee, Clement. *As It Happened.* New York: Viking, 1954.
Beneš, Edvard. *Paměti. Od mnichova k nové válce a k novému vitězství* [Memoirs. From Munich to a new war and a new victory]. Prague: Orbis, 1947.
Bialer, Seweryn, ed. *Stalin and His Generals.* New York: Pegasus, 1969.
Bidault, Georges. *D'une résistance à l'autre.* Paris: Siècle, 1965.
Birse, A. H. *Memoirs of an Interpreter.* London: Michael Head, 1967.
Biryuzov, S. S. *Surovye gody* [The grim years]. Moscow: Nauka, 1965.
Bocca, Giorgio. *Palmiro Togliatti.* Rome: Laterza, 1973.
Bohlen, Charles E. *Witness to History, 1929–1969.* New York: Norton, 1973.
Bondarev, Yurii. *Tishina* [The calm]. Moscow: Sovetskii pisatel', 1962.
Buck, Tim. *Europe's Rebirth.* Toronto: Progress Books, 1947.
Burmeister, Alfred [pseud.]. *Dissolution and Aftermath of the Comintern: Experience and Observations. 1937–1947.* New York: Research Program on the USSR, 1955.
Byrnes, James F. *All in One Lifetime.* New York: Harpers, 1958.
——. *Speaking Frankly.* New York: Harpers, 1947.
Catroux, Maurice. *J'ai vu tomber le rideau de fer.* Paris: Hachette, 1952.
Chuikov, V. I. *The End of the Third Reich.* London: MacGibbon and Kee, 1967.
Churchill, Winston S. *The Second World War.* Vol. III: *The Grand Alliance;* Vol. IV: *The Hinge of Fate;* Vol. V: *Closing the Ring;* Vol. VI: *Triumph and Tragedy.* Boston: Houghton Mifflin, 1950–54.
Clay, Lucius D. *Decision in Germany.* Garden City, N.Y.: Doubleday, 1950.
"Columbia University Research Project: Hungary (CURPH)." New York: Columbia University, Russian Institute, 1958. (Mimeographed interview collection.)
Cretzianu, A. "The Rumanian Armistice Negotiations." *Journal of Central European Affairs,* Vol. XI (1951), pp. 243–58.
Dalton, Hugh. *Memoirs. 1945–1960.* 3 vols. London: Frederick Muller, 1962.
Deane, John R. *The Strange Alliance.* New York: Viking, 1947.
Dedijer, Vladimir. *The Battle Stalin Lost.* New York: Viking, 1971.
——. *Josip Broz Tito. Prilozi za biografiju* [Josip Broz Tito: Contributions to a

biography]. Belgrade: Kultura, 1953. (An abridged translation into English is *Tito Speaks* [London: Weidenfeld and Nicolson, 1954].)

———. *Jugoslovensko-albanski odnosi. 1939–1948* [Yugoslav-Albanian relations]. Belgrade: Borba, 1949.

De Gaulle, Charles. *Mémoires de guerre.* 3 vols. Paris: Plon, 1959.

Dennett, Raymond, and Johnson, Joseph, eds. *Negotiating with the Russians.* Boston: World Peace Foundation, 1951.

Desanti, Dominique. *Les staliniens.* Paris: Fayard, 1975.

Djilas, Milovan. *Conversations with Stalin.* New York: Harcourt-Brace, 1962.

Duclos, Jacques. *Mémoires.* 5 vols. Paris: Fayard, 1969–72.

Dulles, Allen. *The Secret Surrender.* New York: Harper, 1966.

Eden, Anthony. *The Memoirs of Anthony Eden.* Vol. II. Boston: Houghton Mifflin, 1965.

Ehrenburg, Il'ya. *The Postwar Years.* London: MacGibbon and Kee, 1964.

———. *The War.* London: MacGibbon and Kee, 1964.

Eisenhower, Dwight D. *Crusade in Europe.* Garden City, N.Y.: Doubleday, 1948.

Fierlinger, Zdeněk. *Ve službách ČSR* [In the service of Czechoslovakia]. 2 vols. Prague: Orbis, 1947–48.

Fischer, Ernst. *Das Ende einer Illusion. Erinnerungen 1945–1955.* Vienna: Molden, 1973.

Gerö, Ernö. Excerpts from an unpublished memoir, quoted in M. Korom. "Az ideiglenes nemzetgyülés és a kormány létrehozásának elökészítése" [The preparations for the establishment of the provisional national assembly and government]. *Párttörténeti Közlemények,* Vol. XX (1974), pp. 102–35.(See pp. 313–16 above.)

Gladwyn, Lord. *The Memoirs of Lord Gladwyn.* London: Weidenfeld and Nicolson, 1972.

Gniffke, Erich W. *Jahre mit Ulbricht.* Cologne: Wissenschaft und Politik, 1966.

Grossmann, Vassily. *Forever Flowing.* New York: Harper, 1972.

Harriman, Averell, and Abel, Elie. *Special Envoy to Churchill and Stalin.* New York: Random House, 1975.

Hernández, Jesús. *La grande trahison.* Paris: Fasquelle, 1953.

Hottelot, Richard. "Interview with Maxim Litvinov." *Washington Post,* 21 January 1952, p. 1; 22 January, p. B-11; 23 January, p. 13; 24 January, p. 13; 25 January, p. 21.

Hull, Cordell. *Memoirs.* 2 vols. New York: Macmillan, 1948.

Husák, Gustáv. *Svedectvo o Slovenskom národnom povstaní* [Testimony about the Slovak national uprising]. Bratislava: Vyd. Pol. Lit., 1964.

Ismay, Lord. *Memoirs.* New York: Viking, 1960.

Johnson, Hewlett. *Soviet Russia since the War.* New York: Boni and Gaer, 1947.

Kádár, János. "A béképártról" [About the peace party]. *Párttörténeti Közlemények,* Vol. II, nos. 3–4 (1956), pp. 20–26.

Kennan, George. *Memoirs, 1925–1950.* New York: Bantam, 1969.

Kertesz, Stephen D. *Diplomacy in a Whirlpool.* Notre Dame: Notre Dame University Press, 1953.

Khrulev, A. V. "Stanovlenie strategicheskogo tyla v Velikoi Otechestvennoi Voine" [The formation of the strategic rear during the Great Patriotic War]. *Voenno-Istoricheskii Zhurnal,* no. 6 (1961), pp. 64–80.

Khrushchev, N. S. *Khrushchev Remembers.* Boston: Little, Brown, 1970.

———. *The Last Testament.* Boston: Little, Brown, 1974.

King, Ernest J., and Whitehill, Walter M. *Fleet Admiral King. A Naval Record.* New York: Norton, 1952.

Klimov, Gregory. *The Terror Machine.* New York: Praeger, 1953.

Kolotov, V. V. *N. A. Voznesenskii. Biograficheskii ocherk* [Biographical sketch]. 1st ed. Moscow: Politizdat, 1963. 2d rev. ed. Moscow: Politizdat, 1974.

327

Selected Bibliography

Konev, I. S. *Sorok pyatyi* [Forty-five]. Moscow: Voenizdat, 1970.
Kopecký, Václav. *ČSR a KSČ* [Czechoslovakia and the Communist Party of Czechoslovakia]. Prague: SNPL, 1960.
Kuznetsov, N. G. "Na potsdamskoi konferentsii" [At the Potsdam Conference]. *Voprosy Istorii,* no. 8 (1965), pp. 85–88.
Lane, Arthur Bliss. *I Saw Poland Betrayed.* Indianapolis: Bobbs-Merrill, 1948.
Laušman, Bohumil. *Kdo byl vinĕn?* [Who was guilty?]. Vienna: Vorwärts, 1953.
Leahy, William D. *I Was There.* New York: McGraw-Hill, 1950.
Leonhard, Wolfgang. *Die Revolution entlässt ihre Kinder.* Cologne: Kiepenheuer und Witsch, 1955. (A drastically abridged English translation is *Child of the Revolution* [Chicago: Regnery, 1958].)
Loebl, Eugen. *My Mind on Trial.* New York: Harcourt Brace Jovanovich, 1976.
MacDuffie, Marshall. *The Red Carpet.* New York: Norton, 1955.
Maclean, Fitzroy. *Tito.* New York: Ballantine, 1957. (Originally published under the title *The Heretic.*)
Maiskii, Ivan. *Vospominaniya sovetskogo posla. Voina* [Memoirs of a Soviet envoy. The war]. Moscow: Nauka, 1965.
Malinovskii, R. Ya. *Budapesht, Vena, Praga* [Budapest, Vienna, Prague]. Moscow: Voenizdat, 1969.
Mandelstamm, Nadezhda. *Hope Abandoned.* New York: Atheneum, 1974.
Mikołajczyk, Stanislaw. *The Rape of Poland. The Pattern of Soviet Aggression.* New York: McGraw-Hill, 1948.
Milosz, Czeslaw. *The Captive Mind.* New York: Vintage, 1953.
Montgomery, Bernard L. *Memoirs.* Cleveland: World, 1958.
Moran, Charles M. W. *Churchill: The Struggle for Survival, 1940–1963.* Boston: Houghton-Mifflin, 1960.
Mosely, Philip E. "Across the Green Table from Stalin." *Current History,* Vol. XV (1948), pp. 120ff.
Murphy, Robert. *Diplomat among Warriors.* Garden City, N.Y.: Doubleday, 1964.
Nagy, Ferenc. *The Struggle behind the Iron Curtain.* New York: Macmillan, 1948.
Nĕmec, František, and Moudrý, Vladimír. *The Soviet Seizure of Subcarpathian Ruthenia.* Toronto: William B. Anderson, 1955.
Nyaradi, Nicholas. *My Ringside Seat in Moscow.* New York: Crowell, 1952.
Orbán, Gyula. "A tíz év elötti nagy pér" [The great trial ten years ago]. *Új Látóhatar,* Vol. II (1959), pp. 371–74.
Pasternak, Boris. *Doctor Zhivago.* New York: Pantheon, 1958.
Pigurnov, A. "Deyatel'nost voennykh sovetov po ukrepleniyu edinonachaliyu v period Velikoi Otechestvennoi Voiny" [The role of military councils in strengthening leadership during the Great Patriotic War]. *Voenno-Istoricheskii Zhurnal,* no. 4 (1961), pp. 47–56.
Robrieux, Philippe. *Maurice Thorez. Vie secrète et vie publique.* Paris: Fayard, 1975.
Ripka, Hubert. *Czechoslovakia Enslaved. The Story of the Communist Coup d'État.* London: Gollancz, 1950.
Rokossovskii, K. K. *Soldatskii dolg* [A soldier's duty]. Moscow: Voenizdat, 1964.
Roosevelt, Elliott. *As He Saw It.* New York: Duell, Sloan and Pearce, 1946.
Rudolph, Vladimir. "The Agencies of Control" and "The Execution of Power." In *Soviet Economic Policy in Postwar Germany: A Collection of Papers by Former Soviet Officials.* Edited by Robert Slusser. New York: Research Program on the USSR, 1953.
Salisbury, Harrison. *Russia on the Way.* New York: Macmillan, 1946.
Samsonov, A. M. *9 maya 1945 goda* [9 May 1945]. Moscow: Nauka, 1970.
Schöpflin, Gyula. "Dokumentum: A Magyar Kommunista Párt útja, 1945–1950" [Document: The course of the Hungarian Communist Party, 1945–1950]. *Látóhatár* [Horizon], Vol. VI (1955), pp. 238–42.

Sherwood, Robert E. *Roosevelt and Hopkins. An Intimate History.* New York: Harper, 1948.

Shtemenko, S. M. *General'nyi shtab v gody voiny* [The general staff in the war years]. 2 vols. Moscow: Voenizdat, 1968–73.

Slusser, Robert, ed. *Soviet Economic Policy in Postwar Germany: A Collection of Papers by Former Soviet Officials.* New York: Research Program on the USSR, 1953.

Smith, Walter Bedell. *My Three Years in Moscow.* New York: Lippincott, 1949.

Snow, Edgar. *The Pattern of Soviet Power.* New York: Random House, 1945.

Solzhenitsyn, A. I. *The First Circle.* New York: Bantam, 1969.

———. *The Gulag Archipelago.* 2 vols. New York: Harper, 1973, 1976.

Starobin, Joseph R. *American Communism in Crisis.* Cambridge, Mass.: Harvard University Press, 1972.

Stettinius, Edward R. *Roosevelt and the Russians. The Yalta Conference.* Garden City, N.Y.: Doubleday, 1949.

Stimson, Henry L., and Bundy, McGeorge. *On Active Service in Peace and War.* New York: Harper, 1948.

Strang, William. *Home and Abroad.* London: André Deutsch, 1956.

Strassenreiter, Erzsébet, and Sipos, Péter. *Rajk László.* Budapest: Akadémiai kiadó, 1974.

Stypułkowski, Z. *Invitation à Moscou.* Paris: Iles d'Or, 1951.

Táborský, E. "Benes and the Soviets." *Foreign Affairs,* Vol. XXIX (1949), pp. 302–14.

———. "Beneš and Stalin. Moscow, 1943 and 1945." *Journal of Central European Affairs,* Vol. XIII (1953), pp. 154–81.

Tedder, Arthur W. T. *With Prejudice.* London: Cassell, 1966.

Tillon, Charles. *Les FTP. La guérilla en France.* Paris: Julliard, 1962.

———. *On chantait rouge.* Paris: Laffont, 1977.

Tokaev, G. A. *Comrade X.* London: Harvill, 1956.

Tolmagev, A. *M. I. Kalinin.* Moscow: Molodaya Gvardiya, 1963.

Truman, Harry S. *Year of Decisions, 1945.* Garden City, N.Y.: Doubleday, 1955.

Tuominen, Arvo. "The North European Communist Parties." *Occidente,* Vol. XI (1955), pp. 193–209.

Tyulenev, I. V. *Cherez tri voiny* [Through three wars]. Moscow: Voenizdat, 1960.

Vas, Zoltán. *Hazatérés, 1944* [Homecoming, 1944]. Budapest: Szépirodalmi könyvkiadó, 1970.

Vasilevskii, A. M. *Delo vsei zhizni* [Lifetime commitment]. Moscow: Voenizdat, 1974.

———. "K voprosu o rukovodstve vooruzhennoi bor'boi v Velikoi Otechestvennoi Voine" [On the question of the leadership of the armed struggle during the Great Patriotic War]. In *9 maya 1945 goda.* Edited by A. M. Samsonov. Moscow: Nauka, 1970.

Voronov, N. N. *Na sluzhbe voennoi* [On military service]. Moscow: Voenizdat, 1963.

Werth, Alexander. *Musical Uproar in Moscow.* London: Turnstyle, 1949.

———. *Russia. The Postwar Years.* London: Robert Hale, 1971.

———. *Russia at War, 1941–1945.* London: Barrie and Rockliff, 1964.

Zhukov, G. K. *Vospominaniya i razmyshleniya* [Memories and reflections]. Moscow: Voenizdat, 1969.

329

Notes

Abbreviations Used in the Notes

BSE	*Bol'shaya sovetskaya entsiklopediya*
FRUS	United States, Department of State, *Foreign Relations of the United States*
Khrushchev, *Crimes of the Stalin Era*	Nicolaevsky, ed., *Crimes of the Stalin Era*
Khrushchev, *Memoirs*	*Khrushchev Remembers; The Last Testament*
PS	*Partiinoe Stroitel'stvo*
Potsdam Papers	United States, Department of State, *The Conference of Berlin (Potsdam)*
PZh	*Partiinaya Zhizn'*
Roosevelt-Churchill Correspondence	Loewenheim et al., eds. *Roosevelt and Churchill*
Rothstein, *SFP*	USSR, Ministry of Foreign Affairs, *Vneshnyaya politika SSSR*
Stalin, *Correspondence*	USSR, Ministry of Foreign Affairs, *Perepiska*
Stalin, *Soch.*	CPSU, CC, Marx-Engels Institute, *I. V. Stalin. Sochineniya;* McNeal, *I. V. Stalin. Sochineniya*
Teheran Papers	United States, Department of State, *The Conferences at Cairo and Teheran*
VPSS	USSR, Ministry of Foreign Affairs, *Vneshnyaya politika SSSR*
VPSS VOV	USSR, Ministry of Foreign Affairs, *Vneshnyaya politika SSSR v period VOV*
Yalta Papers	United States, Department of State, *The Conferences at Malta and Yalta*

Notes to Chapter 1

Bibliographical Note

Recent scholarly attempts at a Stalin biography are Robert C. Tucker, *Stalin as Revolutionary* (the first volume of a three-volume project) (New York: Norton, 1973); Adam Ulam, *Stalin. The Man and His Era* (New York: Viking, 1973); Ronald Hingley, *Joseph Stalin: Man and Legend* (London: Hutchinson, 1974); and H. Montgomery Hyde, *Stalin: The History of a Dictator* (London: Hart-Davis, 1971). Useful older works are Boris Souvarine, *Staline. Aperçu historique du Bolshevisme* (Paris: Plon, 1935); Victor Serge, *Portrait de Staline* (Paris: B. Grasset, 1940); Leon Trotsky, *Stalin. An Appraisal of the Man and His Influence* (New York: Grosset and Dunlap, 1962); and Isaac Deutscher, *Stalin. A Political Biography*, rev. ed. (New York: Oxford University Press, 1967). Other satisfying portraits of Stalin are in Bertram D. Wolfe, *Three Who Made a Revolution* (Boston: Beacon Press, 1948), chs. 23ff.; Richard Pipes, *The Formation of the Soviet Union*, rev. ed. (New York: Atheneum, 1968), ch. 6; and the survey works by E. H. Carr, *Socialism in One Country*, 3 vols. (New York: Macmillan, 1958–64), Vol. I, pp. 189ff.; Robert V. Daniels, *The Conscience of the Revolution* (Cambridge, Mass.: Harvard University Press, 1960); Stephen Cohen, *Bukharin and the Bolshevik Revolution* (New York: Knopf, 1973); and Leonard Schapiro, *The Communist Party of the Soviet Union* (New York: Random House, 1959).

The only Western studies which review the whole range of Soviet politics in the period at the end of the war in any detail are John A. Armstrong, *The Politics of Totalitarianism* (New York: Random House, 1961), chs. 11–15; Boris Meissner, *Russland im Umbruch*, Vol. IX of *Dokumente und Berichte des Europa-Archivs* (Frankfurt am Main: Verlag für Geschichte und Politik, 1951); Meissner's *Sowjetrussland zwischen Revolution und Restauration* (Cologne: Verlag für Politik und Wirtschaft, 1956); and Thomas B. Trout, "Soviet Policy Making and the Cold War, 1945–1947" (Ph.D. dissertation, Indiana University, 1972). Some new interpretations are suggested by William Zimmerman, "Choices in the Postwar World," in *Caging the Bear*, ed. Charles Gati (New York: Praeger, 1974), pp. 84–108.

The Soviet literature about Soviet politics under Stalin is much less useful. Mines of information are the six-volume official history of the war edited by P. Pospelov et al., *Istoriya Velikoi Otechestvennoi Voiny Sovetskogo Soyuza*, and Volumes IV and V of the recent five-volume official diplomatic history edited by A. Gromyko et al., *Istoriya diplomatii*. Shorter and occasionally interesting surveys of the war period are found in I. G. Viktorov et al., eds., *SSSR v Velikoi Otechestvennoi Voine* [The USSR in the Great Patriotic War] (Moscow: Voenizdat, 1970); and P. Pospelov et al., eds., *Velikaya Otechestvennaya Voina Sovetskogo Soyuza* [The Great Patriotic War of the Soviet Union] (Moscow: Voenizdat, 1970). Most of the material in this chapter will be discussed in greater detail at a later point. The notes, therefore, make no attempt at complete coverage.

1. Comment by the Czech historian Jan Křen, published in the minutes of the conference (Pero Morača, ed., *Narodni front i komunisti. Jugoslavija, Čehoslovačka, Poljska, 1938–1945*, p. 614). Stalin's "statism" is described in other terms by Klaus Mehnert in *Stalin versus Marx* (London: Allen and Unwin, 1952); and by Richard Lowenthal in "Stalin and Ideology. The Revenge of the Superstructure," *Soviet Survey*, no. 33 (1960), pp. 31–37.

2. Testimony about Stalin's fears is in Khrushchev, *Memoirs*, Vol. II, pp. 38ff., 53, 58–59, 188, 191, 354–56, 375; and Djilas, *Conversations with Stalin*, p. 182. Some historians doubt the reliability of Khrushchev's memoirs and Djilas' book. I agree that Khrushchev is untrustworthy when reporting specific incidents, and I use him when (as in the present instance) he reports attitudes or background material. Djilas, on the other

hand, strikes me as reliable despite his obviously narrow perception of events and his anti-Soviet bias.

3. Stalin used these expressions in his "Letter to Razin" (*Soch.*, Vol. XVI, p. 32), and in his "Interview with H. Stassen" (*Soch.*, Vol. XVI, pp. 77–78).

4. This terminology is from Arno J. Mayer, *Wilson versus Lenin* (Cleveland: World Publishing Company, 1959), p. vii.

5. A fine discussion of the many uses of the word "revolution" in 1945 is found in Joseph R. Starobin, *American Communism in Crisis*, ch. 4 and pp. 102ff., 236–37.

6. The classic statement of this view is by "Historicus" (George A. Morgan), "Stalin on Revolution," originally published in *Foreign Affairs*, Vol. XVII (1949). For a critique of Morgan's essay, see Jonathan Harris, "Historicus on Stalin," *Soviet Union*, Vol. I (1974), pp. 54–73.

7. See, for example, Robert C. Tucker's caustic remarks in *The Soviet Political Mind* (New York: Praeger, 1963), p. 161n.

8. See, for example, Marshal D. Shulman, *Stalin's Foreign Policy Reappraised* (Cambridge, Mass.: Harvard University Press, 1963), ch. 1; and the formulas of T. Trout in "Soviet Policy Making," ch. 1, and of John Armstrong, "The Domestic Roots of Soviet Foreign Policy," in *The Conduct of Soviet Foreign Policy*, ed. Erik P. Hoffman and Frederic Fleron, Jr. (New York: Aldine-Atherton, 1971), pp. 50–60. In the latter volume William Zimmerman discusses recent literature ("Elite Perspectives and the Explanation of Soviet Foreign Policy," pp. 18–30), and Alexander Dallin argues that the relationship between Soviet domestic politics and foreign policy is important, suggesting categories and channels ("Soviet Foreign Policy and Domestic Politics. A Framework for Analysis," pp. 36–49).

9. See Stalin's "Response to a Correspondent of *Pravda*," 13 June 1944, in *Soch.*, Vol. XV, p. 150.

10. See, for example, Alexander Werth, *Russia. The Postwar Years*, chs. 1–2. Werth's study is weak history but contains interesting reportage.

11. Frederick Barghoorn records the details of this change in *The Soviet Image of the United States* (New York: Harcourt Brace, 1953).

12. Armstrong (*Politics of Totalitarianism*, pp. 133–35) lists the variations in the membership of the GOKO. Its operation is described by General A. V. Khrulev, "Stanovelnie strategicheskogo tyla v Velikoi Otechestvennoi Voine," pp. 66ff.; and by Marshal A. M. Vasilevskii in "K voprosu o rukovodstve vooruzhennoi bor'boi v Velikoi Otechestvennoi Voine," pp. 45ff.

13. The Politburo's resumption of leadership is documented in Yu. P. Petrov, *Stroitel'stvo politorganov, partiinykh i komsomol'skykh organizatsii armii i flota* [The development of the political organs, the Party, and the Komsomol organizations of the army and the fleet] (Moscow: Voenizdat, 1961), p. 389.

14. Khrushchev documented the establishment of the "septet" in his secret speech to the Twentieth Congress of the CPSU: see *Crimes of the Stalin Era*, p. S62.

15. See the memoir by Vladimir Rudolph in *Soviet Economic Policy in Postwar Germany*, ed. Robert Slusser, pp. 18–61.

16. Cf. Robert C. Tucker, "Autocrats and Oligarchs," in *Russian Foreign Policy*, ed. Ivo Lederer (New Haven: Yale University Press, 1962), pp. 185–95.

17. J. A. Newth, "The Soviet Population. The Wartime Losses and the Postwar Recovery," *Soviet Studies*, Vol. XV (1964), pp. 345–57; Robert Hutchings, "Comment on the Soviet Population," *Soviet Studies*, Vol. XVII (1966), pp. 81–82.

18. *Gulag Archipelago*, Vol. I, p. 19: cf. p. 69, which suggests conditions in 1938.

19. *The War*, pp. 74, 132–33.

20. *Doctor Zhivago*, p. 519.

21. In 1960 Khrushchev told the Supreme Soviet that in May 1945 the Soviet armed forces numbered 11,365,000 (*Pravda*, 15 January 1960). For an evaluation of this

statistic, see Thomas W. Wolfe, *Soviet Power and Europe, 1945–1970* (Baltimore: Johns Hopkins University Press, 1970), pp. 10–11.

22. A picturesque eyewitness account is in Alexander Werth, *Russia at War*, pp. 384ff., 674ff. Cf. Roman Kolkowicz, *The Soviet Military and the Communist Party* (Princeton: Princeton University Press, 1967), pp. 64–71.

23. Striking evidence of the wartime army's independence from political constraints is in Yu. P. Petrov, *Stroitel'stvo politorganov*, p. 379, and in his *Partiinoe stroitel'stvo v sovetskoi armii i flote, 1918–1961 gg.* [Party development in the Soviet army and the fleet], esp. p. 451.

24. Werth, *Russia at War*, pp. 879ff.; Djilas, *Conversations with Stalin*, p. 55; K. K. Rokossovskii, *Soldatskii dolg*, p. 92.

25. Jerry F. Hough, *The Soviet Prefects* (Cambridge, Mass.: Harvard University Press, 1969), pp. 108–9.

26. On the problem of the subjection of the Party to the GOKO, see Sanford R. Lieberman, "The CPSU and Its Response to Stress: The Impact of World War II," a presentation at the AAASS convention at Atlanta in October 1975, based on his Harvard dissertation (1973).

27. Petrov, *Stroitel'stvo politorganov*, p. 389.

28. Meissner, *Sowjetrussland*, pp. 38ff.; Boris Nicolaevsky, "Na komandnykh vysotakh Kremlya. G. M. Malenkov i malenkovtsy" [On the commanding heights of the Kremlin. G. M. Malenkov and his followers], *Sotsialisticheskii Vestnik*, no. 6 (1946), pp. 142–46; and the official Malenkov biography in *BSE*, 2d ed., Vol. XXVI, pp. 145–46.

29. Shcherbakov's official biography is in *BSE*, 2d ed., Vol. XLVIII, pp. 262–63.

30. Fascinating details are in M. I. Likhomanov, *Organizatorskaya rabota partii v promyshlennosti v pervii period Velikoi Otechestvennoi Voiny* [The organizational work of the Party in industry during the first period of the Great Patriotic War] (Leningrad: Leningrad University, 1969).

31. See, for example, the remarks by N. Patolichev in *PS*, no. 6 (1945), pp. 25ff.; the striking editorial in the first issue of *PZh*, 15 November 1946, pp. 18ff.; and the editorial in *Pravda*, 13 February 1948, p. 1 (which is cited in an American Embassy report as "typical": see *FRUS 1948*, Vol. VI, p. 817); and such *oblast* Party histories as A. V. Bakunin et al., *Kommunisty Sverdlovska vo glave mass* [The Sverdlovsk Communists lead the masses] (Sverdlovsk: SUKI, 1967), pp. 254–55.

32. T. Rigby, *Communist Party Membership* (Princeton: Princeton University Press, 1968), pp. 241ff.

33. See, for example, F. L. Aleksandrov et al., eds., *Ocherki istorii moskovskoi organizatsii KPSS* [Outline history of the Moscow organization of the CPSU] (Moscow: Mosk. Rabochii, 1966), pp. 601ff.

34. Petrov, *Partiinoe stroitel'stvo*, p. 451.

35. *PS*, nos. 3–4 (1944), p. 42; no. 10 (1944), p. 16; nos. 11–12 (1944), p. 48.

36. Leonhard, *Die Revolution entlässt ihre Kinder*, pp. 234ff.

37. *Ibid.*, p. 340.

38. S. S. Biryuzov, *Surovye gody*, p. 362.

39. On the comparatively relaxed intellectual atmosphere in the Soviet Union at the end of the war, see David Joravsky, *The Lysenko Affair* (Cambridge, Mass.: Harvard University Press, 1970), pp. 130ff.; and Harold Swayzee, *Political Control of Literature in the USSR* (Cambridge, Mass.: Harvard University Press, 1962), ch. 2.

40. This debate concerned a book by Eugen Varga, published early in 1946, which proposed that the major capitalist states had acquired some ability to regulate their economies and thus, possibly, might survive. The debate was published as a supplement to the journal *Mirovoe Khozyaistvo i Mirovaya Politika* in December 1947.

41. Such hints were conspicuous as early as August 1942, when Churchill visited

334

Stalin in Moscow, and they recurred during his later visits: see Winston S. Churchill, *The Second World War,* Vols. IV, *The Hinge of Fate,* pp. 490–91, and VI, *Triumph and Tragedy,* p. 238. Comparable hints were dropped in Stalin's toast at the Yalta conference, recorded in Churchill, *Triumph and Tragedy,* pp. 362–63; in Stalin's letter of 3 April about the Berne affair (Stalin, *Correspondence,* Vol. II, p. 206); in his talks in May with Harry Hopkins about the Soviet reaction to the cutoff of Lend-Lease (R. Sherwood, *Roosevelt and Hopkins,* pp. 893ff.); and in his talk about "isolationism" with Harriman at Gagry in October (*FRUS 1945,* Vol. VI, p. 792). Cf. Adam Ulam, *Expansion and Coexistence,* 2d ed. (New York: Praeger, 1974), pp. 379ff., 451ff.

42. These extracts are from a report published in 1968 in *Slavic Review,* Vol. XXVII, pp. 482–83.

43. Ambassador Harriman was also firmly convinced, both during and after the war, that Stalin's lieutenants had a great deal of influence on Soviet policy. He was reinforced in this belief by his talks with Soviet Deputy Foreign Commissar Maksim Litvinov (W. Averell Harriman and Elie Abel, *Special Envoy to Churchill and Stalin,* pp. 241, 344, 517ff.; and Vojtěch Mástný, "The Cassandra in the Foreign Commissariat," *Foreign Affairs,* Vol. LIV [1976], pp. 370ff.). The first major postwar Western textbook on Soviet politics also adopted a "prisoner of the Politburo" view of Stalin: see Julian Towster, *Political Power in the USSR* (New York: Oxford University Press, 1948), p. 392.

44. *Tygodnik Powszechny* [General weekly], 6 July 1958, quoted by Robert Conquest in *Power and Policy in the USSR* (London: Macmillan, 1961), p. 51. Basic problems in the evaluation of Communist public statements are discussed by Conquest in the opening chapters of the book just cited; by Myron Rush in *The Rise of Khrushchev* (Washington: Public Affairs Press, 1958), app. 2; by Donald Zagoria in "Note on Methodology," in *The Sino-Soviet Conflict, 1956–1961* (Princeton: Princeton University Press, 1962); and by Sydney Ploss in his introduction to *Conflict and Decision Making in Soviet Russia. A Case Study in Agriculture* (Princeton: Princeton University Press, 1965). Max E. Mote cites the extensive recent literature on this subject in *Would a Communication Model Add to Soviet Lore,* Division of East European Studies, University of Alberta, Occasional Papers, no. 1 (Alberta: University of Alberta, 1976). Before the publication of Rush's study, Western historians in general considered Communist public statements to be wholly unreliable evidence. Since 1965, the use of such statements has become so common among Western students of Soviet affairs as to require no justification.

45. Letter from Julian Schöpflin to the author, 10 June 1961.

46. In the 1940s and 1950s Western scholars tended to argue the question of whether Communists really believed in their ideology or merely used it as propaganda to deceive outsiders. The more knowing recent discussions have centered around the functions of the ideology in Communist political systems. A basic study in the new vein was Barrington Moore's *Soviet Politics—The Dilemma of Power* (Cambridge, Mass.: Harvard University Press, 1950), esp. ch. 18. Pioneering later studies were Zbigniew Brzezinski's *Ideology and Power in Soviet Politics* (New York: Praeger, 1962), pt. 1; Robert V. Daniels' *The Nature of Communism* (New York: Random House, 1962), chs. 1 and 9; and Alfred G. Meyer's "The Functions of Ideology in the Soviet Political System," *Soviet Studies,* Vol. XVII (1966), pp. 273–85.

47. This is a reply to the blanket objections David Joravsky raises against all "kremlinology" in *The Lysenko Affair,* pp. 329ff.

48. Cf. Khrushchev, *Memoirs,* Vol. II, pp. 171–74, and the report in Mikołajczyk, *The Rape of Poland: The Pattern of Soviet Aggression,* pp. 170–71.

49. Related problems of interpretation face historians who study the Nazi movement. They, of course, possess not only the public documents of the movement but also the minutes of Hitler's dinner conversation. With such a plenitude of sources they

should, by traditional scholarly standards, be able to tell us the "truth" about Hitler's intentions, yet they have had to recognize an implemental aspect of the Nazi use of ideological terms, quite similar to that which we perceive in Stalinist usage. Whereas this aspect affords students of Stalinism an entry into the councils of the regime, ironically it prevents the students of Nazism from determining finally whether Hitler actually "intended" war in August and September 1939. See H. W. Koch, "Hitler and the Origins of the Second World War. Second Thoughts on the Status of Some of the Documents," *Historical Journal*, Vol. XI (1968), pp. 125–43.

50. Cf. Meyer, "Functions of Ideology," pp. 279–81.

51. The record of Stalin's known publications is in Robert H. McNeal, *Stalin's Works. An Annotated Bibliography* (Stanford, Calif.: Hoover Institution, 1963).

52. *Propagandist,* no. 14 (1944), p. 5.

53. *PS,* no. 4 (1946), p. 9.

54. Mátyás Rákosi, *A magyar demokráciáért,* p. 41. In October 1976, just after the death of Mao Tse-tung, charges were made in China which cast light on the relation between the public statements and the secret politics of Stalin's and Mao's Communism. In the words of the *New York Times* (27 October 1976, p. 3; 19 December 1976, p. 17):

Hua [Kuo-Feng] brought Prime Minister Robert Muldoon of New Zealand to see [Mao] on April 30 [1976]. Mao asked Mr. Hua to stay after Mr. Muldoon was ushered out, and Mr. Hua delivered a report on progress in the campaign to criticize Teng Hsiao Ping, the ousted deputy prime minister. Mao then wrote out: "Act gradually and don't be in a hurry. Act according to the principles known in the past. With you in charge I am at ease." . . . Mr. Hua reported this to a national conference on economic planning [during the] summer, [but] somehow it got into the minutes of the conference as "Act according to the principles laid down." Although small, the distinction seemed to be that in Mao's original version, he meant principles generally known in the past. But in the altered version, the "principles laid down," only some limited officials might know what those were and could interpret them. After Mao's death, [his widow, Chiang Ching] went to the archives of the Party Central Committee and told the archivist to give her certain documents relating to Mao. The archivist was afraid to refuse but told . . . a Politburo member . . . [who] was upset and told the archivist to get the documents back. Miss Chiang scolded the archivist, so [the Politburo member] had to call Mr. Hua for help. Mr. Hua telephoned Miss Chiang and this time she complied. . . . Mr. Hua discovered [then] that two of the documents had been tampered with.

55. Stalin used this term in his "Marxism and Problems of Linguistics" of 1950 (*Soch.,* Vol XVI, pp. 126, 130). Cf. V. Dedijer, *The Battle Stalin Lost,* p. 94.

56. J. R. Fiszman, "Poland: Continuity and Change," in *The Changing Face of Communism in Eastern Europe,* ed. Peter A. Toma (Tucson: University of Arizona Press, 1970), p. 81.

57. *The First Circle,* pp. 428–29.

58. *Soch.,* Vol. VI, pp. 46–51.

59. It is true that at the 19th Congress of the CPSU, in his last public speech, Stalin mentioned neither Marx nor Lenin and conveyed to the Communist and democratic parties of the world "banners" (as he called them) that were explicitly liberal and nationalist. But in the paper "Economic Problems of Socialism in the USSR," also written for that congress, his inability to break with his ideology was painfully evident.

60. See Leonard Schapiro's "Conclusions" in his *Origins of the Communist Autocracy* (Cambridge, Mass.: Harvard University Press, 1955), and R. V. Daniels' "Introduction" to *The Conscience of the Revolution.*

61. This is the thesis of Tucker's *Stalin as Revolutionary.*

62. Vasily Grossman suggests, in a fascinating Samizdat novel, that Stalin had a

lasting fear of freedom, that he never dared declare himself free of the Revolution, and that it was for such reasons that he launched the great purges: see *Forever Flowing*, pp. 188–89, 230ff.

Notes to Chapter 2

Bibliographical Note
The volume of secondary literature about Stalin's foreign Communist parties is enormous. But because many Communists had little time for theoretical work during the war and because the Communist central organization in Moscow withered after 1943, historians have paid little attention to inter-party relations during our period. A most valuable source of information and understanding is the record of the Karlovy Vary conference of Communist Party historians in 1966: see Pero Morača, ed., *Narodni front i komunisti*. Also very interesting are the recent surveys by Norbert Kołomejczyk, *Rewolucja ludowa w Europie, 1939–1948* [Popular revolution in Europe, 1939–1948] (Warsaw: Wiedza Powszechna, 1973); and W. Góra et al., eds., *Rewolucja i władza ludowa w krajech europejskich, 1944–1948* [Revolution and people's government in the European countries, 1944–1948] (Warsaw: Książka i Wiedza, 1972). Franz Borkenau's *European Communism* (London: Faber and Faber, 1953) remains the only extended Western treatment of wartime international Communism but is very out of date and replete with errors. Joseph Starobin, Zbigniew K. Brzezinski, and Richard Lowenthal have constructed effective models for approaching the subject (J. R. Starobin, "The Origins of the Cold War," *Foreign Affairs*, Vol. XLVII [1969], pp. 681–96; Z. K. Brzezinski, *The Soviet Bloc*, rev. ed. [Cambridge, Mass.: Harvard University Press, 1967], pt. 1; and Richard Lowenthal, *World Communism. The Disintegration of a Secular Faith* [New York: Oxford University Press, 1964]), but none of them gives the war more than summary treatment. For the prewar history of Communism in Europe, see the surveys by Franz Borkenau, *World Communism* (Ann Arbor: University of Michigan Press, 1962); Branko Lazitch, *Les partis communistes de l'Europe* (Paris: Îles d'Or, 1956); and Hugh Seton-Watson, *From Lenin to Khrushchev*, rev. ed. (New York: Praeger, 1960). François Fejtö (*Histoire des démocraties populaires* [Paris: Seuil, 1952]) and Hugh Seton-Watson (*The East European Revolution*, rev. ed. [New York: Praeger, 1961]) afford still useful perspectives on the postwar period.

1. Alfred Rieber analyses the motives of the CPF in *Stalin and the French Communist Party* (New York: Columbia University Press, 1962), pp. 57ff.
2. V. Suchopar discusses the history of coalitionism in "O hesle 'nové demokracie' v Kommunistické Internacionale" [Regarding the "New Democracy" slogan in the Comintern], *Příspěvky k Dějinám KSČS*, Vol. II (1962), pp. 163–91. See also Kermit E. McKenzie, *Comintern and World Revolution, 1929–1943. The Shaping of Doctrine* (New York: Columbia University Press, 1964), pp. 153ff., 174ff. Communists entered the openly revolutionary coalition "governments" of Saxony and Thuringia in 1923, but the Comintern soon condemned their efforts (which in any case proved impermanent). At Wuhan in 1927 Chinese Communists, urged on by Stalin, participated in a coalition government of sorts with non-proletarian groups. However, they suffered such disastrous setbacks when Chiang Kai-shek attacked Wuhan and repressed them that they never repeated the tactic. In 1936, when the Falange attacked the popular front government of Spain, the Communists said they were prepared to enter that government. They seem never to have done so, however, and in France, Chile, and other countries where the popular front was strong, the Communists excused themselves from governmental participation, allegedly so as not to scare off conservative political elements. In March 1943, a Cuban Communist entered the Battista government, but this was only after his Party had imitated the collaborationist policies of the

Communist Party of the United States to the extent of altering its name. Cf. Robert J. Alexander, *Communism in Latin America*, rev. ed. (New Brunswick, N.J.: Rutgers University Press, 1969), p. 284. It seems beyond question that by 1944 most foreign Communists in Russia and many in the resistance movements around the world looked forward with equanimity to their parties' participation in bourgeois governments because of the Soviet alliance with the West. This need not mean, however, as the Yugoslav experience makes amply clear, that they expected the "new type governments" to appear even in countries where the Communists already held power.

3. Recently published documents have demonstrated just how "democratic" Beneš was prepared to be, in the sense of collaborating with Stalin. See Vojtěch Mástný, "The Beneš-Stalin-Molotov conversations," pp. 367–402. Beneš' own account of his dealings with the Communists is in his *Paměti*, pp. 391ff.

4. C. F. Delzell, *Mussolini's Enemies* (Princeton: Princeton University Press, 1961), pp. 338ff.; and S. J. Woolf, ed., *The Rebirth of Italy, 1943–1950* (London: Longman, 1972), pp. 23–24.

5. D. George Kousoulas, *Revolution and Defeat* (London: Oxford University Press, 1965), pp. 193ff.

6. The Chinese Communists announced their acceptance of a coalition policy on 15 September 1944, after several months of negotiation with the Kuomintang: see Jacques Guillermaz, *History of the Chinese Communist Party* (New York: Random House, 1972), pp. 350ff.

7. Harry Pollitt; his speech was reported in *Pravda*, 1 November 1944, p. 4.

8. The text is in *Soch.*, Vol. XV., pp. 107–27.

9. This was Stalin's most positive reference to the Party during the war and, as will appear in a later chapter, it anticipated the launching of the Party revival just two months later. However, Stalin incorporated it in a panegyric about the state which was as enthusiastic as any he had ever uttered.

10. It was in 1943 that the Soviet Union began constructing the state-to-state bonds with the democratic countries of Europe which eventually served as a foundation for the Soviet bloc: see the detailed analysis of this process in Květa Kořalková, *Vytváření systému dvoustranných spojeneckých smluv mezi evropskými socialistickými zeměmi* [The formation of the bilateral alliance system among the European socialist countries], in *Rozpravy Československé Akademie Věd* [Transactions of the Czechoslovak Academy of Sciences], Vol. LXXVI, no. 3 (Prague: Akademia, 1966).

11. "Interview with Mr. King," 23 May 1943, *Soch.*, Vol. XV, pp. 104–5. For background see McKenzie, *Comintern and World Revolution*, ch. 8.

12. Arvo Tuominen, "The North European Communist Parties," p. 204.

13. For background, see Fred S. Burin, "The Communist Doctrine of the Inevitability of War," *American Political Science Review*, Vol. LXII (1963), pp. 334–54. Cf. Roy Medvedev, *Let History Judge* (New York: Knopf, 1971), p. 469, which refers to Soviet expectations of revolution after World War II. One may recall also Stalin's well-known election speech of February 1946, which described the late war in terms of the Leninist theory of imperialism, and his "Interview with a *Pravda* Correspondent" a few weeks later in which he stated that there was a "law of History" (*zakonomernost*) behind the rising influence of Communism in Europe: see *Soch.*, Vol. XVI, pp. 2, 42. A brilliant but far too schematic Western attempt to depict the events of 1944 and 1945 as a "revolutionary crisis" is Gabriel Kolko's *The Politics of War* (New York: Random House, 1968). A useful corrective is Starobin's short but incisive "Origins of the Cold War."

14. *Társadalmi Szemle*, Vol. VII (1952), p. 121.

15. Gyula Schöpflin, "Dokumentum: A Magyar Kommunista Párt útja, 1945–1950," p. 241; and my dissertation, "Communism and Hungary, 1944–1946" (Columbia University, 1965), pp. 244–57.

16. On Stalin's parochialism, see Pipes, *The Formation of the Soviet Union,* ch. 6 and p. 281; Tucker, *Stalin as Revolutionary,* pp. 245ff.

17. One may distinguish between the period before 1928, when Soviet foreign policies were still collegial, and the period from 1928 on, when Stalin was dominant. In the first period, Stalin from time to time threw his weight, as did his colleagues, behind "participationist" efforts to break out of the Soviet Union's diplomatic isolation—for example, in 1926 and 1927 in China. After 1928, Stalin was firm in his isolationist battle against "social Fascism." A survey of these developments is in Ulam, *Expansion and Coexistence,* ch. 4.

18. For Stalin's reluctance to participate in the popular front policies, see Cohen, *Bukharin,* pp. 360 and 469. Cohen argues, perhaps with exaggeration, that Stalin secretly wanted an entente with Berlin. It is possible he wanted no entanglement abroad at all.

19. Good reviews of the Hitler-Stalin rapprochement are found in Trumbull Higgins, *Hitler and Russia* (New York: Macmillan, 1966), ch. 1; and in James E. McSherry, *Stalin, Hitler and Europe,* 2 vols. (Cleveland: World, 1968–70), Vol. I.

20. For the following, see Higgins, *Hitler and Russia,* ch. 4, esp. pp. 113ff.; John Erickson, *The Road to Stalingrad* (New York: Harper and Row, 1975), ch. 2; and Albert Seaton, *The Russo-German War, 1941–1945* (London: Arthur Barker, 1971), chs. 1–2.

21. The most accusatory account of Stalin's suspicions of Great Britain is in Aleksandr M. Nekrich, *1941 22 Iyunya* [22 June 1941] (Moscow: Nauka, 1965), ch. 3. At the time they were known as far away as Yenan, where Mao Tse-tung was expecting a war not between the Soviet Union and Germany but between the Soviet Union and the Western Powers: see Stuart Schram, *Mao Tse-Tung* (London: Penguin, 1967), p. 224.

22. *Soch.,* Vol. XIV, pp. 2–10. The statement was published in *Bol'shevik,* no. 9 (1941), but has attracted little attention because of its esoteric form—it is a commentary, dated July 1934, on an article by Engels written in 1890. Medvedev (*Let History Judge,* p. 515) shows its worthlessness as scholarship. However, this only emphasizes that it was published not as scholarship, but as a clue to Stalin's foreign policy views of May 1941.

23. *Soch.,* Vol. XV, p. 22. Cf. Stalin's first wartime letter to Churchill, which crudely describes the new international situation in terms of imperialist "interests" (Stalin, *Correspondence,* Vol. I, pp. 12–13).

24. *Soch.,* Vol. XV, p. 70.

25. See Vojtěch Mástný, "Stalin and the Prospects of a Separate Peace in World War II," *American Historical Review,* Vol. LXXVII (1972), pp. 43–66; and H. W. Koch, "The Spectre of a Separate Peace in the East," *Journal of Contemporary History,* Vol. X, no. 3 (1975).

26. *Soch.,* Vol. XV, pp. 86ff., esp. p. 91.

27. William H. McNeill, *America, Britain and Russia* (London: Oxford University Press, 1953), p. 275.

28. Bodo Scheurig, *Free Germany. The National Committee and the League of German Officers* (Middletown, Conn.: Wesleyan University Press, 1969), pp. 42ff.; and the more recent detailed account in Horst Duhnke, *Die KPD von 1933 bis 1945* (Cologne: Kiepenheuer und Witsch, 1972), ch. 7.

29. Leonhard, *Die Revolution entlässt ihre Kinder,* pp. 299ff.

30. *Pravda,* 17 January 1944, p. 4. Cf. McNeill, *America, Britain and Russia,* p. 413; and Harriman and Abel, *Special Envoy,* p. 295.

31. Duhnke, *Die KPD,* p. 388.

32. *Pravda* published extensive figures on these supplies in the issue of 11 June 1944. For full discussion, see George C. Herring, Jr., *Aid to Russia* (New York:

Columbia University Press, 1973), esp. pp. 116–20; and Robert H. Jones, *The Roads to Russia. United States Lend Lease to the Soviet Union* (Norman: University of Oklahoma Press, 1969), pp. 245ff.

33. *Soch.,* Vol. XV, p. 93. Under the rubric of "Soviet territory" Stalin mentioned Estonia, Latvia, Lithuania, Moldavia, the Crimea, Karelia, and the Ukraine and Belorussia. The Soviet territorial demands on Poland were not publicly known until a TASS communiqué on 11 January 1944, but Stalin had told the British and the Poles privately of Soviet desires in 1941. For further discussion of Stalin's war aims, see Vojtěch Mástný, "Soviet War Aims at the Moscow and Teheran Conferences of 1943," *Journal of Modern History,* Vol. XLVII (1975), pp. 481–504.

34. For the development of the Soviet-Polish dispute, see S. Biegański, ed., *Documents on Polish-Soviet Relations, 1939–1945,* Vol. I. Also useful is the detailed account from an anti-Communist point of view by Edward J. Rozek, *Allied Wartime Diplomacy. A Pattern in Poland* (New York: John Wiley, 1958), chs. 4–6, and the recent skillful analysis by Jan M. Ciechanowski, *The Warsaw Uprising of 1944* (Cambridge: Cambridge University Press, 1974), chs. 1–3.

35. The relevant documents are in Winston S. Churchill, *Closing the Ring,* pp. 361ff.; and *Teheran Papers,* pp. 512, 594–603.

36. The texts are in Rothstein, *SFP,* Vol. II, pp. 39–41.

37. *Soch.,* Vol. XV, p. 140.

38. By this I mean that before the Ribbentrop-Molotov Pact the Comintern at least went through the motions of formulating a theoretical line before changing its policies: not so afterward (McKenzie, *Comintern and World Revolution,* pp. 164, 169ff.).

39. Morača, *Narodni front i komunisti,* p. 464.

40. See M. K. Dziewanowski, *The Communist Party of Poland,* rev. ed. (Cambridge, Mass.: Harvard University Press, 1975), pp. 149–54; and the detailed account by Marian Malinowski in *Z Pola Walki,* no. 3 (1968).

41. Cf. McKenzie, *Comintern and World Revolution,* p. 171; Morača, *Narodni front i komunisti,* p. 615; Dedijer, *The Battle Stalin Lost,* pp. 48ff., 101ff.; and Jesús Hernández, *La grande trahison,* pp. 246ff. Memories of annexationism were still strong enough in 1945 to stimulate inquires by the Yugoslav Communists about whether Moscow expected Yugoslavia to enter the Soviet Union and to produce strong denials by the Polish Communists that they had a plan whereby Poland would join the Soviet Union: see the Soviet letter of 4 May 1948 to the Yugoslav Central Committee in Royal Institute of International Affairs, *The Soviet-Jugoslav Dispute,* pp. 37–38; W. Gomułka, *W walce o demokrację ludową,* p. 160; and Khrushchev, *Memoirs,* Vol. II, p. 158.

42. Max Jacobson, *The Diplomacy of the Winter War* (Cambridge, Mass.: Harvard University Press, 1961), esp. pp. 145ff., 165–70; McKenzie, *Comintern and World Revolution,* pp. 171–72.

43. Max Beloff, *The Foreign Policy of the Soviet Union, 1924–1941,* 2 vols. (London: Oxford University Press, 1955), Vol. II, pp. 322ff.; Boris Meissner, *Die Sowjetunion, die baltischen Staaten, und das Völkerrecht* (Cologne: Verlag für Politik und Wirtschaft, 1956), ch. 2; and Georg Von Rauch, *The Baltic States, 1917–1940* (London: Hurst, 1974), pt. 5.

44. Eugen Steiner (*The Slovak Dilemma* [Cambridge: Cambridge University Press, 1973], ch. 6) tells of the Soviet recognition of independent Fascist Slovakia in 1940. Paul Shoup (*Communism and the Yugoslav National Question* [New York: Columbia University Press, 1968], pp. 49ff.) attempts to elucidate the devious shifts in Soviet and Yugoslav CP lines between 1939 and 22 June 1941. Cf. also Morača, *Narodni front i komunisti,* pp. 510–15, and 34ff. Titoist historiography claims that in general the Yugoslav Communists supported the unity of Yugoslavia during the Nazi-Soviet period. Shoup (p. 49n) agrees with this assessment, while pointing out that Moscow was not

against the separatist movements. The Communists' ambivalence toward Yugoslav unity is suggested, however, by the swift emergence of an apparently independent Slovene Communist Party immediately after the collapse of Yugoslavia in April 1941.

45. Morača, *Narodni front i komunisti*, p. 609.

46. Djilas claims to have gotten this information from Dimitrov (*Conversations with Stalin*, p. 33).

47. A. A. Grechko, ed., *Osvoboditel'naya missiya sovetskikh vooruzhennykh sil vo Velikoi Otechestvennoi Voine* [The liberating mission of the Soviet armed forces in the Great Patriotic War] (Moscow: Politizdat, 1971), pp. 62ff.; and I. Z. Zakharov, *Druzhba zakalennaya v boyakh* [Friendship steeled in battle] (Moscow: Mysl, 1970), ch. 5.

48. Starobin, *American Communist Party in Crisis*, ch. 2; Philip J. Jaffe, "Rise and Fall of Earl Browder," *Survey*, Vol. XVIII (1972), pp. 83ff.

49. For relevant texts, see Rothstein, *SFP*, Vol. II, pp. 42–50.

50. See Robert S. Sullivant, *Soviet Politics and the Ukraine* (New York: Columbia University Press, 1962), pp. 245–46, 380; Harriman and Abel, *Special Envoy*, pp. 303ff.

51. Rothstein, *SFP*, p. 45.

52. For further information about the Muscovites, see Annie Kriegel, "La dissolution du 'Komintern,' " *Revue d'histoire de la deuxième guerre mondiale*, no. 68 (1967), pp. 33–43; the memoirs of Alfred Burmeister [pseud.], *Dissolution and Aftermath of the Comintern: Experience and Observations;* and Leonhard, *Die Revolution entlässt ihre Kinder*, chs. 1–6.

53. Djilas, *Conversations with Stalin*, pp. 80–81.

54. Duhnke, *Die KPD*, p. 379.

55. See Paul E. Zinner, *Communist Strategy and Tactics in Czechoslovakia* (New York: Praeger, 1962), ch. 5, esp. pp. 85–87, and the recent essay by Thomas Hammond in his *The Anatomy of Communist Takeovers* (New Haven: Yale University Press, 1975), pp. 20ff.

56. Heinz Kühnreich, *Der Partisanenkrieg in Europa* (Berlin: Dietz, 1968), esp. pp. 407–23.

57. Charles B. Maclean, *Soviet Policy and the Chinese Communists, 1931–1946* (New York: Columbia University Press, 1958), pp. 117ff.; Tang Tsou, *America's Failure in China* (Chicago: University of Chicago Press, 1963), pp. 127–41; and Lyman P. Van Slyke, ed., *The Chinese Communist Movement* (Stanford: Stanford University Press, 1968), pp. 217ff.

58. Marian Malinowski, *Geneza PPR* [The genesis of the Polish Worker's Party] (Warsaw: Książka i Wiedza, 1972), chs. 1–2.

59. A classic expression of the Titoist point of view is in Fitzroy Maclean, *Tito*, pp. 88–89. Cf. Morača, *Narodni front i komunisti*, pp. 26ff.

60. Canada, Government of, *Report of the Royal Commission . . . to Investigate the Facts Relating to and the Circumstances Surrounding the Communication . . . of Secret and Confidential Information to Agents of a Foreign Power, June 27, 1946.*

61. Many of these are published in Jane Degras, ed., *The Communist International, 1919–1943*, Vol. III.

62. Djilas, *Conversations with Stalin*, pp. 10–13.

63. See "A békepártról," a memoir by János Kádár in *Párttörténeti Közlemények*, Vol. II, nos. 3–4 (1956), pp. 20–26.

64. Robert Aron, *Histoire de la libération de la France* (Paris: Fayard, 1959), pp. 573ff.

65. See Robert L. Wolff, *The Balkans in Our Time* (Cambridge, Mass.: Harvard University Press, 1956), and, in particular, the fascinating study by Dominique Eudes, *The Kapetaneios: Partisans and Civil War in Greece, 1943–1949* (New York: Monthly Review Press, 1972).

66. Kousoulas, *Revolution and Defeat*, pp. 160–64.

67. Fernand Gambery, *La libération de la Corse* (Paris: Hachette, 1973).

68. Dušan Plenča, *Medjunarodni otnosi Jugoslavije u toku Drugog Svjetskog Rata* [International relations of Yugoslavia during World War II] (Belgrade: Inst. Društ. Nauka, 1962), pp. 214ff.; Dedijer, *Tito. Prilozi*, p. 358.

69. Mástný, "The Beneš-Stalin-Molotov Conversations"; Edouard Táborský, "Beneš and Stalin, Moscow, 1943 and 1945," pp. 154–81; USSR, Ministry of Foreign Affairs, *Sovetsko-chekhoslovatskie otnosheniya vo vremya Velikoi Otechestvennoi Voiny;* and the survey by Josef Korbel, *The Communist Subversion of Czechoslovakia* (Princeton: Princeton University Press, 1959), ch. 6.

70. See the contribution by A. Rupen in T. Hammond, *Anatomy of Communist Takeovers*, pp. 145ff. This annexation symptomized a deep interconnection between Soviet foreign and domestic policies. As Rupen suggests, it accommodated the interests of Soviet atomic energy explorations, which were managed by the secret police. Further, as a "rectification" of the ethnic situation in a frontier zone, it was analogous to the various deportations of nationalities carried out by the secret police in 1943–1944, especially the deportation of the Meskhetian Turks from Soviet Armenia in November 1944 (see R. Conquest, *The Soviet Deportation of Nationalities* [London: Macmillan, 1960], and S. Enders Wimbush and Ronald Wixman, "The Meskhetian Turks," *Canadian Slavonic Papers*, Vol. XVII [1975], pp. 320–40). Finally, one may note that the annexation of Tannu Tuva sparked a reorganization of the industrial *oblasty* of western Siberia and the Urals which, as will appear in a later chapter, launched the domestic political conflicts of the postwar years.

71. Rieber, *Stalin and the French Communist Party*, pp. 44ff.; Robert Murphy, *Diplomat among Warriors*, ch. 14; and Kolko, *Politics of War*, ch. 4.

72. USSR, Ministry of Foreign Affairs, *Sovetsko-frantsuzskie otnosheniya vo vremya Velikoi Otechestvennoi Voiny, 1941–1945. Dokumenty i materialy*, p. 241. This Soviet intelligence report was, presumably, mistaken.

73. When De Gaulle visited Moscow in December 1944, Stalin displayed an extensive interest in the possible existence of a Western bloc: see Charles de Gaulle, *Mémoires de guerre*, Vol. III, pp. 385–86.

74. For the unpublicized but very bitter French Communist debate about this compromise, see D. Desanti, *Les staliniens* (Paris: Fayard, 1975), esp. pp. 9ff. Outwardly, the argument focuses on the disarmament of the resistance forces during the last months of 1944, with the "left" (Marty, Tillon) hinting that the Party leadership went too far in collaborating with De Gaulle, and the "orthodox" wing (Thorez) insisting that the Party was "correct." Below the surface, of course, lies a romantic regret among the "leftists" that despite all the adverse circumstances there was no Communist insurrection during the liberation of France.

75. For the following, see Delzell, *Mussolini's Enemies*, pp. 336ff.; Norman Kogan, *Italy and the Allies* (Cambridge, Mass.: Harvard University Press, 1956), ch. 5; and, recently, Antonio Gambino, *Storia del dopoguerra* (Rome: Laterza, 1975), pp. 31–45.

76. Vyshinsky's remarks are printed in Rothstein, *SFP*, Vol. II, pp. 67–68.

77. The Italians have debated about Togliatti's *svolta* ("turn") much more openly than the French about the compromises of Maurice Thorez. Togliatti himself averred that the *svolta* was not a turnabout at all but a logical continuation of the Italian CP policy which he had pursued in exile after 1935, and that in any case it was necessitated by the economic, social, and political devastation of Italy, which made sectarianism inappropriate. "Revolutionaries" on his left, however, claim he sold out; and on the "right" it is said that he crudely accommodated the CPI to Stalin's diplomacy. The literature is cited in Bocca, *Togliatti*, pp. 313ff.; Guido Quazzi, *La resistenza italiana* (Turin: Giappichelli, 1966), pp. 20–25. Cf. Paolo Spriano, *Storia del Partito Comunista Italiano*, 5 vols. (Turin: Einaudi, 1967–75), Vol. V, chs. 11–12.

78. Leonard Lundin, *Finland in the Second World War* (Bloomington: Indiana University Press, 1957), ch. 9.

79. Herbert Feis, *Churchill, Roosevelt, Stalin* (Princeton: Princeton University Press, 1957), pp. 336ff.; John A. Lukacs, *The Great Powers and Eastern Europe* (New York: American Book Company, 1953), pp. 576–77; and A. Cretzianu, "The Rumanian Armistice Negotiations."

80. Rothstein, *SFP*, Vol. II, p. 65.

81. Leonhard, *Die Revolution entlässt ihre Kinder,* p. 318.

82. *Soch.,* Vol. XV, p. 146.

83. CPSU, *Istoriya KPSS,* Vol. V., pp. 588–90.

84. Kousoulas, *Revolution and Defeat,* pp. 182ff.

Notes to Chapter 3

1. Dedijer, *Tito. Prilozi,* pp. 414–15. For speculation that Tito was ready to work with the Germans to keep the British out of Yugoslavia, see Ernst Halperin, *Der siegreiche Ketzer* (Cologne: Politik und Wirtschaft, 1957), pp. 31ff. A recent and detailed study documents some negotiations between the Partisans and the Germans in 1943, but not in 1944: see Walter R. Roberts, *Tito, Mihailović and the Allies, 1941–1945* (New Brunswick, N.J.: Rutgers University Press, 1973), pp. 106ff.

2. Feis, *Churchill, Roosevelt, Stalin,* pp. 445–46, 485. Cf. *FRUS 1944,* Vol. IV, p. 1007; and Churchill, *Triumph and Tragedy,* p. 230.

3. For details, see Kousoulas, *Revolution and Defeat,* pp. 183ff.

4. See Woodward, *British Foreign Policy in the Second World War,* Vol. III, pp. 115ff.

5. Plenča, *Medjunarodni odnosi Jugoslavije,* pp. 271ff.; Woodward, *British Foreign Policy,* Vol. III, chs. 42–43.

6. Feis, *Churchill, Roosevelt, Stalin,* chs. 39–40.

7. *Soch.,* Vol. XV, pp. 150–51.

8. Djilas, *Conversations with Stalin,* p. 73.

9. Molotov was wont to use the word "peanut" to refer to East European countries he considered insignificant (Djilas, *Conversations with Stalin,* p. 155).

10. The armistice agreement of 12 September with Rumania specified the return of Bessarabia to the Soviet Union; the text is found in Rothstein, *SFP,* Vol. II, pp. 123–27.

11. On 14 September *Pravda* published reports on negotiations between the Ukrainian and Belorussian Soviet Republican governments and the Polish Committee of National Liberation at Lublin about frontier questions and population exchanges.

12. The armistice terms of 19 September with Finland specified the return of Karelia to the Soviet Union and made a number of other frontier adjustments; the text is found in Rothstein, *SFP,* Vol. II, pp. 128–37.

13. Late in November, allegedly "popular" elements in the Soviet-occupied Carpatho-Ukraine abruptly requested Czechoslovak officials, who had arrived in the region, to depart so that the Ukraine might be "reunited." Who exactly these "popular" elements were has never been clarified, but it seems probable that they came from the Soviet partisan center at Kiev. The Polish, Czech, Slovak, Magyar, and even some Balkan Communist partisan movements all seem to have had links with that center, which in 1944 appears to have generated a certain amount of pressure for the unification of the Ukraine. President Beneš himself opened the door for the Carpatho-Ukrainian action in Moscow in December 1943, when he told Stalin that he was willing to consider a territorial concession. Stalin reminded him of his words in a letter of 23 January 1945, and as a result the Czechoslovak government agreed to relinquish the territory in March 1945; it actually did so by treaty in June. On these matters, see the eyewitness accounts by František Němec and Vladimír Moudrý, *The Soviet Seizure of*

Subcarpathian Ruthenia; and Zdeněk Fierlinger, *Ve sluzhbách ČSR,* Vol. II, pp. 371ff. A recent account is in Radomir Luža, "Czechoslovakia between Democracy and Communism," in *A History of the Czechoslovak Republic,* ed. Victor S. Mamatey and Radomir Luža (Princeton: Princeton University Press, 1973), pp. 387ff.

14. Among recent studies of the Warsaw uprising, Jan M. Ciechanowski (*The Warsaw Uprising of 1944*) attributes the disaster ultimately to Polish illusions and irresponsibility, and George L. Bruce, in *The Warsaw Uprising* (London: Hutchinson, 1972), passionately blames the Russians. Hanns von Krannhals' *Der Warschauer Aufstand, 1944* (Frankfurt am Main: Bernard und Graefe, 1962) is based on German materials and stresses the importance of the reinforcements brought in by the Germans. Aleksander Skarzynski's *Polityczni przyczny powstanie Warszawskiego* [The political origins of the Warsaw uprising] (Warsaw: Państwo, 1964) reflects the views of the Warsaw government. As Ciechanowski says (p. 250), the documents regarding Soviet motivation are inaccessible to historians, and, consequently, the question of responsibility cannot really be resolved.

15. Mikołajczyk tells his own story in *The Rape of Poland,* ch. 6.

16. On 13 August TASS published a communiqué blaming the uprising on the Polish émigrés in London and denying that there had been any consultation with the Red Army. On 15 August Vyshinsky used the term "adventurism," replete with ideological connotations, in rejecting an American request for airlift facilities behind Soviet lines. On 16 August Stalin called the uprising an "adventure" in a telegram to Mikołajczyk. See the documents in Biegański, *Polish-Soviet Relations,* Vol. II, pp. 340–47.

17. The conscious surrender of the Allies is nowhere more evident than in Loewenheim et al., eds., *The Roosevelt-Churchill Correspondence,* pp. 563ff.

18. Relevant texts are published in Biegański, *Polish-Soviet Relations,* Vol. II, pp. 367ff. Eyewitness reports are in Churchill, *Triumph and Tragedy,* pp. 226ff.; Eden, *The Reckoning,* pp. 555ff.; and Harriman and Abel, *Special Envoy,* pp. 356ff.

19. For literature on and discussion of the "percentage agreement" see John O. Iatrides, *Revolt in Athens* (Princeton: Princeton University Press, 1972), pp. 78ff.; and C. F. Woodhouse, *The Struggle for Greece, 1941–1949* (London: Hart-Davis, MacGibbon, 1976), pp. 92–94. As Soviet historians indicate, the "percentage agreement" was not an agreement because nothing was said, much less signed, on the Soviet side. However, their claim that Churchill's proposed percentage division of the Balkans was to Stalin merely a dirty piece of paper, expressing only British willingness to compromise, is dubious. The "agreement" clearly influenced Soviet policy toward Greece later in the year.

20. Ghita Ionescu, *Communism in Rumania* (London: Oxford University Press, 1964), pp. 94ff. According to a Rumanian "revelation" in 1961, the Rumanian Muscovite Communists hoped in August and September 1944 that the Russians would reject King Michael's "leap out of the war," that they would conquer Rumania, and that they would then place the Communists in power. Molotov firmly rejected this project. Cf. Stephen Fischer-Galati, *The New Rumania* (Cambridge, Mass.: MIT Press, 1967), pp. 23–25.

21. See A. F. Upton, *The Communist Parties of Scandinavia and Finland* (London: Weidenfeld and Nicolson, 1973), pp. 237ff.; James Billington, "Finland," in *Communism and Revolution: The Strategic Uses of Political Violence,* ed. Cyril Black (Princeton: Princeton University Press, 1964), pp. 117–44; and John H. Hodgson, *Communism in Finland* (Princeton: Princeton University Press, 1967), ch. 7.

22. H. P. Krosby, "The Communist Power Bid in Finland in 1948," *Political Science Quarterly,* Vol. LXXV (1960), pp. 229–43; and Djilas, *Conversations with Stalin,* p. 155.

23. Nissan Oren provides details in *Bulgarian Communism: The Road to Power, 1934–1944* (New York: Columbia University Press, 1971), pp. 251–58.

24. Cf. Wolff, *The Balkans in Our Time*, pp. 292–305.
25. Leonhard, *Die Revolution entlässt ihre Kinder*, p. 333; Djilas, *Conversations with Stalin*, pp. 116–17.
26. The semi-official CPF history accepts the judgment of Robert Aron that only a few provincial Communists favored such a bid: see Jacques Fauvet, *Histoire du Parti Communiste Français*, 2 vols. (Paris: Fayard, 1965), Vol. II, pp. 139ff. That this was not the case is strongly suggested in such works as Charles Tillon's *Les FTP. La guérilla en France*, p. 374, and by the record of the Tillon-Marty affair of 1952. Cf. Desanti, *Les staliniens*, pp. 9ff.; F. Fejtö, *The French Communist Party* (Cambridge, Mass.: MIT Press, 1967), pp. 21–24.
27. For the Muscovite position, see M. Thorez, *Oeuvres*, Vol. XX, pp. 13–15, 67ff. Cf. the warning against adventurism by J. Duclos, cited in Rieber, *Stalin and the French Communist Party*, p. 149. Tillon, in his autobiography, charges that he was ready to launch an insurrection of the entire resistance on 5 August 1944, but that Moscow, with Thorez' consent, asked Duclos to keep the CPF out of it (*On chantait rouge*, p. 387).
28. Thorez attempted to go to Algiers in March 1944, at about the same time as Togliatti returned to Italy, but the Gaullist regime refused him amnesty from the criminal charges the French government laid against him late in 1939. The amnesty was finally granted on 31 October 1944, and Thorez returned to France on 27 November. Fauvet (*Histoire du PCF*, pp. 173–74) denies that Thorez showed interest in the weapons question until January 1945, but this denial seems to be based on technicalities: it is widely reported that Thorez not only urged the weapons decision in France but helped calm the Communist revolt late in November in Belgium. See Desanti, *Les staliniens*, pp. 15ff.; and Rieber, *Stalin and the French Communist Party*, pp. 188ff.
29. One may follow the developments in Slovakia in Vilém Prečan, ed., *Slovenské národne povstanie. Dokumenty*, and in the eyewitness account by Gustáv Husák, *Svedectvo o Slovenskom národnom povstaní*. The best Western accounts are in Steiner, *The Slovak Dilemma*, ch. 7, and Wolfgang Venohr, *Aufstand für die Tschechoslovakei: Der slovakische Freiheitskampf von 1944* (Hamburg: Ch. Wegner, 1969).
30. See the memoir by the Czech Muscovite Communist Václav Kopecký (*ČSR a KSČ*, p. 348), and Venohr, *Aufstand*, p. 143.
31. See my "Communism and Hungary," pp. 102–3. It seems noteworthy that at the beginning of November 1944, Stalin arbitrarily overrode his military advisers and forced a premature—and unsuccessful—Soviet offensive against Budapest. See Malinovsky, *Budapesht, Vena, Praga*, pp. 81–83.
32. G. Dimitrov, *S'chineniya*, Vol. XI, pp. 151–58; cf. pp. 164–67.
33. The derivation of the slogan "people's democracy" is unclear. According to Hungarian historians, it originated with the CPH theorist József Révai in 1938 (Ernö Gondos, "A 'Gondolatról' " [About the journal "Thought"], *Párttörténeti Közlemények*, Vol. X [1964], p. 103). An authority on the Chinese CP, on the other hand, claims that it derives from Mao Tse-tung's "new democracy," which dates from about 1940 (Benjamin Schwartz, "China and the Soviet Theory of People's Democracy," *Problems of Communism*, September–October 1954). Given Stalin's dislike of Mao, I doubt this explanation. My own inclination is to agree with the Czech historian V. Suchopar, who points out that both "people's" and "democracy" were used as slogans by the Bolsheviks in the early days of the formation of the Soviet state (for example, both Khiva and Tannu Tuva were at one time "people's republics"), and that the later European "people's democracies" were just hybrids (*Příspěvky k Dějinám KSČS*, Vol. II, no. 2 [1962], pp. 163–91). It seems relevant that in the early 1920s the Austrian Social Democrat Otto Bauer used the phrase "people's republic" to justify his Party's participation in the government after the bloodless "revolution" of 1918 in Vienna: see *Der Kampf* (Vienna), Vol. VIII (1924), pp. 57–67. In any case, Dimitrov's

Notes to pages 58–61

use of the slogan "people's democracy" in September 1944 antedates any reference hitherto cited by Western historians and must be the first postwar use of the term.

34. A Bulgarian Communist explains the applicability of the "people's democracy" slogan to Bulgaria in Voin Bozhinov, *Zashchitata na natsionalnata nezavisimost na B'lgaria* [The defense of national independence in Bulgaria] (Sofia: Akad. Nauk, 1962), pp. 6ff.

35. *Ibid.*

36. For the Yugoslav model see G. W. Hoffman and F. W. Neal, *Yugoslavia and the New Communism* (New York: Twentieth Century Fund, 1962), p. 84.

37. Rothstein, *SFP*, p. 141; Dedijer, *Tito. Prilozi*, pp. 412–13.

38. For details of these and the following Yugoslav demands, see Shoup, *Communism and the Yugoslav National Question*, pp. 125–28, 150ff.

39. Billington ("Finland," in Black, ed., *Communism and Revolution*, p. 124) notes the Finnish CP's use of the term in October 1944.

40. József Révai used the term on 19 November 1944 and frequently thereafter: see László Dér et al., eds., *Felszabadulás 1944 . . . Dokumentumok*, p. 178, and Révai, *Élni tudtunk a szabadsággal*, pp. 439ff. Cf. the extensive background information in Bálint Szabó, *Népi demokrácia és forradalomelmélet* [People's democracy and revolutionary theory] (Budapest: Kossuth könyvkiadó, 1970), ch. 2, esp. pp. 106ff.

41. Djilas, *Conversations with Stalin*, pp. 114–15.

42. *Ibid.*, pp. 87–97.

43. The affair of the Bulgarian army illustrates how deeply Stalin had involved himself in Balkan politics during 1944 in order to thwart the Yugoslavs. In May, while he was in Moscow, Djilas (*ibid.*, p. 37) sensed that Dimitrov somehow did not feel that the state apparatus of royalist Bulgaria would have to be entirely smashed during the country's liberation. The reason came to light in the fall, when Stalin ordered the Red Army not to disarm the soldiers of the Bulgarian army. According to Zhukov, who received the order, Stalin was indulging Dimitrov's notion that the Bulgarian common man, a Slav, and by tradition a Russophile, might be presumed to be progressive in his political attitudes and to be trustworthy (Zhukov, *Vospominaniya i razmyshleniya*, pp. 579–81). Just after the liberation of Bulgaria and Stalin's display of trust for its people, Tito came to Moscow boasting about how the Yugoslav partisans were liberating their own country. Stalin urged him to let the Bulgarian army, now no longer "Fascist," participate in the final expulsion of the Germans from Yugoslavia. On his way home, Tito met and discussed this matter with a delegation of the Bulgarian Fatherland Front, reluctantly agreeing that the Bulgarians were "democratic" and might therefore help (*Vjesnik* [Zagreb], 10 May 1975, reported in Radio Free Europe, "Yugoslav Background Report," 6 June 1975, p. 4). From that time and throughout the winter, Stalin taunted the Yugoslavs about the superiority of the Bulgarian army over the Partisans.

44. Djilas, *Conversations with Stalin*, p. 112.

45. *Ibid.*, p. 113.

46. *Ibid.*, pp. 113–14.

47. "Interview with Ralph Parker," *Soch.*, Vol. XV, p. 201.

48. T. Stanojević, ed., *Tito, govori i članci*, Vol. I, pp. 325–26.

49. *Deset let*, p. 284.

50. Dimitrov claimed as early as 14 January 1945 that "people's democracy" already existed in Bulgaria: see *S'chineniya*, Vol. XI, pp. 164–67. However, his original use of the slogan, and early Hungarian use of it in general, was put in the future tense. Dimitrov's decision to equate "people's democracy" not with some future form of state but with what actually existed in East European countries in 1945 caused Marxists endless confusion in 1948, when all these countries, without ceasing to be people's democracies, became proletarian dictatorships as well. Ever since then the slogan "people's democracy" has been applied both to the egg (the stage of transition

346

to proletarian dictatorship) and to the chicken (the dictatorship itself). The trend today is to escape the confusion by dating the creation of the dictatorships at the start of the people's democracies—in 1944 or 1945 (see Władisław Góra, in *Z Pola Walki*, no. 3 [1974], pp. 69–84, and the discussion in *Párttörténeti Közlemények*, nos. 2–3 [1964]). This revision eliminates the logical inconsistency between the terms but is historically nonsensical.

51. A sharp dispute between the Soviet government and that of Yugoslavia just a few weeks before Gottwald spoke affords one reason for suspecting that Stalin was Gottwald's inspiration and Tito among his targets. On 27 May 1945 Tito publicly denounced great power "barter and bargaining" with Yugoslav interests in the Trieste region. As a result, on 5 June he received a sharp rebuke from Moscow for allegedly "insulting the Soviet Union": see Clissold, *Yugoslavia and the Soviet Union, 1939–1973. A Documentary Survey*, p. 45. It is also important to note that Stalin retained control over the European Communists by refusing to let Dimitrov leave Moscow for Bulgaria, as he desired, and that ideological developments were taking place. In June 1945 German Communists going home from Moscow sharply changed the theory behind their Party's policies, and at the same moment all the European Communists altered their trade union policies: see Leonhard, *Die Revolution entlässt ihre Kinder*, pp. 397ff.; Borkenau, *European Communism*, p. 464–65. It is notable, finally, that from 21 to 30 June a Czechoslovak government delegation, including Gottwald, was in Moscow to sign the treaty relinquishing the Carpatho-Ukraine to the Soviet Union and to negotiate with a delegation of leading Polish statesmen about frontier problems. Stalin received both delegations. One may add that in the Czechoslovak, as well as in the international Communist context, Gottwald's statement constituted a defense of his coalitionist Party line against "leftists" who wished to proceed to socialism immediately. He defined "people's democracy" as a stage of development which was specifically not yet socialist. See Jaroslav Opat, *O novou demokracii* [About new democracy] (Prague: Akademia, 1966), pp. 220ff.

52. For the dispute, see Adam Ulam, *Titoism and the Cominform* (Cambridge, Mass.: Harvard University Press, 1952); and, more recently, Clissold's introduction to his *Yugoslavia and the Soviet Union*, pp. 42ff.

53. See the commentary in *FRUS 1944*, Vol. IV, pp. 929–30. Among historians, only Starobin ("Origins of the Cold War," p. 283) seems sensitive to the significance of this speech.

54. Although the Red Army was successful throughout 1943 and 1944, Stalin called 1943 a year of "radical breakthrough," whereas 1944 became the year of "decisive victories"—an empty distinction (*Soch.*, Vol. XV, pp. 152–53).

55. Specifically, Stalin declared that the Soviet armies would not have been able to do what they did without the opening of the second front (p. 158) or without the home front (p. 159). Deprecation of the army, even on this subtle level, is not to be found in the speech of 6 November 1943.

56. *Soch.*, Vol. XV, p. 162.

57. *Ibid.*, pp. 163–64 (italics added).

58. *Ibid.*, p. 22.

59. *Ibid.*, pp. 69ff.

60. Leonhard, *Die Revolution entlässt ihre Kinder*, p. 234.

61. *Soch.*, Vol. XV, pp. 168–69 (italics added). As more than one historian has pointed out, Stalin's "law of history" went a good way toward justifying his own unpreparedness in 1941.

62. For background, see R. R. Russell, *History of the United Nations* (Washington, D.C.: Brookings Institution, 1958), and D. Clemens, *Yalta* (New York: Oxford University Press, 1970), pp. 44ff. Some Western historians consider that Stalin had no real interest in the UNO. V. Mástný argues effectively against this view, saying: "Pre-

cisely because of the central role of the [UN] Organization in the American scheme of things, the issue involved the entire pattern of future [Soviet] relations with the most powerful nation in the world" ("The Cassandra in the Foreign Commissariat," p. 368).

63. For the dating, see H. Salisbury, *The 900 Days* (New York: Harper and Row, 1969), p. 576.

64. He published a letter in *Pravda* on 29 June 1939 in which he expressed his personal view that the British and French were not negotiating seriously with Moscow but were stalling until they could smooth things over with the Germans. This was perhaps the bluntest top-level statement of Soviet distrust for *all* imperialists in the prewar era.

65. Interview with the author, Brussels, May 1964.

66. Djilas, *Conversations with Stalin*, pp. 130–33.

67. Khrushchev, *Memoirs*, Vol. II, p. 167.

68. By far the most articulate of the "planners" were the Czech Gottwald and the Hungarian Rákosi. Gottwald referred to his party's plans in his speech of 9 July 1945, published two years later in his *Deset let*, pp. 286–87. He may have simply been referring to some very thorough discussions of postwar tactics which he and his comrades held in Moscow in 1943 and 1944 (see Zinner, *Communist Strategy and Tactics in Czechoslovakia*, pp. 85ff.). As noted above, however, he was countering "leftist" criticism of his coalitionary tactics in that speech; the mention of secret "plans" therefore gave him a certain tactical advantage which historians cannot ignore. Rákosi is reported to have spoken of plans in May 1945, at a closed gathering of Party leaders (see Schöpflin, "Dokumentum: A Magyar Kommunista Párt útja," p. 241), and he publicly hinted at their existence in March 1946, in his commentary on Stalin's polemic against Churchill (*A magyar demokráciáért*, pp. 301ff.). In both cases Rákosi's reference was to Stalin's wish to delay a Communist takeover in Eastern Europe for ten or more years, during which time the Soviet Union would manipulate the splits between the Western imperialists; in the first case, Rákosi explicitly aimed his remarks at Communist "leftists." In 1947, while Rákosi was completing the piece-by-piece demolition of the political opposition in Hungary—his famous "salami" operations—he published a speech, allegedly delivered on 22 February 1945, which seemed to predict this mode of operation. This sort of evidence of "planning" was unmistakably produced in order to overawe the opposition. Later still on 21 and 29 November 1948, Rákosi went further, indicating in his party's daily newspaper, *Szabad Nép,* that the entire takeover had been planned in advance. In 1949, Rákosi's comrade József Révai published an article (widely reprinted and translated) in the CPH theoretical journal *Társadalmi Szemle* (Vol. IV, nos. 3–4) which confirmed that the takeover had been carefully planned. Rákosi repeated this assertion in a well-known speech in 1952 (*Társadalmi Szemle,* Vol. VII, nos. 2–3). In my opinion, these after-the-fact assertions by Rákosi and Révai must be interpreted primarily as a coverup for their own behavior of 1945–1948, which by the standards of 1949–1953 was rightist, nationalist, and un-Leninist deviationism.

69. Elliot R. Goodman, *The Soviet Design for a World State* (New York: Columbia University Press, 1961) treats many Soviet ideological statements, exaggeratedly, as "blueprint plans." A more recent Western discussion of this problem is found in T. T. Hammond's introduction to his *Anatomy of Communist Takeovers*, pp. 20ff. On the Soviet side, the recent and massive fifth volume of Gromyko et al., eds., *Istoriya diplomatii*, pp. 30–34, claims that behind the foreign policy of the Soviet Union during 1945 lay a great "democratic plan" worked out during the war by the Communist Party. We will discuss this claim further in Chapter 9 below.

70. There is great controversy about who to blame for the Communist revolt at Athens and the consequent civil war in Greece. The most scholarly indictment of the Communists is in Stephen G. Xydis' *Greece and the Great Powers, 1944–1947* (Thes-

salonika: Institute for Balkan Studies, 1963). The case against the British may be found in André Kedros' *La résistance grecque* (Paris: Robert Laffont, 1966). Recent studies tend to recognize some British responsibility for the eruption of fighting, and they acknowledge that Belgrade encouraged Greek Communist militancy, but they place most of the blame on the independent spirit of the Greek Communists. See Kousoulas, *Revolution and Defeat*, pp. 173ff., 182ff.; Iatrides, *Revolt in Athens*, p. 279; the long review of Iatrides' book by C. M. Woodhouse in *Balkan Studies*, Vol. XIII (1972), pp. 353–61; Woodhouse's own *The Struggle for Greece, 1941–1949*, pp. 109–10 and ch. 5; and Heinz Richter, *Griechenland zwischen Revolution und Konterrevolution* (Frankfurt am Main: Europäische Verlagsanstalt, 1973), pp. 513ff.

71. T. Trout ("Soviet Policy Making," p. 162) argues that some Soviet journals, including *New Times*, did criticize British policy in Greece. *Pravda* and *Izvestiya* did not press the issue, however, and Stalin and Molotov remained silent—in striking contrast to the British press and the American secretary of state. This is what mattered to Churchill at the time (*Triumph and Tragedy*, pp. 292–93, 305). Further, Moscow gave concrete help: on 30 December 1944, at the height of the Greek civil war, the Soviet government appointed an ambassador to the Greek government against which the Greek Communists were fighting (Kousoulas, *Revolution and Defeat*, p. 214).

72. For a detailed account of this maneuver, see M. Korom, "Az ideiglenes nemzetgyülés és a kormány létrehozásának elökészítése." See also the final chapters of C. A. Macartney, *October Fifteenth*, rev. ed. (Edinburgh: Edinburgh University Press, 1961); and the last chapter of György Ránki, *Emlékiratok és valóság Magyarország második világháborús szerepéröl* [Memoirs and reality about Hungary's role in World War II] (Budapest: Kossuth könyvkiadó, 1964).

73. *Teheran Papers*, p. 486.

74. Djilas, *Conversations with Stalin*, p. 81.

75. *Soch.*, Vol. XVI, pp. 230–31.

Notes to Chapter 4

1. *Soch.*, Vol. XV, pp. 203–4.

2. *Ibid.*, Vol. XVI, pp. 19–20.

3. *Ibid.*, p. 206.

4. For the background of the following account see D. Fedotov-White, *The Growth of the Red Army* (Princeton: Princeton University Press, 1944); John Erickson, *The Soviet High Command* (New York: St. Martin's Press, 1962); and the useful survey in Kolkowicz, *The Soviet Military and the Communist Party*, ch. 3.

5. Robert Conquest, *The Great Terror*, rev. ed. (London: Pelican, 1971), pp. 300–302.

6. Erickson, *The Soviet High Command*, pp. 504–6.

7. It is estimated that at least a quarter of the entire Party membership was lost in the first months of the war (Rigby, *Communist Party Membership*, pp. 241, 251; Armstrong, *Politics of Totalitarianism*, p. 131). All the *oblast* Party histories mention huge leadership turnovers in the early war period.

8. A. V. Khrulev, "Stanovlenie strategicheskogo tyla," pp. 66–67.

9. Petrov, *Stroitel'stvo politorganov*, p. 321.

10. Petrov, *Partiinoe stroitel'stvo*, p. 451. Petrov treats this limitation of the Party's "rights" as the greatest indignity suffered by the Party during the war; he blames it on the "cult of personality." Kolkowicz (*The Soviet Military*, p. 69) depicts the establishment of the company-level Party organizations as the start of the Party's revanche. Petrov (*Stroitel'stvo politorganov*, pp. 311–12) denies this interpretation.

11. Robert Conquest, *The Soviet Police System* (New York: Praeger, 1968), p. 20.

12. See General A. Pigurnov's "Deyatel'nost voennykh sovetov," pp. 47–56; and Dedijer, *Battle Stalin Lost*, p. 98.

13. Leonhard, *Die Revolution entlässt ihre Kinder*, p. 425.
14. Werth, *Russia at War*, pp. 903–4.
15. O. P. Chaney, Jr., *Zhukov* (Norman: University of Oklahoma Press, 1971), pp. 95, 155–57; Werth, *Russia at War*, p. 904; Djilas, *Conversations with Stalin*, p. 55; and Seweryn Bialer, *Stalin and His Generals*, ch. 4, esp. pp. 459–61.
16. Tyulenev, *Cherez tri voiny*, p. 141.
17. Letter of 18 July 1941 to Churchill, *Stalin Correspondence*, Vol. I, p. 13.
18. Quoted in Robert Murphy, *Diplomat among Warriors*, p. 239.
19. Matthew P. Gallagher, *The Soviet History of World War II* (New York: Praeger, 1963), ch. 1.
20. For the first ten days of the war Stalin did not appear in public. On 30 June the GOKO was formed. On 3 July he finally addressed the nation. On 10 July he became chief of the General Staff. On 19 July he replaced Timoshenko as defense commissar. See the discussion of the sources in Salisbury, *The 900 Days*, pp. 80, 139–41.
21. Examples are given in Bialer, *Stalin and His Generals*, esp. pp. 236, 421ff.
22. Rokossovskii, *Soldatskii Dolg*, p. 92.
23. *Soch.*, Vol. XV, pp. 14ff.; Raymond Garthoff, *Soviet Military Doctrine* (Glencoe, Ill.: Free Press, 1953), p. 34.
24. On these matters see Garthoff, "The Marshals and the Party," in H. L. Coles, ed., *Total War and Cold War* (Columbus: Ohio State University Press, 1962), pp. 241–65; the detailed discussion of the "Stalingrad" group in Kolkowicz, *The Soviet Military*, ch. 7; and Kolkowicz' contribution in H. G. Skilling and F. Griffiths, eds., *Interest Groups in Soviet Politics* (Princeton: Princeton University Press, 1971), ch. 5.
25. *Bol'shevik*, no. 16 (1945), pp. 12ff.
26. *Vedomosti Verkhovnogo Soveta SSSR*, nos. 61 (388) and 71 (398) (1945).
27. V. N. Donchenko, "Demobilizatsiya sovetskoi armii" [The demobilization of the Soviet army], *Istoriya SSSR*, no. 3 (1970), p. 97.
28. Raymond Garthoff, *Soviet Strategy in the Nuclear Age* (New York: Praeger, 1958), ch. 2. These changes are discussed in Chapter 10 below.
29. *Propagandist*, no. 18 (1944).
30. Petrov, *Stroitel'stvo politorganov*, p. 379.
31. See in particular the speech by Major General Isaev and the article by Marshal Vasilevskii, monitored by the BBC Soviet Service, 22 February 1946.
32. Petrov, *Stroitel'stvo politorganov*, pp. 393ff.
33. *Ibid.*, p. 397.
34. Kolkowicz, *The Soviet Military*, p. 70; Malcolm Mackintosh, *Juggernaut: The Russian Forces, 1918–1966* (New York: Macmillan, 1967), pp. 271ff.
35. The standard biography of Bulganin is in *BSE*, 2d ed., Vol. VI, p. 260. See also the sketches in B. Meissner, *Sowjetrussland zwischen Revolution und Restauration*, pp. 117–27; B. Nicolaevsky, *Power and the Soviet Elite* (New York: Praeger, 1965), pp. 229ff. The promotions were announced in *Pravda*, 19 November 1944, p. 1, and 22 November 1944, p. 4.
36. Prior to Shcherbakov's death Shikin was deputy chief of the GPUKA and head of its propaganda section: see G. Sredin, "Rukovodstvo Gla PURKKA partiino-politicheskoi raboty v voiskakh v zavershayushchem period voiny" [The leadership of the chief political administration of the Red Army in the Party political work in the army in the closing period of the war], *Voenno-Istoricheskii Zhurnal*, no. 5 (1975), p. 54.
37. Khrushchev ridicules Bulganin's military capacities in his *Memoirs*, Vol. II, p. 12. General S. M. Shtemenko has described the entirely political background of Bulganin's rise. Apparently Stalin was feeling "irritated" at the army at about this time; he therefore "discovered" that generals Voronov and Zhukov had issued some regulations without his knowledge, took the matter to the Politburo, and had that body reprimand

the generals and appoint Bulganin to make an investigation. See Shtemenko, *General'nyi shtab v gody voiny,* Vol. I, p. 297.

38. Chaney, *Zhukov,* pp. 348–50.
39. Garthoff, "The Marshals and the Party," pp. 243ff.
40. Petrov, *Partiinoe stroitel'stvo,* p. 446.
41. Khrushchev, *Crimes of the Stalin Era,* pp. S42–S43.
42. For a recent discussion of the problems of group conflicts within Soviet totalitarianism, see the essays in Skilling and Griffiths, *Interest Groups in Soviet Politics.* The classic study of the Soviet system as "totalitarianism" is Carl J. Friedrich and Zbigniew Brzezinski, *Totalitarian Dictatorship and Autocracy* (Cambridge, Mass.: Harvard University Press, 1956). An important debate on this subject between Carl Linden, T. Rigby, R. Conquest, R. Tucker, and Wolfgang Leonhard appeared in *Problems of Communism,* nos. 5–6 (1963). See also Paul Hollander, "Observations on Bureaucracy, Totalitarianism and the Comparative Study of Communism," *Slavic Review,* Vol. XXVI (1967), pp. 302–7.
43. The histories of the Soviet police all have to be revised in the light of Solzhenitsyn's *Gulag Archipelago.* Useful, however, are Ronald Hingley, *The Russian Secret Police* (London: Hutchinson, 1970), chs. 7–13; Conquest, *The Soviet Police System;* and S. Wolin and R. M. Slusser, eds., *The Soviet Secret Police* (New York: Praeger, 1957).
44. See Conquest, *The Great Terror,* pp. 275–76; and the paper delivered by Robert Slusser at the San Francisco meeting of the American Historical Association in December 1973.
45. The size of the slave labor force in Russia at the end of the war has been the subject of much debate because, as Hingley points out (*The Russian Secret Police,* p. 230), there are no available statistics. At the start of the Cold War, David Dallin and Boris Nicolaevsky estimated ten to twenty million (*Forced Labor in Soviet Russia* [New Haven: Yale University Press, 1948]). Somewhat later, the economist Naum Jasny estimated three and a half million on the basis of the 1941 state plan ("Labor and Output in Soviet Concentration Camps," *Journal of Political Economy,* Vol. LIX, no. 5 [1951], p. 410). The recent study by Conquest doubles this figure (*The Soviet Secret Police,* pp. 80–81). Solzhenitsyn guesses that there were never at one time more than twelve million, perhaps half of which were "politicals" (*Gulag Archipelago,* Vol. I, p. 595).
46. Jasny, "Labor and Output," p. 413.
47. Conquest, *Power and Policy,* pp. 136ff. The official biography of Beria is in *BSE,* 2d ed., Vol. V (1950), pp. 23–24.
48. For an account of Stalin's distrust of Beria in 1941 and later, see Svetlana Alliluyeva, *Only One Year,* p. 376.
49. Marshal N. N. Voronov, *Na sluzhbe voennoi,* pp. 194–95.
50. This information is enshrined in the *BSE* biography. Molotov and Voznesensky both held the same title, and its significance is not known.
51. R. Conquest, *The Soviet Deportation of Nationalities,* chs. 4–7.
52. *Pravda,* 11 July 1945, p. 1.
53. For documentation, see Conquest, *The Soviet Police System,* p. 22. The division between "economic" and "police" functions was not really clear-cut until further reforms were made in 1949 and 1950. In April 1943 V. N. Merkulov became head of the NKGB. *Pravda* recorded Beria's replacement in the NKVD by S. N. Kruglov on 16 January 1946 (p. 6). The Supreme Soviet authorized Merkulov's replacement by V. S. Abakumov on 18 October 1946.
54. Hingley, *The Russian Secret Police,* pp. 197–99, 201.
55. Khrushchev, *Crimes of the Stalin Era,* p. S45.
56. Nicolaevsky, *Power and the Soviet Elite,* p. 109.
57. *Ibid.,* p. 162; Conquest, *Power and Policy,* ch. 5.

Notes to pages 85–88

58. *Khrushchev Remembers,* pp. 295–96.
59. Conquest, *Power and Policy,* ch. 7.
60. Classic attempts at defining the manager group include those of James Burnham, *The Managerial Revolution* (New York: John Day, 1941); Milovan Djilas, *The New Class* (New York: Praeger, 1957); and Alfred Meyer, *The Soviet Political System* (New York: Random House, 1965). Meyer offers the analogy of a complex of giant corporations "owned" centrally by the Communist Party (pp. 112–13). A recent critique of this and other formulations is in David Lane, *Politics and Society in the USSR* (London: Weidenfeld and Nicolson, 1970), ch. 6. Lane describes the leading stratum in terms of a cluster of groups, or elites (ch. 8). In this he parallels Skilling and Griffiths, *Interest Groups in Soviet Politics.* For consideration of the managers as just one such interest group, see J. R. Azrael, *Managerial Power and Soviet Politics* (Cambridge, Mass.: Harvard University Press, 1966). For an analysis of the terminological troubles Soviet scholars encounter in discussing these matters, see Mervyn Matthews, *Class and Society in Soviet Russia* (London: Allen Lane Penguin, 1972), pp. 142–48.
61. A recent history of the managerial elite is in William J. Conyngham, *Industrial Management in the Soviet Union* (Stanford, Calif.: Hoover Institution, 1973), chs. 2–3. I have been helped here by Vera Dunham, *In Stalin's Time* (New York: Cambridge University Press, 1976), and by Sanford Lieberman's paper on the Soviet Party during the war, read at the AAASS national convention in Atlanta in October 1975.
62. Cf. N. S. Timasheff, *The Great Retreat* (New York: Dutton, 1946).
63. *Bol'shevik,* nos. 3–4 (1941), pp. 11–35.
64. Hough, *The Soviet Prefects,* pp. 108–9.
65. Likhomanov, *Organizatorskaya rabota partii v promyshlennosti v pervii period voiny,* chs. 1–2; A. F. Vasil'ev, "Iz praktiki partiino-organizatsionnoi raboty v sovetskom tylu, 1941–1943g" [From the practice of the Party's organizational work in the Soviet rear], *Voprosy Istorii KPSS,* no. 6 (1964), pp. 97–107; and A. Polyakov, ed., *Eshelony idut na vostok: Sbornik statei* [The echelons go east: A collection of articles] (Moscow: Nauka, 1966).
66. Likhomanov, "Organizatorskaya rabota," pp. 103–5. Soviet statistics on the evacuation of personnel seem to lump the managers discussed here with factory workers in the category "workers and employees." In late 1942 the number of these persons in the East had increased 1,069,000 over the 1940 level. In the Urals and the Volga the rise in industrial workers and employees was 65 percent. See I. A. Gladkov, ed., *Sovetskaya ekonomika v period voiny* [The Soviet economy in the war period] (Moscow: Nauka, 1970), p. 197; cf. Hough, *The Soviet Prefects,* p. 45.
67. See Petrov, *Stroitel'stvo politorganov,* p. 279, for the following.
68. See Gerald Segal, "Economics, Politics, and Party Control," *Problems of Communism,* Vol. XV, no. 2 (1966), p. 4ff., and the commentary on his article by Abraham Katz, "The Politics of Economic Reform in the Soviet Union" (Ph.D. diss., Harvard University, 1967), pp. 114–16. Cf. the eulogy to Voznesensky by G. Sorokin in *Pravda,* 1 December 1963, p. 4.
69. The contrast is clear, for example, in Yurii Bondarev's novel *Tishina,* pt. 1, ch. 12; it was a major theme in the election speeches of Malenkov and Molotov in February 1946. Cf. the literary references in Dunham, *In Stalin's Time,* pp. 137ff., 176ff., 195.
70. The *locus classicus* is Voznesensky's *Voennaya ekonomika SSSR,* published in 1948 and available in English as *The Economy of the USSR during World War II* (Washington, D.C.: Public Affairs Press, 1948), esp. ch. 5. Of the several updatings and revisions of Voznesensky since 1956, the most recent are Yu. A. Vasil'ev, *Sibirskii arsenal* [Siberian arsenal] (Sverdlovsk: SUKI, 1965); G. S. Kravchenko, *Ekonomika SSSR v gody voiny* [The economy of the USSR in the war period] (Moscow: Ekonomika, 1970), esp. chs. 7–8; and Gladkov, *Sovetskaya ekonomika.*
71. *Voennaya ekonomika SSSR,* pp. 28–29.

72. *Zasedaniya Verkhovnogo Soveta SSSR, Stenograficheskii Otchet,* Vol. X (1944), p. 62.
73. See, for example, A. Lavrishchev, "Promyshlennost Urala v otechestvennoi voine" [The Urals industry in the fatherland war], *Planovoe Khozyaistvo,* no. 3 (1944), pp. 33ff., which ends with a plea for continued concentration in the Urals in the future; see also *PS,* no. 9 (1944), p. 8.
74. *Zasedaniya Verkhovogo Soveta,* Vol. XII (1946), p. 309; V. A. Malyshev is speaking.
75. *Ibid.,* p. 310.
76. Gladkov, *Sovetskaya ekonomika,* pp. 164ff.
77. See, for example, F. N. Kashinskaya, ed., *Chelyabinskaya oblastnaya partiinaya organizatsiya v gody Velikoi Otechestvennoi Voiny* [The Chelyabinsk *oblast* Party organization in the war] (Chelyabinsk: Rabochii, 1966), p. 82: "Starting in 1943 a significant number of leaders in the liberated west came from the eastern provinces."
78. See in particular the complaints, which are discussed in a later chapter, of the delegates from Leningrad and the Ukraine in *Zasedaniya Verkhovnogo Soveta,* Vol. XI (1945). Note also that according to Voznesensky's biographer, V. Kolotov, "The central idea of the postwar Five Year Plan was that heavy industry and transportation must take precedence over reconstruction" (*N. A. Voznesenskii* [Moscow: Politizdat, 1963], p. 40).
79. The major biography of Malenkov is in *BSE,* 2d ed., Vol. XXVI, pp. 145–46. The most extensive Western account is Martin Ebon's *Malenkov* (New York: McGraw-Hill, 1953), which is based largely on research by Lazar M. Pistrak, published in the *New Leader* for 16 March 1953. See also B. Nicolaevsky, "Na kommananykh vysotakh," pp. 142–46; Meissner, *Sowjetrussland zwischen Revolution und Restauration,* pp. 74–89.
80. This seems to be the implication of such well-known developments as Malenkov's dispatch to Leningrad late in the summer of 1941, his mediation between Stalin and Khrushchev in 1941 and 1942, and his appearance at Stalingrad in mid-1942 to keep tank production going despite the approach of the Germans.
81. See *Sobranie postanovlenii i rasporyazhenii pravitel'stva SSSR,* issued intermittently during the war. The economic decrees for 1941 and 1942 were all signed by Stalin for the government and by Andreev for the Party. In later years signatures on such documents became very rare, and there were none on the decrees published in the daily press. However, the harvest decree of 13 July 1945 was signed by Malenkov.
82. The following account is based on the pertinent biographies in *BSE,* 2d ed., save for the data pertaining to Voznesensky, for which see Kolotov, *Voznesenskii.*
83. *Pravda,* 19 August 1945, p. 1.
84. For details, see Boris Meissner, "Die Entwicklung der Ministerien in Russland," *Europaarchiv,* April 1948, pp. 1257–58.
85. *Pravda,* 6 October 1945, p. 1.
86. One may recall that from mid-1946 to mid-1947 alone almost two million Communist Party members were demobilized (see Petrov, *Partiinoe stroitel'stvo,* p. 442). As a result of the first waves of demobilization, in the middle of 1946 the Smolensk Party organization had grown by 9,305 members, Bryansk by 10,200, Vinitsa by 10,180, Poltava by 11,303, Kursk by 20,942, and Voronezh by 28,166; in each case the size of the organization was almost doubled (see *PS,* nos. 9–10 [1946], p. 25).
87. Ivanovo Melanzh Enterprise resolution of 31 September 1946, in P. V. Fedoseev and K. V. Chernenko, eds., *KPSS v resolyutsiakh i resheniyakh,* Vol. VI, p. 181.
88. Salskii *raikom* resolution of August 1946, *PZh,* no. 1 (1946), p. 18.
89. On these matters see the intelligent discussion in Hough, *The Soviet Prefects,* ch. 4. In his more recent essay in Skilling and Griffiths, *Interest Groups in Soviet Politics,* Hough emphasizes the complexity of the relationship between the local Party

secretary and local manager, and the fact that in practice they seldom represent systematically "opposed" interests. However, the point remains valid that in the postwar years a systematic effort was made to pry them apart.

90. *Ocherki istorii Moskovskoi organizatsii KPSS,* p. 641.

91. *Kommunisty Sverdlovska vo glave mass,* pp. 256–57.

92. As noted in Chapter 2, n. 70, this shakeup began with the annexation of Tannu Tuva in the early autumn of 1944, followed by a revision of the West Siberian *oblast* frontiers (Tomsk and Tyumen were created out of Novosibirsk and Omsk). Late in 1944 the first secretary of the Tatar (Kazan) Autonomous District fell, coincident with the publication of a major Central Committee criticism of Tatar nationalism. By early 1946, the first secretaries of the Bashkir region and the Chelyabinsk, Chkalov, Gorky, Kemerovo, Kuibyshev, Molotov, Novosibirsk, and Sverdlovsk *oblasty* had all been shifted. Not all the secretaries in question fell into disgrace—on the contrary, many of them ended up in the Central Committee bureaucracy in Moscow—but it is clear that the Urals Party network was going through an extensive upheaval.

93. *Pravda,* 21 December 1944, p. 4. This commissariat "spontaneously" began the nation-wide campaign of February 1945 to restore Party discipline in the government bureaucracy: see *Pravda,* 1 February 1945, p. 3. According to Roy Medvedev, Kaganovich had decimated his commissariat through arrests of employees on 16 March 1944 (*Let History Judge,* p. 467).

94. One thinks in this connection of V. A. Malyshev, I. P. Tevosyan, I. I. Nosenko, K. M. Sokolov, S. A. Akopov, A. I. Yefrimov, P. I. Parshin, D. F. Ustinov, P. N. Goremykin, M. Z. Saburov, and M. G. Pervukhin, for example.

95. See Fainsod, *How Russia Is Ruled,* rev. ed. (Cambridge, Mass.: Harvard University Press, 1963), pp. 196–200; L. A. Malenko (*sic*), "Iz istorii razvitii apparata partiinykh organov" [From the history of the development of the Party's organs], *Voprosy Istorii KPSS,* no. 2 (1976), pp. 111–22; and Jonathan Harris, "The Origins of the Conflict between Malenkov and Zhdanov," *Slavic Review,* Vol. XXXV, no. 2 (1976), pp. 287–303.

96. A. N. Larionov, who became deputy chief of the Cadre Administration in August 1946, succeeded Patolichev as first secretary of the Yaroslavl *obkom* [*oblast* committee] in 1942. The Leningraders sent out to the Crimea and to Yaroslavl in August 1946 were N. V. Solovev and I. N. Turko: see Armstrong, *Politics of Totalitarianism,* p. 394, n. 14.

97. Until 1946 it was called Org-Instrukt Otdel. Now it became an *upravlenie* (directorate). The exact date of the reform is not known, but according to Petrov the new *upravlenie* was extant by August 1946 (*Stroitel'stvo politorganov,* p. 410); it was described in *PZh,* no. 3 (1946), p. 55.

98. This chain of events was first remarked by Louis Nemzer, in "The Kremlin's Professional Staff," *American Political Science Review,* Vol. XLIV, no. 1 (1950), pp. 64–85.

99. See Conquest, *Power and Policy,* pp. 74–75, 96ff.

100. Patolichev was on the team sent to the Ukraine in March 1947. Andrianov was the Leningrad Party secretary from 1949 until 1953.

101. This compromise is spelled out in some detail by Vera Dunham in *In Stalin's Time,* where it is labeled "the Big Deal" and is treated (without much reference to the Party revival) as Stalin's response to the insecurities created in Soviet society by the war. She probably overlooks the role of the Party revival in sparking the "Big Deal" because the literary materials she uses as evidence, by their very nature, do not reflect yearly fluctuations in Stalin's policies.

102. *Soch.,* Vol. XVI, pp. 126, 130.

103. Conquest, *Power and Policy,* ch. 8.

Notes to Chapter 5

1. *Crimes of the Stalin Era,* p. S45.
2. Medvedev, *Let History Judge,* p. 480.
3. Imre Nagy, *On Communism,* p. 251.
4. *Pravda,* 28 January 1944. This was the only announced meeting of the Central Committee during the war, and doubts have been expressed as to whether it actually took place. No protocol of the meeting has ever been published or referred to. Its alleged business was preparation of the forthcoming decentralization of the Foreign and Defense commissariats, "organizational" matters to be considered by the Supreme Soviet (which met two weeks later for the second time since 1941), and abolition of the "Internationale" as the Soviet national anthem. An early view of the Party revival from outside is provided by Boris Nicolaevsky, "Ideologicheskaya perestroika VKP(b)" [The ideological reorientation of the CPSU(b)], *Sotsialisticheskii Vestnik,* Vol. XXVI, no. 2 (1946), pp. 35–39. Cf. Armstrong, *The Politics of Totalitarianism,* ch. 13, and the exhaustive survey of the Soviet literature by G. P. Polozov, "Partiinoe rukovodstvo deyatel'nost intelligentsii v gody Velikoi Otechestvennoi Voiny" [The Party's leadership of the intelligentsia during the war years], *Voprosy Istorii KPSS,* no. 9 (1976), pp. 116–25.
5. See *Ocherki istorii Moskovskoi organizatsii KPSS,* pp. 603ff., for this and the following references to Moscow's initiative.
6. *Bol'shevik,* no. 2 (1944), pp. 56–64.
7. *Bol'shevik,* nos. 7–8 (1944), pp. 15–19; and the follow-up essays by P. Fedoseev, M. Iovchuk, and M. Mitin in *Bol'shevik,* no. 9, pp. 8–19, no. 11, pp. 16–29, and no. 11, pp. 39–48.
8. *Pravda,* 5 June 1944, p. 2.
9. *Partiinoe Stroitel'stvo,* nos. 15–16 (went to press on 14 September), 1944, pp. 29–35.
10. *Propagandist,* no. 18 (1944).
11. Petrov, *Stroitel'stvo politorganov . . . armii i flota,* p. 379.
12. See P. E. Corbett, "The Aleksandrov Story," *World Politics,* Vol. I, no. 2 (1949), pp. 161–74.
13. On Pospelov, see the biography in *BSE,* 2d ed., Vol. XXXIV, pp. 247–48.
14. The published descriptions of Agit-Prop all seem to relate either to its condition before the war or to the postwar Zhdanovite reconstruction of it. Accounts of the Party's activities during the war are strangely silent about what the Central Apparatus then looked like: see, for example, the booklet by N. M. Kononikin on the press in the war, which refers only to Sovinformburo and the GPUKA, discussed below, *Partiinaya i sovetskaya pechat' v period VOV* [The Party and the Soviet press in the war period] (Moscow: Ts. K. KPSS, 1960). A more recent text speaks of a rapid proliferation of Agit-Prop departments just after the war began, but then makes no further mention of them, stressing instead the vast powers of Sovinformburo. See V. M. Savel'ev and V. P. Savvin, *Sovetskaya intelligentsiya v VOV* [The Soviet intelligentsia during the Great Patriotic War] (Moscow: Mysl', 1974), pp. 208–10. To repair the condition of Agit-Prop during the war, regular short courses in Leninism had to be re-established in provincial centers during the spring of 1944, and the Party high school attached to the Central Committee had to be established on 1 October 1944: see *PS,* nos. 3–4 (1944), p. 42, 10, p. 16, and 11–12, pp. 48ff.
15. Some major evidence of this is in *PS,* no. 19 (1945), pp. 44–45.
16. See his biography in *BSE,* 2d ed., Vol. XLVIII, pp. 262–63.
17. Kononikin, *Partiinaya . . . pechat',* p. 8.
18. Petrov, *Stroitel'stvo politorganov,* p. 298.
19. *Ibid.,* p. 305.
20. *Ibid.,* p. 301.

21. The evidence is summarized by L. Gouré in his essay in *Communism and the Russian Peasant; Moscow in Crisis*, ed. H. S. Dinerstein and L. Gouré (Glencoe, Ill.: Free Press, 1955). This quote is from G. A. Tokaev, *Stalin Means War* (London: Weidenfeld and Nicolson, 1951), pp. 36ff. See also Tokaev's broader narrative in *Comrade X* (London: Harvill, 1956), ch. 10.

22. David Dallin, *The Real Soviet Russia* (New Haven: Yale University Press, 1950), pp. 43ff.

23. Cf. Ehrenburg, *The War*, pp. 39–41, 54–55.

24. *Ibid.*, pp. 17ff.; Leonhard, *Die Revolution entlässt ihre Kinder*, ch. 4.

25. *Twenty Letters to a Friend*, pp. 197–98. It is interesting in this connection to note A. Meyer's guess (*Soviet Political System*, p. 87) that *partiinost* is comparable to the pragmatism of certain Americans—"an axiomatic truth . . . against which all rational findings must be measured," but which, I would suggest, is so much taken for granted as to prevent self-assessment.

26. *Memoirs, 1925–1950*, p. 206.

27. Bondarev, *Tishina*, p. 24.

28. For numerous literary vignettes illustrating this polarity, see Dunham, *In Stalin's Time*, chs. 8–10.

29. Extremely interesting Soviet justifications of the wartime condition of the Party are found in Likhomanov, *Organizatorskaya rabota partii*, esp. chs. 1–2; Vasil'ev, "Iz praktiki partiino-organizatsionnoi rabota," esp. pp. 101ff.; and the two works by Yu. Petrov, frequently cited above, on the Party organization in the army. All three authors subscribe to the legend that the Party "really" won the war, but then they go on to describe the wartime Party situation as a perfectly rational alternative to the prewar and postwar forms assumed by the Party. Far less helpful are the assorted documentary collections which have tried to prove that the Party in its postwar form won the war: P. P. Andreev, *Kommunisticheskaya Partiya v period Velikoi Otechestvennoi Voiny;* V. S. Vasilenko and E. D. Orekhova, *Kommunisticheskaya Partiya v period Velikoi Otechestvennoi Voiny;* and V. V. Kalinin et al., eds., *KPSS—vdokhnovitel i organizator pobedy sovetskogo naroda v Velikoi Otechestvennoi Voine*. Suggestive of the sensitivity of this whole problem is the criticism in 1976 of Likhomanov, Vasil'ev and others, commanding them to identify more clearly the Party's direct leadership of the economy during the war: see A. L. Ugryumov, "Partiinyi organizatsii Urala v gody Velikoi Otechestvennoi Voiny" [The Party organizations of the Urals during the Great Patriotic War], *Voprosy Istorii KPSS*, no. 6 (1976), pp. 146ff.

30. *PS*, no. 1 (1944), pp. 7–8.

31. Ehrenburg suggests that at the start of the war, at least, Shcherbakov was less than receptive to nationalism, but he then indicates that he himself in 1941–1942 was by no means so "un-Communist" in his hate literature as some people thought (*The War*, pp. 13–20; 176ff.). Khrushchev gives an extremely hostile portrait of Shcherbakov in his memoirs, and since he leaned toward the Party, one may guess that Shcherbakov did not (Khrushchev, *Memoirs*, Vol. I, pp. 171–72, 203–4).

32. Armstrong, *Politics of Totalitarianism*, p. 146.

33. See Nicolaevsky, "Na kommandnykh vysotakh," p. 144.

34. Lozovskii was actually attached to the Foreign Commissariat (Werth, *Russia at War*, pp. 185–86).

35. N. Shatalin, *PS*, no. 20 (1943), p. 12.

36. *Ocherki istorii moskovskoi organizatsii KPSS*, p. 601.

37. Cf. *Pravda*, 23 August 1944, p. 3.

38. *PS*, no. 23 (1943), pp. 12ff.

39. *PS*, nos. 2 (1944), pp. 7ff., 10, pp. 11ff., and 21, pp. 18ff.

40. A perceptive account of the Zoshchenko case is Rebecca A. Demar, "The Tragedy of a Soviet Satirist," in *Through the Looking Glass of Soviet Literature*, ed.

Ernest J. Simmons (New York: Columbia University Press, 1953), pp. 235ff. A second Party attack on a literary figure occurred in June 1944 and was more critical of "apoliticism"; see Swayzee, *Political Control of Literature in the USSR,* pp. 30ff.

41. *Bol'shevik,* nos. 7–8 (1944), pp. 15–19.

42. M. Iovchuk in particular at this time was devoting his attention to Stalin's ambivalent thesis that "Leninism is the highest expression of Russian culture," and suggesting that Marxist ideas only became a "beacon" for the laboring masses of the world after they were detached from their German origins and imbedded in a specifically Russian cultural setting (*Bol'shevik,* no. 11 [1944], pp. 16–29). See also, on this general subject, F. C. Barghoorn, *Soviet Russian Nationalism* (New York: Oxford University Press, 1956), chs. 7–8.

43. *Pravda,* 5 June 1944, p. 2.

44. The official biography of Zhdanov is in *BSE,* 2d ed., Vol. XV (1952), pp. 604ff. See also B. Meissner's sketch of ideological work before the war in *Sowjetrussland zwischen Revolution und Restauration,* pp. 38ff. (originally published in *Osteuropa,* 1952), and Armstrong, *Politics of Totalitarianism,* p. 109.

45. *XVIII S'ezd VKP(b), Stenograficheskii otchet,* pp. 515ff.

46. See his letter in *Pravda* on 29 June 1939.

47. Recently published information about Zhdanov's role on the eve of the war is summarized in Salisbury, *The 900 Days,* ch. 13.

48. *Ocherki istorii moskovskoi organizatsii KPSS,* p. 603.

49. *Vechernyaya Moskva* [Evening Moscow], 4 December 1944, p. 3; *ibid.,* 11 December, p. 2. Popov seems to have been acting as both secretary of the Moscow *gorkom* [City Committee] and mayor on this occasion.

50. See Armstrong, *Politics of Totalitarianism,* pp. 186–87.

51. This rumor is recorded by Gregory Klimov in *The Terror Machine,* pp. 8–19. The rehabilitationist literature recently published in the Soviet Union makes no mention of such a revolt but does indicate that the Leningrad partisans were disgraced (retroactively) during Stalin's last years. See especially the contribution by A. Andrianov in the special Leningrad issue of *Voenno-Istoricheskii Zhurnal,* no. 1 (1964), pp. 25–26. The whole problem is complicated by the appearance of a laudatory article on the partisan groups in question by their leader, M. N. Nikitin, in *PS,* no. 9 (1944) (issue went to press 20 May), approximately two months after the supposed revolt.

52. Salisbury estimates that this event took place between April and August 1944 (*The 900 Days,* p. 576).

53. *Propagandist,* no. 5 (1945), pp. 34–38.

54. Two recent Soviet articles dramatize the escalation of the Party revival during the early months of 1945: A. F. Vasil'ev, "Partorganizatsii Urala v borbe za ekonomiyu i snizhenie sebestoimosti promyshlennoi produktsii, 1941–1945" [The Urals Party organizations' economic struggle and the lowering of industrial production costs], *Voprosy Istorii KPSS,* no. 8 (1973), pp. 91–100; and G. Sredin, "Rukovodstvo Gla PURKKA," pt. 1, pp. 59–60, pt. 2, pp. 33ff.

55. *Pravda,* 13 January 1953.

56. Those of Salomon Mikhoels and Jan Masaryk.

57. *Bol'shevik,* nos. 18–19 (1944), pp. 10ff.

58. *Soch.,* Vol. XV, p. 163.

59. The issue went to press on 6 December.

60. *PS,* no. 21 (1944), p. 16. The quotations which follow are consecutive, with one short omission, until the end of the leader article. Italics have been added.

61. *Bol'shevik,* no. 21 (1944).

62. *PS,* no. 1 (1945), p. 1. Italics have been added.

63. *Ibid.,* p. 2.

64. *Ibid.,* p. 3.

65. *Ibid.*, p. 41.
66. *PS*, no. 4 (1946), pp. 24–25.
67. Cf. *Propagandist*, no. 16 (1945), last page, and no. 17, last page; see also *Bol'shevik*, nos. 17–18 (1945), p. 9.
68. The revival resulted in an enormous increase in the number of pamphlets and texts which had to be written and distributed all over the country, and in an almost greater output of teaching aids for the new Party schools and lecture courses, not to speak of the lectures, etc., which the propagandists had to go out and deliver themselves.
69. The extent of this problem is evident in the article cited above in *PS*, no. 1 (1945), entitled "Lenin and Stalin on the Qualities of Bolshevik Leadership." This ten-page essay was little more than a patchwork of quotations from the two leaders designed to give provincial Party speakers an authoritative excuse for a break with their wartime "lack of *printsipnost.*" Objectively, it is obvious that the most convenient material for this sort of article would be recent quotations from Stalin, yet in the whole collection of some fifty quotes, only two came from Stalin's war speeches, and the great majority dated from before 1930.
70. See the section on ideological-political leadership in the speech at the 17th Party Congress in February 1934 (*Soch.*, Vol. XIII, pp. 291ff.).
71. *Bol'shevik*, nos. 3–4 (1941), pp. 31–32.
72. *Pravda*, 8 February 1946, p. 2.

Notes to Chapter 6

1. *Crimes of the Stalin Era*, pp. S42–S44.
2. Boris Nicolaevsky, *Power and the Soviet Elite*, pp. 161ff.
3. John A. Armstrong, *The Soviet Bureaucratic Elite: A Case Study of the Ukrainian Apparatus* (New York: Praeger, 1959), ch. 9.
4. These statistics are based on a collection of names of *oblast* Party first secretaries culled from *Pravda* and from other contemporary CPSU(b) journals. The exact figures are as follows. *War zone:* of 26 secretaries in the Ukraine, 19 (73 percent) were removed between 1947 and mid-1949; of 18 secretaries in Western regions of the Russian Republic, 12 (66 percent) were removed between mid-1948 and late 1949. *Home front:* of 22 secretaries in the unoccupied regions of European Russia, 9 (40 percent) were removed between mid-1948 and late 1949; of 17 secretaries in the Volga-Urals-West Siberian industrial region, 9 (53 percent) were removed between mid-1948 and late 1949, and this included 4 of 9 new secretaries who had been installed in this region during 1946; of 10 secretaries in the Far Eastern *oblasty*, only 3 (30 percent) were removed between mid-1948 and late 1949. The Belorussian Party organization, though in the war zone, was not purged extensively during 1948–1949, though it was purged on a small scale during 1947 and received a new first secretary in 1949. The reason for this immunity was probably the strong link established during the war between the Belorussian partisan organization (which provided the bulk of the postwar Party first secretaries on the *oblast* level) and the secret police.
5. *Ocherki istorii Leningradskoi organizatsii KPSS* [Outline history of the CPSU Leningrad organization], 2 vols. (Leningrad: Lenizdat, 1968), Vol. II, p. 673.
6. V. I. Yurchuk, "Vosstanovlenie i ukreplenie partiinykh organizatsii na Ukraine v 1945–1953 gg." [The restoration and strengthening of the Party organizations in the Ukraine], *Voprosy Istorii KPSS*, no. 6 (1962), p. 74.
7. Z. P. Antonova, ed., *Ocherki istorii Pskovskoi organizatsii KPSS* [Outline history of the CPSU Pskov organization] (Leningrad: Lenizdat, 1971), p. 322. In January 1945 there were 9,653 Communists in the Orel *oblast* and 8,000 in the Kaluga *oblast*, most of them raw recruits: see N. E. Afanas'ev, ed., *Ocherki istorii Orlovskoi partiinoi organizatsii* [Outline history of the Orel Party organization] (Tula: PKI, 1967), p. 276;

and *Ocherki istorii Kaluzhskoi organizatsii KPSS* [Outline history of the CPSU Kaluga organization] (Tula: PKI, 1967), p. 282. For other such data see N. I. Kondakova, "Odbudowa, konsolidacja ideowa i organizaczina szeregow partijnych w rejonach RSFSR wyzwolenych . . . 1941–1945" [The re-establishment and ideological and organizational consolidation of the Party ranks in regions of the RSFSR liberated during 1941 and 1945], *Dzieje Najnowsze,* Vol. III (1971), pp. 369–80.

8. An overview of this vast subject is found in John A. Armstrong, ed., *Soviet Partisans in World War II* (Madison: University of Wisconsin Press, 1964), pp. 3–72.

9. A. P. Matveev, G. Kh. Bumagin, N. G. Ignatov, and G. M. Boikachev.

10. F. A. Baranov, V. E. Chernyshev, P. Z. Kalinin, K. T. Mazurov, I. F. Klimov, and A. E. Kleshchev.

11. For Ponomarenko's biography, see *BSE,* 2d ed., Vol. XXXIV, pp. 142–43.

12. Armstrong, *Soviet Bureaucratic Elite,* pp. 129, 136.

13. This point is rather heavily underlined in I. D. Nazarenko, ed., *Ocherki istorii Kommunisticheskoi Partii Ukrainy* [Outline history of the Ukrainian Communist Party], 2d rev. ed. (Kiev: Izd. Pol. Lit. Uk., 1964), pp. 509ff.

14. P. I. Doronin, L. M. Antyufeev, and A. S. Chuyanov.

15. An exemplary NKVD partisan was A. P. Matveev, whose obituary appeared in *Pravda,* 2 August 1946, p. 4. Other cases are noted in CPBR, Party History Institute, *Podpl'nye partiinye organy KPBR v gody Velikoi Otechestvennoi Voiny, 1941–1944* [The underground Party organs of the CPBR] (Minsk: Belarus, 1975).

16. Armstrong, *Soviet Bureaucratic Elite,* p. 140, n. 28.

17. Petrov, *Stroitel'stvo politorganov,* p. 312.

18. See, for these two decrees, *Resheniya partii i pravitel'stva po khozyaistvennym voprosam,* Vol. III, pp. 195–200.

19. See, for example, the Belorussian resolution reprinted in *KPSS v resolyutsiyakh i resheniyakh,* Vol. VI, pp. 107–12. Other such resolutions are published or referred to in *Partiinoe Stroitel'stvo* and *Propagandist* for the latter months of 1944. Armstrong (*Politics of Totalitarianism,* p. 179) presents evidence of the considerable attention given to ideological and political as opposed to economic matters in the liberated *oblast* plena. On the home front, more attention was paid to economic matters.

20. Khrushchev's speech to the June 1945 plenum of the CPUK, *PS,* no. 11 (1945), p. 20.

21. See *PS,* nos. 9–10 (1946), pp. 13ff., where Khrushchev complains bitterly about the lack of Party personnel in the villages.

22. *PS,* no. 10 (1944), pp. 27ff.

23. *Pravda,* 15 August 1944, p. 2; *PZh,* nos. 17 (1947), pp. 6–15, 1 (1948), pp. 20–24. Sydney Ploss (*Conflict and Decision Making,* p. 32) attempts to make Doronin's position seem identical with those of Andreev and Khrushchev in the postwar period. Both Khrushchev and Doronin did indeed take a basically sympathetic attitude toward the unhappy peasants, and it is also true that both served on the same front during the war and collaborated for a time in the post-Stalin years. But a reading of all the speeches they published in *Pravda* and *PS* in the postwar years strongly suggests that they favored different policies then. Doronin invariably mentioned the "link" (*zveno*) system, which would have made collective farming more attractive to peasants by generally equating the basic labor unit in the *kolkhozy* with the peasant family. Khrushchev seldom referred to that system, apparently preferring educational or structural reforms. For example, on one occasion he actually claimed that the peasants longed for a chance to attend good lectures by Party agitators on Sunday mornings in their free time (*PS,* no. 11 [1945], pp. 24–25). One may recall in this connection that Doronin's "link" policy was advocated by Andreev and accepted by the Party (i.e., Stalin) in 1947–1948, at a time when Khrushchev was being shoved aside in the Ukraine by

Kaganovich. After 1949, on the other hand, when Khrushchev returned to the seats of power, the "link" policy gave way to his aggressively "Communist" agricultural towns (*agrogorody*), and Doronin spent four years without a job.

24. One may deduce the reluctance of the Party cadres to go out to the villages from the statistics on *kolkhoz* Party organizations. In 1946 there were a mere 1,431 in the entire agricultural Ukraine. Only after a great drive in 1947 did the figure go up to 13,280 (*Ocherki istorii KPUK*, p. 580).

25. *Zasedaniya Verkhovnogo Soveta*, Vol. X, p. 61.

26. Another factor which may have kept the conflict under wraps up to this point was the appointment of Malenkov in August 1943 as chairman of the newly established Committee for Reconstruction of the Liberated Territories. Malenkov was good at silencing complaints.

27. *Vedomosti Verkhovnogo Soveta*, 30 April 1945, pt. 1, p. 4, and pt. 2, p. 3.

28. *Ibid.*, appendix.

29. *Vedomosti*, 20 June 1945, appendix.

30. Nedosikin's speech, *ibid.*, p. 7.

31. M. I. Safronov in *Leningradskaya Pravda*, 8 June 1945, p. 2, demands sums very much larger than those granted in the published budget.

32. Speeches of Kapustin and Popkov to the *gorkom* plenum of July, published in *Propaganda i Agitatsiya* (Leningrad), nos. 14–15 (1945), pp. 15–34.

33. Vasil'ev, "Iz praktiki," p. 102.

34. Much may be learned about the Leningrad Party organization from the highly critical commentary in *Propagandist*, no. 5 (1945), pp. 34–38. See also the rehabilitationist Leningrad *Ocherki*, Vol. II, ch. 8; the articles in *Leningrad. Entsiklopedicheskii spravochnik;* the recent *Ocherki istorii Leningrada* [Outline history of Leningrad], 6 vols. (Leningrad: Nauka, 1970); and the collection of studies about the links between the Leningrad Party and the front in *Voenno-Istoricheskii Zhurnal*, no. 1 (1964). Cf. Yu. P. Petrov, *Partizanskaya dvizhenie v Leningradskoi oblasti, 1941–1944* [The partisan movement in the Leningrad *oblast*] (Leningrad: Lenizdat, 1973).

35. For biographies of Kuznetsov and Popkov, see *Leningrad. Ents. spravochnik*, pp. 565 and 675.

36. Examples of the glorification of Leningrad's past will be given below. Suffice it to say that Kirov's speeches, highly laudatory of Leningrad, were republished in the autumn of 1944 and were advertised, with the specific blessing of Zhdanov, as the product of "the Party's ideal, a bearer of the best tradition of the Party, beloved of the whole Soviet people" (see *PS*, no. 21 [1944], pp. 28–30).

37. Salisbury, *The 900 Days*, pp. 573ff.

38. *Leningradskaya Pravda*, 30 May 1945, p. 4.

39. See, for example, the sonnet by A. Prokovev in *Zvezda*, no. 1 (1945), which opens with the line "Lucky, that I live in this city, that my windows open onto the Neva" and ends with a vision of the hero-city—"a symbol of Russia's greatness"— wearing the Order of Lenin, just then awarded, on a velvet ribbon. In no. 3 of the same journal there is a "cino-scenario" featuring a socialist-realist but highly romantic love story set during the Leningrad siege in which symphonic music periodically expresses "the voice of Leningrad."

40. Armstrong, *Soviet Bureaucratic Elite*, ch. 9; Sullivant, *Soviet Politics*, chs. 5–6.

41. See the testimonies of Djilas, *Conversations with Stalin*, pp. 117–24; and Marshall MacDuffie, *The Red Carpet*, pp. 198–200. Cf. Kolkowicz's account of the formation of the "Stalingrad group" in the Red Army, in *Soviet Military*, pp. 220ff., and Borys Lewytzkyj, "Besonderheiten," *Osteuropa*, no. 10 (1962), pp. 670ff.

42. For the record, see Sullivant, *Soviet Politics*, chs. 2–4.

43. Cf. the lengthy analysis in John A. Armstrong, *Ukrainian Nationalism*, rev.ed. (New York: Columbia University Press, 1963).

44. Yaroslav Bilinsky, *The Second Soviet Republic. The Ukraine after World War II* (New Brunswick, N.J.: Rutgers University Press, 1964), ch. 4.

45. Sullivant, *Soviet Politics,* pp. 245ff.

46. Khrushchev suggests that some Ukrainians were unhappy that the Curzon Line was used as a boundary instead of the Soviet-German frontier of 1939; see his *Memoirs,* Vol. II, p. 158. This seems insignificant information until one learns that from 1941 to 1942 Ukrainian Communist partisans were active around Lwow and by 1943 had managed to become the transmission point between Dimitrov in Moscow and the Polish Communists underground in Warsaw: cf. M. I. Brechak et al., *Pod proporom internatsionalizmu* [Under the banner of internationalism] (Kiev: KPU, 1970), p. 197; and, more generally, M. Juchniewicz, *Polacy w radzieckim ruchu podziemnym, 1941–1945* [Poles in the Soviet underground movement] (Warsaw: MON, 1973). The Ukrainian partisan movement was evidently deeply immersed in East European Communist politics. Cf. Stalin's remarks to Roosevelt about Ukrainian Communist nationalism, quoted in Sullivant, *Soviet Politics,* p. 380.

47. See Djilas, *Conversations with Stalin,* p. 118, for this Ukrainian desire.

48. Beneš, *Paměti,* pp. 391–94.

49. *Zvezda,* no. 11 (1945), pp. 11–14.

50. Sullivant, *Soviet Politics,* pp. 246–47.

51. Bilinsky, *Second Soviet Republic,* p. 101.

52. *Ibid.,* pp. 127–29.

53. Rylskii was removed as chairman of the Ukrainian Writers' Union, according to the newspaper accounts of 15 November 1946. Khrushchev later attributed the massive attack on this poet to Kaganovich (see *Kommunist,* no. 12 [1957], p. 26, and the commentary in Lazar Pistrak, *The Grand Tactician* [New York: Praeger, 1961], p. 183).

54. *Propagandist,* no. 5 (1945), pp. 34–38; *PS,* no. 2 (1945), pp. 20–28.

55. See A. Tolmagaev, *M. I. Kalinin,* esp. pp. 256–58. Djilas, in an often-cited passage, suggests that Kalinin was senile by early 1945 (*Conversations with Stalin,* p. 105), and he did die in June 1946. But many Soviet memorialists suggest that he was still competent and also respected in 1945: see Zhukov's tale about an encounter in May in *Vospominaniya i razmyshleniya,* pp. 707ff. Further, in the public press during 1945 Kalinin was by far the most vocal Party revivalist in the top leadership, and since his death, his fortunes have followed the Party's. For example, in 1946 the Ukrainian Party enthusiastically published his recent speeches, but a Russian edition ran into obstacles. From 1947, when the Party revival faltered, until Stalin's death, Kalinin received little public attention. After Khrushchev's revival of the Party in 1953, however, Kalinin became one of its heroes, and he is the only wartime and postwar Stalinist political leader who still regularly receives accolades in the Soviet Union.

56. *Pravda,* 29 January 1945, p. 2.

57. *Pravda,* 27 January 1945, p. 3.

58. *Pravda,* 22 September 1946, p. 2.

59. See the admissions by Kuznetsov, in *PS,* nos. 23–24 (1945), p. 17; by Popkov, in *PS,* nos. 9–10 (1946), p. 19; and *Pravda,* 2 January 1947, p. 2.

60. Salisbury, *The 900 Days,* pp. 575ff.

61. Khrushchev, *Memoirs,* Vol. I, p. 240.

62. *Soch.,* Vol. XVI, pp. 93–96.

63. See the biography in *Leningrad. Ents. spravochnik,* p. 565. The following remarks are impressionistic, based on the speeches printed in *PS* in 1945 and 1946 and in *PZh* in 1947.

64. Khrushchev, *Crimes of the Stalin Era,* p. S45.

65. *PS,* no. 4 (1946), pp. 9–10 (italics added).

66. See, in particular, the "Leningrad" issue of *PZh,* no. 10 (1947), pp. 28–53, and the final issue, no. 7 (1948), pp. 14ff.

67. Even in the "secret speech" of 1956 Khrushchev insisted that Stalin did what he did in the interests of the Party: "In this lies the whole tragedy" (*Crimes of the Stalin Era,* p. S64).

68. Medvedev, *Let History Judge,* p. 481.

69. Djilas, *Conversations with Stalin,* p. 12.

70. These men were removed from their ministries at the March 1949 session of the Supreme Soviet and made deputy chairmen of the USSR Council of Ministers. At the same session of the Supreme Soviet Voznesensky was removed from the Gosplan and Rodionov from the RSFSR chairmanship. For the later "danger" of Molotov and Mikoyan, see *Crimes of the Stalin Era,* p. S63.

71. See Khrushchev, *Memoirs,* Vol. I, p. 263, and the biographies of Kosygin by J. Marin, in *Porträts der UdSSR Prominenz* (Munich: Inst. zur Erforschung, 1960), and Grey Hodnett, in *Soviet Leaders,* ed. George Simmonds (New York: Crowell, 1967), pp. 40–50.

72. Khrushchev, *Memoirs,* Vol. I, pp. 248–49.

73. Kolotov, *Voznesenskii,* pp. 18ff.

74. See the biographies cited in n. 71. Kosygin, alongside Kalinin and Zhdanov, was one of the three Politburo members who stood for election in Leningrad in the campaign for the Supreme Soviet in January and February 1946.

75. *Istoriya KPSS,* Vol. V, pp. 220ff. All three men were members of the special GOKO task force sent to "help" Zhdanov defend the city late in August 1941. Mikoyan was put in charge of provisioning the city and of the rationing system; Kosygin was charged with the evacuation. There are differing versions of this episode, which seem to vary according to who was in power at the time of writing.

76. Shikin's biography is in *BSE Ezhegodnik, 1962,* p. 622. Cf. Petrov, *Stroitel'stvo politorganov,* p. 301.

77. For the possibility that Stalin sent the task force of August 1941 to Leningrad as a reprimand to Zhdanov, see Salisbury, *900 Days,* pp. 264–66.

78. Rodionov was Party first secretary in the Gorky *oblast* from 1938 until 1946 and had lived there before 1938. Zhdanov was secretary in Gorky before he went to Leningrad. Voznesensky stood for election in 1946 in Gorky; Shikin received his early training in Gorky (see Khrushchev, *Memoirs,* Vol. I, p. 250). In 1949 the Central Committee attacked the Gorky Party organization with a vehemence approaching that of the attack on Leningrad (*KPSS v resolyutsiyakh,* Vol. VI, pp. 277–80).

79. Likhomanov, *Organizatorskaya Rabota Partii,* chs. 1–2.

80. Khrushchev remarked in 1956 that the main result of the rehabilitations in the Leningrad affair was "restoration" of the honor of the Leningrad Party organization (*Crimes of the Stalin Era,* p. S46).

81. *Bol'shevik,* no. 21 (1947), p. 29.

82. Cf. G. Sorokin's essay in *Pravda,* 1 December 1963, p. 4. A perceptive discussion of Voznesensky as an economist is in A. Katz, "The Politics of Economic Reform in the Soviet Union," pp. 114ff. Voznesensky's views are still subject to political coverup by elements in the Soviet leadership: see *Radio Liberation Dispatches,* nos. 381 (1973), 274 and 338 (1974).

83. *Bol'shevik,* no. 6 (1946), pp. 81ff. The Western authority on Soviet economics Naum Jasny on many occasions, though especially in his *Soviet Industrialization, 1928–1952* (Chicago: University of Chicago Press, 1961), p. 249, bitterly mocked Voznesensky's "plan" of 1946 as a travesty on economic science and as a coverup for uninhibited concentration on heavy industry at the expense of consumer production. Indeed, one of the purposes of the plan was to support heavy industry, and heavy industry was in practice its sole beneficiary. But it seems possible that Jasny confuses

the "intention" behind the plan with the results. Consumer production and reconstruction had a clear place in Voznesensky's plan alongside heavy industry, but it so happened that the consumer program failed in practice, whereas the heavy industrial goals were overfulfilled. See the detailed analysis by Katz, "Politics of Economic Reform," pp. 118–119 and esp. p. 139.

84. Kosygin's experience both before the war and after 1949 was entirely in the area of light industry and consumer goods. Rodionov spoke out emphatically for consumer and civilian interests in each of the numerous speeches and statements he published in *Pravda, PS, PZh,* and *Bol'shevik* in the period at the end of the war.

85. "The Party has always insisted that when there are possibilities—and there are many in our country—they must be broadly and persistently utilized for satisfying the urgent need to better the living conditions of the population. The Party has always waged a merciless struggle against bureaucratic neglect of the so-called 'minor questions' " (Molotov, in *Pravda,* 7 February 1946, p. 2).

86. See, for example, the essay by V. Malyshev in *Pravda,* 16 April 1945, p. 3.

87. *Pravda,* 8 February 1946, p. 2.

88. This statement is based on Rodionov's speeches at the Supreme Soviet sessions of February 1944 and March and October 1946; his articles in *Pravda* for 21 December 1944 and 18 April 1945; in *Kul'tura i Zhizn'*, no. 11 (1946), pp. 1–2; in *PZh*, no. 12 (1947), pp. 6–13; and in *Bol'shevik*, nos. 1 (1947), pp. 38–55, and 21 (1947), pp. 18–32. The first *Bol'shevik* article particularly emphasizes the leading role of the Russians, and none of these statements can be called notably "revivalist."

89. During 1946 and 1947, for example, the Russian Republic blossomed with ministries for technical culture, cinematography, luxury goods, delicatessen products, light industry, and the like. It is difficult to generalize about such matters without a comprehensive study of republican legislative activity in the USSR. At present, the most useful guide to the creation of new ministries is E. Crowley et al., *Party and Government Officials of the Soviet Union, 1917–1960.* This is unreliable for our period and lists only All-Union ministries.

90. See Conquest, *Power and Policy,* p. 103, and Nicolaevsky, *Power and the Soviet Elite,* p. 167, for speculations on this subject.

91. *Soch.,* Vol. XVI, pp. 93–96; *Pravda,* 7 September 1947, p. 1.

92. *Bol'shevik,* no. 21 (1947), p. 29.

93. See the criticism of the Gorky Party organization in *KPSS v rezolyutsiyakh,* Vol. VI, pp. 277–80.

94. The report is found in Slusser, ed., *Soviet Economic Policy in Postwar Germany,* pp. 18–61.

95. Djilas, *Conversations with Stalin,* p. 105; Khrushchev, *Memoirs,* Vol. II, pp. 300ff.

96. The Politburo speeches appeared in *Pravda* from 6 to 10 February 1946. Most of them were immediately republished in brochure form. In the final months of its existence, the GOKO included Stalin, Beria, Kaganovich, Malenkov, Bulganin, Mikoyan, Molotov, and Voznesensky. The last four, constituting half of the membership, were public advocates of the Party's revival during 1945 and 1946 and were purged between 1947 and 1949. In 1945 the Politburo included as full members Stalin, Andreev, Kaganovich, Voroshilov, Kalinin, Khrushchev, Mikoyan, Molotov, and Zhdanov. The last five, constituting a majority, were public advocates of the Party's revival during 1945 and 1946. Kalinin died in 1946 and the rest were victims of the purging in 1947, 1948, and 1949. (Of the candidate members of the Politburo in 1945—Beria, Malenkov, Shcherbakov, Shvernik, and Voznesensky—only the last was a revivalist, and he was purged in 1949.)

97. According to *PS,* no. 14 (1944), p. 28, the study of the rules was to be a major theme in the newly established Party high school. *PS,* nos. 21 and 22 (1944), pp. 37ff.

and 26ff., contained a long two-part discussion of the rules together with a convenient "question and answer" section which agitators could look at when asked questions. This interest in the rules was maintained in the publications of the Party revival until the end of 1946. See, for example, the two-part discussion of them by Abalin in *PZh,* nos. 2 and 3 (1946), pp. 51ff. and 48ff. This last piece, which was published, as we will see in a later chapter, at the turning point of Zhdanov's career, specifically discussed the functions of the Party's central organs and referred pointedly to the fact that in the past a congress had been held at the start of each "new period" in the Party's history.

98. Petrov, *Stroitel'stvo politorganov,* p. 389. Petrov, who is the leading Soviet authority on Party affairs in the army, seems to have gotten the information about these discussions of the leading Party organs from the protocols of the postwar Politburo meetings, which were kept as part of the reform of 1946 and to which he had access.

99. According to Dedijer, Malenkov told the Cominform delegates in September 1947 that there would shortly be a Soviet Party congress: see *Tito. Prilozi,* p. 475. According to an article in *Pravda* on 28 April 1964 the Politburo voted twice between 1946 and 1948 to hold a congress but was overriden both times by Stalin.

100. *Bol'shevik,* nos. 23–24 (1944), p. 47 (italics added). The original version of this lecture was published in *Propagandist,* no. 18 (1944), pp. 8–19.

101. The term "voluntarist" does not precisely describe the philosophical view under discussion because "freedom of the will" is here obtained through extreme economic determinism. The term is convenient for two reasons, however. First, it was used in subsequent years to describe (and deprecate) the Voznesensky school of economists: see, for example, the well-known reference by Suslov in *Pravda,* 24 December 1952, and the remarks by Yu. P. Denik, in *Materialy Konferentsii Instituta po Izucheniyu Istorii i Kultury SSSR,* pp. 24–28. Second, "voluntarist" does seem to describe better than any other term the optimistic, expectant, enthusiastic spirit of the Party revival at the end of the war. For background, see R. V. Daniels, "Soviet Thought in the Nineteen-Thirties," *Indiana Slavic Studies,* no. 1 (1956), pp. 97–135; R. V. Daniels, "Soviet Power and Marxist Determinism," *Problems of Communism,* Vol. IX (1960), pp. 12–18; D. P. Costello, "Voluntarism and Determinism in Bolshevist Doctrine," *Soviet Studies,* Vol. XII, no. 4 (1961), pp. 394–403; Gustav A. Wetter, *Dialectical Materialism* (New York: Praeger, 1958), p. 172ff.; and Henri Chambre, *Le Marxisme en l'Union Sovietique* (Paris: Seuil, 1955), p. 405.

102. *Bol'shevik,* nos. 23–24 (1944), p. 47.

103. *Voprosy Istorii KPSS,* no. 6 (1963), pp. 96–98.

104. *Bol'shevik,* no. 6 (1946), p. 71.

105. See Conquest, *Power and Policy,* pp. 88ff., for further speculation as to the Voznesensky-Ostrovityanov association.

106. "Nekotorye voprosy prepodavaniya politicheskoi ekonomii" [Some questions regarding the teaching of political economy], *Pod Znamenem Marksizma* [Under the banner of Marxism], nos. 7–8 (1943), pp. 56–78. This article was translated in the *American Economic Review,* Vol. XXXIV (1944), pp. 531ff., and was widely discussed among American economists as evidence of an emerging "rationality" in Soviet economics. See, for example, Norman Kaplan, "The Law of Value and Soviet Economic Planning," Rand Corporation Research Memorandum RM-488, November 1950.

107. Katz ("Politics of Economic Reform," pp. 130ff.) discusses the "Nekotorye voprosy" article in detail and points out its similarity to the postwar work of Ostrovityanov, Stalin, and "other economists." However, he tends to overlook, perhaps because he ignores the Ostrovityanov lecture, the sharp contrast between the article and the Voznesenskyite postwar school of thought.

108. See Katz's conclusion, arrived at independent of my own, in *ibid.,* p. 139. Cf. Kolotov's evaluation of Voznesensky's economic theories in *Voprosy Istorii KPSS,* no. 6 (1963), p. 97: "[they] were conditioned to a considerable extent by a spirit of dogma-

tism and voluntarism that dominated many researches by economists in the period of the cult of the personality." Further revelations about Voznesensky and his views are found in a revised edition of Kolotov's biography (Moscow: Politizdat, 1974) (excerpts were published in *Znamya* [Banner], no. 6 [1974]) and in the review of it by G. Sorokin in *Pravda*, 25 September 1974.

109. For comments, see Abram Bergson, "The Fourth Five-Year Plan," *Political Science Quarterly*, Vol. LXII (1947), pp. 195–227, and the scornful retrospective analysis by Jasny, "A Close-up of the Soviet Fourth Five-Year Plan," *Quarterly Journal of Economics*, Vol. LXII, no. 2 (1952), pp. 139–71.

110. Molotov's prominence among the Party revivalists who challenged Stalin in 1945—indeed, his very presence among them—will surprise the outside witnesses who felt that Molotov was the most trusted of all Stalin's lieutenants in the years after the war. It is clear, however, that by 1949, when Stalin had Molotov's wife sent to a camp, a trusting relationship no longer existed. In a recent report, the Soviet historian Aleksandr Nekrich dates Stalin's distrust as far back as 1942, when Molotov, on a visit to the United States, had an opportunity (in Stalin's opinion) to become an "imperialist spy" ("The Arrest and Trial of I. M. Maisky," *Survey*, Vol. XXII [1976], pp. 318–19).

111. *Pravda*, 8 February 1946, p. 2.

112. For Molotov's pooh-poohing of the atomic bomb during the autumn of 1945, see A. Kramish, *Atomic Energy and the Soviet Union* (Stanford: Stanford University Press, 1959), pp. 86ff.; *FRUS 1945*, Vol. V, pp. 922ff.

113. Trout ("Soviet Policy Making," pp. 95ff.) recalls the press discussion starting in March 1945 about whether the new plan would be for reconstruction of the country or just for a continuation of prewar construction efforts. He points out also that the plan's exalted production goals and its potential fifteen-year span were both adumbrated in talks Stalin had with Western visitors early in 1944.

114. *Soch.*, Vol. XV, p. 199.

115. These were short letters to the journals *Komsomol'skaya Pravda*, published on 24 May 1945, and *Pionerskaya Pravda*, published on 10 June (*Soch.*, Vol. XV, pp. 203 and 205).

116. It seems relevant that in July *Bol'shevik* published its first essay in some time directly encouraging the cult of "leading personalities" in history; see no. 14, pp. 45ff.

117. *PS*, nos. 9–10 (1945) (to press 4 June), pp. 7ff.

Notes to Chapter 7

Bibliographical Note

By far the most important Soviet work on Soviet foreign policy in the period of 1945 is A. A. Gromyko et al., eds., *Istoriya diplomatii*. Also useful is V. G. Trukhanovskii, ed., *Istoriya mezhdunarodnykh otnoshenii i vneshnei politiki SSSR* [History of international relations and the foreign policy of the USSR], 3 vols. (Moscow: Izdat. Mezhd. Otnosh., 1967). Volume II, edited by V. B. Ushakov, covers 1939–1945; volume III, edited by I. A. Kirilin, covers 1945–1960. Additional information can be found in N. N. Inozemtsev, ed., *Mezhdunarodnye otnosheniya posle Vtoroi Mirovoi Voiny* [International relations after World War II], 2 vols. (Moscow: Gospolitizdat, 1962). Volume I, edited by A. G. Mileikovskii, covers the immediate postwar period. Of older Soviet works the most interesting are V. L. Israelyan's *Diplomaticheskaya istoriya Velikoi Otechestvennoi Voiny* [Diplomatic history of the Great Patriotic War] (Moscow: Inst. Mezhd. Otnosh., 1959), and G. A. Deborin, ed., *Mezhdunarodnye otnosheniya i vneshnyaya politika Sovetskogo Soyuza, 1945–1949 gg.* [International relations and the foreign policy of the Soviet Union, 1945–1949] (Moscow: Inst. Mezhd. Otnosh., 1958). Israelyan revised his book as *Antigitlerovskaya koalitsiya. Diplomaticheskoe sotrudnichestvo SSSR, SShA i Anglii v gody Vtoroi Mirovoi Voiny* [The anti-Hitler coalition.

The diplomatic cooperation of the Soviet Union, the USA, and Britain during World War II] (Moscow: Izdat. Mezhd. Otnosh., 1964). It appeared in English in 1971.

Recent well-documented Western accounts of the Soviet foreign policies of 1945 are in Lynn E. Davis, *The Cold War Begins. Soviet-American Conflict over Eastern Europe* (Princeton: Princeton University Press, 1974); John L. Gaddis, *The United States and the Origins of the Cold War* (New York: Columbia University Press, 1972); Thomas G. Paterson, *Soviet-American Confrontation* (Baltimore: The Johns Hopkins University Press, 1973); and John W. Wheeler-Bennett and Anthony Nichols, *The Semblance of Peace. The Political Settlement after the Second World War* (New York: St. Martins, 1972). See also Wolfe, *Soviet Power and Europe, 1945–1970*, ch. 1. Forthcoming is a major study of Soviet policy by Vojtěch Mástný, *Russia's Road to the Cold War: Stalin's War Aims, 1941–1945* (New York: Columbia University Press, 1978). The standard older work is the series by Herbert Feis which began with *Churchill, Roosevelt, Stalin* (1957) and continued with *Between War and Peace* (Princeton: Princeton University Press, 1960); *Japan Subdued* (Princeton: Princeton University Press, 1961); and *From Trust to Terror* (New York: W. W. Norton, 1970). Indispensable interpretations are W. H. McNeill's *America, Britain and Russia* (1953); and Gabriel Kolko's brilliant but one-sided *Politics of War* (1968). Extensive reviews of American revisionist literature can be found in Christopher Lasch, "The Cold War, Revisited and Re-Visioned," *The New York Times Magazine,* 14 January 1968, pp. 26ff., and Robert J. Maddox, *The New Left and the Origins of the Cold War* (Princeton: Princeton University Press, 1973). For a critique of Maddox's criticisms, see Warren F. Kimball, "The Cold War Warmed Over," *American Historical Review,* Vol. LXXIX (1974), pp. 1119–36.

On the patterns in Soviet diplomacy, see Guy Hentsch, *Staline négotiateur* (Neuchâtel: La Baconnière, 1969); Philip E. Mosely, "Some Soviet Techniques of Diplomacy," in *Negotiating with the Russians,* ed. Raymond Dennett and Joseph E. Johnson, pp. 227–303; and the interesting appendix to Robert Strausz-Hupé et al., *Protracted Conflict* (New York: Harpers-Colophon, 1963), pp. 210–29.

1. *Soch.,* Vol. XV, pp. 163–70.

2. Schöpflin, "Dokumentum: A Magyar Komunista Párt útja, 1945–1950," p. 241. Cf. the discussion in Chapter 3, n. 68, above.

3. P. Chuvikov, "Uchenie Lenina-Stalina o voinakh spravedlivykh i nespravedlivykh" [The Lenin-Stalin teaching about just and unjust wars], *Bol'shevik,* nos. 7–8 (1945) (to press 29 April), pp. 14–26.

4. P. Fedoseev, "Marksizm-Leninizm ob istochkakh i kharaktere voin" [Marxism-Leninism on the sources and character of wars], *Bol'shevik,* no. 16 (1945) (to press 9 October), pp. 31–59.

5. Cf. the recent analysis in T. Trout, "Soviet Foreign Policy Making," esp. p. 137. Trout fully recognizes the importance of the Chuvikov and Fedoseev articles just cited *(ibid.,* pp. 69ff.).

6. See in particular the interviews with Eddie Gilmore and Alexander Werth in 1946 *(Soch.,* Vol. XVI, pp. 45–46, 53–56).

7. *Soch.,* Vol. XVI, pp. 226–32.

8. A useful analysis of the theory behind Soviet foreign policy is Jonathan Harris's "Ideology and International Relations," mimeographed (Pittsburgh: University Center for International Studies, 1970), esp. ch. 7.

9. *FRUS 1945,* Vol. V, p. 232.

10. Undated memorandum, probably of May 1945, in *FRUS 1945,* Vol. V, p. 860.

11. *FRUS 1946,* Vol. V, pp. 696–98.

12. The most satisfying and knowledgeable account of Anglo-American discords during the war is in Woodward, *British Foreign Policy.* McNeill's *America, Britain and*

Russia is also admirable from this point of view, and inter-Allied arguments are the backbone of Robert Beitzell's *The Uneasy Alliance. America, Britain and Russia, 1941–1943* (New York: Knopf, 1972). American historians in general, however, have exhibited a profound inability to recognize either the reality of the "splits" or the seriousness with which Marxists might regard them. Herbert Feis, in particular, errs in this respect, although the American diplomatic reports from Moscow, to which he had the first access, were clear enough on the subject. For example, in *Churchill, Roosevelt, Stalin*, p. 531, when writing of Roosevelt's remarks to Stalin at Yalta, Feis says: "Stalin by then had probably learned not to take Roosevelt's sallies about Churchill's wiles to be other than what they were."

13. Robert Sherwood, *Roosevelt and Hopkins*, pp. 572–73. Even Feis considers this exchange to have been "premature" and "careless" (*Churchill, Roosevelt, Stalin*, pp. 67–68).

14. *Teheran Papers*, p. 486. According to the Soviet version of this conversation, Roosevelt simply suggested that the question of India could be solved best by people who were not "directly involved" (*Tegeran, Yalta, Potsdam*, p. 36).

15. For these disputes, see Woodward, *British Foreign Policy*, (1962 ed.), chs. 21–23, and Harriman and Abel, *Special Envoy*, p. 356.

16. *Sovetsko-frantsuzskie otnoshenie*, pp. 382ff.; De Gaulle, *Mémoires de guerre*, Vol. III, pp. 385–86.

17. Woodward, *British Foreign Policy*, Vol. III, pp. 460–64.

18. At Yalta Stalin charged that 212 members of the Soviet armed forces had been killed by "agents" of the London government (*Yalta Papers*, p. 681). In later years the Polish Communist government admitted to having lost 14,876 men in the struggle with the remnants of the London dominated underground army: see Dziewanowski, *Communist Party of Poland*, p. 194; Khrushchev, *Memoirs*, Vol. II, pp. 175ff.; and W. Góra and R. Halaba, eds., *1944–1947 W walce o utrwalenie wladzy ludowej w Polsce* [In the struggle for the consolidation of a people's government in Poland] (Warsaw: Książka i Wiedza, 1967).

19. Biegański, *Documents on Polish-Soviet Relations*, Vol. II, pp. 485–505; Rozek, *Allied Wartime Diplomacy*, pp. 318ff.; and Clemens, *Yalta*, pp. 8ff.

20. De Gaulle, *Mémoires de guerre*, Vol. III, pp. 379ff., 91–92.

21. Letters to Churchill dated 8 December 1944 and 5 January 1945, letters to Roosevelt dated 27 December 1944 and 1 January 1945, *Correspondence*, Vol. I, pp. 282–83, 293; Vol. II, pp. 180–84.

22. *Pravda*, 24 December 1944, p. 3, and 25 December, p. 3. For the comparability of developments in Hungary and Poland, see Korom, "Az ideiglenes nemzetgyülés," pp. 116ff. Evidently, the Kremlin leadership was worried at this time less by questions of practical power in Eastern Europe than by the theoretical problem of whether governments should be established in liberated countries prior to the emergence of a popular or legal mandate. As manifestations of a new policy, Korom links the establishment of governments in Dimitrov's Bulgaria in September 1944, in Hungary in December, in Poland in January 1945, and in Austria later in 1945.

23. *Yalta Papers*, pp. 78–82, 849, and the Stalin letters to Churchill and Truman on 24 April 1945 in *Correspondence*, Vol. I, p. 331, and Vol. II, p. 220.

24. The Polish delegation was in the Soviet Union from 22 to 25 January 1945, and the record of its movements was daily published.

25. *FRUS 1945*, Vol. V, pp. 942–45. For background, see Martin F. Herz, *Beginnings of the Cold War* (Bloomington: Indiana University Press, 1966), ch. 10; Paterson, *Soviet-American Confrontation*, ch. 2; and Harriman and Abel, *Special Envoy*, p. 384.

26. Such expectations loomed large in Eugen Varga's *Changes in the Economy of Capitalism*, published in 1945, which will be discussed shortly. See also the articles by V. Linetsky in *New Times*, no. 7 (1945), pp. 5–9; by S. Vishnev in *Propagandist*, no. 1

(1946), pp. 48ff.; and Stalin's interview with Stassen in 1947 (*Soch.*, Vol. XVI, esp. pp. 85ff.). American official opinions also sometimes tended in these directions: see, for example, Roosevelt's remarks to Stalin at their first meeting in Teheran (*Tegeran, Yalta, Potsdam*, p. 34); Clayton's report to Stettinius (*Yalta Papers*, pp. 318ff.); and Feis, *From Trust to Terror*, p. 72.

27. *Istoriya KPSS*, Vol. V, pp. 588–90.

28. The relative weakness of the British position emerges clearly in the *Roosevelt-Churchill Correspondence*, pp. 631ff.

29. *Correspondence*, Vol. I, p. 294. For comment, see Bialer, *Stalin and His Generals*, p. 615, n. 16.

30. Khrushchev found Stalin in these days "in the highest spirits" (Khrushchev, *Memoirs*, Vol. II, p. 167). Field Marshal Tedder likewise found him in extraordinarily fine form (*With Prejudice*, pp. 642–52).

31. A recent and well-documented account of the Yalta Conference is in Diane Clemen's *Yalta* (extensive bibliography, pp. 336ff.). Memoirs most revealing about Soviet negotiating techniques at the conference are: Bohlen, *Witness to History*, ch. 11; Byrnes, *Speaking Frankly*, ch. 2; Churchill, *Triumph and Tragedy*, bk. 2, chs. 2–4; Eden, *The Reckoning*, ch. 15; Harriman and Abel, *Special Envoy*, ch. 17; Lord Ismay, *Memoirs*, ch. 31; King and Whitehill, *Fleet Admiral King*, pp. 587ff.; Leahy, *I Was There*, ch. 18; Moran, *Churchill*, ch. 24; Sherwood, *Roosevelt and Hopkins*, ch. 33; and Stettinius, *Roosevelt and the Russians. The Yalta Conference.*

32. *Yalta Papers*, p. 667; *Tegeran, Yalta, Potsdam*, pp. 140–41.

33. *Yalta Papers*, p. 668; *Tegeran, Yalta, Potsdam*, pp. 142–43.

34. *Yalta Papers*, pp. 726–28. This letter was, of course, prepared in consultation with Churchill and incorporated the latter's suggestions, but it was signed only by Roosevelt.

35. For the abruptness of his shift, see the accounts in Feis, *Churchill, Roosevelt, Stalin*, p. 573; Woodward, *British Foreign Policy*, p. 488ff.; and Clemens, *Yalta*, p. 226.

36. Clemens emphasizes the contrast between the lack of preparation of the Western members of the conference, particularly Roosevelt, and the careful planning of the Russians. She also draws on Ivan Maiskii's memoirs to indicate that throughout the war Stalin systematically manipulated Allied guilt feelings over the absence of a second front to extract political concessions (*Yalta*, pp. 74ff.).

37. Kolko holds that "only" fear of mutual enemies held the United States and Britain together at this time (*Politics of War*, pp. 312, 346), a claim which is difficult to accept. Clemens' estimate of the friction in the Anglo-American relationship seems more reasonable (*Yalta*, pp. 176–77ff.).

38. *Yalta Papers*, pp. 572–73. The interview is omitted from the Soviet version.

39. *Ibid.*, p. 769.

40. See in particular the records of the third, fourth, and sixth plenary sessions in *Yalta Papers*, pp. 664ff., 776 ff., and 849ff., and *Tegeran, Yalta, Potsdam*, pp. 139ff., 151ff., and 168ff.

41. This is the conclusion of André Fontaine, *History of the Cold War* (New York: Vintage, 1970), Vol. I, p. 256: Yalta and Potsdam "strengthened [Stalin's] conviction that he was dealing with weaklings and hypocrites forever ready to yield to pressure and happy to settle with empty promises. This experience probably explains his postwar conduct."

42. Chapters published for discussion purposes appeared in *Mirovoe Khozyaistvo i Mirovaya Politika*, nos. 12 (1944), 1 (1945), and 9 (1945). The journal announced the publication of the work in its December 1945 issue, although the volume itself is dated 1946.

43. By far the most effective discussion of Varga's ideas is in László Tikos, *E. Vargas Tätigkeit als Wirtschaftsanalytiker und Publizist* (Tübingen: Böhlau, 1965). A

recent analysis of Varga's work is Richard Nordahl's "Stalinist Ideology," *Soviet Studies,* Vol. XXVI (1974), pp. 239–59. See also the forthcoming paper by Paul Morantz, "The Inevitability of War Controversy." It may be mentioned that some of the best-known Western commentaries on Varga have been misleading: see F. C. Barghoorn, "The Varga Discussion," *American Slavic and East European Review,* Vol. VII (1948), pp. 214–36, and Rieber, *Stalin and the French Communist Party,* pp. 361ff. (which is in other respects a very important book).

44. *Pravda,* 8 February 1946, p. 4.

45. *Pravda,* 6 February 1946, p. 2.

46. This is the version monitored by the BBC and given in the daily report for 8 February. The published text in *Pravda,* 8 February, p. 2, tones down the last few lines.

47. The Malenkov speech was published in *Pravda,* 9 December 1947, but it is known also from the booklet *Informatsionoe soveshchanie predstavitelei nekotorykh kompartii v Polshe v kontse sentyabrya 1947 g.* and from the stenographic notes in Reale, *Avec Jacques Duclos.* The various texts differ.

48. *PS,* no. 4 (1946), p. 10.

49. *PS,* no. 16 (1945), p. 11.

50. *PS,* no. 5 (1945), p. 32.

51. See, for example, Konev's statement in Bialer, *Stalin and His Generals,* p. 521. The development of this hostility in the press is traced by Barghoorn in *The Soviet Image of the United States,* pt. 3.

52. The record is in *FRUS 1945,* Vols. IV, pp. 567ff., and VI, p. 782. Many Western observers perceived the basic split in Soviet foreign policy between "isolationism" and "participation" quite accurately, but there seems to have been very great confusion at the time and ever since about which group advocated what. Kennan's "kremlinological" memorandum of late 1945, published over twenty years later (*Slavic Review,* no. 3 [1968]), is a good example. Kennan associates the "isolationist" trend with "hard-lineism" and "the Party," by which he means Malenkov and Beria. He seems unaware of Zhdanov's return to power, and Molotov in his eyes is little different from Malenkov and "the Party." If we may judge from Harriman's reports of the period, the United States Embassy associated Soviet "participation" in the Grand Alliance with Litvinov (who, of course, was totally out of the "Kremlin" picture). Actually, as we will see, though Malenkov was certainly in favor of "isolationism," he also advocated extreme caution—and an early withdrawal from Europe. Molotov and Zhdanov, on the other hand, were very much for "participation," but on the assumption that it would result in a considerable spread of socialism.

53. *Pravda,* 7 November 1945, pp. 1–2. Central though this speech was to Molotov's thinking, it was omitted from his collected speeches of the postwar era, *Voprosy Vneshnei Politiki.*

54. *Pravda,* 7 November 1945, p. 2.

55. Trout ("Soviet Policy Making," pp. 140–46) recognizes and stresses the significance of the "anti-blocist" stand. Many other Western commentators ignore it.

56. For another example of Molotov's "populism," see Djilas, *Conversations with Stalin,* p. 156.

57. *FRUS 1945,* Vol. V, p. 921.

58. *Washington Post,* 21 January 1952, pp. 1, 4.

59. *Ibid.* For background and discussion of Litvinov's person, see Mástný, "The Cassandra in the Foreign Commissariat." For discussion of Litvinov's interview with Richard Hottelot, during which he made these remarks, see Chapter 11, n. 76 below.

60. *Bol'shevik,* nos. 17–18 (1946), p. 18.

61. *Ibid.*

62. The first of these abusive speeches was delivered on 24 June 1947 and pub-

lished in *Voprosy Filozofii*, no. 1 (1947), and in *Bol'shevik*, no. 16 (1947). The second was delivered in mid-January 1948 and was published as a pamphlet in March 1948.

63. One of the rare observations of this parallel in the Western literature is in Wolfe, *Soviet Power and Europe*, p. 20.

64. *Bol'shevik*, nos. 17–18 (1946), pp. 17–19.

65. *Pravda*, 7 November 1946, pp. 1–2 (italics added).

66. *Soch.*, Vol. XVI, p. 53.

Notes to Chapter 8

1. For details, see *FRUS 1945*, Vol. V, pp. 487–88; Ionescu, *Communism in Rumania*, pp. 103ff.; and Henry L. Roberts, *Rumania* (New Haven: Yale University Press, 1951), pp. 258ff.

2. Lynn Davis (*The Cold War Begins*, pp. 256ff.) and Kolko (*The Politics of War*, pp. 404–6) cite reports from American representatives in Rumania that the disturbances verged on civil war. Kolko goes on to say that the Russians intervened to halt a revolutionary polarization and to keep order. Davis, using the same documents, believes that Soviet authorities encouraged disturbances by disarming the police and stresses that the importance of the coup lay in Vyshinsky's rude exclusion of Western influence. Roberts (*Rumania*, p. 293) says he toured the country for two months between December 1944 and February 1945 and saw no evidence of peasant disorders. He claims it was only after the February events that peasant demonstrations and land seizures became widespread. It is interesting that Rumanian Communist historians downplay the rural revolution, which so interests Westerners, and completely ignore Vyshinsky in explaining the rise of the Groza government. They give exclusive credit to the Rumanian Communist Party's ability to mobilize the urban masses. See G. Zaharia et al., eds., *România în anii revoluţiei democrat-populare, 1944–1947* [Rumania in the years of the popular-democratic revolution] (Bucharest: Ed. Politică, 1971), ch. 2; Aron Petric, "6 Martie—eveniment memorabil în istoria poporului român" [The 6th of March—a memorable event in the history of the Rumanian people], *Anale de istorie*, Vol. XVI (1970), pp. 3–20.

3. The most extended such inquiry is in Roberts, *Rumania*, pp. 269–73. Fischer-Galati (*The New Rumania*, pp. 28ff.) discusses recently revealed Rumanian Communist evidence about the coup, but does not touch on the international background. He shows that the Rumanian CP was split, with one wing (led by Ana Pauker) hoping for a Soviet placement of the Communists in power by coup d'état and a moderate wing (led by Gheorghiu-Dej) backing the idea of a coalition government under Groza. Consequently, he makes Vyshinsky's action seem milder than it does in the international context.

4. See Churchill, *Triumph and Tragedy*, bk. 2, ch. 7; the Harriman and Kennan reports in *FRUS 1945*, Vol. V, pp. 821–24, 853ff., 846–947; and the account in Herz, *Beginnings of the Cold War*, pp. 87–88.

5. In the post-Yalta arguments over Poland Roosevelt himself seems to have felt that the West was drawing back from its commitments: see Herz, *Beginnings*, pp. 90–91; Gar Alperovitz, *Atomic Diplomacy* (New York: Random House, 1965), p. 21; and Kolko, *Politics of War*, pp. 390ff.

6. In March Harriman attempted to explain what was happening in terms of a "discovery" by Stalin and the Polish Communists after Yalta that they were weaker inside Poland than they imagined and consequently needed to push (*FRUS 1945*, Vol. V, p. 840), but even before this, he believed that Molotov was acting on orders not to budge (*ibid.*, p. 136).

7. An eyewitness account is in Z. Stypułkowski, *Invitation à Moscou*. A show trial was held for these Poles in June 1945 in the Soviet Union.

8. See Stephen G. Xydis, "The 1945 Crisis over the Turkish Straits," *Balkan Studies*, Vol. I (1960), pp. 65–90.

9. The most extensive account of the Berne affair is in Allen Dulles, *The Secret Surrender.*

10. American revisionist historians habitually denounce the United States for the Berne affair and many other sins, but practically none of them come to grips with Vyshinsky's coup. D. Clemens, in her *Yalta,* for example, praises Stalin for deliberately holding back Soviet troops from Berlin in early February out of politeness, so as not to embarrass the Allies, but her study stops short of the March crisis. Alperovitz (*Atomic Diplomacy*) and David Horowitz (*The Free World Colossus* [New York: Hill and Wang, 1965]) avoid discussion of the Vyshinsky coup by beginning their narratives with Roosevelt's death, a full six weeks later. Kolko, as noted above, overwhelms the story with tendentious detail. The most honest of the revisionist accounts in this respect (as in many others) is that of D. F. Fleming, *The Cold War and Its Origins,* 2 vols. (Garden City, N.Y.: Doubleday, 1961), Vol. I, pp. 208ff. Like Kolko, Fleming buries the implications of the coup in a mass of detail, but he points out far more clearly than Kolko that it was a calculated act of aggression which was a complete contradiction of Stalin's position at Yalta. By way of explanation, he cites Stettinius, *Roosevelt and the Russians,* pp. 295–303, where there is talk of Stalin being a prisoner of the Politburo.

11. The Finnish election took place on 18 March but was heavily publicized in the Soviet press in the preceding weeks.

12. *Soch.,* Vol. XV, p. 182. This was just three days after the Groza regime was finally installed.

13. Stalin, *Correspondence,* Vol. II, pp. 211–12.

14. *FRUS 1945,* Vol. V, pp. 235–36, 257; Stalin, *Correspondence,* Vol. II, pp. 219–20.

15. *Pravda,* 16 March 1945, p. 4.

16. *Pravda,* 14 April 1945, p. 2.

17. See the evaluations by Ehrenburg, *The War,* pp. 176ff., and Harriman, *FRUS 1945,* Vol. V, pp. 829–31. Wolfgang Leonhard told me in an interview in 1964 that travelers in eastern Germany in mid-1945 could tell exactly where the Red Army had been on 14 April. East of that line the propaganda posters reflected hatred for the Germans; west of the line they proclaimed respect for the German people.

18. *Pravda,* 20 April 1945, p. 4. The matter came up again because Lippmann wrote a letter to *Pravda* protesting its criticism of him. There was a parallel shift in attitudes in two criticisms of Herbert Hoover which *Pravda* published on 5 April, at the height of the Berne affair, and on 22 April.

19. *Die Revolution entlässt ihre Kinder,* p. 340. Leonhard says that hitherto "even the slightest criticism of the Western Allies, even the lightest jokes, could be judged political mistakes." Note also in this connection E. Varga's recollection of how one still had to be discreet in 1945 about calling the Allies "imperialists" ("Diskussiya po knige E. Vargy," appendix to *Mirovoe Khozyaistvo i Mirovaya Politika,* no. 11 [1947], p. 5).

20. *Bol'shevik,* nos. 7–8 (1945), pp. 14–26.

21. *Soch.,* Vol. XV, p. 101.

22. For background, see Duhnke, *Die KPD,* pp. 394ff.

23. There is a controversy here. Henry Krisch, in a recent careful study, denies that there was a change in policy in Germany at this point; he asserts that the re-establishment of political parties in June was implicit in the "front" policy of the Ulbricht group in April (*German Politics under Soviet Occupation* [New York: Columbia University Press, 1974], pp. 51, 232). Leonhard, on the other hand, claims there was a two-stage development. The first, which was operational for the Ulbricht group when it returned home about 30 April, denied the Germans any partisan political activity outside a "national bloc of militant democracy." The second, brought home by Wilhelm

Pieck early in June, placed the whole stress on activity through the parties. See *Die Revolution entlässt ihre Kinder*, ch. 8. I am inclined to believe Leonhard, who was there at the time and was suitably sensitive to ideological currents. Krisch seems to miss the ideological signals, and he also overlooks the operational difference between mere re-establishment of parties on paper (which was perhaps compatible with the "national bloc" policy) and the wholesale shift to reliance *mainly* on the parties, which Pieck instituted.

24. For Stalin's German policy after April 1945, see such memoirs as those of Erich W. Gniffke, *Jahre mit Ulbricht*, pp. 250–51; and Djilas, *Conversations with Stalin*, p. 153; Boris Meissner, *Russland, die Westmächte und Deutschland* (Hamburg: Nolke, 1953), pp. 150ff.; John Gimbel, *The Origins of the Marshall Plan* (Stanford: Stanford University Press, 1976), passim, but esp. pp. 127–29; and Wolfe, *Soviet Power and Europe*, pp. 14–15. Westerners have been extremely puzzled by the odd patterns of Soviet practice in Germany (see, for example, the remark of Charles Bohlen, *Witness to History*, p. 274). One pioneering study depicted it as an effort from the start to establish a separate Communist-dominated state in the Soviet zone (Peter Nettl, *The Eastern Zone and Soviet Policy in Germany, 1945–1950* [New York: Oxford University Press, 1951]). Manuel Gottlieb (*The German Peace Settlement and the Berlin Crisis* [New York: Paine Whitman, 1960], pp. 178–81) and Hans-Peter Schwarz (*Vom Reich zur Bundesrepublik* [Neuwied: Luchterhand, 1966], pp. 203ff.) describe Stalin as simultaneously pursuing several systematic but contradictory policies—i.e., the extraction of heavy reparations, the construction of a Communist satellite, the establishment of Soviet military security, etc. Perhaps in fact Stalin, under the influence of Voznesensky, did this, seriously anticipating the fulfillment of all his goals at once. But it seems certain that the theoretical cover policy was anti-blocism.

25. *Soch.*, Vol. XV, pp. 184–87.

26. The Duclos article appeared originally in *Cahiers du communisme*, n.s., no. 6 (1945), pp. 21–38. For comment, see Starobin, *American Communism in Crisis*, pp. 78–79, 269–71; and the surprisingly acute interpretation by Kolko, *Politics of War*, pp. 439–44.

27. Chuikov gives his version of these events at greatest length in his *The End of the Third Reich*, ch. 5. For a sound evaluation of the controversy, see Albert Seaton, *Stalin as Military Commander* (New York: Praeger, 1976), pp. 238ff.

28. Zhukov, *Vospominaniya i razmyshleniya*, pp. 640–43.

29. Konev (*Sorok pyatyi*, ch. 4) says that Stalin showed him not a letter but a telegram, and that it specifically stated that the British (as opposed to the Americans) were about to attack Berlin. Bialer (*Stalin and His Generals*, pp. 620–21) suggests that Konev confuses the "well-wisher's" letter with Eisenhower's telegram, which he learned about only years after the event.

30. Cf. Eisenhower, *Crusade in Europe*, pp. 398ff.; Stephen E. Ambrose, *Eisenhower and Berlin, 1945* (New York: W. W. Norton, 1967), ch. 3, esp. pp. 54ff.; and Forrest C. Pogue, "The Decision To Halt at the Elbe," in *Command Decisions*, ed. Kent R. Greenfield (New York: Department of the Army, 1959), pp. 479–93.

31. *Roosevelt-Churchill Correspondence*, pp. 696ff.

32. The date of delivery has often been construed as 28 March, the date of expedition. But see John R. Deane, *The Strange Alliance*, p. 158; and Feis, *Churchill, Roosevelt, Stalin*, pp. 604ff., which document the three-day delay.

33. Stalin's reply is reproduced in part in Pospelov, ed., *Istoriya Velikoi Otechestvennoi Voiny*, Vol. V, p. 257, and in full in Chandler, *The Papers of Dwight D. Eisenhower*, Vol. IV, p. 2584. Ambrose has suggested (in *Eisenhower and Berlin*, ch. 3) that Konev's swift breakthrough into Saxony after the start of the 16 April Soviet offensive reflected not (as most historians hold) a weakness in the German defenses on

his front but a special Soviet build-up there because the main Soviet objective was to meet the Americans. It would follow that Stalin did not lie to Eisenhower on 1 April. Unfortunately, it would follow also that all the Soviet generals and all the Soviet histories of the war are lying when they state that the staff conference of 1 and 2 April decided, as a matter of first priority, to attack Berlin. This is not impossible, but I find it improbable.

34. Shtemenko, *General'nyi shtab v gody voiny,* pp. 329–30. For evaluation, see Seaton, *Stalin as Military Commander,* pp. 246–48; and Kolkowicz, *The Soviet Military and the Communist Party,* pp. 218ff.

35. Stalin, *Correspondence,* Vol. II, pp. 205–6.

36. See the Stalin letters to Churchill of 8 November 1941, 13 August 1942, 16 February 1943, 15 March 1943, 2 April 1943, and 24 June 1943, which may be found in his *Correspondence,* Vol. I.

37. See the comments in *FRUS 1945,* Vol. V, pp. 119ff., esp. p. 1123. Kennan says that a concert of religious music attended by the new patriarch was held on 7 February at the Moscow Conservatory and that the use of such a hall for religious purposes seemed incomprehensible in Communist circles. The announcer, he writes, was noticeably nervous and seemed overcome by the "shattering quality" of a statement he had to read about this religious music being an expression of the emotional experience of the Russian people in the war.

38. *Pravda,* 20 April 1945, p. 1.

39. *Izvestiya,* 29 May 1945, p. 4; *FRUS 1945,* Vol. V, pp. 903, 1124.

40. *Soch.,* Vol. XV, pp. 183–87.

41. *Soch.,* Vol. XV, pp. 203–4.

42. *Pravda,* 21 April, p. 3, 22 April, p. 3.

43. This periodical appeared before the war but ceased publication between 1941 and January 1946. For its social significance, see Solzhenitsyn, *The First Circle,* p. 422.

44. *Pravda,* 22 April, pp. 3–4, 23 April, p. 3.

45. *Pravda,* 23 April, p. 3.

46. *Bol'shevik,* no. 14, p. 78 (italics added).

47. *Bol'shevik,* nos. 23–24 (1945), p. 25.

48. *Bol'shevik,* no. 1 (1946), pp. 1–2. This was no obscure speech: it was the annual eulogy spoken on the anniversary of Lenin's death, and the entire Soviet leadership was present at its delivery.

49. *Bol'shevik,* nos. 23–24 (1945) (published 14 January 1946), pp. 8ff. This article was paired in *Bol'shevik* with one of the Aleksandrov articles cited above. The comparison of the two was thus intentional. The Pospelov essay was given broad radio coverage on 14 January, so it was fresh in the public memory when Aleksandrov spoke on 21 January.

50. *Pravda,* 8 February 1946, p. 2.

51. *Pravda,* 7 February 1946, p. 2.

52. For Vyshinsky's biography see *BSE,* 2d ed., Vol. 9, p. 540.

53. See Nicolaevsky, "Ideologicheskaya perestroika VKP(b)," pp. 37–38; Khrushchev, *Memoirs,* Vol. II, pp. 295–96.

54. Stalin, *Correspondence,* Vol. II, pp. 201, 206.

55. *PS,* no. 5 (to press 4 April), 1945, p. 26; *Sputnik Agitatora,* no. 6, pp. 18ff. This "vigilance" campaign later became the ostensible reason for a Party revivalist witch-hunt against wartime editors of various inner-Party journals; see *PS,* no. 19 (24 November 1945), pp. 44–45.

56. Djilas, *Conversations with Stalin,* p. 114.

57. The editors of the *Roosevelt-Churchill Correspondence* state their conviction (p. 709n) that at the time of his death Roosevelt was determined to pursue a tougher line with the Russians. The fact remains that the president's last message to Stalin (in

Stalin, *Correspondence*, Vol. II, p. 214) was conciliatory, and that notwithstanding Roosevelt's firm letters of 1 April about Poland and 5 April about the Berne affair, five weeks of aggressive Soviet probing had not elicited decisive Allied resistance.

58. Unless otherwise noted, the following events were recorded on the front pages of *Pravda* or the *New York Times* for the period in question.

59. Stalin, *Correspondence*, Vol. II, pp. 200–201.

60. *Ibid.*, Vol. II, pp. 201–4.

61. Chaney, *Zhukov*, pp. 306ff.

62. Stalin, *Correspondence*, Vol. II, pp. 205–6.

63. *FRUS 1945*, Vol. VII, pp. 338–40; Feis, *The China Tangle* (Princeton: Princeton University Press, 1952), ch. 26.

64. *FRUS 1945*, Vol. V, p. 828.

Notes to Chapter 9

1. The American records of the conference are printed in *FRUS 1945*, Vol. II, pp. 99ff. The major Soviet speeches are in *VPSS 1945*, pp. 19–31. For background, see Gaddis, *The United States and the Origins of the Cold War*, pp. 263ff., and Davis, *The Cold War Begins*, chs. 8–9.

2. For Molotov's catalogue of wrongs, see in particular his press conferences of 19 September and 3 October in *VPSS 1945*, pp. 64ff., 74ff.

3. See William B. Bader, *Austria between East and West* (Stanford: Stanford University Press, 1966), chs. 1–3; M. Balfour and John Mair, *Four Power Control in Germany and Austria, 1945–1946* (London: Oxford University Press, 1956); Douglas W. Houston, "Karl Renner and Austria in 1945," *Austrian History Yearbook*, Vol. I (1965), pp. 122–49; and Ernst Fischer, *Das Ende einer Illusion*, pp. 23ff.

4. Feis, *Between War and Peace*, ch. 33; Wheeler-Bennett and Nichols, *The Semblance of Peace*, pp. 333ff.; Alperovitz, *Atomic Diplomacy*, pp. 164ff.

5. Byrnes, *Speaking Frankly*, p. 99.

6. *Ibid.*, p. 101.

7. Cf. Feis, *From Trust to Terror*, pp. 6, 16–17.

8. Herring, *Aid to Russia*, ch. 7.

9. Gaddis, *The United States and the Origins of the Cold War*, pp. 328–30.

10. Kolko, *Politics of War*, pp. 422ff., presents these arguments with the exaggeration of an outsider. For more realism, see Davis, *The Cold War Begins*, ch. 8, esp. p. 281, n. 66, where the lack of coordination of American policy is made clear.

11. Byrnes based his plans for the London Conference on an expectation that the Russians would be overawed by America's atomic strength. He was thrown off balance when Molotov refused to be impressed and instead joked about the bomb. Alperovitz (*Atomic Diplomacy*, chs. 6–7) suggests that even the original dropping of the bombs at Hiroshima and Nagasaki was intended above all to impress the Russians, but recent historians show that his interpretation is incorrect and exaggerated: see Martin J. Sherwin, *A World Destroyed. The Atomic Bomb and the Grand Alliance* (New York: Knopf, 1975), chs. 8–9; and B. J. Bernstein, "Roosevelt, Truman and the Atomic Bomb," *Political Science Quarterly*, Vol. XC (1975), pp. 23–69.

12. Molotov is said to have expressed himself to this effect to a friendly journalist in London.

13. Harry S. Truman, *Year of Decisions*, p. 82.

14. Feis, *Between War and Peace*, pp. 84ff.

15. The record is described with clarity in Woodward, *British Foreign Policy*, condensed ed., chs. 29–30; in McNeill, *America, Britain, and Russia*, pp. 652ff.; and in Wheeler-Bennett and Nichols, *Semblance of Peace*, ch. 14.

16. Feis, *Between War and Peace*, ch. 19.

17. Quoted in Sherwood, *Roosevelt and Hopkins*, p. 921.

18. Alperovitz suggests that Truman remained anti-Soviet but, on the advice of Secretary of War Stimson, dropped any *show* of anti-Sovietism, reserving his fire until the atomic bomb was operational (*Atomic Diplomacy,* ch. 3). Even Kolko (*Politics of War,* pp. 421–22) points out that such a conspiratorial move would not have been Truman's style, and that it could have been counterproductive because the Russians, uninformed about the bomb, might have misinterpreted Truman's behavior as a sign of weakness. Harriman calls the Alperovitz thesis "utter nonsense" (*Special Envoy,* p. 490), and both Sherwin (*A World Destroyed,* ch. 7) and Bernstein ("Roosevelt, Truman and the Atomic Bomb," pp. 35ff.) reject it. See also Thomas Hammond, "Did the United States Use Atomic Diplomacy?" in *From the Cold War to Detente,* ed. Potichnyi and Jane Shapiro (New York: Praeger, 1976), pp. 26–56.

19. Sherwood, *Roosevelt and Hopkins,* pp. 897–98, 910ff.; Feis, *Between War and Peace,* chs. 15–17.

20. *Potsdam Papers,* Vol. I, p. 1584. This and the following manipulations have been recounted recently by Charles L. Mee, Jr., in *Meeting at Potsdam* (New York: M. Evans, 1974).

21. Churchill, *Triumph and Tragedy,* p. 636.

22. Transparent efforts to create a split between Britain and America are recorded in the minutes of the first and third plenary sessions and of the foreign ministers' meeting on 20 July: see *Potsdam Papers,* Vol. II, pp. 55, 59, 126, 150–52.

23. In the third, fourth, sixth, and eighth plenary sessions, Stalin was able to witness and mediate acrid Anglo-American disputes, mainly over colonial matters, the seeds of which he himself had planted (*Potsdam Papers,* Vol. II, pp. 129, 174ff., 253ff., 362ff.).

24. Particularly outrageous Soviet attempts at "horse-trading" took place at the 20 July and 23 July foreign ministers' sessions: see *Potsdam Papers,* Vol. II, pp. 145, 277.

25. *Bol'shevik,* no. 16, pp. 31–59.

26. *Ibid.,* p. 57.

27. *Ibid.,* p. 56.

28. *FRUS 1945,* Vol. II, pp. 357–58, 381. According to Byrnes' account, Molotov raised the issue of Japan at a private meeting on 22 September, just before his announcement that the conference had been incorrectly organized. According to the United States documents, he did so only on 24 September. The effect was the same. Cf. Gaddis, *The United States and the Origins of the Cold War,* p. 266n.

29. Byrnes, *Speaking Frankly,* pp. 102–3.

30. For the early stages of the CCP-CPSU(b) dispute, see Jacques Guillermaz, *History of the Chinese Communist Party;* Schram, *Mao Tse-tung.*

31. Stalin called the Chinese Communists "margarine Communists" in a talk with Harriman in August 1944. At about the same time, Molotov informed Patrick Hurley, the future United States ambassador to China, that some people in China called themselves Communists "as a way of expressing economic discontent" (see *United States Relations with China,* p. 72). According to a lower-ranking Soviet official, these labels were still operational in August 1945: see *FRUS 1945,* Vol. VII, p. 448.

32. Guillermaz, *History of the CCP,* pp. 354ff.; Tang Tsou, *America's Failure in China,* p. 297.

33. Schram, *Mao Tse-tung,* pp. 228ff.; and Okabe Tatsumi, "The Cold War and China," in *The Origins of the Cold War in Asia,* ed. Nagai Yōnosuke and Iriye Akira (Tokyo: University of Tokyo Press, 1977), p. 226. Cf. John S. Service's reports from Yenan of 23 March and 1 April 1945 in J. W. Esherick, ed., *Lost Chance in China. The World War II Dispatches of John S. Service,* pp. 350ff.

34. Mao, *Selected Works,* Vol. III, p. 292.

35. *Ibid.,* pp. 282–85.

36. Liu Shao-chi, "About the Party," quoted in the recent official Soviet record of

the Sino-Soviet dispute, O. B. Borisov and B. T. Koloskov, *Sovetsko-Kitaiskie otno-sheniya 1945–1970* (Moscow: Mysl, 1971), translated in *Soviet-Chinese Relations, 1945–1970*, ed. Vladimir Petrov (Bloomington: Indiana University Press, 1975), p. 117. Although the CCP had been touting Mao's "special contribution to Marxism-Leninism" since the anti-Soviet "rectification campaign" of 1940, such boasts were little known outside China until 1945.

37. *FRUS 1945*, Vol. VII, pp. 338–40; Feis, *The China Tangle*, ch. 26.

38. Wheeler-Bennett and Nichols, *Semblance of Peace*, p. 359.

39. On 26 July, which was altogether too late, Molotov attempted to obtain a delay in the publication of the ultimatum to the Japanese "by two or three days" (*Potsdam Papers*, Vol. II, pp. 355ff.). Military logistics probably played some role in Molotov's plea: in May Stalin told Hopkins that the Red Army would be ready in the Far East by 8 August, but at Potsdam he and the chief of the Soviet general staff, A. I. Antonov, told the Allies that readiness would be achieved "in the latter half of August" (Seaton, *Stalin as Military Commander*, pp. 260ff.). I cannot see that two or three days would have made much difference from a military standpoint, however. Molotov's request smells of politics.

40. Lacking a treaty with China, on 29 July the Russians attempted to justify their break with Japan by asking the Western Allies for a formal invitation to enter the war. The maneuver failed. Details are found in Wheeler-Bennett and Nichols, *Semblance of Peace*, pp. 382–84.

41. Mao, *Selected Works*, Vol. IV, pp. 15ff. Guillermaz, *History of the CCP*, p. 376; Schram, *Mao Tse-Tung*, pp. 236–37. Immediately after the Soviet declaration of war Mao claimed for his armies the right to receive the Japanese surrender together with the Nationalists. On 10 August his general, Chu Teh, ordered the Communist troops to act accordingly. The Nationalists vigorously rejected this claim, whereupon Mao turned against them.

42. On 18 August and 31 August Stalin addressed messages to Chiang Kai-shek, and on 29 August he sent one to Prime Minister Choi Bal San of Mongolia. The gist of them was that "this victory has a world historic meaning as a great landmark in the progressive development of all humanity," and that the victory was due to the coopera-tion of the Allied states and armies (*Soch.*, Vol. XV, pp. 209–11).

43. *FRUS 1945*, Vol. VII, p. 448.

44. Grechko et al., eds., *Osvoboditel'naya missiya sovetskykh vooruzhennykh sil*, p. 425. Cf. I. I. Galgov, "Kommunisticheskaya partiya—Organizator pobedy nad mili-taristicheskoi Japoneia" [The CP—the organizer of the victory over militaristic Japan], *Voprosy Istorii KPSS*, no. 9 (1975), pp. 13ff., which cites other literature and ventures that, far from not helping the CCP (as the Chinese claim), the Red Army rescued the Communists from a very embarrassing military position.

45. For Mao's disappointment over the pact, see the document from Yenan cited in Warren I. Cohen, "American Observers and the Sino-Soviet Friendship Treaty of August 1945," *Pacific Historical Review*, Vol. XXXVI (1966), pp. 347–49; also Feis, *The China Tangle*, p. 358; Max Beloff, *Soviet Policy in the Far East, 1944–1949* (New York: Oxford University Press, 1953); and the recent suspect but interesting account in Peter Vladimirov, *The Vladimirov Diaries: Yenan, China, 1942–1945*, pp. 507–8. For Mao's turnabout, see Schram, *Mao Tse-Tung*, p. 236; Okabe, "The Cold War and China," p. 229.

46. A still useful survey of Far Eastern developments is David Dallin, *Soviet Russia and the Far East* (New Haven: Yale University Press, 1948), pt. 4. See also Beloff, *Soviet Policy in the Far East*, ch. 2. For the Mongolian developments, see Robert A. Rupen, *Mongols of the Twentieth Century*, 2 vols. (Bloomington: Indiana University Press, 1964), Vol. I, pp. 257ff.

47. Gregory Henderson, *Korea: Politics of the Vortex* (Cambridge, Mass.: Harvard University Press, 1968), pp. 115, 413.

48. Korea might have been treated as a liberated ally somewhat like Czechoslovakia and France, but there had been no native government for some decades, and since 1943 the Americans had been pressing for the establishment of a Great Power trusteeship after the war so that the Koreans might have favorable conditions for learning about democracy. As late as midsummer 1945, Molotov could still observe with surprise that the American project was "unparalleled" (*FRUS 1945*, Vol. III, p. 913). Nonetheless, in August, when Soviet troops were actually in Korea, the Americans proposed dividing the peninsula at the 38th parallel, and to their great surprise the Russians accepted (see the account by Dean Rusk in *FRUS 1945*, Vol. VI, pp. 39–40). By mid-autumn the Russians were preparing to set up a special Communist organization just for the north of Korea; and in December 1945, at the Moscow Conference of Allied Foreign Ministers, to the horror of all Koreans regardless of their political complexion, the Allies finalized the trusteeship plan. A general discussion is in Robert A. Scalapino and Chong Sik Lee, *Communism in Korea*, 2 vols. (Berkeley: University of California Press, 1974), Vol. I. Robert Slusser has argued recently that the inspiration behind Stalin's policies in Korea and in the entire Far East at the end of the war was a desire for territory, and specifically for ice-free ports: see "Soviet Policy in the Far East 1945–1950," in Nagai and Iriye, *Origins of the Cold War*, pp. 123–46. Slusser's careful argument rests, ultimately, on his belief that Stalin was silent regarding Korea during the great wartime conferences because he was extremely interested in Korea. Like so many other Western speculations about Stalin's precise territorial war aims, this one cannot be verified (though evident briefing papers doubtless exist in the Moscow archives). I prefer to locate the mainspring of Stalin's policies in Korea in his distrust of the Chinese Communists. There is a good deal of documentation that in 1945–1946 he took many steps to make sure that Korean Communism purified itself of CCP influences: see Robert R. Simmons, *The Strained Alliance* (New York: The Free Press, 1975), chs. 1–3.

49. See Robert A. Scalapino, *The Japanese Communist Movement* (Berkeley: University of California Press, 1967), ch. 4; and the documentary record in *FRUS 1945*, Vol. VI, pp. 782ff.

50. Allen S. Whiting and Shih Tsai Sheng, *Sinkiang, Pawn or Pivot* (East Lansing: Michigan State University Press, 1958), ch. 6.

51. For the following, see Davis, *The Cold War Begins*, chs. 8–9.

52. See my dissertation, "Communism and Hungary," pp. 268ff.

53. Wolff, *Balkans in Our Time*, pp. 284–87; and Ionescu, *Communism in Rumania*, p. 114.

54. For recent reviews of the evidence see Davis, *The Cold War Begins*, pp. 306ff.; Jerzy Tomaszewski, "Wybory 1945 roku w Bulgarii" [The elections of 1945 in Bulgaria], *Kwartalnik Historyczny*, Vol. LXXIX (1972), pp. 87–113; and the essay by M. MacKintosh, "Stalin's Policies towards Eastern Europe, 1939–1948," in Hammond, *The Anatomy of Communist Takeovers*, pp. 239–40. Tomaszewski examined the available Bulgarian records and found that the Bulgarian government received no direct instructions or advice from Moscow to postpone the voting but acted on its own in response to Western pressures. Davis has examined the American documents and finds that pressure from the United States representative in Bulgaria was strong, but that it was not authorized by the State Department. MacKintosh, who was a British representative at the Allied Control Council in Bulgaria at the time, says he was present during a phone call from Stalin to the Soviet commander-in-chief in Bulgaria, during which Stalin ordered that the election be cancelled.

55. It was at this time that the Austrian Communists (and the Soviet occupation

authority) agreed to strip the Interior Ministry of its police powers—and thus lost the opportunity to build up a Communist-controlled national police force, comparable to those which afforded the other East European Communist parties a road to state power (Balfour and Mair, *Four Power Control*, pp. 311–20; William L. Stearman, *The Soviet Union and the Occupation of Austria 1945–1955* [Bonn: Siegler, 1960], p. 35).

56. Cf. Guillermaz, *History of the CCP*, p. 380; Geoffrey Jukes, *The Soviet Union in Asia* (Berkeley: University of California Press, 1973), pp. 215–16; E. W. Pauley, *Report on Japanese Assets in Manchuria* (Washington, D.C.: U.S. Government Printing Office, 1946).

57. Many historians, Western and Soviet alike, have argued that the Soviet Union gave massive help to the Chinese Communists in 1945–1946 in Manchuria. Discussing the details of 1945, however, even anti-Communist accounts acknowledge "confusion" and "lack of realism" in Soviet policy rather than purposeful help to the Communists: see Tang Tsou, *America's Failure in China*, pp. 324ff. Adam Ulam admits that the CCP was "bitterly disappointed" when the Russians would not let it have all of Manchuria right away (*Stalin*, p. 627). Vladimirov indicates that Mao really wanted the Red Army to head for Peking and liberate northern China for him (*Vladimirov Diaries*, pp. 488ff.). Many years later Mao claimed that Stalin had deliberately prevented the CCP from "making revolution" in 1945: see Okabe, "The Cold War and China," p. 229.

58. Byrnes, *Speaking Frankly*, p. 108.

59. For general background, see Rouhollah K. Ramazani, *Iran's Foreign Policy 1941–1973* (Charlottesville: University of Virginia Press, 1975), chs. 4–5; Ramazani's "The Republic of Azerbaijan and the Kurdish People's Republic," in Hammond, *The Anatomy of Communist Takeovers*, pp. 448–74; Firuz Kazemzadeh, "Soviet-Iranian Relations," in *The Soviet Union and the Middle East*, ed. Ivo Lederer and Wayne Vucinich (Stanford: Stanford University Press, 1974), pp. 56–62; Sapehr Zabih, *The Communist Movement in Iran* (Berkeley: University of California Press, 1966), chs. 4–5; and William Eagleton, Jr., *The Kurdish Republic of 1946* (London: Oxford University Press, 1963). For the dating of the start of the action, see *FRUS 1945*, Vol. VIII, pp. 400, 417.

60. *Ibid.*, pp. 56–57. A Soviet review of this interesting subject appeared in *New Times*, no. 18 (1946), pp. 8–11.

61. I am unable to determine how directly Moscow brought the relevance of the Iranian action to the attention of Mao Tse-tung and his comrades, but anyone interested in Asian tribal movements must have noticed that Azerbaijan flared up exactly at the time that the "East Turkistan Republic" in Sinkiang was being torpedoed. Further, there was a precise synchronism all through the winter of 1945–1946 between the behavior of the Red Army in Iran and in Manchuria—first promises to leave, then procrastination, finally reluctant evacuation. The Chinese Communist delegation in Moscow in November and December could not have missed the extensive press coverage of Iran. For a comparison between the two rebellions, see Whiting and Sheng, *Sinkiang*, pp. 128–30.

62. *FRUS 1945*, Vol. VII, pp. 420–22.

63. *Bol'shevik*, nos. 17–18 (1945), p. 9. A purge at this time and in the following months affected the editorial boards of *Bol'shevik, Propagandist, Sputnik Agitatora*, and *Agitator i Propagandist Krasnoi Armii*. See the last page of the September issues of each journal.

64. Trout ("Soviet Policy Making," pp. 69–70) underlines the importance of the shift.

65. The attitude of the Soviet press toward the atomic bomb was from the start extraordinarily ambivalent. For example, *Pravda* on 7 and 11 August published objective accounts of what had happened. But on 13 August it published an authoritative foreign policy survey which made no mention of the new weapon, and meanwhile, on 7 August, it started a series of articles stressing the importance of "forces" in the win-

ning of wars and calling the Western press to task for overrating the bomb. Moreover, Soviet military doctrine did not change because of the bomb: until Stalin's death, the five principles of modern warfare, which he had laid down in 1942, remained in force, as if the new weapons had not "really" made any difference. See on this subject Harriman's report in *FRUS 1945*, Vol. V, pp. 922ff.; and Herbert S. Dinerstein, *War and the Soviet Union*, rev. ed. (New York: Praeger, 1962), pp. 6–8. There is a scholarly consensus that the Soviet Union rushed to manufacture a nuclear bomb after August 1945, building on scientific work done during the war (see Kramish, *Atomic Energy and the Soviet Union*, pp. 86ff.); but there is disagreement as to how much Stalin knew about the bomb before Truman spoke to him at Potsdam on 24 July. Shtemenko (*General'nyi shtab*, Vol. I, p. 349) says that Stalin did not comprehend until later the significance of what had been said. Zhukov, on the other hand, (*Vospominaniya i razmyshleniya*, p. 732) claims that Stalin knew very well what Truman was talking about. This is confirmed by the obituaries of Igor Kurchatov, the leading Soviet nuclear scientist, which claim that the Soviet step-up in 1945 followed the American "announcement" of the successful explosion at Alamogordo, not Hiroshima. Since there was no public announcement of Alamogordo, this must refer to Truman's words (see Eugene Rabinowitch, "Igor Kurchatov, 1903–1960, An Introduction," *Bulletin of the Atomic Scientists*, Vol. XXIII [1967], p. 16). Ulam (*Stalin*, p. 625) mocks the numerous Western historians who follow Zhukov, saying Shtemenko is more reliable. But as Seaton (*Stalin as Military Commander*, p. 260ff.) points out, if Stalin was not aware of the power of the bomb by late July, it is difficult to understand his rush to get into the war immediately after 6 August, when it was dropped. One may wonder also why his spies had not long since warned him what was coming.

66. *FRUS 1945*, Vol. V, p. 891.

67. *PS*, no. 16 (1945), p. 11 (to press 4 September). The speech was published also in the Leningrad Party journal, *Propaganda i Agitatsiya*, no. 18 (1945).

68. *PS*, no. 5 (1945), p. 26.

69. *Soch.*, Vol. XV, p. 214.

70. Deutscher, *Stalin*, p. 528. Stalin's insult to the Party was all the more pronounced because in March 1945 the Party had launched a campaign to make Soviet writing of history more *partiinyi* and, implicitly, less nationalist. Stalin's references to the nationalist character of Russia's history sabotaged this campaign. See Konstantin F. Shteppa, *Russia Historians and the Soviet State* (New Brunswick, N.J.: Rutgers University Press, 1962), ch. 9; and Cyril E. Black, ed., *Rewriting Russian History*, 2d rev. ed. (New York: Vintage, 1962), pp. 124ff., 281ff.

71. Djilas, *Conversations with Stalin*, p. 152, speaking of 1947.

72. *Pravda*, 27 July 1945, p. 1. There is a persistent report that in the late spring of 1944 Malenkov and Beria caused portraits which revealed Stalin's age to be distributed in Moscow; that these were removed as soon as he found out about them; and that his anger over the incident caused Malenkov trouble later on.

73. Svetlana Alliluyeva claims that her father was in robust health until very late in his life (*Only One Year*, pp. 359ff.). This seems decisive testimony and throws into relief Stalin's artifice in pleading ill health so as not to go abroad to meet Roosevelt and Churchill in 1944 and 1945 and in starting the widespread discussion of his health during 1945. See N. Gradoboev, "Lyudi v Kremle" [People in the Kremlin], *Posev* (Limburg an der Lahn), no. 13 (1948), pp. 2–5.

74. Admiral N. G. Kuznetsov, "Na potsdamskoi konferentsii," pp. 87–88. Cf. Zhukov, *Vospominaniya i razmyshleniya*, p. 709.

75. For example, the recollections of Hewlett Johnson, the "Red Dean" of Canterbury, who saw Stalin on 12 July 1945 (*Soviet Russia since the War*, pp. 64–74).

76. Deane, *Strange Alliance*, pp. 272–74; Seaton, *Stalin as Military Commander*, p. 259.

77. Truman, *Year of Decisions*, pp. 341–42; *Potsdam Papers*, Vol. II, p. 43.
78. Harriman thinks (and thought at the time) that Stalin was in good health (see *Special Envoy*, p. 502, and the contemporary reports in *FRUS 1945*, Vol. II, pp. 567ff., Vol. VI, pp. 789ff.). Cf. Alliluyeva, *Twenty Letters to a Friend*, p. 188.
79. See *FRUS 1945*, Vol. V, pp. 929–30; Salisbury, *Russia on the Way*, pp. 386–88; and Stalin's remark to Harold Stassen in *Soch.*, Vol. XV, p. 83. For examples of the extensive speculation about Stalin's illness and retirement, see the *Times* (London), 11 October, p. 1; the *New York Times*, 24 October, p. 8, 8 November, p. 13, and 1 December, p. 1; *Time*, 5 November, p. 36; *Newsweek*, 22 October and 19 November. It is characteristic of the journalism about Russia in 1945 that both Salisbury (*Russia on the Way*) and Snow (*The Pattern of Soviet Power*) each saw fit to devote a chapter of their books to Stalin's coming retirement.
80. Soviet press for 5 September 1945.
81. *Pravda* on 10 October 1945 surrounded the announcement on page 1 of Stalin's vacation with reports of how Molotov was carrying out the functions of head of the government.
82. Petrov, *Stroitel'stvo politorganov*, p. 389.
83. These were announced on 6 October, just a few days before Stalin's departure on vacation.
84. Soviet press for 20 March 1946.
85. Petrov, *Stroitel'stvo politorganov*, p. 389.
86. A detailed analysis by B. Meissner is in "Die Entwicklung der Ministerien in Russland, Part III." An interpretation of the increase in the number of ministries is in Alec Nove, *An Economic History of the USSR* (London: Penguin, 1972), pp. 293–95.
87. According to Khrushchev, the Politburo virtually ceased to function in Stalin's last years, and the Central Committee met not at all (*Crimes of the Stalin Era*, p. S61).
88. Gromyko et al., eds., *Istoriya diplomatii*, pp. 30–34.
89. Deborin, *Mezhdunarodnye otnosheniya 1945–1949*, pp. 21–26.
90. See, for example, the suggestion of Mark Ethridge and Cyril Black in Dennett and Johnson, eds., *Negotiating with the Russians*, p. 184; the official British analysis noted in *FRUS 1945*, Vol. V, pp. 914–15; and Kennan's analysis in *ibid.*, pp. 888ff. All of these accounts indicate that Moscow was vastly surprised and caught off guard, in terms of domestic propaganda, by the Western refusal to make concessions at London. By these accounts, the break in the Alliance was exclusively tactical, and the Russians felt that they were operating from a position not of weakness but of great strength.
91. *Bol'shevik*, nos. 17–18 (1946), pp. 18ff.
92. Djilas, *Conversations with Stalin*, p. 83.
93. Notes of Ernö Gerö, *Párttörténeti Közlemények*, Vol. XX (1974), p. 116.
94. See my dissertation, "Communism and Hungary," pp. 390–91.
95. Rieber, *Stalin and the French Communist Party*, p. 166.
96. Dziewanowski, *Communist Party of Poland*, pp. 192, 347.
97. The following remarks on the sociology of Communism after the war are derived from my own studies of the Hungarian CP and from such classic studies as Jules Monnerot, *Sociology and Psychology of Communism* (Boston: Beacon Press, 1953); Gabriel Almond, *The Appeals of Communism* (Princeton: Princeton University Press, 1954); Hugh Seton-Watson, *Neither War nor Peace*, rev. ed. (New York: Praeger, 1960); and Richard V. Burks, *The Dynamics of Communism in Eastern Europe* (Princeton: Princeton University Press, 1961).
98. Tang Tsou (*America's Failure in China*, pp. 333ff.) provides details.
99. How formal the negotiations were between Yenan and Moscow over these matters late in 1945 is not clear from the available sources. In 1946 the Soviet Union denied that Mao had come to Moscow, but Borisov and Koloskov indicate that a delegation from the Northeastern Bureau headed by Liu Shao-chi, Mao's close adviser,

visited Moscow late in 1945, and Stalin referred to such a delegation in talks with the Yugoslav Communists in 1948 (see Beloff, *Soviet Policy in the Far East*, pp. 48–49; Borisov and Koloskov, *Soviet-Chinese Relations*, pp. 52–53; and Djilas, *Conversations with Stalin*, p. 182). The existence of the Northeastern Bureau (though not the precise date of its establishment) is revealed by Borisov and Koloskov (*Soviet-Chinese Relations*, p. 52), but it has long been known that Moscow sent Li Li-san, an old Comintern rival of Mao, to Manchuria as early as September 1945, and that until after Stalin's death Kao Kang, who had specially close relations with Moscow, possessed powers in northeastern China which were in some ways independent of Mao (see Schram, *Mao Tse-Tung*, pp. 284–85; and Nakajima Mineo, "The Sino-Soviet Confrontation," in Nagai and Iriye, *The Origins of the Cold War*, p. 223, n. 15).

100. Mao, *Selected Works*, Vol. IV, pp. 81–85.

101. Djilas, *Conversations with Stalin*, p. 83.

102. On 30 November Molotov pointed out to Ambassador Harriman that the British note to Moscow on 25 November did not mention the withdrawal of *all* foreign troops from Iran, as proposed in an American note of the 24th. Harriman could not explain this divergence, but Molotov got an answer on 8 December, when a new British note said the British were abandoning their earlier plan to evacuate Iran by January 1946 and would stay on (*FRUS 1945*, Vol. VIII, pp. 468–69, 484–85).

103. A good survey of events is Charles B. McLane, *Soviet Strategies in Southeast Asia* (Princeton: Princeton University Press, 1966), ch. 5. On Indonesia, where a native radical Communism ran wild in the winter of 1945–1946 until some Stalinists returned from Europe, see Arnold Brackman, *Indonesian Communism* (New York: Praeger, 1963), chs. 5–7.

104. Communists acting within a people's front seized control of much of Indo-China in 1945, when the Japanese collapsed. In November of that year, in order to avoid scaring the Americans and having to relinquish power, these Communists went so far as to dissolve their separate party organization (of course, maintaining control behind the scenes within the front). When Ho Chih Minh visited Paris during that winter a certain coordination emerged between his Party line and Moscow's. But by the end of 1946, this had evaporated again. Ho's front (the Viet Minh) then became the first Communist-dominated organization to take up openly the standard of revolutionary war. See Bernard Fall, *The Two Viet-Nams* (New York: Praeger, 1963), ch. 5; Robert F. Turner, *Vietnamese Communism. Its Origins and Development* (Stanford: Hoover Institution, 1975), chs. 1–2.

105. See the authoritative accounts in Krisch, *German Politics under Soviet Occupation*, pp. 191ff., 213; Leonhard, *Die Revolution enlässt ihre Kinder*, pp. 429ff., 453ff. Both date serious talk of such a doctrine in November 1945 and associate it with the new political line of "socialist unity" which began late in November 1945 and culminated in the unification of the Communist and Social-Democratic parties in April 1946. By the spring of 1946, the new "separate road" thesis had Moscow's explicit published approval. Leonhard and several other commentators have attributed the new campaign in part to the CP's perception of a need for popularity after the Communist losses in the Austrian and Hungarian elections of November 1945. See also Melvin Croan, "Soviet Uses of the Doctrine of the 'Parliamentary Road' to Socialism: East Germany, 1945–1946," *American Slavic and East European Review*, Vol. XVII (1958), pp. 302–15. On the merger movement in Germany, see the revealing eyewitness account by Erich W. Gniffke, *Jahre mit Ulbricht*, pp. 93ff.

106. For details of the Hungarian "separate road" doctrine, see my dissertation, "Communism and Hungary, 1944–1946." The key document in its development was a lecture by Rákosi in January 1946.

107. There is description of the general phenomenon of "separate roadism" in Brzezinski, *The Soviet Bloc*, ch. 2. The postwar theoretical developments in Poland,

Czechoslovakia, France, and Italy may best be followed in the collected works of Gomułka, Gottwald, Thorez, and Togliatti. On Poland, see also Adam Bromke, *Poland's Politics* (Cambridge, Mass.: Harvard University Press, 1967), pp. 57–65. On Czech developments, see, in particular, Gordon Skilling, "People's Democracy, the Proletarian Dictatorship, and the Czechoslovak Path to Socialism," *American Slavic and East European Review*, Vol. X (1951), pp. 100–116, and his more recent study, "People's Democracy and the Socialist Revolution," *Soviet Studies*, Vol. XII (1961), pp. 241–62, 420–31. For developments in France, see Fauvet, *Histoire du Parti Communiste Français*, p. 175ff., esp. p. 182. For Italy, see Galli, *Storia del Partito Comunista Italiano* (Milan: Schwartz, 1958), p. 256ff., and the same author's contribution on the PCI in *Communism in Europe*, ed. William E. Griffith (Cambridge, Mass.: MIT Press, 1964), Vol. I, pp. 305–6.

108. The failure of the Rumanian Muscovite Communists to develop a "separate road to socialism" theory in this period may perhaps be explained in terms of inner-Party rivalries. The domestic comrade, L. Patrascanu, was rather aggressive in 1945 and 1946 in developing a "separate road" theory which might exclude Soviet influence. The late H. L. Roberts, who was present in Rumania at the time, told me that Patrascanu was not above consulting with Western observers on this subject. Perhaps, therefore, the Muscovites abstained from "separate roadism" because they feared it would give the Party into Patrascanu's hands.

109. Dimitrov, *S'chineniya*, Vol. 12, pp. 62ff.

110. *Příspěvky k Dějinám KSČS*, no. 1 (1964), p. 13. These words were quoted by K. Gottwald to the Central Committee of the Czechoslovak CP in a speech in August 1946 to justify continuation of the Party's mild, coalitional line. During the 1950s the memory of the quotation was suppressed, and it does not appear in the reproduction of Gottwald's speech in his *Spisy* (1955–57), Vol. XIII. But Gottwald said similar things in an interview with the London *Times*, printed on 18 November 1946, as did Maurice Thorez and Władisław Gomułka at about the same time. Further, Stalin told Morgan Philips, the secretary of the British Labor Party, who visited him in September 1946, that many roads to socialism were possible, and Philips revealed this to the public in an interview with the London *Daily Herald* when he got home: see the interesting article by Jaroslav Opat, "K metodě studia a výkladu některých problémů v období 1945–1948" [On the method of studying and elucidating certain problems of the 1945–1948 period], *Příspěvky k Dějinám KSČS*, no. 1 (1965), pp. 68ff.

111. Djilas, *Conversations with Stalin*, p. 113. The record of Stalin's talk with the British Laborites is in *Pravda*, 26 January 1945.

112. See the citation by M. Kruzhkov in *Bol'shevik*, nos. 15–16 (1945), p. 38. The original idea is from Lenin, *Sochinenie*, Vol. V, p. 3.

113. *Bol'shevik*, no. 22 (1945), p. 64.

114. Fedoseev, in *Bol'shevik*, no. 22 (1945), pp. 27ff. Fedoseev, it may be recalled, was the new editor of *Bol'shevik*, and came to that office in August 1945 as a spokesman for the Party revival. His contribution on the Yugoslav "people's democracy" thus represents an early example of the converging interests of Soviet *partiinost* and "Titoism" abroad.

115. Djilas, *Conversations with Stalin*, p. 113. Djilas claims that Stalin never put in writing his idea that socialism could now be achieved under an English king, but the "correction" mentioned here came pretty close to it.

116. *FRUS 1945*, Vol. V, pp. 881–84.

117. The reports from the Moscow Embassy strongly fostered the "prisoner" image of Stalin at this time: see *FRUS 1945*, Vol. V, pp. 754, 763, 891ff.; and Harriman, *Special Envoy*, pp. 516–17, 521–22. For the impact of these reports, see the Truman-Stettinius conversation of 22 October 1945, documented in the Stettinius calendar notes, Box 247 Stettinius Papers, University of Virginia Library. (I am indebted to

T. Hammond for calling my attention to this document, which is quoted in Gaddis, *The United States and the Origins of the Cold War*, p. 275.)

118. One may note in this connection Stalin's frank indication to certain Americans at Potsdam that he simply could not allow free elections in Eastern Europe if he was to preserve the Soviet state's interest in having "friendly" neighbors there. This was false: Stalin already had allowed entirely free elections in Finland, and subsequently allowed them in Austria, Hungary, and Czechoslovakia. The point, however, is that Stalin was "honest" and "approachable": Philip Mosely, who reported the incident, was impressed in exactly the way intended ("Across the Green Table from Stalin," pp. 129ff., 130–31).

119. *FRUS 1945*, Vol. V, pp. 929–30; H. Salisbury, *Russia on the Way*, pp. 386–88.

120. *Bol'shevik*, no. 17–18 (1946), p. 18.

121. *Soch.*, Vol. XVI, p. 83.

122. Eisenstein's film received preliminary approval in 1940–1941. It was filmed with considerable publicity during the war, so that there can be no question of Stalin's ignorance of it. Part I, the climax of which is Ivan's retreat from Moscow to Aleksandrovskaya Sloboda in 1564, was shown in January 1945 and was awarded a Stalin prize on 26 January 1946. Part II went into production in February 1945, after the script had received Central Committee approval. It was ready for showing by the middle of 1946. Eisenstein here made Ivan far less heroic and far more neurotic a figure. Consequently, on 4 September 1946, the Central Committee sharply criticized the weakness attributed to Ivan and the wickedness attributed to the *oprichniky* in the film, and it had to be redone. See Marie Seton, *S. M. Eisenstein* (New York: A. A. Wyn, 1953), ch. 15.

Notes to Chapter 10

1. *Soch.*, Vol. XVI, p. 2.

2. For representative comment, see *FRUS 1946*, Vol. VI, p. 695; Feis, *From Trust to Terror*, pp. 63, 71–75.

3. *FRUS 1945*, Vols. II, pp. 576ff., VI, pp. 789ff.

4. For the American record, see *FRUS 1945*, Vol. II, pp. 800ff.

5. The atmosphere of the early winter is captured remarkably well in Fleming, *The Cold War*, Vol. I, pp. 338ff.

6. *Soch.*, Vol. XVI, p. 42.

7. Interview with Eddie Gilmore, *ibid.*, pp. 45–46.

8. *FRUS 1945*, Vol. VI, p. 792.

9. Gaddis, *The United States and the Origins of the Cold War*, pp. 273–74.

10. At this time the Americans were debating whether to withdraw the Marines, thus abandoning Chiang Kai-shek, or to increase their military commitment to Chungking and thus get involved in a civil war and a confrontation with the Russians. There is some evidence that this debate contributed to Byrnes' decision to hold a new conference of the Allied foreign ministers. On 23 November, some hours before he sent his cable to Molotov requesting a new meeting of the Foreign Ministers Council, he received an urgent cable from the United States Embassy in Chungking: Chiang Kai-shek was writing to President Truman personally, asking him to intervene in some fashion to end Soviet collusion with the Communists in northern China. Top-level discussions in the American government during the following weeks resulted in the Great Power-backed mediation effort by General Marshall. See *FRUS 1945*, Vol. II, p. 578, Vol. VII, pp. 663ff., 666, 685; and Paul E. Varg, *The Closing of the Door* (East Lansing: Michigan State University Press, 1973), pp. 219–27.

11. Kennan, *Memoirs, 1925–1950*, pp. 301–3. Harriman's opinion was similar: see *Special Envoy*, pp. 523ff.

12. Byrnes, *Speaking Frankly*, p. 109.

13. The financial talks were completed on 6 December 1945, and the resulting agreement was pushed through a reluctant Parliament a week later: see D. C. Watt, "American Aid to Britain and the Problem of Socialism," *American Review*, Vol. II (1963), pp. 46–67; Richard Gardner, *Sterling-Dollar Diplomacy* (Oxford: Oxford University Press, 1956), ch. 10; and Paterson, *Soviet-American Confrontation*, ch. 8. For the British response to Byrnes' unilateral overture to Moscow, see Ambassador Winant's panic-stricken cable to Byrnes from London on 26 November (*FRUS 1945*, Vol. II, pp. 501ff.).

14. Hugh Dalton, *Memoirs, 1945–1960*, Vol. III, ch. 8.

15. Byrnes, *Speaking Frankly*, pp. 111–12.

16. *Ibid.*, p. 114.

17. *Ibid.*, pp. 116–17.

18. *Ibid.*, pp. 120–21. Byrnes doctors the evidence at this point. According to the American minutes of the 26 December meeting, Byrnes suggested dropping the Iranian discussion *before* Bevin's plaintive question, and Molotov's response was not only a triumphant acknowledgment of Soviet success in obtaining American collusion but was also the closing word of the conference. Byrnes' reversal of the order of events minimizes the significance of what he did (*FRUS 1945*, Vol. II, pp. 805, 813–14).

19. Some representative British responses are quoted in Feis, *From Trust to Terror*, p. 54, and in Wheeler-Bennett, *Semblance of Peace*, pp. 424–30.

20. "The Anglo-American Financial Agreement," *New Times*, no. 1 (1946), pp. 5–10. There is a comparable essay in *Propagandist*, no. 1 (1946) pp. 48ff. For Kennan's confirmation of the importance of the Varga article as a sign of Soviet thinking, see *FRUS 1946*, Vol. VI, p. 684. In Stalin's last talk with Harriman on 23 January 1946 and in his first talk with the new American ambassador to Moscow, Walter Bedell Smith, on 4 April the British loan formed the background for discussion of an American credit to the Soviet Union, such as had been proposed by Molotov in January 1945. Harriman has the impression that Stalin was then still willing in principle to accept American money, which seems probable if, as I believe, he was, at all costs, following a "participationist" foreign policy (not, as Harriman calls it, "isolationism") (*Special Envoy*, p. 533). That Stalin was "jealous" of the British, as Paterson (*Soviet-American Confrontation*, p. 172) speculates, seems improbable.

21. Byrnes, *Speaking Frankly*, p. 121.

22. *Soch.*, Vol. XVI, pp. 19–20.

23. Voznesensky's Five Year Plan speech was published in *Bol'shevik*, no. 6 (1946).

24. See the comment of Alec Nove in *An Economic History of the USSR*, p. 290. Actually, all this should not have come as such a surprise. At least as early as 1944 Stalin was telling outsiders—for example, the American Eric Johnston—of his plans for a fifteen-year industrial push and his hope for an annual production of 60 million tons of steel (*FRUS 1945*, Vol. V, pp. 994–95).

25. Kolkowicz, *The Soviet Military*, pp. 224ff., esp. p. 237; Chaney, *Zhukov*, pp. 306ff.; Bialer, *Stalin and His Generals*, pp. 493–94.

26. See the election speeches of Bulganin and Vasilevskii in *Pravda*, 4 and 6 February 1946; the editorial by Major General Isaev in *Krasnaya Zvezda*, 31 January; and Isaev's speech and Vasilevskii's editorial in the press for 22 February.

27. *Soch.*, Vol. XVI, p. 10.

28. *Soch.*, Vol. XVI, pp. 24–27.

29. Meissner, *Russland im Umbruch*, pp. 42ff. Petrov (*Stroitel'stvo politorganov*, pp. 391ff.) describes the reform as the result of a Politburo decision and gives an account of the politicization of the Stavka at this time.

30. Petrov, *Stroitel'stvo politorganov*, p. 392. Shikin's fairly extensive publicist activities in these years focused entirely on the virtues of "education"—i.e., the repetition of Marxist-Leninist slogans. On these developments, see Boris Nicolaevsky,

"Opala Marshala Zhukova" [The fall of Marshal Zhukov], *Sotsialisticheskii Vestnik*, nos. 7–8 (1946), pp. 168–71.

31. Beria was replaced in the NKVD by S. N. Kruglov on 14 January 1946. His deputy, V. N. Merkulov, was replaced in the MGB by V. S. Abakumov on 18 October 1946.

32. Every member of the Orgburo of March 1946 except Suslov can be identified with an office which at some time had earlier been represented in the Orgburo. All the major Party administrative interests were represented in this Orgburo except the "Special Section" of the Central Committee apparatus, which supervised the police. It follows that Suslov probably represented the "Special Section." Khrushchev, in his secret speech to the 20th Congress of the CPSU, confirms that after the war the Party did supervise the police (*Crimes of the Stalin Era*, p. S45); as explained in Chapter 12, the supervisor Khrushchev mentions, A. A. Kuznetsov, probably replaced Suslov in this function in September 1947.

33. For Poskrebyshev, see Nicolaevsky, *Power and the Soviet Elite*, pp. 109ff.

34. See the daily press and Nicolaevsky's articles in *Sotsialisticheskii Vestnik*, Vol. XXVI (1946), pp. 87–89, 143–46.

35. See Chapter 4 above.

36. For details see Chapter 11.

37. *Bol'shevik*, no. 6 (1946), p. 71.

38. *Pravda*, 8 February 1946, p. 2.

39. See Kennan's remarks on this subject in *FRUS 1946*, Vol. VI, pp. 719–20.

40. The colorlessness of Popov may account for one of the more puzzling aspects of postwar Soviet politics, namely, the extraordinary prominence which Leningrad not only sought but achieved in the leading Party publications from 1945 to 1948. It may be added that when Popov fell in 1949, he was given a minor economic ministry, which he held until 1951, and did not share in the tribulations of the Leningraders. Furthermore, he was succeeded by Khrushchev, a man of political strength comparable to that of his predecessor, Shcherbakov.

41. Zhdanov became chairman of the Soviet of the Union in March 1946 and kept the office for just one year. This hardly seems to count, however, in the power context we are discussing.

42. Petrov, *Stroitel'stvo politorganov*, p. 389.

43. See Harris, "On the Origins of the Conflict between Malenkov and Zhdanov, 1939–1941," pp. 287–303.

44. The introduction is dated January 1946 and appeared in *Soch.*, Vol. I, pp. xi–xx, which was in print in June 1946.

45. *Soch.*, Vol. I, pp. xix–xx.

46. For the record of these publications, see McNeal, *Stalin's Works*, introductions to pts. 1 and 2.

47. The reply to Razin was first published in *Bol'shevik*, no. 3 (1947), pp. 6–8. There is no way to establish that Stalin really wrote it in February 1946.

48. *Soch.*, Vol. XVI, p. 30.

49. *Soch.*, Vol. XVI, pp. 31–32.

50. This phrase is from Malenkov's election speech, published in *Pravda*, 8 February 1946, p. 2.

51. This is from Aleksandrov's speech on the anniversary of Lenin's death, reported in *Bol'shevik*, no. 1 (1946), pp. 1–2.

52. See Gary R. Hess, "The Iranian Crisis of 1945–1946 and the Cold War," *Political Science Quarterly*, Vol. LXXXIX (1974), pp. 117–46; Peter Avery, *Modern Iran* (New York: Praeger, 1965), ch. 24; and George Lenczowski, *Russia and the West in Iran* (Ithaca, N.Y.: Cornell University Press, 1949), chs. 8 and 11.

53. Byrnes, *Speaking Frankly*, p. 119.

54. The United States Embassy report on this matter makes it clear that Stalin waited until he was sure what the effect of the "iron curtain" speech on world opinion would be before responding to Churchill (*FRUS 1946*, Vol. VI, pp. 712–13, 716–17)— this despite the "insider" reports that leaked out about his pain and agitation when he first heard of the speech (see Lord Gladwyn Jebb, *Memoirs of Lord Gladwyn*, p. 185). Perhaps the clearest evidence that Stalin was playacting in March 1946 is the contrast between his heated response to the remarks of Churchill, who held no public office, and his entirely passive response just a year later to President Truman's messianic appeal in the United States Congress for aid to Greece and Turkey.

55. *Soch.*, Vol. XVI, p. 46.

56. See the analysis of Zhdanov's speeches in Chapter 7 above.

57. The thesis that imperialists, reactionaries, and atomic bombs are "paper tigers" is generally attributed to Mao Tse-tung (interview with Anna Louise Strong, August 1946, *Selected Works*, Vol. IV, p. 100). As we have observed, however, the phrase, felicitous though it may be, reflects attitudes which lay at the root of the Soviet Party revival in 1944 and 1945. Mao's "genius" lay in the capsulization of the idea, not in its invention.

Notes to Chapter 11

1. *Soch.*, Vol. XVI, pp. 45–46.

2. *Soch.*, Vol. XVI, pp. 53–56.

3. *Soch.*, Vol. XVI, pp. 65ff. The interview actually took place on 21 December 1947.

4. *Ibid.*, p. 68. Stalin used the term *narod*, which implies rather more than just "people" and which he had used during the war in the sense of "country." He went on to say that there had been a worsening in the relations between "governments," but that this had resulted from "misunderstandings" and caused him no concern.

5. See Daniel Yergin, *Shattered Peace. The Origins of the Cold War and the National Security State* (Boston: Houghton Mifflin, 1977), pp. 264–72, chs. 11–13. Yergin's work, which appeared too late for use in the present study, contains an often illuminating, picturesque, and extensively documented narrative of American foreign policy in the sociological context of the emerging military-industrial clique. It is far more balanced than the revisionist literature of the late 1960s and is broader than the studies by John Gaddis (*The United States and the Origins of the Cold War*) and Lynn Davis (*The Cold War Begins*). Yergin makes no effort to investigate Soviet and Communist sources, nor does he cite materials not in the English language (as Gaddis and Davis both do), and consequently he makes significant errors of judgment.

6. See George Kousoulas, "The Truman Doctrine and the Stalin-Tito Rift," *South Atlantic Quarterly*, Vol. LXXII (1973), p. 428. When a leading Greek Communist visited Moscow in January 1946, Molotov and Zhdanov told him that the Soviet government was committed to the existing Greek government, and that his party should form a broad democratic front. The Greek CP had already decided to boycott the 31 March election, however, and, after soul-searching debate, ignored this information about Soviet policy, treating it as a suggestion, not a directive.

7. See Samuel Sharp, *Poland: White Eagle on Red Field* (Cambridge, Mass.: Harvard University Press, 1953), pp. 306ff. Khrushchev (*Memoirs*, Vol. II, pp. 172ff.) expresses the Soviet view of the election in unvarnished terms. For the traditional Western understanding, see Mikołajczyk, *The Rape of Poland*, ch. 14; and Arthur Bliss Lane, *I Saw Poland Betrayed*, ch. 19.

8. *Soch.*, Vol. XVI, pp. 76–78.

9. See the reply to Wallace, 17 May 1948, and the reply to a *Pravda* correspondent on 28 October 1948 (*Soch.*, Vol. XVI, pp. 102–6). Stalin's other two public statements of 1948 described a friendship treaty with Finland as "proof" of the possibility of cooperation between states with different systems.

10. *Soch.*, Vol. XVI, p. 106. For appraisal, see the comments by the Moscow Embassy in *FRUS 1946*, Vol. VI, p. 783, and *FRUS 1948*, Vol. IV, p. 824.

11. Nove, *Economic History*, pp. 293ff.; E. Yu. Lokshin, *Pomyshlennost' SSSR* [Industry of the USSR] (Moscow: Izdat. Sots.-Ekon. Lit., 1964), pp. 147ff.

12. Quoted in *Pravda*, 21 January 1961: "In 1946 the drought didn't smash us: it finished off the economy which had been smashed by the war." For an economist's view of the agricultural crisis of 1946–1947, see Jasny, *Soviet Industrialization*, chs. 13–14.

13. Yu. V. Arutyunyan, *Sovetskoe krest'yanstvo v gody Velikoi Otechestvennoi Voiny* [The Soviet peasantry during the Great Patriotic War], 2d rev. ed. (Moscow: Nauka, 1970), p. 323. The original edition of this important book is significantly different from the revised edition (Moscow: Akad. Nauk, 1963).

14. Nove, *Economic History*, p. 296. For insights into village life at the end of the war, see the short novel by F. Abramov in *Novyi Mir*, nos. 1–3 (1968).

15. For the production estimates of the time, see the Central Committee resolution of February 1947 in *KPSS v Rezolyutsiyakh*, Vol. VI, p. 211. Statistics were not published until much later in USSR, Central Statistical Administration, *Narodnoe khozyaistvo SSSR. Statisticheskii spravochnik 1965*, p. 311.

16. Details are scattered throughout the memoir of the leader of the UNRRA mission in the Ukraine, Marshall MacDuffie, *The Red Carpet*, esp. ch. 12.

17. *New Times*, no. 20 (1946), pp. 3ff.

18. See Khrushchev's remarks in *Pravda*, 10 December 1963.

19. *Resheniya Partii i Pravitel'stva po Khozyaistvennym Voprosam*, Vol. III, pp. 336–41.

20. For the full text see the Soviet press for 9 and 21 October 1946.

21. Earlier in 1946 the Ministry for Agriculture was split into separate ministries for food products, industrial crops, and livestock (Nove, *Economic History*, pp. 296–97).

22. The members were P. I. Doronin (Kursk), G. B. Pal'tsev (Vladimir), U. Yu. Yusupov (Uzbekistan), Khrushchev, I. A. Benediktov (minister of Food Products), Patolichev and Andrianov (Central Committee secretaries), and G. V. Perov, I. S. Yegorov, and T. I. Sokolov (minor agricultural officials). Perov was secretary of the council.

23. Patolichev was from Chelyabinsk and would be sent to help Kaganovich purge the Ukraine in February 1947. Andrianov was from Sverdlovsk and would figure in Leningrad after 1949 as Zhdanov's successor and purger of his men. These two can be said to have "characterized" the new council because they and Andreev were its original members, announced on 8 October. The other members were announced on 21 October.

24. See, for example, Fainsod, *How Russia Is Ruled*, pp. 453–54; Ploss, *Conflict and Decision Making*, p. 30.

25. Arutyunyan, *Sovetskoe krest'yanstvo*, 1970 ed., p. 9.

26. See the disquisition on the new decree by Professor I. D. Laptev, a well-known Zhdanovite, in *Kul'tura i Zhizn'*, 24 October 1946. One may note that Laptev did not predict an immediate upsurge of enthusiasm: he admitted that the process of developing it would be long and difficult. But the basic notion of his article was that by reestablishing "correct" socialist institutional frameworks the regime could eventually persuade the peasantry to see the light. On the importance of such an argument for Soviet middle-level bureaucrats, see Joravsky's illuminating remarks in *The Lysenko Affair*, p. 305.

27. Arutyunyan, *Sovetskoe krest'yanstvo*, 1963 ed., pp. 4–8.

28. See Andreev's report to the Central Committee plenum in February 1947 (*PZh*, no. 4 [1947], pp. 50–76); *Pravda*, 18 September 1947, p. 1; and the accumulated evidence cited in L. Volin, *A Survey of Soviet Agriculture*, Agricultural Monograph no. 5 (Washington, D.C.: U.S. Government Printing Office, n.d.), p. 32.

29. This statement was made by Doronin at the September 1953 Central Committee plenum, according to Khrushchev's account at the plenum of December 1958.

30. *Pravda*, 4 February 1947; Nove, *Economic History*, p. 297.

31. The major Khrushchevian revelations about this plenum are in Khrushchev, *Stroitel'stvo kommunizma v SSSR i razvitie sel'skogo khozyaistva*, Vol. I, pp. 137–39, Vol. II, p. 107, Vol. VI, pp. 57–58, 177–80.

32. The development of the *kolkhoz* market actually dated from a decision of 9 November 1946: see *Pravda*, 11 November 1946, p. 1; John T. Whitman, "The Kolkhoz Market," *Soviet Studies*, Vol. VII, pp. 384–98.

33. See Jasny, *Soviet Industrialization*, ch. 13; Ploss, *Conflict and Decision Making*, ch. 1.

34. Zhores Medvedev, *The Rise and Fall of T. D. Lysenko* (Garden City, N.Y.: Doubleday, 1971), pp. 105–6; Joravsky, *The Lysenko Affair*, pp. 132–33.

35. Joravsky, *The Lysenko Affair*, pp. 239–44; Loren Graham, *Science and Philosophy in the Soviet Union* (New York: Knopf, 1972), app. 1, pp. 443–50.

36. Khrushchev has told his own story (*Memoirs*, Vol. I, pp. 234ff.). The assignment of Malenkov to agricultural responsibilities is recorded (briefly and enigmatically) in a speech in *Pravda*, 23 November 1947, p. 2.

37. *Soch.*, Vol. XVI, pp. 29ff.

38. Arutyunyan, *Sovetskoe krest'yanstvo*, 1970 ed., pp. 321–22. This figure is a low estimate. The entire non-urban population was rather larger than 66 million.

39. *Ibid.*, pp. 360–61.

40. Alec Nove, "Rural Taxation in the USSR," *Soviet Studies*, Vol. V (1953), pp. 159–66.

41. See Conquest, *Power and Policy*, pp. 126–27, and, more generally, Ploss, *Conflict and Decision Making*, chs. 1–2.

42. For background, see Moshe Lewin, *Russian Peasants and Soviet Power* (London: Allen and Unwin, 1968).

43. The advantages and difficulties of the "necessity" argument are explored by T. Von Laue in his essay "Problems of Modernization" (in Lederer, ed., *Russian Foreign Policy*, pp. 69–108), and in his *Why Lenin, Why Stalin?* (Philadelphia: Lippincott, 1964).

44. Ehrenburg, *The War*, pp. 132–33.

45. *Ibid.*, p. 74.

46. For the following, see Werth, *Russia at War*, passim; his *Russia. The Postwar Years*, passim; the sensitive essay on Zoshchenko by R. Demar, in Simmons, ed., *Through the Looking Glass of Soviet Literature;* Swayzee, *Political Control of Literature*, ch. 2; Sheila Fitzpatrick, "Culture and Politics under Stalin," *Slavic Review*, Vol. XXXV (1976), pp. 211–31; and the dated collection of texts in George S. Counts and Nina Lodge, eds., *The Country of the Blind. The Soviet System of Mind Control* (Boston: Houghton Mifflin, 1949).

47. N. Mandelstamm, *Hope Abandoned*, p. 375, gives the lie to other versions of this episode.

48. See the critique of the novel in *Kul'tura i Zhizn'*, December 1947, and in Klaus Mehnert, "An Moskau's literarischer Front," *Osteuropa*, Vol. IV (1954), p. 345. Fadeev had to rewrite the book, excising those parts which emphasized the ingenuity, enthusiasm, and local initiative of Party members and introducing a motif of planning and direction by the Party center.

49. For the Zhdanovshchina, see Armstrong, *Politics of Totalitarianism*, ch. 13; Swayzee, *Political Control of Literature*, passim; and Werth, *The Postwar Years*, ch. 11. The first issue of *Kul'tura i Zhizn'* was announced in *Pravda*, on 30 June 1946, p. 2.

50. Petrov, *Stroitel'stvo politorganov*, pp. 393–95.

51. *KPSS v Rezolyutsiyakh*, Vol. VI, pp. 154–61.

52. *Ibid.*, pp. 162–72.

53. *Bol'shevik*, nos. 17–18 (1946), pp. 18–19.

54. *Ibid.*, p. 18.

55. For the Central Committee resolution, see *Bol'shevik*, no. 15 (1946), pp. 11–13. The exact course of events is not clear from the available sources and is often confused in secondary accounts. Zhdanov seems to have made two speeches attacking the Leningrad literati, one at a Leningrad Party activists' meeting and the other at the Leningrad Writers' Union. The former was probably the basis for the Central Committee resolution of 14 August. On 21 August the speeches were mentioned in *Pravda* as "recent." They were published in various forms but are most widely known through a "combined" text published in *Pravda* and other journals on 21 September and later in *Bol'shevik*, nos. 17–18 (1946), pp. 4–19.

56. Djilas, *Conversations with Stalin*, p. 150. For some eyewitness impressions, see Werth, *The Postwar Years*, pp. 208–9; Mandelstamm, *Hope Abandoned*, ch. 31, pt. 5.

57. *Bol'shevik*, no. 16 (1946), pp. 45–53.

58. Both V. Rudolph's account and those of the Western authorities who have studied the matter—Nicolaevsky, Meissner, Gradoboev, Armstrong, and Conquest—agree that Malenkov's power declined in this period but are unclear about details. One useful index may be the rise of Malenkov's successor in the secretariat, N. S. Patolichev. The latter's first major appearance in the Soviet top leadership was at Kalinin's funeral: see *Pravda*, 6 June 1946, pp. 1, 3, and the major celebrations recorded in that journal all summer. At official functions recorded in *Pravda* on 19 August and 9 September, Malenkov's name was no longer ranked so high as it had been earlier. On 8 October *Pravda* recorded Patolichev's appointment to the new Collective Farm Council. On 18 and 19 October the Supreme Soviet endorsed Malenkov's appointment to the government as deputy prime minister. On 2 November *Pravda* mentioned that Patolichev was a Central Committee secretary.

59. *Partiinaya Stroitel'stvo, Propagandist,* and certain other inner Party journals ceased publication on 1 August 1946 to make way for a new central journal, *Partiinaya Zhizn';* the latter did not start publication until late in November. See *Kul'tura i Zhizn'*, no. 6 (1946), p. 1, for details. There is some internal evidence that *PZh* was from the start intended to be the house organ not of Zhdanov's Agit-Prop people but of the Cadre and Checking Party Organs Administrations, where he had less influence; after less than a year of publication, its editorial control was placed in the hands of Malenkov's aide in the Cadre Administration, N. Shatalin: see *PZh*, no. 10 (1947), p. 72.

60. Both in these speeches on literature and in his election speech of February 1946, Zhdanov was effusive in his praise of Leningrad, of her "revolutionary" traditions, and of her special *partiinyi* mission. These speeches rank, indeed, among the most fulsome statements of Leningrad Party patriotism in the entire period of the Party revival. Under such circumstances there seems no reason to consider Zhdanov's attacks on his city's intelligentsia as anything but self-critical.

61. In August two of the most prominent secretaries of the Leningrad Party organization, N. V. Solovev and I. N. Turko, were transferred to the Crimea (which had just then been "given" by the RSFSR to the Ukrainian Republic) and to the not particularly important Yaroslavl *oblast*. See *Pravda*, 15 August 1946, p. 1, and 28 August, p. 1. For comment on the highly unusual fashion in which these transfers were announced, see Armstrong, *Politics of Totalitarianism*, p. 394.

62. *Crimes of the Stalin Era*, p. S62.

63. The session had originally been scheduled for September. See *Pravda*, 6 September 1946, p. 1.

64. The Supreme Soviet pointedly relieved Malenkov of membership in its presidium, then appointed him a deputy chairman in the Council of Ministers, a title he lost in

March 1946. During the war Malenkov's power derived from holding both key government and key Party posts. I calculate that in March he was ousted from the government and in October was given a government sinecure in exchange for relinquishing his Party offices.

65. See the announcement of the opening of the Party Academy of Social Sciences in *Pravda,* 2 November 1946, p. 2.

66. V. S. Abakumov was made head of the MGB on 18 October. Very little is known about him. He became notorious after 1949 as a principal prosecutor of the Leningrad case and was tried and shot in 1954 for falsification of the evidence used there. Clearly, he was in an overall sense no "enemy" of Beria. In 1946, however, he was far less clearly associated with Beria than his predecessor, Merkulov, and he was dropped from the MGB considerably before the fall of Beria (probably in 1951). My guess is that he was installed in office in 1946 by the Zhdanovites to counter Beria and then led the purge against them in 1949 in order to save his own neck. This interpretation would be consistent with the portrait of him in Solzhenitsyn, *The First Circle,* ch. 20. For the available evidence, see Conquest, *Power and Policy,* pp. 87, 100–101, 187, 448–49; Nicolaevsky, *Power and the Soviet Elite,* pp. 158–74; and Hingley, *The Russian Secret Police,* ch. 11.

67. On 4 November 1946 the press announced the discontinuation of the Ukrainian Party journals *Propagandist i Agitator* and *Partrabotnik Ukrainy.* In their place, the prewar journal *Bol'shevik Ukrainy* was to resume publication, on the model of the Moscow *Bol'shevik,* and a Ukrainian version of *Partiinaya Zhizn'* was launched.

68. See the review of events in Yurchuk, "Vostanovlenie i ukreplenie partiinykh organizatsii na Ukraine," pp. 83–87; Sullivant, *Soviet Politics and the Ukraine,* pp. 255–67; Bilinsky, *Second Soviet Republic,* pp. 234–35; and Conquest, *Power and Policy,* pp. 87, 97–101, which cites Zhdanov's initiative.

69. It may be noted that the February 1947 Central Committee plenum made Voznesensky a full member of the Politburo, thus in an obscure sense repairing the injustice the Party revivalists did to the full members of the Politburo in September 1946, when they "let" Stalin appoint Voznesensky, a candidate member, to the "septet."

70. Ehrenburg, *The Postwar Years,* pp. 46–47.

71. *FRUS 1946,* Vol. VI, pp. 768ff.

72. Byrnes, *Speaking Frankly,* p. 154.

73. A major de-Stalinizing account of postwar Soviet foreign policy mentions the Turkish affair of August 1946 as a mistake made by Molotov personally. The charge is all the more remarkable since this is the only reference to Molotov in the entire two-volume study: see Mileikovskii, *Mezhdunarodnye otnosheniya posle vtoroi mirovoi voiny,* Vol. I, pp. 254–55.

74. A long and detailed anti-Communist account of the crisis is in Xydis, *Greece and the Great Powers,* pp. 296–359, 626ff. More balanced is Jonathan Knight's "American Statecraft and the 1946 Black Sea Straits Controversy," *Political Science Quarterly,* Vol. XXX (1975), pp. 451–75.

75. Molotov returned to Paris on 5 September and immediately requested postponement of the imminent UNO session. *Pravda* announced the postponement of the Supreme Soviet session on 6 September.

76. One of the oddest incidents of the period suggests both the background of this "hesitation" and the extreme intensity of the conflicts within the Soviet leadership over foreign policy. In the first week of June 1946, an American reporter, Richard Hottelot, arrived in Moscow and telephoned Deputy Foreign Minister Maksim Litvinov requesting an interview. Litvinov consented. Despite the fact that Hottelot was in close contact with the American Embassy, the interview took place in Litvinov's (presumably "bugged") office on 18 June. Three days earlier, on 15 June, Molotov had resumed a position of stubborn virtue at the Foreign Ministers' Conference in Paris, insisting that

the West could and should make concessions. Yet now Litvinov informed Hottelot in no uncertain terms that the "wrong people" were in charge of Soviet policy, that Soviet secret intentions were of the worst, and that any concessions made by the West would result in further Soviet demands. Hottelot immediately reported this to the Embassy, which passed on the information to Secretary of State Byrnes, who then stood firm against Molotov. Litvinov, as is known, was frequently indiscreet in these years, secure (according to a CIA report) in the knowledge that a manuscript of his memoirs was secreted in the West and would be published if anything happened to him. Nonetheless, I find the Hottelot interview wholly mystifying unless it is assumed that Litvinov was acting with the sanction of someone higher up (for example, Stalin, Malenkov, or Beria) who wanted to see Molotov in trouble. See Hottelot's report on the interview in the *Washington Post* for 21 January 1952, pp. 1, 4, and subsequent issues; and Vojtěch Mástný's study of Litvinov in "The Cassandra in the Foreign Commissariat." It should be noted that Molotov also at this time went outside accepted channels to make his views known to people in the West. Earl Browder, the deposed head of the American Communist Party, was in Moscow in May and June 1946. He had made his name during the war as an advocate of Soviet-American cooperation as a road to socialism. Since his fall in June 1945, the CPUSA had become dogmatically militant and "blocist." It is of interest, therefore, that Molotov, who, as an anti-blocist, was committed to Party methods, went out of his way to receive Browder and talked with him at great length about the opportunities for Soviet-American friendship. Browder was not so effective a communications link with America as Hottelot, but he too passed on Molotov's remarks when he got home (Starobin, *American Communism in Crisis,* p. 278).

77. On the Wallace affair, see two recent careful studies: Richard J. Walton, *Henry Wallace, Harry Truman and the Cold War* (New York: Viking, 1976), pp. 99ff., and J. Samuel Walker, *Henry A. Wallace and American Foreign Policy* (Westport, Conn.: Greenwood Press, 1976), ch. 11.

78. See the commentary in *FRUS 1946,* Vol. VI, pp. 782–84.

79. *Soch.,* Vol. XVI, pp. 53–56.

80. Rieber, *Stalin and the French Communist Party,* p. 266; Feis, *From Trust to Terror,* p. 166; *FRUS 1946,* Vol. VI, pp. 786ff.

81. See *Pravda,* 7 November 1946, pp. 2–3.

82. On 10 February 1947, Under Secretary of State Dean Acheson in a congressional hearing labeled Soviet policy "aggressive." This was the first time an American official had said this in public. It led to immediate—and vain—Soviet diplomatic protests (*FRUS 1947,* Vol. IV, p. 431).

83. "The issue which vexed the Soviet leadership toward the end of World War II was not the desirability of an empire—that was taken for granted . . . but rather the ways and means of its possible integration into an international order compatible with the Western notions" (Mástný, "The Cassandra in the Foreign Commissariat," p. 375).

84. Stalin's line during and even after the "thaw" was marked by extraordinary resentment of "blocism" in the West. See, for example, his remarks to Montgomery on 10 January (Viscount Montgomery, *Memoirs,* pp. 399–408); his correspondence with Bevin about the revision of the Anglo-Soviet treaty in February (which started with a *Pravda* attack on Bevin for abandoning the wartime alliance system); and his talk with Bevin on 24 March (*FRUS 1947,* Vol. II, pp. 278–84).

Notes to Chapter 12

Bibliographical Note

The official record of the meeting was published in the first three issues of *For a Lasting Peace, For a People's Democracy* late in 1947 and in *Informatsionnoe sovesh-*

chanie predstavitelei nekotorykh kompartii v Polshe v kontse sentyabrya 1947 g. An indispensable eyewitness account, together with notes on the proceedings, is Eugenio Reale, *Avec Jacques Duclos au banc des accusés* (but see the caveat in Bocca, *Togliatti,* pp. 447ff.). Yugoslav eyewitness material is in Dedijer, *Tito. Prilozi,* pp. 412ff.; brief references by some Polish witnesses may be found in *Nowe Drogi,* nos. 9–10 (1948), p. 138 (Gomułka) and no. 10 (1956), p. 90 (Berman). A summary of parts of the official Hungarian report on the meeting is in Agnes Ságvári, *Népfront és koalíció Magyarországon 1936–1948* [Popular front and coalition in Hungary] (Budapest: Kossuth könyvkiadó, 1967), pp. 276–82. Jacques Duclos gives a short and unrevealing account in his *Mémoires,* Vol. IV, pp. 217–220. The standard secondary study of the meeting is Adam Ulam, *Titoism and the Cominform* (Cambridge, Mass.: Harvard University Press, 1952). For background see the older narratives in H. F. Armstrong, *Tito and Goliath* (New York: Macmillan, 1951), and Peter Calvocoressi, *Survey of International Affairs, 1947–1948* (London: Oxford University Press, 1952), pp. 52ff. The very interesting study by Lilly Marcou, *Le Kominform* (Paris: Presses de la Fondation Nationale des Sciences Politiques, 1977), appeared too late for integration here.

1. Some of the material in this chapter has been published, in different form, in my article, "Domestic Politics and Soviet Foreign Policy at the Cominform Conference in 1947," *Slavic and Soviet Series* (Russian and East European Research Center, Tel Aviv University), Vol. II, no. 1 (1977), pp. 1–30.

2. Robert Lovett, *Department of State Bulletin,* 19 October 1947, p. 769. The first *Pravda* editorial appeared on 10 October. Cf. the latter-day definitions by W. S. Sworakowski in his *World Communism. A Handbook, 1918–1965* (Stanford: Hoover Institution, 1973), p. 77.

3. *Soch.,* Vol. XVI, p. 80.

4. The extraordinarily complex Allied postwar negotiations about Germany have been analyzed tangentially, but very carefully, by John Gimbel, first in *The American Occupation of Germany. Politics and the Military, 1945–1949* (Stanford: Stanford University Press, 1968), and recently in his *Origins of the Marshall Plan.* He finds that the main reason for the breakdown of the negotiations was not the unilateral Soviet behavior in the first months of the peace (population and frontier shifting and industrial dismantlements) nor Soviet obstruction, but a diplomatic impasse created by the French. In 1945 and 1946 the Russians, the British, and the Americans were all willing to set up central economic institutions for a united Germany, as had been agreed at Potsdam, but they were blocked by the French, who were not bound by the Potsdam agreements but who had a veto in Germany and refused to take any step toward the restoration of a German government until a possible French acquisition of the Saar, the Rhineland, and the Ruhr had been settled one way or the other. Such a settlement could not be made because of Soviet insistence that the Potsdam agreements be made operative prior to peace treaty negotiations. In the ensuing paralysis of the occupation regime, other issues arose, and by the Moscow peace treaty conference of March-April 1947, the original rights and wrongs of the situation were obscured. There are other versions of what happened; for example, Bruce Kuklick argues that the Americans had been conspiring ever since the spring of 1945 to deny the Russians reparations and to rescue Germany from socialization (*American Policy and the Division of Germany. The Clash with the Russians over Reparations* [Ithaca, N.Y.: Cornell University Press, 1972]). Gimbel (*Origins of the Marshall Plan,* p. 55) mocks this argument. Traditional Western historians have accepted General Marshall's charges that it was Soviet obstructionism at the Moscow conference and Soviet aid to the Communists in eastern Germany that finally split the country (see, for example, Feis, *From Trust to Terror,* ch. 27). Gimbel indicates (*Origins of the Marshall Plan,* pp. 138–40) that these charges are not entirely correct. It is clear from the American records of the Moscow confer-

ence, however, that Molotov, for whatever reason, was very irritating (*FRUS 1947,* Vol. II). For Stalin's interview with Marshall, see *FRUS 1947,* Vol. II, pp. 337ff.

5. Molotov told some Yugoslav Communists at Paris that Stalin was planning to reject the plan eventually but that meanwhile, for propaganda reasons, he might arrange to have all the East European countries accept it so that they could walk out later, with dramatic effect. In retrospect, this sounds more like a bizarre excuse than an explanation. See Djilas, *Conversations with Stalin,* p. 128.

6. For Molotov's arguments, see *VPSS 1947,* Vol. II, pp. 118ff., and *FRUS 1947,* Vol. III, pp. 297–307.

7. Fresh details on the Czech decision to countermand the acceptance of the Paris invitation are in an archival study by J. Belda, M. Bouček, Z. Deyl, and M. Klimeš, "K otázce účastí Československa na Marshallově plánu" [Regarding the participation of Czechoslovakia in the Marshall Plan], *Revue Dějin Socializmu,* Vol. III (1968), pp. 81–101. The Soviet chargé d'affaires in Prague told Czechoslovak Foreign Minister Masaryk three times on 6 July that he had no instructions on the subject of Czechoslovak participation in the Marshall Plan. Privately he assured Masaryk that Czechoslovakia could go ahead. It has been said that this was an example of Soviet inefficiency and that Stalin's mind was clear, but if so, one must ask why even Gottwald, the Communist prime minister of Czechoslovakia, received no instructions through Party channels.

8. The Hungarian position is reported by Gy. Heltai, at the time the highest ranking Communist in the Foreign Ministry. He attended an enlarged Hungarian CP Politburo meeting in July 1947 to discuss Hungarian participation in the plan. Finding the top Party leadership perplexed, he suggested asking Moscow. Rákosi replied to the effect that: "that's not the way we do things" (interview with the author, March 1964). For the similar position of the Polish and Rumanian Communists, see Fontaine, *History of the Cold War,* Vol. I, pp. 329–30.

9. For French Communist ignorance of Stalin's intentions at this time, see Rieber, *Stalin and the French Communist Party,* pp. 361–62.

10. *For a Lasting Peace,* no. 1 (1947), p. 1.

11. *Ibid.*

12. *Ibid.,* p. 2.

13. Reale's notes make it seem that there were six speakers on 23 September, among them Gomułka and Longo, whose talks he does not transcribe, and then only two reports on one of the following days. This schedule leaves a gap at the end of the conference. It seems more reasonable to think that there were two speakers each morning and afternoon.

14. Reale (*Avec Jacques Duclos,* pp. 34–35) says that Kardelj confessed to the Italians many years later that this was so. Cf. Dedijer, *Tito. Prilozi,* p. 475.

15. Reale, *Avec Jacques Duclos,* pp. 178, 176.

16. For Duclos' attitudes, see Desanti, *Les staliniens,* p. 86. Another such journal was issued by the Soviet Trade Union Organization under the title *New Times* (during the war this was called *War and the Working Class*).

17. "Stalin explained that at no congress and at no central committee meeting of the Communist Party had he, J. V. Stalin, ever spoken about the *impossibility* of cooperation between two [different economic] systems, nor could he have spoken about that. He, J. V. Stalin, did say in 1937 that there existed a capitalist encirclement of, and a great danger of attack on, the USSR. Clearly, if one side does not want to cooperate, that means that there exists a danger of attack. In fact, Germany, not desiring to cooperate with the USSR, did attack the USSR. But was it possible for the USSR to cooperate with Germany? Yes . . . just as with any other country" (*Soch.,* Vol. XVI, pp. 77–78).

18. Khrushchev, *Memoirs,* Vol. II, pp. 38ff., 53, 58–59, 188, 191, 354–56, 375; *FRUS 1948,* Vol. IV, pp. 821; Djilas, *Conversations with Stalin,* p. 182.

19. Mao at this time developed his theory that in the countries of the "intermediate zone" between the Soviet Union and the United States, it was legitimate—indeed, necessary—to fight liberation wars without regard either for the coalition between the two Great Powers or for the danger of war between them. In other words, he sought to divorce completely the definition of his own Party's struggle from that of Stalin's grand strategy. See Okabe, "The Cold War and China," pp. 230–36.

20. Starobin, *American Communism in Crisis,* p. 156.

21. Tim Buck, *Europe's Rebirth,* p. 97. Interesting remarks on this general development are in the pan-European surveys by N. Kołomejczyk, *Rewolucja ludowe w Europie, 1939–1948,* and in W. Góra et al., *Rewolucja i władze ludowe w krajech europejskich 1944–1948* [Revolution and people's government in the European countries, 1944–1948] (Warsaw: Książka i Wiedza, 1972).

22. Rákosi's "commitment" did not, of course, mean any moral obligation to, or love of, the other political parties, but simply public identification of himself, as leader of the Hungarian CP, with anti-blocism, "separate roadism," and the expectation of a long-term coalitional takeover. For details, see my doctoral dissertation, "Communism and Hungary," passim. For Marshal Voroshilov's commitment as chief of the Allied Control Commission to the Smallholders, see F. Nagy, *Struggle behind the Iron Curtain,* p. 184. The only Western attempt at a scholarly study of these Hungarian events of 1946 and 1947 is Peter Horvath's now very outdated dissertation, "Communist Tactics in Hungary" (New York University, 1956). Horvath's view is that the Smallholder Party was both powerful and virtuous, and that all the force of the Communist "salami tactic" was needed to overthrow it. He also sees Communism as monolithic. All this I find untenable. The Communists shared a siege mentality which made them *think* the opposition was more formidable than it actually was, and which made them *believe* they were united. But the top leaders (and especially the Rákosi clique) knew perfectly well that the political parties were flabby and that there were differences over policy within the CP. A recent biography of Rajk published in Budapest tells, for example, that during 1947 in Politburo circles Mihály Farkas and Gábor Péter, Rákosi's closest collaborators, referred to Rajk as "the enemy" and that they brought formal charges against him in January 1948, eighteen months before his arrest. See Strassenreiter and Sipos, *Rajk László,* pp. 167ff. and 184ff. The other reports of discord upon which my reconstruction is based are in Ferenc Nagy, *Struggle behind the Iron Curtain,* p. 305; François Honti, *Le drame hongrois* (Paris: Triolet, 1949), p. 251; François Fejtö, "L'affaire Rajk est une affaire Dreyfus internationale," *L'Ésprit,* Vol. XVII (1949), pp. 719ff.; Gyula Schöpflin, "Dokumentum," pp. 246ff.; and journalistic reports in *Nyugati Hirnök* [Western herald] (Paris), 20 December 1947; *New York Herald Tribune* (Paris), 11 May 1948; *Manchester Guardian,* 17 May 1949; and by John MacCormac in the *New York Times,* 30 June 1948. The transcript of the Rajk trial (*László Rajk and His Accomplices before the People's Court,* esp. pp. 47ff.) has also been useful, as have the files of the Hungarian desk of Radio Free Europe in Munich and a number of conversations with historians and eyewitnesses in Hungary.

23. The impurity of Rákosi's road to socialism was, from a Bolshevik point of view, great. For an example see the pamphlet "A MKP szervezési feladatai" [The organizational tasks of the CPH] (Budapest: Szikra, 1947), which tells of a CPH *apparatchik* conference at which Rákosi's second-in-command, Mihály Farkas, advised village Communist recruiters to lure local Catholic choirmasters into the Communist Party. His reasoning was that where the choirmaster goes, the whole congregation will follow.

24. Similar judgments appear in Starobin, *American Communism in Crisis,* pp. 155ff.; Rieber, *Stalin and the French Communist Party,* pp. 358ff.; and Ulam, *Stalin,* p. 660.

25. Interview with Gy. Heltai, Brussels, March 1964.

26. See Dedijer, *Tito. Prilozi*, p. 472; Roy Macridis, "Stalinism and the Meaning of Titoism," *World Politics*, Vol. IV (1952), pp. 219ff.

27. Reale, *Avec Jacques Duclos*, pp. 178, 176.

28. See Gomułka's own account in *Nowe Drogi*, nos. 9–10 (1948), pp. 138ff.; and Dedijer, *Tito. Prilozi*, pp. 475–76. The conference initially resolved to situate the information bureau at Prague, but Stalin countermanded this decision and, to the pleasure of the Yugoslavs, chose Belgrade (Djilas, *Conversations with Stalin*, p. 129).

29. For Gomułka's deviation, see Ulam, *Titoism and the Cominform*, pp. 159ff.; Samuel Sharp, *Poland: White Eagle on Red Field*, pp. 207ff.; Bromke, *Poland's Politics*, ch. 4; and Nicholas Bethell, *Gomułka. His Poland and His Communism* (London: Pelican, 1972), chs. 7–9.

30. See Reale's comment in *Avec Jacques Duclos*, p. 19. Cf. Dedijer, *Tito. Prilozi*, p. 475, where it is claimed that Duclos was so idealistic that he wept when criticism came his Party's way. Longo, the Italian, on the other hand, is said to have been defiant.

31. For other examples of this institution, see Leonhard, *Die Revolution entlässt ihre Kinder*, pp. 224ff.; Yu. Bondarev, *Tishina*, pt. 2, ch. 12; and N. Mandelstamm, *Hope Abandoned*, pp. 380ff.

32. Tito, for example, was loud in his criticism of the French and Italian comrades in a talk with a French journalist well over a year before Szklarska Poręba: see Desanti, *Les staliniens*, pp. 85, 92, 149; Reale, *Avec Jacques Duclos*, p. 14.

33. An Italian CC letter to the CPSU(b) dated 16 August 1947, in which nation-wide demonstrations were proposed, was mentioned at the meeting (Reale, *Avec Jacques Duclos*, pp. 131, 135, 178). Duclos in his initial presentation warned that a CPF policy of violence would play into the hands of De Gaulle, but he went on to propose an "ardent" campaign against "war-mongers" (*ibid.*, pp. 87, 85). One may recall in this connection that the CPF led a massive strike wave in May 1947, after it dropped out of the government.

34. *Pravda*, 9 September 1947, p. 1.

35. Nicolaevsky, *Power and the Soviet Elite*, p. 109.

36. Suslov was identified as having communicated greetings in the name of the CPSU(b) to the congress of the East German SED, then in session. It is often supposed that Suslov at this time took over the leadership of the Agit-Prop Directorate from G. F. Aleksandrov, thus acquiring an interest in Zhdanov's second bailiwick, Soviet culture. This happened before January 1948, but Suslov's first recorded "promotion" was into international Communist affairs.

37. *Soch.*, Vol. XVI, p. 93.

38. *Soch.*, Vol. XVI, p. 96.

39. See Khrushchev, *Crimes of the Stalin Era*, p. S45.

40. It stopped publication with no. 7. The last issue contained an article on Leningrad which recalled the special issue on Leningrad published in no. 10 for 1947. There was a brief attempt late in 1950 and early in 1951 to produce an inner-Party journal entitled *Partiinoe Prosveshchenie* [Party education] for the Bolshevik Party, but in the long run it was left to Stalin's successors to restore such a journal, which one might think would be indispensable to the smooth functioning of such a huge organization.

41. In *Bol'shevik*, no. 21 (1947), pp. 29ff., Rodionov quoted the martyred Leningrad leader Kirov to the effect that Leningrad was a "great forge of cadres for our new socialist system," and that "in industrial affairs, Leningrad plays a uniquely responsible role." Rumors circulated at this time that an international Russian fair be held in Leningrad and that the capital of the Russian Republic might be shifted there from Moscow. See Conquest, *Power and Policy*, p. 103, and Nicolaevsky, *Power and the Soviet Elite*, p. 167, for the speculations on this subject.

42. See the characterization by Medvedev, *Let History Judge*, p. 481.

43. A condensed version appeared as "O sovetskoi demokratii," *Bol'shevik*, no. 22 (1946), pp. 9–37. The lecture was also published in full as a pamphlet.
44. See especially M. Mitin's essay on Soviet democracy in *Bol'shevik*, no. 5 (1947), pp. 22–43, and P. Trainin's two-part study of democracy of a new type in *Sovetskoe Gosudarstvo i Pravo*, nos. 1 and 3 (1947). For background see the dated article by R. A. Rose, "The Soviet Theory of People's Democracy," *World Politics*, Vol. I (1949), pp. 489–510; Samuel Sharp, "People's Democracy in Soviet Theory," *Soviet Studies*, Vol. II (1951), nos. 7, pp. 16–33, and 10, pp. 131–49.
45. See Tikos, *E. Vargas Tätigkeit*, pp. 78–81.
46. *Soch.*, Vol. XVI, p. 90.
47. *Mirovoe Khozyaistvo i Mirovaya Politika*, no. 5 (1947), p. 126. The minutes of the debate were published as an appendix to the final issue of *MKhMP* in December 1947 and are available in English under the title *Soviet Views on the Post-War World Economy* (Washington, D.C.: Public Affairs Press, 1948).
48. Molotov agreed to go to Paris on 23 June and arrived there on 26 June. Zhdanov addressed the philosophers on 24 June. For details see P. E. Corbett, "The Aleksandrov Story," pp. 161–74, and J. N. Miller, "Zhdanov's Speech to the Philosophers," *Soviet Studies*, Vol. I (1949), pp. 40–51. The speech may be found in *Bol'shevik*, no. 16 (1947), pp. 7–23.
49. Malenkov's speech was published in *Pravda*, after a long delay, on 9 December 1947, and in the second number of *For a Lasting Peace*.
50. Zhdanov's distinction between the Slavic countries of the "new democracy" and the other East Europeans went back to various Stalin statements of March and April 1945 and emphasized the many extant "types" of democracy. It is interesting in this connection that the Soviet head of the international Slavic Committee after the war was A. A. Voznesensky, brother of N. A. Voznesensky, the Politburo economist, and that his committee was most active in the autumn of 1947. See the recent collection of essays *Uchenyi Kommunist: A. A. Voznesenskii* [A scholarly Communist] (Leningrad: Izdat. Len. Univ., 1973), ch. 12.
51. *For a Lasting Peace*, no. 1 (1947), p. 1.
52. The speeches may be found in *For a Lasting Peace*, nos. 1–2 (1949).
53. A. A. Kuznetsov, *PS*, no. 4 (1946), p. 1.
54. Rákosi, *A magyar demokráciáért*, p. 41.
55. O. Utis [pseud. for D. J. R. Scott], "Generalissimo Stalin and the Art of Government," *Foreign Affairs*, Vol. XXX (1952), pp. 197–214.
56. Medvedev has argued (*Let History Judge*, pp. 362–64) that the cult of personality was created by Stalin's underlings and has become a part of their psychology. I do not disagree with this, but feel that Stalin used the cult for his own purposes. Cf. Khrushchev's agonized discussion of Stalin's responsibility in *Crimes of the Stalin Era*, pp. S46ff.
57. It is obvious from the elaborateness of the security arrangements that the Poles, as hosts, were not without warning of the planned meeting. But Reale (*Avec Jacques Duclos*, pp. 4, 7) indicates that the Italian Party was informed by special courier on 13 or 14 September, and that the French also were invited late. The Hungarian Party press announced on 16 September that its secretary, M. Farkas, would attend the SED Congress at Berlin, which was to start on 20 September. Farkas in fact showed up at the Cominform meeting instead (*Szabad Nép*, 16 September 1947, p. 3). Some members of the German SED Politburo learned about the meeting as late as 8 October from the newspapers (Gniffke, *Jahre mit Ulbricht*, p. 264). The juxtaposition of the Szklarska Poręba conference with the long-planned SED congress also suggests a somewhat last-minute arrangement. If the Cominform event had resulted from a long-standing plan, surely such an overlap would have been avoided.
58. Anyone who read the Soviet press in Stalin's day will recall not only the

overt attention paid to birthdays and anniversaries of revolutionary and political events and dates of death but also the uncanny "silent" anniversaries. I have mentioned the occurence of a "March crisis" in 1946, just a year after that of 1945, and the publication of Stalin's letter to Razin exactly a year after it was written. Yaakov Ro'i has called my attention to an extreme case: the announcement of the "doctors' plot" in January 1953, on the anniversary of the murder of the Jewish leader Salomon Mikhoels on 13 January 1948. Such coincidences were typical of the late Stalinist terror and should not be ignored. Cf. Alliluyeva's account of Stalin's dread of 8 November each year, the anniversary of her mother's suicide (*Twenty Letters to a Friend,* p. 193).

59. *Only One Year,* pp. 384–85.

60. "The Cold War from the Soviet Point of View," paper delivered at the AAASS Conference, St. Louis, October 1976, pp. 28ff. Dinerstein argues that Stalin characteristically showed a great deal of reluctance when he had to abandon a policy; that he hated to admit failure and would grasp at virtually any sort of objective evidence to justify continued adherence to a worn-out policy; and that he would often not adopt a new policy explicitly until the debate in his entourage about the old one had been completely resolved. It adds spice to Dinerstein's hypothesis that Stalin himself pointed in 1947 to the parallels with 1941 and that in May 1941, at the height of his indecision, he published a document he had allegedly written at his moment of indecision in July 1934 (*Soch.,* Vol. XIV, pp. 2ff.).

61. These extraordinary sayings are reported in the *Times* (London), 24 October 1947, p. 4.

62. See especially the sarcastic treatment of the two texts in the same issue of the *Times.*

Notes to Chapter 13

1. See the account in Henderson, *Politics of the Vortex,* pp. 122ff.

2. For discussions of the rise of Kim Il Sung, his elimination of Communists who came from the south and Yenan from the Korean CP, and his development of a theory whereby Korea's road to socialism would have a military character, see Scalapino and Lee, *Communism in Korea,* Vol. I, pp. 318ff., 359ff.; Simmons, *The Strained Alliance,* ch. 2; and the final chapters of Dae-Suk Suh, *The Korean Communist Movement 1918–1948* (Princeton: Princeton University Press, 1967).

3. See *FRUS 1947,* Vol. VI, pp. 793ff., for a discussion of American intentions.

4. On 24 September the American political adviser in Seoul recorded that he had received three written Soviet requests for a meeting since 17 September; he set up the meeting for 26 September. It was at this meeting that the Russians announced their change of policy (*FRUS 1947,* Vol. VI, p. 815).

5. In *New Times,* no. 43 (1947), dated 26 October, a "historical" essay depicted the tsarist intrigues in Korea prior to 1904 as "Russia" 's fifty-year-old effort to "rescue" the Koreans from Japanese and American imperialism. "Blocism" could hardly have been expressed more bluntly. The previous article about Korea in *New Times* appeared in issue no. 32 (6 August) and concerned the Soviet desire to "democratize" all of Korea through participation in the Joint Soviet-American Commission in Seoul.

6. For background, see Elizabeth Monroe, *Britain's Moment in the Middle East* (Baltimore: Johns Hopkins University Press, 1963), ch. 7; William R. Polk, D. M. Stamler, and Edmund Asfour, *Backdrop to Tragedy* (Boston: Beacon Press, 1957); and W. Laqueur, *Communism and Nationalism in the Middle East* (New York: Praeger, 1956), pt. 3.

7. On Soviet policy see the careful study by Yaacov Ro'i, "Soviet-Israeli Relations," in *The USSR and the Middle East,* ed. M. Confino and Shimon Shamir (New York: John Wiley, 1973), esp. pp. 123–33; Arnold Krammer, *The Forgotten Friendship*

(Urbana: University of Illinois Press, 1974), ch. 2; and the contribution by Nadav Safran in Lederer and Vucinich, *The Soviet Union and the Middle East,* pp. 157–62.

    8. See, for example, the article by L. Sedin in *New Times,* no. 11 (1948), pp. 8–12. I am indebted in this discussion to an unpublished study of Soviet attitudes toward Third World questions by Professor Jon Harris of the University of Pittsburgh.

    9. Harriman, *Special Envoy,* p. 297.

    10. Gniffke, *Jahre mit Ulbricht,* pp. 250–51.

    11. See Djilas' comment in *Conversations with Stalin,* p. 153.

    12. The SED leadership decided to hold a Volkskongress on 24 November, the day before the Council of Foreign Ministers met at London, and issued a public call for the congress on the 26th. It met from 6 to 8 December. See Gniffke, *Jahre mit Ulbricht,* pp. 268ff.

    13. *Pravda,* 7 November 1947, pp. 1–2.

    14. The records of the conference at London are in *FRUS 1947,* Vol. II, pp. 726ff.

    15. For details, see Boris Meissner, *Das Ostpaktsystem. Dokumentensammlung;* Kořalková, *Vytváření systému dvoustranných . . . smluv;* and Brzezinski, *The Soviet Bloc,* ch. 6.

    16. The classic account of the Berlin blockade is in the memoirs of General Lucius Clay, *Decision in Germany,* which has recently been supplemented by Volume II of Jean Edward Smith's *The Papers of General Lucius D. Clay. Germany 1945–1949.* Monographs on the subject are W. Philipps Davison, *The Berlin Blockade* (Princeton: Princeton University Press, 1958); and Hans Herzfeld, *Berlin in der Weltpolitik* (Berlin: De Gruyter, 1973).

    17. Gimbel (*American Occupation of Germany,* pp. 194ff.) discusses these events.

    18. Djilas, *Conversations with Stalin,* p. 153.

    19. Clay, *Decision in Germany,* p. 350.

    20. Gniffke, *Jahre mit Ulbricht,* p. 281; Meissner, *Russland, die Westmächte und Deutschland,* p. 158.

    21. See especially the speech on the occasion of the signing of the pact with Finland on 7 April and his extraordinarily fatuous reply to a letter from Henry Wallace published on 18 May (*Soch.,* Vol. XVI, pp. 99–104).

    22. Reported in W. Bedell Smith, *My Three Years in Moscow,* p. 244.

    23. *Pravda,* 7 November 1948, pp. 1–2.

    24. Reale, *Avec Jacques Duclos,* pp. 55–56.

    25. See Meissner, *Russland, die Westmächte und Deutschland,* p. 174; the suggestive figures in Jasny, *Soviet Industrialization,* pp. 362–63; and Wolfe, *Soviet Power in Europe,* pp. 10–11.

    26. *Pravda,* 9 November 1947, p. 2. The speech was also published at this time in the second issue of *For a Lasting Peace,* which came out unaccountably late.

    27. Both the reference to Malenkov and the Suslov biography appeared in *Pravda,* 23 November, p. 2, the former buried in an election speech. It was most unusual for biographical material about any Soviet official to be published elsewhere than in an obituary.

    28. *Pravda,* 19 November, p. 1; cf. the similar appeal from Moscow in *Pravda,* 29 November, p. 1.

    29. Khrushchev, *Crimes of the Stalin Era,* p. S45.

    30. Tikos, *E. Vargas Tätigkeit,* pp. 87–89.

    31. *Pravda,* 15 December 1947, pp. 1ff.; Werth, *The Postwar Years,* pp. 339ff.

    32. F. Kozlov attributed the currency reform to Voznesensky's ideas in *Pravda,* 7 January 1948, p. 2.

    33. Khrushchev speaks of Malenkov's prominence in the prosecution of Voznesensky in his *Memoirs,* Vol. I, p. 221.

    34. Werth, *The Postwar Years,* pp. 338–39.

35. *Pravda,* 22 November 1946.

36. See Salo W. Baron, *The Russian Jew under Tsars and Soviets* (New York: Macmillan, 1964), and the essays in Lionel Kochan, ed., *The Jews in Russia since 1917* (London: Oxford University Press, 1972).

37. Yehoshua A. Gilboa, *The Black Years of Soviet Jewry* (Boston: Little, Brown, 1971), pp. 381–82.

38. Shimon Redlich, "The Jewish Anti-Fascist Committee in the Soviet Union," *Jewish Social Studies,* Vol. XXXI (1969), pp. 25–36.

39. Djilas, *Conversations with Stalin,* pp. 154, 170; Alliluyeva, *Only One Year,* pp. 153–54; and the account by Mikhoels' daughter in the *New York Times,* 13 January 1974, p. 15. It is indicative of the extreme complexity of Soviet political trends in January 1948 that Mikhoels was reportedly Beria's "man" in the Jewish Anti-Fascist Committee. This means that the murder was not (as it might seem at first) a symptom that Beria was regaining Stalin's favor, but rather that he was under intensified attack. Yaacov Ro'i, of the University of Tel Aviv, who provided me with this information from a forthcoming book on the Anti-Fascist Committee, suggests that Stalin at this time was driving a wedge into the community of interest which may once have linked Beria and Malenkov. For other suggestions, see Medvedev, *Let History Judge,* p. 484.

40. The highlighting of Suslov as an index of Zhdanov's decline followed the precedent of the highlighting of Patolichev in 1946 as an index of Malenkov's decline. The exact sequence of events is, of course, not known. It is clear only that Zhdanov attacked the chief of Agit-Prop, G. F. Aleksandrov, late in June and managed to oust him; that Suslov was a CC Secretary by 24 September with responsibilities for foreign Communism; and that on 21 January 1948 Suslov delivered the speech on the anniversary of Lenin's death, a task traditionally the responsibility of the chief of Agit-Prop.

41. On the musical affair, see Werth, *Musical Uproar in Moscow,* which gives many contemporary anecdotes, and Boris Schwarz, *Music and Musical Life in Soviet Russia* (London: Barrie and Jenkins, 1972), pp. 213ff. Schwarz refutes a report in Werth's account that Stalin heard the opera in December 1947 and arbitrarily took a dislike to it.

42. There were a great many ambiguities both in Zhdanov's speech and in Suslov's 21 January address about Soviet cultural policy. Patently both men were trying to muffle the sharpness of the change, which is nonetheless clear even in the biographies of Zhdanov in *BSE,* 2d ed., Vol. XV, pp. 604–7; 3d ed., Vol. IX, pp. 127–28.

43. The Central Committee resolution on this subject was dated 10 February 1948, was reported in the press on 14 February, and was published in *Bol'shevik,* no. 3 (1948), pp. 10–14. Zhdanov's speech and some records of the meeting were published in March 1948 in a pamphlet entitled *Soveshchanie deyatelei sovetskoi muziky v TsKVKP(b),* whose appearance was noted in *Bol'shevik,* no. 6, pp. 63ff. The speech was not considered important enough to be published either in that journal or in *PZh,* as earlier Zhdanov speeches had been.

44. *Pravda,* 25 January 1948, p. 1. Cf. the commentary in *FRUS 1948,* Vol. IV, pp. 800–801.

45. See, for example, *PZh,* no. 2 (1948), pp. 35–37.

46. Khrushchev's recovery and the return of Kaganovich from the Ukraine to Moscow were reported in *Pravda* on 14, 16, and 26 December 1947. Cf. Georg Paloczi-Horvath, *Chruschtschow* (Frankfurt am Main: Fischer, 1961), pp. 128–31; Armstrong, *Politics of Totalitarianism,* pp. 204–5; and Khrushchev, *Memoirs,* Vol. II, p. 240.

47. Fainsod (*How Russia Is Ruled,* p. 339) and Nove (*The Soviet Economy* [New York: Praeger, 1961], pp. 66–67) give details. On 9 January the State Planning Commission was reconstituted into a State Planning Committee, and two new departments were created. It is possible that Voznesensky himself precipitated this reorganization; one of his more romantic ideas seems to have entailed a "fading away" of the Planning

Office through decentralization after it had been given total economic power. At any rate, in Stalin's entourage a massive reorganization of a lieutenant's empire usually meant the undermining of his power, and this certainly happened in Voznesensky's case during 1948 and 1949. According to their *BSE* biographies, both Bulganin and Kosygin were admitted to the Politburo in February 1948, although no announcement was made at the time.

48. For a confirmation of Zhdanov's disgrace in the months before his death, see Medvedev, *Let History Judge,* p. 484.

49. This is noted in the summaries to the *BBC Soviet Monitoring Reports,* nos. 83–84 (8 and 12 December 1947).

50. See Kousoulas, *Revolution and Defeat,* pp. 246, 248; Woodhouse, *The Struggle for Greece,* ch. 8, esp. pp. 216–18, 222. The background of these events is very murky. As Kousoulas puts it: "Greek, Bulgarian, Titoist, Bulgaro-Macedonian, Soviet and Albanian influences were often working at cross-purposes" (p. 231). The war became the subject of bitter factional strife within the Greek CP between Markos, who remained in the mountains, and Zachariades, who went behind the iron curtain. Characteristically, even though Stalin in February 1948 suggested the winding up of the revolt, it was Zachariades who insisted on a struggle to the end, whereas Markos, who may have sided with Tito, favored a shift to a less militant stance (see Clissold, *Yugoslavia and the Soviet Union,* p. 48).

51. In the following account, I have relied on Shoup, *Communism and the Yugoslav National Question,* pp. 128ff., and the *BBC East European Monitoring Reports* for the period.

52. Dedijer, *Jugoslovensko-albanski odnosi, 1939–1948,* p. 126.

53. I have been told by György Heltai and by a source in Hungary that Tito's visit to Budapest was welcomed not because the CPH had any special love for Tito, nor because it had received instructions from Moscow, but because Tito's welcome in Sofia and elsewhere had been so overwhelming as to imply Kremlin approval. It may be noted that political tensions in the Hungarian CP leadership were extremely high at this time: the radicals around Rajk were in the ascent; Rákosi had found it expedient to take a two-month-long "vacation" abroad, so despite Communist power, there had been no político "progress" since early autumn; and the advice which Tito was indiscriminately bestowing on all his neighbors was finding an audience in Budapest (even though Rajk personally appears to have disliked Tito's egotism). All this was reflected later in Rajk's trial, when Tito's visit was construed as a critical moment in the formation of Rajk's conspiracy against Hungary's democracy. See Fejtö, "L'affaire Rajk," pp. 719ff., and the interview with Gyula Orbán, "A tíz év elötti nagy pér," pp. 371–74.

54. Andrije Hebrang's removal as chief of the Yugoslav Planning Office was made public on 8 January 1948, but both Dedijer and Djilas indicate that it was one of the factors leading to Djilas' invitation to Moscow—a summons which arrived in Belgrade "late in December." Djilas by his own account left for Moscow on 8 January.

55. According to Dedijer, the CCP representative came to Belgrade in mid-1948, after the Cominform criticism of Yugoslavia, to investigate what was happening (see *The Battle Stalin Lost,* p. 122). It now appears that the visit took place in 1947, however, and Liu Ning-yi reported on it in *Jen-min jih-pao* on 26 October and 20 December of that year (see Okabe, "The Cold War and China," pp. 241, 250, n. 65). This means that what Dedijer considers the first concrete Yugoslav-Chinese Party contact—a mission he himself received from Tito in January 1948—was really a response to the Chinese initiative, and that the whole question of Yugoslav-Chinese and Greek-Chinese Communist relations before 1948 may be reconsidered. See *The Battle Stalin Lost,* ch. 1, and Woodhouse, *Struggle for Greece,* p. 217.

56. Mao, *Selected Works,* Vol. IV, pp. 157ff.

57. Bhabam Sen Gupta [pseud. for Chanakya Sen], *Communism in Indian Politics*

(New York: Columbia University Press, 1972), p. 28; Eugene Overstreet and Marshall Windmuller, *Communism in India* (Berkeley: University of California Press, 1959), p. 260.

58. There has been a great deal of controversy about the spread of Communist militancy in Asia during late 1947 and 1948. During the 1950s and early 1960s many Western scholars, reflecting Cold War pressures, considered that Moscow had systematically propagated Zhdanov's two-camp line at the Congress of the Communist Party of India and the Southeast Asia Youth Conference at Calcutta in February 1948—in other words, that the spread of militancy was centrally directed. See, for example, A. Doak Barnett, *Communist China and Asia: Challenge to American Policy* (New York: Harper, 1960), p. 152. More recent scholars have felt that there existed no Moscow line for Southeast Asia at that time; that the Calcutta conference was certainly not the kind of assembly where it could have been propagated, had it existed; and, finally, that the revolts which took place in 1948 were generally not against imperialists but against local "bourgeois" regimes, and thus worked against Moscow's probable interest. See the excellent survey in McLane, *Soviet Strategies in Southeast Asia,* pp. 355ff.; and Tanigawa Yoshihiko, "The Cominform and Southeast Asia," in Nagai and Iriye, *The Origins of the Cold War in Asia,* pp. 362ff.

59. The Yugoslavs had been involved in the year-long preparations for the Calcutta youth conference and were represented there by Vladimir Dedijer. Dedijer later visited Burma during a Communist turn toward insurrectionism there and was supposed to go on to China, but was stopped by a Soviet political intervention. See Dedijer, *The Battle Stalin Lost,* pp. 25ff.

60. Djilas, *Conversations with Stalin,* pt. 3.

61. *Pravda,* 6 January, pp. 3–4.

62. Djilas, *Conversations with Stalin,* pp. 159–61.

63. It may be added that in 1949, while Communist troops were conquering China, the Soviet ambassador to Chiang Kai-shek's Republican government followed the Nationalists each time they moved their capital, negotiating all the while to obtain concessions in Sinkiang. See Nakajima, "Sino-Soviet Confrontation," p. 208.

64. Our knowledge of this meeting is based on Dedijer's propagandistic *Tito. Prilozi,* written from the Yugoslav minutes, and on Djilas' more sensitive *Conversations with Stalin,* written from distant memory. Various authors have expressed doubts about the reliability of this evidence—for example, Adam Ulam (*Expansion and Coexistence,* p. 483). Since Djilas corroborates Dedijer, however, although he writes from a position of political opposition, their joint version of the events of that night seems acceptable.

65. For the aftermath in Greece, see Kousoulas, *Revolution and Defeat,* ch. 17.

66. See Korbel, *Communist Subversion of Czechoslovakia,* ch. 11; Zinner, *Communist Strategy and Tactics in Czechoslovakia,* pt. 3; Gordon M. Skilling, "Revolution and Continuity in Czechoslovakia 1945–1946," *Journal of Central European Affairs,* Vol. XX (1961), pp. 357–77; Gordon M. Skilling, "The Breakup of the Czechoslovak Coalition 1947–1948," *Canadian Journal of Economics and Social Sciences,* Vol. XXVI (1960), pp. 396–412; Gordon M. Skilling, "The Prague Overturn of 1948," *Canadian Slavonic Papers,* Vol. IV (1959), pp. 88–114; and the review of the recent literature by Pavel Tigrid, "The Prague Coup of 1948," in T. Hammond, *Anatomy of Communist Takeovers,* pp. 399ff.

67. Fejtö, *Le coup de Prague* (Paris: Seuil, 1976), p. 149. Fejtö's admirable book draws extensively on an unpublished manuscript by an anonymous Czech historian which is based on archival research and was smuggled out of Czechoslovakia after 1968 (Jan Švec [pseudonym], "Československý únor 1948" [Czechoslovak February 1948]). Neither Švec's manuscript nor Fejtö's work was available to me during the preparation of this book. Both contain information about the importance of radicalism in the

Czechoslovak Party in 1947–1948 which entirely confirms my findings about radicalism in the Hungarian CP.

68. It was extensively rumored early in 1948 that the Cominform was concocting a plan for the subversion of Czechoslovakia, and that it held a meeting for this purpose at Milan, during the Italian Communist Party Congress in January. In effect, the Czecho- slovak CP Politburo decided to notify the Cominform headquarters at Belgrade as soon as the political crisis got under way on 13 February (see Bohumil Lausman, *Kdo byl vinĕn,* pp. 106–7). Considering what we now know about the unimportance of the Cominform organization, these rumors seem insubstantial and the Politburo action seems laughable. Fejtö reports nothing beyond these rumors (p. 131), so perhaps one may assume that nothing occurred.

69. Zorin played a consequential role in that he conveyed a message from Stalin to Gottwald that the Soviet Union "would not allow the West to interfere in Czechoslova- kia's internal affairs." This was not an "order" to seize power, but it was an assurance that a seizure of power would not be reversed, if it happened. See J. Belda et al., *Na rozhrani dvou epoch* [At the crossroads of two epochs] (Prague: Svoboda, 1968), pp. 264–65.

70. *Soch.,* Vol. XVI, pp. 96–97.

71. Finland and its Communist Party were closely associated with Zhdanov, who had his base in nearby Leningrad and who was chairman of the Allied Control Commis- sion in Helsinki after 1944. As noted in an earlier chapter, moreover, the Finnish CP's separate road to socialism between 1945 and 1948 stressed political moderation and educational measures in a fashion which might be called Zhdanovist. For such reasons the start of the Soviet action in February 1948 may have reflected Zhdanov's initiative in the Kremlin. It is certainly interesting in this light that as Zhdanov's star declined, the Russians simply did not follow through with pressure, and that at the height of the political crisis in March, the Finnish Communist who was in charge of the police tipped off the government that a coup was impending. See the discussion of this incident in Kevin Devlin's "Finland in 1948," in Hammond, *Anatomy of Communist Takeovers,* p. 443. Devlin presents the convincing thesis that the Finnish coup failed because Moscow was uninterested in pursuing it. See also Hans P. Krosby, "The Communist Power Bid in Finland, 1948"; J. Billington, "Finland," in Black, ed., *Communism and Revolution,* pp. 117–44.

72. One may follow the development of the Soviet-Yugoslav controversy through the correspondence, published in English in 1948 by the Royal Institute of International Affairs; through the surveys by Dedijer and Fitzroy Maclean; and most recently through the book by Savo Krzhavats, *Shta je to IB—Informbiro* [What is the IB—the Informburo] serialized for fifteen issues in the magazine *NIN* (Belgrade) from 2 Novem- ber 1975 to April 1976.

Notes to Chapter 14

1. *Pravda,* 20 July 1948, p. 2; Ebon, *Malenkov,* p. 57. Soviet policy toward Com- munism in the Far East had been markedly more "annexationist" and "statist" than in Europe during the later war years. Perhaps one may hypothesize that the Central Committee Foreign Department had Asiatic and European sections, which were united in September 1945 under Zhdanov and now were separated again.

2. See Medvedev, *The Rise and Fall of T. D. Lysenko,* pp. 111ff.; Joravsky, *The Lysenko Affair,* pp. 135ff.; Ploss, *Conflict and Decision-Making,* pp. 38–39.

3. Gilboa, *The Black Years,* pp. 205ff.; Ulam, *Stalin,* pp. 678ff. The inside story of Stalin's attack on the "Zionists" in the last months of 1948 is reflected in Alliluyeva, *Twenty Letters to a Friend,* pp. 65, 196–97.

4. Nemzer, "The Kremlin's Professional Staff," pp. 64ff.

5. Conquest, *Power and Policy,* ch. 5.

6. Alliluyeva, *Twenty Letters to a Friend*, p. 192.

7. An announcement in *Pravda*, 13 January 1953, laid the murder of Zhdanov at the door of the Kremlin doctors.

8. Such themes were adumbrated even in such Cold War studies as Carl Friedrich and Zbigniew Brzezinski, *Totalitarian Dictatorship and Autocracy* (1956), and in Brzezinski's *The Permanent Purge* (Cambridge, Mass.: Harvard University Press, 1956).

9. The theme of Khrushchev's secret speech at the CPSU 20th Congress in 1956 was that Beria had somehow hoodwinked Stalin into suspecting the Leningrad people.

10. Khrushchev became leader of the Moscow Party organization in December 1949, assumed some of Malenkov's responsibilities in agriculture during 1950, and by 1952 was probably the single most important functionary in the central Party bureaucracy.

11. It is worthy of note that the first essay on linguistics appeared just a few days before the outbreak of the Korean war, and that Stalin's subsequent remarks, each of which shifted focus on the question of "pedantry," coincided with the changes at the front during the summer.

12. Conquest, *Power and Policy in the USSR*, chs. 7–8; Nicolaevsky, *Power and the Soviet Elite*, pt. 3. I am indebted to Robert Slusser for numerous suggestions about the extent to which the police were beyond Stalin's absolute control during his last years.

13. *Twenty Letters to a Friend*, p. 200.

14. Hoffman and Neal (*Yugoslavia and the New Communism*, p. 140) list this and other psychosomatic disturbances.

15. Bethell, *Gomułka*, ch. 9.

16. Leonhard, *Die Revolution entlässt ihre Kinder*, ch. 9; Desanti, *Les staliniens*, ch. 6; Flora Lewis, *Red Pawn* (Garden City, N.Y.: Doubleday, 1965), p. 191.

17. In 1951 the exiled Polish poet Czeslav Milosz published a series of character sketches stressing the importance of psychological factors in inducing voluntary compliance with Stalinism by intellectuals (*The Captive Mind*, esp. chs. 4–7). Unlike many other East European émigré publications of that period, which explained Stalinism in terms of moral wickedness, Milosz' book was later confirmed by eyewitnesses, for example, by numerous respondents of the "Columbia University Research Project: Hungary," by Tamás Aczél and Tibor Méray in *The Revolt of the Mind;* and by Eugen Loebl, *My Mind on Trial*.

18. The record has been documented in Jiří Pelikan, ed., *The Czechoslovak Political Trials, 1950–1954*.

19. Annie Kriegel, *Les Communistes français. Essai d'ethnographie politique* (Paris: Seuil, 1968), pt. 2; Ronald Tiersky, *French Communism, 1920–1972* (New York: Columbia University Press, 1974), chs. 6 and 9, esp. p. 322; and Desanti, *Les staliniens*, pt. 2.

20. A classic example of this independence was the rebellion at Madiun in Indonesia in September 1948. Since a leading Indonesian Communist, Musso, returned from a long stay in Moscow in August and assumed command of the Party, Westerners took this disastrous rebellion as evidence that Stalin had adopted an insurrectionist line. In reality, the contrary was true: the rebellion reflected the wishes of local Communists, and Musso was drawn into it (see George McT. Kahin, *Nationalism and Revolution in Indonesia* [Ithaca, N.Y.: Cornell University Press, 1952], ch. 9, esp. pp. 269ff.).

21. A good survey is in McLean, *Soviet Strategies in Southeast Asia*, ch. 6.

22. Schram, *Mao Tse-Tung*, pp. 253ff.; Nakajima, "The Sino-Soviet Confrontation," pp. 203ff.

23. For evidence of Stalin's responsibility, see n. 11 above. But the trend in scholarly opinion today is that the war broke out as a result of the inner political strains in Korea and in the North Korean Communist Party, although Stalin probably opened the door for it: see Simmons, *The Strained Alliance*, pp. 176–79; and Okonogi Masao,

"The Domestic Roots of the Korean War," in Nagai and Iriye, *The Origins of the Cold War in Asia,* pp. 316–17, 320.

24. Nakajima, "Sino-Soviet Confrontation," pp. 219–20.

25. Marshall Shulman emphasizes the importance of the peace movement in *Stalin's Foreign Policy Reappraised,* pp. 85ff., 131ff., 155ff.

Notes to Addendum

1. Dekanozov was the deputy foreign commissar responsible for European affairs, which included both France and Eastern Europe. See Catroux, *J'ai vu tomber le rideau de fer,* p. 41.

2. The excerpts are embedded in M. Korom's "Az ideiglenes nemzetgyűlés," pp. 112–25. I have translated them (save for one minor transposition) in the order in which he presents them and in full, but have summarized his text in my own words.

Index

Page numbers in italics indicate the first citation of a source in notes and bibliography.

405

Index

Bohlen, Charles E., 220, *326*
Bol'shevik, 99, 112, 114, 378 n. 63
Bondarev, Yurii, 103, *326*
Borisov, C. B., *376 n. 36*
Borkenau, Franz, *337*
Bozhinov, Voin, *346 n. 35*
Brackman, Arnold, *381 n. 103*
Brechak, M. I., *361 n. 46*
Bromke, Adam, *382 n. 107*
Bruce, George L., *344 n. 14*
Brussels Pact of 1948, 291
Brzezinski, Zbigniew K., *335 n. 46, 337, 403 n. 8*
Buck, Tim, *326*
Budapest, 57, 345 n. 31
Bukovina, 169
Bulganin, N. A.: background, 80; leads Party assault on Army, 80–81, 224, 350 n. 37, 384 n. 26; in top leadership, 108, 229–30, 400; in 1949, 132, 305
Bulgaria: liberation of, 54, 56, 169, 188, 367 n. 22; election of 1945, 198–99, 377 n. 54; peace settlement 59, 188, 190, 220–22; army of, 59, 346 n. 43
—Communist Party of: during liberation, 57–58; "separate roadism" of, 213; at Cominform meeting of 1947, 261, 271; in 1948–1949, 299–300, 308. *See also* Dimitrov, Georgi
Burin, Fred S., *338 n. 13*
Burks, Richard V., *380 n. 97*
Burma, 309, 401 n. 59
Burmeister, Alfred, *326*
Burnham, James, *352 n. 60*
Byrnes, James F., *326;* at London Conference, 193, 200, 208, 374 n. 11, 375 n. 28; at Moscow Conference, 219–22, 383 n. 10, 384 nn. 13 and 18; Stuttgart speech, 256
Byrnes, Robert F., *320*

Cadogan, Sir Alexander, *322*
Calcutta youth conference, 1948, 401 nn. 58–59
Calvocoressi, Peter, *392*
Canada: Communist Party of, 45
Carr, E. H., *332*
Casablanca Conference of 1943, 38
Catroux, Maurice, *326*
Caucasus, 83–85, 122, 125, 180
Censorship, Soviet, 216
Central Committee, CPSU: plenum of January 1944, 98, 104, 355 n. 4; decrees

of 1944–1945, 79, 114, 203; plenum of March 1946, 138, 206, 228–32; decrees of 1946, 79, 91, 226, 249–53, 383 n. 122, 389 n. 55 (*see also* Zhdanovshchina); plenum of February 1947, 246–47, 390 n. 69 (*See also* Agriculture); in 1948 and later, 296, 305, 380 n. 87, 399 n. 43. *See also* Orgburo; Politburo; Secretariat, CPSU
—Agit-Prop Administration, 99–100, 102, 115, 230, 278, 295
—Cadre Administration, 90, 93–94, 230–31
—Department for Checking Party Organs, 94, 230–31, 354 n. 97, 389 n. 59
—foreign section, 18, 273, 304, 402 n. 1
—police section, 85, 225, 230, 274, 285 n. 32
—science section, 304
Chambre, Henri, *364 n. 101*
Chandler, Alfred D., *322*
Chaney, O. P., Jr., *350 n. 15*
Chelyabinsk, 87–88, 124, 230, 354 n. 92
Chervenkov, Vlko, 271
Chiang Kai-shek, 196, 298, 310, 376 n. 42, 383 n. 10
China, 194–200, 202, 211–13, 219, 255, 299, 339 n. 17, 383 n. 10, 401 n. 63
Chinese Communist Party: Soviet assessments of, 194, 196, 245, 337 n. 2, 375 n. 31, 377 n. 48; in war, 32, 45, 194–97, 199–200, 338 n. 6, 376 nn. 41, 44–45, 378 n. 57; Northeastern Bureau established, 211–12, 380 n. 99; "separate roadism" of, 194–96, 201, 212; link with Yugoslavs, 1947, 400 n. 48, 401 n. 59; march to victory, 1946–1949, 242, 266–67, 298–99, 310, 394 n. 19. *See also* Mao Tse-tung
Chuikov, V. I, 176, *326,* 372 n. 27
Churchill, Winston S., *323, 324, 326;* as wartime prime minister, 38, 53, 55, 78, 152, 154–56, 170, 187, 191, 335 n. 41, 344 n. 19; intimacy with Stalin, 215; as postwar leader, 210; "iron curtain" speech, 218, 235–36, 262, 386 n. 54. *See also* Grand Alliance; Great Britain; "Percentage agreement" of 1944
Chuvikov, P., *366 nn. 3 and 5*
Ciechanowski, Jan M., *340 n. 34*
Clausewitz, Karl von, 233–34
Clay, Lucius D., *324, 326*
Clemens, Diane, *347 n. 62*

407

Index

Index

Index

Zhdanov in 1946–1948, 17, 231–32, 253, 278–79, 282, 306; agricultural involvement in 1947, 247, 353 n. 81, 388 n. 36, 403 n. 10; at Cominform meeting in 1947, 93, 265, 278, 281, 293, 364 n. 99, 369 n. 47; political revanche in 1947–1949, 137, 281, 294, 304; evades Stalin, 93–95, 307. *See also* Economic policy; Home Front; Managerial class
Malinovskii, R. Ya., *328*
Malinowski, Marian, *341 n. 58*
Mamatey, Victor S., 344 n. 13
Managerial class, 86–95, 100–103, 352 nn. 60 and 66, 354 n. 101. *See also* Home front; Industry; Malenkov, G. M.
Manchuria, 197, 199–200, 211–12, 242, 378 nn. 57 and 61
Mandelstamm, Nadezhda, 250, *328*
Manuilsky, D. Zh., 127
Mao Tse-tung, *323;* in World War II, 194–95, 339 n. 21; "separate roadism" of, 195, 202, 211–12; and liberation crisis, 196–97, 211–12, 376 n. 41, 378 nn. 57 and 61, 380 n. 99; theories in 1944–1947, 212, 298, 345 n. 36, 366 n. 54, 386 n. 57, 394 n. 19 (*see also* "Paper tiger" slogan); in 1947–1948, 298–99, 394 n. 19; victory of 1949, 309–10
Marcou, Lilly, *392*
Marin, J., *362 n. 71*
Marshall, George C., 255, 262, 291, 383 n. 10, 392 n. 4
Marshall Plan, 262–63, 266, 278, 287
Marxism-Leninism: as communications vehicle, 22–28, 65, 279–82; as Stalin's weak point, 27–28, 143–45, 150, 217–18, 231–35, 279–82, 308; as Russian culture in 1941–1945, 106, 143, 357 n. 42; as "truth" in 1944–1946, 109–16, 139–42, 144–45, 181–83, 245; as foreign policy guide in 1945, 156–59, 162–67, 190–94, 222; as "pedantry" and "talmudism" in 1944–1953, 116–17, 182–83, 233–34, 247, 275–79, 307; great debate about, in 1947, 181–85, 275–79; vs. technology in 1947–1948, 106, 246–47, 304–5. *See also* Anti-sectarian campaign; Communist movement; Ideology; Imperialism, Leninist theory of; Mao Tse-tung; Voluntarism
Masaryk, Jan, 357 n. 56, 393 n. 7
Mástný, Vojtěch, *323, 335 n. 43, 339 n. 25, 340 n. 33, 366*

Matthews, Mervyn, *352 n. 60*
Mayer, Arno, *333 n. 4*
Medvedev, Roy, 131, *338 n. 13*
Medvedev, Zhores, *388 n. 34*
Mee, Charles L., Jr., *375 n. 20*
Mehnert, Klaus, *332 n. 1, 388 n. 48*
Meissner, Boris, *323, 332, 340 n. 43, 353 n. 84, 372 n. 24*
Merkulov, V. N., 351 n. 53, 385 n. 31, 390 n. 66
Meskhetian Turks, 342 n. 70
Meyer, Alfred G., *335 n. 46, 352 n. 60*
Michael, King of Rumania, 54, 168–69, 198, 344 n. 20
Middle East: Soviet demands in, 192; Greek revolts in, 46, 54; Turkish crisis of 1945–1946, 170, 180, 184, 242, 255, 260; Iranian crisis of 1945–1946, 200–202, 212, 221–22; Palestinian crisis of 1947, 288–89. *See also names of individual countries*
Mikhoels, Solomon, 295, 299, 357 nn. 56 and 58, 399 n. 39
Mikołajczyk, Stanisław, 54, *328*, 344 n. 16
Mikoyan, A. I.: as top leader, 132, 229, 253; Leningrad association of, 133, 362 n. 75; postwar role of, 134, 136–37, 253; fall of, in 1949, 132, 305, 362 n. 70
Mileikovskii, A. G., *365 n. 48*
Miller, J. M., *396 n. 48*
"Millerandism," 32, 269. *See also* Communist movement: coalition tactics of
Millis, Walter, *323*
Milosz, Czeslaw, *328*
Ministries: commissariats renamed as, in 1946, 207; multiplicity of, 380 n. 86. *See also name of individual ministry*
Mitin, M., 110, 355 n. 7, 396 n. 44
Moldavia, 122, 164, 340 n. 33, 343 n. 10
Molotov, V. M., *323;* as top leader, 17, 229, 351 n. 50, 363 n. 96; as Stalin's adviser, 44, 51, 161, 186, 343 n. 9, 369 n. 52; in 1939, 107; in 1941–1942, 133, 152, 365 n. 110; in February 1944, 42, 49; negotiations of 1944, 49, 153, 313–16, 344 n. 20; as Party revivalist in 1944–1947, 134–35, 141, 185, 227, 229, 259, 278, 281, 365 n. 112; against isolationism, 42, 161–63, 166, 278, 292, 369 nn. 52 and 56, 386 n. 6, 390 nn. 73 and 76; negotiations of 1945, 154–56, 170–72, 175, 185, 188, 190–93, 196, 200–202, 219–22, 374 n. 11, 384 n. 18; as Stalin's

415

Stalin, J. V.—*continued*
  power of, in last years, 306; success of, in Communist movement, 307–10; fails to achieve peace, 310–12
—public statements: significance of, 23–28, 279–82, 336 n. 51, 358 n. 69; *Problems of Leninism*, 133, 233; *prikazy* and statements of 1941–1944, 34, 37–41, 49, 53, 64, 98, 339 nn. 22–23; correspondence with Allies, *324;* speech of 6 November 1943, 32–34, 63, 338 n. 9; speech of 6 November 1944, 62–68, 94, 110–12, 149–52, 162–63, 193, 280, 283, 347 n. 53; toast to the Russian people of May 1945, 75–76, 128, 143–45; speech about Japan, 204–5; other statements of 1945, 60, 76, 143, 172, 174–76, 180, 197, 365 n. 115, 376 n. 42; election speech of 1946, 131, 150, 217–18, 223–24, 227, 235, 280–81, 338 n. 13; *Collected Works*, 232–33, *322, 323,* 385 n. 44; reply to Razin, 233–34, 247, 280, 385 n. 47; reply to Churchill, 218, 236, 262, 386 n. 54; Gilmore interview, 231, 218, 236, 241; Werth interview, 150, 166, 241, 256; interview with Elliot Roosevelt, 241–42, 257; Stassen interview, 14, 24, 216, 243, 262, 266, 277, 746 n. 17; toast to Moscow, 130–31, 273–74, 287; *Problems of Linguistics*, 95, 281, 307, 336 n. 55, 403 n. 11; *Economic Problems of Socialism*, 70, 150, 281, 336 n. 59
Stalingrad, 19, 38, 121–22, 125
Stanojević, T., *324*
Starobin, Joseph R., *329, 337*
Stassen. Harold, 14, 24, 216, 243, 262, 266, 277, 746 n. 17
State Control, Ministry of, 230–31
State Defense Committee. *See* GOKO
State Planning Commission. *See* Gosplan
State Secrets Decree of 1947, 263
"Statism," 13. *See also* Stalin: "statism" of
Stavropol *krai,* 225, 230
Stearman, William L., *378 n. 55*
Steiner, Eugen, *340 n. 44*
Stettinius, Edward, 153, *329*
Stimson, Henry L., *329*
Strang, William, *329*
Strassenreiter, Erzsébet, *329*
Strausz-Hupé, Robert, *366*
Strong, Anna Louise, *386 n. 57*

Stypułkowski, Z., *329*
"Substitution," 20–21, 87, 91–93, 104, 106, 126, 166, 353 n. 89. *See also* Communist Party of the Soviet Union (CPSU)
Suchopar, V., *337 n. 2*
Suh, Dae-Suk, *397 n. 2*
Sullivant, Robert S., *341 n. 50*
Supreme Soviet: award to Leningrad, 129–30; abolishes GOKO, 92, 203, 225; election campaign of 1945, 159–63, 203, 223
—meetings: January 1944, 42, 124, 355 n. 4; April 1945, 124–25, 143, 186; March 1946, 141–42, 206–7, 225, 389 n. 64; October 1946, 253, 255, 389 n. 64; spring 1947, 263; March 1949, 362 n. 70
Suslov, M. I.: during war, 123, 225; in Orgburo in 1946, 225, 230–31, 385 n. 32; rise in 1947–1948, 273, 281, 293, 295, 302, 364 n. 101, 399 nn. 40 and 42
Svec, Jan, *401 n. 67*
Sverdlovsk, 88, 92, 230, 354 n. 92
Swayzee, Harold, *334 n. 39*
Sworakowski, Witold S., *392 n. 2*
Syria, 278
Szabó, Bálint, *346 n. 40*
Szálasi, Ferenc, 68, 313–14

Táborský, Edouard, *329,* 342 n. 69
"Talmudism." *See* Marxism-Leninism
Tanigawa, Yoshikiko, 401 n. 58
Tannu Tuva, 47, 201, 342 n. 70, 345 n. 33, 354 n. 92
Tatar Republic, 99, 354 n. 92
Tedder, Arthur W. T., *329*
Teheran Conference of 1943, 34, 38–39, 46, 152, 156, 195
Tel'pukhovskii, Boris S., *324*
Thaw of 1946. *See* Foreign policy, Soviet
Thorez, Maurice, *325;* as Muscovite, 43, 342 nn. 74 and 77; returns home in 1945, 57, 62, 345 n. 28; as separate roadist, 271, 382 n. 110; as Stalinist in 1949, 309
Tiersky, Ronald, *403 n. 19*
Tigrid, Pavel, *401 n. 66*
Tikos, László, *368 n. 43*
Tillon, Charles, *329,* 342 n. 74. 345 n. 26
Timasheff, N. S., *352 n. 62*
Tito, Josip Broz, *324;* in World War II, 343 n. 1; in Moscow in 1944, 51–52, 57, 346 n. 43; and the West, 52–53, 55, 242;

William O. McCagg, Jr., is director of the Russian and East European Program and professor of history at Michigan State University. He received the A.B. degree from Harvard College and the M.A. and Ph.D. degrees from Columbia University. His publications include Jewish Nobles and Geniuses in Modern Hungary (1972) and An Atlas of Russian and East European History (with A. Adams and I. Matley) (1967).

The manuscript was edited by Jean Owen. The book was designed by Donald R. Ross. The typeface for the text is Times Roman, designed under the supervision of Stanley Morison; and the display face is Egyptian Bold Condensed, originally a nineteenth-century Miller & Richard's design.

The text is printed on S. D. Warren's "66" paper. The book is bound in Joanna Mills Arrestox cloth over binder's boards. Manufactured in the United States of America.